marketing
strategy
4e

O. C. **Ferrell**
University of New Mexico

•

Michael D. **Hartline**
Florida State University

THOMSON
—————✳—————™
SOUTH-WESTERN

Australia · Brazil · Canada · Mexico · Singapore · Spain · United Kingdom · United States

THOMSON
™

SOUTH-WESTERN

Marketing Strategy, 4th Edition
O. C. Ferrell and Michael D. Hartline

VP/Editorial Director:
Jack W. Calhoun

VP/Editor-in-Chief:
Dave Shaut

Publisher:
Neil Marquadt

Developmental Editor:
Elizabeth Lowry

Marketing Manager:
Nicole Moore

Assoc. Content Project Manager:
D. Jean Buttrom

Manager of Technology, Editorial:
John Barans

Technology Project Manager:
Pam Wallace

Manufacturing Coordinator:
Diane Gibbons

Production House:
International Typesetting and
Composition

Printer:
Edwards Brothers
Ann Arbor, MI

Art Director:
Stacy Jenkins Shirley

Internal Designer:
c miller design

Cover Designer:
c miller design

Cover Images:
© Getty Images

Photography Manager:
Don Paris Schlotman

Photo Researcher:
Don Paris Schlotman

Library of Congress Control Number:
2006938699

For more information about our
products, contact us at:
**Thomson Learning Academic Resource
Center**
1-800-423-0563

Thomson Higher Education
5191, Natorp Boulevard
Mason, OH 45040.
USA

To my wife, Linda Ferrell

O. C. Ferrell

To mentors everywhere,
especially those who have influenced me the most:
my parents (Maril and Martha Hartline),
my wife (Marsha Wood Hartline),
Wilma Roby, Guy Anderson, P. J. Forrest,
O. C. Ferrell, and Dennis Cradit

Michael D. Hartline

Brief Contents

Contents

CHAPTER 5

Developing Competitive Advantage and Strategic Focus   117

CHAPTER 6

Customers, Segmentation, and Target Marketing   148

CHAPTER 7

Product Strategy   186

CHAPTER 8

Pricing Strategy   221

CHAPTER 9

Distribution and Supply Chain Management   255

CHAPTER 10

Integrated Marketing Communications   282

CHAPTER 11

Marketing Implementation and Control   311

CHAPTER 12

Developing and Maintaining Long-Term Customer Relationships   341

CASES

APPENDIX A

Marketing Plan Worksheets   639

APPENDIX B

Example Marketing Plan   650

Preface

Welcome to one of the most interesting, challenging, and important topics in your business education. What makes marketing strategy so interesting, challenging, and important, you ask? To begin, marketing strategy is interesting because (1) it is inherently people driven and (2) it is never stagnant. A distinct blend of both art and science, marketing strategy is about people (inside an organization) finding ways to deliver exceptional value by fulfilling the needs and wants of other people (customers, shareholders, business partners, and society at large), as well as the needs of the organization itself. Marketing strategy draws from psychology, sociology, and economics to better understand the basic needs and motivations of these people—whether they are the organization's customers (typically considered the most critical), its employees, or its stakeholders. In short, marketing strategy is about people serving people.

For this reason, marketing strategy is interesting because it is never stagnant. The simple fact is that people change. What works today might not work tomorrow. Products that are popular today are forgotten next week. These are truisms in marketing. This is important because truly understanding marketing strategy means accepting the fact that there are few concrete rules for developing and implementing marketing activities. Given the constant state of change in the marketing environment, it is virtually impossible to say that given "this customer need" and "these competitors" and "this level of government regulation" that Product A, Price B, Promotion C, and Distribution D will produce the best results. Marketing simply doesn't work this way. The lack of concrete rules and the ever-changing economic, sociocultural, competitive, technological, and political/legal landscapes make marketing strategy a wonderful, fascinating subject.

Now that you know why marketing strategy is so interesting, it should be easy to see why it is also challenging. A perfect marketing strategy that is executed perfectly can still fail. Sometimes, organizations get lucky and are successful despite having a terrible strategy and/or execution. The nature of marketing can make marketing planning frustrating.

Finally, the importance of marketing strategy is undeniable. No other business function focuses on developing relationships with customers—the lifeblood of all organizations (even nonprofits). This statement does not diminish the importance of other business functions because they all are necessary for an organization to be successful. In fact, coordination with other functions is critical to marketing success. However, without customers and marketing programs in place to cultivate customer relationships, no organization can survive.

Our Focus

Given this marketing landscape, *Marketing Strategy*, Fourth Edition, provides a practical, straightforward approach to analyzing, planning, and implementing marketing strategies. Our focus is based on the creative process involved in applying the knowledge and concepts of marketing to the development and implementation of marketing strategy. Our goal is to encourage students of marketing to think and act like a marketer. By discussing the key concepts and tools of marketing strategy, our emphasis on critical thinking, both analytical and creative, allows students to understand the essence of how marketing decisions fit together to create a coherent strategy.

Our approach in this edition of *Marketing Strategy* is also grounded in the development and execution of the marketing plan. Throughout the text, we provide a comprehensive planning framework based on conducting sound background research, developing market capabilities and competitive advantages, designing integrative marketing programs, and managing customer relationships for the long term. We also emphasize the need for integrity in the strategic planning process, as well as the design of marketing programs that are both ethical and socially responsible. We also stress the integration and coordination of marketing decisions with other functional business decisions as the key to achieving an organization's overall mission and vision. Throughout the text, we offer examples of successful planning and implementation to illustrate how firms face the challenges of marketing strategy in today's economy.

Purpose

We view strategic marketing planning not only as a process for achieving organizational goals but also as a means of building long-term relationships with customers. Creating a customer orientation takes imagination, vision, and courage, especially in today's rapidly changing economic and technological environments. To help meet these challenges, our text approaches marketing strategy from both "traditional" and "cutting-edge" practices. We cover topics such as segmentation, creating a competitive advantage, marketing program development, and the implementation process with a solid grounding in traditional marketing but with an eye toward emerging practices. Lessons learned from the rise, fall, and reemergence of the dot-com sector illustrate the importance of balancing the traditional and emerging practices of marketing strategy. Our text never loses sight of this balance.

Although our approach allows for the use of sophisticated research and decision-making processes, we have employed a practical perspective that permits marketing managers in any size organization to develop and implement a marketing plan. We have avoided esoteric, abstract, and highly academic material that does not relate to typical marketing strategy decisions in most organizations. The marketing plan framework that we utilize throughout the text has been used by a number of organizations to successfully plan their marketing strategies. Many companies report great success in using our approach, partially due to the ease of communicating the plan to all functional areas of the business.

Target Audience

Our text is relevant for a number of educational environments, including undergraduate, graduate, and corporate training courses. At the undergraduate level, our text is appropriate for the capstone course or any upper-level integrating course such as Marketing

Management, Marketing Strategy, or Marketing Policy. At this level, the text provides an excellent framework to use with our included text-based cases, live-client cases, or a computer simulation. At the graduate level, our text is appropriate for courses addressing strategic marketing planning, competitive marketing strategies, or as a supplement for any simulation-based course. A growing segment of the market, corporate training, can use our text when educating business professionals interested in developing marketing plans of their own or interpreting and implementing the plans of others.

Each of the twenty cases included in our text describes the strategic situations of real-world, identifiable organizations. Because these cases feature real situations, instructors have the option of using the case material as published, or they may give students the opportunity to update the cases by conducting research to find the latest information. In addition to the cases provided in our text, instructors can order a customized casebook through TextChoice and Thomson Custom Publishing. Many additional resources for students and instructors can be found at our text's companion website, http://www.thomsonedu.com/marketing/ferrell.

Key Features of the Fourth Edition

The key features of this edition include the following:

- A completely revised and updated text:

  - A new feature, Beyond the Pages, has been added to each chapter. This boxed material offers a vignette of key issues or current marketing practices at many well-known companies. Some of the topics discussed in Beyond the Pages (there are two in each chapter) include social networking, innovation, the growing Chinese market, rebranding, media fragmentation, podcasting, and the changing rules of corporate leadership.

  - We have added coverage of additional marketing planning tools where appropriate. For example, a discussion of the balanced-performance scorecard has been added to Chapter 2, "Strategic Marketing Planning." In addition, the concept of Blue Ocean Strategy and its planning tools are discussed in Chapter 5, "Developing Competitive Advantage and Strategic Focus."

  - Our discussion of ethics and social responsibility has been moved to Chapter 3, "Marketing Ethics and Social Responsibility in Strategic Planning." These important topics are now more prominently placed within the text and more tightly integrated into our overall strategic planning framework.

  - We have relocated and integrated related concepts that formerly appeared in separate chapters. For example, our discussion of customer relationship management has been expanded and moved to Chapter 12, "Developing and Maintaining Long-Term Customer Relationships," where it now serves as a means to integrate and summarize the entire text. Likewise, the discussion of product positioning has been moved to Chapter 7, "Product Strategy." These changes allow for a tighter discussion of customer behavior and market segmentation in Chapter 6, "Customers, Segmentation, and Target Marketing."

- Finally, to improve the visual aspects of our text, we have added photographs for the first time. These photographs are used to further emphasize key concepts within each chapter.

- Our most aggressive case revision program to date. The fourth edition includes seven new cases written specifically for our text:

  - Case 5, "Blockbuster: Movie Rentals in the Digital Era," describes the challenges facing Blockbuster as it strives to stay on top of the movie- and game-rental market. Blockbuster faces the real possibility that the traditional store-based rental industry is coming to an end. Blockbuster must deal with intense competition from Movie Gallery (store-based), Netflix (online and mail), and emerging competitors in the electronic delivery market.

  - Case 6, "Mobile ESPN: The Sports Fan's MVP?," focuses on ESPN's failed brand extension into the MVNO wireless telephone market. Historically, ESPN has been very successful in leveraging its brand in venues such as news, entertainment programming, and shopping. The wireless phone market is lucrative but was too far of a stretch for ESPN. In addition, other, more broadly based media and sports organizations are looking to move into the market. ESPN must search for an alternative strategy to best distribute its branded sports information content.

  - Case 8, "Best Buy," examines the company's conversion to a customer-centric model throughout its chain of stores. Best Buy's strategy is based on a wealth of data that the company has collected about its customers. A refined segmentation program is also part of Best Buy's strategy to fulfill customers' needs more fully.

  - Case 10, "New Belgium Brewing Company (B): Developing a Brand Personality," has been added as a companion to our continuing New Belgium case on ethical and environmental responsibility (Case 9). New Belgium (B) looks at the company's brand management strategies. The case addresses New Belgium's media choices, message development, and the creation of the company's "brand manifesto."

  - Case 12, "PETCO Develops Successful Stakeholder Relationships," describes the company's overall social responsibility and ethical compliance program. PETCO's position in the pet industry demands that the company be mindful of its obligations related to animal care. It also means that PETCO is vulnerable to special-interest organizations that strongly advocate for animal rights.

  - Case 14, "IKEA," discusses the Swedish retailer's production and marketing programs as they relate to the company's expansion around the world. IKEA enjoys strong positioning in the market for affordable, modern, and stylish furniture. However, to more fully expand into the U.S. market, IKEA may have to adapt its products and operating structure—something that does not mesh well with the company's focus on efficiency and low-cost operations.

  - Case 15, "Mistine," explores the direct-selling cosmetics market in Thailand. The Better Way Company pioneered the direct-selling market when it launched its Mistine brand in 1991. The case discusses Mistine's growth via its direct-selling operations and creative message campaigns over time. Although Mistine currently holds the dominant position in the Thai market, the brand faces intense competition from Avon, Amway, and U*Star.

- A complete revision of the eight cases that have been carried over from the third edition of our text. Many have been refocused:

  - Case 2, "*USA Today* and the Future of Information Distribution," has been rewritten to focus on the growing threat of information technology. The case is now written as an analysis of the situation that faces *USA Today* as it prepares for the technological advances that will change the distribution of news and information in the future.

  - Case 7, "Gillette: The Razor Wars Continue," has a much stronger focus on Gillette's battle with Schick as each competes for global share in the razor and blades market. Although Gillette dominates the global market, the company may have reached the end of its impressive string of advancements in shaving technology. Hence, Gillette may have to find other ways of maintaining its dominance.

  - Case 11, "Mattel, Inc.," has added emphasis on Mattel's core brands and their relative weakness in sales growth. Mattel has experienced several years of declining sales for Barbie—its flagship product—as competition from Bratz dolls and cultural changes in the children's market have taken their toll.

- The inclusion of five new outside cases—three from the Harvard Business School and two from the Ivey School of Business at the University of Western Ontario:

  - Harvard Cases:

    Museum of Fine Arts Boston
    G.I. Joe: Marketing an Icon
    Strategic Inflection: TiVo in 2005

  - Ivey Cases:

    The Brand in the Hand: Mobile Marketing at Adidas
    Santa Fe Relocation Services: Regional Brand Management

- A revised set of Marketing Plan Worksheets, provided in Appendix A. The worksheets have been updated to reflect a more concise approach to marketing plan development. However, the worksheets remain comprehensive in scope to help ensure that students and/or managers do not omit important issues in developing strategic marketing plans.

- A new Example Marketing Plan, provided in Appendix B. This marketing plan, based on a virtual case developed by Dr. Hartline, is our most comprehensive example plan to date. Students will find this plan helpful because it illustrates the format and writing style used in creating an actual marketing plan document.

- A continued user-friendly writing style that covers essential points without heavy use of jargon. Although the text has been completely revised, it remains a friendly twelve chapters in length.

Instructor Resources

The Instructor Resource materials for the fourth edition have been updated. These materials include

- A revised PowerPoint package, available on the Instructor's Resource CD-ROM and our text's website (http://www.thomsonedu.com/marketing/ferrell).

- An updated website (http://www.thomsonedu.com/marketing/ferrell) to support the text and cases. In addition to the new PowerPoint package, instructors will find lecture outlines, case teaching notes, and sample syllabi for use in their classes.

- An updated Instructor's Manual, which includes the following:

  - Lecture outlines for each chapter—These outlines may be used to quickly review chapter content before class or to gain an overview of the entire text. The outlines can also be downloaded from our website so that instructors can add their own personal notes and examples before class.

  - Case teaching notes—Our teaching notes use a consistent format to help instructors evaluate cases before use or to assist instructors in leading case analysis and class discussion. These case notes are also available on our website. Although there are many different approaches to using cases, our notes will help instructors identify key issues and alternatives as they relate to the content of the case and corresponding text chapters.

  - Examination materials—These materials include a test bank of multiple-choice and discussion questions for each chapter.

  - PowerPoint thumbnails—Thumbnail images from the PowerPoint package are in the Instructor's Manual to help instructors locate materials more quickly.

Student Resources

Our primary student resources are contained within the text. Appendix A includes a detailed set of marketing plan worksheets that assist students in developing marketing plans. Likewise, Appendix B provides a complete example marketing plan to give students an idea of what a finished plan looks like.

The remaining student resources can be found online at our website:

- A downloadable Microsoft Word version of the Marketing Plan Worksheets found in Appendix A. The worksheets are designed so students can fill-in material and edit the worksheets outside of class.

- A downloadable Microsoft Word version of the lessons from each chapter. This document provides a complete outline of each chapter so that students may add to and edit the lessons outside of class. Alternatively, the file can be used during class as a way to organize note taking.

- Online exercises for each chapter. These exercises allow students to practice the concepts learned in class.

- Online quizzes for each chapter. These quizzes help students prepare for course exams.

- A tutorial on how to perform a case analysis. The tutorial provides a suggested way to conduct cases analyses. Instructors may use this tutorial or provide one of their own.

- Helpful information on choosing a marketing career and resources for locating marketing-related information.

Acknowledgments

Throughout the development of this text, several extraordinary individuals provided their talent and expertise to make important contributions. A number of individuals have made many useful comments and recommendations as reviewers of this text. We appreciate the generous help of these reviewers:

Timothy W. Aurand, *Northern Illinois University*
Fred H. Campbell, *University of North Carolina at Charlotte*
Linda Ferrell, *University of New Mexico*
Lynn Jahn, *University of Iowa*
Keith C. Jones, *North Carolina A&T State University*
Mike McCardle, *Western Michigan University*
Abe Qastin, *Lakeland College*
Donald P. Roy, *Middle Tennessee State University*
Debbie M. Thorne, *Texas State University—San Marcos*

We also deeply appreciate the assistance of several individuals who played a major role in developing cases or other materials. Specifically, we thank the following individuals:

Marie Bell,
Harvard University
Ron Clark,
East Carolina University
Christin Copeland,
Florida State University
Niraj Dawar,
University of Western Ontario
Melanie Drever,
University of Wyoming

Linda Ferrell,
University of New Mexico
Nigel F. J. Goodwin,
Nanyang Technological University (Singapore)
Nuntiya Ittiwattanakorn,
Thammasat University (Thailand)
Keith C. Jones,
North Carolina A&T State University

Geoff Lantos,
Stonehill College
Gail J. McGovern,
Harvard University
Rawadee Mekwichai,
Thammasat University (Thailand)
V. Kasturi Rangan,
Harvard University
Andy Rohm,
Northeastern University
Don Roy,
Middle Tennessee State University
Supishsha Sajjamanochai,
Thammasat University (Thailand)
Alexi Sherrill,
University of Wyoming

Bryan Simpson,
New Belgium Brewing Company
Fareena Sultan,
Northeastern University
Debbie M. Thorne,
Texas State University—San Marcos
Ekachai Wangprapa,
Thammasat University (Thailand)
David Wesley,
Northeastern University
Pai-Ling Yin,
Harvard University
David B. Yoffie,
Harvard University

The editorial, production, and marketing staff at South-Western and Thomson cannot be thanked enough. With a deep sense of appreciation, we thank Elizabeth Lowry, Emma Guttler, Neil Marquardt, Nicole Moore, and Jean Buttrom.

Finally, we express appreciation for the support and encouragement of our families (especially the patience of Dr. Hartline's daughters) and our colleagues at the University of Wyoming, University of New Mexico, and Florida State University.

O. C. Ferrell, Ph.D.

The University of New Mexico

O. C. Ferrell (PhD, Louisiana State University) is Professor of Marketing and Creative Enterprise Scholar at the Anderson Schools of Management at the University of New Mexico. He recently served as the Bill Daniels Distinguished Professor of Business Ethics at the University of Wyoming and was previously Chair of the Marketing Department at Colorado State University (CSU). Prior to his arrival at CSU, Dr. Ferrell was the Distinguished Professor of Marketing and Business Ethics at the University of Memphis. He has also served as a professor at the University of Tampa, Texas A&M University, Illinois State University, and Southern Illinois University. His MBA and BA degrees are from Florida State University.

Dr. Ferrell is past president of the Academic Council of the American Marketing Association and former chair of the American Marketing Association Ethics Committee. Under his leadership, the committee developed the AMA Code of Ethics and the AMA Code of Ethics for Marketing on the Internet. Dr. Ferrell currently chairs a new committee to revise the AMA Code of Ethics. He is a Society for Marketing Advances Fellow and a member of the Board of Governors of the Academy of Marketing Science.

Dr. Ferrell has taught a wide variety of courses, including marketing strategy, principles of marketing, marketing ethics, and international marketing, as well as most undergraduate courses in marketing. Annually, Dr. Ferrell teaches a graduate course in competitive marketing strategies at Thammasat University in Bangkok, Thailand.

Dr. Ferrell is the coauthor of seventeen books and more than seventy articles. His research has been published in the *Journal of Marketing Research, Journal of Marketing, Journal of Business Ethics, Journal of Business Research,* and *Journal of the Academy of Marketing Science,* as well as other journals. His *Marketing: Concepts and Strategies* text, coauthored with Bill Pride, is one of the most widely adopted principles of marketing texts in the world. Furthermore, his *Business Ethics: Decision Making and Cases* text is a leading business ethics text. Dr. Ferrell currently serves as the marketing ethics and values section editor for the *Journal of Macromarketing.*

Dr. Ferrell has served as an expert witness in many high-profile civil litigation cases related to marketing ethics. More recently, he has assisted organizations and worked with state regulatory agencies in modifying marketing programs to maintain compliance with both ethical and legal requirements.

Dr. Ferrell and his wife, Linda (also a faculty member at the University of New Mexico), live in Albuquerque. He enjoys golf, skiing, reading, and travel.

Michael D. Hartline
Florida State University

Michael D. Hartline (PhD, University of Memphis) is Associate Professor, Chair of the Marketing Department, and the Charles A. Bruning Professor of Business Administration in the College of Business at Florida State University (FSU). Prior to joining the FSU faculty in 2001, Dr. Hartline taught at the University of Arkansas at Little Rock, Louisiana State University, and Samford University. His MBA and BS degrees are from Jacksonville State University in Alabama.

Dr. Hartline has taught many different courses but primarily teaches the MBA course in Marketing Strategy and undergraduate courses in Services Marketing and Service Operations Management. He has won many teaching and research awards and has made many presentations to industry and academic audiences. Dr. Hartline has also served as a consultant to several for-profit and nonprofit organizations in the areas of marketing plan development, market feasibility analysis, customer satisfaction measurement, customer service training, and pricing policy. He most recently worked with Pfizer Pharmaceuticals in New York as a faculty intern in Corporate Affairs, Philanthropy, and Government Relations.

Dr. Hartline's research focus addresses marketing implementation issues in service firms. Specifically, his work examines the role of customer-contact employees and work groups in the effective delivery of quality service to customers. Dr. Hartline's research appears in the *Journal of Marketing, Journal of Service Research, Journal of Business Research, Journal of Services Marketing, Cornell Quarterly, Journal of Relationship Marketing, Journal of Strategic Marketing, Journal of Business Ethics,* and *Marketing Science Institute Working Paper Series.* He also serves on the editorial review boards of a number of leading marketing journals.

Dr. Hartline and his wife, Marsha, live in Tallahassee with their daughters, Meghan, Madison, and Mallory. They have two dogs, Bella and Chief (both Japanese Chins), and a cat, Snickers. Dr. Hartline is a self-professed electronics and gadget freak who enjoys travel, music, reading, personal computing, college football (Go Seminoles!), and playing with his children.

CHAPTER 1

Marketing in Today's Economy

Introduction

As noted in Beyond the Pages 1.1, competing in today's economy means finding ways to break out of commodity status to meet customers' needs better than competing firms. All organizations—both for-profit and non-profit—require effective planning and a sound marketing strategy to do this effectively. Without these efforts, organizations could not satisfy customers or meet the needs of other stakeholders. For example, having an effective marketing strategy allows Toyota to develop popular products, such as its line of hybrid vehicles and its new low-cost Scion line. Further, effective planning and strategy allows Procter & Gamble to continually improve the performance of Tide and to make a key acquisition in its purchase of the Gillette Company, all the while continuing its expansion into the lucrative pharmaceuticals market. These and other organizations use sound marketing strategy to leverage their strengths and capitalize on opportunities that exist in the market. Every organization—from your favorite local restaurant to giant multinational corporations; from city, state, and federal governments to charities such as Habitat for Humanity and the American Red Cross—develops and implements marketing strategies.

How organizations plan, develop, and implement marketing strategies is the focus of this book. To achieve this focus, we provide a systematic process for developing customer-oriented marketing strategies and marketing plans that match an organization to its internal and external environments. Our approach focuses on real-world applications and practical methods of marketing planning, including the process of developing a marketing plan. The chapters of this book focus on the steps of this process. Our goal is to give the reader a deeper understanding of marketing planning, the ability to organize the vast amount of information needed to complete the planning process, and an actual "feel" for the development of marketing plans.

Beyond the Pages 1.1

WELCOME TO COMMODITY HELL[1]

Welcome to commodity hell, where your product is just like everyone else's, your profit margins are low, and price is the only true means of differentiation that matters to customers. If this scenario sounds far-fetched, it isn't. Many companies today find themselves in this difficult situation. Commoditization is the curse of mature markets whereby products lack real means of differentiation and customers begin to see all competing products as offering roughly the same benefits. When consumers see competing products as commodities, price is the only thing that matters.

Commoditization is a consequence of mature industries, where slowing innovation, extensive product assortment, excess supply, and fickle, price-conscious consumers force margins to the floor. Since firms have few competitive differences, they cannot increase margins. They must also spend a great deal on promotion to attract new customers. This situation makes firms more vulnerable to the entry of new competitors. Consider the airline industry. Notwithstanding a few minor differences, most air travelers see all airlines as being roughly the same. They all get passengers from Point A to Point B while offering the same basic customer services. This makes price the driving force in consumer decision making and allows discount airlines such as Southwest and Jet Blue to steal customers away from traditional full-service carriers. This same precarious situation exists in a broad range of industries including telephone service, hotels, packaged goods, automobiles, household appliances, and retailing.

As might be expected, low-price leaders can do quite well in commodity hell. Southwest, for example, has been profitable for over 32 years—something no other airline can claim. Wal-Mart and Dell are champions at navigating their way through commodity status. Other firms, however, avoid commodity status through the most basic of

marketing tactics: brand building. Here, firms break free from commodity status by developing a distinctive brand position that separates them and their products from the competition. By offering compelling reasons for consumers to buy products, brand building allows firms to increase margins.

For example, Starbucks clearly sells one of the most commoditized, ubiquitous products of all time: coffee. Starbucks Chairman Howard Schultz, however, does not accept that his firm is in the coffee business. Instead, Schultz sees Starbucks as a "third place" to hang out (with home and work being #1 and # 2, respectively). Through this mentality, Starbucks offers its customers much more than coffee, including wireless Internet access, music, food, and relaxation. In another example, Best Buy has taken steps to improve its customer experience. The company has done extensive marketing research to learn everything it can about its customers. One result is the creation of a boutique store catering to soccer moms. And, unlike other big-box electronic retailers, Best Buy develops its own in-house brands of innovative new products, bringing them to market months ahead of its competitors. As a result, Best Buy has increased its margins by 0.5 percent over the past two years.

Getting out of commodity hell is not an easy feat. To do so, firms must give consumers a compelling reason to buy their products over competing products. Ultimately, winning the commodity game is all about innovation. Consider the ten firms that top *Fortune*'s list of the World's Most Innovative Companies for 2006 (in order): Apple, Google, 3M, Toyota, Microsoft, GE, Procter & Gamble, Nokia, Starbucks, and IBM. Each of these companies offers innovative products that stand apart from the competition; yet each competes in mature industries known for commoditization. These companies prove that innovation and good marketing strategy are the antidotes for commodity hell.

In this first chapter, we review some of the major challenges and opportunities that exist in planning marketing strategy in today's economy. We also review the nature and scope of major marketing activities and decisions that occur throughout the planning process. Finally, we look at some of the major challenges involved in developing marketing strategy.

The Challenges and Opportunities of Marketing in Today's Economy

Although the euphoria over the dot-com bubble and its subsequent demise is long over, the fact remains that advances in computer, communication, and information technology have forever changed the world and the world of marketing. It wasn't that long ago when few people knew the difference between a .com and a .org, much less the names of today's powerhouse companies such as Amazon, Google, Yahoo!, and eBay. Consider these fundamental changes to marketing and business practice, as well as our own personal buying behavior:

- **Power Shift to Customers** The astounding growth of the Internet has shifted power to customers, not marketers. Rather than businesses having the ability to manipulate customers via technology, customers often manipulate businesses because of their access to information and ability to comparison shop. Individual consumers and business customers can compare prices and product specifications in a matter of minutes. In many cases, customers are able to set their own prices, such as purchasing airline tickets at Priceline.com. In addition, customers can now interact with one another because merchants such as Amazon and eBay allow customers to share opinions on product quality and supplier reliability. As power continues to shift to customers, marketers have little choice but to ensure that their products are unique and of high quality, thereby giving customers a reason to purchase their products and remain loyal to them.

- **Massive Increase in Product Selection** The variety and assortment of goods and services offered for sale on the Internet and in traditional stores is staggering. In grocery stores alone, customers are faced with countless options in the cereal and soft-drink aisles. The growth in online retailing now allows customers to purchase a car from CarsDirect.com, handmade, exotic gifts from Mojo Tree (http://www.mojotree.co.uk), or a case of their favorite wine from Wine.com. Increased transaction efficiency (for example, 24/7 access, delivery to home or office) allows customers to fulfill their needs more easily and conveniently than ever before. Furthermore, the vast amounts of information available online has changed the way we communicate, read the news, and entertain ourselves. Customers can now have the news delivered to them via RSS feeds (really simple syndication) from hundreds of sources. This radical increase in product selection and availability has exposed marketers to inroads by competitors from every corner of the globe.

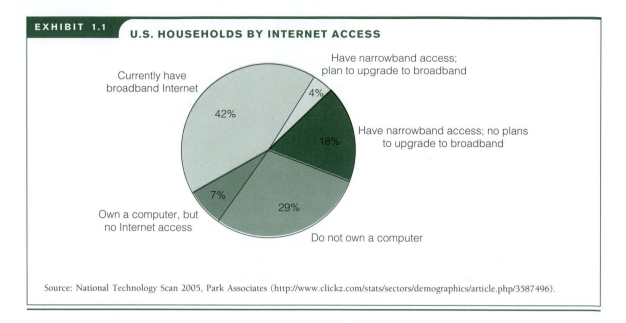

EXHIBIT 1.1   **U.S. HOUSEHOLDS BY INTERNET ACCESS**

Source: National Technology Scan 2005, Park Associates (http://www.clickz.com/stats/sectors/demographics/article.php/3587496).

- **Audience and Media Fragmentation** Since the advent of cable television in the 1970s, mass-media audiences have become increasingly fragmented. Television audiences, for example, shifted from the big three networks (ABC, CBS, NBC) and began watching programming on ESPN, HGTV, Nickelodeon, and the Discovery Channel. When the growth of the Internet, satellite radio, and mobile communication is added to this mix, it becomes increasingly difficult for marketers to reach a true mass audience. Media audiences have become fragmented due to (1) the sheer number of media choices that we have available today and (2) the limited time that we have to devote to any one medium. As shown in Exibit 1.1, a full 42 percent of U.S. households now have broadband Internet access. Across the board, the time that we devote to traditional television, radio, and print media is declining, while the time that we spend with interactive media (online, wireless, gaming) is on the rise. Despite the challenge of reaching mass audiences today, media fragmentation does have a big advantage: It is easier to reach small, highly targeted audiences.

- **Changing Value Propositions** The speed and efficiency of commerce today has changed the way that customers view value. For example, fewer customers automatically turn to travel agents for assistance in booking airline tickets, cruises, or hotel stays. Now, customers turn to travel sites like Expedia.com or book directly at websites operated by travel and lodging providers. A similar change has taken place in the real estate industry as buyers are moving their house hunting online, while sellers are increasingly taking the "for sale by owner" route.[2] Similar changes have occurred in banking, mortgage lending, and car buying. The lesson for marketers is clear: In situations where customers see goods and services as commodities, customers will turn to the most convenient, least-expensive alternative. This fact makes it increasingly difficult for marketers to differentiate their product offering in today's economy.

- **Shifting Demand Patterns** In some cases, changes in technology have shifted customer demand for certain product categories. The explosive growth in the digital distribution of music and video bears this out. The success of Apple's iPod and iTunes, as well as the ongoing issues associated with copyright protection and digital piracy, proves that customers absolutely prefer to get their music and video from the Internet. The repercussions of this demand shift for the recording and movie industries are enormous. For example, in the traditional movie theater business, ticket sales have declined 7 percent in recent years due to the growing popularity of DVD distribution by mail (for example, Netflix) and increasing sales of home theater equipment.[3] Now, an emerging sector devoted to online movie distribution has appeared, with CinemaNow being one of the early pioneers.

- **New Sources of Competitive Advantage** Businesses that link their internal computer networks with the networks of customers, suppliers, and other partners can leverage the advantages of e-commerce. Dell Computer, for example, has seamlessly integrated its supply chain—from suppliers (manufacturers of chips, drives, displays, and so on), to assembly, to product delivery (United Parcel Service). As a result, Dell enjoys reduced costs, operational efficiency, economies of scale, and broad customer reach, which are all key aspects of its leadership in the personal computer industry.[4] Dell's example illustrates that to be successful marketers must be able and willing to network with other firms to create new efficiencies and competitive advantages. In today's economy, some of the best competitive advantages stem from partnerships and alliances with other firms.

- **Privacy, Security, and Ethical Concerns** Changes in technology have made our society much more open than in the past. As a result, these changes have forced marketers to address real concerns about security and privacy, both online and offline. Businesses have always collected routine information about their customers. Now, customers are much more attuned to these efforts and the purposes for which the information will be used. Though customers appreciate the convenience of e-commerce, they want assurances that their information is safe and confidential. Concerns over online privacy and security are especially acute with respect to controversial businesses—such as casinos or pornography—and with respect to children. For example, many well-known and respected companies, including Mrs. Fields Cookies and Hershey Foods, have been fined for violating the standards of the Children's Online Privacy Protection Act.[5] Exhibit 1.2 provides an overview of this law and its standards.

- **Unclear Legal Jurisdiction** When a company does business in more than one country (as virtually all Internet-based firms do), that company often faces a dilemma with respect to differing legal systems. Today, this difference is especially keen for firms that do business in both the United States and China. Google, for example, faced a difficult situation when the Chinese government demanded that Google censor certain types of information from the company's popular search engine. Though Google is a U.S. firm, it complied with the Chinese request by

---

EXHIBIT 1.2   **THE CHILDREN'S ONLINE PRIVACY PROTECTION ACT**

The Children's Online Privacy Protection Act (COPPA) applies to operators of commercial websites and online services that attempt to collect personal information from children under the age of 13. The law explains what must be included in the firm's privacy policy, when and how to seek verifiable consent from a parent or guardian, and the firm's responsibilities to protect children's privacy and safety. Firms cannot evade the law's provisions by claiming that children under 13 cannot visit their sites; nor can they make information optional or ask the visitor's age.

In implementing the provisions of COPPA, the Federal Trade Commission issued the Children's Online Privacy Protection Rule, which is designed to give parents control over the information that is collected from their children. The rule requires website operators to

- post a description of its privacy policy on the site's home page and any other area where personal information is collected.
- provide notice to parents about the site's information collection practices. This full disclosure must describe (1) the type of information collected, (2) why the information is being collected, (3) how the information will be used and stored, (4) whether the information will be disclosed to third parties, and (5) parental rights with regard to information content and usage.
- obtain verifiable parental consent to the collection and use of a child's personal information for internal use. The operator must also give parents the opportunity to choose not to have this information disclosed to third parties.
- give parents access to their child's information, give them the right and means to review and/or delete this information, and give parents the choice to opt out of the future collection or use of the information.
- not require that children provide more information than is reasonably necessary to participate in an activity. Children cannot be required to provide information as a condition of participation.
- maintain the security, confidentiality, and integrity of all personal information collected from children.

Source: U.S. Federal Trade Commission, Kidz Privacy (http://www.ftc.gov/bcp/conline/edcams/kidzprivacy/index.html).

---

launching a new Chinese search engine that censors information considered sensitive by the Chinese government.[6] Doing business in China is also an issue with respect to protection of intellectual-property rights, where Chinese laws do not offer the same protections found in the United States.[7] Another important legal issue involves the collection of sales tax for online transactions. In the early days of e-commerce, most online merchants did not collect sales taxes for online transactions—giving them a big advantage against store-based merchants. States countered that they were losing millions in yearly tax revenue. In 2003, major retailers—including Wal-Mart, Target, and Toys "R" Us—in an agreement with a consortium of thirty-eight states and the District of Columbia agreed to collect online sales taxes.[8] However, many online merchants still do not charge sales tax, especially if they do not have a physical presence in a given state.

Although the full effect of these challenges will not be recognized for some time, circumstances have forced businesses to move ahead by adjusting their marketing activities at both the strategic and tactical levels. As we review the major marketing concepts and activities in this chapter, we will look at how today's challenges have affected strategic planning in these areas.

Basic Marketing Concepts

Marketing is many different things. Many people, especially those not employed in marketing, see marketing as a function of business. From this perspective, marketing parallels other business functions such as production, research, management, human resources, and accounting. As a business function, the goal of marketing is to connect the organization to its customers. Other individuals, particularly those working in marketing jobs, tend to see marketing as a process of managing the flow of products from the point of conception to the point of consumption. The field's major trade organization, the American Marketing Association (AMA), recently changed the definition of *marketing* after 20 years. From 1985 until 2005, the AMA defined marketing this way:

> *Marketing is the process of planning and executing the conception, pricing, promotion, and distribution of ideas, goods, and services to create exchanges that satisfy individual and organizational objectives.*[9]

In 2005 the AMA changed the definition of *marketing* to better reflect the realities of competing in today's marketplace:

> *Marketing is an organizational function and a set of processes for creating, communicating, and delivering value to customers and for managing customer relationships in ways that benefit the organization and its stakeholders.*[10]

Notice that the changes in the definition are not merely cosmetic in nature. The new definition stresses two critical success factors in marketing today: value and customer relationships. The notion of value recognizes that customer satisfaction can be derived from many different aspects of the total product offering, not just from having access to high-quality products at a low price. Customer relationships—which grow and thrive on exceptional value—are an absolute necessity in the commodity-driven status of many product markets. Whereas the former definition of *marketing* had a decidedly transactional focus, the new definition emphasizes long-term relationships that provide value for both customers and the firm.

A final way to think about marketing relates to meeting human and social needs. This broad view links marketing with our standard of living, not only in terms of enhanced consumption and prosperity but also in terms of society's well-being. Through marketing activities, consumers can buy cars from South Korea and wines from South Africa; and organizations can earn a viable profit, making both employees and stockholders happy. However, marketing must also bear responsibility for any negative effects that it may generate. This view demands that marketers consider the social and ethical implications of their actions and whether they practice good citizenship by giving back to their communities. As exemplified in the New Belgium Brewery case at the end of the text, firms can successfully meet human and social needs through socially responsible marketing and business practices.

Let's take a closer look at several basic marketing concepts. As we will see, ongoing changes in today's economy have forever altered our way of thinking about these foundational aspects of marketing.

What Is a Market?

At its most basic level, a *market* is a collection of buyers and sellers. We tend to think of a market as a group of individuals or institutions that have similar needs that can be met by a particular product. For example, the housing market is a collection of buyers and sellers of residential real estate, and the automobile market includes buyers and sellers of automotive transportation. Marketers or sellers tend to use the word *market* to describe only the buyers. This basic understanding of a market has not changed in a very long time. What has changed, however, is not so much the "what" but the "where" of a market—that is, the location of the buyers and sellers. In both consumer markets (like housing and automobiles) and business markets (like replacement parts and raw materials), the answer to the "where" question is quickly becoming "anywhere" as markets become less defined by geography.

Until recently, marketers have considered a market to be a physical location where buyers and sellers meet to conduct transactions. Although those venues (for example, grocery stores, malls, and flea markets) still thrive, technology mediates some of the fastest-growing markets. The term *marketspace* has been coined to describe these electronic marketplaces unbound by time or space.[11] Some of the largest marketspaces, such as Amazon.com, eBay, and Monster.com, are now household names. In fact, Amazon.com has become the marketspace equivalent of a shopping mall as the company now sells shoes, apparel, jewelry, beauty aids, and sporting goods in addition to its traditional offerings of books and electronics. Marketspaces also exist in the business-to-business realm. The shift from marketplaces to marketspaces has significant ramifications for marketers. The fact that customers can shop and place orders 24/7 means that these businesses must be capable of operating in that same time frame. In effect, marketspace operators never take a break at closing time—they never close. Furthermore, the substitution of technology for human interaction can be both a blessing and a curse. Some marketspaces, like CarsDirect.com, are successful because they eliminate the hassle of dealing with another human in the buying process. Many customers, however, have been slow to embrace marketspaces because they lack the human element. In these cases, the design and implementation of the online experience is a serious challenge for marketspace operators. Finally, the wealth of information available through today's marketspaces not only makes customers more educated than ever before but also gives customers increased power through comparison shopping and price negotiation.

Another interesting shift related to markets is the advent of metamarkets and metamediaries. A *metamarket* is a cluster of closely related goods and services that center around a specific consumption activity. A *metamediary* provides a single access point where buyers can locate and contact many different sellers in the metamarket.[12] Assume, for example, that you are engaged to be married. How many different buying decisions will you and your fiancé have to make in the coming months? How many

EXHIBIT 1.3	COMMON METAMARKETS AND PARTICIPANTS		
	Metamarkets		
	Automotive	Home Ownership	Parenting
Metamediaries	http://www.edmunds.com	http://www.realtor.com	http://www.parenting.ivillage.com
	http://autos.msn.com	http://realestate.msn.com	http://www.parenting.com
	http://www.carsdirect.com	http://www.bhg.com	
	http://www.kbb.com		
Metamarket Participants	Buyers	Homeowners	Parents
	Manufacturers	Builders	Doctors
	Car dealerships	Real estate agents	Retailers
	Banks	Mortgage companies	Baby supply manufacturers
	Credit unions	Insurance companies	Insurance firms
	Credit reporting services	Home inspectors and	Financial planners
	Insurance firms	appraisers	Educational providers
	Rating services	Pest control services	Toy manufacturers
	Magazines	Magazines	Television programs
	Television programs	Television programs	Movies
	Aftermarket parts/accessories	Retailers	
	Repair services		
	Car rental firms		
	Auction houses		

newspaper ads, websites, and magazines will you explore? Although the businesses and decisions are diverse, they all converge on the single theme of wedding planning. This is the driving principle behind a metamarket. Exhibit 1.3 shows examples of common metamarkets and metamediaries. Although customers don't use these terms, they fully understand the concept of finding information and solutions in one place. For example, iVillage (http://www.ivillage.com) has become the Internet's preeminent metamediary with respect to women's issues. One of its most popular sections deals with pregnancy and parenting, which has become the first stop for many anxious parents in need of advice. Metamediaries like iVillage fulfill a vital need by offering quick access and one-stop shopping to a wide variety of information, goods, and services.

What Is Exchange?

Closely related to the concept of a market, our ideas about exchange have changed in recent years. *Exchange* is traditionally defined as the process of obtaining something of value from someone by offering something in return; this usually entails obtaining products for money. For exchange to occur, five conditions must be met:

1. *There must be at least two parties to the exchange.* Although this has always been the case, the exchange process today can potentially include an unlimited number of participants. Online auctions provide a good example. Customers who bid on an item at eBay may be one of many participants to the exchange process. Each

participant changes the process for the others, as well as the ultimate outcome for the winning bidder. Some auctions include multiple quantities of an item, so the potential exists for multiple transactions within a single auction process.

2. *Each party has something of value to the other party*. Exchange would be possible but not very likely without this basic requirement. The Internet has exposed us to a vast array of goods and services that we did not know existed previously. Today, we buy a television or stereo receiver from not only a local merchant but also have access to hundreds of online merchants. Furthermore, the ability to comparison shop products and their prices allows customers to seek out the best value.

3. *Each party must be capable of communication and delivery*. The advantages of today's communication and distribution infrastructure are amazing. We can seek out and communicate with potential exchange partners anywhere and anytime via telephone, personal computers, handheld devices, and wireless telephones. We can also conduct arm's-length transactions in real time, with delivery of exchanged items occurring in a matter of hours if necessary.

4. *Each party must be free to accept or reject the exchange*. In the online world, this condition of exchange becomes a bit more complicated. Customers have grown accustomed to the ease with which they can return items to local merchants. Easy return policies are among the major strengths of traditional offline merchants. Returning items is more difficult with online transactions. In some cases, the ability to reject an exchange is not allowed in online transactions. Ordering airline tickets on Priceline.com and winning a bid on an item at eBay are contractually binding acts for the customer. In other words, once the actual purchasing process has started, the customer is not free to reject the exchange.

5. *Each party believes that it is desirable to exchange with the other party*. Customers typically have a great deal of information about or even a history with offline merchants. In online exchange, customers often know nothing about the other party. To help resolve this issue, a collection of third-party firms has stepped in to provide ratings and opinions about online merchants. Sites like BizRate.com and Epinions.com not only provide these ratings but also provide product ratings and serve as shopping portals. eBay goes one step further by allowing its users to rate both buyers and sellers. This gives both parties to the exchange process some assurance that reputable individuals or organizations exist on the other side of the transaction.

The bottom line is that exchange has become all too easy in today's economy. Opportunities for exchange bombard us virtually everywhere we go—even in our own homes. Customers don't even have to trouble themselves with giving credit cards or completing forms for shipping information. Most online merchants will remember this information for us if we let them. For example, Amazon's 1-Click® ordering feature allows customers to purchase products with a single mouse click.[13] The ease with which exchange can occur today presents a problem in that individuals who do not have the authority to exchange can still complete transactions. This is especially true for underage customers.

What Is a Product?

It should come as no surprise that the primary focus of marketing is the customer and how the organization can design and deliver products that meet customers' needs. Organizations create essentially all marketing activities as a means toward this end; this includes product design, pricing, promotion, and distribution. In short, an organization would have no reason to exist without customers and a product to offer them.

But what exactly is a product? A very simple definition is that a *product* is something that can be acquired via exchange to satisfy a need or a want. This definition permits us to classify a broad number of "things" as products:[14]

- **Goods** Goods are tangible items ranging from canned food to fighter jets, from sports memorabilia to used clothing. The marketing of tangible goods is arguably one of the most widely recognizable business activities in the world.

- **Services** Services are intangible products consisting of acts or deeds directed toward people or their possessions. Banks, hospitals, lawyers, package-delivery companies, airlines, hotels, repair technicians, nannies, housekeepers, consultants, and taxi drivers all offer services. Services, rather than tangible goods, dominate modern economies like the U.S. economy.

- **Ideas** Ideas include platforms or issues aimed at promoting a benefit for the customer. Examples include cause-related or charitable organizations such as the Red Cross, the American Cancer Society, Mothers Against Drunk Drivers, or the American Legacy Foundation's campaign against smoking.[15]

- **Information** Marketers of information include websites, magazine and book publishers, schools and universities, research firms, churches, and charitable organizations. In the digital age, the production and distribution of information has become a vital part of our economy.

- **Digital Products** Digital products, such as software, music, and movies, are among the most profitable in our economy. Advancements in technology have also wreaked havoc in these industries because pirates can easily copy and redistribute digital products in violation of copyright law. Digital products are interesting because content producers grant customers a license to use them, rather than outright ownership.

- **People** The individual promotion of people, such as athletes or celebrities, is a huge business around the world. The exchange and trading of professional athletes takes place in a complex system of drafts, contracts, and free agency. Other professions, such as politicians, actors, professional speakers, and news reporters, also engage in people marketing.

- **Places** When we think of the marketing of a place, we usually think of vacation destinations like Rome or Orlando. However, the marketing of places is quite diverse. Cities, states, and nations all market themselves to tourists, businesses, and potential residents. The state of Alabama, for example, has done quite well in attracting direct investment by foreign firms. Over the last decade, Alabama has landed assembly plants from Mercedes, Honda, and Hyundai, as well as many different parts plants and related firms. It's no wonder that some people think of Alabama as the new Detroit.[16]

- **Experiences and Events** Marketers can bring together a combination of goods, services, ideas, information, or people to create one-of-a-kind experiences or single events. Good examples include theme parks such as Disney World and Universal Studios, athletic events like the Olympics or the Super Bowl, or stage and musical performances like *The Phantom of the Opera* or a concert by Madonna.

- **Real or Financial Property** The exchange of stocks, bonds, and real estate, once marketed completely offline via real estate agents and investment companies, now occurs increasingly online. For example, Realtor.com is the nation's largest real estate listing service, with over 2.5 million searchable listings. Likewise, Schwab.com is the world's largest and top-rated online brokerage.

- **Organizations** Virtually all organizations strive to create favorable images with the public—not only to increase sales or inquiries but also to generate customer goodwill. In this sense, General Electric is no different than the United Way: Both seek to enhance their images in order to attract more people (customers, volunteers, and clients) and money (sales, profit, and donations).

We should note that the products in this list are not mutually exclusive. For example, firms that sell tangible goods almost always sell services to supplement their offerings, and vice versa. Charitable organizations simultaneously market themselves, their ideas, and the information that they provide. Finally, special events, like the Daytona 500, combine people (drivers), a place (Daytona), an event (the race), organizations (sponsors), and goods (souvenirs) to create a memorable and unique experience for race fans.

 To effectively meet the needs of their customers and fulfill organizational objectives, marketers must be astute in creating products and combining them in ways that make them unique from other product offerings. Customers' decisions to purchase one product or group of products over another is primarily a function of how well that choice will fulfill their needs and satisfy their wants. Economists use the term *utility* to describe the ability of a product to satisfy a customer's desires. Customers usually seek out exchanges with marketers who offer products that are high in one or more of these five types of utility:

- **Form Utility** Products high in form utility have attributes or features that set them apart from the competition. Often these differences result from the use of high-quality raw materials, ingredients, or components or from the use of highly efficient production processes. For example, Ruth's Chris Steakhouse, considered by many to be one of the nation's top restaurants, provides higher form utility than other national chains because of the quality of beef they use. Papa John's Pizza even stresses form utility in its slogan "Better Ingredients. Better Pizza." In many product categories, higher-priced product lines offer more form utility because they have more features or "bells-and-whistles." Cars are a good example.

- **Time Utility**   Products high in time utility are available when customers want them. Typically, this means that products are available now rather than later. Grocery stores, restaurants, and other retailers that are open around the clock provide exceptional time utility. Often the most successful restaurants around college campuses are those that are open 24/7. Many customers are also willing to pay more for products available in a shorter time frame (such as overnight delivery via Federal Express) or for products available at the most convenient times (such as midmorning airline flights).

- **Place Utility**   Products high in place utility are available where customers want them, which is typically wherever the customer happens to be at that moment (such as grocery delivery to a home) or where the product needs to be at that moment (such as florist delivery to a workplace). Home delivery of anything (especially pizza), convenience stores, vending machines, and e-commerce are examples of good place utility. Products that are high in both time and place utility are exceptionally valuable to customers because they provide the utmost in convenience.

- **Possession Utility**   Possession utility deals with the transfer of ownership or title from marketer to customer. Products higher in possession utility are more satisfying because marketers make them easier to acquire. Marketers often combine supplemental services with tangible goods to increase possession utility. For example, furniture stores that offer easy credit terms and home delivery enhance the possession utility of their goods. In fact, any merchant that accepts credit cards enhances possession utility for customers who do not carry cash or checks. Expensive products, like a home or a new factory, require acceptable financing arrangements to complete the exchange process.

- **Psychological Utility**   Products high in psychological utility deliver positive experiential or psychological attributes that customers find satisfying. Sporting events often fall into this category, especially when the competition is based on an intense rivalry. The atmosphere, energy, and excitement associated with being at the game can all create psychological benefits for customers. Conversely, a product might offer exceptional psychological utility because it lacks negative experiential or psychological attributes. For example, a vacation to the beach or the mountains might offer more psychological

utility to some customers because it is seen as less stressful than a vacation to Disney World.

The strategic and tactical planning of marketing activities involves the important basic concepts that we have explored in this section. Marketers often struggle with finding and reaching the appropriate markets for their products. In other cases, the market is easily accessible, but the product is wrong or does not offer customers a compelling reason to purchase it. The ability to match markets and products in a way that satisfies both customer and organizational objectives is truly an art and a science. Doing so in an environment of never-ending change creates both opportunities and challenges for even the strongest and most respected organizations.

The process of planning marketing activities to achieve these ends is the focus of this book. As we turn our attention to an overview of major marketing activities and decisions, we also want to lay out the structure of the text. The chapters roughly coincide with the major activities involved in developing marketing strategy and writing a marketing plan. Although our approach is orderly and straightforward, it provides a holistic representation of the marketing planning process from one period to the next. As we will see, marketing planning is an evolving process that has no definite beginning or ending point.

Major Marketing Activities and Decisions

Organizations must deal with a number of activities and decisions in marketing their products to customers. These activities vary in both complexity and scope. Whether the issue is a local restaurant's change in copy for a newspaper ad or a large multinational firm launching a new product in a foreign market, all marketing activities have one thing in common: They aim to give customers a reason to buy the organization's product. In this section, we briefly introduce the activities and decisions that will be the focus of the remaining chapters of this book.

Strategic Planning

If an organization is to have any chance of reaching its goals and objectives, it must have a game plan or road map for getting there. A *strategy*, in effect, outlines the organization's game plan for success. Effective marketing requires sound strategic planning at a number of levels in an organization. At the top levels of the organization, planners concern themselves with macro issues such as the corporate mission, management of the mix of strategic business units, resource acquisition and assignments, and corporate policy decisions. Planners at the middle levels, typically a division or strategic business unit, concern themselves with similar issues but focus on those that pertain to their particular product/market. Strategic planning at the lower levels of an organization is much more tactical in nature. Here, planners concern themselves with the development of marketing plans—more specific game plans for connecting products and markets in ways that satisfy both organizational and customer objectives.

Although this book is essentially about strategic planning, it focuses on tactical planning and the development of the marketing plan. *Tactical planning* concerns itself with specific markets or market segments and the development of marketing programs that will fulfill the needs of customers in those markets. The *marketing plan* provides the outline for how the organization will combine product, pricing, distribution, and promotion decisions to create an offering that customers will find attractive. The marketing plan also concerns itself with the implementation, control, and refinement of these decisions.

To stand a reasonable chance for success, marketing plans should be developed with a keen appreciation of how they fit into the strategic plans of the middle- and upper-levels of the firm. In Chapter 2, we discuss the connection among corporate, business-unit, and marketing planning, as well as how marketing plans must be integrated with the plans of other functions in the organization (financial plans, production plans, and others). We also discuss the structure of the marketing plan and some of the challenges involved in creating one.

Social Responsibility and Ethics

The role of social responsibility and ethics in marketing strategy has come to the forefront of important business issues in today's economy. Our society still reverberates from the effects of corporate scandals at Enron, WorldCom, and ImClone, among others. Although these scandals make for interesting reading, many innocent individuals have suffered the consequences from these companies' unethical behavior. *Social responsibility* refers to an organization's obligation to maximize its positive impact on society while minimizing its negative impact. In terms of marketing strategy, social responsibility addresses the total effect of an organization's marketing activities on society. A major part of this responsibility is *marketing ethics,* or the principles and standards that define acceptable conduct in marketing activities. Ethical marketing can build trust and commitment and is a crucial ingredient in building long-term relationships with all stakeholders. Another major component of any firm's impact on society is the degree to which it engages in philanthropic activities. Many firms now make philanthropy a key strategic activity.

In Chapter 3, we discuss the economic, legal, ethical, and philanthropic dimensions of social responsibility, along with the strategic management of corporate integrity in the marketing planning process. Although there are occasional lapses, most firms understand their economic and legal responsibilities. However, ethical responsibilities, by their nature, are not so clearly understood. Consequently, ethical lapses can be quite damaging. For example, consumers and privacy advocates were appalled to learn that many Sony BMG music CDs installed DRM (digital rights management) software on the hard drives of many unsuspecting computer users.[17] When a user played one of these CDs, the software installed itself as a root kit, thereby making itself undetectable. The software connected with Sony's computers, thus allowing Sony to track the user's CD usage. Sony is still reeling from the financial and brand image fallout from this decision.

Research and Analysis

Strategic planning depends heavily on the availability and interpretation of information. Without this lifeblood, strategic planning would be a mindless exercise and a waste of time. Thankfully, today's planners are blessed with an abundance of information due to improving technology and the Internet. However, the challenge of finding and analyzing the right information remains. As many marketing planners have found, having the right information is just as important as having the right product.

Marketers are accustomed to conducting and analyzing research, particularly with respect to the needs, opinions, and attitudes of their customers. Although customer analysis is vital to the success of the marketing plan, the organization must also have access to three other types of information and analysis: internal analysis, competitive analysis, and environmental analysis. *Internal analysis* involves the objective review of internal information pertaining to the firm's current strategy and performance, as well as the current and future availability of resources. Analysis of the competitive environment, increasingly known as *competitive intelligence,* involves analyzing the capabilities, vulnerabilities, and intentions of competing businesses.[18] Analysis of the external environment, also known as *environmental scanning,* involves the analysis of economic, political, legal, technological, and cultural events and trends that may affect the future of the organization and its marketing efforts. Some marketing planners use the term *situation analysis* to refer to the overall process of collecting and interpreting internal, competitive, and environmental information.

The development of a sound marketing plan requires the analysis of information on all fronts. In Chapter 4, we address the collection and analysis of internal, customer, competitive, and environmental information. We also discuss the challenges involved in finding the right information from an overwhelming supply of available information. The uncertainty and continual change in the external environment also create challenges for marketers (as the Internet boom and bust have shown us). As we will see, this type of research and analysis is perhaps the most difficult aspect of developing a marketing plan.

Developing Competitive Advantage

To be successful, a firm must possess one or more competitive advantages that it can leverage in the market in order to meet its objectives. A *competitive advantage* is something that the firm does better than its competitors and gives it an edge in serving customers' needs and/or maintaining mutually satisfying relationships with important stakeholders. Competitive advantages are critical because they set the tone, or strategic focus, of the entire marketing program. When these advantages are tied to market opportunities, the firm can offer customers a compelling reason to buy their products. Without a competitive advantage, the firm and its products are likely to be just one more offering among a sea of commoditized products. Southwest Airlines, for example, maintains a cost-based competitive advantage over its rivals due to its no-frills strategy of high efficiency, limited routes, a uniform fleet of airplanes, online reservation system, low pricing, and dedicated people. Southwest's marketing strategy has allowed the company to remain profitable for over 32 years. Southwest is also the only air carrier to remain consistently profitable since the September 11, 2001 terrorist attacks.[19]

In Chapter 5, we discuss the process of developing competitive advantages and establishing a strategic focus for the marketing program. We also address the role of SWOT analysis as a means of tying the firm's strengths or internal capabilities to market opportunities. Further, we discuss the importance of developing goals and objectives. Having good goals and objectives is vital because these become the basis for measuring the success of the entire marketing program. For example, Hampton Inn has a goal of 100 percent customer satisfaction. Customers do not have to pay for their stay if they don't have complete satisfaction.[20] Goals like these are useful in not only setting milestones for evaluating marketing performance but also motivating managers and employees. This can be especially true when marketing goals or objectives help drive employee evaluation and compensation programs.

Marketing Strategy Decisions

An organization's marketing strategy describes how the firm will fulfill the needs and wants of its customers. It can also include activities associated with maintaining relationships with other stakeholders such as employees or supply chain partners. Stated another way, marketing strategy is a plan for how the organization will use its strengths and capabilities to match the needs and requirements of the market. A marketing strategy can be composed of one or more marketing programs; each program consists of two elements—a target market or markets and a marketing mix (sometimes known as the four Ps of product, price, place, and promotion). To develop a marketing strategy, an organization must select the right combination of target market(s) and marketing mix(es) in order to create distinct competitive advantages over its rivals.

Market Segmentation and Target Marketing   The identification and selection of one or more target markets is the result of the market segmentation process. Marketers engage in *market segmentation* when they divide the total market into smaller, relatively homogeneous groups or segments that share similar needs, wants, or characteristics. When marketers select one or more *target markets,* they identify one or more segments of individuals, businesses, or institutions toward which the firm's marketing efforts will be directed. As described in Beyond the Pages 1.2, marketers increasingly use online social networking as a way to target the lucrative youth market.

Advances in technology have created some interesting changes in the ways that organizations segment and target markets. Marketers can now analyze customer-buying patterns in real time at the point of purchase via barcode or RFID (radio-frequency identification) scanning in retail stores and analyzing clickstream data in online transactions. This allows organizations to target specific segments with product offers or

Beyond the Pages 1.2

TARGETING YOUNG CONSUMERS VIA ONLINE SOCIAL NETWORKING[21]

Social networking sites on the Internet have proved to be very popular with both users and advertisers. Sites like MySpace.com and Facebook.com allow users to "hang out" in an online equivalent of shopping malls, parking lots, and bars. Most users are teens and young adults who use the sites to trade messages, photos, music, and blogs. The largest and most profitable of these sites currently is MySpace, which was acquired by News Corp. in 2005 for $580 million. Other sites like Facebook and LinkedIn are also busy and profitable.

Although social networks are very popular, they have attracted a fair amount of criticism. Many argue that these sites make it easier for predators to reach teens and children through the use of their online profiles. Business experts have been skeptical of the long-term success of social networking as a business model. They argue that younger audiences are fickle and will leave these sites for the next hot thing on the Internet. Others argue that the questionable nature of the content on these sites is a risky proposition when tied to advertising strategies.

Despite these criticisms, online social networking appears to have legs for the long term—forcing media companies and advertisers to take notice. The reason is simple: the demographic profile of the social networking audience is extremely lucrative. MySpace alone reaches over 70 million registered users, mostly in the 12- to 17-year-old age range. Power like that has forced an increasing number of advertisers to consider social networking as a viable media strategy. Target, NBC, Procter & Gamble, Viacom, and Geffen A&M Records are only some of the firms that have run ad campaigns on MySpace.

In addition to the demographic bonanza, social networking also allows firms to carefully target promotions to the right audience and collect a striking amount of information about users. For example, Procter & Gamble launched Secret Sparkle to 16- to 24-year-old girls and women using MySpace. These users were not only exposed to ads for the product but also allowed to participate in a Secret Sparkle sweepstakes. Volkswagen also used MySpace as a part of its "Unpimp Your Auto" campaign for the GTI. The campaign featured Helga, a blond bombshell, and Wolfgang, a German engineer, who both maintained profiles on MySpace. More than 7,500 fans signed up as Helga's friends.

Though the future of social networking sites looks promising, the protection of minor children remains a nagging issue. In early 2006, MySpace began taking aggressive steps to ensure the safety of children, including hiring a former federal prosecutor as its first chief security officer. MySpace and other social networking sites must find a balance between security and free expression. If these firms tighten up too much, users will leave and so will advertisers.

promotional messages.[22] Furthermore, technology now gives marketers the ability to target individual customers through direct mail and e-mail campaigns. This saves considerable time and expense by not wasting efforts on potential customers who may not be interested in the organization's product offering. However, these new opportunities for marketers come at a price: Many potential buyers resent the ability of marketers to reach them individually. Consequently, customers and government authorities have raised major concerns over privacy and confidentiality. This is especially true with respect to RFID, which uses tiny radio-enabled chips to track merchandise. Because RFID chips can be scanned from distances up to 25 feet, many fear that the technology will allow companies to track consumers even after they leave a store.[23]

Chapter 6 discusses the issues and strategies associated with market segmentation and target marketing. In that discussion, we will examine different approaches to market segmentation and look at target marketing in both consumer and business markets. Effective segmentation and target marketing sets the stage for the development of the product offering and the design of a marketing program that can effectively deliver the offering to targeted customers.

Product Decisions   Earlier in the chapter, we discussed the many different types of products that can be offered to customers today. As one of the basic parts of marketing, the product and the decisions that surround it are among the most important aspects of marketing strategy. This importance hinges on the connection between the product and the customers' needs. Even large corporations fail to make this connection at times. McDonald's, for example, spent over $100 million in the mid-1990s to launch the Arch Deluxe—a hamburger designed for adult tastes. The product failed miserably because it was designed for older customers (not the children who are McDonald's core market), was expensive, and had a very high-calorie content. McDonald's customers avoided the Arch Deluxe, and the sandwich was eventually discontinued.[24] As this example illustrates, marketing is unlikely to be effective unless there is a solid linkage between a product's benefits and customers' needs.

In Chapter 7, we will discuss the decisions that marketers make about products and their total product offering. Product decisions include much more than issues regarding design, style, or features. Marketers must also make decisions regarding package design, branding, trademarks, warranties, new product development, and product positioning. *Product positioning* involves establishing a mental image, or position, of the product offering relative to competing offerings in the minds of target buyers. The goal of positioning is to distinguish or differentiate the firm's product offering from those of competitors by making the offering stand out among the crowd. For example, the mental image that most customers have about Wal-Mart is associated with everyday low prices. Target has a slightly different position, one that emphasizes value with a stronger sense of style and quality.

Pricing Decisions   Pricing decisions are important for several reasons. First, price is the only element of the marketing mix that leads to revenue and profit. All other elements of the marketing mix, such as product development and promotion, represent expenses. Second, price typically has a direct connection with customer demand. This connection makes pricing the most overmanipulated element of the marketing mix. Marketers routinely adjust the price of their products in an effort to stimulate or curb demand. Third, pricing is the easiest element of the marketing program to change. Very few other aspects of marketing can be altered in real time. This is a huge plus for marketers who need to adjust prices to reflect local market conditions or for online merchants who want to charge different prices for different customers based on total sales or customer loyalty. Finally, pricing is a major quality cue for customers. In the absence of other information, customers tend to equate higher prices with higher quality.

Pricing decisions are the subject of Chapter 8, where we will discuss buyer and seller perspectives on pricing, pricing objectives, the issue of price elasticity, and strategies for setting profitable and justifiable prices. One of the reasons that pricing is so interesting is that price represents a major point in marketing strategy where buyer and seller motivations come into conflict. Although other elements of the marketing mix are relatively stable, the price can be negotiated. The ease with which buyers can compare prices among competing firms today makes setting the right price even more challenging for marketers.

Distribution and Supply Chain Decisions   Distribution and supply chain issues are among the least apparent decisions made in marketing, particularly with customers. The goal of *distribution and supply chain management* is essentially to get the product to the right place, at the right time, in the right quantities, at the lowest possible cost. *Supply chain* decisions involve a long line of activities—from the sourcing of raw materials, through the production of finished products, to ultimate delivery to final customers. Most of these activities, which customers take for granted, take place behind the scenes. Few customers, for example, contemplate how their favorite cereal ends up on their grocer's shelf or how Dell can have a made-to-order laptop at your door in days. Customers just expect these things to happen. In fact, most customers never consider these issues until something goes wrong. Suddenly, when the grocer is out of an item or an assembly line runs low on component parts, distribution and supply chain factors become quite noticeable.

As we will discuss in Chapter 9, distribution and supply chain issues are critical for two major reasons: product availability and distribution costs. The importance of product availability is obvious; customers cannot buy your product if it is not available at the right time and place or in the right quantities. Distribution decisions are therefore closely connected to the issues of time, place, and possession utility that we discussed earlier in the chapter. The importance of distribution costs is tied to the firm's profit margin. No matter how you look at it, distribution is expensive. As a result, firms that take the time to build highly efficient and effective distribution systems can lower their operating costs and create a competitive advantage against rival firms. For large companies, even a fractional decrease in costs can lead to big increases in profits.

Promotion Decisions   Modern marketing has replaced the term *promotion* with the concept of *integrated marketing communication* (IMC), or the coordination of all promotional activities (media advertising, direct mail, personal selling, sales promotion, public relations, packaging, store displays, website design, personnel) to produce a unified, customer-focused message. Here, the term *customers* not only refers to customers in the traditional sense but also includes employees, business partners, shareholders, the government, the media, and society in general. IMC rose to prominence in the 1990s as businesses realized that traditional audiences for promotional efforts had become more diverse and fragmented. IMC can also reduce promotional expenses by eliminating the duplication of effort among separate departments (marketing, sales, advertising, public affairs, and information technology) and by increasing efficiencies and economies of scale.

As we will see in Chapter 10, the goals of IMC are the same as traditional promotion—namely, to inform, persuade, and remind customers (that is, all stakeholders) about the organization and its product offerings so as to influence their behavior. Promotional decisions are the most noticeable and among the most expensive of all marketing activities. In today's society, it is virtually impossible to not be exposed to promotional messages. Some of these messages, like Nike's "Just Do It," have become ingrained into modern culture. However, even a good message cannot overcome poor decisions regarding other marketing program elements.

Implementation and Control

Once a marketing strategy has been selected and the elements of the marketing mix are in place, the marketer must put the plan into action. *Marketing implementation,* the process of executing the marketing strategy, is the "how" of marketing planning. Rather than being an add-on at the end of the marketing strategy and marketing plan, implementation is actually a part of planning itself. That is, when planning a marketing strategy, the organization must always consider how the strategy will be executed. Sometimes, the organization must revisit the strategy or plan to make revisions during the strategy's execution. This is where marketing control comes into play. Adequate control of marketing activities is essential to ensure that the strategy stays on course and focused on achieving its goals and objectives.

The implementation phase of marketing strategy calls into play the fifth P of the marketing program: people. As we will learn in Chapter 11, many of the problems that occur in implementing marketing activities are "people problems" associated with the managers and employees on the frontline of the organization who have responsibility for executing the marketing strategy. Many organizations understand the vital link between people and implementation by treating their employees as indispensable assets. Aflac, for example, has been named eight consecutive times by *Fortune* magazine to its list of the "100 Best Companies to Work for in America." The Georgia-based company has developed a corporate culture that focuses on caring for employees and providing for their needs.[25] Other companies cited as having good relationships with their employees include The Container Store, J.M. Smucker, and S.C. Johnson & Son.

Developing and Maintaining Customer Relationships

Over the last decade, marketers have come to the realization that they can learn more about their customers and earn higher profits if they develop long-term relationships with them. This requires that marketers shift away from transactional marketing and embrace a relationship marketing approach. The goal of *transactional marketing* is to complete a large number of discrete exchanges with individual customers. The focus is on acquiring customers and making the sale, not necessarily on attending to customers' needs and wants. In *relationship marketing,* the goal is to develop and maintain long-term, mutually satisfying arrangements where both buyer and seller focus on the value obtained from the relationship. As long as this value stays the same or increases, the relationship is likely to deepen and grow stronger over time. Exhibit 1.4 lists the basic characteristics of transactional versus relationship marketing. Relationship marketing promotes customer trust and confidence in the marketer, who can then develop a deeper understanding of

EXHIBIT 1.4	MAJOR CHARACTERISTICS OF TRANSACTIONAL AND RELATIONSHIP MARKETING	
	Transactional Marketing	Relationship Marketing
Marketing focus	Customer acquisition	Customer retention
Time orientation	Short term	Long term
Marketing goal	Make the sale	Mutual satisfaction
Relationship focus	Create exchanges	Create value
Customer service priority	Low	High
Customer contact	Low to moderate	Frequent
Commitment to customers	Low	High
Characteristics of the interaction	Adversarial, manipulation, conflict resolution	Cooperation, trust, mutual respect, confidence
Source of competitive advantage	Production, marketing	Relationship commitment

customers' needs and wants. This puts the marketer in a position to respond more effectively to customers' needs, thereby increasing the value of the relationship for both parties.

The principles and advantages of relationship marketing are the same in both business-to-business and consumer markets. Relationship marketing activities also extend beyond customers to include relationships with employees and supply chain partners. In Chapter 12, we will discuss these and other aspects of relationship marketing in greater depth. Long-term relationships with important stakeholders will not materialize unless these relationships create value for each participant. This is especially true for customers faced with many different alternatives among firms competing for their business. Because the quality and value of a marketer's product offering typically determine customer value and satisfaction, Chapter 12 will also explore the role of quality, value, and satisfaction in developing and maintaining customer relationships. Issues associated with quality, value, and satisfaction cut across all elements of the marketing program. Hence, we discuss these issues in our final chapter as a means of tying all marketing program elements together.

Taking on the Challenges of Marketing Strategy

One of the greatest frustrations and opportunities in marketing is change—customers change, competitors change, and even the marketing organization changes. Strategies that are highly successful today will not work tomorrow. Customers will buy products today that they will have no interest in tomorrow. These are truisms in marketing. Although frustrating, challenges like these also make marketing extremely interesting and rewarding. Life as a marketer is never dull.

Another fact about marketing strategy is that it is inherently people driven. Marketing strategy is about people (inside an organization) trying to find ways to deliver exceptional value by fulfilling the needs and wants of other people (customers, shareholders, business partners, society at large), as well as the needs of the organization itself. Marketing strategy draws from psychology, sociology, and economics to better understand the basic needs and motivations of these people—whether they are the organization's customers (typically considered the most critical), its employees, or its stakeholders. In short, marketing strategy is about people serving people.

The combination of continual change and the people-driven nature of marketing makes developing and implementing marketing strategy a challenging task. A perfect strategy that is executed perfectly can still fail. This happens because there are very few rules for how to do marketing in specific situations. In other words, it is impossible to say that given "this customer need" and these "competitors" and this "level of government regulation" that Product A, Price B, Promotion C, and Distribution D should be used. Marketing simply doesn't work that way. Sometimes, an organization can get lucky and be successful despite having a terrible strategy and/or execution. The lack of rules and the ever-changing economic, sociocultural, competitive, technological, and political/legal landscapes make marketing strategy a terribly fascinating subject.

Most of the changes that marketers have faced over the past 20 years deal with the basic evolution of marketing and business practice in our society. One of the most basic shifts involves the increasing demands of customers. Today, customers have very high expectations about basic issues such as quality, performance, price, and availability. American customers in particular have a passion for instant gratification that marketers struggle to fulfill. Some evidence suggests that marketers have not met this challenge. The American Customer Satisfaction Index, computed by the National Quality Research Center at the University of Michigan, indicates that customer satisfaction has trended downward since the Center first computed the index in 1994. As shown in Exhibit 1.5, some industries such as newspapers and airlines have suffered large declines in customer satisfaction. Satisfaction in other industries, such as the automotive industry, has remained fairly high and stable.

The decline in satisfaction can be attributed to several reasons. For one, customers have become much less brand loyal than in previous generations. Today's customers are very price sensitive, especially in commoditized markets where products lack any real means of differentiation. Consequently, customers constantly seek the best value and thrive on their ability to compare prices among competing alternatives. Customers are also quite cynical about business in general and are not that trusting of marketers. In short, today's customers have not only more power but also more attitude. This combination makes them a formidable force in the development of contemporary marketing strategy.

Marketers have also been forced to adapt to shifts in markets and competition. In terms of their life cycles, most products compete today in very mature markets. Many firms also compete in markets where product offerings have become commoditized by a lack of differentiation (for example, customers perceive competing offerings as essentially the same). Some examples include airlines, wireless phone service, department stores, laundry supplies, and household appliances. Product commoditization

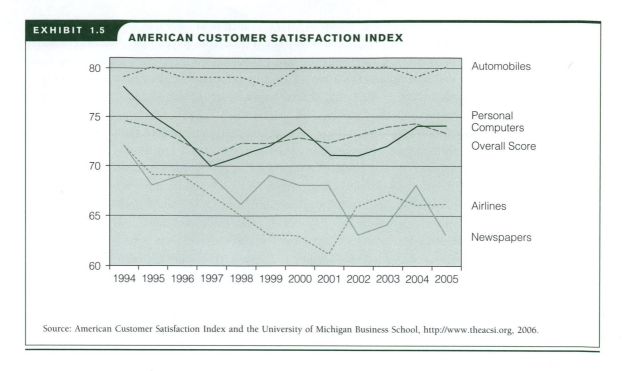

EXHIBIT 1.5

AMERICAN CUSTOMER SATISFACTION INDEX

Automobiles

Personal Computers

Overall Score

Airlines

Newspapers

Source: American Customer Satisfaction Index and the University of Michigan Business School, http://www.theacsi.org, 2006.

pushes margins lower and reduces brand loyalty even further. To meet this challenge, U.S. firms have moved aggressively into foreign markets in an effort to increase sales and find new growth opportunities. At the same time, however, foreign firms have moved into U.S. markets to meet the challenges of maturing markets in their own countries. It is interesting to watch Wal-Mart move aggressively into China while British retailer Tesco launches a chain of large convenience stores in California.[26] The end result of these changes is that firms around the globe face new competition and new challenges.

In the face of increasing competition and maturing markets, businesses have been forced to cut expenses to remain competitive. Some businesses do this by eliminating products or product lines, such as when GM recently dropped the Hummer H1. Others have maintained their product mix but have aggressively sought ways to lower their distribution costs. The growth in direct distribution (manufacturer to end user) is a result of these efforts. Still, other firms have been forced to take drastic measures such as downsizing and laying off employees to trim expenses. Fortunately, the news is not all gloomy. Firms have found that success often comes from aggressive cooperation rather than competition. Today, businesses have formed alliances and partnerships at a record pace. For example, many considered the 2001 service agreement between Federal Express (FedEx) and the U.S. Postal Service a triumph in the extremely competitive package-delivery market. Under the agreement, FedEx placed drop boxes in post offices, while the postal service turned its Express Mail service over to FedEx.[27] Recent agreements between U.S. automakers to produce alternative-fuel vehicles (AFVs) are also a testament to this booming trend.

Developing a viable and effective marketing strategy has become extremely challenging. Even the most admired marketers in the world like McDonald's, Procter & Gamble, Anheuser-Busch, and Toyota occasionally have problems meeting the demands of the strategic planning process and developing the "right" marketing strategy. Our goal in this book is not to teach you to develop the "right" strategy. Rather, our approach will give you a framework for organizing the planning process and the ability to see how all of the pieces fit together. Think of it as a mind-set or way to think about marketing strategy. The remainder of this text dedicates itself to these goals.

Lessons from Chapter 1

Marketing challenges and opportunities in the new economy include

- a shift in power to customers caused by increased access to information.

- a massive increase in product selection due to line extensions and global sourcing.

- greater audience and media fragmentation as customers spend more time with interactive media and less time with traditional media.

- changing customer perceptions of value and demands for greater convenience.

- shifting demand patterns for certain product categories, especially those delivered electronically.

- new sources of competitive advantage such as partnerships and alliances.

- new concerns over privacy, security, and ethics.

- unclear legal jurisdictions, especially in global markets.

Marketing

- is parallel to other business functions such as production, research, management, human resources, and accounting. The goal of marketing is to connect the organization to its customers.

- is defined as an organizational function and a set of processes for creating, communicating, and delivering value to customers and for managing customer relationships in ways that benefit the organization and its stakeholders.

- has changed in focus over the past 20 years. Today, marketing stresses value and customer relationships.

- is linked with our standard of living not only in terms of enhanced consumption and prosperity but also in terms of society's well-being.

Basic marketing concepts include

- market—a collection of buyers and sellers.

- marketplace—a physical location where buyers and sellers meet to conduct transactions.

- marketspace—an electronic marketplace not bound by time or space.

- metamarket—a cluster of closely related goods and services that centers around a specific consumption activity.

- metamediary—a single access point where buyers can locate and contact many different sellers in the metamarket.

- exchange—the process of obtaining something of value from someone by offering something in return; this usually involves obtaining products for money. There are five conditions of exchange:

  1. There must be at least two parties to the exchange.
  2. Each party has something of value to the other party.
  3. Each party must be capable of communication and delivery.
  4. Each party must be free to accept or reject the exchange.
  5. Each party believes that it is desirable to exchange with the other party.

- product—something that can be acquired via exchange to satisfy a need or a want.

- utility—the ability of a product to satisfy a customer's needs and wants. The five types of utility provided through marketing exchanges are form utility, time utility, place utility, possession utility, and psychological utility.

Major marketing activities and decisions include

- strategic and tactical planning.

- social responsibility and ethics.

- research and analysis.

- developing competitive advantages and a strategic focus for the marketing program.

- marketing strategy decisions, including decisions related to market segmentation and target marketing, the product, pricing, distribution, and promotion, which will create competitive advantages over rival firms.

- implementing and controlling marketing activities.

- developing and maintaining long-term customer relationships, including a shift from transactional marketing to relationship marketing.

Some of the challenges involved in developing marketing strategy include

- unending change—customers change, competitors change, and even the marketing organization changes.

- the fact that marketing is inherently people driven.

- the lack of rules for choosing appropriate marketing activities.

- the basic evolution of marketing and business practice in our society.

- the increasing demands of customers.

- an overall decline in brand loyalty and an increase in price sensitivity among customers.

- increasing customer cynicism about business and marketing activities.

- competing in mature markets with increasing commoditization and little real differentiation among product offerings.

- increasing expansion into foreign markets by U.S. and foreign firms.

- aggressive cost-cutting measures in order to increase competitiveness.

- increasing cooperation with supply chain partners and competitors.

Questions for Discussion

1. Increasing customer power is a continuing challenge to marketers in today's economy. In what ways have you personally experienced this shift in power; either as a customer or as a businessperson? Is this power shift uniform across industries and markets? How so?

2. How concerned are you about privacy and security in today's economy? Are you more concerned about online security or about the potential ramifications of RFID technology? Will these issues still be important in 10 years? Explain.

3. The text argues that marketing possesses very few rules for choosing the appropriate marketing activities. Can you describe any universal rules of marketing that might be applied to most products, markets, customers, and situations?

Exercises

1. The pace of change in our economy was frenetic from 1999 to 2001 (the so called dot-com boom). Shortly thereafter, the bubble burst and the boom collapsed. Perform some research to discover the reasons for this collapse. Are there signs that the same thing is happening again today? If so, what are they? How can firms prevent another collapse?

2. Log on to a metamediary in the automobile metamarket (for example, http://www.edmunds.com, http://www.autos.msn.com, or http://www.carsdirect.com). What aspects of the car buying experience does the metamediary offer? Which aspects of the experience are missing? How does the metamediary overcome these missing aspects?

3. Think about all of the exchanges that you participate in on a weekly or monthly basis. How many of these exchanges have their basis in long-term relationships? How many are simple transaction-based exchanges? Which do you find most satisfying? Why?

CHAPTER 2

Strategic Marketing Planning

Introduction

The process of strategic marketing planning can be either complex or relatively straightforward. As evidenced in Beyond the Pages 2.1, strategic planning for a multinational corporation like General Motors, with its multiple divisions and business units, is more intricate than planning the marketing strategy of a sole-proprietorship. Although the issues differ, the planning process is the same in many ways. Ultimately, the goals and objectives can be similar. Large or small, all marketers strive to meet the needs of their customers while meeting their own business and marketing objectives.

One way to think about the marketing planning process is to picture it as a funnel.[1] At the top are important corporate decisions dealing with the firm's mission, vision, goals, and the allocation of resources among business units. Planning at this level also involves decisions regarding the purchase or divestment of the business units themselves. Procter & Gamble's acquisition of Gillette is a good example of the decision-making complexity that is often typical of major corporate decisions. These decisions trickle down the funnel to the business-unit level where planning focuses on meeting goals and objectives within defined product markets. Planning at this level must take into account and be consistent with decisions made at the corporate level. However, in organizations having only one business unit, corporate and business-unit strategy are the same. The most specific planning and decision making occurs at the bottom of the funnel. It is at this level where organizations make and implement tactical decisions regarding marketing strategy (target markets and the marketing mix) as well as marketing plans.

In this chapter, we examine the planning process at different points in this process. We begin by discussing the overall process by considering the hierarchy of decisions that must be made in strategic marketing planning. Next, we introduce the marketing plan and look at the marketing plan framework used throughout the text. We also discuss the role and importance of the marketing plan in marketing strategy.

Beyond the Pages 2.1

GM'S NEW STRATEGY[2]

After years of dismal sales, financial losses, and market losses to Japanese automakers, General Motors (GM) in 2006 began taking bold moves to restructure its operating philosophy. CEO Richard Wagoner, the architect of GM's new strategy, had to do something to stop the bleeding. GM was losing just under $11 billion per year. Its parts supplier, Delphi, was going through bankruptcy reorganization. And, GM's U.S. market share had fallen 1 percent as car buyers began to shy away from GM products, fearing that the company was headed for its own day in bankruptcy court.

Wagoner's plan has two fronts: aggressive cost cutting and new auto designs. Cost cutting is not new to GM. However, years of downsizing were not enough to solve GM's problems. One of the biggest reasons is GM's bloated $5.3 billion retirement program. So many former GM employees are supported on the program that each active GM employee supports 3.2 retirees and spouses. Overall, the retirement program costs GM roughly $1,500 per vehicle—an amount that quickly cancels out profit on most models.

Wagoner's tactic is to shrink GM to a market defensible size until 2010 when retiree costs will drop as more of them qualify for Social Security and Medicare. To get to that point, GM is closing twelve factories, cutting 30,000 jobs, and offering buyout packages to its entire North American workforce. To raise cash, GM plans to sell a 51 percent controlling interest in its GMAC financing division to Cerberus Capital for $14.1 billion. The sale of GMAC is widely criticized because it has been the main source of GM's revenue for decades. In total, GM's cost-cutting moves are expected to result in a net income of $1.6 billion in 2007.

GM's new strategy also involves new auto designs. GM recently adopted Toyota's strategy of globalization whereby parts, platforms, and production are synchronized around the world. These changes, along with a new development and design team, have lead to more Asian- and European-designed cars appearing in U.S. showrooms. Some recent winning designs include the Saturn Aura and Sky, the redesigned Chevy Tahoe, the Buick Lucerne, the Chevy Equinox and HHR, and many Cadillac offerings. GM will also drop some of its seventy models, including the original Hummer H1. However, GM remains hesitant to trim less successful brands. In particular, many investors are pushing GM to drop its Pontiac division entirely, as the company did with its Oldsmobile division several years ago.

So far, Wagoner's strategy is working. The company reported a $445 million profit in the first quarter of 2006—pushing GM's stock price up more than 32 percent. However, two major issues worry many at GM: oil prices and labor relations. GM will have to renegotiate its master contract with the United Auto Workers when the current contract expires in September 2007. To put GM on more secure financial footing, Wagoner needs significant union concessions. Despite these looming issues, Wagoner and industry analysts are cautiously optimistic. And for now at least, Wall Street has stopped using the "B" word when it discusses GM's future.

Finally, we explore recent developments in strategic planning such as the balanced-performance scorecard.

The Strategic Planning Process

Whether at the corporate, business-unit, or functional level, the planning process begins with an in-depth analysis of the organization's internal and external environments— sometimes referred to as a *situation analysis*. As we will discuss in Chapter 4, this analysis focuses on the firm's resources, strengths, and capabilities vis-à-vis competitive, customer, and environmental issues. Based on an exhaustive review of these relevant environmental issues, the firm establishes its mission, goals, and/or objectives; its

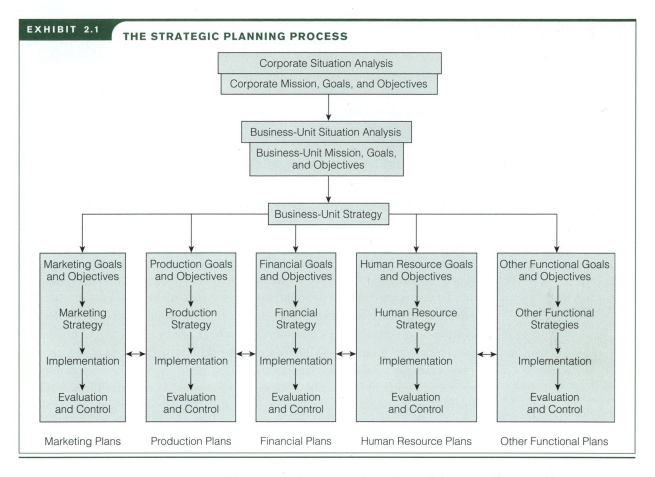

EXHIBIT 2.1

THE STRATEGIC PLANNING PROCESS

Corporate Situation Analysis

Corporate Mission, Goals, and Objectives

Business-Unit Situation Analysis

Business-Unit Mission, Goals, and Objectives

Business-Unit Strategy

Marketing Goals and Objectives	Production Goals and Objectives	Financial Goals and Objectives	Human Resource Goals and Objectives	Other Functional Goals and Objectives
Marketing Strategy	Production Strategy	Financial Strategy	Human Resource Strategy	Other Functional Strategies
Implementation	Implementation	Implementation	Implementation	Implementation
Evaluation and Control	Evaluation and Control	Evaluation and Control	Evaluation and Control	Evaluation and Control
Marketing Plans	Production Plans	Financial Plans	Human Resource Plans	Other Functional Plans

strategy; and several functional plans. As indicated in Exhibit 2.1, planning efforts within each functional area will result in the creation of a strategic plan for that area. Although we emphasize the issues and processes concerned with developing a customer-oriented marketing strategy and marketing plan, we should stress that organizations develop effective marketing strategies and plans in concert with the organization's mission and goals, as well as the plans from other functional areas. Senior management must coordinate these functional plans in a manner that will achieve the organization's mission, goals, and objectives.

In this text, we are interested in a particular type of functional plan—the marketing plan. A *marketing plan* is a written document that provides the blueprint or outline of the organization's marketing activities, including the implementation, evaluation, and control of those activities. The marketing plan serves a number of purposes. For one, the marketing plan clearly explains how the organization will achieve its goals and objectives. This aspect of marketing planning is vital—not having goals and objectives is like driving a car without knowing your destination. In this sense, the marketing plan serves as the "road map" for implementing the marketing strategy. It instructs employees as to their roles and functions in fulfilling the plan. It also provides specifics regarding the allocation of resources and includes the specific marketing tasks, responsibilities of individuals, and the timing of all marketing activities.

Although our focus is on marketing planning and strategy, we cannot emphasize enough that marketing decisions must be made within the boundaries of the organization's overall mission, goals, and objectives. The sequencing of decision stages outlined in the following sections begins with broad decisions regarding the organizational mission, followed by a discussion of the corporate or business-unit strategy. It is within these contexts that marketing goals/objectives and marketing strategies must be developed and implemented.

Organizational Mission Versus Organizational Vision

To adequately address the role of the organizational mission in strategic planning, we must first understand the subtle differences between the organization's mission and its vision. A *mission*, or *mission statement*, seeks to answer the question "What business are we in?" It is a clear and concise statement (a paragraph or two at most) that explains the organization's reason for existence. By contrast, a *vision*, or *vision statement*, seeks to answer the question "What do we want to become?" For example, Pfizer—the world's largest research-based pharmaceutical company—defines its mission this way: "We dedicate ourselves to humanity's quest for longer, healthier, happier lives through innovation in pharmaceutical, consumer, and animal health products." Compare this to the company's vision: "We will become the world's most valued company to patients, customers, colleagues, investors, business partners, and the communities where we work and live."[3] Similarly, Google's mission is "to organize the world's information and make it universally accessible and useful." Google's vision is "Never settle for the best." Note that an organization's vision tends to be future oriented, in that it represents where the organization is headed and where it wants to go.

If you ask many businesspeople "What is your reason for existence?" their response is likely to be "To make money." Although that may be their ultimate objective, it is not their raison d'être. Profit has a role in this process, of course, but it is a goal or objective of the firm, not its mission or vision. The mission statement identifies what the firm stands for and its basic operating philosophy. Profit and other performance outcomes are ends and thus are out of place and tend to confuse the mission statement.

Elements of the Mission Statement   A well-devised mission statement for any organization, unit within an organization, or single-owner business should answer the same five basic questions. These questions should clarify for the firm's stakeholders (especially employees):

1. Who are we?

2. Who are our customers?

3. What is our operating philosophy (basic beliefs, values, ethics, and so on)?

4. What are our core competencies or competitive advantages?

5. What are our responsibilities with respect to being a good steward of our human, financial, and environmental resources?

A mission statement that delivers a clear answer to each of these questions installs the cornerstone for the development of the marketing plan. If the cornerstone is weak, or not in line with the foundation laid in the preliminary steps, the entire plan will have no real chance of long-term success. Exhibit 2.2 outlines several mission statements considered to be among the best. As you read these statements, consider how well they answer those five questions.

The mission statement is the one portion of the strategic plan that should not be kept confidential. It should tell everyone—customers, employees, investors, competitors, regulators, and society in general—what the firm stands for and why it exists. Mission statements facilitate public relations activities and communicate to customers and others important information that can be used to build trust and long-term relationships. The mission statement should be included in annual reports and major press releases, framed on the wall in every office, and personally owned by every employee of the organization. Goals, objectives, strategies, tactics, and budgets are not for public viewing. A mission statement kept secret, however, is of little value to the organization.

Mission Width and Stability   In crafting a mission statement, management should be concerned about the statement's width. If the mission is too broad, it will be meaningless to those who read and build upon it. A mission to "make all people happy around the world by providing them with entertaining products" sounds splendid but provides no useful information. Overly broad missions can lead companies to establish plans and strategies in areas where their strengths are limited. Such endeavors almost always result in failure. Exxon's past foray into office products and Sears' expansion into real estate and financial services serve as reminders of the problems associated with poorly designed mission statements. Although a well-designed mission statement should not stifle an organization's creativity, it must help keep the firm from moving too far from its core competencies.

Overly narrow mission statements that constrain the vision of the organization can prove just as costly. Early in the twentieth century, the railroads defined their business as owning and operating trains. Consequently, the railroad industry had no concerns about the invention of the airplane. After all, they thought, the ability to fly had nothing to do with trains or the railroad business. Today, we know that firms such as American Airlines, Southwest Airlines, and Federal Express, rather than Burlington, Union Pacific, or Santa Fe, dominate the passenger and time-sensitive freight business. The railroads missed this major opportunity because their missions were too narrowly tied to railroads, as opposed to a more appropriate definition encompassing the transportation business.

EXHIBIT 2.2   THE BEST MISSION STATEMENTS

In their book, *Say It and Live It: The 50 Corporate Mission Statements That Hit the Mark,* Patricia Jones and Larry Kahaner identify 50 companies that possess outstanding mission statements. This exhibit lists several of these companies, along with their 1995, 2000, and 2006 mission statements. Remember that these organizations customized their mission statements to fit their own needs and goals, not to match the criteria established in this chapter.

Boeing

1995   To be the number one aerospace company in the world and among the premier industrial concerns in terms of quality, profitability, and growth.

2000   Our mission is bigger and broader than ever. It is to push not just the envelope of flight, but the entire envelope of value relating to our customers and shareholders.

2006   People working together as a global enterprise for aerospace leadership.

Leo Burnett

1995   The mission of the Leo Burnett Company is to create superior advertising. In Leo's words: "Our primary function in life is to produce the best advertising in the world, bar none. This is to be advertising so interrupting, so daring, so fresh, so engaging, so human, so believable and so well-focused as to themes and ideas that, at one and the same time, it builds a quality reputation for the long haul as it produces sales for the immediate present."

2000   Our Vision: To be an indispensable source of our clients' competitive advantage. Our Mission: We will work with our clients as a community of star-reachers whose ideas build leadership brands through imagination and a sensitive and deeper understanding of human behavior.

2006   We are Leo Burnett. Our aspiration is simply to be the best marketing communications company in the world, bar none.

Celestial Seasonings

1995   Our mission is to grow and dominate the U.S. specialty tea market by exceeding consumer expectations with the best tasting, 100 percent natural hot and iced teas, packaged with Celestial art and philosophy, creating the most valued tea experience. Through leadership, innovation, focus, and teamwork we are dedicated to continuously improving value to our consumers, customers, employees, and stakeholders with a quality-first organization.

2000   We believe in creating and selling healthful, naturally oriented products that nurture people's bodies and uplift their souls. Our products must be

- superior in quality,
- of good value,
- beautifully artistic, and
- philosophically inspiring.

Our role is to play an active part in making this world a better place by unselfishly serving the public. We believe we can have a significant impact on making people's lives happier and healthier through their use of our products.

2006   To create and sell healthful, naturally oriented products that nurture people's bodies and uplift their spirits. Our products must be:

- superior in quality
- of good value
- beautifully artistic
- philosophically inspiring

Our role is to play an active part in making this world a better place by unselfishly serving the public. We can have a significant impact on making people's lives happier and healthier through their use of our products.

Intel Corporation

1995   Do a great job for our customers, employees and stockholders by being the preeminent building block supplier to the computing industry.

2000   Intel's mission is to be the preeminent building block supplier to the worldwide Internet economy.

2006   Intel's corporate mission is to "Do a great job for our customers, employees and stockholders by being the preeminent building block supplier to the worldwide Internet economy."

Source: Patricia Jones and Larry Kahaner, *Say It and Live It: The 50 Corporate Mission Statements That Hit the Mark* (New York: Doubleday, 1995); and the websites of these companies.

Mission stability refers to the frequency of modifications in an organization's mission statement. Of all the components of the strategic plan, the mission should change the least frequently. It is the one element that will likely remain constant through multiple rounds of strategic planning. Goals, objectives, and marketing plan elements will change over time, usually as an annual or quarterly event. When the mission changes, however, the cornerstone has been moved and everything else must change as well. The mission should change only when it is no longer in sync with the firm's capabilities, when competitors drive the firm from certain markets, when new technology changes the delivery of customer benefits, or when the firm identifies a new opportunity that matches its strengths and expertise. As we discussed in Chapter 1, the growth of the Internet and electronic commerce has affected many industries. The importance and role of travel agents, stockbrokers, and car dealers have changed dramatically as customers changed the way that they shop for travel, financial products, and automobiles. Organizations in these and other industries have been forced to refocus their efforts by redefining their mission statements.

Customer-Focused Mission Statements   In recent years, firms have realized the role that mission statements can play in their marketing efforts. Consequently, mission statements have become much more customer oriented. People's lives and businesses should be enriched because they have dealt with the organization. A focus on profit in the mission statement means that something positive happens for the owners and managers of the organization, not necessarily for the customers or other stakeholders. For example, a focus on customers is one of the leading reasons for the long-running success of Southwest Airlines. The company's mission has not changed since 1988:

> *The mission of Southwest Airlines is dedication to the highest quality of Customer Service delivered with a sense of warmth, friendliness, individual pride, and Company Spirit.*[4]

The mission statement of cultural icon Ben & Jerry's Ice Cream consists of three interrelated parts and is a good example of how an organization can work to have a positive impact on customers and society:[5]

> *Product Mission: To make, distribute & sell the finest quality all natural ice cream & euphoric concoctions with a continued commitment to incorporating wholesome, natural ingredients and promoting business practices that respect the Earth and the Environment.*

> *Economic Mission: To operate the Company on a sustainable financial basis of profitable growth, increasing value for our stakeholders & expanding opportunities for development and career growth for our employees.*

> *Social Mission: To operate the company in a way that actively recognizes the central role that business plays in society by initiating innovative ways to improve the quality of life locally, nationally & internationally.*

The infamous 1982 Tylenol cyanide tragedy illustrated the importance of a customer-oriented mission statement. After several deaths occurred as a result of outside tampering with Tylenol capsules, McNeilab and Johnson & Johnson immediately pulled all Tylenol capsules from the market at a direct cost of $100 million. When asked about the difficulty of this decision, executives said that the choice was obvious given Johnson & Johnson's mission statement. That statement, developed decades earlier by the firm's founders, established that Johnson & Johnson's primary responsibility is to the doctors, nurses, patients, parents, and children who prescribe or use the company's products. Because the mission dictated the firm's response to the crisis, Tylenol became an even more dominant player in the pain-reliever market after the tragedy.[6]

Customer-focused mission statements are the norm for charities and humanitarian organizations. These nonprofit organizations—just like their for-profit counterparts—strive to fulfill their missions through effective marketing programs. For instance, the mission of the American Red Cross reads this way:

> *The American Red Cross, a humanitarian organization led by volunteers, guided by its Congressional Charter and the Fundamental Principles of the International Red Cross Movement, will provide relief to victims of disasters and help people prevent, prepare for, and respond to emergencies.*

Unlike other charitable organizations, the American Red Cross holds a key competitive advantage: its congressional charter. This gives the American Red Cross the authority needed to respond no matter the nature or complexity of the crisis. During the aftermath of Hurricanes Katrina, Rita, and Wilma in 2005, the American Red Cross initiated its single largest disaster response in the organization's 125-year history. Through a massive promotional campaign and significant corporate sponsorships, the American Red Cross was able to raise the $2.1 billion needed for relief efforts.[7]

Corporate or Business-Unit Strategy

All organizations need a *corporate strategy*, the central scheme or means for utilizing and integrating resources in the areas of production, finance, research and development, human resources, and marketing, to carry out the organization's mission and achieve the desired goals and objectives. In the strategic planning process, issues such as competition, differentiation, diversification, coordination of business units, and environmental issues all tend to emerge as corporate strategy concerns. In small businesses, corporate strategy and business-unit strategy are essentially the same. Although we use both terms, corporate and business-unit strategy apply to all organizations, from large corporations to small businesses and nonprofit organizations.

Larger firms often find it beneficial to devise separate strategies for each strategic business unit (SBU), subsidiary, division, product line, or other profit center within the parent firm. Business-unit strategy determines the nature and future direction of each business unit, including its competitive advantages, the allocation of its resources, and the coordination of the functional business areas (marketing, production, finance, human resources, and so on). Many organizations manage their differing SBUs in ways that create synergies by providing customers a single-branded solution across multiple markets. Sony, for example, has a number of SBUs and joint ventures, including Sony Electronics (televisions, DVD, mobile electronics, computers), Sony BMG Music Entertainment (record labels such as Arista, Epic, Columbia, and LaFace), Sony Pictures Entertainment (Columbia TriStar studios, movie distribution), Sony Ericsson (mobile multimedia and cell phones), and Sony Computer Entertainment (the PlayStation family of games and consoles).[8]

An important consideration for a firm determining its corporate or business-unit strategy is the firm's capabilities. When a firm possesses capabilities that allow it to serve customers' needs better than the competition, it is said to have a *competitive,* or *differential advantage.* Although a number of advantages come from functions other than marketing—such as human resources, research and development, or production— these functions often create important competitive advantages that can be exploited through marketing activities. For example, Wal-Mart's long-running strategic investments in logistics allow the retailer to operate with lower inventory costs than its competitors—an advantage that translates into lower prices at retail. The 3M Company is highly regarded for its expertise in research and development. The company's advantage in research and innovation allows its thirty-five business units to excel in six different business segments: consumer and office, display and graphics, electro and communications, health care, industrial and transportation, and safety, security, and protection services.[9]

Competitive advantages cannot be fully realized unless targeted customers see them as valuable. The key issue is the organization's ability to convince customers that its advantages are superior to those of the competition. Wal-Mart has been able to convey effectively its low price advantage to customers by adhering to an everyday low-price policy. The company's advertising plays on this fact by using a happy face to "roll back" prices. Interestingly, Wal-Mart's prices are not always the lowest for a given product in a given geographic area. However, Wal-Mart's perception of offering low prices translates into a key competitive advantage for the firm.

Functional Goals and Objectives

Marketing and all other business functions must support the organization's mission and goals, translating these into objectives with specific quantitative measurements. For example, a corporate or business-unit goal to increase return on investment might translate into a marketing objective to increase sales, a production objective to reduce the cost of raw materials, a financial objective to rebalance the firm's portfolio of investments, or a human resources objective to increase employee training and productivity. All functional objectives should be expressed in clear, simple terms so that all personnel understand what type and level of performance that the organization desires. In other words, objectives should be written so that their accomplishment can be measured accurately. In the case of marketing objectives, units of measure might include sales volume (in dollars or units), profitability per unit, percentage gain in market share, sales per square foot, average customer purchase, percentage of customers in the firm's target market who prefer its products, or some other measurable achievement.

It is also important for all functional objectives to be reconsidered for each planning period. Perhaps no strategy arose in the previous planning period to meet the stated objectives. Or perhaps the implementation of new technology allowed the firm to greatly exceed its objectives. In either case, realism demands the revision of functional objectives to remain consistent with the next edition of the functional area plan.

Functional Strategy

Organizations design functional strategies to provide a total integration of efforts that focus on achieving the area's stated objectives. In production, this might involve strategies for procurement, just-in-time inventory control, or warehousing. In human resources, strategies dealing with employee recruitment, selection, retention, training, evaluation, and compensation are often at the forefront of the decision-making process. In marketing strategy, the process focuses on selecting one or more target markets and developing a marketing program that satisfies the needs and wants of members of that target market. AutoZone, for example, targets do-it-yourself "shade-tree mechanics" by offering an extensive selection of automotive replacement parts, maintenance items, and accessories at low prices.

Functional strategy decisions do not develop in a vacuum. The strategy must (1) fit the needs and purposes of the functional area with respect to meeting its goals and objectives, (2) be realistic given the organization's available resources and environment, and (3) be consistent with the organization's mission, goals, and objectives. Within the context of the overall strategic planning process, each functional strategy must be evaluated to determine its effect on the organization's sales, costs, image, and profitability.

Implementation

Implementation involves activities that actually execute the functional area strategy. One of the more interesting aspects of implementation is that all functional plans have at least two target markets: an external market (customers, suppliers, investors, potential employees, the society at large) and an internal market (employees, managers, executives). This occurs because functional plans, when executed, have repercussions both inside and outside the firm. Even seemingly disconnected events in finance or human resources can have an effect on the firm's ultimate customers—the individuals and businesses that buy the firm's products.

For a functional strategy to be implemented successfully, the organization must rely on the commitment and knowledge of its employees—its internal target market. After all, employees have a responsibility to perform the activities that will implement the strategy. For this reason, organizations often execute internal marketing activities designed to gain employee commitment and motivation to implement functional plans.

Evaluation and Control

Organizations design the evaluation and control phase of strategic planning to keep planned activities on target with goals and objectives. In the big picture, the critical issue in this phase is coordination among functional areas. For example, timely distribution and product availability almost always depend on accurate and timely production. By maintaining contact with the production manager, the marketing manager helps ensure effective marketing strategy implementation (by ensuring timely production) and, in the long run, increased customer satisfaction. The need for coordination is especially keen in marketing where the fulfillment of marketing strategy always depends on coordinated execution with other functional strategies.

The key to coordination is to ensure that functional areas maintain open lines of communication at all times. Although this can be quite a challenge, it is helpful if the organizational culture is both internally and externally customer oriented. Maintaining a customer focus is extremely important throughout the strategic planning process but especially so during the implementation, evaluation, and control phases of the process. Functional managers should have the ability to see the interconnectedness of all business decisions and act in the best interests of the organization and its customers.

In some ways, the evaluation and control phase of the planning process is an ending and a beginning. On one hand, evaluation and control occur after a strategy has been implemented. In fact, the implementation of any strategy would be incomplete without an assessment of its success and the creation of control mechanisms to provide and revise the strategy or its implementation—or both, if necessary. On the other hand, evaluation and control serve as the beginning point for the planning process in the next planning cycle. Because strategic planning is a never-ending process, managers should have a system for monitoring and evaluating implementation outcomes on an ongoing basis.

The Marketing Plan

The result of the strategic planning process described in the first portion of this chapter is a series of plans for each functional area of the organization. For the marketing department, the marketing plan provides a detailed formulation of the actions necessary to carry out the marketing program. Think of the marketing plan as an action document—it is the handbook for marketing implementation, evaluation, and control. With that in mind, it is important to note that a marketing plan is not the same as a business plan. Business plans, although they typically contain a marketing plan, encompass other issues such as business organization and ownership, operations, financial strategy, human resources, and risk management. Although business plans and marketing plans are not synonymous, many small businesses will consolidate their corporate, business-unit, and marketing plans into a single document.

A good marketing plan requires a great deal of information from many different sources. An important consideration in pulling all this information together is to maintain a big-picture view while keeping an eye on the details. This requires looking at the marketing plan holistically rather than as a collection of related elements. Unfortunately, adopting a holistic perspective is rather difficult in practice. It is easy to get deeply involved in developing marketing strategy only to discover later that the strategy is inappropriate for the organization's resources or marketing environment. The hallmark of a well-developed marketing plan is its ability to achieve its stated goals and objectives.

In the following sections, we explore the marketing plan in more detail, including the structure of a typical marketing plan. This structure matches the marketing plan worksheets in Appendix A and the sample marketing plan in Appendix B. As we work through the marketing plan structure, keep in mind that a marketing plan can be written in many different ways. Marketing plans can be developed for specific products, brands, target markets, or industries. Likewise, a marketing plan can focus on a specific element of the marketing program such as a product development plan, a promotional plan, a distribution plan, or a pricing plan.

Marketing Plan Structure

All marketing plans should be well organized to ensure that all relevant information is considered and included. Exhibit 2.3 illustrates the structure, or outline, of a typical marketing plan. We say that this outline is "typical," but there are many other ways to organize a marketing plan. Although the actual outline used is not that important, most plans will share common elements described here. Regardless of the specific outline that you use to develop a marketing plan, keep in mind that a good marketing plan outline is all of the following:

- **Comprehensive** Having a comprehensive outline is essential to ensure that there are no omissions of important information. Of course, every element of the outline may not be pertinent to the situation at hand, but at least each element receives consideration.

- **Flexible** Although having a comprehensive outline is essential, flexibility should not be sacrificed. Any outline that you choose must be flexible enough to be modified to fit the unique needs of your situation. Because all situations and organizations are different, using an overly rigid outline is detrimental to the planning process.

- **Consistent** Consistency between the marketing plan outline and the outline of other functional area plans is an important consideration. Consistency may also include the connection of the marketing plan outline to the planning process used at the corporate or business-unit levels. Maintaining consistency ensures that executives and employees outside of marketing will understand the marketing plan and the planning process.

- **Logical** Because the marketing plan must ultimately sell itself to top managers, the plan's outline must flow in a logical manner. An illogical outline could force top managers to reject or underfund the marketing plan.

The marketing plan structure that we discuss here has the ability to meet all four of these points. Although the structure is comprehensive, you should freely adapt the outline to match the unique requirements of your situation.

EXHIBIT 2.3	MARKETING PLAN STRUCTURE

I. Executive Summary

   a. Synopsis
   b. Major aspects of the marketing plan

II. Situation Analysis

   a. Analysis of the internal environment
   b. Analysis of the customer environment
   c. Analysis of the external environment

III. SWOT Analysis (Strengths, Weaknesses, Opportunities, and Threats)

   a. Strengths
   b. Weaknesses
   c. Opportunities
   d. Threats
   e. Analysis of the SWOT matrix
   f. Developing competitive advantages
   g. Developing a strategic focus

IV. Marketing Goals and Objectives

   a. Marketing goals
   b. Marketing objectives

V. Marketing Strategy

   a. Primary (and secondary) target market
   b. Product strategy
   c. Pricing strategy
   d. Distribution/supply chain strategy
   e. Integrated marketing communication (promotion) strategy

VI. Marketing Implementation

   a. Structural issues
   b. Tactical marketing activities

VII. Evaluation and Control

   a. Formal controls
   b. Informal controls
   c. Implementation schedule and timeline
   d. Marketing audits

Executive Summary The *executive summary* is a synopsis of the overall marketing plan, with an outline that conveys the main thrust of the marketing strategy and its execution. The purpose of the executive summary is to provide an overview of the plan so that the reader can quickly identify key issues or concerns related to his or her role in implementing the marketing strategy. Therefore, the executive summary does not provide detailed information found in the following sections or any other detailed information that supports the final plan. Instead, this synopsis introduces the major aspects of the marketing plan, including objectives, sales projections, costs, and performance evaluation measures. Along with the overall thrust of the marketing strategy, the executive summary should also identify the scope and time frame for the plan. The idea is to give the reader a quick understanding of the breadth of the plan and its time frame for execution.

Individuals both within and outside the organization may read the executive summary for reasons other than marketing planning or implementation. Ultimately, many users of a marketing plan ignore some of the details because of the role that they play. The CEO, for example, may be more concerned with the overall cost and expected return of the plan and less interested in the plan's implementation. Financial institutions or investment bankers may want to read the marketing plan before approving any necessary financing. Likewise, suppliers, investors, or others who have a stake in the success of the organization sometimes receive access to the marketing plan. In these cases, the executive summary is critical because it must convey a concise overview of the plan and its objectives, costs, and returns.

Although the executive summary is the first element of a marketing plan, it should always be the last element to be written because it is easier (and more meaningful) to write after the entire marketing plan has been developed. There is another good reason to write the executive summary last: It may be the only element of the marketing plan read by a large number of people. As a result, the executive summary must accurately represent the entire marketing plan.

Situation Analysis   The next section of the marketing plan is the *situation analysis,* which summarizes all pertinent information obtained about three key environments: the internal environment, the customer environment, and the firm's external environment. The analysis of the firm's internal environment considers issues such as the availability and deployment of human resources, the age and capacity of equipment or technology, the availability of financial resources, and the power and political struggles within the firm's structure. In addition, this section summarizes the firm's current marketing objectives and performance. The analysis of the customer environment examines the current situation with respect to the needs of the target market (consumer or business), anticipated changes in these needs, and how well the firm's products presently meet these needs. Finally, the analysis of the external environment includes relevant external factors—competitive, economic, sociocultural, political/ legal, and technological—that can exert considerable direct and indirect pressures on the firm's marketing activities.

A clear and comprehensive situation analysis is one of the most difficult parts of developing a marketing plan. This difficulty arises because the analysis must be both comprehensive and focused on key issues in order to prevent information overload—a task actually made more complicated by advances in information technology. The information for a situation analysis may be obtained internally through the firm's marketing information system, or it may have to be obtained externally through primary or secondary marketing research. Either way, the challenge is often having too much data and information to analyze rather than having too little.

SWOT (Strengths, Weaknesses, Opportunities, and Threats) Analysis SWOT *analysis* focuses on the internal factors (strengths and weaknesses) and external factors (opportunities and threats)—derived from the situation analysis in the preceding section—that give the firm certain advantages and disadvantages in satisfying the needs of its target market(s). These strengths, weaknesses, opportunities, and threats should be analyzed relative to market needs and competition. This analysis helps the company determine what it does well and where it needs to make improvements.

SWOT analysis has gained widespread acceptance because it is a simple framework for organizing and evaluating a company's strategic position when developing a marketing plan. However, like any useful tool, SWOT analysis can be misused unless one conducts the appropriate research to identify key variables that will affect the performance of the firm. A common mistake in SWOT analysis is the failure to separate internal issues from external issues. Strengths and weaknesses are internal issues unique to the firm conducting the analysis. Opportunities and threats are external issues that exist independently of the firm conducting the analysis. Another common mistake is to list the firm's strategic alternatives as opportunities. However, alternatives belong in the discussion of marketing strategy, not in the SWOT analysis.

At the conclusion of the SWOT analysis, the focus of the marketing plan shifts to address the strategic focus and competitive advantages to be leveraged in the strategy. The key to developing strategic focus is to match the firm's strengths with its opportunities to create capabilities in delivering value to customers. The challenge for any firm at this stage is to create a compelling reason for customers to purchase its products over those offered by competitors. It is this compelling reason that then becomes the framework or strategic focus around which the strategy can be developed. As explained in Beyond the Pages 2.2, even perennial successes like Dell Computer shift their strategic thinking to stay fresh and competitive.

Marketing Goals and Objectives Marketing goals and objectives are formal statements of the desired and expected outcomes resulting from the marketing plan. *Marketing goals* are broad, simple statements of what will be accomplished through the marketing strategy. The major function of goals is to guide the development of objectives and to provide direction for resource allocation decisions. *Marketing objectives* are more specific and are essential to planning. Objectives should be stated in quantitative terms to permit reasonably precise measurement. The quantitative nature of marketing objectives makes them easier to implement after development of the strategy.

DELL'S MAKEOVER[10]

Dell, the onetime bedrock of growth for investors, made a surprising announcement in May 2006 that it would not meet its earning projections for the first quarter. The announcement pushed Dell shares down to around $25—a point more than 40 percent less than a year earlier. This was the third time in four quarters that Dell had failed to meet revenue expectations. Of course, Dell was not losing money. Still, investors were left wondering what had happened to the consistent double-digit growth posted by Dell over the past several years.

Competition is what happened. Dell's chief U.S. rival—Hewlett-Packard—had completed its cost restructuring and was now able to offer PCs at prices that either matched or beat Dell's. Foreign, low-cost producers—such as Lenovo and Acer—were also stealing market share away from Dell. Not only had Dell lost its edge in pricing, but the quality of the company's customer service was also in decline. The end result: Dell's share of the worldwide PC market fell from 18.6 percent to 18.1 percent, while its U.S. share fell from 33.9 percent to 32.3 percent.

Increasing competition had forced Dell to cut prices—often to rock-bottom levels. In the past, this strategy wouldn't have been a problem for Dell. But cost improvements throughout the industry had cut Dell's pricing advantage in half to roughly 5 percent. This small pricing advantage was not enough to maintain Dell's edge in the highly competitive market. Analysts argued that Dell's price cutting went too far and that the company did not invest enough in the "customer experience" as it attempted to maintain margins.

To break away from its price-cutting strategy, Dell underwent a makeover. To protect the brand, Dell planned to spend $100 million to improve customer service and technical support. In the initial part of this effort, Dell added more than 2,000 workers to cut phone waiting times by 50 percent. The company also began aggressively pushing its mid- and high-end machines, most notably its XPS line of desktops and notebooks. Part of this strategy was Dell's acquisition of Alienware—a Miami-based PC maker known for its high-end gaming machines and hip styling. Dell also announced that it would begin using AMD processor chips in its line of high-end servers, a move that ended Intel's dominance in Dell machines. Both analysts and computer experts hailed this move because AMD processors are considered by many to be more powerful and energy efficient than Intel's chips. Some speculate that Dell will eventually offer AMD processors in desktops and notebooks because AMD chips are used in many Alienware machines.

Dell executives believe that the company's makeover will return it to double-digit growth. However, industry experts don't expect Dell to end its bargain pricing anytime soon. They argue that the key to Dell's success is to give consumers a compelling nonprice reason to buy its machines.

This section of the marketing plan has two important purposes. First, it sets the performance targets that the firm seeks to achieve by giving life to its strategic focus through its marketing strategy (that is, what the firm hopes to achieve). Second, it defines the parameters by which the firm will measure actual performance in the evaluation and control phase of the marketing plan (that is, how performance will actually be measured). At this point, it is important to remember that neither goals nor objectives can be developed without a clearly defined mission statement. Marketing goals must be consistent with the firm's mission, and marketing objectives must flow naturally from the marketing goals.

Marketing Strategy This section of the marketing plan outlines how the firm will achieve its marketing objectives. In Chapter 1, we said that marketing strategies involve selecting and analyzing target markets and creating and maintaining an appropriate marketing program (product, distribution, promotion, and price) to satisfy the needs of those target markets. It is at this level where the firm will detail how it will gain a competitive advantage by doing something better than the competition: Its products must be of higher quality than competitive offerings, its prices must be consistent with the level of quality (value), its distribution methods must be as efficient as possible, and its promotions must be more effective in communicating with target customers. It is also important that the firm attempt to make these advantages sustainable. Thus, in its broadest sense, marketing strategy refers to how the firm will manage its relationships with customers in a manner that gives it an advantage over the competition.

Marketing Implementation The implementation section of the marketing plan describes how the marketing program will be executed. This section of the marketing plan answers several questions with respect to the marketing strategies outlined in the preceding section:

1. What specific marketing activities will be undertaken?

2. How will these activities be performed?

3. When will these activities be performed?

4. Who is responsible for the completion of these activities?

5. How will the completion of planned activities be monitored?

6. How much will these activities cost?

Without a good plan for implementation, the success of the marketing strategy is seriously jeopardized. For this reason, the implementation phase of the marketing plan is just as important as the marketing strategy phase. You should remember, too, that implementation hinges on gaining the support of employees: Employees implement marketing strategies, not organizations. As a result, issues such as leadership, employee motivation, communication, and employee training are critical to implementation success.

Evaluation and Control The final section of the marketing plan details how the results of the marketing program will be evaluated and controlled. Marketing control involves establishing performance standards, assessing actual performance by comparing it with these standards, and taking corrective action if necessary to reduce discrepancies between desired and actual performance. Performance standards should be tied back to the objectives stated earlier in the plan. These standards can be based on increases in sales volume, market share, or profitability or even advertising standards such as brand-name recognition or recall. Regardless of the standard selected, all performance standards must be agreed upon before the results of the plan can be assessed.

The financial assessment of the marketing plan is also an important component of evaluation and control. Estimates of costs, sales, and revenues determine financial projections. In reality, budgetary considerations play a key role in the identification of alternative strategies. The financial realities of the firm must be monitored at all times. For example, proposing to expand into new geographic areas or alter products without financial resources is a waste of time, energy, and opportunity. Even if funds are available, the strategy must be a "good value" and provide an acceptable return on investment to be a part of the final plan.

Finally, should it be determined that the marketing plan has not lived up to expectations; the firm can use a number of tools to pinpoint potential causes for the discrepancies. One such tool is the *marketing audit*—a systematic examination of the firm's marketing objectives, strategy, and performance. The marketing audit can help isolate weaknesses in the marketing plan and recommend actions to help improve performance. The control phase of the planning process also outlines the actions that can be taken to reduce the differences between planned and actual performance.

Using the Marketing Plan Structure

In Appendix A are marketing plan worksheets that expand the marketing plan structure into a comprehensive framework for developing a marketing plan. These worksheets are designed to be *comprehensive, flexible,* and *logical.* The consistency of this framework with other planning documents will depend on the planning structure used in other functional areas of an organization. However, this framework is certainly capable of being consistent with the plans from other functional areas.

Although you may not use every single portion of the worksheets, you should at least go through them in their entirety to ensure that all important information is present. You should note that the sample marketing plan provided in Appendix B uses this same framework. However, this plan does not match the framework *exactly* because the framework was adapted to match the characteristics of a unique planning situation. You will also find additional marketing plan examples on our text's website (http://www.thomsonedu.com/marketing/ferrell).

Before we move ahead, we offer the following tips for using the marketing plan framework to develop a marketing plan:

- **Plan ahead**   Writing a comprehensive marketing plan is very time consuming, especially if the plan is under development for the first time. Initially, most of your time will be spent on the situation analysis. Although this analysis is very demanding, the marketing plan has little chance for success without it.

- **Revise, then revise again**   After the situation analysis, you will spend most of your time revising the remaining elements of the marketing plan to ensure that they mesh with each other. Once you have written a first draft of the plan, put it away for a day or so. Then, review the plan with a fresh perspective and fine-tune sections that need changing. Because the revision process always takes more time than expected, it is wise to begin the planning process far in advance of the due date for the plan.

- **Be creative**   A marketing plan is only as good as the information that it contains and the effort and creativity that go into its creation. A plan developed half-heartedly will collect dust on the shelf.

- **Use common sense and judgment**   Writing a marketing plan is an art. Common sense and judgment are necessary to sort through all of the information, weed out poor strategies, and develop a sound marketing plan. Managers must always weigh any information against its accuracy, as well as their own intuition, when making marketing decisions.

- **Think ahead to implementation**   As you develop the plan, always be mindful of how the plan will be implemented. Great marketing strategies that never see the light of day do little to help the organization meet its goals. Good marketing plans are those that are realistic and doable given the organization's resources.

- **Update regularly**   Once the marketing plan has been developed and implemented, it should be updated regularly with the collection of new data and information. Many organizations update their marketing plans on a quarterly basis to ensure that the marketing strategy remains consistent with changes in the internal, customer, and external environments. Under this approach, you will always have a working plan that covers 12 months into the future.

- **Communicate to others**   One critical aspect of the marketing plan is its ability to communicate to colleagues, particularly top managers who look to the marketing plan for an explanation of the marketing strategy, as well as for a justification of needed resources, like the marketing budget.[11] The marketing plan also communicates to line managers and other employees by giving them points of reference to chart the progress of marketing implementation. A survey of marketing executives on the importance of the marketing plan revealed that

> *the process of preparing the plan is more important than the document itself. . . . A marketing plan does compel attention, though. It makes the marketing team concentrate on the market, on the company's objectives, and on the strategies and tactics appropriate to those objectives. It's a mechanism for synchronizing action.*[12]

Research indicates that organizations that develop formal, written strategic marketing plans tend to be more tightly integrated across functional areas, more specialized, and more decentralized in decision making. The end result of these marketing plan efforts is improved financial and marketing performance.[13] Given these benefits, it is surprising that many firms do not develop formal plans to guide their marketing efforts. For example, a survey of CEOs done by the American Banking Association found that only 44 percent of community banks have a formal marketing plan.[14]

Purposes and Significance of the Marketing Plan

The purposes of a marketing plan must be understood to appreciate its significance. A good marketing plan will fulfill these five purposes in detail:

1. It explains both the present and future situations of the organization. This includes the situation and SWOT analysis and the firm's past performance.

2. It specifies the expected outcomes (goals and objectives) so that the organization can anticipate its situation at the end of the planning period.

3. It describes the specific actions that are to take place so that the responsibility for each action can be assigned and implemented.

4. It identifies the resources that will be needed to carry out the planned actions.

5. It permits the monitoring of each action and its results so that controls may be implemented.

Feedback from monitoring and control provides information to start the planning cycle again in the next time frame.

These five purposes are very important to various persons in the firm. Line managers have a particular interest in the third purpose (description of specific actions) because they are responsible for ensuring the implementation of marketing actions. Middle-level managers have a special interest in the fifth purpose (monitoring and control) because they want to ensure that tactical changes can be made, if needed. These managers must also be able to evaluate why the marketing strategy does or does not succeed.

The most pressing concern for success, however, may lie in the fourth purpose: identifying needed resources. The marketing plan is the means of communicating the strategy to top executives who make the critical decisions regarding the productive and efficient allocation of resources. Very sound marketing plans can prove unsuccessful if implementation of the plan is not adequately funded. It is important to remember that marketing is not the only business function competing for scarce resources. Other functions such as finance, research and development, and human resources have strategic plans of their own. It is in this vein that the marketing plan must sell itself to top management.

Organizational Aspects of the Marketing Plan

Who writes the marketing plan? In many organizations, the marketing manager, brand manager, or product manager writes the marketing plan. Some organizations develop marketing plans through committees. Others will hire professional marketing consultants to write the marketing plan. However, in most firms, the responsibility for planning lies at the level of a marketing vice president or marketing director.[15] The fact that top managers develop most marketing plans does not necessarily refute the logic of having the brand or product manager prepare the plan. However, except in small organizations where one person both develops and approves the plan, the authority to approve the marketing plan is typically vested in upper-level executives. At this stage, top managers usually ask two important questions:

1. Will the proposed marketing plan achieve the desired marketing, business-unit, and corporate goals and objectives?

2. Are there alternative uses of resources that would better meet corporate or business-unit objectives than the submitted marketing plan?

In most cases, *final* approval actually lies with the president, chairman, or CEO of the organization.[16] Many organizations also have executive committees that evaluate and screen marketing plans before submission to the approving executive. In the end, regardless of who writes the marketing plan, the plan must be clear and persuasive to win the approval of the decision makers who make the evaluation. It is also critical that these individuals make efficient and timely decisions with respect to the marketing plan. To give the plan every chance for success, very little time should elapse between the completion of the plan and its implementation.

Once a marketing plan has been approved, it still faces many obstacles before its marketing programs can come to fruition. Exhibit 2.4 outlines some of these obstacles. One major hurdle involves the relative time horizon of the organization's key stakeholders, particularly its managers and investors. It is quite common for American firms to ignore long-range strategy and focus on the near term. Typically, this is caused by a compensation structure that rewards executives for short-term financial results such as profit, market capitalization, or stock price. Unfortunately, this mind-set can play havoc on many marketing activities—such as advertising to build brand awareness—because their results are only apparent over longer time horizons. Consequently, many firms will shift strategies "midstream" rather than wait for results to emerge.

Maintaining Customer Focus and Balance in Strategic Planning

In the past two decades, many firms have changed the focus and content of their strategic planning efforts and marketing plans. Of these changes, two stand out: (1) renewed emphasis on the customer and (2) the advent of balanced strategic planning. These changes require shifting focus from the company's products to the unique requirements of specific target market segments. Firms have also had to become more astute at linking marketing activities to other functional areas.

Customer-Focused Planning

Focusing on the customer has not been the hallmark of strategic planning through out history. Early in the twentieth century, planning focused on production ideals

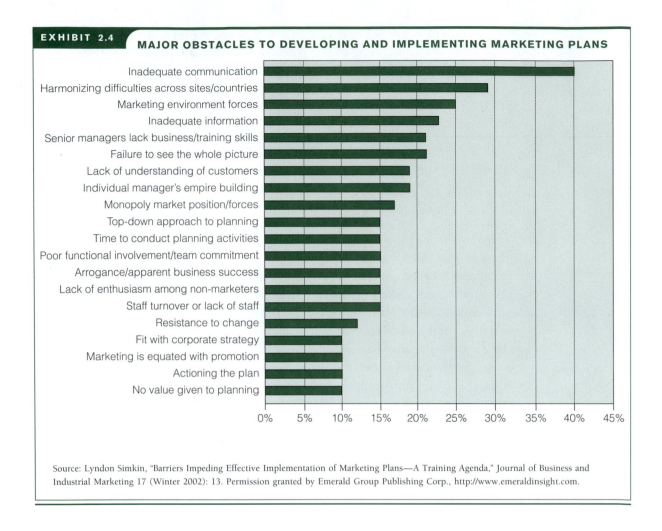

EXHIBIT 2.4

MAJOR OBSTACLES TO DEVELOPING AND IMPLEMENTING MARKETING PLANS

Source: Lyndon Simkin, "Barriers Impeding Effective Implementation of Marketing Plans—A Training Agenda," Journal of Business and Industrial Marketing 17 (Winter 2002): 13. Permission granted by Emerald Group Publishing Corp., http://www.emeraldinsight.com.

such as efficiency and quality. Automobile pioneer Henry Ford has long been credited with the statement that customers could have any color car that they wanted as long as it was black. This mentality, though it worked well in its day, meant that strategic planning proceeded with little regard for customer needs and wants. Today, cars, trucks, and SUVs (sport utility vehicles) come in an array of colors that Henry Ford would have never contemplated. By the middle of the twentieth century, strategic planning focused on *selling* products to customers rather than making products for customers. Marketing strategies during this time concentrated on overcoming customer resistance and convincing them to buy products whether they needed them or not. Today, we no longer see door-to-door sales of vacuum cleaners, brushes, or encyclopedias.

The cornerstone of marketing thought and practice during the mid-to-late twentieth century was the marketing concept, which focused on customer satisfaction and the achievement of the firm's objectives. Having a market or customer orientation meant putting customers' needs and wants first. This shift in thinking led to the growth of marketing research to determine unmet customer needs and systems for satisfying those needs. Today's twenty-first-century marketing organizations move one step beyond the marketing concept to focus on long-term, value-added relationships with customers, employees, suppliers, and other partners. The focus has shifted from customer transactions to customer relationships and from competition to collaboration.

Market-oriented firms are those that successfully generate, disseminate, and respond to market information. These firms focus on customer analysis, competitor analysis, and integrating the firm's resources to provide customer value and satisfaction as well as long-term profits.[17] To be successful, the firm must be able to focus its efforts and resources toward understanding their customers in ways that enhance the firm's ability to generate sustainable competitive advantages.[18] By creating organizational cultures that put customers first, market-oriented firms tend to perform at higher levels and reap the benefits of more highly satisfied customers. Exhibit 2.5 depicts the difference between a traditional and market-oriented organizational structure. Where traditional structures are very authoritative, with

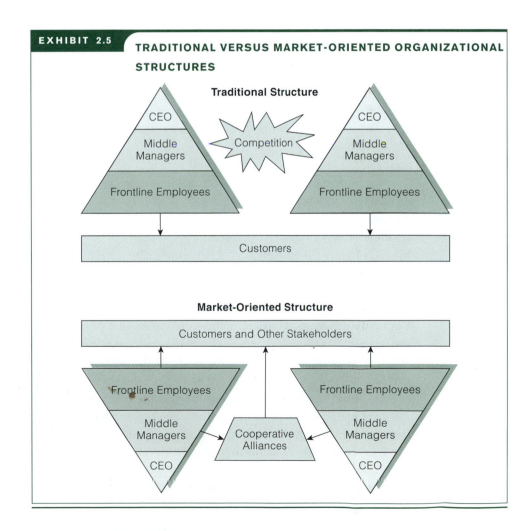

EXHIBIT 2.5

TRADITIONAL VERSUS MARKET-ORIENTED ORGANIZATIONAL STRUCTURES

Traditional Structure

CEO — Middle Managers — Frontline Employees — Competition

Customers

Market-Oriented Structure

Customers and Other Stakeholders

Frontline Employees — Middle Managers — CEO — Cooperative Alliances decision-making authority emanating from the top of the hierarchy, market-oriented structures decentralize decision making.

In a market-oriented organization, every level of the organization has its focus on serving customer needs. Each level serves the levels above it by taking any actions necessary to ensure that each level performs its job well. In this case, the role of the CEO is to ensure that his or her employees have everything they need to perform their jobs well. This same service mentality carries through all levels of the organization, including customers. Thus, the job of a frontline manager is to ensure that frontline employees are capable and efficient. The end result of the market-oriented design is a complete focus on customer needs.

In today's business environment, an orientation toward customers also requires that the organization's suppliers and even competitors be customer oriented as well. Though competing firms can continue to serve customers separately, customers can also be served through cooperative efforts that place customers ahead of competitive interests. For example, Toyota has a number of partnerships with rival automakers, particularly focused on emerging hybrid technology. Nissan is using Toyota's hybrid fuel system in its vehicles, while GM is collaborating with Toyota in developing new fuel-cell technologies. GM and Toyota have a long-standing relationship in the joint production of vehicles including the Toyota Corolla, the Pontiac Vibe, and the Toyota Tacoma.[19]

Balanced Strategic Planning

The shift to balanced strategic planning was borne out of necessity. As firms approached the twenty-first century, they realized that traditional planning and measurement approaches could not capture value created by the organization's intangible assets. These assets—including such vital issues as customer relationships, processes, human resources, innovation, and information—were becoming increasingly important to business success, but they were not being reported through traditional financial measures. One solution to this problem was the development of the balanced-performance scorecard by Robert Kaplan and David Norton of Harvard University.[20] Their approach to strategic planning is illustrated in Exhibit 2.6.

The basic tenet of the balanced-performance scorecard is that firms can achieve better performance if they align their strategic efforts by approaching strategy from four complementary perspectives: financial, customer, internal process, and learning and growth. The financial perspective is the traditional view of strategy and performance. This perspective is vital but should be balanced by the other components of the scorecard. The customer perspective looks at customer satisfaction metrics as a key indicator of firm performance, particularly as the firm moves ahead. Financial measures are not suited to this task because they report past performance rather than current performance. The internal process perspective focuses on the way that the business is running by looking at both mission-critical and routine processes that drive day-to-day activity. Finally, the learning and growth perspective focuses on people and includes such vital issues as corporate culture, employee training, communication, and knowledge management.[21]

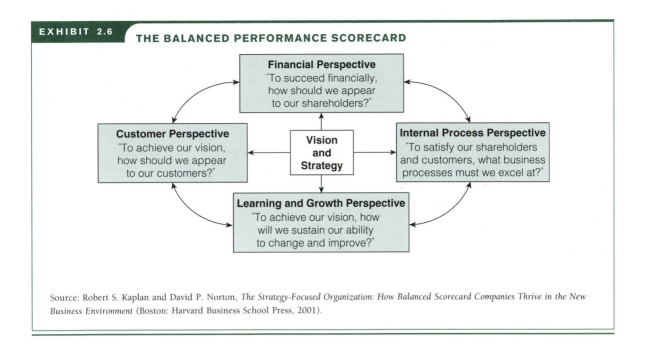

EXHIBIT 2.6   **THE BALANCED PERFORMANCE SCORECARD**

Financial Perspective
"To succeed financially, how should we appear to our shareholders?"

Customer Perspective
"To achieve our vision, how should we appear to our customers?"

Vision and Strategy

Internal Process Perspective
"To satisfy our shareholders and customers, what business processes must we excel at?"

Learning and Growth Perspective
"To achieve our vision, how will we sustain our ability to change and improve?"

Source: Robert S. Kaplan and David P. Norton, *The Strategy-Focused Organization: How Balanced Scorecard Companies Thrive in the New Business Environment* (Boston: Harvard Business School Press, 2001).

The balanced scorecard has been used successfully by many public- and private-sector organizations. Kaplan and Norton found that these successful firms typically adhered to five common principles when implementing the balanced scorecard:[22]

1. *Translate the strategy into operational terms.* Successful firms can illustrate the cause-and-effect relationships that show how intangible assets are transformed into value for customers and other stakeholders. This provides a common frame of reference for all employees.

2. *Align the organization to strategy.* Successful firms link different functional areas through common themes, priorities, and objectives. This creates synergy within the organization that ensures that all efforts are coordinated.

3. *Make strategy everyone's everyday job.* Successful firms move the strategy from the executive boardroom to the front lines of the organization. They do this through communication, education, allowing employees to set personal objectives, and tying incentives to the balanced scorecard.

4. *Make strategy a continual process.* Successful firms hold regular meetings to review strategy performance. They also establish a process whereby the firm can learn and adapt as the strategy evolves.

5. *Mobilize change through executive leadership.* Successful firms have committed energetic leaders who champion the strategy and the balanced scorecard. This ensures that the strategy maintains momentum. Good leaders also prevent the strategy from becoming an obstacle to future progress.

The balanced scorecard doesn't refute the traditional approach to strategic planning. It does, however, caution business leaders to look at strategy and performance as a multidimensional issue. Financial measures, though important, simply cannot tell the whole story. One of the major benefits of the balanced scorecard is that it forces organizations to explicitly consider *during strategy formulation* those factors that are critical to strategy execution. We cannot stress this point enough. Good strategy is always developed with an eye toward how it will be implemented. Issues within the balanced scorecard such as employee training, corporate culture, organizational learning, and executive leadership are critical to the implementation of any strategy.

Lessons from Chapter 2

Strategic marketing planning

- begins with broad decisions and then flows into more specific decisions as the process proceeds through subsequent planning stages.

- involves establishing an organizational mission, corporate or business-unit strategy, marketing goals and objectives, marketing strategy, and ultimately a marketing plan.

- must be consistent with the organization's mission and the corporate or business-unit strategy.

- must be coordinated with all functional business areas to ensure that the organization's goals and objectives will be considered in the development of each functional plan, one of which is the marketing plan.

- establishes marketing-level goals and objectives that support the organization's mission, goals, and objectives.

- develops a marketing strategy, which includes selecting and analyzing target markets and creating and maintaining an appropriate marketing program to satisfy the needs of customers in those target markets.

- ultimately results in a strategic market plan that outlines the activities and resources required to fulfill the organization's mission and achieve its goals and objectives.

The organizational mission

- answers the broad question "What business are we in?"

- identifies what the firm stands for and its basic operating philosophy by answering five basic questions:

    1. Who are we?

    2. Who are our customers?

    3. What is our operating philosophy (basic beliefs, values, ethics, and so on)?

    4. What are our core competencies or competitive advantages?

5. What are our responsibilities with respect to being a good steward of our human, financial, and environmental resources?

- is not the same as the organization's vision, which seeks to answer the question "What do we want to become?"

- should not be too broad or too narrow, thereby rendering it useless for planning purposes.

- should be customer oriented. People's lives and businesses should be enriched because they have dealt with the organization.

- should never focus on profit. A focus on profit in the mission means that something positive happens for the owners and managers of the organization, not necessarily for the customers or other stakeholders.

- must be owned and supported by employees if the organization has any chance of success.

- should not be kept secret but instead communicated to everyone—customers, employees, investors, competitors, regulators, and society in general.

- should be the least changed part of the strategic plan.

Business-unit strategy

- is the central scheme or means for utilizing and integrating resources in the areas of production, finance, research and development, human resources, and marketing to carry out the organization's mission and achieve the desired goals and objectives.

- is associated with developing a competitive advantage where the firm leverages its capabilities in order to serve customers' needs better than the competition.

- determines the nature and future direction of each business unit, including its competitive advantages, the allocation of its resources, and the coordination of functional business areas (marketing, production, finance, human resources, and so on).

- is essentially the same as corporate strategy in small businesses.

The marketing plan

- provides a detailed explanation of the actions necessary to execute the marketing program and thus requires a great deal of effort and organizational commitment to create and implement.

- should be well organized to ensure that it considers and includes all relevant information. The typical structure or outline of a marketing plan includes these elements:

> Executive summary
> Situation analysis

SWOT analysis
Marketing goals and objectives
Marketing strategies
Marketing implementation
Evaluation and control

- should be based on an outline that is comprehensive, flexible, consistent, and logical.

- fulfills five purposes:

    Explains both the present and future situations of the organization.
    Specifies expected outcomes (goals and objectives).
    Describes the specific actions that are to take place and assigns responsibility for each action.
    Identifies the resources needed to carry out the planned actions.
    Permits the monitoring of each action and its results so that controls may be implemented.

- serves as an important communication vehicle to top management and to line managers and employees.

- is an important document, but not nearly as important as the knowledge gained from going through the planning process itself.

- is most often prepared by the director or vice president of marketing but is ultimately approved by the organization's president, chairman, or CEO.

Customer-focused strategic planning

- requires that organizations shift focus from products to the requirements of specific target market segments, from customer transactions to customer relationships and from competition to collaboration.

- puts customers' needs and wants first and focuses on long-term, value-added relationships with customers, employees, suppliers, and other partners.

- must be able to focus its efforts and resources toward understanding customers in ways that enhance the firm's ability to generate sustainable competitive advantages.

- instills a corporate culture that places customers at the top of the organizational hierarchy.

- finds ways to cooperate with suppliers and competitors to serve customers more effectively and efficiently.

Balanced strategic planning

- was borne out of necessity because traditional planning and measurement approaches could not capture value created by an organization's intangible assets (customer relationships, processes, human resources, innovation, and information).

- was advocated strongly by Kaplan and Norton with their creation of the balanced-performance scorecard.

- considers traditional financial indicators of performance but also looks at planning from three additional perspectives: customers, internal processes, and learning and growth.

- is used successfully by many public- and private-sector organizations. Successful firms are those that adhere to five principles when implementing the balanced scorecard:

    Translate the strategy into operational terms.
    Align the organization to strategy.
    Make strategy everyone's everyday job.
    Make strategy a continual process.
    Mobilize change through executive leadership.

- does not refute the traditional approach to strategic planning, but it does caution business leaders to look at strategy and performance as a multidimensional issue.

- forces organizations to explicitly consider *during strategy formulation* those factors that are critical to strategy execution. Good strategy is always developed with an eye toward how it will be implemented.

Questions for Discussion

1. In many organizations, marketing does not have a place of importance in the organizational hierarchy. Why do you think this happens? What are the consequences for a firm that gives little importance to marketing relative to other business functions?

2. Defend or contradict this statement: Developing marketing strategy is more important than implementing marketing strategy because if the strategy is flawed its implementation doesn't matter.

3. What are some of the potential difficulties in approaching strategic planning from a balanced perspective? Isn't financial performance still the most important perspective to take in planning? Explain.

Exercises

1. Review each of the mission statements listed in Exhibit 2.2. Do they follow the guidelines discussed in this chapter? How well does each answer the five basic questions? What do you make of the changes or lack thereof in these mission statements over time?

2. Talk with a small-business owner about the strategic planning process that he or she uses. Do they have a mission statement? Marketing goals and objectives?

A marketing plan? What are the major issues that he or she faces in implementing their marketing program?

3. Palo Alto Software maintains a website devoted to business and marketing plans. Log on to http://www.bplans.com/ma/ and take a look at a few of the sample marketing plans available. Do these plans use the same framework discussed in this chapter?

3

Marketing Ethics and Social Responsibility in Strategic Planning

Introduction

The importance of marketing ethics and social responsibility has been growing over the last few years. The role of ethics and social responsibility in the strategic planning process has become even more important as many firms have seen their image, reputation, and marketing efforts destroyed by problems in these areas. The failure to see ethical conduct as strategic market planning can destroy trust and customer relationships that are necessary for success. Ethical and social responsibility is a necessity in light of stakeholder demands and changes in federal law. In addition to this necessity, being ethical and socially responsible also improves marketing performance and profits. Marketing ethics does not just happen by hiring ethical people; it requires implementation of an effective ethics and compliance program.

Motivated by news reports of scandals and misconduct, customers have increasingly demanded that marketers behave responsibly. Marketers can be judged based on their actions or, as shown in Beyond the Pages 3.1, the social responsibility of the products they offer for sale. Even the world's most respected brands are not immune. Coca-Cola, for example, has struggled with many ethical issues in recent years. One highly publicized event took place when Matthew Whitley, a middle-level Coca-Cola executive, filed a whistle-blowing suit against the company alleging retaliation for revealing fraud in a market study performed on behalf of Burger King. To increase sales, Coca-Cola suggested that Burger King invest in and promote frozen Coke as a kid's snack. Coca-Cola exaggerated the number of frozen Cokes sold in a market test. Coca-Cola eventually paid $21 million to Burger King, $540,000 to the whistle-blower, and a $9 million pretax write-off had to be taken.[1] Coca-Cola also settled a regulatory probe related to allegations of channel stuffing. The Securities and Exchange Commission (SEC) concluded that Coke repeatedly inflated sales and misled investors by shipping extra beverage concentrate to bottlers. The SEC said Coca-Cola executives participated in the scheme to avoid profit shortfalls that would have rattled investors.[2] More recently, Coca-Cola bottlers who serve as the

Beyond the Pages 3.1

THE AUTO INDUSTRY TRIES TO GO GREEN[3]

Toyota dealers now estimate that, in the face of rising gas prices and more environmental awareness, their hybrid Prius only remains on the lot a maximum of 20 hours before being sold. Many people buy hybrid cars with the intention of doing something positive for the environment; but with gas prices soaring, some are now turning to hybrids as a possible money-saving opportunity. It is true that hybrid owners may buy less gas and be required to do less maintenance on their cars, but hybrids generally cost more than conventional cars and the initial cost plus higher insurance costs can seriously add up. A case in point: The hybrid Honda Accord costs around $3,800 more than the conventional Accord. Given this, the only way for a hybrid owner to make up the cost difference (given an estimated 15,000 miles of driving each year) is for gas prices to soar to and stay at $9.20 for at least five years. In the case of the Ford Escape, gas prices would have to rise to $5.60 to make up the difference between the hybrid and conventional Escape. Another way for hybrid purchasers to save is to take advantage of new 2006 tax breaks. According to the American Council for an Energy-Efficient Economy, it is estimated that hybrid purchasers could save up to $3,150 on taxes.

Although the average hybrid may not be the best financial buy, purchasing one may very well be an excellent environmental choice. A hybrid car has a bifurcated system that uses both an electric motor and a gasoline engine. A hybrid car's gasoline engine can be much smaller than that of a conventional car, making the hybrid's engine more efficient. Some hybrids are designed to get the best

possible gas mileage, but the Prius is designed to reduce emissions in urban areas. The Prius can accelerate to about 40 miles per hour before the gasoline engine switches on. However, it turns out that getting the best gas mileage and reducing emissions are closely linked.

Two of the pollutants that cars emit are carbon monoxide and carbon dioxide. A car that burns twice as much gas to travel a mile will also emit twice the amount of carbon monoxide pollution. There would seem to be no argument that a hybrid car's engine would produce fewer pollutants. The bottom line: If you're interested in going green in support of the environment, a hybrid vehicle may be for you. However, if you're interested in saving the green in your wallet, you may want to explore other options.

One option that you may have heard about is ethanol. Many in the auto industry are looking at the grain-based fuel as a means of reducing our demand on oil. However, ethanol has issues of its own. The biggest challenge is that it takes a great deal of corn or other grains to make ethanol. In fact, the grain needed to fill a 25-gallon fuel tank could feed one person for a year. This unfortunate fact pits drivers against the two billion poorest people in the world who rely on grain resources for survival. Currently, ethanol distilleries are taking over the U.S. corn supply, and commodity prices are increasing. For example, world corn and wheat prices are up 25 percent since the ethanol craze began. In the end, however, ethanol is *not* a solution. If the entire U.S. grain supply was converted to ethanol, it would satisfy less than one-sixth of U.S. demand for fuel.

firms' wholesalers sued Coca-Cola, claiming that the plan to send the Powerade product directly to retailers such as Wal-Mart was a breach of contract.[4] Finally, a Coca-Cola administrative secretary and two accomplices were arrested in 2006 and charged in a criminal complaint with wire fraud and attempts to steal and sell trade secrets to PepsiCo.[5] Pepsi immediately reported the plan to Coca-Cola and criminal investigators. Interestingly, after this event, *Advertising Age* conducted an online poll and asked, "if there were no repercussions, would you read a competitor's marketing plan?" While some respondents voiced concerns, 67 percent said if given a competitor's marketing plan, they would read it.[6]

The willingness of marketers to use stolen confidential information should be a concern for all of us. In this chapter, we look at ethics and social responsibility, their connection to marketing strategy, and the challenges of being ethical. Then we discuss deceptive practices in marketing as well as organizational and self-regulating methods of preventing deception. Finally, we examine the organizational context of marketing ethics, including codes of ethics and the role of ethics and social responsibility in improving marketing performance.

The Role of Ethics and Social Responsibility in Marketing Strategy

In response to customer demands, along with the threat of increased regulation, more and more firms have incorporated ethics and social responsibility into the strategic market planning process. Reputation can be damaged by poor performance or ethical misconduct. Poor marketing performance is easier to recover from than ethical misconduct. Obviously, stakeholders who are most directly affected by negative events will have a corresponding shift in their perceptions of a firm's reputation. On the other hand, even those indirectly connected to negative events can shift their reputation attributions. In many cases, those indirectly connected to the negative events may be more influenced by the news media or general public opinion than those who are directly connected to an organization.[7] Some scandals may lead to boycotts and aggressive campaigns to dampen sales and earnings. Nike experienced such a backlash from its use of offshore subcontractors to manufacture its shoes and clothing. When Nike claimed no responsibility for the subcontractors' poor working conditions and extremely low wages, some consumers demanded greater accountability and responsibility by engaging in boycotts, letter-writing campaigns, and public-service announcements. Nike ultimately responded to the growing negative publicity by changing its practices and becoming a model company in managing offshore manufacturing.[8] Due to the links between reputation, ethics, and marketing, we explore the dimensions of social responsibility and marketing ethics, examine research that relates ethics and social responsibility to marketing performance, and discuss their roles in the strategic marketing planning process.

Dimensions of Social Responsibility

Social responsibility is a broad concept that relates to an organization's obligation to maximize its positive impacts on society while minimizing its negative

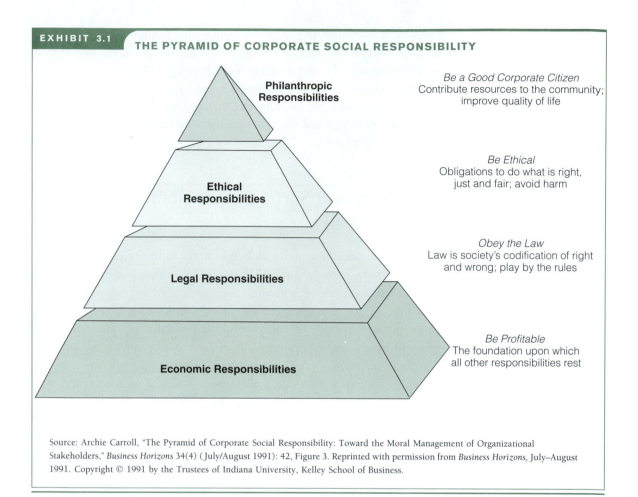

EXHIBIT 3.1

THE PYRAMID OF CORPORATE SOCIAL RESPONSIBILITY

Philanthropic Responsibilities

Be a Good Corporate Citizen
Contribute resources to the community; improve quality of life

Ethical Responsibilities

Be Ethical
Obligations to do what is right, just and fair; avoid harm

Legal Responsibilities

Obey the Law
Law is society's codification of right and wrong; play by the rules

Economic Responsibilities

Be Profitable
The foundation upon which all other responsibilities rest

Source: Archie Carroll, "The Pyramid of Corporate Social Responsibility: Toward the Moral Management of Organizational Stakeholders," *Business Horizons* 34(4) (July/August 1991): 42, Figure 3. Reprinted with permission from *Business Horizons,* July–August 1991. Copyright © 1991 by the Trustees of Indiana University, Kelley School of Business.

impacts. As shown in Exhibit 3.1, social responsibility consists of four dimensions or responsibilities: economic, legal, ethical, and philanthropic.[9]

From an economic perspective, all firms must be responsible to their shareholders, who have a keen interest in stakeholder relationships that influence reputation of the firm and, of course, earning a return on their investment. The economic responsibility of making a profit also serves employees and the community at large due to its impact on employment and income levels in the area that the firm calls home. Marketers also have expectations, at a minimum, to obey laws and regulations. This is a challenge because the legal and regulatory environment is hard to navigate and interpretations of the law change frequently. Economic and legal concerns are the most basic levels of social responsibility for good reason: Without them, the firm may not survive long enough to engage in ethical or philanthropic activities.

At the next level of the pyramid, *marketing ethics* refers to principles and standards that define acceptable marketing conduct as determined by the public, government regulators, private-interest groups, competitors, and the firm itself. The most basic of these principles have been codified as laws and regulations to induce marketers to conform to society's expectations of conduct. However, it is important to understand that marketing ethics goes beyond legal issues: Ethical marketing decisions foster trust, which helps build long-term marketing relationships.

Marketing ethics includes decisions about what is right or wrong in the organizational context of planning and implementing marketing activities in a global business environment to benefit (1) organizational performance, (2) individual achievement in a work group, (3) social acceptance and advancement in the organization, and (4) stakeholders. This definition of *marketing ethics* recognizes that ethical decisions occur in a complex social network environment of a marketing organization. Marketers are often asked by upper-level management to help make the numbers by reaching almost impossible sales targets. In fact, most marketing misconduct is done to help the organization. Being a team player and bending the rules to make targets may result in a promotion. On the other hand, it has destroyed the career of some of those willing to do anything that they are asked to do.

Ample evidence shows that ignoring these issues can destroy trust with customers and prompt government intervention. When firms engage in activities that deviate from accepted principles to further their own interests, continued marketing exchanges become difficult, if not impossible. The best way to deal with such problems is during the strategic planning process, not after major problems materialize. For example, at HCA, The Hospital Corporation of America, allegations of health-care fraud made the company a target of federal and state investigations of its Medicare and home-health-care billing practices. Now, HCA spends roughly $4 million a year on its ethics program, which includes an external ethical compliance committee, two internal committees that draft ethics policies and monitor ethical compliance, and a twenty-member department that implements the entire program. HCA also uses extensive training programs to help employees understand the firm's focus on ethics and legal compliance. In addition to a formal ethical compliance orientation that occurs during initial employment, all HCA employees must complete a 1-hour refresher course on HCA's code of ethical conduct each year.[10]

Being ethical and responsible requires commitment. For this reason, many firms simply ignore these issues and focus instead on satisfying their economic and legal responsibilities, with an eye toward the overall bottom line of profit maximization. Although the firm may do nothing wrong, it misses out on the long-term benefits that can be derived from satisfying ethical and philanthropic responsibilities. Firms that choose to take these extra steps concern themselves with increasing their overall positive impact on society, their local communities, and the environment, with the bottom line of increased goodwill toward the firm, as well as increased profits.

Many firms try hard to align their philanthropy with marketing and brand image. During major disasters, like Hurricane Katrina, firms are given an opportunity to make their philanthropic programs more responsive and visible to the public. For example, Wal-Mart has been given credit for responding to the needs of Hurricane Katrina victims better than the federal government. Wal-Mart's response to Hurricane Katrina was fast, efficient, and significant. Wal-Mart contributed $17 million in cash, more than $3 million in merchandise, $15 million to the Bush–Clinton Katrina Fund, $1 million to the Salvation Army, and $1 million to the American Red Cross. Wal-Mart also provided more than $8.5 million in cash assistance to impacted associates through Wal-Mart's Associate Disaster Relief Fund. Wal-Mart donated 100 truckloads of water and other supplies to the afflicted area. They also donated food for 100,000 meals and the promise of a job for every one of its displaced workers. Cliff Brumfield, executive vice president of the Brookhaven–Lincoln County Chamber of Commerce, said he was impressed with Wal-Mart's preparations: "They were ready before FEMA was." H. Lee Scott, Wal-Mart's CEO, appeared on *Larry King Live* to discuss the chain's response to the storm and was singled out and praised by former presidents George H. W. Bush and Bill Clinton. As Wal-Mart has demonstrated, being socially responsible is not only good for customers, employees, and the community but also makes good business sense.

Philanthropic activities make very good marketing tools. Thinking of corporate philanthropy as a marketing tool may seem cynical, but it points out the reality that philanthropy can be very good for a firm. Nike, for example, sponsors sporting events at local Boys and Girls Clubs and then features these events in its national advertising. This approach has been called "strategic philanthropy," or financially sound goodwill. Firms that engage in philanthropic activities win the trust and respect of their employees, customers, and society, thus allowing them to earn higher profits in the long run. Many firms focus their philanthropic efforts on education. Acknowledging that today's students are tomorrow's customers and employees, firms such as Kroger, Campbell's Soup, Kodak, American Express, Apple Computer, and the Coca-Cola Company have donated money, equipment, and employee time to help improve local schools around the nation. McDonald's, for example, provides college scholarship money to high school students who work part time in its restaurants. Although some members of the public fear strategic philanthropy initiatives in education and other social areas, business participation is necessary in helping to educate future employees and customers.

Marketing Ethics and Strategy

Marketing ethics includes the principles and standards that guide the behavior of individuals and groups in making marketing decisions. Marketing strategy must consider stakeholders—including managers, employees, customers, industry associations, government regulators, business partners, and special-interest groups—all of whom contribute to accepted standards and society's expectations. The most basic of these standards have been codified as laws and regulations to encourage companies to conform to society's expectations of business conduct.[11] Exhibit 3.2 lists some of the more common ethical issues that occur in marketing.

The standards of conduct that determine the ethics of marketing activities require both organizations and individuals to accept responsibility for their actions and to comply with established value systems.[12] As Exhibit 3.3 indicates, the vast majority of consumers support existing government regulation of marketing or want more regulation. Without a shared view of which values and conduct are appropriate and

EXHIBIT 3.2   **POTENTIAL ETHICAL ISSUES IN MARKETING**

Overall

Misrepresenting the firm's capabilities
Manipulation or misuse of data or information
Exploitation of children or disadvantaged groups
Invasion of privacy
Anticompetitive activities
Abusive behavior

Product Issues

Misrepresentation of goods or services
Failing to disclose product defects
Counterfeit or gray-market products
Misleading warranties
Failure to disclose important product information
Reducing package contents without reducing package size

Pricing Issues

Price deception
Reference pricing claims
Price discrimination
Price fixing between competitors
Predatory pricing
Fraudulent refund policies

Distribution Issues

Opportunistic behavior among members of the supply chain
Exclusive distribution arrangements
Tying contracts
Withholding product availability
Withholding product or promotional support

Promotion Issues

Bait-and-switch advertising
False or misleading advertising
High-pressure salespeople
False or misleading selling techniques
Bribery of salespeople or purchasing agents
Entertainment and gift giving
Lying
Stereotypical portrayals of women, minorities, or senior citizens
Sexual innuendo in advertising
Fine print in newspaper advertising

acceptable, companies may fail to balance their desires for profits against the wishes and needs of society. As illustrated in Beyond the Pages 3.2, maintaining this balance often demands changes, compromises, or trade-offs in marketing strategy. If a balance is not maintained, more regulation can result to require responsible behavior of all

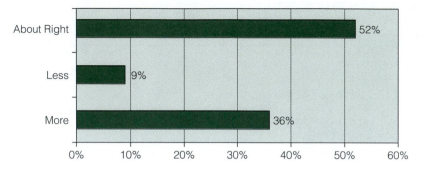

EXHIBIT 3.3   **GOVERNMENT REGULATION OF MARKETING ACTIVITIES**

Do you think that government should do more or less to regulate the types of activities that organizations use to market to consumers?

About Right — 52%
Less — 9%
More — 36%

Source: Harris Interactive/Public Relations Society of America Foundation telephone survey of 1,015 adults ages 18 and older in *USA Today Snapshots,* "Government Regulation of Marketing Activities," April 6, 2006, B1.

marketers. Therefore, many best practices evolve to ensure ethical conduct that avoids the inflexibility and expense of regulation. Society has developed rules—both legal and implied—to guide firms in their efforts to earn profits through means that do not harm individuals or society at large.

When companies deviate from the prevailing standards of industry and society, the result is customer dissatisfaction, lack of trust, and legal action. Indeed, 78 percent of U.S. consumers say they avoid certain businesses or products because of negative perceptions about them.[13] Consumers in other countries also avoid businesses or products because of negative perceptions. According to one survey, two-thirds of consumers in their 30s and 40s in the United Kingdom boycott brands because of "unethical behavior" by the manufacturers. Ninety-five percent of the 1,000 consumers surveyed indicated they would never purchase the brand.[14]

A firm's reputation is one its greatest intangible assets. The value of a positive reputation is difficult to quantify, but it is very important. A single negative incident can influence perceptions of a firm's image and reputation for years afterwards. Corporate reputation, image, and branding are more important than ever and are among the most critical aspects of sustaining relationships with key stakeholders. Although an organization does not control its reputation in a direct sense, its actions, choices, behaviors, and consequences do influence its reputation. Companies such as ExxonMobil, Chevron, and Royal Dutch Shell receive low ratings from the public for what the public perceives as a "heartless" spike in gasoline prices at a time when these companies are enjoying record profits. Despite corporate–governance reforms and a growing commitment to ethics and social responsibility, the overall reputation of American corporations continues to slip. Seventy-one percent of the public rates the

Beyond the Pages 3.2

MARKETING LINKED TO OBESITY[15]

Most companies operate within socially acceptable guidelines. However, from time to time, companies are found to operate outside these guidelines. To be socially responsible, a firm must work to emphasize its positive effects and avoid any negative effects it or its products may have on society. One growing area of concern involves the combination of advertising and nutrition. Today, many firms are being criticized for aggressively marketing foods that are high in fat, sugar, and calories. The issue is especially intense with respect to marketing toward children.

Studies conducted by the Kaiser Family Foundation have found that the average child sees around 40,000 television advertisements per year—most of these encourage children to eat candy, cereal, and fast food and drink soft drinks. The Institute of Medicine also released a compilation report of 123 research studies over 30 years, saying there is "strong evidence" that advertising is linked with obesity in young children. A particularly problematic issue is the use of popular licensed children's cartoon characters (such as SpongeBob SaqurePants and Scooby Doo) to advertise unhealthy foods.

Obesity can greatly impact children's health. According to the Centers for Disease Control and Prevention, since 1980 the number of overweight children between the ages of 6 and 11 (the group most largely targeted by advertisements containing cartoon characters) has more than doubled. The Kaiser findings indicate that food advertisements may influence the food choices/requests that

children make and confuse them regarding what is nutritious and what is not. Companies have been using cartoon characters in advertising since Mickey Mouse appeared on Post Toasties in 1935. The Institute of Medicine recommended that food companies stop using licensed characters to advertise their high-sugar, high-calorie, low-nutrient foods and to use these characters to market only healthy food choices. The Kaiser study also indicated that companies could have a positive impact on children by using their favorite characters to advertise healthful foods.

Although the food industry has long denied the connection between advertising and obesity, the recent evidence is pretty clear in supporting the connection. Although some companies, such as General Mills, are remaining silent on the issue, others are making some positive changes. Kraft Foods has begun limiting its use of cartoon characters in a promise to promote better nutritional standards for children under the age of 12. Kellogg's has placed information on its cereal boxes that teach children how to choose healthy breakfast foods. Viacom recently agreed to place SpongeBob SquarePants on spinach packages.

Although some companies are making efforts to promote healthier food choices for children, those in the food industry will need to agree on a definition for what makes a healthy food. The information is out there regarding this issue. The question is whether or not companies choose to be socially responsible in advertising to children or whether they keep the focus on the bottom line.

reputation of American businesses as "not good" or "terrible," up from 68 percent in only two years.[16]

Some businesspeople choose to behave ethically because of enlightened self-interest or the expectation that "ethics pays." They want to act responsibly, be good citizens, and assume that the public and customers will reward the company for its ethical behavior. Avon, for example, is a company that achieves success, contributes to society, and has ethical management. Andrea Jung, CEO, and Susan Kropf, COO, operate in the high-risk area of direct selling without scandals or major ethical issues. In 2004 Jung was named one of *Fortune*'s 100 most powerful women.[17] According to *BusinessWeek*, Jung gave Avon a much needed facelift as revenues increased from $5.3

billion to $7.7 billion. Avon has also won approval to conduct direct selling in China—the first approval for a U.S. company since China banned the practice in 1998.[18]

The Challenges of Being Ethical and Socially Responsible

Although most consider the values of honesty, respect, and trust to be self-evident and universally accepted, business decisions involve complex and detailed discussions in which correctness may not be so clear cut. Both employees and managers need experience within their specific industry to understand how to operate in gray areas or to handle close calls in evolving areas, such as Internet privacy. For example, how much personal information should be stored on a firm's website without customers' permission? In Europe, the European Union Directive on Data Protection prohibits selling or renting mailing lists—consumers' data cannot be used without their permission.[19] In the United States, firms have more freedom to decide how to collect and use customers' personal data, but advancing technology raises new questions every day. Issues related to personal privacy, unsolicited e-mail, and misappropriation of copyrighted intellectual property cause ethical problems. Protecting trademarks and brand names becomes more difficult as e-marketing has advanced.

Individuals who have limited business experience often find themselves required to make sudden decisions about product quality, advertising, pricing, sales techniques, hiring practices, privacy, and pollution control. For example, how do advertisers know when they make misleading statements as opposed to simple puffery or exaggeration? Bayer claims to be "the world's best aspirin," Hush Puppies are "the earth's most comfortable shoes," and Firestone (before recalling 6.5 million tires) promised "quality you can trust."[20] The personal values learned through socialization from family, religion, and school may not provide specific guidelines for these complex business decisions. In other words, a person's experiences and decisions at home, in school, and in the community may be quite different from the experiences and the decisions that he or she has to make at work. Moreover, the interests and values of individual employees may differ from those of the company in which they work, from industry standards, and from society in general. When personal values are inconsistent with the configuration of values held by the work group, ethical conflict may ensue. It is important that a shared vision of acceptable behavior develop from an organizational perspective to cultivate consistent and reliable relationships with all concerned stakeholders. A shared vision of ethics that is part of an organization's culture can be questioned, analyzed, and modified as new issues develop. However, marketing ethics should relate to work environment decisions and should not control or influence personal ethical issues.[21]

It is imperative that firms become familiar with many of the ethical and social issues that can occur in marketing so that these issues can be identified and resolved when they occur. Essentially, any time that an activity causes managers, employees, or customers in a target market to feel manipulated or cheated, an ethical issue exists regardless of the legality of the activity. Many ethical issues can develop into legal problems if they do not become addressed in the planning

EXHIBIT 3.4	TYPES OF MISCONDUCT OBSERVED IN ORGANIZATIONS	
Abusive or intimidating behavior toward employees		21%
Lying to employees, customers, vendors or the public		19%
A situation that places employee interests over organizational interests		18%
Violations of safety regulations		16%
Misreporting of actual time worked		16%
E-mail and Internet abuse		13%
Discrimination on the basis of race, color, gender, age or similar categories		12%
Stealing or theft		11%
Sexual harassment		9%
Provision of goods or services that fail to meet specifications		8%
Misuse of confidential information		7%
Alteration of documents		6%
Falsification or misrepresentation of financial records or reports		5%
Improper use of competitors' inside information		4%
Price fixing		3%
Giving or accepting bribes, kickbacks or inappropriate gifts		3%

Source: Ethics Resource Center, *2005 National Business Ethics Survey: How Employees View Ethics in Their Organizations* (Washington, DC: Ethics Resource Center, 2005), 25. Reprinted with permission.

process. Once an issue has been identified, marketers must decide how to deal with it. Exhibit 3.4 provides an overview of types of observed misconduct in organizations. All marketers are subject to observing and preventing these types of ethical issues. Although Exhibit 3.4 documents many types of issues that exist in organizations, due to the almost infinite number of ways that misconduct can occur, it is impossible to list every conceivable ethical issue. Any type of manipulation, deceit, or even just the absence of transparency in decision making can create harm to others.

Deceptive Practices In Marketing

When a marketing decision results in deception in order to advance individual or organizational interests over those of another individual, group, or organization, charges of fraud may result. In general, *fraud* is any false communication that deceives, manipulates, or conceals facts in order to create a false impression. It can be considered a crime, and convictions may result in fines, imprisonment, or both. Fraud costs U.S. organizations more than $600 billion a year; the average company loses about 6 percent of total revenues to fraud and abuses committed by its own employees.[22] Some of the most common fraudulent activities reported by employees include stealing office supplies and employee shoplifting, claiming to have worked extra hours, and stealing money or products.[23] In recent years, both marketing and accounting fraud have become major ethical issues and front-page news stories. The negative publicity has taken its toll on public opinion of the marketing profession. Telemarketers, car salespeople, and advertising executives are now among the lowest-ranked marketing professions in terms of the public's perceptions of honesty and ethics.[24]

Deceptive Communication and Promotion

Marketing practices that are false or misleading can destroy customers' trust in an organization. Although the most famous examples of deception occur at the national or global level, the problems of marketing deception are not limited to these large and well-known firms. In fact, a great deal of marketing deception occurs at the county or local level. According to the National Association of Consumer Agency Administrators, local home-improvement contractors are among the most frequent abusers of deceptive marketing. Not keeping promises, offering faulty warranties and service contracts, and going out of business before completing a job are the most common abuses. In many states, there are few licensing requirements for contractors, which make it much easier for consumers to be duped by anyone with a hammer and saw.[25]

False and deceptive communication and promotion are the most common and recurring issues in marketing deception. Abuses in promotion can range from exaggerated claims and concealed facts to outright lying. *Exaggerated claims* are those that cannot be substantiated, such as when a commercial states that a certain product is superior to any other on the market. For example, Papa John's International, Inc., invested years and millions of dollars into its "Better Ingredients, Better Pizza" advertising campaign. However, a Texas jury found that the slogan constituted deceptive advertising, and the judge ordered the company to stop using the claim in future advertising.[26] The decision was eventually overturned on appeal.

Another form of advertising abuse involves making *ambiguous statements,* in which claims are so weak that the viewer, reader, or listener must infer the advertiser's intended message. Because it is inherently vague, using ambiguous wording enables the advertiser to deny any intent to deceive. The verb *help* is a good example (as in expressions such as "helps prevent," "helps fight," "helps make you feel").[27] Consumers may view such advertisements as unethical because they fail to communicate all the information needed to make a good purchasing decision or because they deceive the consumer outright. In another example, the Federal Trade Commission (FTC) and other agencies now monitor more closely the promotions for work-at-home business ventures. Consumers lose millions of dollars each year responding to ads for phony business opportunities such as those promising $50,000 a year for doing medical billing from a home computer.[28]

Product-labeling issues can be even murkier than advertising. For example, Mott's, Inc., the nation's leading producer of applesauce and apple juice, agreed to revise the labels of some of its fruit products after New York's attorney general claimed they were misleading consumers. The products—often made by blending apple juice with enough grape or cherry juice to make the designated flavor—had labels with the words "100% Juice" and a picture of grapes and cherries and the fruits' names in large lettering underneath. The attorney general argued that placing the fruit's name under "100% Juice" could lead consumers to assume that the products were 100 percent grape juice or cherry juice. Mott's admitted no wrongdoing but agreed to pay $177,500 to cover the investigation costs and to institute a minor change to the labels in question.[29]

In another case, a jury awarded $50 million in compensatory damages to Gerald Barnett who suffered a heart attack and quadruple bypass surgery after taking Vioxx for 31 months. The decision was the latest in a string of verdicts against Merck's assertion that it acted responsibly in developing and marketing Vioxx, which it took off the market in September 2004 after a study linked the drug to an increased risk of heart attacks and strokes in patients who took it for 18 months or longer. The jury also awarded $1 million in punitive damages, arguing that Merck had acted with neglect because the company knew about Vioxx's risks years before it withdrew the drug from the market. So far, Merck has won three of the six cases that have gone to trial in both federal and state courts. However, the losses have been expensive. There are an estimated 14,200 pending Vioxx-related cases against Merck.[30] As a result of Merck's challenges, the pharmaceutical industry adopted new guidelines for direct-to-consumer advertising in the United States. At issue was the ability of direct-to-consumer advertising to encourage patients to use drugs that they may not have needed.[31]

Communication in the context of personal selling can also mislead by concealing facts within a message. For instance, a salesperson anxious to sell a medical insurance policy might list a large number of illnesses covered by the policy but fail to mention that it does not cover some commonly covered illnesses. Fraudulent activity has rapidly increased in the area of direct marketing, in which companies use the telephone and nonpersonal media to communicate information to customers, who then purchase products via mail, telephone, or the Internet. In 2005 consumers reported losses of $680 million resulting from direct-marketing fraud. Of the 685,000 complaints received by the FTC that year, 255,565 concerned identity theft, and 431,118 were about other forms of fraud. Internet-related complaints accounted for 46 percent of fraud reports and $335 million of reported losses.[32]

Regulating Deceptive Marketing Practices

Many firms attempt to regulate themselves in an effort to demonstrate ethical responsibility and to preclude further regulation by federal or state governments. In addition to complying with all relevant laws and regulations, many firms choose to join trade associations that have self-regulatory programs. Although such programs are not a direct outgrowth of laws, many became established to stop or delay the development of laws and regulations that would restrict the associations' business practices. Some trade associations establish codes of conduct by which their members must abide or risk rebuke or expulsion from the association.

Perhaps the best-known self-regulatory association is the Better Business Bureau (BBB), an organization supported by over 300,000 local member businesses. More than 150 local bureaus extending over 98 percent of the nation help millions of consumers and businesses each year.[33] Each bureau works to champion good business practices within a community although it usually does not have strong tools for enforcing its rules of business conduct. When a firm violates what the BBB believes to be good business practice, the bureau warns consumers through local newspapers or broadcast media. If the offending organization is a member if the BBB, it may be expelled from the local bureau. For example, a Connecticut BBB revoked the membership of Priceline.com after the online retailer failed to address numerous complaints related to misrepresentation of products, failed to provide promised refunds, and failed to correct billing problems.[34] The BBB has also developed a website (http://www.bbb.org) to help consumers identify businesses that operate in an ethical manner. BBB members who use the site agree to binding arbitration with regard to online privacy issues.

Self-regulatory programs like the BBB have a number of advantages over government regulation. Establishment and implementation of such programs are usually less costly, and their guidelines or codes of conduct are generally more practical and realistic. Furthermore, effective self-regulatory programs reduce the need to expand government bureaucracy. However, self-regulation also has several limitations. Nonmember firms are under no obligation to abide by a trade association's industry guidelines or codes. Moreover, most associations lack the tools or authority to enforce their guidelines. Finally, these guidelines are often less strict than the regulations established by government agencies.

Organizational Determinants of Marketing Ethics and Social Responsibility

Although individuals can and do make ethical decisions, they do not operate in a vacuum. Ethical choices in business are most often made jointly in committees and work groups or in conversations with coworkers. Moreover, people learn to settle ethical issues not only from their individual backgrounds but also others with whom they associate in the business environment. The outcome of this learning process depends on the strength of each individual's personal values, the opportunity for unethical behavior, and the exposure to others who behave ethically or unethically. Consequently, the culture of the organization—as well as superiors, peers, and subordinates—can have a significant impact on the ethical decision-making process.[35]

Corporate or organizational culture may be conveyed formally in employee handbooks, codes of conduct, memos, and ceremonies, but it is also expressed informally through dress codes, extracurricular activities, and anecdotes. A firm's culture gives its members meaning and offers direction about how to behave and deal with problems within the firm. The corporate culture at American Express, for example, includes numerous anecdotes about employees who have gone beyond the call of duty to help customers in difficult situations. This strong tradition of customer service might encourage an American Express employee to take extra steps to help a customer who encounters a problem while traveling overseas.

On the other hand, a firm's, or even an industry's, culture may also encourage employees to make decisions that others may judge as unethical or it may not discourage actions that may be viewed as unethical. For example, increasing competition in the beer industry has led many firms to use more provocative advertising. These ads depict younger-looking consumers enjoying beer and fun at parties. Coors at one time used an ad that asked "Why do we party? Because we can-can-can!" Many consumer advocacy organizations have complained that beer industry ads push too hard to attract younger consumers under the legal drinking age. Coors agreed to pull its ad after several complaints. However, the attention attracted increased scrutiny from the FTC, which began an investigation into beer and alcohol marketing practices.[36]

In marketing, we think of *ethical climate* as that part of a corporate culture that relates to an organization's expectations about appropriate conduct. To some extent, ethical climate is the character component of an organization. Corporate policies and codes, the conduct of top managers, the values and moral philosophies of coworkers, and opportunity for misconduct all contribute to a firm's ethical climate. When top managers strive to establish an ethical climate based on responsibility and citizenship, they set the tone for ethical decisions. Such is the case at the White Dog Café in Philadelphia, where owner Judy Wicks infuses social responsibility throughout her entire business operation. The restaurant operates using 100 percent wind-powered electricity, with 20 percent of all profits donated to charity. Wicks purchases only organic produce and meats from humanely raised animals.[37] The responsibility and citizenship exhibited by Wicks has established an ethical climate that promotes responsible conduct. Ethical climate also determines whether an individual perceives an issue as having an ethical component. Recognizing ethical issues and generating alternatives to address them are manifestations of a firm's ethical climate.

To meet the public's escalating demands for ethical marketing, firms need to develop plans and structures for addressing ethical considerations. Some directions for the improvement of ethics have been mandated through regulation, but firms must be willing to have in place a values and ethics system that exceeds minimum regulatory requirements. Although there are no universal standards that can be applied to organizational ethics programs, most companies develop codes, values, or policies to guide business behavior. It would be very naïve to think that simply having a code of ethics would solve any ethical dilemmas a firm might face.[38] In fact, the majority of firms that experience ethical or legal problems usually have stated ethics codes and programs. Often, the problem is that top management, as well as the overall corporate culture, has not integrated these codes, values, and standards into daily decision making. For example, before its troubles ensued, Tyco had an ethics program and was a member of the Ethics Officers Association. Unfortunately, the program was never active at Tyco, and top management involved themselves in misconduct that resulted in a complete loss of public confidence in the company.

Codes of Conduct

Most firms begin the process of establishing organizational ethics programs by developing *codes of conduct* (also called *codes of ethics*), which are formal statements that describe what an organization expects of its employees. According to an Ethics Resource Center survey, 86 percent of employees reported that their firm has written standards of ethical business conduct such as codes of ethics, policy statements on

---

EXHIBIT 3.5   **KEY CONSIDERATIONS IN DEVELOPING AND IMPLEMENTING A CODE OF ETHICAL CONDUCT**

1. Examine high-risk areas and issues.
2. State values and conduct necessary to comply with laws and regulations. Values are an important buffer in preventing serious misconduct.
3. Identify values that specifically address current ethical issues.
4. Consider values that link the organization to a stakeholder orientation. Attempt to find overlaps among organizational and stakeholder values.
5. Make the code of conduct understandable by providing examples that reflect values.
6. Communicate the code frequently and in language that employees can understand.
7. Revise the code every year with input from a wide variety of internal and external stakeholders.

---

ethics, or guidelines on proper business conduct.[39] These codes may address a variety of situations from internal operations to sales presentations and financial disclosure practices.

A code of ethical conduct has to reflect the board of directors' and senior management's desire for organizational compliance with the values, rules, and policies that support an ethical climate. Development of a code of conduct should involve the board of directors, president, and senior managers who will be implementing the code. Legal staff should be called upon to ensure that the code has correctly assessed key areas of risk and that standards contained in the code buffer potential legal problems. A code of conduct that does not address specific high-risk activities within the scope of daily operations is inadequate for maintaining standards that can prevent misconduct. Exhibit 3.5 lists the key considerations in developing and implementing a code of ethical conduct.

As a large multinational firm, Texas Instruments (TI) manufactures computers, calculators, and other high-technology products. Its code of ethics resembles that of many other organizations. The code addresses issues related to policies and procedures; government laws and regulations; relationships with customers, suppliers, and competitors; the acceptance of gifts, travel, and entertainment; political contributions; expense reporting; business payments; conflicts of interest; investment in TI stock; handling of proprietary information and trade secrets; use of TI employees and assets to perform personal work; relationships with government officials and agencies; and the enforcement of the code. TI's code emphasizes that ethical behavior is critical to maintaining long-term success and that each individual is responsible for upholding the integrity of the company. The preamble to TI's code of conduct puts it this way:

> *Our reputation at TI depends upon all of the decisions we make and all the actions we take personally each day. Our values define how we will evaluate our decisions and actions . . . and how we will conduct our business. We are working in a difficult and demanding, ever-changing business environment. Together we are building a work environment on the foundation of Integrity, Innovation and Commitment. Together we are moving our company into a new century . . . one good decision at a time. Our high*

standards have rewarded us with an enviable reputation in today's marketplace . . . a reputation of integrity, honesty and trustworthiness. That strong ethical reputation is a vital asset . . . and each of us shares a personal responsibility to protect, to preserve and to enhance it. Our reputation is a strong but silent partner in all business relationships. By understanding and applying the values presented on the following pages, each of us can say to ourselves and to others, "TI is a good company, and one reason is that I am a part of it." Know what's right. Value what's right. Do what's right.[40]

To ensure that its employees understand the nature of business ethics and the ethical standards that the company expects them to follow, TI offers an "ethics quick test" to help them when they have doubts about the ethics of specific situations and behaviors:

- Is the action legal?

- Does it comply with our values?

- If you do it, will you feel bad?

- How will it look in the newspaper?

- If you know it's wrong, don't do it!

- If you're not sure, ask.

- Keep asking until you get an answer.

TI provides a toll-free number (1-800-33-ETHIC) for employees to call, anonymously, to report incidents of unethical behavior or to simply ask questions.[41]

Research has found that corporate codes of ethics often have five to seven core values or principles in addition to more detailed descriptions and examples of appropriate conduct.[42] Six core values are considered to be highly desirable in any code of ethical conduct: (1) trustworthiness, (2) respect, (3) responsibility, (4) fairness, (5) caring, and (6) citizenship.[43] These values will not be effective without distribution, training, and the support of top management in making them a part of the corporate culture and the ethical climate. Employees need specific examples of how these values can be implemented.

Codes of conduct will not resolve every ethical issue encountered in daily operations, but they help employees and managers deal with ethical dilemmas by prescribing or limiting specific activities. Many firms have a code of ethics, but sometimes they do not communicate their code effectively. A code placed on a website or in a training manual is useless if the company doesn't reinforce it on a daily basis. By communicating both the expectations of proper behavior to employees, as well as punishments they face if they violate the rules, codes of conduct curtail opportunities for unethical behavior and thereby improve ethical decision making. Codes of conduct do not have to be so detailed that they take into account every situation, but they should provide guidelines and principles capable of helping employees achieve organizational ethical objectives and address risks in an accepted manner.[44]

Marketing Ethics and Leadership

There is increasing support that ethical cultures emerge from strong leadership. Many agree that the character and success of the most admired companies emanates from their leaders. The reason is simple: Employees look to the leader as a model of acceptable behavior. As a result, if a firm is to maintain ethical behavior, top management must model its policies and standards. In fact, maintaining an ethical culture is near impossible if top management does not support ethical behavior. For example, in an effort to keep earnings high and boost stock prices, many firms have engaged in falsifying revenue reports. Top executives in these firms encouraged the behavior because they held stock options and could receive bonus packages tied to the company's performance. Thus, higher reported revenues meant larger executive payoffs.

In the realm of marketing ethics, great leaders (1) create a common goal or vision for the company; (2) obtain buy-in, or support, from significant partners; (3) motivate others to be ethical; (4) use the resources that are available to them; and (5) enjoy their jobs and approach them with an almost contagious tenacity, passion, and commitment.[45] Along with strong ethical leadership, a strong corporate culture in support of ethical behavior can also play a key role in guiding employee behavior. A study of 330,000 employees at 72 U.S. companies indicated that problems in corporate belief and value systems cause "ethical lapses" more often than individual unethical behavior.[46] Organizational culture, coworkers and supervisors, and the opportunity to engage in unethical behavior influence ethical decision making. Ethics training can affect all three types of influence. Full awareness of the philosophy of management, rules, and procedures can strengthen both the organizational culture and the ethical stance of peers and supervisors. Such awareness, too, arms employees against opportunities for unethical behavior and lessens the likelihood of misconduct. If adequately and thoughtfully designed, ethics training can ensure that everyone in the firm (1) recognizes situations that might involve ethical decision making, (2) understands the values and culture of the firm, and (3) can evaluate the impact of ethical decisions on the firm in the light of its value structure.[47]

Stakeholders, Market Orientation, and Marketing Performance

One of the most powerful arguments for including ethics and social responsibility in the strategic planning process is the increasing evidence of a link between social responsibility, stakeholders, and marketing performance.[48] An ethical climate calls for organizational members to incorporate the interests of all stakeholders, including customers, in their decisions and actions. Hence, employees working in an ethical climate will make an extra effort to better understand the demands and concerns of customers. One study found that ethical climate is associated with employee commitment to quality and intrafirm trust.[49] Employee commitment to the firm, customer loyalty, and profitability have also been linked to increased social responsibility.[50]

These findings emphasize the role of an ethical climate in building a strong competitive position.

As employees perceive an improvement in the ethical climate of their firm, their commitment to the achievement of high-quality standards also increases. They become more willing to personally support the quality initiatives of the firm. These employees often discuss quality-related issues with others both inside and outside of the firm, and gain a sense of personal accomplishment from providing quality goods and services.[51] These employees exhibit effort beyond both expectations and requirements in order to supply quality products in their particular job or area of responsibility. Conversely, employees who work in less ethical climates have less committment to providing such quality. These employees tend to work only for the pay, take longer breaks, and are anxious to leave everyday whether or not they completed their work.[52]

Market Orientation

An ethical climate is also conducive to a strong market orientation. *Market orientation* refers to the development of an organizational culture that effectively and efficiently promotes the necessary behaviors for the creation of superior value for buyers and, thus, continuous superior performance of the firm.[53] Market orientation places the customer's interests first, but it does not exclude the interests of other stakeholders. Being market oriented means fostering a sense of cooperation and open information exchange that gives the firm a clearer view of the customer's needs and desires. Without a strong ethical climate, a competitive workplace orientation can emerge. A competitive orientation encourages personal success, which may come at the expense of openness and cooperation. Internal competition between employees may encourage the achievement of financial performance levels, without regard for their potential effects on other stakeholders both inside and outside the firm. Consequently, employees are unlikely to incorporate the demands and concerns of society, business, or customers in their decisions.

Stakeholder Orientation

The degree to which a firm understands and addresses stakeholder demands can be referred to as a *stakeholder orientation*. This orientation contains three sets of activities: (1) the organization-wide generation of data about stakeholder groups and assessment of the firm's effects on these groups, (2) the distribution of this information throughout the firm, and (3) the organization's responsiveness as a whole to this intelligence.[54]

Generating data about stakeholders begins with identifying the stakeholders who are relevant to the firm. Relevant stakeholder communities should be analyzed on the basis of the power that each enjoys as well as by the ties between them. Next, the firm should characterize the concerns about the business's conduct that each relevant stakeholder group shares. This information can be derived from formal research, including surveys, focus groups, Internet searches, or press reviews. For example, Ford Motor Company obtains input on social and environmental responsibility issues from company representatives, suppliers, customers, and community leaders. Shell

has an online discussion forum where website visitors are invited to express their opinions on the company's activities and their implications. Employees and managers can also generate this information informally as they carry out their daily activities. For example, purchasing managers know about suppliers' demands, public relations executives about the media, legal counselors about the regulatory environment, financial executives about investors, sales representatives about customers, and human resources advisers about employees. Finally, the company should evaluate its impact on the issues that are important to the various stakeholders who it has identified.[55]

A stakeholder orientation is not complete unless it includes activities that address stakeholder issues. For example, The Gap reported that although factory inspections are improving, it is still struggling to wipe out deep-seated problems such as discrimination and excessive overtime. In 2004 The Gap revoked approval for seventy factories that violated its code of vendor conduct. The Gap also realized that it sometimes contributes to problems by making unreasonable demands on factories; it is becoming stricter about its own deadlines to ensure that dumping rush jobs on factories does not occur.[56]

The responsiveness of the organization as a whole to stakeholder intelligence consists of the initiatives that the firm adopts to ensure that it abides by or exceeds stakeholder expectations and has a positive impact on stakeholder issues. Such activities are likely to be specific to a particular stakeholder group (for example, family-friendly work schedules) or to a particular stakeholder issue (for example, pollution-reduction programs). These responsiveness processes typically involve the participation of the concerned stakeholder groups. Kraft, for example, includes special-interest groups and university representatives in its programs to become sensitized to present and future ethical issues.

A stakeholder orientation can be viewed as a continuum in that firms are likely to adopt the concept to varying degrees. To gauge a given firm's stakeholder orientation, it is necessary to evaluate the extent to which the firm adopts behaviors that typify both the generation and dissemination of stakeholder intelligence and responsiveness to it. A given organization may generate and disseminate more intelligence about certain stakeholder communities than about others and, as a result, may respond to that intelligence differently.[57]

Marketing Performance

A climate of ethics and social responsibility also creates a large measure of trust among a firm's stakeholders. The most important contributing factor to gaining trust is the perception that the firm and its employees will not sacrifice their standards of integrity.[58] In an ethical work climate, employees can reasonably expect to be treated with respect and consideration by their coworkers and superiors.

Furthermore, trusting relationships with key external stakeholders can contribute to greater efficiencies and productivity in the supply chain, as well as a stronger sense of loyalty among the firm's customers. A study by Cone/Roper reported that three out of four customers say they avoid or refuse to buy from certain businesses. Poor service is the number one reason cited, but business conduct is the second reason that customers give for avoiding specific companies.[59] After the Exxon *Valdez* oil spill, certain groups and individual citizens aggressively boycotted Exxon because of its response to the environmental disaster. Likewise, many consumers stopped buying Chicken of the Sea and competing tuna products when those companies initially refused to require that their tuna suppliers adopt dolphin-friendly fishing practices.[60]

Research indicates a strong association between social responsibility and customer loyalty in that customers are likely to keep buying from firms perceived as doing the right thing. A survey by Walker Research revealed that 88 percent of customers are more likely to buy from a firm that is socially responsible and a good corporate citizen if the quality, service, and price are equal to that of competitors.[61] One explanation for this observation may be that good-citizen firms are responsive to customers' concerns and have a sense of dedication to treating them fairly. By gauging customer satisfaction, continuously improving the quality and safety of products, and by making customer information easily accessible and understandable, ethical and socially responsible firms are more likely to serve customers' needs satisfactorily.

Firms that do not develop strategies and programs to incorporate ethics and social responsibility into their organizational cultures will pay the price with potentially poor marketing performance, the potential costs of civil or criminal litigation, and damaging negative publicity when the public discovers questionable activities. On the other hand, firms that do incorporate ethics and social responsibility into their strategic plans are likely to experience improved marketing performance. Unfortunately, because many firms do not view marketing ethics and social responsibility as organizational performance issues, many firms do not believe that these issues need to be considered in the strategic planning process. Individuals also have different ideas as to what is ethical or unethical, leading them to confuse the need for workplace ethics with the right to maintain their own personal values and ethics. Although the concept of ethics is controversial, it is possible and desirable to incorporate ethics and social responsibility into the planning process.

Incorporating Ethics and Social Responsibility into Strategic Planning

Many firms integrate ethics and social responsibility into their strategic planning through ethics compliance programs or integrity initiatives that make legal compliance, ethics, and social responsibility an organization-wide effort.[62] Such programs establish, communicate, and monitor a firm's ethical values and legal requirements through codes of conduct, ethics offices, training programs, and audits. Although many firms take considerable time and effort in creating their own codes of conduct, many do not. Krispy Kreme, once a high-flying company, experienced a meltdown when two executives tried to manage earnings to meet Wall Street expectations. The company's stock, which had traded for $105/share in November 2000 before two-for-one stock splits, traded at $5/share in January 2006.[63] A poll by Harris Interactive found many scandal-plagued firms at the bottom of its annual survey of perceived corporate reputation, including Enron, Global Crossing, WorldCom, Andersen Worldwide, and Adelphia. The survey, which ranks companies according to how respondents rate them on twenty attributes, also found that public perceptions of trust had declined considerably as a result of the accounting scandals of the early twenty-first century. Joy Sever, a Harris vice president, reported, "The scandals cost many companies their emotional appeal, the strongest driver of reputation."[64]

The marketing plan should include distinct elements of ethics and social responsibility as determined by top-level marketing managers. Marketing strategy and implementation plans should be developed that reflect an understanding of (1) the risks associated with ethical and legal misconduct, (2) the ethical and social consequences of strategic choices, and (3) the values of organizational members and stakeholders.[65] To help ensure success, top managers must demonstrate their commitment to ethical and socially responsible behavior through their actions—words are simply not enough. In the end, a marketing plan that ignores social responsibility or is silent about ethical requirements leaves the guidance of ethical and socially responsible behavior to the work group, which risks ethical breakdowns and damage to the firm.

Lessons from Chapter 3

Marketing ethics and social responsibility

- have grown in importance over the last few years because many firms have seen their image, reputation, and marketing efforts destroyed by problems in these areas.

- have become necessities in light of stakeholder demands and changes in federal law.

- improve marketing performance and profits.

- are important considerations in the development of marketing strategy.

Social responsibility

- is a broad concept that relates to an organization's obligation to maximize its positive impacts on society while minimizing its negative impacts.

- includes the economic responsibility of making a profit to serve shareholders, employees, and the community at large.

- includes the legal responsibility of obeying all laws and regulations.

- includes the ethical responsibility to uphold principles and standards that define acceptable conduct as determined by the public, government regulators, private-interest groups, competitors, and the firm itself.

- includes the philanthropic responsibility to increase the firm's overall positive impact on society, the local community, and the environment.

Marketing ethics

- contains the principles and standards that guide the behavior of individuals and groups in making marketing decisions.

- requires that both organizations and individuals accept responsibility for their actions and comply with established value systems.

- can lead to violations of public trust when ethical standards are not upheld.

- involves complex and detailed decisions in which correctness may not be so clear cut.

- deals with experiences and decisions made at work, which may be quite different from the ethical decisions made away from work.

- comes into play any time that an activity causes managers, employees, or customers in a target market to feel manipulated or cheated.

Deceptive practices in marketing

- include fraud, or any false communication that deceives, manipulates, or conceals facts in order to create a false impression.

- include exaggerated claims or statements about a product or firm that cannot be substantiated.

- include ambiguous statements in which claims are so weak that the viewer, reader, or listener must infer the advertiser's intended message.

- include product-labeling issues such as false or misleading claims on a product's package.

- include selling abuses such as intentionally misleading customers by concealing facts.

- are typically regulated by the firms themselves or by industry and trade associations.

Ethical decision making

- is determined not only by an individual's background but also from others with whom the individual associates in the business environment.

- is affected by the combination of personal values, the opportunity for unethical behavior, and the exposure to others who behave ethically or unethically.

- is intricately tied to the firm's culture and its ethical climate.

- can only be improved when a firm develops plans and structures for addressing ethical considerations.

- is more likely to occur when a strong leader models ethical standards.

A code of ethical conduct

- is a formal statement that describes what an organization expects of its employees.

- is not an effective means of controlling ethical behavior unless it becomes integrated into daily decision making.

- is not truly effective unless it has the full support of top management.

- must reflect senior management's desire for organizational compliance with the values, rules, and policies that support an ethical climate.

- should have six core values: (1) trustworthiness, (2) respect, (3) responsibility, (4) fairness, (5) caring, and (6) citizenship.

- will not resolve every ethical issue encountered in daily operations, but it can help employees and managers deal with ethical dilemmas by prescribing or limiting specific activities.

Marketing ethics and leadership

- are intricately connected because employees look to the leader as a model of acceptable behavior.

- become closely intertwined when the leader (1) creates a common goal or vision for the company; (2) obtains buy-in, or support, from significant partners; (3) motivates others to be ethical; (4) uses the resources that are available to them; and (5) enjoys their jobs and approach them with an almost contagious tenacity, passion, and commitment.

Market orientation

- is strongly tied to ethics and social responsibility.

- refers to the development of an organizational culture that effectively and efficiently promotes the necessary behaviors for the creation of superior value for buyers and, thus, continuous superior performance of the firm.

- means fostering a sense of cooperation and open information exchange that gives the firm a clearer view of the customer's needs and desires.

Stakeholder orientation

- is strongly tied to ethics and social responsibility.

- refers to the degree to which a firm understands and addresses stakeholder demands.

- is composed of three sets of activities: (1) the organization-wide generation of data about stakeholder groups and assessment of the firm's effects on these groups, (2) the distribution of this information throughout the firm, and (3) the organization's responsiveness as a whole to this intelligence.

- consists of the initiatives that the firm adopts to ensure that it abides by or exceeds stakeholder expectations and has a positive impact on stakeholder issues.

The connection between ethics/social responsibility and marketing performance

- can cause employees to become more motivated to serve customers, more committed to the firm, more committed to standards of high quality, and more satisfied with their jobs.

- can cause customers to become more loyal to the firm and increase their purchases from the firm.

- can lead to increased trust among the firm's stakeholders. The most important contributing factor to gaining trust is the perception that the firm and its employees will not sacrifice their standards of integrity.

- is so strong that firms not developing strategies and programs to incorporate ethics and social responsibility into their organizational cultures will pay the price with potentially poor marketing performance, the potential costs of civil or criminal litigation, and damaging negative publicity when the public discovers questionable activities.

The connection between ethics and strategic planning

- is typically done through ethical compliance programs or integrity initiatives that make legal compliance, ethics, and social responsibility an organization-wide effort.

- is vested in the marketing plan, which should include distinct elements of ethics and social responsibility as determined by top-level marketing managers.

- is based on an understanding of (1) the risks associated with ethical and legal misconduct, (2) the ethical and social consequences of strategic choices, and (3) the values of organizational members and stakeholders.

- is manifested in a commitment to ethical and socially responsible behavior through actions—words are simply not enough.

Questions for Discussion

1. Why is marketing ethics a strategic consideration in organizational decisions? Who is most important in managing marketing ethics: the individual or the firm's leadership? Explain your answer.

2. Why have we seen more evidence of widespread ethical marketing dilemmas within firms today? Is it necessary to gain the cooperation of marketing managers to overstate revenue and earnings in a corporation?

3. What is the relationship between marketing ethics and organizational performance? What are the elements of a strong ethical compliance program to support responsible marketing and a successful marketing strategy?

Exercises

1. Visit the Federal Trade Commission website (http://www.ftc.gov). What is the FTC's current mission? What are the primary areas for which the FTC has responsibility? Review the last two months of press releases from the FTC. Based on these releases, what appear to be the major marketing ethical issues of concern at this time?

2. Visit the Better Business Bureau website (http://www.bbb.org). Review the criteria for the BBB Marketplace Torch Awards. What are the most important marketing activities necessary for a firm to receive this award?

3. Look at several print, broadcast, online, or outdoor advertisements and try to find an ad that you believe is questionable from an ethical perspective. Defend why you believe the ad is ethically questionable.

CHAPTER 4

Collecting and Analyzing Marketing Information

Introduction

In this chapter, we begin the process of developing a marketing plan by examining key issues in collecting and structuring marketing information to assist in the formulation of marketing strategies. Managers in all organizations, large and small, devote a major portion of their time and energy to developing plans and making decisions. As shown in Beyond the Pages 4.1, continuous tracking of the buying preferences of target consumers over time is critical. However, the ability to do so requires access to and analysis of data to generate usable information in a timely manner. Staying abreast of trends in the marketing environment is but one of several tasks performed by marketing managers. However, it is perhaps the most important task because practically all planning and decision making depends on how well this analysis is conducted.

One of the most widely used approaches to the collection and analysis of marketing information is situation analysis. The purpose of situation analysis is to describe current and future issues and key trends as they affect three key environments: the internal environment, the customer environment, and the external environment. As shown in Exhibit 4.1, many issues need to be considered in a situation analysis. When viewed together, the data collected during the situation analysis give the organization a big picture of the issues and trends that affect its ability to deliver value to stakeholders. These efforts drive the development of the organization's competitive advantages and strategic focus as discussed in the next chapter.

In this chapter, we examine several issues related to conducting a situation analysis, the components of a situation analysis, and the collection of marketing data and information to facilitate strategic marketing planning. Although situation analysis has traditionally been one of the most difficult aspects of market planning, recent advances in technology have made the collection of market data and information much easier and more efficient. A wealth of valuable data and information are free for the asking. This chapter examines the different types of marketing data and

Beyond the Pages 4.1

A FRESH LOOK AT BABY BOOMERS[1]

Baby boomers—the 77 million people born between 1946 and 1964—have long been the holy grail of marketers aimed at growing their business. The simple raw numbers have always made boomers a powerful force and a favored target of marketers for decades. However, 2006 was a milestone year for boomers and the marketers that pursue them. As the oldest boomers turn 60, over half of all baby boomers are now over the age of 50. These numbers are significant because 50 is the typical age at which marketers give up on consumers. Tradition says that by the age of 50, a consumer has developed deeply entrenched buying preferences and brand loyalty that no amount of marketing can undo. Today's marketers, however, are finding that tradition is wrong.

Marketers are rediscovering baby boomers for a number of reasons. One reason is the incredible buying potential. Thanks to better health and longer life expectancies, most boomers plan to continue working well into their 60s in order to fatten their retirement savings. Today, boomers account for over $1 trillion in spending power every year. A second reason is that today's consumers who are 50 years and older are much more active than their parents. Unlike previous generations, boomers are much more likely to change careers, have more children, go back to school, remarry, pursue new hobbies, and inherit more money from their parents. Consequently, marketers are finding that boomers' brand preferences and shopping habits are not as entrenched as once thought. Finally, marketers cannot give up on boomers due to the relatively smaller number of Generation X consumers—only 50 million strong—who are following behind them. In the years ahead, businesses must continue to reach out to boomers until the 74 million Generation Y consumers (teens and 20-somethings) reach their peak earning potential.

Reaching out to boomers has become a challenge for many marketers because they have to throw out their stereotypical ideas about consumers who are 50 years and older. The Gap, for example, tried to reach out to boomers using advertising featuring well-known boomer celebrities. That strategy backfired, however, because The Gap's clothes do not suit boomers' tastes. To solve the problem, the company launched a new chain called Forth & Towne, which sells career wear and casual clothing. Other marketers have found success simply by catering to boomers' ideals and needs. For example, Dove saw its sales increase 3.4 percent after it dropped attractive models from its advertising in favor of ordinary, 40-something women. Cover Girl adopted a similar strategy by launching its first line of makeup targeted at older women. The Home Depot is adding renovation services to its mix in addition to its assortment of products for do-it-yourselfers. And even Honda was surprised when it learned that 40 percent of its minivan buyers were older customers who needed to haul grandchildren rather than their own children. As a result, Honda introduced a luxury version of its popular Odyssey minivan to cater to the needs of older consumers.

In addition to discarding traditional ideas about older consumers, experts also agree that marketers must not assume that the 50+ market is of one mind. Researchers at Duke University have discovered that boomers are the most diverse of all current generations. Consequently, marketers must segment this market carefully to ensure that their marketing resonates with the correct boomer segment.

information needed for planning, as well as many sources where such data may be obtained.

Conducting a Situation Analysis

Before we move forward in our discussion, it is important to keep in mind four important issues regarding situation analysis. We hope our advice helps you overcome potential problems throughout the situation analysis.

EXHIBIT 4.1   **ISSUES TO BE CONSIDERED IN A SITUATION ANALYSIS**

The Internal Environment

Review of current objectives, strategy, and performance
Availability of resources
Organizational culture and structure

The Customer Environment

Who are our current and potential customers?
What do customers do with our products?
Where do customers purchase our products?
When do customers purchase our products?
Why (and how) do customers select our products?
Why do potential customers not purchase our products?

The External Environment

Competition
Economic growth and stability
Political trends
Legal and regulatory issues
Technological advancements
Sociocultural trends

Analysis Alone Is Not a Solution

Although it is true that a comprehensive situation analysis can lead to better planning and decision making, analysis itself is not enough. Put another way, situation analysis is a necessary but insufficient prerequisite for effective strategic planning. The analysis must be combined with intuition and judgment to make the results of the analysis useful for planning purposes. Situation analysis should not replace the manager in the decision-making process. Its purpose is to empower the manager with information for more effective decision making.

A thorough situation analysis empowers the marketing manager because it encourages both analysis and synthesis of information. From this perspective, situation analysis involves taking things apart: whether it's a customer segment (to study the heavy users), a product (to understand the relationship between its features and customers' needs), or competitors (to weigh their strengths and weaknesses against your own). The purpose of taking things apart is to understand why people, products, or organizations perform the way they do. After this dissection is complete, the manager can then synthesize the information to gain a big-picture view of the complex decisions to be made.

Data Are Not the Same as Information

Throughout the planning process, managers regularly face the question "How much data and information do I need?" The answer sounds simple, but in practice it is not. Today, there is no shortage of data. In fact, it is virtually impossible to know everything about a specific topic. Thankfully, the cost of collecting and storing vast amounts of data has dropped dramatically over the past decade. Computer-based marketing information systems are commonplace. Online data sources allow managers to retrieve data in a matter of seconds. The growth of wireless technology now gives managers access to vital data while in the field. The bottom line is that managers are more likely to be overwhelmed with data rather than face a shortage.

Although the vast amount of available data is an issue to be resolved, the real challenge is that good, useful information is not the same as data. Data are easy to collect and store, but good information is not. In simple terms, *data* are a collection of numbers or facts that have the potential to provide information. Data, however, do not become informative until a person or process transforms or combines them with other data in a manner that makes them useful to decision makers. For example, the fact that your firm's sales are up 20 percent is not informative until you compare it with the industry's growth rate of 40 percent. It is also important to remember that information is only as good as the data from which it comes. As the saying goes, "Garbage in, garbage out." It is a good idea to be curious about, perhaps even suspicious of, the quality of data used for planning and decision making.

The Benefits of Analysis Must Outweigh the Costs

Situation analysis is valuable only to the extent that it improves the quality of the resulting marketing plan. For example, data that cost $4,000 to acquire but improve the quality of the decision by only $3,999 should not be part of the analysis process. Although the costs of acquiring data are easy to determine, the benefits of improved decisions are quite difficult to estimate. Managers must constantly ask such questions as, "Where do I have knowledge gaps?"; "How can these gaps be filled?"; "What are the costs of filling these gaps?"; and "How much improvement in decision making will be gained by acquiring this information?" By asking these questions, managers can find a balance between jumping to conclusions and "paralysis by analysis," or constantly postponing a decision due to a perceived lack of information. Perpetually analyzing data without making any decisions is usually not worth the additional costs in terms of time or financial resources.

Conducting a Situation Analysis Is a Challenging Exercise

Situation analysis is one of the most difficult tasks in developing a marketing plan. Managers have the responsibility of assessing the quality, adequacy, and timeliness of the data and information used for analysis and synthesis. The dynamic nature of internal and external environments often creates breakdowns in the effort to develop effective information flows. This dynamism can be especially troubling when the firm attempts to collect and analyze data in international markets.

It is important that any effort at situation analysis be well organized, systematic, and supported by sufficient resources (for example, people, equipment, information,

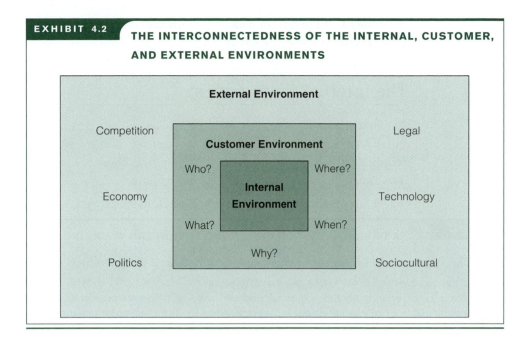

EXHIBIT 4.2   **THE INTERCONNECTEDNESS OF THE INTERNAL, CUSTOMER, AND EXTERNAL ENVIRONMENTS**

and budget). However, the most important aspect of the analysis is that it should be an ongoing effort. The analysis should not only take place in the days and weeks immediately preceding the formation of strategies and plans, but the collection, creation, analysis, and dissemination of pertinent marketing data and information must also be ingrained in the organization's culture. This is not an easy task, but if the organization is going to be successful, it must have the ability to assess its current situation in real time. This type of live data is especially important when tracking customers and competitors.

A final challenge is the task of tracking all three environments (internal, customer, and external) simultaneously. Although the rapid pace of change in today's economy is one cause of this difficulty, the interconnectedness of all three environments creates challenges as well. As shown in Exhibit 4.2, the internal, customer, and external environments do not exist independently. Changes in one portion of the external environment can cause subsequent shifts in the customer environment or the internal environment. For example, due to a patent infringement lawsuit, it appeared that Research in Motion would have to shut down the system behind its incredibly popular Blackberry wireless handheld device. This single challenge from its legal environment not only threatened the Blackberry's existence but also affected competitors' stances toward the market. Although Research in Motion eventually settled the suit, it is likely to face additional legal hurdles in the future.[2]

As we turn our attention to the three major components of the situation analysis, keep in mind that data and information about these environments will come from both internal and external sources. Even information about the firm's internal environment can be collected via external sources such as third-party analysis and ratings, financial commentaries, or customer opinion ratings. Finally, it is important to remember that the type of data and information source is not as important as having ready access to a wide variety of sources.

The Internal Environment

The first aspect of a situation analysis involves the critical evaluation of the firm's internal environment with respect to its objectives, strategy, performance, allocation of resources, structural characteristics, and political climate. Exhibit 4.3 provides a framework for analyzing the internal environment.

EXHIBIT 4.3   **A FRAMEWORK FOR ANALYZING THE INTERNAL ENVIRONMENT**

Review of Current Marketing Objectives, Strategy, and Performance

1. What are the current marketing goals and objectives?
2. Are the marketing goals and objectives consistent with the corporate or business-unit mission, goals, and objectives? Are they consistent with recent changes in the customer or external environments? Why or why not?
3. How are current marketing strategies performing with respect to anticipated outcomes (for example, sales volume, market share, profitability, communication, brand awareness, customer preference, customer satisfaction)?
4. How does current performance compare with other organizations in the industry? Is the performance of the industry as a whole improving or declining? Why?
5. If performance is declining, what are the most likely causes? Are marketing objectives inconsistent? Is the strategy flawed? Was the strategy poorly implemented?
6. If performance is improving, what actions can be taken to ensure that performance continues to improve? Is the improvement in performance due to a better-than-anticipated environment or superior planning and implementation?

Review of Current and Anticipated Organizational Resources

1. What is the state of current organizational resources (for example, financial, human, experience, relationships with key suppliers or customers)?
2. Are these resources likely to change for the better or worse in the near future? How?
3. If the changes are for the better, how can these added resources be used to meet customer needs better than competitors?
4. If the changes are for the worse, what can be done to compensate for these new resource constraints?

Review of Current and Anticipated Cultural and Structural Issues

1. What are the positive and negative aspects of the current and anticipated organizational culture?
2. What issues related to internal politics or management struggles might affect the organization's marketing activities?
3. What is the overall position and importance of the marketing function as seen by other functional areas? Are key executive positions expected to change in the future?
4. How will the overall market- or customer-orientation of the organization (or lack thereof) affect marketing activities?
5. Does the organization emphasize a long- or short-term planning horizon? How will this emphasis affect marketing activities?
6. Currently, are there positive or negative issues with respect to motivating employees, especially those in frontline positions (for example, sales and customer service)?

Review of Current Objectives, Strategy, and Performance

First, the marketing manager must assess the firm's current marketing objectives, strategy, and performance. A periodic assessment of marketing objectives is necessary to ensure that they remain consistent with the firm's mission and the changing customer and external environments. It may also be necessary to reassess the firm's marketing goals if the objectives prove to be out-of-date or ineffective. This analysis serves as an important input to later stages of the marketing planning process.

The marketing manager should also evaluate the performance of the current marketing strategy with respect to sales volume, market share, profitability, and other relevant measures. This analysis can take place at many levels: by brand, product line, market, business unit, division, and so on. It is also important to analyze the marketing strategy relative to overall industry performance. Poor or declining performance may be the result of (1) holding on to marketing goals or objectives inconsistent with the current realities of the customer or external environments, (2) a flawed marketing strategy, (3) poor implementation, or (4) changes in the customer or external environments beyond the control of the firm. The causes for poor or declining performance must be pinpointed before marketing strategies can be developed to correct the situation.

For example, in the mid-1990s Pepsi was locked in a seemingly endless market-share battle with Coca-Cola. By all accounts, the battle was not going well for Pepsi: Its profits trailed Coca-Cola's by 47 percent while its market value was less than half of its chief rival.[3] But losing out to Coca-Cola in the cola wars was just the kick that Pepsi needed to regroup. Forced to look outside of the soft-drink industry for new growth opportunities, Pepsi moved aggressively into noncarbonated and sports beverages, food, and snacks. Today, Pepsi's Aquafina bottled water and Gatorade are dominant over Coke's Dasani bottled water and PowerAde in their respective markets. In addition, Pepsi's Frito-Lay division commands over 60 percent of the U.S. snack-food market. Since 2000 Pepsi's profits have climbed more than 100 percent.

Availability of Resources

Second, the marketing manager must review the current and anticipated levels of organizational resources that can be used for marketing purposes. This review includes an analysis of financial, human, and experience resources, as well as any resources the firm might hold in key relationships with supply chain partners, strategic alliance partners, or customer groups. An important element of this analysis is to gauge whether the availability or level of these resources is likely to change in the near future. Additional resources might be used to create competitive advantages in meeting customer needs. If the marketing manager expects resource levels to decline, he or she must find ways to compensate when establishing marketing goals, objectives, and strategies for the next planning period.

In bad economic times, financial shortfalls get most of the attention. However, many experts predict that a shortage of skilled labor will be a major problem in the U.S. over the next few years. The problem is not the raw number of workers but the skill set that each one brings to the job. After years of increasing technological innovation, workers must now possess the right set of skills to work with technology. Likewise, workers of today must possess knowledge-related skills such as abstract reasoning, problem solving, and communication. Firms in many industries—most notably services—have turned to moving jobs offshore to other countries where highly educated, English-speaking employees will work for less pay than their U.S. counterparts. Of all white-collar jobs that have been sent offshore, a full 90 percent are now located in India. An interesting irony is that the same technology that demands increased skills from employees allows these jobs to be sent offshore to other countries.[4]

Organizational Culture and Structure

Finally, the marketing manager should review current and anticipated cultural and structural issues that could affect marketing activities. One of the most important issues in this review involves the internal culture of the firm. In some organizations, marketing does not hold a prominent position in the political hierarchy. This situation can create challenges for the marketing manager in acquiring resources and gaining approval of the marketing plan. The internal culture also includes any anticipated changes in key executive positions within the firm. The marketing manager, for example, could have difficulty in dealing with a new production manager who fails to see the benefits of marketing. Other structural issues to be considered include the overall customer orientation of the firm (or lack thereof), issues related to employee motivation and commitment to the organization (particularly among unionized employees), and the relative emphasis on long- versus short-term planning. Top managers who concern themselves only with short-term profits are unlikely to see the importance of a marketing plan that attempts to create long-term customer relationships.

For most firms, culture and structure are relatively stable issues that do not change dramatically from one year to the next. In fact, changing or reorienting an organization's culture is a difficult and time-consuming process. In some cases, however, the culture and structure can change swiftly, causing political and power struggles within the organization. Consider the effects when two organizations combine their separate cultures and structures during a merger. For example, the merger of Chrysler Corporation and Daimler Benz AG in a deal of so-called equals resulted in culture conflicts, with the German component of the merged firm taking over most management positions. Management issues continued under former CEO Juergen Schrempp to the point that DaimlerChrysler lost sight of the importance of the Mercedes brand. After several years of declining quality, lower sales, and declining profits for Mercedes, new CEO Dieter Zetsche overhauled the management structure at DaimlerChrysler to reinstate the Mercedes division to its dominant position as the core business of the company.[5]

The Customer Environment

In the second part of a situation analysis, the marketing manager must examine the current and future situation with respect to customers in the firm's target markets. During this analysis, information should be collected that identifies (1) the firm's current and potential customers, (2) the prevailing needs of current and potential customers, (3) the basic features of the firm's and competitors' products perceived by customers as meeting their needs, and (4) anticipated changes in customers' needs.

In assessing the firm's target markets, the marketing manager must attempt to understand all relevant buyer behavior and product usage characteristics. One method that the manager can use to collect this information is the 5W Model: Who, What, Where, When, and Why. We have adapted and applied this model to customer analysis, as shown in Exhibit 4.4. Organizations that are truly market or customer oriented should know their customers well enough that they have easy access to the types of information that answer these questions. If not, the organization may need to conduct primary marketing research to fully understand its target markets.

Who Are Our Current and Potential Customers?

Answering the "who" question requires an examination of the relevant characteristics that define target markets. This includes demographic characteristics (gender, age, income, and so on), geographic characteristics (where customers live, density of the target market, and so on), and psychographic characteristics (attitudes, opinions, interests, and so on). Depending on the types of products sold by the firm, purchase influencers or users, rather than actual purchasers, may be important as well. For example, in consumer markets it is well known that the influence of children is critical for purchases such as cars, homes, meals, toys, and vacations. In business markets, the analysis typically focuses on the buying center. Is the buying decision made by an individual or by a committee? Who has the greatest influence on the purchase decision?

The analysis must also assess the viability of potential customers or markets that may be acquired in the future. This involves looking ahead to situations that may increase the firm's ability to gain new customers. For example, firms around the world are particularly excited about the further opening of the Chinese market and its 1.4 billion potential consumers. Many firms, including Procter & Gamble, Wal-Mart, Starbucks, and Pepsi have established a presence in China that they hope to leverage for future growth opportunities. German-based Adidas went so far as to spend roughly $100 million to become the official footwear sponsor of the 2008 Beijing Olympics.[6]

What Do Customers Do with Our Products?

The "what" question entails an assessment of how customers consume and dispose of the firm's products. Here the marketing manager might be interested in identifying the rate of product consumption (sometimes called the usage rate), differences between heavy and light users of products, whether customers use complementary products during consumption, and what customers do with the firm's products after consumption. In business markets, customers typically use the firm's products in the creation of their own products. As a result, business customers tend to pay very close attention to product specifications and quality.

In some cases, marketers cannot fully understand how customers use their products without looking at the complementary products that go with them. In

EXHIBIT 4.4   **THE EXPANDED 5W MODEL FOR CUSTOMER ANALYSIS**

Who Are Our Current and Potential Customers?

1. What are the demographic, geographic, and psychographic characteristics of our customers?
2. Who actually purchases our products?
3. Do these purchasers differ from the users of our products?
4. Who are the major influencers of the purchase decision?
5. Who is financially responsible for making the purchase?

What Do Customers Do with Our Products?

1. In what quantities and in what combinations are our products purchased?
2. How do heavy users of our products differ from light users?
3. Do purchasers use complementary products during the consumption of our products? If so, what is the nature of the demand for these products, and how does it affect the demand for our products?
4. What do our customers do with our products after consumption?
5. Are our customers recycling our products or packaging?

Where Do Customers Purchase Our Products?

1. From what types of vendors are our products purchased?
2. Does e-commerce have an effect on the purchase of our products?
3. Are our customers increasing their purchasing from nonstore outlets?

When Do Customers Purchase Our Products?

1. Are the purchase and consumption of our products seasonal?
2. To what extent do promotional events affect the purchase and consumption of our products?
3. Do the purchase and consumption of our products vary based on changes in physical/social surroundings, time perceptions, or the purchase task?

Why (and How) Do Customers Select Our Products?

1. What are the basic features provided by our products and our competitors' products? How do our products compare to those of competitors?
2. What are the customer needs fulfilled by our products and our competitors' products? How well do our products meet these needs? How well do our competitors' products meet these needs?
3. Are the needs of our customers expected to change in the future? If so, how?
4. What methods of payment do our customers use when making a purchase? Is the availability of credit or financing an issue with our customers?
5. Are our customers prone to developing close long-term relationships with us and our competitors, or do they buy in a transactional fashion (primarily based on price)?
6. How can we develop, maintain, or enhance the relationships we have with our customers?

Why Do Potential Customers Not Purchase Our Products?

1. What are the basic needs of noncustomers that our products do not meet?
2. What are the features, benefits, or advantages of competing products that cause noncustomers to choose them over our products?
3. Are there issues related to distribution, promotion, or pricing that prevent noncustomers from purchasing our products?
4. What is the potential for converting noncustomers into customers of our products?

Source: Adapted from Donald R. Lehmann and Russell S. Winer, *Analysis for Marketing Planning*, 6th ed. (Boston: McGraw-Hill/Irwin, 2005).

these cases of *derived demand*—where the demand for one product depends on (is derived from) the demand of another product—the marketer must also examine the consumption and usage of the complementary product. For example, tire manufacturers concern themselves with the demand for automobiles, and makers of computer accessories closely watch the demand for desktop and laptop computers. By following the demand for and consumption of complementary products, marketers are in a much better position to understand how customers use their own products.

Before customers and marketers became more concerned about the natural environment, many firms looked only at how their customers used products. Today, marketers have become increasingly interested in how customers dispose of products, such as whether customers recycle the product or its packaging. Another postconsumption issue deals with the need for reverse channels of distribution to handle product repairs. Car manufacturers, for example, must maintain an elaborate network of certified repair facilities (typically through dealers) to handle maintenance and repairs under warranty.

Sometimes recycling and repair issues come into conflict. The relatively low cost of today's home electronics leads many customers to buy new televisions, radios, computers, or cell phones rather than have old ones repaired. This causes a problem: What do consumers do with e-waste, or broken and obsolete electronic devices? Though e-waste makes up only 1 percent of our country's garbage volume, state governments and local communities have struggled for years with the roughly five million tons of e-waste that enters landfills each year. The problem has also created environmental concerns with respect to the lead, cadmium, mercury, and other hazardous materials contained in e-waste. Many states have responded to these concerns by implementing bans on the dumping of e-waste in landfills and incinerators or by creating recycling programs specifically aimed at e-waste. As a result of these initiatives, schools, churches, and charities have been inundated with donations of obsolete electronics.[7]

Where Do Customers Purchase Our Products?

The "where" question is associated mainly with distribution and customer convenience. Until recently, most firms looked solely at traditional channels of distribution such as brokers, wholesalers, and retailers. Thus, the marketing manager would have concerns about the intensity of the distribution effort and the types of retailers that the firm's customers patronized. Today, however, many other forms of distribution are available. The fastest growing form of distribution today is nonstore retailing—which includes vending machines; direct marketing through catalogs, home sales, or infomercials; and electronic merchandising through the Internet, interactive television, and video kiosks.[8] Business markets have also begun to capitalize on the lower costs of procurement via the Internet. Likewise, many manufacturers have bypassed traditional distribution channels in favor of selling through their own outlet stores or websites. Disney, for example, has begun selling many of its movies via online download for use on computers and portable devices.[9] The move allows Disney to close the time gap between DVD release and cable on-demand availability by several months.

When Do Customers Purchase Our Products?

The "when" question refers to any situational influences that may cause customer purchasing activity to vary over time. This includes broad issues such as the seasonality of the firm's products and the variability in purchasing activity caused by promotional events or budgetary constraints. Everyone knows that consumer-purchasing activity increases just after payday. In business markets, budgetary constraints and the timing of a firm's fiscal year often dictate the "when" question. For example, many schools and universities buy large quantities of supplies just before the end of their fiscal years.

The "when" question also includes more subtle influences that can affect purchasing behavior such as physical and social surroundings, time perceptions, and the purchase task. For example, a consumer may purchase a domestic brand of beer for regular home consumption but purchase an import or microbrew when visiting a bar (physical surroundings), going out with friends (social surroundings), or throwing a party. Customers can also vary their purchasing behavior based on the time of day or how much time they have to search for alternatives. Variation by purchase task depends on what the customer intends to accomplish with the purchase. For example, a customer may purchase Brand A for her own use, brand B for her children, and brand C for her coworker as a gift.

Why (and How) Do Customers Select Our Products?

The "why" question involves identifying the basic need-satisfying benefits provided by the firm's products. The potential benefits provided by the features of competing products should also be analyzed. This question is important because customers may purchase the firm's products to fulfill needs that the firm never considered. For example, most people think of vinegar as an ingredient in salad dressings. However, vinegar boasts many other uses, including cleaning floors, loosening rusted screws or nuts, tenderizing meat, and softening hard paint brushes.[10] The answer to the "why" question can also aid in identifying unsatisfied or undersatisfied customer needs. During the analysis, it is also important to identify potential changes in customers' current and future needs. Customers may purchase the firm's products for a reason that may be trumped by newly launched competitive products in the future.

The "how" part of this question refers to the means of payment that customers use when making a purchase. Although most people use cash (which also includes checks and debit cards) for most transactions, the availability of credit makes it possible for customers to take possession of high-priced products like cars and homes. The same is true in business markets where credit is essential to the exchange of goods and services in both domestic and international transactions. Recently, a very old form of payment has reemerged in business markets—barter. Barter involves the exchange of goods and services for other goods or services; no money changes hands. Barter arrangements are very good for small businesses short on cash. According to the International Reciprocal Trade Association, over $8.4 billion of international trade in goods and services is conducted on a noncash basis—a number that represents 15 percent of the global economy. Barter has grown at the rate of roughly eight percent each year, thanks in part to the advent of barter networks on the Internet.[11]

Why Do Potential Customers Not Purchase Our Products?

An important part of customer analysis is the realization that many potential customers choose not to purchase the firm's products. Although there are many potential reasons why customers might not purchase a firm's products, some reasons include the following:

- Noncustomers have a basic need that the firm's product does not fulfill.

- Noncustomers perceive that they have better or lower-priced alternatives such as competing substitute products.

- Competing products actually have better features or benefits than the firm's product.

- The firm's product does not match noncustomers' budgets or lifestyles.

- Noncustomers have high switching costs.

- Noncustomers do not know that the firm's product exists.

- Noncustomers have misconceptions about the firm's product (weak or poor image).

- Poor distribution makes the firm's product difficult to find.

Once the manager identifies the reasons for nonpurchase; he or she should make a realistic assessment of the potential for converting noncustomers into customers. Although conversion is not always possible, in many cases converting noncustomers is as simple as taking a different approach. For example, Australian-based Casella Wines was able to convert noncustomers into wine drinkers by fundamentally changing their approach to the wine industry. Through its [yellow tail] brand, Casella converted nonwine drinkers by positioning itself as being easy to drink, easy to understand, easy to buy, and fun. [yellow tail] ignored long-held wine attributes such as prestige and complexity to make wine more approachable to the masses. The end result is that [yellow tail] is now the number-one imported wine in the United States.[12]

Once the marketing manager has analyzed the firm's current and potential customers, the information can be used to identify and select specific target markets for the revised marketing strategy. The firm should target those customer segments where it can create and maintain a sustainable advantage over its competition.

The External Environment

The final and broadest issue in a situation analysis is an assessment of the external environment, which includes all the external factors—competitive, economic, political, legal/regulatory, technological, and sociocultural—that can exert considerable direct and indirect pressures on both domestic and international marketing activities. Exhibit 4.5 provides a framework for analyzing factors in the external environment. As this framework suggests, the issues involved in examining the external environment can be divided into separate categories (that is, competitive, economic, political, and so on). However, some environmental issues can fall into multiple categories.

One such example is the explosive growth in direct-to-consumer (DTC) advertising in the pharmaceutical industry. In 2005 the industry spent roughly $3 billion on DTC advertising through "ask your doctor" style ads aimed at encouraging consumers to request drugs by name from their physicians. This promotional strategy has been praised and criticized on a number of fronts. Some argue that DTC advertising plays an important role in educating the population about both disease and available treatments. Critics—including the U.S. Congress—argue that DTC advertising encourages consumers to self-diagnose and is often misleading about a drug's benefits and side effects. In response to these criticisms, the pharmaceutical industry developed a set of guiding principles for DTC advertising. However, most expect Congress to eventually pass legislation curtailing or barring the practice.[13]

Issues in the external environment can often be complex. For example, a 1997 strike by UPS employees not only put UPS employees out of work but also led to economic slowdowns in UPS hub cities. The strike also became a political issue for President Bill Clinton because he was continually pressured to invoke the Taft–Hartley Act to force striking UPS employees back to work. Although the effects of the UPS strike were short lived, some changes have a lasting impact. The tragic events of September 11, 2001 led to many changes in the competitive, economic, political, legal, technological, and sociocultural environments that will be felt for decades to come. Thankfully, complex situations like these occur infrequently. As we examine each element of the external marketing environment, keep in mind that issues arising in one aspect of the environment are usually reflected in other elements as well.

Competition

In most industries, customers have choices and preferences in terms of the goods and services that they can purchase. Thus, when a firm defines the target markets it will serve, it simultaneously selects a set of competing firms. The current and future actions of these competitors must be constantly monitored and, hopefully, even anticipated. One major problem in analyzing competition is the question of identification. That is, how does the manager answer the question "Who are our current and

EXHIBIT 4.5   **A FRAMEWORK FOR ANALYZING THE EXTERNAL ENVIRONMENT**

Competition

1. Who are our major brand, product, generic, and total budget competitors? What are their characteristics in terms of size, growth, profitability, strategies, and target markets?
2. What are our competitors' key strengths and weaknesses?
3. What are our competitors' key capabilities and vulnerabilities with respect to their marketing program (for example, products, distribution, promotion, and pricing)?
4. What response can we expect from our competitors if environmental conditions change or if we change our marketing strategy?
5. How is our set of competitors likely to change in the future? Who are our new competitors likely to be?

Economic Growth and Stability

1. What are the general economic conditions of the country, region, state, and local area in which our firm operates?
2. What are the economic conditions of our industry? Is our industry growing? Why or why not?
3. Overall, are customers optimistic or pessimistic about the economy? Why?
4. What are the buying power and spending patterns of customers in our industry? Are our industry's customers buying less or more of our products? Why?

Political Trends

1. Have recent elections changed the political landscape within our domestic or international markets? If so, how?
2. What type of industry regulations do elected officials favor?
3. What are we doing currently to maintain good relations with elected officials? Have these activities been effective? Why or why not?

Legal and Regulatory Issues

1. What proposed changes in international, federal, state, or local laws and regulations have the potential to affect our marketing activities?
2. Do recent court decisions suggest that we should modify our marketing activities?
3. Do the recent rulings of federal, state, local and self-regulatory agencies suggest that we should modify our marketing activities?
4. What effect will changes in global trade agreements or laws have on our international marketing opportunities?

Technological Advancements

1. What impact has changing technology had on our customers?
2. What technological changes will affect the way that we operate or manufacture our products?
3. What technological changes will affect the way that we conduct marketing activities such as distribution or promotion?
4. Are there any current technologies that we do not use to their fullest potential in making our marketing activities more effective and efficient?
5. Do any technological advances threaten to make our products obsolete? Does new technology have the potential to satisfy previously unmet or unknown customer needs?

Sociocultural Trends

1. How are society's demographics and values changing? What effect will these changes have on our customers, products, pricing, distribution, promotion, and our employees?
2. What challenges or opportunities have changes in the diversity of our customers and employees created?
3. What is the general attitude of society about our industry, company, and products? Could we take actions to improve these attitudes?
4. What social or ethical issues should we be addressing?

EXHIBIT 4.6	MAJOR TYPES OF COMPETITION			
Product Category (Need Fulfilled)	Brand Competitors	Product Competitors	Generic Competitors	Total Budget Competitors
Sport utility vehicles (transportation)	Ford Escape Toyota RAV4 Honda CR-V	Trucks Passenger cars Minivans	Rental cars Motorcycles Bicycles	Vacation Debt reduction Home remodeling
Soft drinks (refreshment)	Coca-Cola Classic Pepsi Cola Dr. Pepper	Tea Orange juice Bottled water	Tap water	Candy Gum Potato chips
Movies (entertainment)	*Harry Potter* *The Matrix* *Star Wars*	Cable TV Pay-Per-View Video rentals	Athletic events Arcades Concerts	Shopping Reading Fishing
Colleges (education)	New Mexico Florida State LSU	Trade school Community college Online programs	Books CD-ROMs Apprenticeships	New cars Vacations Investments

future competitors?" To arrive at an answer, the manager must look beyond the obvious examples of competition. Most firms face four basic types of competition:

1. *Brand competitors*, which market products with similar features and benefits to the same customers at similar prices

2. *Product competitors*, which compete in the same product class but with products that are different in features, benefits, and price

3. *Generic competitors*, which market very different products that solve the same problem or satisfy the same basic customer need

4. *Total budget competitors*, which compete for the limited financial resources of the same customers

Exhibit 4.6 presents examples of each type of competition for selected product markets. In the fast-growing, small-SUV segment of the automobile industry, for example, the Ford Escape, Toyota RAV4, Honda CR-V, and Subaru Forester are brand competitors. However, each faces competition from other types of automobile products such as midsize SUVs, trucks, minivans, and passenger cars. Some of this product competition comes from within each company's own product portfolio (for example, Ford's Explorer SUV, Taurus car, Freestar minivan, and F-150 truck). Small SUVs also face generic competition from Honda motorcycles, Schwinn bicycles, Hertz rental cars, and public transportation—all of which offer products that satisfy the same basic customer need for transportation. Finally, customers have many alternative uses for their money rather than purchasing a small SUV: They can take a vacation, install a pool in the backyard, buy a boat, start an investment fund, or pay off debt.

All four types of competition are important, but brand competitors rightfully receive the greatest attention because customers see different brands as direct substitutes for each other. For this reason, strategies aimed at getting customers to switch brands are a major focus in any effort to beat brand competitors. For example, Gatorade, far and away the dominant sports drink, has taken steps to convince soft-drink consumers to switch to noncarbonated beverages. The company has introduced many new flavors including Frost, Fierce, Xtremo, and All-Stars; Gatorade has also developed a low-calorie fitness water called Propel. These additions, along with the introduction of new bottles, multipacks, and refreshed labeling, has placed Gatorade squarely alongside other drink choices in supermarkets and convenience stores. Gatorade's popularity was also behind its recent partnership with Comcast to develop programming for a new on-demand service called Exercise[tv]. Gatorade's bold moves into the mainstream have made the brand a formidable product competitor among branded competition in the soft-drink market.[14]

Competitive analysis has received greater attention recently for several reasons: more intense competition from sophisticated competitors, increased competition from foreign firms, shorter product life cycles, and dynamic environments, particularly in the area of technological innovation. A growing number of companies have adopted formalized methods of identifying competitors, tracking their activities, and assessing their strengths and weaknesses—a process referred to as competitive intelligence. *Competitive intelligence* involves the legal and ethical observation, tracking, and analysis of the total range of competitive activity including competitors' capabilities and vulnerabilities with respect to sources of supply, technology, marketing, financial strength, manufacturing capacities and qualities, and target markets. It also attempts to predict and anticipate competitive actions and reactions in the marketplace.[15] Competitive analysis should progress through the following stages:

1. **Identification** Identify all current and potential brand, product, generic, and total budget competitors.

2. **Characteristics** Focus on key competitors by assessing the size, growth, profitability, objectives, strategies, and target markets of each one.

3. **Assessment** Assess each key competitor's strengths and weaknesses, including the major capabilities and vulnerabilities that each possesses within its functional areas (marketing, research and development, production, human resources, and so on).

4. **Capabilities** Focus the analysis on each key competitor's marketing capabilities in terms of its products, distribution, promotion, and pricing.

5. **Response** Estimate each key competitor's most likely strategies and responses under different environmental situations as well as its reactions to the firm's own marketing efforts.

Many sources are available for gathering information on current or potential competitors. Company annual reports are useful for determining a firm's current performance and future direction. An examination of a competitor's mission statement can also provide information, particularly with respect to how the company defines itself. A thorough scan of a competitor's website can also uncover information—such as product specifications and prices—that can greatly improve the competitive analysis. Other, clever ways to collect competitive information include data-mining techniques, patent tracking to reveal technological breakthroughs, creating psychological profiles of competitor's key executives, searching consumer review and blog websites, and attending trade shows and conferences.[16] Other valuable information sources include business periodicals and trade publications that provide newsworthy tidbits about companies. There are also numerous commercial databases, such as ABI/INFORM, InfoTrac, EBSCO, Hoover's, and Moody's, which provide a wealth of information on companies and their marketing activities. The information contained in these databases can be purchased in print form, on CD-ROM, or through an online connection with a data provider such as a school or public library.

Economic Growth and Stability

If there is one truism about any economy, it is that it will inevitably change. Therefore, current and expected conditions in the economy can have a profound impact on marketing strategy. A thorough examination of economic factors requires marketing managers to gauge and anticipate the general economic conditions of the nation, region, state, and local area in which they operate. These general economic conditions include inflation, employment and income levels, interest rates, taxes, trade restrictions, tariffs, and the current and future stages of the business cycle (prosperity, stagnation, recession, depression, and recovery). After a downward trend in inflation since 1990's 5+ percent rate, evidence suggests that inflation may be on the rise again. Since 2002 annual inflation has increased from just above one percent to roughly 3.5 percent today.[17]

Equally important economic factors include consumers' overall impressions of the economy and their ability and willingness to spend. Consumer confidence (or lack thereof) can greatly affect what the firm can or cannot do in the marketplace. In times of low confidence, consumers may not be willing to pay higher prices for premium products, even if they have the ability to do so. In other cases, consumers may not have the ability to spend, regardless of the state of the economy. Another important factor is the current and anticipated spending patterns of consumers in the firm's target market. If consumers buy less (or more) of the firm's products, there could be important economic reasons for the change.

One of the most important economic realities in the United States over the last 50 years has been a steady shift away from a tangibles-dominant economy (goods, equipment, and manufacturing) to one dominated by intangibles such as services and information. In fact, virtually everyone is aware that the U.S. economy is a knowledge-based economy. However, our methods of measuring and reporting on the economy have not kept pace with this change. Our methods are very good at capturing manufacturing output, capital expenditures, and investments in other tangible assets; but they cannot capture investments in intangibles such as innovation, employee training, brand equity, or product design. Consequently, the true nature of our economy is underreported by virtually all current statistics such as the revered gross domestic product (GDP). Innovation, creativity, and human assets—the main drivers behind the success of most U.S. businesses—are not counted as a part of yearly GDP statistics. One of the major challenges moving forward is finding ways of capturing these intangibles in our regular reporting and economic analyses.[18]

Political Trends

Although the importance will vary from firm to firm, most organizations should track political trends and attempt to maintain good relations with elected officials. Organizations that do business with government entities, such as defense contractors, must be especially attuned to political trends. Elected officials who have negative attitudes toward a firm or its industry are more likely to create or enforce regulations unfavorable for the firm. For example, the antitobacco trend in the United States has been in full swing since the late 1990s. Today, many states and local communities have passed laws to prevent smoking in public places. One of the most hotly contested political issues in 2006 was the status of illegal immigrants crossing the U.S. border, especially from Mexico. This single issue had potential ramifications for the U.S. economy (employment, health care, and trade), society (language and culture), and political relations with other nations. As these examples show, political discussions can have serious, lasting consequences for an industry or firm.

Many organizations view political factors as beyond their control and do little more than adjust the firm's strategies to accommodate changes in those factors. Other firms, however, take a more proactive stance by seeking to influence elected officials. For example, some organizations publicly protest legislative actions, while others seek influence more discreetly by routing funds to political parties or lobbying groups. Whatever the approach, managers should always stay in touch with the political landscape.

Legal and Regulatory Issues

As you might suspect, legal and regulatory issues have close ties to events in the political environment. Numerous laws and regulations have the potential to influence marketing decisions and activities. The simple existence of these laws and regulations causes many firms to accept this influence as a predetermined aspect of market planning. For example, most firms comply with procompetitive legislation rather than face the penalties of noncompliance. In reality, most laws and regulations are fairly vague (for instance, the Americans with Disabilities Act), which often forces firms to test the limits of certain laws by operating in a legally questionable manner. The vagueness of laws is particularly troubling for e-commerce firms who face a number of ambiguous legal issues involving copyright, liability, taxation, and legal jurisdiction.

For reasons such as these, the marketing manager should carefully examine recent court decisions to better understand the law or regulation in question. New court interpretations can point to future changes in existing laws and regulations. The marketing manager should also examine the recent rulings of federal, state, local and self-regulatory trade agencies to determine their effects on marketing activities.

One of the most profound legislative shifts in recent times occurred with President George Bush's signing of the Sarbanes–Oxley Act on July 30, 2002. Sarbanes–Oxley was essentially the federal government's response to a string of corporate scandals—most notably Enron, Tyco, and WorldCom. The law introduced very stringent rules for financial practice and corporate governance designed to protect investors by increasing the accuracy and reliability of corporate disclosures of financial information. An interesting result of Sarbanes–Oxley is the intense media and public attention that it garnered. The accuracy of corporate disclosures is now such a closely watched issue that organizations are forced into compliance both legally and practically. It is estimated that compliance with the law—in the form of new information and reporting systems—has cost U.S. businesses more than $30 billion.[19]

Organizations that engage in international business should also be mindful of legal issues surrounding the trade agreements among nations. The implementation of the North American Free Trade Agreement (NAFTA), for example, created an open market of roughly 374 million consumers. Since NAFTA went into effect, many U.S. firms have begun or expanded operations in Canada and Mexico. Conversely, national governments sometimes use trade agreements to limit the distribution of certain products into member countries. Recurring disagreements between the United States, Canada, and Argentina and the European Union over genetically modified foods, for example, prompted the United States to file a complaint with the World Trade Organization in 2003. The European Union had banned all genetically modified food and crops since 1998. The complaint argued that the ban lacked scientific support and amounted to an unfair trade barrier. The WTO ruled against the European Union in 2006, opening the way for genetically modified foods to enter the European Union. Despite the ruling, market access for producers of genetically modified foods may not be enough: Over 54 percent of European consumers believe that these foods are unsafe for consumption.[20]

Technological Advancements

When most people think about technology, they tend to think about new high-tech products such as wireless telephones, broadband Internet access, medical breakthroughs, or interactive television. However, technology actually refers to the way that we accomplish specific tasks or the processes that we use to create the "things" we consider as new. Of all the new technologies created in the past 30 years, none has had a greater impact on marketing than advances in computer and information technology. These technologies have changed the way that consumers and employees live and the way that marketers operate in fulfilling their needs. In some cases, changes in technology can be so profound that they make a firm's products obsolete, such as with vinyl long-playing (LP) records, typewriters, cassette tapes, and pagers.

Many changes in technology assume a frontstage presence in creating new marketing opportunities. By *frontstage technology,* we mean those advances that are most noticeable to customers. For example, products such as wireless telephones, DVDs, microwave ovens, and genetic engineering have spawned entirely new industries aimed at fulfilling previously unrecognized customer needs. Many frontstage technologies, such as smart phones and GPS satellite navigation systems, aim to increase customer convenience. Likewise, companies continue to push toward even more substantial changes in the ways that marketers reach customers through the use of interactive marketing via computers and digital television.

These and other technological changes can also assume a backstage presence when their advantages are not necessarily apparent to customers. Advances in backstage technology can affect marketing activities by making them more efficient and effective. For example, advances in computer technology have made warehouse storage and inventory control more efficient and less expensive. Similar changes in communication technology have made field sales representatives more efficient and effective in their dealings with managers and customers.

In some cases, technology can have both a frontstage and a backstage presence. One of the most promising breakthroughs is radio-frequency identification (RFID), which involves the use of tiny radio-enabled chips that can be attached to a product or its packaging. The radio signals emitted or reflected from the chip can be used to track inventory levels, detect product spoilage, or prevent theft. They can also be used for the instantaneous checkout of an entire shopping cart of items. RFID is also used in other applications such as patient tracking in hospitals, real-time data analysis in Indy racecars, and EZ-Pass systems on the nation's toll roads. Many retailers and packaged goods manufacturers fund research to develop RFID, which is expected to replace barcode technology by 2016.[21]

Sociocultural Trends

Sociocultural factors are those social and cultural influences that cause changes in attitudes, beliefs, norms, customs, and lifestyles. These forces profoundly affect the way that people live and help determine what, where, how, and when customers buy a firm's products. The list of potentially important sociocultural trends is far too long to examine each one here. Exhibit 4.7 lists examples of some of these trends. Two of the more important trends, however, are changes in demographics and customer values.

Many changes are taking place in the demographic makeup of the U.S. population. For example, most of us know that the population as a whole has grown older as a result of advances in medicine and healthier lifestyles. Research suggests that the number of Americans age 65 years and older will increase 147 percent between 2000 and 2050, from 12.4 to 21 percent of the population.[22] Experts project that by 2050, the worldwide population of older people will be larger than the population of children ages 0–14 for the first time in human history. As a result, marketers of health care, recreation, tourism, and retirement housing can expect large increases in demand over the next several decades. Other important changes include a decline in the teenage population, an increasing number of singles and single-parent households,

---

EXHIBIT 4.7   **TRENDS IN THE SOCIOCULTURAL ENVIRONMENT**

Demographic Trends

Aging of the American population

Decline in the teen population (as a percentage of the total population)

Population growth in Sun Belt states

Increasing number of single-member/individual households

Increasing participation of women in the workforce

Increasing number of single-parent families

Increasing population diversity, especially in the number of Hispanic Americans

Increasing immigration (legal and illegal)

Increasing number of wealthy Americans

Lifestyle Trends

Clothing has become more casual, especially at work

Clothing has become more revealing, especially for women

Growing participation in body modification (for example, tattoos and piercings)

Americans have less time for leisure activities

Vacationing at home is more common

Less shopping in malls, more shopping from home

Continuing focus on health, nutrition, and exercise

Increasing importance of leisure time versus work time

Time spent watching television and reading newspapers has declined

Time spent using computers and talking on cell phones has increased

Growing popularity of fuel-efficient hybrid vehicles

Growing ubiquity of digital music and portable music players

Value Trends

Shorter attention spans and less tolerance for waiting

Less focus on "me-oriented" values

More value-oriented consumption (good quality, good price)

Importance of maintaining close, personal relationships with others

Increasing importance of family and children

Increasing concerns about the natural environment

Greater focus on ethics and social responsibility

Increased interest in giving back to the community

Less tolerance of smoking in public places

More tolerance of individual lifestyle choices

Growing disconnect with government

---

and still greater participation of women in the workforce. The increase in the number of two-income and single-parent families has, for example, led to a massive increase in demand and retail shelf space for convenient frozen entrees and meals. Our growing focus on health and nutrition has led many of the marketers of these meals to offer lower-calorie and lower-carbohydrate content in their products.

One of the other most important demographic changes taking place is the increasing diversity of the U.S. population. The number of legal immigrants coming to the United States has risen steadily since 1975. Between 2006 and 2050, minority population growth will account for a full 90 percent of the growth of the total U.S. population. This trend is especially true among the Hispanic population, which will grow by 188 percent. By 2050 almost one-quarter of the U.S. population will be of Hispanic decent.[23] These changes in diversity will create both threats and opportunities for most organizations. A diverse population means a diverse customer base. Firms must alter their marketing practices, including the way they recruit and select employees, to match these changing customer segments. For example, women of color, ignored by cosmetics companies for a long time, used to have a very difficult time finding makeup in shades appropriate for their skin tones. Now, virtually all cosmetics companies offer product lines designed specifically for these previously unserved markets. Furthermore, discount retailer Kmart has moved toward a multicultural customer base, especially Hispanics, in the heavily populated urban areas where its stores are located. Over 40 percent of Kmart's sales come from this customer group.[24]

Changes in our cultural values—the guiding principles of everyday life—can also create opportunities and challenges for marketers. Values influence our views of how to live, the decisions we make, the jobs we do, and the brands we buy. In a major study of American values, researchers found that the three most important values regardless of age, gender, race, income, or region are (1) having close relationships with other people, (2) being secure and stable, and (3) having fun. In fact, despite what we often see depicted on television and in advertising, few Americans actually concern themselves with "me-oriented" values like power, influence, or developing themselves personally.[25] Astute marketers can use this information to reflect our prevailing values in the products they design and the advertising they create.

As you can see, the external environment encompasses a wide array of important factors that must be analyzed carefully before developing the marketing plan. These issues are so important that most firms have specialists on staff to track emerging trends and develop strategies for dealing with external concerns. These specialists are typically housed in corporate affairs departments as outlined in Beyond the Pages 4.2. Although the external environment is the largest of the three environments that we have discussed, it is not necessarily the most important. Depending on the firm, its industry, and the timing, the internal and/or customer environments can be much more important in developing marketing strategy. The important issue is that all three environments must be analyzed prior to developing a marketing strategy and marketing plan. Good analysis requires the collection of relevant data and information, our next topic in this chapter.

Collecting Marketing Data and Information

To perform a complete situation analysis, the marketing manager must invest time and money to collect data and information pertinent to the development of the marketing plan. This effort will always involve the collection of secondary data, which must be compiled inside or outside the organization for some purpose other than the current analysis. However, if the required data or information is unavailable, primary data may have to be collected through marketing research. Accessing secondary data sources is usually preferable as a first option because these sources can be obtained more quickly and at less cost than collecting primary data. In this section, we examine the different sources of environmental data and challenges in collecting this data.

Beyond the Pages 4.2

A CORPORATE AFFAIRS PRIMER[26]

What is corporate affairs? In its broadest sense, *corporate affairs* is a collection of strategic activities aimed at marketing an organization, its issues, and its ideals to potential stakeholders (consumers, general public, shareholders, media, government, and so on). One way to think about corporate affairs is that it includes all of the organization's marketing activities not directed at the end users of its products. The activities that define corporate affairs vary; however, most organizations maintain departments that engage in the following strategic activities:

• *Corporate communication* includes activities aimed at telling the organization's story and promoting goodwill among a variety of stakeholders. It includes such activities as public relations, employee relations, corporate image advertising, public affairs, and media relations.

• *Government relations* are activities aimed at educating and influencing elected officials, government officials, and regulatory agencies with respect to key issues that are pertinent to the firm. The most visible form of government relations is lobbying.

• *Investor relations* are activities designed to promote investment in the organization through the sale of financial instruments such as stocks and bonds. It includes such activities as developing the annual report, planning shareholders' meetings, and other customer service activities directed at corporate shareholders.

• *Corporate philanthropy* includes activities aimed at serving the needs of the community at large (either domestically or globally) through product or cash donations, volunteerism, or support of humanitarian initiatives.

• *Policy analysis* involves activities designed to influence the national or international dialogue with respect to public or economic policy in an industry-related area. It includes research and analysis designed to provide needed information for making policy decisions.

Perhaps the best way to understand corporate affairs is to see what organizations themselves have to say about it. Here are a few examples:

Microsoft

Public policy influences everyone's daily life. Good public policy requires that everyone's voice be heard. Often found at the intersection where government, corporate, community and private interests meet, decisions must be reached on myriad issues: What's the role of government in ensuring Internet safety for children? How can Microsoft and other business leaders help to address the growing threat of identity theft? What do elected officials and community leaders need to understand about the impact of the digital divide on people's lives?

Microsoft's Global Corporate Affairs group, which includes professionals focused on government relations and public policy advocacy, industry outreach, regulatory counsel, and compliance advice and community engagement programs, is our public voice on important issues.

(continued)

Secondary Information Sources

There are four basic sources of secondary data and information: internal, government, periodicals/books, and commercial. Most of these sources are available in both print and electronic formats. Let's look at the major strengths and weaknesses of these sources.

Internal Sources The firm's own records are the best source of data on current objectives, strategy, performance, and available resources. Internal sources may also be a good source of data on customer needs, attitudes, and buying behavior. Internal data also has the advantage of being relevant and believable because the organization itself has responsibility for its collection and organization.

Government, industry and regulatory affairs employees are corporate ambassadors to every level of government—local, state, national and international. They contribute knowledgeable insights required for sound public policy decision-making, cultivate mutually beneficial relationships and advocate on technology-related policy issues.

Our community engagement professionals manage nearly $500 million in corporate community investments in thousands of inter-governmental and nonprofit organizations around the world. This group also oversees employee engagement programs that encourage Microsoft's workforce to give generously of their time and money to improve the lives of others.

Philip Morris International

In Corporate Affairs, we work with governments and other stakeholders to secure comprehensive regulation of all aspects of the tobacco business so that there are clear rules established and enforced for all tobacco companies.

We seek to understand what our stakeholders expect from us, and to respond to those expectations where our products are sold.

We communicate with our consumers and others about our products, the health risks of smoking, and our efforts to pursue solutions to important issues such as the harm caused by smoking, and how to tackle the complex issue of youth smoking.

Pfizer

Corporate Affairs' seasoned professionals employ their skills and knowledge in the fields of government relations; media relations; communications; corporate advertising; public affairs; philanthropy; and economic, science, and healthcare policy to help create the social and political conditions essential for Pfizer to sustain its industry leadership.

BlueScope Steel (Australia)

BlueScope Steel Corporate Affairs manages BlueScope Steel's corporate relationships with a number of key external stakeholders including media, governments, industry bodies, and other steelmakers. Corporate Affairs produces regular media releases and announcements, and is responsible for managing the production of corporate reports, including the Annual Report and the Community, Safety & Environment Report.

Corporate Affairs is also responsible for the management of communications with the company's 17,000-plus employees around the globe, including production of the company-wide employee newspaper, Steel Connections.

BlueScope Steel maintains a sophisticated electronic communications system, including regular 'Stop Press' email announcements and an extensive corporate intranet site, in addition to the company's external Internet sites.

Given the complexity of the external environment in today's economy, strategic planning regarding corporate affairs is every bit as important as developing sound strategy for reaching the organization's customers. No organization exists in isolation. Consequently, all organizations must actively manage their relationships with potential stakeholders to ensure continued success.

One of the biggest problems with internal data is that they are often not in a readily accessible form for planning purposes. Boxes of printed company records that sit in a warehouse are hardly useful for marketing planning. To overcome this problem, many organizations maintain corporate intranets or virtual private networks (VPNs) that make data easily accessible and interactive. These systems enable employees to access internal data, such as customer profiles and product inventory, and to share details of their activities and projects with other company employees across the hall or the world. Intranets and VPNs provide an opportunity for company-wide marketing intelligence that permits coordination and integration of efforts to achieve a true market orientation.

Government Sources   If it exists, the U.S. government has collected data about it. The sheer volume of available information on the economy, population, and business activities is the major strength of most government data sources. Government sources also have the added advantages of easy accessibility and low cost—most are even free. The major drawback to government data is timeliness. Although many government sources have annual updates, some are done much less frequently (for example, the census every decade). As a result, some government sources may be out-of-date and not particularly useful for market planning purposes.

Still, the objectivity and low cost of government sources make them an attractive answer to the data needs of many organizations. Some of the best government sources available on the Internet include the following:

- Federal Trade Commission (http://www.ftc.gov) provides reports, speeches, and other facts about competitive, antitrust, and consumer protection issues.

- *FedWorld* (http://www.fedworld.gov) offers links to various federal government sources of industry and market statistics.

- Edgar Database (http://www.sec.gov/edgarhp.htm) provides comprehensive financial data (10K reports) on public corporations in the United States.

- U.S. Small Business Administration (http://www.sba.gov) offers numerous resources for small businesses, including industry reports, maps, market analyses (national, regional, or local), library resources, and checklists.

Book and Periodical Sources   The articles and research reports available in books and periodicals provide a gamut of information about many organizations, industries, and nations. Forget any notion about books and periodicals appearing only in print. Today, many good sources exist only in electronic format. Timeliness is a major strength of these sources because most are about current environmental trends and business practices. Some sources, such as academic journals, provide detailed results of research studies that may be pertinent to the manager's planning efforts. Others, such as trade publications, focus on specific industries and the issues that characterize them.

Many of these sources are freely available on the Internet. Most, however, require paid subscriptions. Some of the better examples include the following:

- Subscription services such as *Moody's* (http://www.moodys.com), *Hoover's* (http://www.hoovers.com), *Standard and Poor's* (http://www.standardandpoors.com/), and *Dismal Scientist* (http://www.dismal.com) offer in-depth analyses and current statistics about major industries and corporations.

- Major trade associations (such as the American Marketing Association http://www.marketingpower.com/ and Sales and Marketing Executives http://www.smei.org) and trade publications (such as *Adweek* http://www.adweek.com and *Chain Store Age* http://www.chainstoreage.com) offer a wide range of news and information to their membership and readers.

- Academic journals, such as the *Harvard Business Review* (http://www.hbr.org) and the *Sloan Management Review* (http://sloanreview.mit.edu/smr), are good sources of cutting-edge thinking on business and marketing.

- General business publications, such as the *Wall Street Journal* (http://www.wsj.com), *Fortune* (http://www.fortune.com), and *BusinessWeek* (http://www.businessweek.com), offer a wealth of information on a wide variety of industries and companies.

The two biggest drawbacks to book and periodical sources are information overload and relevance to the specific problem at hand. That is, despite the sheer volume of information that is available, finding data or information that pertains to the manager's specific and unique situation can feel like looking for that proverbial needle in a haystack.

Commercial Sources   Commercial sources are almost always relevant to a specific issue because they deal with the actual behaviors of customers in the marketplace. Firms such as Nielsen monitor a variety of behaviors from food purchases in grocery stores to media usage characteristics. Commercial sources generally charge a fee for their services. However, their data and information are invaluable to many companies. Some commercial sources provide limited information on their websites:

- A. C. Nielsen Company (http://www.acnielsen.com) and Information Resources, Inc. (http://www.infores.com) supply data and reports on point-of-purchase sales.

- Mediamark Research, Inc. (http://www.mediamark.com/) and Arbitron (http://www.arbitron.com) specialize in multimedia audience research by providing a wealth of customer demographic, lifestyle, and product usage data to major media and advertising companies.

- The Audit Bureau of Circulations (http://www.accessabc.com) provides independent, third-party audits of print circulation, readership and website activity.

- Surveys.com (http://www.surveys.com) uses an online consumer panel to provide information to businesses about the products and services they provide.

The most obvious drawback to these and other commercial sources is cost. Although this is not a problem for large organizations, small companies often cannot afford the expense. However, many commercial sources provide limited, free access to some data and information. Additionally, companies often find "off-the-shelf" studies less costly than conducting primary research.

Primary Data Collection

The situation analysis should always begin with an examination of secondary data sources due to their availability and low cost. Each secondary data source has its advantages and disadvantages, so the best approach is one that blends data and information from a variety of sources. However, if the needed secondary data are not available, out of date, inaccurate, unreliable, or irrelevant to the specific problem at hand, an organization may have little choice but to collect primary data through marketing research. Primary marketing research has the major advantages of being relevant to the specific problem, as well as trustworthy due to the control that the manager has over data collection. However, primary research is extremely expensive and time consuming. There are four major types of primary data collection:

- *Direct observation,* where the researcher records the overt behaviors of customers, competitors, or suppliers in natural settings. Historically, researchers have used direct observation to study the shopping and buying behaviors of customers. However, behavior can be observed today through the use of technology such as bar-code scanners and RFID tags. The main advantage of observation research is that it accurately describes behavior without influencing the target under observation. However, the results of observation research are often overly descriptive and subject to a great deal of bias and researcher interpretation.

- *Focus groups,* where the researcher moderates a panel discussion among a gathering of six to ten people who openly discuss a specific subject. Focus group research is an excellent means of obtaining in-depth information about a particular issue. Its flexibility also allows it to be used in a variety of settings and with different types of panel members (that is, customers, suppliers, and employees). Focus groups are also very useful in designing a large-scale survey to ensure that questions have the appropriate wording. The main disadvantage is that focus groups require a highly skilled moderator to help limit the potential for moderator bias.

- *Surveys,* where the researcher asks respondents to answer a series of questions on a particular topic. Surveys can be administered using the paper-and-pencil method, either in person or through the mail; or they can be administered interactively via telephone, e-mail, or the Internet. Although surveys are a very useful and time-efficient way to collect primary data, it has become increasingly difficult to convince people to participate. Potential respondents have become skeptical of survey methods due to overly long questionnaires and the unethical practices of many researchers. These concerns are one of the reasons behind the creation of the national Do Not Call Registry for telemarketers.[27]

- *Experiments,* where the researcher selects matched subjects and exposes them to different treatments while controlling for extraneous variables. Because experiments are well suited to testing for cause-and-effect relationships, researchers use them often in test-marketing programs. Marketers can experiment with different combinations of marketing-mix variables to determine which combination has the strongest effect on sales or profitability. The major obstacles to effective experimentation in marketing are the expense and the difficulty of controlling for all extraneous variables in the test.

As with secondary data, often the best approach to primary data collection is to use a combination of data sources. Focus groups and direct observation can be used to gain a more complete understanding of a particular issue or marketing phenomenon. Surveys can then be used to further test for certain tendencies or effects before launching into a full-scale test-marketing program. At this point, the process comes full circle because observation and focus groups can be used to explore the outcomes of the test-marketing program.

Overcoming Problems in Data Collection

Despite the best intentions, problems usually arise in collecting data and information. One of the most common problems is an incomplete or inaccurate assessment of the situation that the gathering of data should address. After expending a great degree of effort in collecting data, the manager may be unsure of the usefulness or relevance of what has been collected. In some cases, the manager might even suffer from severe information overload. To prevent these problems from occurring, the marketing problem must be accurately and specifically defined before the collection of any data. Top managers who do not adequately explain their needs and expectations to marketing researchers often cause the problem.

Another common difficulty is the expense of collecting environmental data. Although there are always costs associated with data collection (even if the data are free), the process need not be prohibitively expensive. The key is to find alternative data collection methods or sources. For example, an excellent way for some businesses to collect data is to engage the cooperation of a local college or university. Many professors seek out marketing projects for their students as a part of course requirements. Likewise, to help overcome data collection costs, many researchers have turned to the Internet as a means of collecting both quantitative and qualitative data on customer opinions and behaviors.

A third issue is the time it takes to collect data and information. Although this is certainly true with respect to primary data collection, the collection of secondary data can be easy and fast. Online data sources are accessible. Even if the manager has no idea where to begin the search, the powerful search engines and indexes available on the Internet make it easy to find data. Online data sources have become so good at data retrieval that the real problem involves the time needed to sort through all of the available information to find something that is truly relevant.

Finally, it can be challenging to find a way to organize the vast amount of data and information collected during the situation analysis. Clearly defining the marketing problem and blending different data sources are among the first steps toward finding all the pieces to the puzzle. A critical next step is to convert the data and information into a form that will facilitate strategy development. Although a variety of tools can be used to analyze and organize environmental data and information, one of the most effective tools is SWOT analysis. As we will see in the next chapter, SWOT analysis which involves classifying data and information into strengths, weaknesses, opportunities, and threats—can be used to organize data and information and used as a catalyst for strategy formulation.

Lessons from Chapter 4

Collecting and analyzing marketing information through a situation analysis

- is perhaps the most important task of the marketing manager because practically all decision making and planning depends on how well he or she conducts the analysis.

- should be an ongoing effort that is well organized, systematic, and supported by sufficient resources.

- involves analysis and synthesis to understand why people, products, and organizations perform the way they do.

- is not intended to replace the marketing manager in the decision-making process but to empower him or her with information for decision making.

- recognizes that data and information are not the same. Data are not useful until converted into information.

- forces managers to ask continually, "How much data and information do I need?"

- is valuable only to the extent that it improves the quality of the resulting decisions. Marketing managers must avoid "paralysis by analysis."

- should provide as complete a picture as possible about the organization's current and future situation with respect to the internal, customer, and external environments.

Analysis of the internal environment

- includes an assessment of the firm's current goals, objectives, performance, and how well the current marketing strategy is working.

- includes a review of the current and anticipated levels of organizational resources.

- must include a review of current and anticipated cultural and structural issues that could affect marketing activities.

Analysis of the customer environment

- examines the firm's current customers in its target markets, as well as potential customers that currently do not purchase the firm's product offering.

- can be conducted by using the expanded 5W model:

  Who are our current and potential customers?
  What do customers do with our products?

Where do customers purchase our products?
When do customers purchase our products?
Why (and how) do customers select our products?
Why do potential customers not purchase our products?

Analysis of the external environment

- examines the competitive, economic, political, legal and regulatory, technological, and sociocultural factors in the firm's external environment.

- includes an examination of the four basic types of competitors faced by all businesses: brand competitors, product competitors, generic competitors, and total budget competitors.

- is often handled by a team of specialists within an organization's corporate affairs department.

Marketing data and information

- can be collected from a wide array of internal, government, periodical, book, and commercial sources, as well as through primary marketing research.

- are often collected through four different types of primary research: direct observation, focus groups, surveys, and experiments.

- must be blended from many different sources to be the most useful for planning purposes.

Problems that can occur during data collection include

- an incomplete or inaccurate definition of the marketing problem.

- ambiguity about the usefulness or relevance of the collected data.

- severe information overload.

- the expense and time associated with data collection.

- finding ways to organize the vast amount of collected data and information.

Questions for Discussion

1. Of the three major environments in a situation analysis (internal, customer, and external), which do you think is the most important in a general sense? Why? What are some situations that would make one environment more important than the others?

2. Understanding the motivations of a firm's noncustomers is often just as important as understanding its customers. Look again at the reasons why an individual would not purchase a firm's products. How can a firm reach out to noncustomers and successfully convert them into customers?

3. Do you think that the Internet has made it easier or more difficult to collect marketing data and information? Why? How might the major data collection issues of today compare to the issues that occurred in the pre-Internet era?

Exercises

1. Choose a specific product that you use on a daily basis (such as food items, toiletries, or your car) and apply the 5W model in Exhibit 4.4 to yourself:

    a. Who are you (demographics, psychographics, and so on)?

    b. What do you do with the product (consumption, storage, disposal, and so on)?

    c. Where do you purchase the product? Why?

    d. When do you purchase the product? Why?

    e. Why and how do you select the product?

    f. Why do you not purchase competing products?

    Assume that your responses are similar to millions of other consumers. Given this profile, how would you approach the marketing strategy for this particular product?

2. Consider the last purchase you made (maybe it was lunch or a soft drink). List all of the brand, product, generic, and total budget competitors for that product. In a general sense, what would it take for you to switch to another type of competitor? Are there situations that would encourage you to switch to a generic competitor? When would total budget competitors become more relevant to your decision making?

3. Review the sociocultural trends in Exhibit 4.7. What other trends could be added to the list? What trends are specific to your generation that do not universally apply to all Americans?

CHAPTER

Developing Competitive Advantage and Strategic Focus

Introduction

Situation analysis, as discussed in Chapter 4, can generate a great deal of data and information for marketing planning. But information in and of itself provides little direction to managers in preparing a marketing plan. If the analysis does not structure the information in a meaningful way that clarifies both present and anticipated situations, the manager cannot see how the pieces fit together. This synthesis of information is critical in developing competitive advantages and the strategic focus of the marketing plan. As illustrated in Beyond the Pages 5.1, this synthesis often comes from enhanced innovation, a stronger focus on customer needs, and tighter integration within the firm. Understanding the connectedness of the external environment is vital to enhanced innovation across a number of industries.

How should the marketing manager organize and use the information collected during the situation analysis? One widely used tool is SWOT analysis (strengths, weaknesses, opportunities, and threats). A SWOT analysis encompasses both the internal and external environments of the firm. Internally, the framework addresses a firm's strengths and weaknesses on key dimensions such as financial performance and resources, human resources, production facilities and capacity, market share, customer perceptions, product quality, product availability, and organizational communication. The assessment of the external environment organizes information on the market (customers and competition), economic conditions, social trends, technology, and government regulations.

As shown in Exhibit 5.1, many consider SWOT analysis to be one of the most effective tools in the analysis of marketing data and information. SWOT analysis is a simple, straightforward framework that provides direction and serves as a catalyst for the development of viable marketing plans. It fulfills this role by structuring the assessment of the fit between what a firm can and cannot do (strengths and weaknesses), and the environmental conditions working for and against the firm (opportunities and threats). When performed correctly, a SWOT analysis not only organizes data and information but also can be especially useful in uncovering competitive

117

Beyond the Pages 5.1

INNOVATION: THE KEY TO SUCCESS?[1]

Innovation is the buzzword of business in the twenty-first century. Of course, innovation has always been important, especially with respect to developing new products. What has changed, however, is the focus of innovation in most companies. The twentieth-century model of innovation was about quality control, cost cutting, and operational efficiency. Today, innovation is more about reinventing business processes, collaborating and integrating within the firm, and creating entirely new markets to meet untapped customer needs. Increasing globalization, the growth of the Internet, and more demanding customers are forcing marketers to find innovative ways of conducting business.

An important lesson that many companies have learned is that innovation is not always about technology or offering the latest gee-whiz product. Differences in innovation style are apparent in *BusinessWeek*'s second annual list of the World's Most Innovative Companies. The top-ten companies on the list include both cultural icons and manufacturing giants:

Rank	Company	1995–2005 Stock Returns (%)
1	Apple	24.6
2	Google	n/a
3	3M	11.2
4	Toyota	11.8
5	Microsoft	18.5
6	General Electric	13.4
7	Procter & Gamble	12.6
8	Nokia	34.6
9	Starbucks	27.6
10	IBM	14.4
Median of 100 Most Innovative Companies		14.3
Median of S&P 1,200 Global Stock Index		11.1

Several types of innovation are presented in this list. For example, in launching the iPod, Apple combined innovations in product design (the iPod), branding (the white color), strategic alliances (agreements with music companies), and business model (selling songs via iTunes for 99¢ each) to create a cultural phenomenon. Innovation at Starbucks has nothing to do with technology. Instead, the company innovated by seeing itself as more than a coffee company. Toyota makes the top ten due to relentless manufacturing expertise, tight integration within the firm, and advancements in hybrid technology with its Prius.

One thing that all innovative companies have in common is a laserlike focus on customer needs. Innovative companies find new ways of learning from customers in addition to traditional methods. For example, many companies closely watch blogs and online communities to learn what customers are thinking. Focusing on customers may not sound innovative, but increasing competition and shorter product cycles are forcing marketers to shift away from the price- and efficiency-driven approaches of the past. To escape from commodity hell, marketers must find innovation in unfamiliar places. For example, BMW (number sixteen on the list) finds innovation in product design by relocating hundreds of employees from across the globe to a central design studio. Starbucks finds innovation outside of coffee by offering music and movies to its customers. An interesting side effect of innovation is that it often creates a new set of competitors for the firm. For example, Apple competes with Starbucks in music and is soon to compete with Nokia in cell phones. Another example is the chewing gum industry. Wrigley has launched Airwaves Active (a wellness gum that contains vitamins and other ingredients that boost the immune system) and Orbit White (a teeth-whitening gum). Likewise, GumRunners has licensed the Jolt brand to launch a caffeinated gum to capitalize on the increasing popularity of energy drinks.

As reflected in the table, innovation is obviously good for the bottom line. Through increased growth, better collaboration, and a broader product mix, the most innovative companies can pull their products out of commodity status and increase their profit margins. It is clear that innovation has become a key driver of competitive advantage and success in today's market.

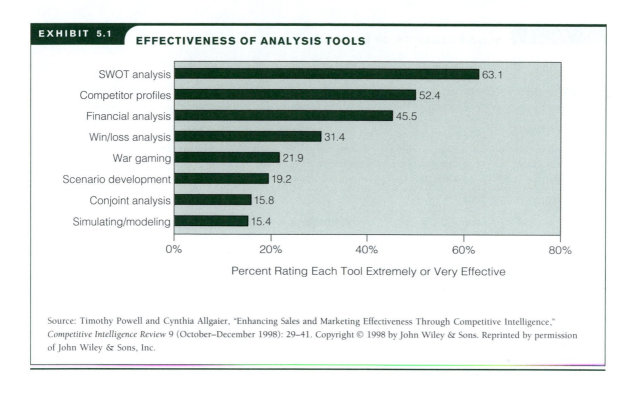

EXHIBIT 5.1

EFFECTIVENESS OF ANALYSIS TOOLS

Percent Rating Each Tool Extremely or Very Effective

- SWOT analysis: 63.1
- Competitor profiles: 52.4
- Financial analysis: 45.5
- Win/loss analysis: 31.4
- War gaming: 21.9
- Scenario development: 19.2
- Conjoint analysis: 15.8
- Simulating/modeling: 15.4

Source: Timothy Powell and Cynthia Allgaier, "Enhancing Sales and Marketing Effectiveness Through Competitive Intelligence," *Competitive Intelligence Review* 9 (October–December 1998): 29–41. Copyright © 1998 by John Wiley & Sons. Reprinted by permission of John Wiley & Sons, Inc.

advantages that can be leveraged in the firm's marketing strategy. These competitive advantages help establish the strategic focus and direction of the firm's marketing plan.

As a planning tool, SWOT analysis has many benefits, as outlined in Exhibit 5.2. In fact, SWOT analysis is so useful and logical that many underestimate its value in planning. However, this simplicity often leads to unfocused and poorly conducted analyses.[2] The most common criticisms leveled against SWOT analysis are that (1) it allows firms to create lists without serious consideration of the issues and (2) it often becomes a sterile academic exercise of classifying data and information. It is important to remember that SWOT analysis by itself is not inherently productive or unproductive. Rather, the way that one uses SWOT analysis will determine whether it yields benefits for the firm.

Making SWOT Analysis Productive

Whether a firm receives the full benefits of SWOT analysis depends on the way that the manager uses the framework. If done correctly and smartly, SWOT analysis can be a viable mechanism for the development of the marketing plan. If done haphazardly or incorrectly, it can be a great waste of time and other valuable resources. To help ensure that the former, not the latter, takes place, we offer the following directives to make SWOT analysis more productive and useful. Exhibit 5.3 outlines these directives.

EXHIBIT 5.2 | **MAJOR BENEFITS OF SWOT ANALYSIS**

Simplicity

SWOT analysis requires no extensive training or technical skills to be used successfully. The analyst needs only a comprehensive understanding of the nature of the company and the industry in which it competes.

Lower Costs

Because specialized training and skills are not necessary, the use of SWOT analysis can actually reduce the costs associated with strategic planning. As firms begin to recognize this benefit of SWOT analysis, many opt to downsize or eliminate their strategic planning departments.

Flexibility

SWOT analysis can enhance the quality of an organization's strategic planning even without extensive marketing information systems. However, when comprehensive systems are present, they can be structured to feed information directly into the SWOT framework. The presence of a comprehensive information system can make repeated SWOT analyses run more smoothly and efficiently.

Integration and Synthesis

SWOT analysis gives the analyst the ability to integrate and synthesize diverse information, both of a quantitative and qualitative nature. It organizes information that is widely known, as well as information that has only recently been acquired or discovered. SWOT analysis can also deal with a wide diversity of information sources. In fact, SWOT analysis helps transform information diversity from a weakness of the planning process into one of its major strengths.

Collaboration

SWOT analysis fosters collaboration and open information exchange between different functional areas. By learning what their counterparts do, what they know, what they think, and how they feel, the marketing analyst can solve problems, fill voids in the analysis, and eliminate potential disagreements before the finalization of the marketing plan.

Stay Focused

Marketing planners often make the mistake of conducting one generic SWOT analysis for the entire organization or business unit. Such an approach produces stale, meaningless generalizations that come from the tops of managers' heads or from press release files. Although this type of effort may make managers feel good and provide a quick sense of accomplishment, it does little to add to the creativity and vision of the planning process.

When we say SWOT analysis, we really mean SWOT *analyses*. In most firms, there should be a series of analyses, each focusing on a specific product–market combination. For example, a single SWOT analysis for the Chevrolet division of General Motors would not be focused enough to be meaningful. Instead, separate analyses for each product category (passenger cars, trucks, minivans) or brand (Corvette, Impala, Avalanche, Tahoe, Uplander) in the division would be more appropriate. Such a focus enables the marketing manager to look at the specific mix of competitors, customers, and external factors that are present in a given market. Chevrolet's Tahoe, for example, competes in the crowded SUV market in which the auto industry releases new models at a staggering pace. Consequently, market planning for the Tahoe should differ substantially from market planning for Chevrolet's Corvette or Uplander minivan. If

---

EXHIBIT 5.3   **DIRECTIVES FOR A PRODUCTIVE SWOT ANALYSIS**

Stay Focused

A single, broad analysis leads to meaningless generalizations. Separate analyses for each product–market combination are recommended.

Search Extensively for Competitors

Although major brand competitors are the most important, the analyst must not overlook product, generic, and total budget competitors. Potential future competitors must also be considered.

Collaborate with Other Functional Areas

SWOT analysis promotes the sharing of information and perspective across departments. This cross-pollination of ideas allows for more creative and innovative solutions to marketing problems.

Examine Issues from the Customers' Perspective

Customers' beliefs about the firm, its products, and marketing activities are important considerations in SWOT analysis. The views of employees and other key stakeholders must also be considered.

Look for Causes, Not Characteristics

Rather than simply list characteristics of the firm's internal and external environments, the analyst must also explore the resources possessed by the firm and/or its competitors that are the true causes for the firm's strengths, weaknesses, opportunities, and threats.

Separate Internal Issues from External Issues

If an issue would exist even if the firm did not exist, the issue should be classified as external. Marketing options, strategies, or tactics are not the same as opportunities in SWOT analysis.

---

needed, separate product–market analyses can be combined to examine the issues relevant for the entire strategic business unit, and business-unit analyses can be combined to create a complete SWOT analysis for the entire organization. The only time a single SWOT analysis would be appropriate is when an organization has only one product–market combination.

Search Extensively for Competitors

Information on competitors and their activities is an important aspect of a well-focused SWOT analysis. The key is not to overlook any competitor, whether a current rival or one on the horizon. As we discussed in Chapter 4, the firm will focus most of its efforts on brand competition. During the SWOT analysis, however, the firm must watch for any current or potential direct substitutes for its products. Product, generic, and total budget competitors are important as well. Looking for all four types of competition is crucial because many firms and managers never look past brand competitors. Although it is important for the SWOT analysis to be focused, it must not be myopic.

Even industry giants can lose sight of their potential competitors by focusing exclusively on brand competition. Kodak, for example, had always taken steps to maintain its market dominance over rivals Fuji, Konica, and Polaroid in the film industry. However, the advent of digital photography added Sony, Nikon, and Canon to Kodak's set of competing firms. And, as digital cameras become better integrated into wireless phones, Kodak will have to add Motorola, LG, Samsung, and Nokia to its competitive set. A similar trend has occurred in financial services as deregulation has allowed brokers, banks, and insurance firms to compete in each other's traditional markets. State Farm, for example, now offers mortgage loans, credit cards, mutual funds, and traditional banking services alongside its well-known insurance products. This shift has forced firms such as Charles Schwab and Citigroup to look at insurance companies in a different light.

Collaborate with Other Functional Areas

One of the major benefits of SWOT analysis is that it generates information and perspective that can be shared across a variety of functional areas in the firm. The SWOT process should be a powerful stimulus for communication outside normal channels. The final outcome of a properly conducted SWOT analysis should be a fusion of information from many areas. Managers in sales, advertising, production, research and development, finance, customer service, inventory control, quality control, and other areas should learn what other managers see as the firm's strengths, weaknesses, opportunities, and threats. This allows the marketing manager to come to terms with multiple perspectives before actually creating the marketing plan.

While combining the SWOT analyses from individual areas, the marketing manager can identify opportunities for joint projects and cross selling of the firm's products. In a large firm, the first time a SWOT takes place may be the initial point at which managers from some areas have ever formally communicated with each other. Such cross-pollination can generate a very conducive environment for creativity and innovation. Moreover, research has shown that the success of introducing a new product, especially a radically new product, is extremely dependent on the ability of different functional areas to collaborate and integrate their differing perspectives. For example, every time that BMW develops a new car, they relocate 200 to 300 engineering, design, production, marketing, and finance employees from their worldwide locations to the company's research and innovation center. For up to three years, these employees work alongside BMW's research and development team in a manner that speeds communication and car development.[3]

Examine Issues from the Customers' Perspective

In the initial stages of SWOT analysis, it is important to identify issues exhaustively. However, all issues are not equally important with respect to developing competitive advantages and strategic focus for the marketing plan. As the analysis progresses, the marketing manager should identify the most critical issues by looking at each one through the eyes of the firm's customers. To do this, the manager must constantly ask questions such as the following:

- What do customers (and noncustomers) believe about us as a company?

- What do customers (and noncustomers) think of our product quality, customer service, price and overall value, convenience, and promotional messages in comparison to our competitors?

- Which of our weaknesses translate into a decreased ability to serve customers (and decreased ability to convert noncustomers)?

- How do trends in the external environment affect customers (and noncustomers)?

- What is the relative importance of these issues; not as we see them, but as customers see them?

Marketing planners must also gauge the perceptions of each customer segment that the firm attempts to target. For example, older banking customers, due to their reluctance to use ATMs and online banking services, may have vastly different perceptions of a bank's convenience than younger customers. Each customer segment's perceptions of external issues, such as the economy or the environment, are also important. It matters little, for example, that managers think the economic outlook is positive if customers have curbed their spending because they think the economy is weak.

Examining issues from the customers' perspective also includes the firm's internal customers: its employees. The fact that management perceives the firm as offering competitive compensation and benefits is unimportant. The real issue is what the employees think. Employees are also a valuable source of information on strengths, weaknesses, opportunities, and threats that management may have never considered. Some employees, especially frontline employees, are closer to the customer and can offer a different perspective on what customers think and believe. For example, research indicates that employees are a valuable source of information regarding the effectiveness of a firm's advertising.[4] Other key stakeholders, such as investors, the general public, and government officials, should also be considered. The key is to examine every issue from the most relevant perspective. Exhibit 5.4 illustrates how taking the customers' perspective can help managers interpret the clichés they might develop and then break them down into meaningful customer-oriented strengths and weaknesses.

Taking the customers' perspective is a cornerstone of a well-done SWOT analysis. Managers have a natural tendency to see issues the way that they think they are (for example, "We offer a high-quality product"). SWOT analysis forces managers to change their perceptions to the way that customers and other important groups see things (for example, "The product offers weak value given its price and features as compared against the strongest brand competitor"). The contrast between these two perspectives often leads to the identification of a gap between management's version of reality and customers' perceptions. As the planning process moves ahead, managers must reduce or eliminate this gap and determine whether their views of the firm are realistic.

Look for Causes, Not Characteristics

Although taking the customers' perspective is important, it often provides just enough information to get into serious trouble. That is, it provides a level of detail that is often very descriptive, but not very constructive. The problem lies in listing strengths, weaknesses, opportunities, and threats as simple descriptions or characteristics of the firm's internal and external environments without going deeper to consider the causes

EXHIBIT 5.4

BREAKING DOWN MANAGERIAL CLICHÉS INTO CUSTOMER-ORIENTED STRENGTHS AND WEAKNESSES

Cliché	Potential Strengths	Potential Weaknesses
"We are an established firm."	Stable after-sales service	Old-fashioned
	Experienced	Inflexible
	Trustworthy	Weak innovation
"We are a large supplier."	Comprehensive product line	Bureaucratic
	Technical expertise	Focused only on large accounts
	Longevity	Impersonal
	Strong reputation	Weak customer service
"We have a comprehensive product line."	Wide variety and availability	Shallow assortment
	One-stop supplier	Cannot offer hard-to-find products
	Convenient	Limited in-depth product expertise
	Customized solutions	
"We are the industry standard."	Wide product adoption	Vulnerable to technological changes
	High status and image	Limited view of competition
	Good marketing leverage	Higher prices (weaker value)
	Extensive third-party support	

Source: Adapted from Nigel Piercy, *Market-Led Strategic Change* (Oxford, UK: Butterworth-Heineman, 1992), 261.

for these characteristics. Although the customers' perspective is valuable, customers do not see behind the scenes to understand the reasons for a firm's characteristics. More often than not, the causes for each issue in a SWOT analysis can be found in the resources possessed by the firm and/or its competitors.

From a resource-based viewpoint, every organization can be considered as a unique bundle of tangible and intangible resources. Major types of these resources include the following:[5]

- **Financial Resources**   Cash, access to financial markets, physical facilities, equipment, raw materials, systems and configurations

- **Intellectual Resources**   Expertise, discoveries, creativity, innovation

- **Legal Resources**   Patents, trademarks, contracts

- **Human Resources**   Employee expertise and skills, leadership

- **Organizational Resources**   Culture, customs, shared values, vision, routines, working relationships, processes and systems

- **Informational Resources**   Customer intelligence, competitive intelligence, marketing information systems

- **Relational Resources**   Strategic alliances, relations with customers, vendors, and other stakeholders, bargaining power, switching costs

- **Reputational Resources**   Brand names, symbols, image

The availability or lack of these resources are the causes for the firm's strengths and weaknesses in meeting customers' needs and determine which external conditions represent opportunities and threats. For example, Wal-Mart's strength in low-cost distribution and logistics comes from its combined resources in terms of distribution, information, and communication infrastructure; committed employees; and strong relationships with vendors. Likewise, 3M's strength in product innovation is the result of combined financial, intellectual, legal, organizational, and informational resources. These resources not only give Wal-Mart and 3M strengths or advantages in serving customers but also create imposing threats for their competitors.

Separate Internal Issues from External Issues

For the results of a SWOT analysis to be truly beneficial, we have seen that the analyst must go beyond simple descriptions of internal and external characteristics to explore the resources that are the foundation for these characteristics. It is equally important, however, for the analyst to maintain a separation between internal issues and external issues. Internal issues are the firm's strengths and weaknesses, whereas external issues refer to opportunities and threats in the firm's external environments. The key test to differentiate a strength or weakness from an opportunity or threat is to ask, "Would this issue exist if the firm did not exist?" If the answer is yes, the issue should be classified as external.

At first glance, the distinction between internal and external issues seems simplistic and immaterial. However, the failure to understand the difference between internal and external issues is one of the major reasons for a poorly conducted SWOT analysis. This happens because managers tend to get ahead of themselves and list their marketing options or strategies as opportunities. However, options and strategies are not the same as opportunities in the SWOT framework. Opportunities (and threats) exist independently of the firm and are associated with characteristics or situations present in the economic, customer, competitive, sociocultural, technological, political, or legal environments in which the firm resides. A manager's options, strategies, or tactics should be based on what the firm intends to do about its opportunities and threats relative to its own strengths and weaknesses. The development of strategic options occurs at a later point within the marketing plan framework.

In summary, a SWOT analysis should be directed by Socrates' advice: "Know thyself." This knowledge should be realistic, based on how customers (external and internal) and other key stakeholders see the company, and viewed in terms of the firm's resources. If managers find it difficult to make an honest and realistic assessment of these issues, they should recognize the need to bring in outside experts or consultants to oversee the process.

SWOT-Driven Strategic Planning

As we discussed in Chapter 4, the collection of marketing information via a situation analysis identifies the key factors that should be tracked by the firm and organizes them within a system that will monitor and distribute information on these factors on an ongoing basis. This process feeds into and helps define the boundaries of a SWOT

EXHIBIT 5.5   POTENTIAL ISSUES TO CONSIDER IN A SWOT ANALYSIS

Potential Internal Strengths

Abundant financial resources
Well-known brand name
Number 1 ranking in the industry
Economies of scale
Proprietary technology
Patented processes
Lower costs (raw materials or processes)
Respected company/product/brand image
Superior management talent
Better marketing skills
Superior product quality
Alliances with other firms
Good distribution skills
Committed employees

Potential External Opportunities

Rapid market growth
Complacent rival firms
Changing customer needs/tastes
Opening of foreign markets
Mishap of a rival firm
New product discoveries
Economic boom
Government deregulation
New technology
Demographic shifts
Other firms seeking alliances
High brand switching
Sales decline for a substitute product
Changing distribution methods

Potential Internal Weaknesses

Lack of strategic direction
Limited financial resources
Weak spending on research and
development
Very narrow product line
Limited distribution
Higher costs (raw materials or processes)
Out-of-date products or technology
Internal operating problems
Internal political problems
Weak market image
Poor marketing skills
Alliances with weak firms
Limited management skills
Undertrained employees

Potential External Threats

Entry of foreign competitors
Introduction of new substitute products
Product life cycle in decline
Changing customer needs/tastes
Declining consumer confidence
Rival firms adopting new strategies
Increased government regulation
Economic downturn
Change in Federal Reserve policy
New technology
Demographic shifts
Foreign trade barriers
Poor performance of ally firm
International political turmoil
Weakening currency exchange rates

---

analysis that will be used as a catalyst for the development of the firm's marketing plan. The role of SWOT analysis then is to help the marketing manager make the transition from a broad understanding of the marketing environment to the development of a strategic focus for the firm's marketing efforts. The potential issues that can be considered in a SWOT analysis are numerous and will vary depending on the particular firm or industry being examined. To aid your search for relevant issues, we have provided a list of potential strengths, weaknesses, opportunities, and threats in Exhibit 5.5. This list is not exhaustive, and these items illustrate only a handful of potential issues that may arise in a SWOT analysis.

Strengths and Weaknesses

Relative to market needs and competitors' characteristics, the marketing manager must begin to think in terms of what the firm can do well and where it may have deficiencies. Strengths and weaknesses exist either because of resources possessed (or not possessed) by the firm or in the nature of the relationships between the firm and its customers, its employees, or outside organizations (for example, supply chain partners, suppliers, lending institutions, and government agencies). Given that SWOT analysis must be customer focused to gain maximum benefit, strengths are meaningful only when they serve to satisfy a customer need. When this is the case, that strength becomes a capability.[6] The marketing manager can then develop marketing strategies that leverage these capabilities in the form of strategic competitive advantages. At the same time, the manager can develop strategies to overcome the firm's weaknesses or find ways to minimize the negative effects of these weaknesses.

A great example of strengths and weaknesses in action occurs in the U.S. airline industry. As a whole, the industry was in trouble even before September 11, 2001. Big carriers—such as American, Delta, Northwest, and US Airways—have strengths in terms of sheer size, passenger volume, and marketing muscle. However, they suffer from a number of weaknesses related to internal efficiency, labor relations, and business models that cannot compensate for changes in customer preferences. These weaknesses are especially dramatic when compared to low-cost airlines such as Southwest, AirTran, and JetBlue. Initially, these carriers offered low-cost service in routes ignored by the big carriers. Their strengths in terms of internal efficiency, flexible operations, and lower-cost equipment gave low-cost carriers a major advantage with respect to cost economies. The differences in operating expenses per available seat mile (an industry benchmark) are eye opening: JetBlue (6.9¢), Southwest (7.7¢), AirTran (9.3¢), and ATA (10.7¢) versus American (12¢), Delta (14¢), US Airways (16.1¢), and Northwest (16.2¢). The ability of low-cost carriers to operate more efficiently and at reduced costs has changed the way customers look at air travel. Today, most customers see air travel as a commodity product, with price being the only real distinguishing feature among competing brands. As a result, many analysts predict that the internal operating weaknesses of the major air carriers will cause one or two carriers to cease operations within five years.[7]

Opportunities and Threats

In leveraging strengths to create capabilities and competitive advantages, the marketing manager must be mindful of trends and situations in the external environment. Stressing internal strengths while ignoring external issues can lead to an organization that, although efficient, cannot adapt when external changes either enhance or impede the firm's ability to serve the needs of its customers. Opportunities and threats exist outside the firm, independently of internal strengths, weaknesses, or marketing options. Opportunities and threats typically occur within the

competitive, customer, economic, political/legal, technological, and/or sociocultural environments. After identifying opportunities and threats, the manager can develop strategies to take advantage of opportunities and minimize or overcome the firm's threats.

Market opportunities can come from many sources. For example, when founder Howard Schultz first envisioned the idea of Starbucks in 1983, he never dreamed that his idea would create an entire industry. Schultz was on a trip to Milan, Italy when he first conceived of a chain of American coffee bars. At that time, there was essentially no competition in coffee because most consumers considered it a commodity. He knew that the demand for coffee was high because it is only second to water in terms of consumption around the world. However, the U.S. coffee market was largely found on grocery store shelves and in restaurants. In fact, only 200 coffeehouses existed in the United States when Starbucks began its expansion. This clear lack of competition gave Schultz the impetus to take Starbucks from its humble Seattle, Washington, beginnings to the rest of the world. Today, there are over 11,000 Starbucks coffeehouses around the world—71 percent of them in the United States. Coffee is now a cultural phenomenon because there are over 14,000 coffeehouses in the United States today, most being mom-and-pop businesses that piggyback on Starbucks' success. Starbucks, customers eagerly spend $3 for a cup of coffee, but they get more than a mere drink. Starbucks is a place to meet friends, talk business, listen to music, or just relax. Starbucks' popularity has spread to grocery store shelves where the brand is now a major threat to traditional in-store competitors. It is clear that Schultz's idea has forever changed the worldwide coffee market.[8]

The SWOT Matrix

As we consider how a firm can use its strengths, weaknesses, opportunities, and threats to drive the development of its marketing plan, remember that SWOT analysis is designed to synthesize a wide array of information and aid the transition to the firm's strategic focus. To address these issues properly, the marketing manager should appraise every strength, weakness, opportunity, and threat to determine their total impact on the firm's marketing efforts. To utilize SWOT analysis successfully, the marketing manager must be cognizant of four issues:[9]

1. The assessment of strengths and weaknesses must look beyond the firm's resources and product offering(s) to examine processes that are key to meeting customers' needs. This often entails offering "solutions" to customers' problems, rather than specific products.

2. The achievement of the firm's goals and objectives depends on its ability to create capabilities by matching its strengths with market opportunities. Capabilities become competitive advantages if they provide better value to customers than competing offerings.

3. Firms can often convert weaknesses into strengths or even capabilities by investing strategically in key areas (for example, customer support, research and development,

EXHIBIT 5.6 **THE SWOT MATRIX**

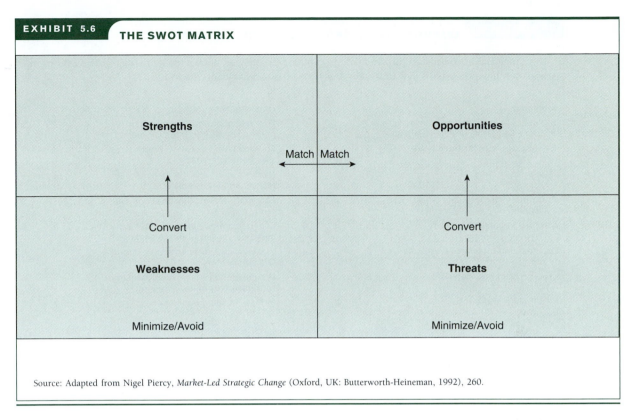

Source: Adapted from Nigel Piercy, *Market-Led Strategic Change* (Oxford, UK: Butterworth-Heineman, 1992), 260.

supply chain efficiency, and employee training). Likewise, threats can often be converted into opportunities if the right resources are available.

4. Weaknesses that cannot be converted into strengths become the firm's limitations. Limitations that are obvious and meaningful to customers or other stakeholders must be minimized through effective strategic choices.

One useful method of conducting this assessment is to visualize the analysis via a SWOT matrix. Exhibit 5.6 provides an example of this four-cell array that can be used to visually evaluate each element of a SWOT analysis. At this point, the manager must evaluate the issues within each cell of the matrix in terms of their magnitude and importance. As we have stated before, this evaluation should ideally be based on customers' perceptions. If customers' perceptions cannot be gathered, managers should base the ratings on the input of employees, business partners, or their own intuition and expertise.

It is not mandatory that the SWOT matrix be assessed quantitatively, but it can be informative to do so. Exhibit 5.7 illustrates how this assessment might be conducted using information from the marketing plan example in Appendix B. The first step is to quantify the magnitude of each element within the matrix. *Magnitude* refers to how strongly each element affects the firm. A simple method is to use a scale of 1 (low magnitude), 2 (medium magnitude), or 3 (high magnitude) for each strength and opportunity and –1 (low magnitude), –2 (medium magnitude), or –3 (high magnitude) for each weakness and threat. The second step is to rate the importance of each element using a scale of 1 (weak importance), 2 (average importance), or 3

EXHIBIT 5.7   **QUANTITATIVE ASSESSMENT OF THE SWOT MATRIX**

This analysis was conducted for the marketing plan example that appears in Appendix B. The ratings in each cell have their basis in a thorough analysis of the company and the industry.

Strengths	M	I	R	Opportunities	M	I	R
BOPREX approved to treat arthritis, migraine headache, and general pain	3	3	9	FDA has approved the transition of prescription NSAIDs into OTC market	3	3	9
Patent exclusivity for three years	3	3	9	Consumers will try new products as they become available	3	3	9
New product entry	3	2	6	NSAIDs can be used as general pain reliever and fever reducer	3	3	9
Prescription-strength pain relief available OTC	3	2	6	Potential market channels not currently exploited	3	3	9
Effective migraine treatment	3	2	6	Competing prescription pain relievers have been pulled from the market	3	2	6
Talented and motivated workforce	2	2	4	Weak product differentiation among OTC competitors	3	2	6
Lower cost of raw materials	3	1	3	U.S. population is increasingly seeking convenience of online shopping	2	3	6
Wide range of products	1	2	2	Increase in aging population	2	2	4

Weaknesses	M	I	R	Threats	M	I	R
Limited marketing budget	−3	3	−9	Competition from both prescription pain relievers and OTC pain relievers	−3	3	−9
Market position (number 6 in market)	−3	3	−9	Extremely crowded OTC market	−3	3	−9
Weak product differentiation	−3	3	−9	Consumer loyalty with existing competitors	−3	2	−6
Current brand name (new to market)	−3	2	−6	Negative publicity regarding NSAIDs	−2	3	−6
Mid-sized company	−2	2	−4	Declining physician recommendation of NSAIDs	−1	3	−3
BOPREX associated with gastrointestinal side effects	−1	3	−3	OTC NSAIDs not indicated for long-term use	−1	2	−2
Variability in offshore suppliers	−1	2	−2	Regulations on drug advertisements could intensify	−1	2	−2

M = magnitude of the element, I = importance of the element, R = total rating of the element.
Magnitude scale ranges from ±1 (low magnitude) to ±3 (high magnitude).
Importance scale ranges from 1 (low importance) to 3 (high importance).

(major importance) for all elements in the matrix. The final step is to multiply the magnitude ratings by the importance ratings to create a total rating for each element. Remember that the magnitude and importance ratings should be heavily influenced by customer perceptions, not just the perceptions of the manager.

Those elements with the highest total ratings (positive or negative) should have the greatest influence in developing the marketing strategy. A sizable strength in an important area must certainly be emphasized in order to convert it into a capability or competitive advantage. On the other hand, a fairly small and insignificant opportunity should not play a central role in the planning process. The magnitude and importance of opportunities and threats will vary depending on the particular product or market. For example, a dramatic increase in new housing starts would be very important for the lumber, mortgage, or real estate industries but inconsequential for industries involving semiconductors or telecommunications. In this example, the magnitude of the opportunity would be the same for all industries; however, the importance ratings would differ across industries.

Developing and Leveraging Competitive Advantages

After the magnitude and importance of each element in the SWOT matrix have been assessed, the manager should focus on identifying competitive advantages by matching strengths to opportunities. The key strengths most likely to be converted into capabilities will be those that have a compatibility with important and sizable opportunities. Remember that capabilities that allow a firm to serve customers' needs better than the competition give it a competitive advantage. As outlined in Exhibit 5.8, competitive advantages can arise from many internal or external sources.

EXHIBIT 5.8 **COMMON SOURCES OF COMPETITIVE ADVANTAGE**

Relational Advantages

- Brand-loyal customers
- High customer-switching costs
- Long-term relationships with supply chain partners
- Strategic alliance agreements
- Comarketing or cobranding agreements
- Tight coordination and integration with supply chain partners
- Strong bargaining power

Legal Advantages

- Patents and trademarks
- Strong and beneficial contracts
- Tax advantages
- Zoning laws
- Global trade restrictions
- Government subsidies

Organizational Advantages

- Abundant financial resources
- Modern plant and equipment
- Effective competitor and customer intelligence systems
- Culture, vision, and shared goals
- Strong organizational goodwill

Human Resource Advantages

- Superior management talent
- Strong organizational culture
- Access to skilled labor
- Committed employees
- World-class employee training

Product Advantages

- Brand equity and brand name
- Exclusive products
- Superior quality or features
- Production expertise
- Guarantees and warranties
- Outstanding customer service
- Research and development
- Superior product image

Pricing Advantages

- Lower production costs
- Economies of scale
- Large-volume buying
- Low-cost distribution
- Bargaining power with vendors

Promotion Advantages

- Company image
- Large promotion budget
- Superior sales force
- Creativity
- Extensive marketing expertise

Distribution Advantages

- Efficient distribution system
- Real-time inventory control
- Extensive supply chain integration
- Superior information systems
- Exclusive distribution outlets
- Convenient locations
- Strong e-commerce capabilities

When we refer to *competitive advantages,* we usually speak in terms of real differences between competing firms. After all, competitive advantages stem from real strengths possessed by the firm or in real weaknesses possessed by rival firms. However, competitive advantages can also be based more on perception than reality. For example, Apple's iPod dominates the market for portable MP3 players despite the fact that it is not technically the best player on the market. In fact, competing products from Toshiba, iRiver, and Creative typically match or beat the iPod in terms of features and expert reviews. Customers who are unaware of better players (or those who simply don't care) buy the iPod because of its slick image, integration with iTunes, and the availability of third-party accessories.[10]

Effectively managing customer's perceptions has been a challenge for marketers for generations. The problem lies in developing and maintaining capabilities and competitive advantages that customers can easily understand and that solve their specific needs. Capabilities or competitive advantages that do not translate into specific benefits for customers are of little use to a firm. In recent years, many successful firms have developed capabilities and competitive advantages based on one of three basic strategies: operational excellence, product leadership, and customer intimacy:

- **Operational Excellence** Firms employing a strategy of operational excellence focus on efficiency of operations and processes. These firms operate at lower costs than their competitors, allowing them to deliver goods and services to their customers at lower prices or a better value. Low-cost airlines, like Southwest Airlines, are a prime example of operational excellence in action. Southwest's no-frills service—no meals or advanced seating—and use of nearly identical Boeing 737 aircraft keep operating costs quite low compared with other air carriers. Other firms that employ operational excellence include Dell and Wal-Mart.[11]

- **Product Leadership** Firms that focus on product leadership excel at technology and product development. As a result, these firms offer customers the most advanced, highest-quality goods and services in the industry. For example, Microsoft, which dominates the market for personal computer operating systems and office productivity suites, continues to upgrade and stretch the technology underlying its software while creating complementary products that solve customers' needs. Pfizer, Intel, and 3M are other examples of companies that pursue a product leadership strategy.

- **Customer Intimacy** Working to know your customers and understand their needs better than the competition is the hallmark of customer intimacy. These firms attempt to develop long-term relationships with customers by seeking their input on how to make the firm's goods and services better or how to solve specific customer problems. Nordstrom, for example, organizes its store layout by fashion and lifestyle rather than by merchandise categories. The company offers high-quality products with impeccable customer service. In fact, Nordstrom is consistently ranked tops in customer service among all retail chains.[12] Other firms that pursue customer intimacy include Amazon, DHL, and Saturn.

EXHIBIT 5.9   **CORE COMPETENCIES NECESSARY FOR COMPETITIVE ADVANTAGE STRATEGIES**

Operational Excellence Strategy

Notable firms using operational excellence: Wal-Mart, Southwest Airlines, and Dell
Core competencies:

- Low-cost operations
- Totally dependable product supply
- Expedient customer service
- Effective demand management

Common attributes:

- Deliver compelling value through the use of low prices, standardized product offerings, and convenient buying processes
- Target a broad, heterogeneous market of price-sensitive buyers
- Invest to achieve scale economies and efficiency-driven systems that translate into lower prices for buyers
- Develop information systems geared toward capturing and distributing information on inventories, shipments, customer transactions, and costs in real time
- Maintain a system to avoid waste and highly reward efficiency improvement

Product Leadership

Notable firms using product leadership: Microsoft, Intel, and 3M
Core competencies:

- Basic research/rapid research interpretation
- Applied research geared toward product development
- Rapid exploitation of market opportunities
- Excellent marketing skills

Common attributes:

- Focus their marketing plans on the rapid introduction of high-quality, technologically sophisticated products in order to create customer loyalty
- Constantly scan the environment in search of new opportunities, often making their own products obsolete through continuous innovation

(continued)

To be successful, firms should be able to execute all three strategies. However, the most successful firms choose one area at which to excel and then actively manage customer perceptions so that customers believe that the firm does indeed excel in that area. To implement any one of these strategies effectively, a firm must possess certain core competencies as outlined in Exhibit . Firms that boast such competencies are more likely to create a competitive advantage than those that do not. However, before a competitive advantage can be translated into specific customer benefits, the firm's target markets must recognize that its competencies give it an advantage over the competition. Exhibit includes a list of attributes that customers might use to describe a company that possesses each particular competitive advantage. The core

- Target narrow, homogeneous market segments
- Maintain organizational cultures characterized by decentralization, adaptability, entrepreneurship, creativity, and the expectation of learning from failure
- Have an attitude of "How can we make this work?" rather than "Why can't we make this work?"

Customer Intimacy

Notable firms using customer intimacy: Nordstrom, Saturn, and Amazon

Core competencies:

- Exceptional skills in discovering customer needs
- Problem-solving proficiency
- Flexible product/solution customization
- A customer-relationship management mind-set
- A wide presence of collaborative (win–win) negotiation skills

Common attributes:

- See customer loyalty as their greatest asset as they focus their efforts on developing and maintaining an intimate knowledge of customer requirements
- Consistently exceed customer expectations by offering high-quality products and solutions without an apology for charging higher prices
- Decentralize most decision-making authority to the customer-contact level
- Regularly form strategic alliances with other companies to address customers' needs in a comprehensive fashion
- Assess all relationships with customers or alliance partners on a long-term, even lifetime, basis

Source: Adapted from Michael Treacy and Fred Wiersema, *The Discipline of Market Leaders* (Reading, MA: Addison-Wesley, 1995).

competencies are internal (strength) issues, and specific attributes refer to activities that customers will notice as they interact with the firm.

Establishing a Strategic Focus

At the conclusion of the SWOT analysis, the marketing manager must turn his or her attention toward establishing the strategic focus of the firm's marketing program. By *strategic focus*, we mean the overall concept or model that guides the firm as it weaves various marketing elements together into a coherent strategy. A firm's strategic focus is typically tied to its competitive advantages. However, depending on the situation, the strategic focus can shift to compensate for the firm's weaknesses or to defend against its vulnerabilities. A firm's strategic focus can change over time to reflect the dynamic nature of the internal and external environments. The direction taken depends on how the firm's strengths and weaknesses match up with its external opportunities and threats. Using the results of the SWOT analysis as a guide, a firm might consider four major directions for its strategic efforts:[13]

- **Aggressive: Many Internal Strengths/Many External Opportunities**   Firms in this enviable position can take an aggressive stance toward their marketing strategies.

Expansion and growth, with new products and new markets, are the keys to an aggressive approach. These firms are often so dominant that they can actually reshape the industry or the competitive landscape to fit their agenda. Good examples of aggressive companies include Google, Apple, Starbucks, Microsoft, and Procter & Gamble.

- **Diversification: Many Internal Strengths/Many External Threats**   Firms in this position have a great deal to offer, but external factors weaken their ability to pursue aggressive strategies. To help offset these threats, firms can use marketing strategy to diversify their portfolio of products, markets, or even business units. A perfect example of this strategy in action is the Altria Group, whose divisions include Philip Morris USA, Philip Morris International, a majority ownership in Kraft Foods, and partial ownership of SABMiller (the world's second largest brewer). Altria's international tobacco and Kraft assets, along with many of the world's most recognizable brands, are its major strengths. Unfortunately, the firm faces innumerable threats from low-cost competitors, taxes, and litigation. Until litigation against the company settles down, Altria plans to remain a diversified concern.[14]

- **Turnaround: Many Internal Weaknesses/Many External Opportunities**   Firms often pursue turnaround strategies because they find themselves in the situation— often temporary—of having too many internal problems to consider strategies that will take advantage of external opportunities. In these cases, firms typically have to put their own house back in order before looking beyond their current products or markets. For example, Vodaphone was once on a quest for global domination in the wireless phone market. The company invested heavily in infrastructure in an effort to offer purely wireless high-speed data and voice services. However, Vodaphone ran into difficulties in integrating its services around the world. And, the market for voice, data, and television began to converge to a point where a wireless-only company like Vodaphone could not compete effectively. To begin its turnaround, Vodaphone began investing in fixed landline infrastructure and created a division to begin offering converged services on both fixed-line and wireless platforms.[15]

- **Defensive: Many Internal Weaknesses/Many External Threats**   Firms take a defensive posture when they become overwhelmed by internal and external problems simultaneously. For example, pharmaceutical giant Merck started reeling in 2004 when it was announced that patients taking the company's pain reliever Vioxx were at an increased risk of heart attacks. Merck withdrew Vioxx from the market, which marked the beginning of a string of potentially damaging litigation against the firm. Further, over the next several years Merck faced the loss of patent protection for many of its most popular drugs including Zocor, Fosamax, and Singulair. These losses are further exacerbated by the fact that Merck's research and development pipeline is very thin. Industry analysts believed that the uncertainty over the Vioxx lawsuits and Merck's weakened product portfolio would hang over the company for 5 to 10 years.[16]

Although these four stances are common, other combinations of strengths, weaknesses, opportunities, and threats are possible. For example, a firm may have few internal strengths but many external opportunities. In this situation, the firm cannot take advantage of opportunities because it does not possess the needed resources to create capabilities or competitive advantages. To resolve this problem, the firm might focus all its efforts toward small-niche markets, or it might consider establishing alliances with firms that possess the necessary resources. It is also possible that a firm will possess many internal strengths but few external opportunities. In this situation, the firm might pursue a strategy of diversification by entering new markets or acquiring other companies. This strategy is dangerous, however, unless these new pursuits are consistent with the mission of the firm. Business history is replete with stories of firms that explored new opportunities that were outside their core mission and values. Sears' expansion into real estate, financial services, and credit cards in the 1980s should remind us all that stepping beyond core strengths is often a bad idea.

Establishing a solid strategic focus is important at this stage of the planning process because it lays the groundwork for the development of marketing goals and objectives that follow. Unfortunately, many firms struggle with finding a focus that translates into a strategy that offers customers a compelling reason for purchasing the firm's products. Firms can use any number of tools and techniques for identifying a compelling strategic focus. We believe that one of the most useful tools is the strategy canvas, which was developed by W. Chan Kim and Renee Mauborgne in their book *Blue Ocean Strategy*.[17]

In essence, a *strategy canvas* is a tool for visualizing a firm's strategy relative to other firms in a given industry. As an example, consider the strategy canvas for Southwest Airlines depicted in Exhibit 5.10.[18] The horizontal axis of a strategy canvas

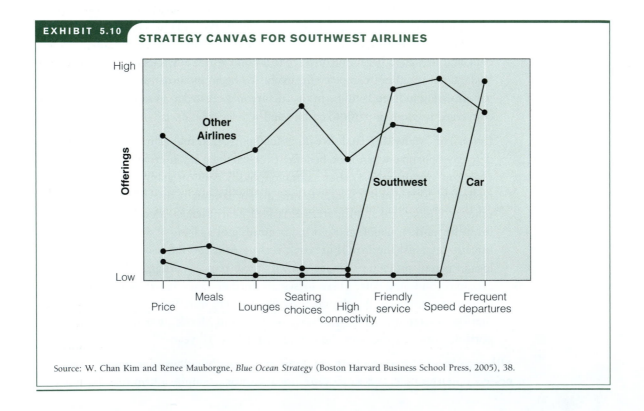

EXHIBIT 5.10   **STRATEGY CANVAS FOR SOUTHWEST AIRLINES**

Source: W. Chan Kim and Renee Mauborgne, *Blue Ocean Strategy* (Boston Harvard Business School Press, 2005), 38.

identifies the key factors that the industry competes on with the products that are offered to customers. In the case of the airline industry, these factors include price, meals, seating choices, and service, among others. The vertical axis indicates the offering level that firms offer to buyers across these factors. The central portion of the strategy canvas is the value curve, or the graphic representation of the firm's relative performance across its industry's factors. The key to using the strategy canvas (and the key to developing a compelling strategic focus) lies in identifying a value curve that stands apart from the competition.

As illustrated in Exhibit 5.10, Southwest's strategic focus is based on downplaying the traditional competitive factors used in the airline industry (price, meals, and so on), stressing other factors (service and speed), and creating a new factor upon which to base its competitive advantage (frequent departures). In doing this, Southwest offers a compelling alternative to customers who dislike making the trade-offs between air travel and car travel. Southwest's strategic focus, then, is offering fast, friendly, and frequent air travel at prices that appeal to customers who would have customarily opted to travel by car. As we have seen earlier in this chapter, Southwest can support this focus through its competitive advantages based on operational excellence. It should be no surprise that Southwest has been successful and profitable for over 30 years.[19]

To use the strategy canvas successfully, the marketing manager must identify a value curve with two major characteristics.[20] First, the value curve should clearly depict the firm's strategic focus. As shown in Exhibit 5.10, Southwest Airlines' focus on service, speed, and frequent departures is clear. All other competitive factors are downplayed in Southwest's strategy. Second, the value curve should be distinctively different from competitors. Again, this is the case for Southwest because its combination of competitive factors clearly separates the firm from the competition. More information on the Blue Ocean approach to developing a strategic focus can be found in Beyond the Pages 5.2.

The combination of the SWOT matrix and the strategy canvas offers a useful and powerful means of visualizing the firm's competitive advantage and strategic focus. Clearly articulating the firm's focus is crucial as the marketing manager moves ahead in developing the marketing plan. In the next phase of the planning process, the manager must identify the firm's marketing goals and objectives in order to connect the strategic focus to the outcomes that are desired and expected. These goals and objectives will also be crucial at the latter stages of planning as the manager identifies standards that will be used to assess the performance of the marketing strategy. In the next section, we look at the development of marketing goals and objectives in more detail.

Developing Marketing Goals and Objectives

After identifying a strategic focus, the marketing manager may have some ideas about potential marketing activities that can be used to leverage the firm's competitive advantages relative to the opportunities available in the market. At this stage, however, there are likely to be many different goals and objectives that coincide with the anticipated strategic direction. Because most firms have limited resources, it is

Beyond the Pages 5.2

A CLOSER LOOK AT BLUE OCEAN STRATEGY[21]

In addition to the strategy canvas discussed in the chapter, Kim and Mauborgne developed a companion tool called the four-actions framework. Whereas the strategy canvas graphically depicts the firm's strategic focus relative to competitors and the factors that define competition within an industry, the four-actions framework is a tool for discovering how to shift the strategy canvas and reorient the firm's strategic focus. As shown in the diagram, the four-actions framework is designed to challenge traditional assumptions about strategy by asking four questions about the firm's way of doing business.

As an example of how the four-actions framework can be used, Kim and Mauborgne drew on the experiences of Casella Wine's successful launch of [yellow tail]. First, Casella *eliminated* traditional competitive factors such as impenetrable wine terminology, aging qualities, and heavy marketing expenditures. Casella reasoned that these factors made wine inaccessible to the mass of buyers who were unfamiliar with wine culture. Second, Casella *reduced* the importance of other factors such as wine complexity, range of wine selections, and prestige. At launch, for example, Casella introduced only two wines: chardonnay and shiraz. They also used a nontraditional label featuring an orange and yellow kangaroo on a black background to reduce the prestige or "snob appeal" common in most wines. Third, Casella *raised* the importance of

competitive factors such as store involvement. Casella involved store employees by giving them Australian clothing to wear at work. This created a laid-back approach to wine that made the employees eager to recommend [yellow tail] to their customers. Finally, Casella *created* easy to drink, easy to buy, and fun as new competitive factors. [yellow tail] has a soft fruity taste that makes it more approachable. Casella also put red and white wines in the same-shaped bottle— an industry first. This simple change greatly reduces manufacturing costs and makes point-of-sale displays simpler and more eye catching.

In addition to Casella, the Blue Ocean approach is used successfully by Southwest Airlines, Cirque du Soleil, and Curves (a chain of women-only fitness centers), among others. Kim and Mauborgne argue that successfully reorienting a firm's strategic focus requires the firm to give up long-held assumptions about how business should be conducted. They caution firms to avoid benchmarking and extensive customer research because these approaches tend to create a typical "more for less" mentality that guides the strategic focus of most firms. Instead, the Blue Ocean approach requires firms to fundamentally alter their strategic logic. Therein lies the challenge of Blue Ocean thinking: It is very, very difficult for most businesses to change. Consequently, true Blue Ocean approaches tend to be a rare occurrence.

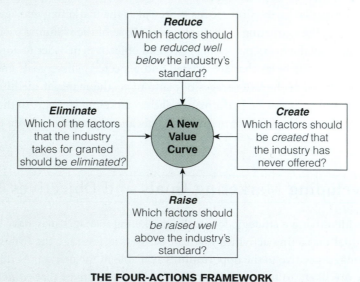

THE FOUR-ACTIONS FRAMEWORK

typically difficult to accomplish everything in a single planning cycle. At this point, the manager must prioritize the firm's strategic intentions and develop specific goals and objectives for the marketing plan.

We reiterate that marketing goals and objectives must be consistent with the overall mission and vision of the firm. Once the firm has a mission statement that clearly delineates what it is, what it stands for, and what it does for others, the marketing manager can then begin to express what he or she hopes to achieve in the firm's marketing program. These statements of desired accomplishments are goals and objectives. Some use the terms *goals* and *objectives* interchangeably. However, failure to understand the key differences between them can severely limit the effectiveness of the marketing plan. *Goals* are general desired accomplishments, whereas *objectives* provide specific, quantitative benchmarks that can be used to gauge progress toward the achievement of the marketing goals.

Developing Marketing Goals

As statements of broad, desired accomplishments, goals are expressed in general terms and do not contain specific information about where the organization presently stands or where it hopes to be in the future. Electronics retailer Circuit City, for example, has a goal of having lower prices than the competition. This goal is not specific, however, because it does not specify a benchmark that defines what a lower price is. To achieve this goal, Circuit City offers a price guarantee that matches then beats competitors' prices by 10 percent.[22] Goals like these are important because they indicate the direction in which the firm attempts to move, as well as the set of priorities it will use in evaluating alternatives and making decisions.

It is also important that all functional areas of the organization be considered in the goal-setting process. In developing goals for the marketing plan, it is important to keep in mind that marketing goals should be attainable, consistent, comprehensive, and involve some degree of intangibility. Failure to consider these issues will result in goals that are less effective and perhaps even dysfunctional. Let's look more closely at these characteristics.

Attainability   Setting realistic goals is important because the key parties involved in reaching them must see each goal as reasonable. Determining whether a goal is realistic requires an assessment of both the internal and external environments. For example, it would not be unrealistic for a firm in second place in market share, trailing the leading brand by just two percent, to set a goal of becoming the industry leader. Other things being equal, such a goal could help motivate employees toward becoming "number one." In contrast, a firm in sixth place, trailing the fifth place firm by five percent and the leader by 30 percent, could set the same goal—but it

would not be realistic. Unrealistic goals can be demotivational because they show employees that management is out of touch. Because one of the primary benefits of having goals is to motivate employees toward better performance, setting unrealistic goals can cause major problems.

Consistency   In addition to being realistic, management must work to set goals that are consistent with one another. Enhancing market share and working to have the highest profit margins in the industry are both reasonable goals by themselves, but together they are inconsistent. Goals to increase both sales and market share would be consistent, as would goals to enhance customer service and customer satisfaction. However, setting goals to reduce inventory levels and increase customer service are usually incompatible. Goals across and within functional areas should also mesh together. This is a major concern in large organizations, and it highlights the need for a great deal of information sharing during the goal-formulation process.

Comprehensiveness   The goal-setting process should also be comprehensive. This means that each functional area should be able to develop its own goals that relate to the organization's goals. For example, if goals are set only in terms of advancing the technology associated with a firm's products, members of the marketing department may wonder what role they will play in this accomplishment. The goal should be stated so that both marketing and research and development can work together to help advance the organizational goal of offering the most technologically advanced products. Marketing will need to work on the demand side of this effort (measuring customer needs and staying attuned to trends in the external environment), while research and development will focus on the supply side (conducting basic and applied research, as well as staying abreast of all major technological innovations). Goals should help clarify the roles of all parties in the organization. Functional areas that do not match any of the organization's goals should question their need for future resources and their ability to acquire them.

Intangibility   Finally, goals should involve some degree of intangibility. Some planners have been known to confuse strategies, and even tactics, with goals. A goal is not some action that the firm can take; rather, it is an outcome that the organization hopes to accomplish. Actions such as hiring 100 new salespeople or doubling the advertising budget are not goals because any firm with adequate resources can accomplish both tasks. However, having "the best-trained sales force in the industry" or "the most creative and effective advertising campaign in the industry" are suitable goals. Note the intangibility associated with the use of terms such as *best-trained, most creative,* and *most effective.* These terms are motivational because they promote comparisons with rival firms. They also continually push for excellence because their open-ended nature always leaves room for improvement.

Developing Marketing Objectives

Objectives provide specific and quantitative benchmarks that can be used to gauge progress toward the achievement of the marketing goals. In some cases, a particular goal may require several objectives for its progress to be adequately monitored, usually across multiple business functions. For example, a goal of "creating a high-quality image for the firm" cannot be accomplished by better inventory control if accounts receivable makes mistakes and customer complaints about the firm's salespeople are on the rise. Similarly, the marketing department alone could not have accomplished The Home Depot's phenomenal growth in stores—up 20 percent in the past two years.[23] Such an endeavor requires a carefully coordinated effort across many departments.

Goals without objectives are essentially meaningless because progress is impossible to measure. A typical marketing objective might be that "the sales division will decrease unfilled customer orders from three percent to two percent between January and June of this fiscal year." Note that this objective contains a high degree of specificity. It is this specificity that sets goals and objectives apart. Objectives involve measurable, quantitative outcomes, with specifically assigned responsibility for their accomplishment and a definite time period for their attainment. Let's look at the specific characteristics of marketing objectives.

Attainability   As with goals, marketing objectives should be realistic given the internal and external environments identified during the situation and SWOT analyses. A good objective is one that is attainable with a reasonable amount of effort. Easily attainable objectives will not motivate employees to achieve higher levels of performance. Likewise, good objectives do not come from false assumptions that everything will go as planned or that every employee will give 110 percent effort. In some cases, competitors will establish objectives that include taking customers and sales away from the firm. Setting objectives that assume inanimate or inept competitors, when history has proven otherwise, creates objectives that quickly lose their value as employees recognize them as being unreasonable.

Continuity   The need for realism brings up a second consideration, that of continuity. Marketing objectives can be either continuous or discontinuous. A firm uses continuous objectives when its current objectives are similar to objectives set in the previous planning period. For example, an objective "to increase market share from 20 to 22 percent in the next fiscal year" could be carried forward in a similar fashion to the next period: "to increase market share from 22 to 24 percent in the next fiscal year." This would be a continuous objective because the factor in question and the magnitude of change are similar, or even identical, from period to period.

An important caveat about continuous objectives: Objectives that are identical or only slightly modified from period to period often do not need new strategies, increased effort, or better implementation to be achieved. Marketing objectives should lead employees to perform at higher levels than would otherwise have been the case. Employees naturally tend to be objective oriented. Once they meet the objective, the level of creativity and effort tends to fall off. There are certainly circumstances where continuous objectives are appropriate, but they should not be set simply as a matter of habit.

Discontinuous objectives significantly elevate the level of performance on a given outcome factor or bring new factors into the set of objectives. If sales growth has been averaging 10 percent and the SWOT analysis suggests that this is an easily obtainable level, an example of a discontinuous objective might be "to increase sales 18 percent during the next fiscal year." This would require new strategies to sell additional products to existing customers, to expand the customer base, or at the very least to develop new tactics and/or enhance the implementation of existing strategies. Discontinuous objectives require more analysis and linkage to strategic planning than continuous objectives.

Developing discontinuous objectives is one of the major benefits a company can gain from applying for the Malcolm Baldrige National Quality Award. Exhibit 5.11 identifies the performance criteria for the Baldrige Award. To demonstrate proficiency in these areas, a firm must first establish benchmarks, which typically are the quantitative

---

EXHIBIT 5.11   2006 BALDRIGE AWARD CRITERIA FOR PERFORMANCE EXCELLENCE

Categories and Items		Point Values
1	**Leadership**	120
	1.1 Senior Leadership	70
	1.2 Governance and Social Responsibilities	50
2	**Strategic Planning**	85
	2.1 Strategy Development	40
	2.2 Strategy Deployment	45
3	**Customer and Market Focus**	85
	3.1 Customer and Market Knowledge	40
	3.2 Customer Relationships and Satisfaction	45
4	**Measurement, Analysis, and Knowledge Management**	90
	4.1 Measurement, Analysis, and Review of Organizational Performance	45
	4.2 Information and Knowledge Management	45
5	**Human Resource Focus**	85
	5.1 Work Systems	35
	5.2 Employee Learning and Motivation	25
	5.3 Employee Well-Being and Satisfaction	25
6	**Process Management**	85
	6.1 Value Creation Processes	45
	6.2 Support Processes and Operational Planning	40
7	**Results**	450
	7.1 Product and Service Outcomes	100
	7.2 Customer-Focused Outcomes	70
	7.3 Financial and Market Outcomes	70
	7.4 Human Resource Outcomes	70
	7.5 Organizational Effectiveness Outcomes	70
	7.6 Leadership and Social Responsibility Outcomes	70
	Total Points	1,000

Source: "2006 Criteria for Performance Excellence," *Malcolm Baldrige National Quality Award Program* (Gaithersburg, MD: National Institute of Standards and Technology, Technology Administration, U.S. Department of Commerce, 2006), 14.

performance levels of the leaders in an industry. The firm then develops objectives that center on improving performance in each area. Many companies feel that simply applying for the Baldrige Award has positive effects on performance, if for no other reason than the process forces the company to set challenging discontinuous objectives. This is also true for organizations that use the Baldrige guidelines as a planning aid.

Time Frame   Another key consideration in setting objectives is the time frame for their achievement. Although companies often establish marketing plans on an annual basis, marketing objectives may differ from this period in their time frame. Sales volume, market share, customer service, and gross margin objectives may be set for terms less than, equal to, or greater than one year. The time frame should be appropriate and allow for accomplishment with reasonable levels of effort. To set a target of doubling sales for a well-established company within six months would likely be unreasonable. On the other hand, objectives having an excessively long time frame may be attained without any increased effort or creativity. The combination of managerial expertise and experience, along with the information acquired during the situation and SWOT analyses, should lead to the establishment of an appropriate time frame.

For objectives with longer time frames, it is important to remind employees of the objective on a regular basis and to provide feedback on progress toward its achievement. For example, employees at Federal Express' (FedEx) terminal in Memphis, Tennessee, can see a real-time accuracy gauge that displays the company's current performance in terms of getting packages to their rightful destinations. FedEx also uses a nightly countdown clock to remind employees of the speed needed to turnaround packages and load them on outbound cargo planes. Whether a weekly announcement, a monthly newsletter, or a real-time gauge on the wall that charts progress toward the objective, feedback is a critical part of the objective-setting process, particularly for longer-term objectives.

Assignment of Responsibility   One final aspect of objectives that sets them apart from goals is that the marketing manager must identify the person, team, or unit responsible for achieving each objective. By explicitly assigning responsibility, the firm can limit the problems of stealing credit and avoiding responsibility. A bank might give the marketing department the responsibility of achieving an objective of "having 40 percent of its customers list the bank as their primary financial institution within one year." If by the end of the year, 42 percent of all customers list the bank as their primary financial institution, the marketing department gets credit for this outcome. If the figure is only 38 percent, the marketing department must provide an explanation.

Moving Beyond Goals and Objectives

Marketing goals and objectives identify the desired ends, both general and specific, that the organization hopes to achieve during the planning period. However, companies do not fulfill properly set goals and objectives automatically or through wishing and hoping. They set into motion a chain of decisions and serve as a catalyst for the subsequent stages in the planning process. Organizational goals and objectives must lead to the establishment of consistent goals and objectives for each functional area of the firm. Having recognized the desired ends, each area, including marketing, must next determine the means that will lead to these targeted results.

As we move forward, we focus our attention on the means issue as we address marketing strategy development. Although a firm might consider the steps of the market planning process sequentially, in reality the firm must move back and forth between steps. If marketing strategies that have the potential to achieve the marketing goals and objectives cannot be developed, the goals and objectives may not be reasonable and need to be reevaluated before the development of the marketing strategy. Given that the marketing plan must be a working document, the cycling among planning steps never truly ends.

Lessons from Chapter 5

SWOT analysis

- is considered to be one of the most useful tools in analyzing marketing data and information.

- links a company's ongoing situation analysis to the development of the marketing plan.

- structures the information from the situation analysis into four categories: strengths, weaknesses, opportunities, and threats.

- uses the structured information to uncover competitive advantages and guide the selection of the strategic focus for the firm's marketing strategy.

To make SWOT analysis as productive as possible, the marketing manager should

- stay focused by using a series of SWOT analyses, each focusing on a specific product–market combination.

- search extensively for competitors, whether they are present competitors or ones in the future.

- collaborate with other functional areas by sharing information and perspectives.

- examine issues from the customers' perspective by asking such questions as "What do customers (and noncustomers) believe about us as a company?" and "Which of our weaknesses translate into a decreased ability to serve customers (and a decreased ability to convert noncustomers)?" This includes examining the issues from the perspective of the firm's internal customers, its employees.

- look for causes, not characteristics, by considering the firm's resources that are the true causes for the firm's strengths, weaknesses, opportunities, and threats.

- separate internal issues from external issues using this key test to differentiate: "Would this issue exist if the firm did not exist?" If the answer is yes, the issue should be classified as external.

Strengths and weaknesses

- exist because of resources possessed (or not possessed) by the firm, or they exist due to the nature of key relationships between the firm and its customers, its employees, or outside organizations.

- must be leveraged into capabilities (in the case of strengths) or overcome (in the case of weaknesses).

- are meaningful only when they assist or hinder the firm in satisfying customer needs.

Opportunities and threats

- are not potential marketing actions. Rather, they involve issues or situations that occur in the firm's external environments.

- should not be ignored as the firm gets caught up in developing strengths and capabilities for fear of creating an efficient but ineffective organization.

- may stem from changes in the competitive, customer, economic, political/legal, technological, and/or sociocultural environments.

The SWOT matrix

- allows the marketing manager to visualize the analysis.

- should serve as a catalyst to facilitate and guide the creation of marketing strategies that will produce desired results.

- allows the manager to see how strengths and opportunities might be connected to create capabilities that are key to meeting customer needs.

- involves assessing the magnitude and importance of each strength, weakness, opportunity, and threat.

Competitive advantage

- stems from the firm's capabilities in relation to those held by the competition.

- can be based on both internal and external factors.

- is based on both reality and customer perceptions.

- is often based on the basic strategies of operational excellence, product leadership, and/or customer intimacy.

Establishing a strategic focus

- is based on developing an overall concept or model that guides the firm as it weaves various marketing elements together into a coherent strategy.

- is typically tied to the firm's competitive advantages.

- involves using the results of the SWOT analysis as the firm considers four major directions for its strategic efforts: aggressiveness, diversification, turnaround, or defensiveness.

- can help ensure that the firm does not step beyond its core strengths to consider opportunities that are outside its capabilities.

- can be visualized through the use of a strategy canvas where the goal is to develop a value curve that is distinct from the competition.

- is often done by downplaying traditional industry competitive factors in favor of new approaches.

- is an important stage of the planning process because it lays the groundwork for the development of marketing goals and objectives and connects the outcomes of the SWOT analysis to the remainder of the marketing plan.

Marketing goals

- are broad, desired accomplishments that are stated in general terms.

- indicate the direction the firm attempts to move in, as well as the set of priorities it will use in evaluating alternatives and making decisions.

- should be attainable, realistic, internally consistent, and comprehensive and help clarify the roles of all parties in the organization.

- should involve some degree of intangibility.

Marketing objectives

- provide specific and quantitative benchmarks that can be used to gauge progress toward the achievement of the marketing goals.

- should be attainable with a reasonable degree of effort.

- may be either continuous or discontinuous, depending on the degree to which they depart from present objectives.

- should specify the time frame for their completion.

- should be assigned to specific areas, departments, or individuals who have the responsibility to accomplish them.

Questions for Discussion

1. Strengths, weaknesses, opportunities, and threats: Which is the most important? Why? How might your response change if you were the CEO of a corporation? What if you were a customer of the firm? An employee? A supplier?

2. Support or contradict this statement: "Given the realities of today's economy and the rapid changes occurring in business technology, all competitive advantages are short lived. There is no such thing as a *sustainable* competitive advantage that lasts over the long term." Defend your position.

3. Is it possible for an organization to be successful despite having a value curve that is not distinct from the competition? In other words, can an organization be successful by selling a me-too product (a product that offers no compelling differences when compared to the competition)? Explain.

Exercises

1. Perform a SWOT analysis using yourself as the product. Be candid about your resources and the strengths and weaknesses you possess. Based on the opportunities and threats you see in the environment, where do you stand in terms of your ability to attend graduate school, get a job, begin a career, or change careers?

2. Choose two companies from the same industry: one that is successful and one that is struggling. For each company, list every strength and weakness that you believe it possesses (both the company and its products). Compare your answers with those of your colleagues. What could these companies learn from your analysis?

3. Using the same companies from Exercise 2, draw a strategy canvas that depicts the value curve of both firms, as well as the "average" firm in the industry (that is, draw three value curves). What does the successful firm offer that the struggling firm does not offer? What might a firm do to break away from the industry's traditional competitive factors?

Customers, Segmentation, and Target Marketing

Introduction

In this chapter, we begin our discussion of marketing strategy by examining customers, segments, and target markets. In Chapter 1, we referred to a market as a collection of buyers and sellers. Now, we focus our attention on the buyers who collectively make up the major portion of most markets. From this perspective, we concern ourselves with markets as individuals, institutions, or groups of individuals or institutions that have similar needs that can be met by a particular product offering. As we will see, firms can attempt to reach all buyers in a market, smaller groups or segments of the market, or even specific buyers on an individual level. Whether the firm aims for the entire market or smaller market segments, the goal of marketing strategy is to identify specific customer needs and then design a marketing program that can satisfy those needs. To do this effectively, the firm must have a comprehensive understanding of its current and potential customers, including their motivations, behaviors, needs, and wants.

The ability to determine in-depth information about customers is a fairly recent phenomenon in marketing. Fifty years ago, for example, technology and marketing know-how were less sophisticated. Marketers of the day couldn't fully understand customers' needs and wants, much less make fine distinctions among smaller segments of the total market. Marketers tended to offer products that came in only one variety, flavor, or style. Today, market segmentation is critical to the success of most firms. Segmentation allows marketers to more precisely define and understand customer needs and gives them the ability to tailor products to better suit those needs. As discussed in Beyond the Pages 6.1, the level of detailed information available about customers today is rapidly changing the way that firms do business. However, the use of such information raises concerns about consumer privacy. Still, without segmentation we would not enjoy the incredible variety of products available today. Consider the number of choices we have in categories such as soft drinks, cereals, packaged goods, automobiles, and clothing. In many respects, segmentation has improved our standard of living. Customers now expect firms to delve into their needs and wants

Beyond the Pages 6.1

DATA, DATA EVERYWHERE[1]

Consider a world where what you eat, read, wear, listen to, watch, buy, and do can be reduced to a mathematical formula. Every move you make is tracked with such a level of specificity that your entire life can be captured in a computer model. Sound far-fetched? It's not. Today, the combination of computer science, mathematics, and business is changing our view of consumers and their behavior. The ability to track consumer behavior has never been more advanced than it is today. The new insights gained from the mathematical modeling of consumer behavior is creating new avenues for business, allowing marketers to develop one-to-one relationships with consumers, and causing a fair amount of anxiety. It is also causing a sharp increase in the hiring of math graduates from our nation's universities.

None of this is really new. Through advanced math, computer modeling, and data mining, businesses have been able to track consumer attitudes and behaviors for some time. The difference today is the unprecedented access to data made available via the Internet and other technologies. Today, a sizable portion of the consuming public has moved its work, play, conversation, and shopping online. These integrated networks collect vast amounts of data and store our lives in databases that can be connected in ways that allow us to capture a more complete picture of consumer behavior. For example, researchers at companies like Yahoo!, Google, and Amazon are developing mathematical models of customers. These firms are also working with other companies and government agencies to develop models that can predict voting behavior, how patients respond to disease intervention, or which employee is best suited for a job assignment.

The advertising and media industries are perhaps the most affected by this shift. As mass-audience advertising has declined, marketers have been looking for ways to target customers more directly. Google is a pioneer in this effort because the company has amassed an unfathomable amount of data on what customers do online. In research conducted with the Interactive Advertising Bureau, for example, Ford learned that it could maximize truck sales by increasing its online ad spending from 2.5 percent to six percent of its total media budget. Ford responded by moving 30 percent of its ad budget into targeted media including online advertising. Harrah's Entertainment (a major player in the casino industry) has used computer models to predict which customers will respond to the company's targeted advertising and promotional offers. From 2001 to 2006, Harrah's has averaged 22 percent annual growth by targeting its customers more precisely.

Of course, all this sophistication comes at a price. The ability of companies to track customers and model their behavior raises a number of privacy concerns. Most companies take great pains to protect individual consumer identities and their private information. However, the continuing erosion of consumer privacy is likely to continue. A key question for marketers is at what point will consumers say enough is enough? How far can firms push the boundaries of data collection and analysis before consumers mount a backlash? These issues will only become more prominent in the years ahead.

and to tailor products accordingly. This fact makes market segmentation a vital part of marketing strategy. Until a firm has chosen and analyzed a target market, it cannot make effective decisions regarding other elements of the marketing strategy.

In this chapter, we examine issues associated with buyer behavior in both consumer and business markets. We also discuss traditional and individualized approaches to market segmentation, the criteria for successful market segmentation, and specific target-marketing strategies. The potential combinations of target markets and marketing programs are essentially limitless. Choosing the right target market from among many possible alternatives is one of the key tests in developing a good marketing strategy.

Buyer Behavior in Consumer Markets

Trying to understand the buyer behavior of consumers is a very trying and challenging task. The behavior of consumers is often irrational and unpredictable. Consumers often say one thing but do another. Still, the effort spent trying to understand consumers is valuable because it can provide needed insight on how to design products and marketing programs that better meet consumer needs and wants. One of the most recent trends in learning about customers is the rising use of ethnography. Computer maker Lenovo, for example, has been using ethnographic research to learn more about how families in India use consumer electronics. One interesting finding is that the family social center in Indian homes is the parents' bedroom. The kitchen serves the same social function in American homes. Lenovo plans to use this type of information to develop consumer electronics that better fit differing family lifestyles in India and the United States.[2]

In this section, we look at key issues with respect to buyer behavior in consumer markets. Here, we examine the consumer buying process and the factors that alter the ways that consumers buy goods and services. As we will see, successful marketing strategy depends on a clear understanding of customers with respect to who they are, what they need, what they prefer, and why they buy. Although this understanding clearly has relevance for designing the product offering, it also impacts the pricing, distribution, and promotion decisions in the marketing program.

The Consumer Buying Process

The consumer buying process shown in Exhibit 6.1 depicts five stages of activities that consumers may go through in buying goods and services. The process begins with the recognition of a need and then passes through the stages of information search,

evaluation of alternatives, purchase decision, and postpurchase evaluation. A marketer's interest in the buying process can go well beyond these stages to include actual consumption behaviors, product uses, and product disposal after consumption. As we consider each stage of the buying process, it is important to keep a few key issues in mind.

First, the buying process depicts the possible range of activities that may occur in making purchase decisions. Consumers, however, do not always follow these stages in sequence and may even skip stages en route to making a purchase. For example, impulse purchases, such as buying a pack of chewing gum or a newspaper, do not involve lengthy

EXHIBIT 6.1 | **THE CONSUMER BUYING PROCESS**

Stages	Key Issues
Need recognition	• Consumer needs and wants are not the same. • An understanding of consumer needs is essential for market segmentation and the development of the marketing program. • Marketers must create the appropriate stimuli to foster need recognition.
Information search	• Consumers trust internal and personal sources of information more than external sources. • The amount of time, effort, and expense dedicated to the search for information depends on: (1) the degree of risk involved in the purchase, (2) the amount of experience that the consumer has with the product category, and (3) the actual cost of the search in terms of time and money. • Consumers narrow their potential choices to an evoked set of suitable alternatives that may meet their needs.
Evaluation of alternatives	• Consumers translate their needs into wants for specific products or brands. • Consumers evaluate products as bundles of attributes that have varying abilities to satisfy their needs. • Marketers must ensure that their product is in the evoked set of potential alternatives. • Marketers must take steps to understand consumers' choice criteria and the importance they place on specific product attributes.
Purchase decision	• A consumer's purchase intention and the actual act of buying are distinct concepts. • Several factors may prevent the actual purchase from taking place. • Marketers must ensure that their product is available and offer solutions that increase possession utility.
Postpurchase evaluation	• Postpurchase evaluation is the connection between the buying process and the development of long-term customer relationships. • Marketers must closely follow consumers' responses (delight, satisfaction, dissatisfaction, or cognitive dissonance) to monitor the product's performance and its ability to meet customers' expectations.

search or evaluation activities. On the other hand, complex purchases like buying a home are often lengthy because they incorporate every stage of the buying process. Likewise, consumers who are loyal to a product or brand will skip some stages and are most likely to simply purchase the same product they bought last time. Consequently, marketers have a difficult time promoting brand switching because they must convince these customers to break tradition and take a look at what their products have to offer.

Second, the buying process often involves a parallel sequence of activities associated with finding the most suitable merchant of the product in question. That is, while consumers consider which product to buy, they also consider where they might buy it. In the case of brand-name products, this selection process may focus on the product's price and availability at different stores or online merchants. A specific model of Sony television, for example, is often available from many different retailers and may even be available at Sony's website (www.sonystyle.com). Conversely, in the case of private-label merchandise, the choice of product and merchant are made simultaneously. If a customer is interested only in Gap-brand clothing, then that customer must purchase the clothing from a Gap store or the Gap website.

Third, the choice of a suitable merchant may actually take precedence over the choice of a specific product. In some cases, customers are so loyal to a particular merchant that they will not consider looking elsewhere. For example, many older consumers are fiercely loyal to American car manufacturers. These customers will limit their product selection to a single brand or dealership, greatly limiting their range of potential product choices. In other cases, customers might be loyal to a particular merchant because they hold that merchant's credit card or are a member of its frequent customer program. Finally, some merchants become so well known for certain products that customers just naturally execute their buying process with that merchant. Sears, for example, is well known for its selection of brand-name appliances. For many customers, Sears is the natural place to go when they are in the market for a new refrigerator, washer, or dryer.

Need Recognition   The buying process begins when consumers recognize that they have an unmet need. This occurs when consumers realize that there is a discrepancy between their existing situation and their desired situation. Consumers can recognize needs in a variety of settings and situations. Some needs have their basis in internal stimuli such as hunger, thirst, and fatigue. Other needs have their basis in external stimuli such as advertising, window shopping, interacting with salespeople, or talking with friends and family. External stimuli can also arouse internal responses such as the hunger you might feel when watching an advertisement for Pizza Hut.

Typically, we think of needs as necessities, particularly with respect to the necessities of life (food, water, clothing, safety, shelter, health, or love). However, this definition is limited because everyone has a different perspective on what constitutes a need. For example, many people would argue that they need a car when their real need is for transportation. Their need for a car is really a "want" for a car. This is where we draw the distinction between needs and wants. A *need* occurs when an individual's current level of satisfaction does not equal his or her desired level of satisfaction. A *want* is a consumer's desire for a specific product that will satisfy the need. Hence, people need transportation, but they choose to fulfill that need with a car rather than with alternative products like motorcycles, bicycles, pubic transportation, a taxi, or a horse.

The distinction between needs and wants is not simply academic. In any marketing effort, the firm must always understand the basic needs fulfilled by its products. For example, people do not need drills; they need to make holes or drive screws. Similarly, they do not need lawnmowers; they need shorter, well-manicured grass. Understanding these basic needs allows the firm to segment markets and create marketing programs that can translate consumer needs into wants for their specific products. An important part of this effort involves creating the appropriate stimuli that will foster need recognition among consumers. The idea is to build on the basic need and convince potential consumers to want your product because it will fulfill their needs better than any competing product.

It is also important to understand that wants are not the same thing as demand. Demand occurs only when the consumer's ability and willingness to pay for specific products backs up the wants for those products.[3] Many customers want a luxury yacht, for example, but only a few are able and willing to buy one. In some cases, consumers may actually need a product but not want it. So-called "unsought products" like life insurance, cemetery plots, long-term health insurance, and continuing education are good examples. In these cases, the marketer must first educate consumers on the need for the product, and then convince consumers to want its products over competing products.

Understanding consumers' needs and wants is an important consideration in market segmentation. Some markets can be segmented on the basis of needs alone. College students, for example, have needs that are very different from senior citizens; and single consumers have very different needs than families with small children. However, most marketing of products does not occur on the basis of need-fulfillment alone. In the automobile market, for example, essentially no manufacturers promote their products as being the best to get you from Point A to Point B (the basic need of transportation). Rather, they market their products on the basis of consumer wants such as luxury (Lexus), image (Mercedes), sportiness (Pontiac), durability (Ford trucks), fuel economy (Honda Civic), and value (Kia). These wants are the hot buttons for consumers and the keys to promoting further activity in the buying process.

Information Search   When done correctly, marketing stimuli can prompt consumers to become interested in a product, leading to a desire to seek out additional information. This desire can be passive or active. In a passive information search, the consumer becomes more attentive and receptive to information such as noticing and paying attention to automobile advertisements if the customer has a want for a car. A consumer engages in active information search when he or she purposely seeks additional information such as surfing the Internet, asking friends, or visiting dealer showrooms. Information can come from a variety of sources. Internal sources, including personal experiences and memories, are typically the first type of information that consumers search. Information can also come from personal sources including advice from friends, family, or coworkers. External sources of information include advertising, magazines, websites, packaging, displays, and salespeople. Although external sources are the most numerous, consumers typically trust these sources less than internal and personal sources of information.

The amount of time, effort, and expense dedicated to the search for information depends on a number of issues. First, and perhaps most important, is the degree of risk involved in the purchase. Consumers by nature are naturally risk-adverse; they use their search for information to reduce risk and increase the odds of making the right choice. Buying risk comes in many forms, including financial risk (buying a home), social risk (buying the right clothing), emotional risk (selecting a wedding photographer), and personal risk (choosing the right surgeon). In buying a car, for example, consumers regularly turn to *Consumer Reports* magazine, friends, and government safety ratings to help reduce these types of risk. A second issue is the degree of expertise or experience that the consumer has with the product category. If a first-time buyer is in the market for a notebook computer, they face a bewildering array of choices and brands. This buyer is likely to engage in extensive information search to reduce risk and narrow the potential set of product choices. The same buyer, several purchases later, will not go through the same process. Finally, the actual cost of the search in terms of time and money will limit the extent to which consumers search for information. In some situations, such as time deadlines or emergencies, consumers have little time to consult all sources of information at their disposal.

Throughout the information search, consumers learn about different products or brands and begin to remove some from further consideration. They evaluate and reevaluate their initial set of products or brands until their list of potential product choices has been narrowed to only a few products or brands that can meet their needs. This evoked set of suitable alternatives represents the outcome of the information search and the beginning of the next stage of the buying process.

Evaluation of Alternatives   In evaluating the alternative product or brand choices among the members of the evoked set, the consumer essentially translates his or her need into a want for a specific product or brand. The evaluation of alternatives is the "black box" of consumer behavior because it is typically the hardest for marketers to understand, measure, or influence. What we do know about this stage of the buying process is that consumers base their evaluation on a number of different criteria, which usually equate with a number of product attributes.

Consumers evaluate products as bundles of attributes that have varying abilities to satisfy their needs. In buying a car, for example, each potential choice represents a bundle of attributes including brand attributes (for example, image, reputation, reliability, and safety), product features (for example, power windows, automatic transmission, and fuel economy), aesthetic attributes (for example, styling, sportiness, roominess, and color), and price. Each consumer has a different opinion about the relative importance of these attributes—some put safety first, while others consider price the dominant factor. Another interesting feature of the evaluation stage is that the priority of each consumer's choice criteria can change during the process. Consumers may visit a dealership with price as their dominant criterion, only to leave the dealership with price dropping to third on their list of important attributes.

There are several important considerations for marketers during the evaluation stage. First and foremost, the marketer's products must be in the evoked set of potential alternatives. For this reason, marketers must constantly remind consumers of his or her company and its product offerings. Second, it is vital that marketers take steps to understand consumers' choice criteria and the importance that they place on specific product attributes. As we will see later in this chapter, understanding the connection between customers' needs and product attributes is an important consideration in market segmentation and target-marketing decisions. Finally, marketers must often design marketing programs that change the priority of choice criteria or change consumers' opinions about a product's image. Cadillac, for example, has moved aggressively to combat the erosion of its once-dominant share of the luxury car market. Since 1980, Cadillac sales have dropped roughly 50 percent as affluent car buyers have migrated toward BMW, Mercedes, Lexus, and Infiniti. Cadillac has countered by targeting younger consumers and greatly enhancing the technological sophistication of its products. The company has also rolled out several new vehicles in recent years, including the Escalade, CLS, XTS, SRX, and the XLR roadster.[4]

Purchase Decision   After the consumer has evaluated each alternative in the evoked set, he or she forms an intention to purchase a particular product or brand. However, a purchase intention and the actual act of buying are distinct concepts. A consumer may have every intention of purchasing a new car, for example, but several factors may prevent the actual purchase from taking place. The customer may postpone the purchase due to unforeseen circumstances such as an illness or job loss. The salesperson or the sales manager may anger the consumer, leading him or her to walk away from the deal. The buyer may not be able to obtain financing for his or her purchase due to a mistake in his or her credit file. Or the buyer may simply change his or her mind. Marketers can often reduce or eliminate these problems by reducing the risk of purchase through warranties or guarantees, making the purchase stage as easy as possible, or finding creative solutions to unexpected problems.

Assuming these potential intervening factors are not a concern, the key issues for marketers during the purchase stage are product availability and possession utility. Product availability is critical. Without it, buyers will not purchase from you but from someone else who can deliver the product. The key to availability—which is closely related to the distribution component of the marketing program—is convenience. The goal is to put the product within the consumer's reach wherever that consumer happens to be. This task is closely related to possession utility (that is, ease of taking possession). To increase possession utility, the marketer may have to offer financing or layaway for large dollar purchases, delivery and installation of products like appliances or furniture, home delivery of convenience items like pizza or newspapers, or the proper packaging and prompt shipment of items through the mail.

Postpurchase Evaluation   In the context of attracting and retaining buyers, postpurchase evaluation is the connection between the buying process and the development of long-term customer relationships. Marketers must closely follow consumers' responses during this stage to monitor the product's performance and its ability to meet consumers' expectations. In the postpurchase stage, buyers will experience one of these four outcomes:

- **Delight**   The product's performance greatly exceeds the buyer's expectations.
- **Satisfaction**   The product's performance matches the buyer's expectations.
- **Dissatisfaction**   The product's performance falls short of the buyer's expectations.
- **Cognitive Dissonance (Postpurchase Doubt)**   The buyer is unsure of the product's performance relative to his or her expectations.

Consumers are more likely to experience dissatisfaction or cognitive dissonance when the dollar value of the purchase increases, the opportunity costs of rejected alternatives are high, or the purchase decision is emotionally involving. Firms can manage these responses by offering liberal return policies, providing extensive postpurchase support, or reinforcing the wisdom of the consumer's purchase decision. The firm's ability to manage dissatisfaction and dissonance is not only a key to creating customer satisfaction but also has a major influence on the consumer's intentions to spread word-of-mouth information about the company and its products.

Factors That Affect the Consumer Buying Process

As we mentioned previously, the stages in the buying process depict a range of possible activities that may occur as consumers make purchase decisions. Consumers may spend relatively more or less time in certain stages, they may follow the stages in or out of sequence, or they may even skip stages entirely. This variation in the buying process occurs because consumers are different, the products that they buy are different, and the situations in which consumers make purchase decisions are different. A number of factors affect the consumer buying process, including the complexity of the purchase and decision, individual influences, social influences, and situational influences. Let's briefly examine each factor.

Decision-Making Complexity   The complexity of the purchase and decision-making process is the primary reason why the buying process will vary across consumers and with the same consumer in different situations. For example, highly complex decisions—like buying a first home, buying a first car, selecting the right college, or choosing elective surgery—are very involving for most consumers. These purchases are often characterized by high personal, social, or financial risk; strong emotional involvement; and the lack of experience with the product or purchase situation. In these instances, consumers will spend a great deal of time, effort, and even money to help ensure that they make the right decision. In contrast, purchase tasks that are low in complexity are relatively noninvolving for most consumers. In some cases, these purchase tasks can become routine in nature. For example, many consumers buy groceries by selecting familiar items from the shelf and placing them in their carts without considering alternative products.

For marketers, managing the decision-making complexity is an important consideration. Marketers of highly complex products must recognize that consumers are quite risk adverse and need a great deal of information to help them make the right decision. In these situations, access to high-quality and useful information should be an important consideration in the firm's marketing program. Firms that sell less-complex products do not have to provide as much information, but they do face the challenges of creating a brand image and ensuring that their products are easily recognizable. For these marketers, issues like branding, packaging, advertising, and point-of-purchase displays are key considerations in the marketing program.

Individual Influences   The range of individual influences that can affect the buying process is extensive. Some individual factors, such as age, life cycle, occupation, and socioeconomic status, are fairly easy to understand and incorporate into the marketing strategy. For the most part, these individual factors dictate preferences for certain types of products or brands. Married consumers with three children will clearly have different needs and preferences than young, single consumers. Likewise, more affluent consumers will have the same basic needs as less affluent consumers; however, their "wants" will be quite different. These individual factors are useful for marketers in target market selection, product development, and promotional strategy.

Other individual factors, such as perceptions, motives, interests, attitudes, opinions, or lifestyles, are much harder to understand because they do not clearly coincide with demographic characteristics like age, gender, or income levels. These individual factors are also very difficult to change. For that reason, many marketers adapt their products and promotional messages to fit existing attitudes, interests, or lifestyles. For example, Honda introduced the Fit subcompact car in the United States to appeal to a younger, nonconformist demographic that loves digital music, ring tones, video games, and graphic movies. The Fit's quirky style and flexible interior is appealing to this target market. Honda's promotional strategy is nonconformist as well. The Fit's television ads are just five seconds long and run in "pods" of three for a total commercial length of 15 seconds. Honda placed the ads on cable networks favored by the target market (for example, Cartoon Network and Nick at Nite) but avoided the broadcast networks (ABC, NBC, and CBS).[5]

Social Influences   Like individual influences, there is a wide range of social influences that can affect the buying process. Social influences such as culture, subculture, social class, reference groups, and family have a profound impact on what, why, and how consumers buy. Among these social influences, none is more important than the family. From birth, individuals become socialized with respect to the knowledge and skills needed to be an effective consumer. As adults, consumers typically exhibit the brand and product preferences of their parents. The influence of children on the buying process has grown tremendously over the last 50 years.

Reference groups and opinion leaders also have an important impact on consumer buying processes. Reference groups act as a point of comparison and source of product information. A consumer's purchase decisions tend to fall in line with the advice, beliefs, and actions of one or more reference groups. Opinion leaders can be part of a reference group or may be a specific individual who exists outside of a reference group. When consumers feel that they lack personal expertise, they seek the advice of opinion leaders, whom they view as being well informed in a particular field of knowledge. In some cases, marketers will seek out opinion leaders before trying to reach more mainstream consumers. Software manufacturers, for example, release beta (test) versions of their products to opinion leaders before a full-scale launch. This practice not only works the bugs out of the product but also starts a word-of-mouth buzz about the upcoming software release.

Situational Influences   A number of situational influences can affect the consumer buying process. Exhibit 6.2 illustrates some of the most common situational influences, many of which affect the amount of time and effort that consumers devote to the purchase task. For example, hungry consumers who are in a hurry often grab the quickest lunch that they can find—even if it comes from a vending machine. This fact accounts for the quick success of Pret A Manger, a chain of fast-food restaurants that offers prepackaged fare focusing on fresh, all-natural, and organic foods.[6]

EXHIBIT 6.2 **COMMON SITUATIONAL INFLUENCES IN THE CONSUMER BUYING PROCESS**

Situational Influences	Examples	Potential Influences on Buying Behavior
Physical and spatial influences	Retail atmospherics Retail crowding Store layout and design	A comfortable atmosphere or ambience promotes lingering, browsing, and buying. Crowded stores in terms of people or spatial layout may cause customers to leave or buy less than planned.
Social and interpersonal influences	Shopping in groups Salespeople Other customers	Consumers are more susceptible to the influences of other consumers when shopping in groups. Rude salespeople can end the buying process. Obnoxious "other" customers may cause the consumer to leave or be dissatisfied.
Temporal (time) influences	Lack of time Emergencies Convenience	Consumers will pay more for products when they are in a hurry or face an emergency. Lack of time greatly reduces the search for information and the evaluation of alternatives. Consumers with ample time can seek information on many different product alternatives.
Purchase task or product usage influences	Special occasions Buying for others Buying a gift	Consumers may buy higher-quality products for gifts or special occasions. The evoked set will differ when consumers are buying for others as opposed to themselves.
Consumer dispositional influences	Stress Anxiety Fear Fatigue Emotional involvement Good/bad mood	Consumers suffering from stress or fatigue may not buy at all, or they may indulge in certain products to make themselves feel better. Consumers who are in a bad mood are exceptionally difficult to please. An increase in fear or anxiety over a purchase may cause consumers to seek additional information and take great pains to make the right decision.

Consumers facing emergency situations have little time to reflect on their product choices and whether they will make the right decision. Consumers may also devote less time and effort to the buying process if they are uncomfortable. For this reason, sit-down restaurants should be inviting and relaxing to encourage longer visits and add-ons such as dessert or coffee after the meal.

Other situational influences can affect specific product choices. For example, if you have your boss over for dinner, your product choices would likely differ from those you make in everyday purchases of food and drink. Likewise, customers may purchase more expensive items for gifts or when they shop with friends. Product choices also change when customers make the purchase for someone else, such as buying clothing for children. In fact, many parents will purposely buy less expensive clothing for their children if they are growing rapidly or are exceptionally active. These parents want to save money on clothing that will quickly wear out or become too small.

Buyer Behavior in Business Markets

As we shift our attention to buyer behavior in business markets, keep in mind that business markets and consumer markets have many things in common. Both contain buyers and sellers who seek to make good purchases and satisfy their personal or organizational objectives. Both markets use similar buying processes that include stages associated with need identification, information search, and product evaluation. Finally, both processes focus on customer satisfaction as the desired outcome. However, as discussed next, business markets differ from consumer markets in important ways. One of the most important differences involves the consumption of the purchased products. Consumers buy products for their personal use or consumption. In contrast, organizational buyers purchase products for use in their operations. These uses can be direct, as in acquiring raw materials to produce finished goods, or indirect, as in buying office supplies or leasing cars for salespeople.

There are four types of business markets: producer markets, reseller markets, government markets, and institutional markets. *Producer markets* (also called commercial markets) buy raw materials for use in producing finished goods, and they buy facilitating goods and services used in the production of finished goods. Producer markets include a variety of industries such as aerospace, agriculture, mining, construction, transportation, communication, and utilities. *Reseller markets* consist of channel intermediaries such as wholesalers, retailers, or brokers that buy finished goods from the producer market and resell them at a profit. As we will see in Chapter 9, channel intermediaries have the responsibility for creating the variety and assortment of products offered to consumers. Therefore, they wield a great deal of power in the supply chain. *Government markets* include federal, state, county, city, and local governments. Governments buy a wide range of finished goods ranging from aircraft carriers to fire trucks to office equipment. However, most government purchases are for the services provided to citizens, such as education, fire and police protection, maintenance and repair of roads, and water and sewage treatment. *Institutional markets* consist of a diverse group of noncommercial organizations such as churches, charities, schools, hospitals, or professional organizations. These organizations primarily buy finished goods that facilitate their ongoing operations.

Unique Characteristics of Business Markets

Business markets differ from consumer markets in at least four ways. These differences concern the nature of the decision-making unit, the role of hard and soft costs in making and evaluating purchase decisions, reciprocal buying relationships, and the dependence of the two parties on each other. As a general rule, these differences are more acute for firms attempting to build long-term client relationships. In business markets, buying needed products at the lowest possible price is not necessarily the most important objective. Because many business transactions are based on long-term relationships, trust, reliability, and overall goal attainment are often much more important than the price of the product.

The Buying Center The first key difference relates to the role of the *buying center*—the group of people responsible for making purchase decisions. In consumer markets, the buying center is fairly straightforward: The adult head-of-household tends to make most major purchase decisions for the family, with input and assistance from children and other family members as applicable. In an organization, however, the buying center tends to be much more complex and difficult to identify, in part because it may include three distinct groups of people—economic buyers, technical buyers, and users—each of which may have its own agenda and unique needs that affect the buying decision.

Any effort to build a relationship between the selling and buying organization must include economic buyers—those senior managers with the overall responsibility of achieving the buying firm's objectives. In recent years, economic buyers have become increasingly influential as price has become less important in determining a product's true value to the buying firm. This has made economic buyers a greater target for promotional activities. Technical buyers—employees with the responsibility of buying products to meet needs on an ongoing basis—include purchasing agents and materials managers. These buyers have the responsibility of narrowing the number of product options and delivering buying recommendations to the economic buyer(s) that are within budget. Technical buyers are critical in the execution of purchase transactions and are also important to the day-to-day maintenance of long-term relationships. Users—managers and employees who have the responsibility of using a product purchased by the firm—comprise the last group of people in the buying center. The user is often not the ultimate decision maker but frequently has a place in the decision process, particularly in the case of technologically advanced products. For example, the head of information technology (IT) often has a major role in computer and IT purchase decisions.

Hard and Soft Costs The second difference between business and consumer markets involves the significance of hard and soft costs. Consumers and organizations both consider *hard costs,* which include monetary price and associated purchase costs such as shipping and installation. Organizations, however, must also consider *soft costs* such as downtime, opportunity costs, and human resource costs associated with the compatibility of systems in the buying decision. The purchase and implementation of a new payroll system, for example, will decrease productivity and increase training costs in the payroll department until the new system has been fully integrated.

Reciprocity   The third key difference involves the existence of reciprocal buying relationships. With consumer purchases, the opportunity for buying and selling is usually a one-way street: The marketer sells and the consumer buys. Business marketing, however, is more often a two-way street, with each firm marketing products that the other firm buys. For example, a company may buy office supplies from another company that in turn buys copiers from the first firm. In fact, such arrangements can be an upfront condition of purchase in purely transaction-based marketing. Reciprocal buying is less likely to occur within long-term relationships unless it helps both parties achieve their respective goals.

Mutual Dependence   Finally, in business markets, the buyer and seller are more likely to be dependent on each other. For consumer–marketer relationships, this level of dependence tends to be low. If a store is out of a product or a firm goes out of business, customers simply switch to another source to meet their needs. Likewise, the loss of a particular customer through brand switching, relocation, or death is unfortunate for a company but not in of itself particularly damaging. The only real exception to this norm is when consumers are loyal to a brand or merchant. In these cases, consumers become dependent on a single brand or merchant, and the firm can become dependent on the sales volume generated by these brand-loyal consumers.

This is not the case in business markets where sole-source or limited-source buying may leave an organization's operations severely distressed when a supplier shuts down or cannot deliver. The same is true for the loss of a customer. The selling firm has invested significantly in the client relationship, often modifying products and altering information or other systems central to the organization. Each client relationship represents a significant portion of the firm's profit, and the loss of a single customer can take months or even years to replace. For example, after Rubbermaid's relationships with Wal-Mart, Lowe's, and The Home Depot soured, these retailers pulled Rubbermaid products from their shelves and turned to Sterilite, a small Massachusetts-based manufacturer, to supply plastic products (storage bins, containers, and the like) for their stores. Along with damaging Rubbermaid's reputation and profits, the considerable buying power of Wal-Mart, Lowe's, and The Home Depot turned Sterilite into a major competitor for Rubbermaid. Rubbermaid was able to recover somewhat by lavishing its buying partners with exceptional service.[7]

The Business Buying Process

Like consumers, businesses follow a buying process. However, given the complexity, risk, and expense of many business purchases, business buyers tend to follow these stages in sequence. Some buying situations are routine such as the daily or weekly purchase and delivery of raw materials or the purchase of office consumables like paper and toner cartridges. Nonetheless, business buyers often make even routine purchases from prequalified or single-source suppliers. Consequently, virtually all business purchases have gone through the following stages of the buying process at one time or another:

1. **Problem Recognition**   The recognition of needs can stem from a variety of internal and external sources such as employees, members of the buying center, or outside salespeople. Business buyers often recognize needs due to special circumstances such as when equipment or machinery breaks or malfunctions.

2. **Developing Product Specifications**   Detailed product specifications often define business purchases. This occurs because new purchases must be integrated with current technologies and processes. Developing product specifications is typically done by the buying center.

3. **Vendor Identification and Qualification**   Business buyers must ensure that potential vendors can deliver on needed product specifications, within a specified time frame, and in the needed quantities. Therefore, business buyers will conduct a thorough analysis of potential vendors to ensure they can meet their firm's needs. The buyers then qualify and approve the vendors that meet their criteria to supply goods and services to the firm.

4. **Solicitation of Proposals or Bids**   Depending on the purchase in question, the buying firm may request that qualified vendors submit proposals or bids. These proposals or bids will detail how the vendor will meet the buying firm's needs and fulfill the purchase criteria established during the second stage of the process.

5. **Vendor Selection**   The buying firm will select the vendor or vendors that can best meet its needs. The best vendor is not necessarily the one offering the lowest price. Other issues such as reputation, timeliness of delivery, guarantees, or personal relationships with the members of the buying center are often more important.

6. **Order Processing**   Often a behind-the-scenes process, order processing involves the details of processing the order, negotiating credit terms, setting firm delivery dates, and any final technical assistance needed to complete the purchase.

7. **Vendor Performance Review**   The final stage of the buying process involves a review of the vendor's performance. In some cases, the product may flawlessly fulfill the needed specifications, but the vendor's performance is poor. In this stage, both product and vendor specifications can be reevaluated and changed if necessary. In the end, the result of these evaluations will affect future purchase decisions.

As in consumer markets, a number of factors can influence the business buying process. Environmental conditions can have a major influence on buyer behavior by increasing the uncertainty, complexity, and risk associated with a purchase. In situations of rapid environmental change, business buyers may alter their buying plans, postpone purchases, or even cancel purchases until things settle down. Environmental conditions affect not only the purchase of products but also decisions regarding the recruitment and hiring of employees.

Organizational factors can also influence business buying decisions. These factors include conditions within the firm's internal environment (resources, strategies, policies, and objectives), as well as the condition of relationships with business or supply chain partners. A shift in the firm's resources can change buying decisions, such as a temporary delay in purchasing until favorable credit terms can be arranged. Likewise, if a supplier suddenly cannot provide needed quantities of products or cannot meet a needed delivery schedule, the buying firm will be forced to identify and qualify new suppliers. Internal changes in IT can also affect the buying process, such as when technicians integrate electronic procurement systems with the legacy systems of the firm and its vendors. Finally, interpersonal relationships and individual factors can affect the buying process. A common example occurs when members of the buying center are at odds over purchase decisions. Power struggles are not uncommon in business buying, and they can bring the entire process to a halt if not handled properly. Individual factors, such as a manager's personal preferences or prejudices, can also affect business buying decisions. The importance of interpersonal and individual factors depends on the specific buying situation and its importance to the firm's goals and objectives. Major purchases typically create the most conflict among members of the buying center.

Market Segmentation

Understanding the processes that consumers and businesses use to make purchase decisions is critical to the development of long-term, mutually beneficial relationships with customers. It is also a necessary first step in uncovering similarities among groups of potential buyers that can be used in market segmentation and target-marketing decisions. From a strategic perspective, we define *market segmentation* as the process of dividing the total market for a particular product or product category into relatively homogeneous segments or groups. To be effective, segmentation should create groups where the members within the group have similar likes, tastes, needs, wants, or preferences but where the groups themselves are dissimilar from one another.

In reality the most fundamental segmentation decision is really whether to segment at all. When a firm makes the decision to pursue the entire market, it must do so on the basis of universal needs that all customers possess. However, most firms opt to target one or more segments of the total market because they find that they can be more successful when they tailor products to fit unique needs or requirements. In today's economy, segmentation is often mandated by customers due to their search for unique products and their changing uses of communication media. The end result is that customer segments have become even more fragmented and more difficult to reach. Many firms today take segmentation to the extreme by targeting small niches of a market or even the smallest of market segments: individuals.

Traditional Market Segmentation Approaches

Many segmentation approaches are traditional in the sense that firms have used them successfully for decades. It is not our intention to depict these approaches as old or out of date, especially when compared to individualized segmentation strategies, which we discuss later. In fact, many of today's most successful firms use these tried-and-true approaches. Some organizations actually use more than one type of segmentation, depending on the brand, product, or market in question.

Mass Marketing   It seems odd to call mass marketing a segmentation approach because it involves no segmentation whatsoever. Companies aim *mass-marketing* campaigns at the total (whole) market for a particular product. Companies that adopt mass marketing take an undifferentiated approach that assumes that all customers in the market have similar needs and wants that can be reasonably satisfied with a single marketing program. This marketing program typically consists of a single product or brand (or, in the case of retailers, a homogeneous set of products), one price, one promotional program, and one distribution system. Duracell, for example, offers a collection of different battery sizes (D, C, A, AA, AAA, 9-volt, Prismatics), but they are all disposable batteries marketed to consumers for use in toys and small electronic devices. Likewise, the WD-40 Company offers an assortment of brands—including WD-40, 3-IN-ONE Oil, Lava Soap, 2000 Flushes, Carpet Fresh, and X14 Cleaner—used in a variety of household tasks.

Mass marketing works best when the needs of an entire market are relatively homogeneous. Good examples include commodities like oil and agricultural products. In reality, very few products or markets are ideal for mass marketing if for no other reason than companies, wanting to reach new customers, often modify their product lines. For most of its existence, Vaseline manufactured and offered a single product. To reach new customers, Vaseline modified this strategy by launching its Intensive Care line of products and extending customers' perception of Vaseline's uses to various needs in the home including in the garage/workshop. Furthermore, think of the many products that contain Arm & Hammer Baking Soda, a product that at one time was sold only as a baking ingredient.

Although mass marketing is advantageous in terms of production efficiency and lower marketing costs, it is inherently risky. By offering a standard product to all customers, the organization becomes vulnerable to competitors that offer specialized products that better match customers' needs. In industries where barriers to entry are low, mass marketing runs the risk of being seen as too generic. This situation is very inviting for competitors who use more targeted approaches. Mass marketing is also very risky in global markets where even global brands like Coca-Cola must be adapted to match local tastes and customs.

Differentiated Marketing   Most firms use some form of market segmentation by (1) dividing the total market into groups of customers having relatively common or homogeneous needs and (2) attempting to develop a marketing program that appeals to one or more of these groups. This approach may be necessary when customer needs are similar within a single group, but their needs differ across groups. Through well-designed and carefully conducted research, firms can identify the particular needs of each market segment to create marketing programs that best match those needs and expectations. Within the differentiated approach, there are two options: the multisegment approach and the market concentration approach.

Firms using the *multisegment approach* seek to attract buyers in more than one market segment by offering a variety of products that appeal to different needs. Firms using this option can increase their share of the market by responding to the heterogeneous needs of different segments. If the segments have enough buying potential and the product is successful, the resulting sales increases can more than offset the increased costs of offering multiple products and marketing programs. The multisegment approach is the most widely used segmentation strategy in medium- to large-sized firms. It is extremely common in packaged goods and grocery products. Maxwell House, for example, began by marketing one type of coffee and one brand. Today, this division of Kraft Foods offers forty different brand varieties under the Maxwell House label, in addition to providing private-label brands for retailers. A walk down the cereal aisle of your local supermarket offers additional examples. Firms such as Kellogg's and Nabisco offer seemingly hundreds of brands of breakfast cereals targeted at specific segments including children (for example, Fruity Pebbles and Apple Jacks), health-conscious adults (for example, Shredded Wheat and Total), parents looking for healthier foods for their children (for example, Life and Kix), and so on.

Firms using the *market concentration* approach focus on a single market segment. These firms often find it most efficient to seek a maximum share in one segment of the market. For example, Armor All markets a well-known line of automotive cleaners, protectants, and polishes targeted primarily at young male consumers of driving age. The main advantage of market concentration is specialization because it allows the firm to focus all its resources toward understanding and serving a single segment. Specialization is also the major disadvantage of this approach. By "putting all of its eggs in one basket," the firm can be vulnerable to changes in its market segment, such as economic downturns and demographic shifts. Still, the market concentration approach can be highly successful. In the arts, where market concentration is almost universal, musical groups hone their talents and plan their performances to satisfy the tastes of one market segment, divided by genres of music such as country, rock, or jazz.

Niche Marketing   Some companies narrow the market concentration approach even more and focus their marketing efforts on one small, well-defined market segment, or niche, that has a unique, specific set of needs. Customers in niche markets will typically pay higher prices for products that match their specialized needs. One example of successful niche marketing is found in the spa industry. Industry growth has slowed in recent years, however, so many firms have launched highly specialized fitness, medical, and skin-care spas. Men-only spas, the fastest-growing niche, now account for 25 percent of spa revenue worldwide.[8] As the spa industry has learned, the key to successful niche marketing is to understand and meet the needs of target customers so completely that, despite the small size of the niche, the firm's substantial share makes the segment highly profitable. An attractive market niche is one that has growth and profit potential but is not so appealing that it attracts competitors. The firm should also possess a specialization or provide a unique offering that customers find highly desirable.

Individualized Segmentation Approaches

Due to advances in communication and Internet technology, individualized segmentation approaches have emerged. These approaches are possible because organizations now have the ability to track customers with a high degree of specificity. By combining demographic data with past and current purchasing behavior, organizations can tweak their marketing programs in ways that allow them to precisely match customers' needs, wants, and preferences. Three types of individualized segmentation approaches are one-to-one marketing, mass customization, and permission marketing.

One-to-One Marketing   When a company creates an entirely unique product or marketing program for each customer in the target segment, it employs one-to-one marketing. This approach is common in business markets where companies design unique programs and/or systems for each customer. For example, providers of enterprise software—such as Oracle, SAP, and Business Objects—create customized solutions that allow firms to track customers, business processes, and results in real time. Insurance companies or brokers, such Britain's Sedgwick Group, design insurance and pension programs to meet a corporation's specific needs. The key to one-to-one marketing is personalization where every element of the marketing program is customized to meet the specifics of a particular client's situation.

Historically, one-to-one marketing has been used less often in consumer markets although Burger King was an early pioneer in this approach with its "Have It Your Way" effort that continues today. One-to-one marketing is common in luxury and custom-made products such as large sailboats, airplanes, or custom-built homes. In such instances, the product has significant modifications made to it to meet unique customer needs and preferences. Many service firms—such as hairstylists, lawyers, physicians, and educational institutions—also customize their marketing programs to match individual consumer needs. One-to-one marketing has grown rapidly in e-commerce where customers can be targeted very precisely.[9] Amazon, for example, maintains complete profiles on customers who browse and buy from its site. These profiles assist Amazon with the customization of web pages in real time, product suggestions, and reminder e-mails sent to customers.

Mass Customization   An extension of one-to-one marketing, mass customization refers to providing unique products and solutions to individual customers on a mass scale. Along with the Internet, advances in supply chain management—including real-time inventory control—have allowed companies to customize products in ways that are both cost effective and practical. For example, Dell and Gateway build thousands of custom-ordered computers every day. 1-800-Flowers.com can create a custom flower arrangement, plant, or other gift and deliver it to family and friends in the same day. Likewise, customers of the Build-A-Bear Workshop retail stores can select, stuff, wash, and dress a teddy bear or other animal of their choice. Customers can even include their own voice greeting with the stuffed animal.

Mass customization also occurs in business markets. Through a buying firm's electronic procurement system, employees can order products ranging from office supplies to travel services. The system allows employees to requisition goods and services via a customized catalog—unique to the firm—where the buying firm has negotiated the products and prices. E-procurement systems like these have become popular for good reason: They allow firms to save a great deal of money—not only on prices but also on the costs of placing orders. Selling firms benefit as well by customizing their catalogs to specific buying firms, allowing them to sell more goods and services at a reduced cost.

Permission Marketing   Permission marketing, although similar to one-to-one marketing, is different in that customers choose to become part of a firm's market segment. In permission marketing, customers give companies permission to specifically target them in their marketing efforts. The most common tool used in permission marketing is the opt-in e-mail list where customers permit a firm—or a third-party partner of the firm—to send periodic e-mail about goods and services that they have interest in purchasing. This scenario is ubiquitous in business-to-consumer e-commerce, so much so that many consumers fail to notice it. When customers order products online, they receive the option of receiving or not receiving future e-mail notifications about new products. In many cases, customers must deselect a box at the end of the order form, or they will be added to the e-mail list.

Permission marketing has a major advantage over other individualized segmentation approaches: Customers who opt-in have already shown interest in the goods and services offered by the firm. This allows the firm to precisely target only those individuals with an interest in their products, thereby eliminating wasted marketing effort and expense. For example, many airlines have the permission of their customers to send weekly e-mail notices of airfare and other travel-related specials. This system is in stark contrast to traditional mass-media advertising where only a portion of the viewing or reading audience has a real interest in the company's product.

One-to-one marketing, mass customization, and permission marketing will become even more important in the future because their focus on individual customers makes them critical to the development and maintenance of long-term relationships. The simple truth is that customers will maintain relationships with firms that best fulfill their needs or solve their problems. Unfortunately, individualized segmentation approaches can be prohibitively expensive. To make these approaches viable, firms must be mindful of two important issues. First, the delivery of the marketing program must be automated to a degree that makes it cost efficient. The Internet makes this possible by allowing for individual customization in real time. Second, the marketing program must not become so automated that the offering lacks personalization. Today, personalization means much more than simply calling customers by name. We use the term *personalization* to describe the idea of giving customers choices—in terms of not only product configuration but also the entire marketing program. Firms like Dell and Amazon offer a great deal of personalization by effectively mining their customer databases. Customers can choose payment terms, shipping terms, delivery locations, gift wrapping, and whether to opt-in to future e-mail promotions. Also, by monitoring clickstream data in real time, the best e-commerce firms can offer product suggestions on the fly—while customers visit their sites. This sort of customized point-of-sale information not only increases sales but also better fulfills customers' needs and increases the likelihood of establishing long-term customer relationships.

Criteria for Successful Segmentation

It is important to remember that not all segmentation approaches or their resulting market segments are viable in a marketing sense. For example, it makes little sense to segment the soft-drink market based on eye color or shoe size because these characteristics have nothing to do with the purchase of soft drinks. Although markets can be segmented in limitless ways, the segmentation approach must make sense in terms of at least five related criteria:

- **Identifiable and Measurable**   The characteristics of the segment's members must be easily identifiable. This allows the firm to measure identifying characteristics including the segment's size and purchasing power.

- **Substantial**   The segment must be large and profitable enough to make it worthwhile for the firm. The profit potential must be greater than the costs involved in creating a marketing program specifically for the segment.

- **Accessible**   The segment must be accessible in terms of communication (advertising, mail, telephone, and so on) and distribution (channels, merchants, retail outlets, and so on).

- **Responsive**   The segment must respond to the firm's marketing efforts including changes to the marketing program over time. The segment must also respond differently than other segments.

- **Viable and Sustainable**   The segment must meet the basic criteria for exchange including being ready, willing, and able to conduct business with the firm. The segment must also be sustainable over time to allow the firm to effectively develop a marketing strategy for serving the needs of the segment.

It is possible for a market segment to meet these criteria yet still not be viable in a business sense. Markets for many illegal products, such as illicit drugs or pornography, can easily meet these criteria. However, ethical and socially responsible firms would not pursue these markets. Other markets, like gaming or gambling, may not be illegal in some cases or geographic areas but are often not in the best interests of the firm. More commonly, firms will identify perfectly viable market segments; however, these

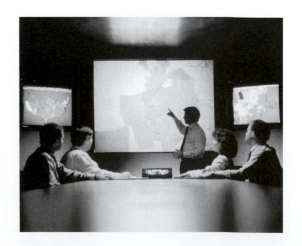

segments will rest outside the firm's expertise or mission. Just because a market segment is viable or highly profitable does not mean the firm should pursue it.

Identifying Market Segments

A firm's segmentation strategy and its choice of one or more target markets depend on its ability to identify the characteristics of buyers within those markets. This involves selecting the most relevant variables to identify and define the target market(s). Many of these variables, including demographics, lifestyles, product usage, or firm size, derive from the situation analysis section of the marketing plan. However, a new or revised marketing strategy often requires changes in target market definition to correct problems in the previous marketing strategy. Target markets also shift in response to required changes in specific elements of the marketing program, such as reducing price to enhance value, increasing price to connote higher quality, adding a new product feature to make the benefits more meaningful, or selling through retail stores instead of direct distribution to add the convenience of immediate availability. In short, the target market and the marketing program are interdependent, and changes in one typically require changes in the other. Beyond the Pages 6.2 outlines the challenges and changes faced by companies as they attempt to capture a share of the lucrative Chinese market.

Beyond the Pages 6.2

THE LUCRATIVE AND CHALLENGING CHINESE MARKET[10]

It's hard to ignore a market that numbers 1.4 billion consumers in size. China is the world's most populous country and its second largest economy. And, though the size is appealing (China has 20 percent of the world's population compared to only 4.5 percent for the United States), it is China's growing middle class that gets U.S. firms excited about its market potential. In contrast to the United States where the middle class is declining, China's middle class is growing rapidly. Experts estimate that the number of middle-class households in China will triple by 2010 and will account for over $500 billion in spending power.

Despite the enormous potential, China is a very challenging market for most firms. Some reasons are obvious: the sheer size of the country, its complicated language with multiple dialects, and its relatively low personal incomes compared to Western standards. Despite these and other challenges, the market potential is so enticing that many U.S. firms are moving boldly into the Chinese market. Here, we examine the challenges faced by Pepsi, Wal-Mart, and Starbucks in reaching the lucrative Chinese consumer.

Pepsi

Pepsi faces a number of challenges in the Chinese market. The first is demand. Chinese citizens consume only one-twentieth of the soft drinks per capita than their American counterparts do. One reason is that most Chinese prefer tea to soft drinks. A second challenge is competition. Coca-Cola, which has been in China a lot longer than Pepsi, controls 24 percent of the market. China's own Wahaha Future Cola, which generated over $1 billion in sales in 2005, is extremely popular in the rural areas of China. A third challenge is that Pepsi is forced to work with local companies. Pepsi has more than thirty joint ventures and partnerships in China, a network that proves to be very challenging to manage effectively. Until recently, Pepsi has struggled to turn a profit. Now the company plans to invest $850 million in China over a 3-year period— almost as much as the company invested in China over the last 25 years. Pepsi expects sales growth of roughly 25 percent each year for the following several years.

(continued)

Wal-Mart

The retail market in China is attractive for many reasons. It is currently the seventh largest retail market in the world and will soon pass Italy and France to move into the number-five position. Further, China's retail market is growing at roughly seven percent per year, as opposed to the five percent annual growth rate in the United States. It is no surprise then that Wal-Mart has moved aggressively into the Chinese market. However, Wal-Mart faces intense competition from a number of European retailers. French retailer Carrefour operates more than 240 supermarkets and discount stores in China. Tesco, a U.K. supermarket chain, operates 50 hypermarkets with plans to open 15 additional stores by 2007. By comparison, Wal-Mart operates 56 supercenters and Sam's Club stores, with plans to open 20 more by 2007. Competition from local retailers, which account for 90 percent of retail sales in China, is also intense. These local merchants include traditional supermarkets as well as street markets (local vendors who sell everything from fresh produce to live animals). Chinese consumers favor local merchants because of their low prices and freshness of food. In addition to competition, Wal-Mart also faces a unique problem in the shortage of skilled employees. Wal-Mart currently employs 30,000 people but plans to add 150,000 employees to its payroll by 2011. To ease the crunch, Wal-Mart is considering the creation of a university degree program to train the accountants, bakers, and other employees that the company needs for future growth.

Starbucks

To raise awareness in the Chinese market, Starbucks plans to donate a total of $5 million to charity projects within the country. The first was a $1.5 million donation to train 3,000 schoolteachers and provide books and computers to schools in China's poor western provinces. Starbucks is making a commitment to China— the company's number-one growth market outside the United States— despite the many challenges faced by the company. In addition to Chinese preferences for tea, Starbucks faces a daunting economic situation: Its $6 a cup coffee costs more than the average Chinese worker earns in one day. Despite this stark reality, Starbucks' 220 locations in eighteen cities have been successful. The company's success has bred a great deal of imitation by local competitors, many of which have pirated the Starbuck's brand name and logo.

Segmenting Consumer Markets

The goal in segmenting consumer markets is to isolate individual characteristics that distinguish one or more segments from the total market. The key is to segment the total market into groups with relatively homogeneous needs. As you may recall from our earlier discussion, consumers buy products because the benefits they provide can fulfill specific needs or wants. The difficulty in segmenting consumer markets lies in isolating one or more characteristics that closely align with these needs and wants. For example, marketers of soft drinks do not necessarily concern themselves with the age or gender of their customers but rather in how age and gender relate to customers' needs, attitudes, preferences, and lifestyles.

In the discussion that follows, we look more closely at segmentation in consumer markets by examining the different factors that can be used to divide these markets into homogeneous groupings. As Exhibit 6.3 illustrates, these factors fall into one of four general categories: behavioral segmentation, demographic segmentation, psychographic segmentation, and geographic segmentation.

Behavioral Segmentation   Behavioral segmentation is the most powerful approach because it uses actual consumer behavior or product usage to make distinctions among

EXHIBIT 6.3	COMMON SEGMENTATION VARIABLES USED IN CONSUMER MARKETS	

Category	Variables	Examples
Behavioral segmentation	Benefits sought	Quality, value, taste, image enhancement, beauty, sportiness, speed, excitement, entertainment, nutrition, convenience
	Product usage	Heavy, medium, and light users; nonusers; former users; first-time users
	Occasions or situations	Emergencies, celebrations, birthdays, anniversaries, weddings, births, funerals, graduation
	Price sensitivity	Price sensitive, value conscious, status conscious (not price sensitive)
Demographic segmentation	Age	Newborns, 0–5, 6–12, 13–17, 18–25, 26–34, 35–49, 50–64, 65+
	Gender	Male, female
	Income	Under $15,000, $15,000–$30,000, $30,000–$50,000, $50,000–$75,000, $75,000–$100,000, over $100,000
	Occupation	Blue collar, white collar, technical, professional, managers, laborers, retired, homemakers, unemployed
	Education	High school graduate, some college, college graduate, graduate degree
	Family life cycle	Single, married no children, married with young children, married with teenage children, married with grown children, divorced, widowed
	Generation	Generation Y, Generation X, baby boomers, seniors
	Ethnicity	Caucasian, African American, Hispanic, Asian
	Religion	Protestant, Catholic, Muslim, Hindu
	Nationality	American, European, Japanese, Australian, Korean
	Social class	Upper class, middle class, lower class, working class, poverty level
Psychographic segmentation	Personality	Outgoing, shy, compulsive, individualistic, materialistic, civic minded, anxious, controlled, venturesome
	Lifestyle	Outdoor enthusiast, sports-minded, homebody, couch potato, family-centered, workaholic
	Motives	Safety, status, relaxation, convenience
Geographic segmentation	Regional	Northeast, Southeast, Midwest, New England, Southern France, South Africa
	City/county size	Under 50,000; 50,000–100,000; 100,000–250,000; 250,000–500,000; 500,000–1,000,000, over 1,000,000
	Population density	Urban, suburban, rural

market segments. Typically, these distinctions are tied to the reasons that customers buy and use products. Consequently, behavioral segmentation, unlike other types of consumer segmentation, is most closely associated with consumer needs. A common use of behavioral segmentation is to group consumers based on their extent of product usage—heavy, medium, and light users. Heavy users are a firm's "bread-and-butter" customers, and they should always be served well. Marketers often use strategies to increase product usage among light users as well as nonusers of the product or brand. One of the best uses of behavioral segmentation is to create market segments based on specific consumer benefits. Exhibit 6.4 illustrates how benefit segmentation might be applied in the snack-food market. Once different benefit segments have been

EXHIBIT 6.4

BENEFIT SEGMENTATION OF THE SNACK FOOD MARKET

	Nutritional Snackers	Weight Watchers	Guilty Snackers	Party Snackers	Indiscriminant Snackers	Economical Snackers
Benefits Sought	Nutritious, all-natural ingredients	Low calorie, quick energy	Low calorie, good tasting	Can be served to guests, goes well with beverages	Good tasting, satisfies hunger cravings	Low price, best value
Types of Snacks Eaten	Fruits, vegetables, cheeses	Yogurt, vegetables	Yogurt, cookies, crackers, candy	Potato chips, nuts, crackers, pretzels	Candy, ice cream, cookies, potato chips, pretzels, popcorn	No specific products
Snack Consumption Level	Light	Light	Heavy	Average	Heavy	Average
Percentage of Snackers	23%	15%	10%	16%	16%	19%
Demographic Characteristics	Better educated, have young children	Younger, single	Less educated, lower incomes	Middle aged, suburban	Teens	Better educated, larger families
Psychographic Characteristics	Self-assured, controlled	Outdoorsy, influential, venturesome	Anxious, isolated	Sociable, outgoing	Hedonistic, time deprived	Self-assured, price sensitive

Source: Adapted from Charles W. Lamb, Jr., Joseph F. Hair, Jr., and Carl McDaniel, *Marketing*, 7th ed. (Mason, OH: South-Western, 2004), 224.

identified, marketers can conduct research to develop profiles of the consumers in each segment.

Behavioral segmentation is a powerful tool; however, it is also difficult to execute in practice. Conducting research to identify behavioral segments is expensive and time consuming. Also, the personal characteristics associated with behavioral segments are not always clear. For example, although some consumers buy a new car solely for transportation, most buy specific makes and models for other reasons. Some consumers want cars that are sporty, fun to drive, and that enhance their image. The problem lies in identifying the characteristics of these consumers. Are they older or younger, men or women, single or married, and do they live in urban or suburban areas? In some cases, consumer characteristics are easy to identify. Families purchase minivans because they want more room for their children and cargo. Older consumers tend to opt for comfortable and luxurious models. The key to successful behavioral segmentation is to clearly understand the basic needs and benefits sought by different consumer groups. Then this information can be combined with demographic, psychographic, and geographic segmentation to create complete consumer profiles.

Demographic Segmentation   Demographic segmentation divides markets into segments using demographic factors such as gender (for example, Secret deodorant for women), age (for example, Abercrombie & Fitch clothing for teens and young adults), income (for example, Lexus automobiles for wealthy consumers), and education (for example, online executive MBA programs for busy professionals). Demographic segmentation tends to be the most widely used basis for segmenting consumer markets because demographic information is widely available and relatively easy to measure. In fact, much of this information is easily obtainable during the situation analysis through secondary sources.

Some demographic characteristics are often associated with true differences in needs that can be used to segment markets. In these cases, the connection between demographics, needs, and desired product benefits can make demographic segmentation quite easy. For example, men and women have clearly different needs with respect to clothing and health care. Large families with children have a greater need for life insurance, laundry detergent, and food. Children prefer sweeter-tasting food and beverages than do adults. Unfortunately, demographic segmentation becomes less useful when the firm has a strong interest in understanding the motives or values that drive buying behavior. Often, the motives and values that drive actual purchases do not necessarily have anything to do with demographics. For example, how would you describe the demographic characteristics of a price-sensitive, value-conscious consumer? Before you answer, remember that Wal-Mart customers come from all walks of life. Likewise, how would you describe the demographics of an adventuresome, out-door-oriented consumer? Honda was taken by surprise when it targeted its Element utility vehicle to adventuresome, high school and college-aged consumers. Honda quickly discovered that the Element was just as popular with 30- and 40-somethings who used it to haul kids and groceries. The problem in understanding consumer motives and values is that these variables depend more on what consumers *think and feel* rather than who they are. Delving into consumer thoughts and feelings is the subject of psychographic segmentation.

Psychographic Segmentation   Psychographic segmentation deals with state-of-mind issues such as motives, attitudes, opinions, values, lifestyles, interests, and personality. These issues are more difficult to measure and often require primary marketing research to properly determine the makeup and size of various market segments. Once the firm identifies one or more psychographic segments, they can be combined with demographic, geographic, or behavioral segmentation to create fully developed consumer profiles.

One of the most successful and well-known tools of psychographic segmentation is VALS© developed by SRI Consulting.[11] VALS, which stands for "values and lifestyles," divides adult U.S. consumers into one of eight profiles based on their level of resources and one of three primary consumption motives: ideals (knowledge and principles), achievement (demonstrating success to others), or self-expression (social or physical activity, variety, and risk taking). Exhibit 6.5 describes the eight VALS profiles. Many companies use VALS in a variety of marketing activities including new product development, product positioning, brand development, promotional strategy, and media placement. SRI has also developed a geographic version of VALS, called GeoVALS©, which links each consumer profile with geographic information such as ZIP codes. This tool is useful in direct-marketing campaigns and retail site selection.

Psychographic segmentation is useful because it transcends purely descriptive characteristics to help explain personal motives, attitudes, emotions, and lifestyles directly connected to buying behavior. For example, companies such as Michelin

EXHIBIT 6.5 **VALS CONSUMER PROFILES**

Innovators

These consumers have abundant resources and high self-esteem. Innovators are successful, sophisticated consumers who have a taste for upscale, innovative, and specialized goods and services. Innovators are concerned about image as an expression of self but not as an expression of status or power.
Example products: fine wines, upscale home furnishings, lawn maintenance services, recent technology, luxury automobiles

Thinkers

Thinkers are well-educated consumers who value order, knowledge, and responsibility. These consumers like to be as well informed about the products they buy as they are about world and national events. Although Thinkers have resources that give them many choices or options, they tend to be conservative consumers who look for practicality, durability, functionality, and value.
Example products: news and information services, low-emission vehicles, conservative homes and home furnishings

Achievers

The lifestyle of an Achiever is focused and structured around family, a place of worship, and career. Achievers are conventional, conservative, and respect authority and the status quo. These individuals are very active consumers who desire established, prestigious products and services that demonstrate their success. Achievers lead busy lives; hence, they value products that can save them time and effort.
Example products: SUVs, family vacations, products that promote career enhancement, online shopping, swimming pools

Experiencers

Experiencers are young, enthusiastic, and impulsive consumers who are motivated by self-expression. These consumers emphasize variety, excitement, the offbeat, and the risky. Experiencers enjoy looking good and buying "cool" products.
Example products: fashion, entertainment, sports/exercise, outdoor recreation and social activities

Believers

Believers are conservative, conventional consumers who hold steadfast beliefs based on traditional values related to family, religion, community, and patriotism. These consumers are predictable in that they follow

(continued)

and State Farm appeal to consumers motivated by issues such as safety, security, and protection when buying tires or insurance. Other firms, such as Subaru, Kia, and Hyundai, appeal to consumers whose values and opinions about transportation focus more on economy than status. Online degree programs appeal to consumers whose active lifestyles do not allow them to attend classes in the traditional sense.

Geographic Segmentation Geographic characteristics often play a large part in developing market segments. For example, firms often find that their customers are geographically concentrated. Even ubiquitous products like Coke sell better in the southern United States than in other parts of the country. Consumer preferences for certain purchases based on geography are a primary consideration in developing trade areas for retailers such as grocery stores, gas stations, and dry cleaners. For example, geodemographic segmentation, or geoclustering, is an approach that looks at established routines centered on family, community, or organizational membership. Believers prefer familiar and well-known American brands and tend to be very loyal customers.

Example products: membership in social, religious, or fraternal organizations; American-made products; charitable organizations

Strivers

Strivers are motivated by achievement, yet they lack the resources to meet all their desires. As a group, Strivers are trendy, fun loving, and concerned with the opinions and approval of others. These consumers see shopping as a social activity and an opportunity to demonstrate their purchasing power up to the limits imposed by their financial situations. Most Strivers think of themselves as having jobs rather than careers.

Example products: stylish products, impulse items, credit cards, designer "knock-offs," shopping as entertainment

Makers

Makers, like Experiencers, are motivated by self-expression. However, these consumers experience the world by engaging in many do-it-yourself activities such as repairing their own cars, building houses, or growing and canning their own vegetables. Makers are practical consumers who value self-sufficiency and have the skills to back it up. Makers are also unimpressed by material possessions, new ideas, or big business. They live traditional lives and prefer to buy basic items.

Example products: auto parts, home-improvement supplies, gardening supplies, sewing supplies, discount retailers

Survivors

Survivors live narrowly focused lives and have few resources with which to cope. They are primarily concerned with safety, security, and meeting needs rather than fulfilling wants. As a group, Survivors are cautious consumers who represent a fairly small market for most products. They are loyal to favorite brands, especially if they can buy them on sale.

Example products: basic necessities and staples; old, established brands

Source: SRI Consulting Business Intelligence, http://www.sric-bi.com/VALS/types.shtml.

neighborhood profiles based on demographic, geographic, and lifestyle segmentation variables. One of the best-known geoclustering tools is Claritas' PRIZM$_{\text{NE}}$™ segmentation system, which classifies every neighborhood in the United States into one of sixty-six different demographic and behavioral clusters. The "Kids and Cul-de-Sacs" cluster contains upscale, suburban, families living in recently built subdivisions. The adults in this cluster are highly educated professionals working in administrative jobs that pay upper middle–class incomes. They are prime targets for child-centered products, personal services, and travel. PRIZM is useful to marketers because it allows them to focus their marketing programs only in areas where their products are more likely to be accepted. This not only makes their marketing activities more successful but also greatly reduces marketing expenditures.[12]

Segmenting Business Markets

One of the most basic methods of segmenting business markets involves the four types of markets discussed earlier in the chapter: producer markets, reseller markets, government markets, and institutional markets. Marketers may focus on one or more of these markets because each may have different requirements. However, even within one type of market, marketers will discover that buying firms have unique and varying characteristics. In these cases, further segmentation using additional variables might be needed to further refine the needs and characteristics of business customers. For example, Canon launched a line of wide format printers aimed at CAD and architectural design users, as well as emerging segments such as fine art, photography, office, and signage. Each segment has different uses for wide-format printing as well as different requirements with respect to the types of inks used in the printers.[13] In addition to the types of business markets, firms can also segment business buyers with respect to the following:

- **Type of Organization**   Different types of organizations may require different and specific marketing programs such as product modifications, different distribution and delivery structures, or selling strategies. A glass manufacturer, for example, might segment customers into several groups such as car manufacturers, furniture makers, window manufacturers, or repair and maintenance contractors.

- **Organizational Characteristics**   The needs of business buyers often vary based on their size, geographic location, or product usage. Large buyers often command price discounts and structural relationships that are appropriate for their volume of purchases. Likewise, buyers in different parts of the country, as well as in different nations, may have varying product requirements, specifications, or distribution arrangements. Product usage is also important. Computer manufacturers often segment markets based on how their products will be used. For example, K–12 educational institutions have different requirements for computers and software than do major research universities.

- **Benefits Sought or Buying Processes**   Organizations differ with respect to the benefits that they seek and the buying processes that they use to acquire products. Some business buyers seek only the lowest cost provider, while others require extensive product support and service. Additionally, some businesses buy using highly structured processes, most likely through their buying center. Others may use online auctions or even highly informal processes.

- **Personal and Psychological Characteristics**   The personal characteristics of the buyers themselves often play a role in segmentation decisions. Buyers will vary according to risk tolerance, buying influence, job responsibilities, and decision styles.

- **Relationship Intensity**   Business markets can also be segmented based on the strength and longevity of the relationship with the firm. Many organizations structure their selling organization using this approach with one person or team dedicated to the most critical relationships. Other members of the selling organization may be involved in business development strategies to seek out new customers.

As we have seen, segmentation in business markets concerns itself with many of the same issues found in consumer markets. Despite some differences and additional considerations that must be addressed, the foundation remains the same. Marketers

EXHIBIT 6.6 — BASIC STRATEGIES FOR TARGET MARKET SELECTION

Single Segment Targeting

	M_1	M_2	M_3
P_1		●	
P_2			
P_3			

Selective Targeting

	M_1	M_2	M_3
P_1	●		
P_2			●
P_3		●	

Mass Market Targeting

	M_1	M_2	M_3
P_1	●	●	●
P_2	●	●	●
P_3	●	●	●

Product Specialization

	M_1	M_2	M_3
P_1	●	●	●
P_2			
P_3			

Market Specialization

	M_1	M_2	M_3
P_1		●	
P_2		●	
P_3		●	

P = Product Category; M = Market

must understand the needs of their potential customers and how these needs differ across segments within the total market.

Target–Marketing Strategies

Once the firm has completed segmenting a market, it must then evaluate each segment to determine its attractiveness and whether it offers opportunities that match the firm's capabilities and resources. Remember that just because a market segment meets all criteria for viability does not mean the firm should pursue it. Attractive segments might be dropped for several reasons including a lack of resources, no synergy with the firm's mission, overwhelming competition in the segment, an impending technology shift, or ethical and legal concerns over targeting a particular segment. Based on its analysis of each segment, the firm's current and anticipated situation, and a comprehensive SWOT analysis, a firm might consider five basic strategies for target market selection. Exhibit 6.6 depicts the following strategies.[14]

- **Single Segment Targeting** Firms use single segment targeting when their capabilities are intrinsically tied to the needs of a specific market segment. Many consider the firms using this targeting strategy to be true specialists in a particular product category. Good examples include New Belgium Brewing (craft beer), Porsche, and Ray-Ban. These and other firms using single segment targeting are successful because they fully understand their customers' needs, preferences, and lifestyles. These firms also constantly strive to improve quality and customer satisfaction by continuously refining their products to meet changing customer preferences.

- **Selective Targeting** Firms that have multiple capabilities in many different product categories use selective targeting successfully. This strategy has several advantages including diversification of the firm's risk and the ability to "cherry pick" only the most attractive market segment opportunities. Procter & Gamble (P&G) uses selective targeting to offer customers many different products in the family-care, household-care, and personal-care markets. Besides the familiar deodorants, laundry detergents, and hair-care products, P&G also sells products in the cosmetics, snack-food and beverages, cologne, and prescription-drug markets. One of the keys to P&G's success is that the company does not try to be all things for all customers. The company carefully selects product–market combinations where its capabilities match customers' needs. The company's recent acquisition of Gillette further solidifies P&G's standing in these markets.

- **Mass Market Targeting**   Only the largest firms have the capability to execute mass market targeting, which involves the development of multiple marketing programs to serve all customer segments simultaneously. For example, Coca-Cola offers roughly 400 branded beverages across many segments that fulfill different consumer needs in over 200 countries around the world. Likewise, General Motors manufactures and sells different types of transportation to virtually all consumer and business segments around the world.

- **Product Specialization**   Firms engage in product specialization when their expertise in a product category can be leveraged across many different market segments. These firms can adapt product specifications to match the different needs of individual customer groups. For example, many consider Littmann Stethoscopes, a division of 3M, as the worldwide leader in auscultation technology. Littmann offers high-performance electronic stethoscopes for cardiologists, specially designed stethoscopes for pediatric/infant use, lightweight stethoscopes for simple physical assessment, and a line of stethoscopes for nursing and medical students. The company also offers a line of veterinary stethoscopes.[15]

- **Market Specialization**   Firms engage in market specialization when their intimate knowledge and expertise in one market allows them to offer customized marketing programs that not only deliver needed products but also provide needed solutions to customers' problems. The Follett Corporation is a prime example. Follett specializes in the education market by serving over 110,000 schools, colleges, and universities in over sixty countries around the world. The company's slogan "powering education worldwide" is based on the firm's goal to be the leading provider of educational solutions, services, and products to schools, libraries, colleges, students, and lifelong learners.[16]

In addition to targeting a subset of current customers within the product or market, firms can also take steps to target noncustomers. As we discussed in Chapter 4, there are many reasons why noncustomers do not purchase a firm's products. These reasons can include unique customer needs, better competing alternatives, high switching costs, lack of product awareness, or the existence of long-held assumptions about a product. For example, products associated with tooth whitening were at one time associated only with dentists. Consequently, consumers were hesitant to use these products due to the expense, effort, and anxiety involved. Oral-care companies were able to break this tradition and reach out to noncustomers by developing high-quality, low-price, over-the-counter alternatives that were much easier to purchase. Today, these at-home tooth-whitening products— such as Colgate's Simply White and P&G's Crest Whitestrips— are a $300 million market in the United States.[17]

As this example illustrates, the key to targeting noncustomers lies in understanding the reasons that they do not buy and then finding ways to remove these obstacles. Removing obstacles to purchase, whether they exist in product design, affordability, distribution convenience, or product awareness, is a major strategic issue in developing an effective marketing program. Over the next four chapters, we turn our attention to the important strategic issues involved in creating this marketing program by examining product, pricing, distribution/supply chain, and integrated marketing communications strategies.

Lessons from Chapter 6

Buyer behavior in consumer markets

- is often irrational and unpredictable because consumers often say one thing but do another.

- can progress through five stages: need recognition, information search, evaluation of alternatives, the purchase decision, and postpurchase evaluation.

- does not always follow these stages in sequence and may even skip stages en route to the purchase.

- may be characterized by loyalty where consumers simply purchase the same product that they bought last time.

- often involves a parallel sequence of activities associated with finding the most suitable merchant. That is, while consumers consider which product to buy, they also consider where they might buy it.

- may occur with only one merchant for a particular product category if the consumer is fiercely loyal to that merchant.

Keys to understanding consumer needs and wants are the following:

- Defining needs as "necessities" has limitations because everyone has a different perspective on what constitutes a need.

- Needs occur when a consumer's current level of satisfaction does not equal the desired level of satisfaction.

- Wants are a consumer's desire for a specific product that will satisfy a need.

- The firm must always understand the basic needs fulfilled by its products. This understanding allows the firm to segment markets and create marketing programs that can translate consumer needs into wants for their specific products.

- Although some products and markets can be segmented on the basis of needs alone, most product categories are marketed on the basis of wants, not need fulfillment.

- Wants are not the same thing as demand; demand occurs only when the consumer's ability and willingness to pay backs up a want for a specific product.

The information search stage of the consumer buying process

- can be passive—where the consumer becomes more attentive and receptive to information—or active—where the consumer engages in a more aggressive information search by seeking additional information.

- depends on a number of issues including the degree of risk involved in the purchase, the amount of expertise or experience the consumer has with the product category, and the actual cost of the search in terms of time and money.

- culminates in an evoked set of suitable buying alternatives.

During the evaluation of alternatives

- consumers essentially translate their needs into wants for specific products or brands.

- consumers evaluate products as bundles of attributes that have varying abilities to satisfy their needs.

- the priority of each consumer's choice criteria can change.

- marketers must ensure that their product is in the evoked set of potential alternatives by constantly reminding consumers of their company and its product offerings.

During the purchase stage of the buying process

- it is important to remember that the intention to purchase and the actual act of buying are distinct concepts.

- the key issues for marketers are product availability and possession utility.

During postpurchase evaluation

- the outcome of the buying process is linked to the development of long-term customer relationships. Marketers must closely follow customers' responses to monitor the product's performance and its ability to meet customers' expectations.

- consumers will experience one of four potential outcomes: delight, satisfaction, dissatisfaction, or cognitive dissonance.

Overall, the consumer buying process can be affected by

- the complexity of the purchase and decision-making process.

- individual factors such as age, life cycle, occupation, socioeconomic status, perceptions, motives, interests, attitudes, opinions, and lifestyles.

- social influences such as culture, subculture, social class, family, reference groups, and opinion leaders.

- situational influences such as physical and spatial influences, social and inter-personal influences, time, purchase task or usage, and the consumer's disposition.

Business markets

- purchase products for use in their operations, such as acquiring raw materials to produce finished goods or buying office supplies or leasing cars.

- consist of four types of buyers: producer markets, reseller markets, government markets, and institutional markets.

- possess four unique characteristics not typically found in consumer markets:

  - The buying center: Economic buyers, technical buyers, and users comprise this element.
  - Hard and soft costs: Soft costs (downtime, opportunity costs, or human resource costs) are just as important as hard costs (monetary price or purchase costs).
  - Reciprocity: Business buyers and sellers often buy products from each other.
  - Mutual dependence: Sole-source or limited-source buying makes both buying and selling firms mutually dependent.

The business buying process

- follows a well-defined sequence of stages including: (1) problem recognition, (2) development of product specifications, (3) vendor identification and qualification, (4) solicitation of proposals or bids, (5) vendor selection, (6) order processing, and (7) vendor performance review.

- can be affected by a number of factors, including environmental conditions, organizational factors, and interpersonal and individual factors.

Market segmentation

- is the process of dividing the total market for a particular product or product category into relatively homogeneous segments or groups.

- should create groups where the members are similar to one another but where the groups are dissimilar from one another.

- involves a fundamental decision of whether to segment at all.

- typically allows firms to be more successful due to the fact that they can tailor products to meet the needs or requirements of a particular market segment.

Traditional market segmentation approaches

- have been used successfully for decades, are not out of date, and are used by many of today's most successful firms.

- are sometimes used in combination with newer approaches by the same firm, depending on the brand or product or market in question.

Mass marketing

- involves no segmentation whatsoever because it is aimed at the total (whole) market for a particular product.

- is an undifferentiated approach that assumes that all customers in the market have similar needs and wants that can be reasonably satisfied with a single marketing program.

- works best when the needs of an entire market are relatively homogeneous.

- is advantageous in terms of production efficiency and lower marketing costs.

- is inherently risky because a standardized product is vulnerable to competitors that offer specialized products that better match customers' needs.

Differentiated marketing

- involves dividing the total market into groups of customers having relatively common or homogeneous needs and attempting to develop a marketing program that appeals to one or more of these groups.

- may be necessary when customer needs are similar within a single group but their needs differ across groups.

- involves two options: the multisegment approach and the market concentration approach.

Niche marketing

- involves focusing marketing efforts on one small, well-defined market segment or niche that has a unique, specific set of needs.

- requires that firms understand and meet the needs of target customers so completely that, despite the small size of the niche, the firm's substantial share makes the segment highly profitable.

Individualized segmentation approaches

- have become viable due to advances in technology, particularly communication technology and the Internet.

- are possible because organizations now have the ability to track customers with a high degree of specificity.

- allow firms to combine demographic data with past and current purchasing behavior so that they can tweak their marketing programs in ways that allow them to precisely match customers' needs, wants, and preferences.

- will become even more important in the future because their focus on individual customers makes them critical to the development and maintenance of long-term relationships.

- can be prohibitively expensive to deliver.

- depend on two important considerations: automated delivery of the marketing program and personalization.

One-to-one marketing

- involves the creation of an entirely unique product or marketing program for each customer in the target segment.

- is common in business markets where unique programs and/or systems are designed for each customer.

- is growing rapidly in consumer markets, particularly in luxury and custom-made products, as well as in services and electronic commerce.

Mass customization

- refers to providing unique products and solutions to individual customers on a mass scale.

- is now cost effective and practical due to advances in supply chain management including real-time inventory control.

- is used often in business markets, especially in electronic procurement systems.

Permission marketing

- is different from one-to-one marketing because customers choose to become a member of the firm's target market.

- is commonly executed via the opt-in e-mail list where customers permit a firm to send periodic e-mail about goods and services that they have an interest in purchasing.

- has a major advantage in that customers who opt-in are already interested in the goods and services offered by the firm.

- allows a firm to precisely target individuals, thereby eliminating the problem of wasted marketing effort and expense.

Successful segmentation

- requires that market segments fulfill five related criteria; segments must be identifiable and measurable, substantial, accessible, responsive, and viable and sustainable.

- involves avoiding ethically and legally sensitive segments that are profitable but not viable in a business sense.

- involves avoiding potentially viable segments that do not match the firm's expertise or mission.

Identifying market segments

- involves selecting the most relevant variables to identify and define the target market, many of which come from the situation analysis section of the marketing plan.

- involves the isolation of individual characteristics that distinguish one or more segments from the total market. These segments must have relatively homogeneous needs.

- in consumer markets involves the examination of factors that fall into one of four general categories:

  - Behavioral segmentation, the most powerful approach because it uses actual consumer behavior or product usage helps make distinctions among market segments

  - Demographic segmentation, which divides markets using factors such as gender, age, income, and education

  - Psychographic segmentation, which deals with state-of-mind issues such as motives, attitudes, opinions, values, lifestyles, interests, and personality

  - Geographic segmentation, which is often most useful when combined with other segmentation variables

- in business markets is often based on type of market (producer, reseller, government, and institutional) or on other characteristics such as type of organization, organizational characteristics, benefits sought or buying processes, personal or psychological characteristics, or relationship intensity.

Target marketing strategies

- are based on an evaluation of the attractiveness of each segment and whether each offers opportunities that match the firm's capabilities and resources.

- include single segment targeting, selective targeting, mass market targeting, product specialization, and market specialization.

- should also consider issues related to noncustomers such as reasons why they do not buy and finding ways to remove obstacles to purchase.

Questions for Discussion

1. Many people criticize marketing as being manipulative based on the argument that marketing activities create needs where none previously existed. Marketers of SUVs, tobacco products, diet programs, exercise equipment, and luxury products are typically the most criticized. Given what you now know about the differences between needs and wants, do you agree with these critics? Explain.

2. Many consumers and consumer advocates are critical of individualized segmentation approaches due to personal privacy concerns. They argue that technology has made it far too easy to track buyer behavior and personal information. Marketers counter that individualized segmentation can lead to privacy abuses but that the benefits to both consumers and marketers far outweigh the risks. Where do you stand on this issue? What are the benefits and risks associated with individualized segmentation?

3. As we have seen thus far, the size of the consuming population over the age of 50 years continues to grow. What are some of the current ethical issues involved in targeting this age group? As this group gets older, will these issues become more or less important? Explain.

Exercises

1. Consider the last purchase you made in these categories: personal electronics, clothing, and vacation destination. To what extent was your purchase decision influenced by decision-making complexity, individual influences, social influences, and situational influences? What specific issues were the most influential in making the decision? How could a marketer have swayed your decision in each case?

2. One of the most exciting advances in market segmentation is the increasing use of geographic information systems (GIS) to map target markets. Go to http://www.gis.com and get a feel for the use of GIS in business and other fields. Then, enter your ZIP code into "ZIP Code Fast Facts" to learn more about where you live. What are the advantages of using GIS in market segmentation?

3. As discussed in the chapter, VALS is one of the most popular proprietary segmentation tools used in marketing segmentation. Go to the SRI Consulting website (http://www.sric-bi.com/VALS/presurvey.shtml) and take the free VALS survey. Do you agree with the survey results? Why or why not?

7 Product Strategy

Introduction

O f all the strategic decisions to be made in the marketing plan, the design, development, branding, and positioning of the product are perhaps the most critical. At the heart of every organization lie one or more products that define what the organization does and why it exists. As we stated in Chapter 1, the term *product* refers to something that buyers can acquire via exchange to satisfy a need or a want. This is a very broad definition that allows us to classify many different things as products—for example, food, entertainment, information, people, places, and ideas. An important strategic fact about products is that they are not created and sold as individual elements; rather, products are developed and sold as offerings. An organization's product offering is typically composed of many different elements—usually some combination of tangible goods, services, ideas, image, or even people. As Beyond the Pages 7.1 illustrates, individuals who purchase a Steinway piano buy much more than a musical instrument. They also get exceptional craftsmanship, unparalleled customer service, a highly prestigious brand name, and over 150 years of technical innovation.

Given the complex makeup of most products, we prefer to discuss products as offerings, or the bundle of physical (tangible), service (intangible), and symbolic (perceptual) attributes designed to satisfy customers' needs and wants. Good product strategy focuses on all elements of the product offering rather than on only on a single element. We have noted throughout this text how most firms today compete in rather mature markets characterized by commoditization. In these cases, the core product (the element that satisfies the basic customer need) typically becomes incapable of differentiating the product offering from those of the competition. Consequently, most organizations strive to enhance the service and symbolic elements of their product offerings. Note that this means focusing primarily on the intangible aspects of a product, not on its tangible or physical elements. This makes product strategy even more challenging for the firm. It also requires product strategy to be fully integrated with pricing, distribution, and promotion because these components of the marketing program add value to the product offering.

Beyond the Pages 7.1

STEINWAY: MORE THAN A PIANO[1]

One of the most dominant strengths any firm can possess occurs when the firm enjoys an image of superior quality that is backed by patent protection. Such is the case for Steinway and Sons, makers of the world's finest pianos. For over 150 years, Steinway's art and craftsmanship have made it the world's most renowned brand for high-end, "concert hall quality" pianos. In fact, virtually every top pianist in the world performs on a Steinway.

The company holds 120 technical patents and innovations that distinguish its pianos from all others. Each piano made in the Astoria, New York, factory takes 9 to 12 months to complete and is hand assembled from 12,000 parts— most of them also made by hand. Despite this artistry, Steinway is not a large company. It sells roughly $165 million in pianos each year— a number dwarfed by other firms in the industry. Steinway, however, does not define success in terms of numbers but in its reputation. Steinway is the piano of choice for concert halls, composers, professional musicians, and wealthy customers. Although the company accounts for only two percent of piano sales in the United States, it earns 35 percent of the industry's profit. Customers enjoy the quality, beauty, and reputation of a Steinway piano and don't mind paying the $40,000 to $100,000 price tag. In fact, many argue that a Steinway is more akin to a work of art than a musical instrument. The advantages earned from this type of reputation and customer loyalty are hard to beat.

However, Steinway's stellar image and reputation presented a problem for the company at one point in its history. Although Steinway dominated the upper end of the piano market, the company did not compete in the rapidly growing and much larger entry-level and mid-level piano markets. These markets were dominated by Asian brands such as Yamaha and Kawai— good names in their own right but not in the same league as Steinway. Piano dealers were forced to stock these brands alongside Steinways in order to meet the needs of other customer segments. The challenge for Steinway was to find a way to compete in these markets without damaging the brand equity in the Steinway name.

The company's solution involved the launch of two new brands: "Boston, designed by Steinway" for the mid-level market and "Essex, designed by Steinway" for the entry-level market. Both the Boston and the Essex are manufactured in Japan and sold through exclusive channels. The decision to launch these new brands was agonizing for Steinway's management. The company's CEO, Bruce Stevens, once said, "There is no such thing as a cheaper Steinway." With that in mind, the launch of the Boston and Essex represented a real risk for the company.

Reflecting on the company's success, Stevens argues that the only way to maintain brand equity, especially with a name like Steinway, is to take a long-term view and move very slowly. This is the company's strategy with its most recent move into Asian markets— the home turf of Steinway's less expensive rivals. The company opened a Shanghai operation in 2004 and now earns 35 percent of its business from outside the United States. Steinway also raises its prices three to four percent each year— another long-term strategy aimed at maintaining brand equity. Stevens argues that you cannot put a discounted price on the passion associated with a worldwide icon like Steinway.

As we consider product decisions in this chapter, it is important to remember that product offerings in and of themselves have little value to customers. Rather, an offering's real value comes from its ability to deliver benefits that enhance a customer's situation or solve a customer's problems. For example, customers don't buy pest control; they buy a bug-free environment. Lexus customers don't buy a car; they buy luxury, status, comfort, and social appeal. Students who frequent a local nightclub are not thirsty; they want to fulfill their need for social interaction. Likewise, companies do not need computers; they need to store, retrieve, distribute, network, and analyze data and information. Marketers who keep their sights set on developing product offerings that truly meet the needs of the target market are more likely to be successful.

The Product Portfolio

Products fall into two general categories. Products used for personal use and enjoyment are called *consumer products*, and those purchased for resale, to make other products, or for use in a firm's operations are called *business products*. Exhibit 7.1 illustrates examples of each type of product category. Although the distinction may seem simplistic, it is important in a strategic sense because the type of product in question can influence its pricing, distribution, or promotion. For example, marketing strategy for consumer convenience products must maximize availability and ease of purchase—both important distribution considerations. The strategy associated with consumer shopping products often focuses more on differentiation through image and symbolic attributes—both important branding and promotion issues. Marketing strategies for raw materials are especially challenging because these products are commodities by definition. Here, conformance to exacting product specifications and low acquisition costs are the keys to effective strategy. Many business products are also characterized by derived demand where the demand for the product is derived from or dependent upon the demand for other business or consumer products. For example, the demand for business products such as glass, steel, rubber, chrome, leather, and carpeting depends on the demand for automobiles.

It is very rare for a company to sell only one product. Most firms sell a variety of products to fulfill a variety of different needs. In general terms, the products sold by a firm can be described with respect to product lines and product mixes. A *product line* consists of a group of closely related product items. As shown in Exhibit 7.2, Procter & Gamble (P&G) sells a number of famous brands in its line of house and home products, including Tide, Bounty, Pringles, and Folgers. Most companies sell a variety of different product lines. The different product lines at General Motors carry well-known brand names like Corvette, Chevrolet, Cadillac, and Pontiac. Likewise, Federal Express (FedEx) offers a number of logistics and supply chain services in its family of brands, such as FedEx Express, FedEx Ground, and FedEx Freight. A firm's *product mix,* or *portfolio.* is the total group of products offered by the company. For example, P&G's entire product portfolio consists of personal and beauty products, health and wellness products, baby and family products, and pet nutrition and care products in addition to the products in its house and home line.

Decisions regarding product lines and product mixes are important strategic considerations for most firms. One of these important decisions is the number of product lines to offer, referred to as the *width,* or *variety,* of the product mix. By offering a wide variety of product lines, the firm can diversify its risk across a portfolio of product offerings. Also, a wide product mix can be used to capitalize on the strength and reputation of the firm. Sony, for example, enjoys this advantage because it uses its name to stake out a strong position in electronics, music, and movies. The second important decision involves the depth of each product line. Sometimes called

EXHIBIT 7.1	TYPES OF CONSUMER AND BUSINESS PRODUCTS	
	Type of Product	**Examples**
Consumer Products	**Convenience Products** Inexpensive, routinely purchased products that consumers spend little time and effort in acquiring.	Soft drinks Candy and gum Gasoline Dry cleaning
	Shopping Products Products that consumers will spend time and effort to obtain. Consumers shop different options to compare prices, features, and service.	Appliances Furniture Clothing Vacations
	Specialty Products Unique, one-of-a-kind products that consumers will spend considerable time, effort, and money to acquire.	Sports memorabilia Antiques Plastic surgery Luxury items
	Unsought Products Products that consumers are unaware of or a product that consumers do not consider purchasing until a need arises.	True innovations Repair services Emergency medicine Insurance
Business Products	**Raw Materials** Basic natural materials that become part of a finished product. They are purchased in very large quantities based on specifications or grades.	Iron ore Chemicals Agricultural products Wood pulp
	Component Parts Finished items that become part of a larger finished product. They are purchased based on specifications or industry standards.	Spark plugs Computer chips Pane glass Hard drives
	Process Materials Finished products that become unidentifiable upon their inclusion in the finished product.	Food additives Wood sealants Paint colorings
	Maintenance, Repair, and Operating Products Products that are used in business processes or operations but do not become part of the finished product.	Office supplies Janitorial services Building security Bathroom supplies
	Accessory Equipment Products that help facilitate production or operations but do not become part of the finished product.	Tools Office equipment Computers Furniture
	Installations Major purchases, typically of a physical nature, that are based on customized solutions including installation/construction, training, financing, maintenance, and repair.	Enterprise software Buildings Heat and air systems
	Business Services Intangible products that support business operations. These purchases often occur as a part of outsourcing decisions.	Legal services Accounting services Consulting Research services

Source: This material is adapted from William M. Pride and O. C. Ferrell, *Foundations of Marketing* (Boston: Houghton Mifflin, 2004), 210–211.

EXHIBIT 7.2	PROCTER & GAMBLE'S PORTFOLIO OF HOUSE AND HOME PRODUCTS					
	Product Mix Width (Variety)					
	Dish Care	Household Cleaners	Batteries	Laundry	Paper Products	Snacks and Beverages
Product Mix Depth (Assortment)	Dawn	Swiffer	Duracell	Tide	Charmin	Pringles
	Joy	Mr. Clean		Cheer	Bounty	Millstone
	Cascade	Mr. Clean Autodry		Bounce	Puffs	Folgers
	Ivory	Bounty		Gain		Home Cafe
		Febreze ScentStories		Downy		
		Febreze Noticeables		Dreft		
				Era		
				Febreze		
				Ivory		

Source: Taken from the Procter & Gamble website (http://www.pg.com/en_US/products/all_products/index.jhtml).

assortment, product line depth is an important marketing tool. Firms can attract a wide range of customers and market segments by offering a deep assortment of products in a specific line. Each brand or product in the assortment can be used to fulfill different customer needs. For example, Hilton, Inc. offers eight different lodging brands—including Hilton, Hilton Garden Inn, Hampton Inn, Conrad, and Embassy Suites—that cater to different segments of the hospitality market.

Although offering a large portfolio of products can make the coordination of marketing activities more challenging and expensive, it also creates a number of important benefits:[2]

- **Economies of Scale**   Offering many different product lines can create economies of scale in production, bulk buying, and promotion. Many firms advertise using an umbrella theme for all products in the line. Nike's "Just Do It" and Maxwell House's "Good to the Last Drop" are examples of this. The single theme covering the entire product line saves considerably on promotional expenses.

- **Package Uniformity**   When all packages in a product line have the same look and feel, customers can locate the firm's products more quickly. It also becomes easier for the firm to coordinate and integrate promotion and distribution. For example, Duracell batteries all have the same copper look with black and copper packaging. All of Apple's iPods are packaged in black boxes made of high-quality materials.

- **Standardization**   Product lines often use the same component parts. For example, Toyota's Camry and Highlander use many of the same chassis and engine components. This greatly reduces Toyota's manufacturing and inventory-handling costs.

- **Sales and Distribution Efficiency**   When a firm offers many different product lines, sales personnel can offer a full range of choices and options to customers. For the same reason, channel intermediaries are more accepting of a product line than they are of individual products.

- **Equivalent Quality Beliefs** Customers typically expect and believe that all products in a product line are about equal in terms of quality and performance. This is a major advantage for a firm that offers a well-known and respected line of products. For example, Crest's portfolio of oral-care products enjoy the same reputation for high quality.

A firm's product portfolio must be carefully managed to reflect changes in customers' preferences and the introduction of competitive products. Product offerings may be modified to change one or more characteristics that enhance quality, style, or lower the product's price. Firms may introduce product line extensions that allow it to compete more broadly in an industry. The recent trend of flavored soft drinks, such as Vanilla Coke, Vanilla Pepsi, Sprite Remix, and Cherry Vanilla Dr. Pepper, is a good example of this. Sometimes, a firm may decide that a product or product line has become obsolete or is just not competitive against other products. When this happens, the firm can decide to contract the product line, as GM did when it decided to drop the Pontiac TransAm, the Chevrolet Camaro, and the Hummer H1 from its portfolio.

The Challenges of Service Products

It is important to remember that products can be intangible services and ideas as well as tangible goods. Service firms such as airlines, hospitals, movie theaters, and hair stylists, as well as nonprofit organizations, charitable causes, and government agencies, all develop and implement marketing strategies designed to match their portfolio of intangible products to the needs of target markets. In this section, we look at some of the key issues in developing product strategy for services.

Products lie on a continuum ranging from tangible-dominant goods (for example, salt and soap) to intangible-dominant services (for example, education and consulting). Firms lying closer to the intangible end of this spectrum face unique challenges in developing marketing strategy. These challenges are the direct result of the unique characteristics of services as shown in Exhibit 7.3. Obviously, the primary difference between a good and a service is that a service is intangible. Some services, such as business consulting and education, are almost completely intangible, whereas others have more tangible elements. The services provided by United Parcel Service (UPS) and FedEx, for example, include tangible airplanes, trucks, boxes, and air bills. Another challenging characteristic of services is that they cannot be stored for future use. This lack of inventory means that service firms experience major problems in balancing service supply (capacity) and service demand. Likewise, the demand for services is extremely time-and-place dependent because customers must typically be present for service to be delivered. Consider the issues faced by popular restaurants every Friday and Saturday night. The increased demand forces restaurant managers to preschedule the right amount of food ingredients and number of employees to accommodate the increase in guests. And, given that the restaurant's capacity is fixed, the manager and employees must serve guests efficiently and effectively in a crowded,

EXHIBIT 7.3   **UNIQUE CHARACTERISTICS OF SERVICES AND RESULTING MARKETING CHALLENGES**

Service Characteristics	Marketing Challenges
Intangibility	It is difficult for customers to evaluate quality, especially before purchase and consumption.
	It is difficult to convey service characteristics and benefits in promotion. As a result, the firm is forced to sell a promise.
	Many services have few standardized units of measurement. Therefore, service prices are difficult to set and justify.
	Customers cannot take possession of a service.
Simultaneous Production and Consumption	Customers or their possessions must be present during service delivery.
	Other customers can affect service outcomes including service quality and customer satisfaction.
	Service employees are critical because they must interact with customers to deliver service.
	Converting high-contact services to low-contact services will lower costs but may reduce service quality.
	Services are often difficult to distribute.
Perishability	Services cannot be inventoried for later use. Therefore, unused service capacity is lost forever.
	Service demand is very time-and-place sensitive. As a result, it is difficult to balance supply and demand, especially during periods of peak demand.
	Service facilities and equipment sit idle during periods of off-peak demand.
Heterogeneity	Service quality varies across people, time, and place, making it very difficult to deliver good service consistently.
	There are limited opportunities to standardize service delivery.
	Many services are customizable by nature. However, customization can dramatically increase the costs of providing the service.
Client-Based Relationships	Most services live or die by maintaining a satisfied clientele over the long term.
	Generating repeat business is crucial for the service firm's success.

noisy atmosphere. This precarious balance is common across most industries in the services sector of our economy.

Because of the intangibility of service, it is difficult for customers to evaluate a service before they actually purchase and consume it. Third-party evaluations and recommendations for services are not as prevalent as they are with respect to tangible goods. Of course, customers can ask friends and family for recommendations, but in many cases a good assessment of quality is hard to obtain. This forces customers to place some degree of trust in the service provider to perform the service correctly and in the time frame promised or anticipated. One way that companies can address this issue is by providing satisfaction guarantees to customers. For example, Hampton Inn, a national chain of mid-priced hotels, offers guests a free night if they are not 100 percent satisfied with their stay.[3] Midas, H&R Block, and FedEx offer similar guarantees.

Moreover, because most services depend on people (for example, employees and customers) for their delivery, they are susceptible to variations in quality and inconsistency. Such variations can occur from one organization to another, from one outlet to another within the same organization, from one service to another within the same outlet, and even from one employee to another within the same outlet. Service quality can further vary from week to week, day to day, or even hour to hour. Also, because service quality is a subjective phenomenon, it can also vary from customer to customer and for the same customer from one visit to the next. As a result, standardization and service quality are very difficult to control. The lack of standardization, however, actually gives service firms one advantage: Services can be customized to match the specific needs of any customer. Such customized services are frequently very expensive for both the firm and its customers. This creates a dilemma: How does a service firm provide efficient, standardized service at an acceptable level of quality while simultaneously treating every customer as a unique person? This dilemma is especially prevalent in the health-care industry today where care is managed to carefully control both access and cost.

Another major challenge for service marketers is to tie services directly to customers' needs. Although customers typically have few problems in expressing needs for tangible goods, they often have difficulty in expressing or explaining needs for services. In some cases, the need is vague. For example, you may decide that you need a relaxing vacation, but how do you know which services will best meet your need? Which is best for relaxation: a trip to the beach, a cruise, or a stay at a bed-and-breakfast inn? The answer depends on how you personally define *relaxing*. Because different customers have different definitions, the vacation provider has a more difficult job in connecting its service offerings to customers' needs. In other cases, customers may not understand the need for a specific service. For example, business consultants, insurance agents, financial planners, and wedding consultants often have to educate customers on why their services are needed. This is a necessary first hurdle to overcome before these service providers can offer their products as the solution that will best fulfill the need.

New Product Development

One of the key issues in product strategy deals with the introduction of new products. The development and commercialization of new products is a vital part of a firm's efforts to sustain growth and profits over time. The success of new products depends on the product's fit with the firm's strengths and a defined market opportunity. Market characteristics and the competitive situation will also affect the sales potential of new products. For example, despite the growing popularity of electronic books, the format has never really made it to the mainstream. One reason is the lack of suitable technology to make e-books as portable and convenient as traditional paper books. Sony's Reader (a handheld e-book reader) was launched in an effort to resolve this issue. Other technological advances, such as e-paper, are expected in the future. However, the fact that most people prefer paper books is a daunting market characteristic to overcome.

Many firms base their new product introductions on key themes such as product or technological superiority. New product introductions in the electronics, computer, and automotive industries often take this approach. In other firms and industries, new product introductions may stem from only minor tweaking of current products. This approach is common in packaged goods and household items. Truthfully, what is considered to be a new product depends on the point of view of both the firm and its customers. Although some product introductions are actually new, others may only be *perceived* as being new. There are six strategic options related to the newness of products. These options follow, in decreasing degrees of product change:

- **New-to-the-World Products: Discontinuous Innovations**   These products involve a pioneering effort by a firm that eventually leads to the creation of an entirely new market. New-to-the-world products are typically the result of radical thinking by individual inventors or entrepreneurs. For example, Fred Smith's idea for an overnight package delivery service gave us FedEx.

- **New Product Lines**   These products represent new offerings by the firm, but the firm introduces them into established markets. Gateway Computer's move to offer flat-panel televisions and small consumer electronics is an example. New product lines are not as risky as true innovation, and they allow the firm to diversify into closely related product categories.

- **Product Line Extensions**   These products supplement an existing product line with new styles, models, features, or flavors. Anheuser-Busch's introduction of Budweiser Select and Honda's launch of the Civic Hybrid are good examples. Product line extensions allow the firm to keep its products fresh and exciting with minimal development costs and risk of market failure.

- **Improvements or Revisions of Existing Products**   These products offer customers improved performance or greater perceived value. The common "new and improved" strategy used in packaged goods and the yearly design changes in the automobile industry are good examples. Clorox, for example, spiced up sales after adding lemon and floral scents to its perennial bleach product. The common "shampoo plus conditioner" formulas of many shampoos are another example.

- **Repositioning**   This strategy involves targeting existing products at new markets or segments. Repositioning can involve real or perceived changes to a product. An example is Carnival Cruise Line's effort to attract senior citizens to supplement its younger crowd. Likewise, the advent of global positioning technology allows wireless phone manufacturers to promote the safety and security features of their products.

- **Cost Reductions**   This strategy involves modifying products to offer performance similar to competing products at a lower price. Book publishers use this strategy when they convert hardback books to paperbacks. Similarly, a firm may be able to lower a product's price due to improved manufacturing efficiency or a drop in the price of raw materials. All computer manufacturers offer lower-priced products that use standard or slightly dated technology. In fact, computer maker eMachines (now owned by Gateway) was actually founded on this cost-reduction strategy.

The first two options are the most effective and profitable when the firm wants to significantly differentiate its product offering from competitors. The consulting firm of Booz Allen Hamilton found that 30 percent of the product introductions that it studied were innovations or new product lines, and 60 percent of the profitable product changes were of this type.[4] Despite this, there are often good reasons to pursue one of the remaining four options, particularly if resource constraints are an issue or if the firm's management does not want to expose the firm to increased market risk.

A firm's ability to develop new products successfully will hinge on many internal and external factors. However, despite any favorable or unfavorable conditions, the key to new product success is to create a differential advantage for the new product. What unique benefit does the new product offer to customers? Although this benefit can be based on real differences or based entirely on image, it is the customers' *perception* of differentiation that is critical. For example, the razor wars have turned into a game of one-upmanship between P&G's Fusion and Schick's Quattro. At issue is whether the Fusion's five-blade design is truly better than Quattro's four blades (or P&G's Mach three razor) and whether the battery-powered version of each razor really produces better results. Despite *Consumer Reports* tests that battery-powered razors do not provide a closer shave, many consumers believe that they do. In the battle for supremacy in the razor market, customer perceptions are often all that matter.

Customer perceptions are also critical in the process of developing new products. Although the new product development process varies across firms, most firms will go through the following stages:

- **Idea Generation**   New product ideas can be obtained from a number of sources including customers, employees, basic research, competitors, and supply chain partners.

- **Screening and Evaluation**   New product ideas are screened for their match with the firm's capabilities and the degree to which they meet customers' needs and wants. In some cases, prototype products are developed to further test the commercial viability of a product concept. New product concepts are also evaluated with respect to projected costs, revenues, and profit potential.

- **Development**   At this stage, product specifications are set, the product design is finalized, and initial production begins. In addition, the full marketing plan is developed in order to acquire the resources and collaboration needed for a full-scale launch.

- **Test Marketing**   As a final test before launch, the new product is test-marketed in either real or simulated situations to determine its performance relative to customer needs and competing products.

- **Commercialization**   In this final stage, the product is launched with a complete marketing program designed to stimulate customer awareness and acceptance of the new product.

Many firms look to customers for new product ideas. For example, Sirius developed its S50 portable satellite-radio player by shadowing forty-five customers for 4 weeks. Sirius was interested in how these customers listened to music, watched TV, and perused magazines. Because Sirius did its homework, the S50 was a huge success. It proved to be not only more popular than a similar device from rival XM but also led to a large increase in the number of Sirius subscribers.[5] Sirius' success in developing the S50 highlights the importance of taking a proactive stance toward new product development. Truly innovative companies see product development as a continuous effort guided by the ongoing collection of data on emerging market opportunities. As we noted in Chapter 5, many of the world's most powerful brands—like Apple, Microsoft, Toyota, and Nokia—are well known for their continuous efforts at product innovation.

Branding Strategy

One of the most important product decisions that marketers must make relates to branding. A *brand* is a combination of name, symbol, term, or design that identifies a specific product. Brands have two parts: the brand name and the brand mark. The brand name is the part of a brand that can be spoken, including words, letters, and numbers (for example, Honda, 7-Eleven, WD-40, GMC, and BankOne). The brand mark—which includes symbols, figures, or a design—is the part of a brand that cannot be spoken. Good brand marks, like McDonald's golden arches, Nike's swoosh, and Prudential's rock, effectively communicate the brand and its image without using spoken words. Brand marks are also useful in advertising and product placement such as when college football broadcasts clearly depict the Nike logo on the clothing and uniforms of both coaches and players.

Although these technical aspects of branding are important, branding strategy involves much more than developing a clever brand name or unique brand mark. To be truly effective, a brand should succinctly capture the product offering in a way that answers a question in the customer's mind.[6] Good brands are those that immediately come to mind when a customer has a problem to be solved or a need to be fulfilled. Consider these questions that might be asked by a customer:

- Where can I find information quickly?

- Where can I get a quick meal and make my kids happy?

- Where can I buy everything I need, all at decent prices?

- Where can I get the best deal on car insurance?

- How do I find a value-priced hotel in Manhattan?

How do you answer these questions? How many customers do you think would give the following answers: Google, McDonald's, Wal-Mart, GEICO, Expedia.com? To successfully develop a brand, the firm should position the product offering (which includes all tangible, intangible, and symbolic elements) as the answer to questions like these. Customers tend to buy products whose combination of attributes is the best solution to their problems.

Strategic Issues in Branding Strategy

The key advantages associated with branding, as shown in Exhibit 7.4, make branding decisions one of the most important pieces in the development of marketing strategy. Branding offers advantages to both firms and customers. For one, branding makes the customer buying process much more efficient because customers can locate and

EXHIBIT 7.4 **ADVANTAGES OF BRANDING**

Overall Advantages of Branding

Product Identification	Customers can easily identify the brands they like
Comparison Shopping	Assists customers in comparing and evaluating competing products
Shopping Efficiency	Speeds up the buying process and makes repeat purchases easier by reducing search time and effort
Risk Reduction	Allows customers to buy a known quantity, thereby reducing the risk of purchase
Product Acceptance	New products under a known brand name are accepted and adopted more easily
Enhanced Self-Image	Brands convey status, image, or prestige
Enhanced Product Loyalty	Branding increases psychosocial identification with the product

Unique Advantages of Selling Manufacturer (Name) Brands

Reduced Costs	Heavy promotion by the manufacturer reduces the marketing costs of the merchant that carries the brand
Built-In Loyalty	Manufacturer brands come with their own cadre of loyal customers
Enhanced Image	The image and prestige of the merchant are enhanced
Lower Inventory	Manufacturers are capable of time-certain delivery, which allows the merchant to carry less inventory and reduce inventory costs
Less Risk	Poor quality or product failures become attributed to the manufacturer rather than the merchant

Unique Advantages of Selling Private-Label (Store) Brands

Increased Profit	The merchant maintains a higher margin on its own brands and faces less pressure to cut prices to match the competition
Less Competition	Where manufacturer brands are carried by many different merchants, private-label brands are exclusive to the merchant that sells them
Total Control	The merchant has total control over the development, pricing, distribution, and promotion of the brand
Merchant Loyalty	Customers who are loyal to a private-label brand are automatically loyal to the merchant

purchase products more easily than without branding. In this section, we examine some of the key strategic issues to be considered in branding strategy.

Manufacturer Versus Private-Label Brands The distinction between manufacturer brands and private-label brands (brands owned by the merchants that sell them) is an important issue in distribution and supply chain decisions related to branding. Private-label brands, sometimes called store brands, range from well-known products like Gap clothing and Craftsman tools to other products such as Wal-Mart's Ol' Roy dog food, Equate aspirin, or Sam's Choice soft drinks. Strategically, the choices to sell, carry, or distribute manufacturer brands or private-label brands are not either-or decisions. As Exhibit 7.4 illustrates, both types of brands have key advantages. For that reason, many distributors, wholesalers, and retailers carry both types of brands. Due to the increased profit margins associated with private-label brands, many retailers have moved aggressively to increase the number of private brands that they carry. J.C. Penney, for example, recently launched a.n.a.—a line of women's trendy clothing that is the company's largest private-brand initiative to date. Roughly 40 percent of

Penney's sales come from private-label brands, more than any other department store. Seven of its brands—including Arizona, Worthington, and St. John's Bay—individually sell over $1 billion each year.[7] In addition to the advantages of private-label brands, retailers carry manufacturer brands because customers expect to find them in stores. Hence, manufacturer brands are important in driving customer traffic. They also give customers confidence that they are buying a widely known brand from a respected company.

Brand Loyalty   *Brand loyalty* is a positive attitude toward a brand that causes customers to have a consistent preference for that brand over all other competing brands in a product category. There are three degrees of brand loyalty: brand recognition, brand preference, and brand insistence. *Brand recognition* exists when a customer knows about the brand and is considering it as one of several alternatives in the evoked set. This is the lowest form of brand loyalty and exists mainly due to the awareness of the brand rather than a strong desire to buy the brand. *Brand preference* is a stronger degree of brand loyalty where a customer prefers one brand to competitive brands and will usually purchase this brand if it is available. For example, a customer may hold a brand preference for Diet Coke. However, if this brand is not available, the customer will usually accept a substitute such as Diet Pepsi rather than expending extra effort to find and purchase Diet Coke. *Brand insistence,* the strongest degree of brand loyalty, occurs when customers will go out of their way to find the brand and will accept no substitute. Customers who are brand insistent will expend a great deal of time and effort to locate and purchase their favorite brand. For example, there is not a Mercedes dealer in the state of Wyoming. Consequently, a loyal Mercedes customer may have to drive to Colorado to obtain service or purchase a vehicle. Brand loyalty is high in many different product categories including cigarettes, mayonnaise, toothpaste, coffee, photographic film, bath soap, medicines, body lotion, makeup, soft drinks, ketchup, and diapers. Note that most of these examples include products that customers put in their mouths or on their bodies—a common trait of products that enjoy high brand loyalty.

Brand Equity   The value of a brand is often referred to as *brand equity*. Another way of looking at brand equity is the marketing and financial value associated with a brand's position in the marketplace. Brand equity usually has ties to brand-name awareness, brand loyalty, brand quality, and the association with the brand's organization. Although brand equity is hard to measure, it represents a key asset for any firm and an important part of marketing strategy. Exhibit 7.5 lists the world's twenty-five most valuable brands. Brands like these take years to develop and nurture into the valuable assets that they have come to represent. This reality makes it easier and less expensive for firms to buy established brands than to develop new brands from scratch. For example, Johnson & Johnson's acquisition of Pfizer's consumer products unit allowed the company to add several powerful brands to its portfolio—Listerine, Sudafed, Visine, Neosporin, and Nicorette. The equity associated with these brands would have taken Johnson & Johnson decades to develop on its own.[8]

EXHIBIT 7.5	THE WORLD'S TWENTY-FIVE MOST VALUABLE BRANDS				
2005 Brand Rank	Brand Name	2005 Brand Value ($ millions)	2004 Brand Value ($ millions)	Change in Brand Value (%)	Country of Ownership
1	Coca-Cola	67,525	67,394	0	U.S.
2	Microsoft	59,941	61,372	−2	U.S.
3	IBM	53,376	53,791	−1	U.S.
4	GE	46,996	44,111	7	U.S.
5	Intel	35,588	33,499	6	U.S.
6	Nokia	26,452	24,041	10	Finland
7	Disney	26,441	27,113	−2	U.S.
8	McDonald's	26,014	25,001	4	U.S.
9	Toyota	24,837	22,673	10	Japan
10	Marlboro	21,189	22,128	−4	U.S.
11	Mercedes-Benz	20,006	21,331	−6	Germany
12	Citi	19,967	19,971	0	U.S.
13	Hewlett-Packard	18,866	20,978	−10	U.S.
14	American Express	18,559	17,683	5	U.S.
15	Gillette	17,534	16,723	5	U.S.
16	BMW	17,126	15,886	8	Germany
17	Cisco	16,592	15,948	4	U.S.
18	Louis Vuitton	16,077	NA	NA	France
19	Honda	15,788	14,874	6	Japan
20	Samsung	14,956	12,553	19	South Korea
21	Dell	13,231	11,500	15	U.S.
22	Ford	13,159	14,475	−9	U.S.
23	Pepsi	12,399	12,066	3	U.S.
24	Nescafe	12,241	11,892	3	Switzerland
25	Merrill Lynch	12,018	11,499	5	U.S.

Source: *BusinessWeek*, August 1, 2005 (http://www.finfacts.com/brands.htm), based on data from Interbrand Corporation. To make the list, a brand must be worth at least $1 billion, derive a third of its earnings outside the home country, and have publicly available marketing and financial data. Parent companies are not included in the rankings.

Brand equity stems from four elements: brand awareness, brand loyalty, brand quality, and brand associations.[9] *Brand awareness* and *brand loyalty* increase customer familiarity with a brand. Customers familiar or comfortable with a specific brand are more likely to consider the brand when making a purchase. When this familiarity is combined with a high degree of *brand quality,* the inherent risk in purchasing the brand decreases dramatically. *Brand associations* include the brand's image, attributes, or benefits that either directly or indirectly give the brand a certain personality. For example, customers associate 7-Up with "uncola," Charmin tissue with "squeezably soft," Michelin tires with family safety, Allstate insurance with "the good hands," and Honeycomb cereal with a "big, big bite." Associations like these are every bit as important as quality and loyalty, and they also take many years to develop.

Unfortunately, it is also possible for brand associations (and brand equity) to be negative. South Korean carmakers Kia and Hyundai, for example, struggle with a weak quality image associated with their brands. This is despite recent data that rank these brands third in initial quality behind Porsche and Lexus. To counteract their weak quality image, Kia and Hyundai back their products with 10-year, 100,000-mile warranties.[10]

Brand Alliances   As we have stated in previous chapters, relationships with other firms are among the most important competitive advantages that can be held by an organization. Many of these relationships are based on joint branding strategies. For example, *cobranding* is the use of two or more brands on one product. Cobranding leverages the brand equity of multiple brands to create distinctive products with distinctive differentiation. For example, Dell computers actually carry three brands on the cover: Dell, Intel, and Microsoft Windows. Cobranding is common in processed foods and credit cards. For example, General Mills' partners with Hershey's on its Betty Crocker chocolate cake mixes with Hershey's cocoa. This brand alliance gives Betty Crocker a distinct advantage over competitors like Duncan Hines. Likewise, credit card companies like Visa and MasterCard offer cobranded versions of their cards emblazoned with the logos of sports teams, universities, professions, or other firms like American Airlines and Disney World. Cobranding is successful because the complementary nature of the brands used on a single product increases perceived quality and customer familiarity.

Brand licensing is another type of branding alliance. *Brand licensing* involves a contractual agreement where a company permits an organization to use its brand on noncompeting products in exchange for a licensing fee. Although this royalty can be expensive, the instant brand recognition that comes with the licensed brand is often worth the expense. Fashion brands such as Calvin Klein, Ralph Lauren, Bill Blass, and Tommy Hilfiger appear on numerous products in a variety of product categories. Licensing is also common in toys where manufacturers will license the characters and images from popular movies like *Cars* or *Harry Potter* to create a variety of products. Even Jack Daniels and Jim Beam whiskeys have licensed barbeque sauces that bear their famous brands.

As you can see, branding can be a very challenging and complicated part of marketing strategy. However, the value of a good brand to product identification and differentiation is without question. So important are these fundamental roles of branding that marketers go to great lengths to protect their brand names and brand marks. For example, the Beatles' record label Apple Corps has tried several times to stop Apple Computer from using its famous logo, most recently in connection with the iTunes music store. The courts have always upheld Apple's use of its logo, arguing that consumers do not confuse the branding of the separate companies.[11] Companies like Apple expend significant money and effort to monitor potential brand abuses. Although the U.S. legal system provides many laws to protect brands, most of the responsibility for enforcing this protection falls on the company to find and police abuses. Due to the differing and often lax legal systems in other nations, brand abuse is quite common in foreign markets. It is not surprising that patent, copyright, and intellectual-property law has become a growth industry both in the United States and around the world.

In addition to brand misidentification, firms protect their brands if there is any danger that the brand can become synonymous with an entire product category. Examples of brands that constantly fight this battle include Scotch tape, Xerox copiers, Band-Aid adhesive bandages, Coca-Cola, FedEx, and Kleenex. To protect their brands, firms obtain trademarks to legally designate that the brand owner has exclusive use of the brand and to prohibit others from using the brand in any way. Former brand names that their parent companies did not protect sufficiently include aspirin, escalator, nylon, linoleum, kerosene, and shredded wheat.

Packaging and Labeling

At first glance, the issues of packaging and labeling might not seem like important considerations in branding strategy. Although packaging and labeling strategy does involve different goals than branding, the two often go hand in hand in developing a product, its benefits, its differentiation, and its image. Consider, for instance, the number of products that use distinctive packaging as part of their branding strategy. Obvious examples include the brand names and brand marks that appear on all product packaging. The color used on a product's package or label is also a vital part of branding, such as Tide's consistent use of bright orange on its line of laundry detergents. The size and shape of the label is sometimes a key to brand identification; for example, Heinz uses a unique crown-shaped label on its ketchup bottles. The physical characteristics of the package itself sometimes become part of the brand. Coca-Cola's unique 10-ounce glass bottle, Pringles' potato chip canister, and the bottles used by Absolut vodka and Crown Royal whiskey are good examples. Finally, products that use recyclable packaging are gaining favor. For example, NatureWorks (a subsidiary of agricultural giant Cargill), has developed polylactic acid (PLA)—a fully compostable material made from corn. PLA is used by BIOTA Spring Water, whose bottles degrade in 75 to 80 days in commercial composting. Other firms, such as Del Monte and Newman's Own, also use PLA in their packaging. The advantages offered by PLA are dramatic in that traditional plastic bottles and packaging are not biodegradable.[12]

Packaging serves a number of important functions in marketing strategy. Customers take some functions—like protection, storage, and convenience—for granted until the package fails to keep the product fresh or they discover that the package will not conveniently fit in the refrigerator, medicine cabinet, or backpack. Packaging can also play a role in product modifications and repositioning. An improved cap or closure, an "easy-open" package, a more durable box or container, or the introduction of a more conveniently sized package can create instant market recognition and a competitive advantage. Packaging can also be used as a part of a cobranding strategy. Hillshire Farms, for example, repackaged its Deli Select line of lunchmeats in Glad-Ware reusable plastic containers to give the product a more natural and consistent texture. The package is also easy to seal and completely reusable once the lunchmeat has been consumed.[13]

Labeling, in and of itself, is an important consideration in marketing strategy. Product labels not only aid in product identification and promotion but also contain a great deal of information to help customers make proper product selections. Labeling is also an important legal issue because several federal laws and regulations specify the information that must be included on a product's packaging. The Nutritional Labeling and Education Act of 1990 was one of the most sweeping changes in federal labeling law in history. The law mandated that packaged food manufacturers must include detailed nutritional information on their packaging. The law also set standards for health claims such as "low fat," "light," "low calorie," and "reduced cholesterol." Recently, members of Congress introduced the Food Choking Prevention Act, which they designed in order to develop labeling regulations for products that pose a choking hazard for children.[14]

Differentiating and Positioning the Product Offering

Though we have focused solely on product issues to this point in the chapter, it is vital to remember that product strategy is intricately tied to the other elements of the marketing program. This integration with other strategic elements comes to the fore-front when the firm attempts to differentiate and position its product offering relative to competing offerings. People sometimes confuse differentiation and positioning with market segmentation and target marketing. *Product differentiation* involves creating differences in the firm's product offering that set it apart from competing offerings. Differentiation typically has its basis in distinct product features, additional services, or other characteristics. *Positioning* refers to creating a mental image of the product offering and its differentiating features in the minds of the target market. This mental image can be based on real or perceived differences among competing offerings. Whereas differentiation is about the product itself, positioning is about customers' perceptions of the real or imaginary benefits that the product possesses.

Although differentiation and positioning can be based on actual product features or characteristics, the principal task for the firm is to develop and maintain a *relative position* for the product in the minds of the target market. The process of creating a favorable relative position involves several steps:

1. Identify the characteristics, needs, wants, preferences, and benefits desired by the target market.

2. Examine the differentiating characteristics and relative position of all current and potential competitors in the market.

3. Compare the position of your product offering with the positions of the competition for each key need, want, preference, or benefit desired by the target market.

4. Identify a unique position that focuses on customer benefits that the competition does not currently offer.

5. Develop a marketing program to leverage the firm's position and persuade customers that the firm's product offering will best meet their needs.

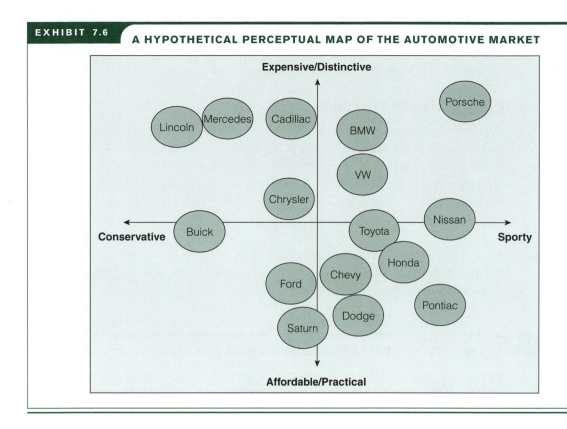

EXHIBIT 7.6

A HYPOTHETICAL PERCEPTUAL MAP OF THE AUTOMOTIVE MARKET

6. Continually reassess the target market, the firm's position, and the position of competing offerings to ensure that the marketing program stays on track and also to identify emerging positioning opportunities.[15]

The concept of relative position is typically addressed using a tool called perceptual mapping. A *perceptual map* represents customer perceptions and preferences spatially by means of a visual display. A hypothetical perceptual map for automotive brands is shown in Exhibit 7.6. The axes represent underlying dimensions that customers might use to form perceptions and preferences of brands. Any number of dimensions can be represented using computer algorithms such as multidimensional scaling or cluster analysis. However, simple two-dimensional maps are the most common form because a limited number of dimensions is typically the most salient for consumers.

Perceptual maps illustrate two basic issues. First, they indicate products/brands that are similar in terms of relative mental position. In the example perceptual map, customers are likely to see the offerings of Toyota and Honda as being very similar. Positioning a brand to coincide with competing brands becomes more difficult when many brands occupy the same relative space. Second, perceptual maps illustrate voids in the current mindscape for a product category. In the map, note the empty space in the bottom-left corner. This indicates that consumers do not perceive any current products to be both conservative and inexpensive. This lack of competition within the mind space might occur because customers have (1) unmet needs or preferences or

(2) no desire for a product offering with this combination of dimensions. Obviously, additional research would be needed to determine whether this lack of perceived competition indicates a viable unmet segment of the market.

Differentiation Strategies

Customer perceptions are of utmost importance in product differentiation because differences among competing products can be based on real qualities (for example, product characteristics, features, or style) or psychological qualities (for example, perception and image). Generally, the most important tool of product differentiation is the brand. However, there are other important bases for differentiation, including product descriptors, customer support services, and image.

Product Descriptors   Firms generally provide information about their products in one of three contexts, as shown in Exhibit 7.7. The first context is *product features,* which are factual descriptors of the product and its characteristics. For example, Dell's E1405

EXHIBIT 7.7   **USING PRODUCT DESCRIPTORS IN PRODUCT DIFFERENTIATION**

Product	Features	Advantages	Benefits
Dell Inspiron E1405 Notebook	Intel Centrino Core Duo processor	Very lightweight and compact	Ultimate mobility
	Only 1.5 in. and 5.3 lbs	Blazingly fast multimedia performance	Rugged entertainment on the road
	14.1-in. TrueLife Display	Multitasking of applications	Watch three two-hour movies on a single charge
	85WHr nine-cell battery	Long-lasting battery	Stay connected wherever you are
	Integrated Wi-Fi and Bluetooth	Hassle-free connectivity	
	RoadReady design technology		
Pontiac Gran Prix GXP	5.3-liter LS4 V8 engine	0 to 60 mph in 5.7 seconds	Enhanced self-image
	Wider front-to-rear track design	Superb handling	Fun to drive
	Near 90-degree opening rear doors	Better road grip	Easy to drive
	Magnasteer II steering assistance	Easy-to-load cargo	Safety
Crest MultiCare Whitening Toothpaste	Dissolving microcleansing Crystals	Fights cavities	Whiter teeth
	Foaming action	Fights tartar buildup	Fresher breath
	Fresh mint flavor	Protects against acids	Teeth stay cleaner longer
Bounty Select-a-Size Paper Towels	Sheets can be torn in varying sizes	Great for any size cleaning job	More control over cleaning
	More sheets per roll	Less waste	Reduces cost of buying paper towels
	Increased wet strength	Superior absorbency	Can be sized for use as placemats
		Won't run out as often	

notebook includes key features such as an Intel Core Duo processor and a 14.1-inch TrueLife display. However, features—although they tell something about the nature of the product—are not generally the pieces of information that lead customers to buy. Features must be translated into the second context, advantages. *Advantages* are performance characteristics that communicate how the features make the product behave, hopefully in a fashion that is distinctive and appealing to customers. The advantages of Dell's E1405 include a lightweight, compact design; fast performance; and long battery life. However, as we have said before, the real reason customers buy products is to gain *benefits*—the positive outcomes or need satisfaction they acquire from purchased products. Thus, the benefits of the E1405 include ultimate mobility and rugged entertainment on the road. Other benefits, like increased productivity and connectivity, might also be implied in Dell's promotional program.

Increasingly, one aspect of a product's description that customers value highly is quality. Product characteristics that customers associate with quality include reliability, durability, ease of maintenance, ease of use, and a trusted brand name. In business markets, other characteristics—such as technical suitability, ease of repair, and company reputation—become included in this list of quality indicators. In general, higher product quality—real or imagined—means that a company can charge a higher price for its product and simultaneously build customer loyalty. This relationship between quality and price (inherent in the concept of value) forces the firm to consider product quality carefully when making decisions regarding differentiation, positioning, and the overall marketing program.

Customer Support Services   A firm may have difficulty differentiating its products when all products in a market have essentially the same quality, features, or benefits. In such cases, providing good customer support services—both before and after the sale—may be the only way to differentiate the firm's products and move them away from a price-driven commodity status. For example, small, locally owned bookstores continue to disappear at an alarming rate as competition from Barnes & Noble, Books-A-Million, and Amazon.com has taken its toll. The local stores that have remained in business thrive because of the exceptional, personalized service that they provide to their customers. Many local bookstores create customer loyalty by being actively involved in the community, including contributing to local schools, churches, and charities. Many customers value this level of personalization so highly that they will pay slightly higher prices and remain loyal to *their* bookstore.

Support services include anything that the firm can provide in addition to the main product that adds value to that product for the customer. Examples include assistance in identifying and defining customer needs, delivery and installation, technical support for high-tech systems and software, financing arrangements, training, extended warranties and guarantees, repair, layaway plans, convenient hours of operation, affinity programs (for example, frequent flier/buyer programs), and adequate parking. If you buy a Kenmore refrigerator, for example, you can expect Sears to provide financing, delivery and installation, and warranty repair service, if necessary. Through research, the firm can discover the types of support services that customers value most. In some cases, customers may want lower prices rather than an array of support services. Airlines and budget hotels are good examples. The importance of having the proper mix of support services has increased in recent years, causing many firms to design their customer services as carefully as they design their products.

Image   The image of a product or organization is the overall impression, positive or negative, that customers have of it. This impression includes what the organization has done in the past, what it presently offers, and projections about what it will do in the future. All aspects of the firm's marketing program, as perceived by customers, will affect this impression. Consider the car rental industry. In the industry's early years, Hertz not only stood in first place but also maintained a vast lead over second-place Avis. The management of Avis, intent on capturing a larger portion of Hertz's customers, asked its advertising agency to develop an effective positioning strategy relative to Hertz. After searching for any advantage that Avis held over Hertz, the agency concluded that the only difference was that Avis was number two. Avis management decided to claim this fact as an advantage, using the theme "We're number two. We try harder!" Avis rentals soared, putting the company in a much stronger number-two position.

In the case of product differentiation, reality is often not as important as perception. Firms that enjoy a solid image or reputation can differentiate their product offerings based solely on the company or brand name alone. Examples of firms that have this ability include BMW, Mercedes, Michelin, Budweiser, Campbell's, Ritz-Carlton Hotels, Disney World, and Princess Cruises. A good image is not only one of the best means of product differentiation but also a major sustainable competitive advantage. However, a good image can also be lost over time—or shattered in an instant.

Positioning Strategies

Firms can design their marketing programs to position and enhance the image of a product offering in the minds of target customers. To create a positive image for a product, a firm can choose from among several positioning strategies, including strengthening the current position, repositioning, or attempting to reposition the competition.

Strengthen the Current Position   The key to strengthening a product's current position is to monitor constantly what target customers want and the extent to which customers perceive the product as satisfying those wants. Any complacency in today's dynamic marketplace is likely to result in lost customers and sales. For example, a firm known for excellent customer service must continue to invest time, money, talent, and attention to its product position to protect its market share and sales from competitive activity. This is especially true for firms such as Ritz-Carlton and Nordstrom that pursue competitive advantage based on customer intimacy.

Strengthening a current position is all about continually raising the bar of customer expectations and being perceived by customers as the only firm capable of reaching this new height. For example, Ford has strived for years to differentiate its

Freestar minivan (formerly called the Windstar) by positioning it on the cutting edge of industry safety. The Windstar was the first minivan in the industry to receive the Quadruple five-Star crash-test rating and the only minivan to earn the rating five years in a row. The Freestar has continued this tradition by being the only minivan to receive a top rating for protection against neck injuries from the Insurance Institute for Highway Safety. The Freestar's position is different from the strategies pursued by Honda's Odyssey (innovation and design), Chrysler's Town and Country (performance and customer loyalty), and Toyota's Sienna (designed by kids). By continuing its safety positioning, Ford understands that it must constantly raise expectations about safety if it is to hold its position and remain competitive.

Repositioning   At times, declining sales or market share may signal that customers have lost faith in a product's ability to satisfy their needs. In such cases, a new position may be the best response because strengthening the current position may well accelerate the downturn in performance. Repositioning may involve a fundamental change in any of the marketing mix elements or perhaps even all of them. J. Crew, for example, dropped its preppy style of clothing in favor of more "urban and hip" merchandise. The traditional catalog-based retailer also expanded its number of retail stores. As its traditional baby-boom customers age, J. Crew has tried to attract younger shoppers who have traditionally favored stores like Banana Republic and Abercrombie & Fitch.

Some of the most memorable marketing programs involve attempts to move to new positions. The "Not Just for Breakfast Anymore" campaign for orange juice and the "Pork: The Other White Meat" campaign are good examples. A continuing example is Cadillac's attempt to reposition the brand because of the aging of its traditional target. The erosion of Cadillac's share of the luxury car market has forced the company to focus on and attract younger audiences to the brand. Cadillac's recent marketing programs have been headlined by the "Fusion of Design and Technology," "Heritage Reborn," and "Break Through" campaigns. In some cases, repositioning requires a focus on new products. Sony, for example, recently launched the Alpha 100, the company's first digital SLR (single-lens reflex) camera aimed at the high end of the market. Although Sony is the second-largest camera manufacturer in the world, it has not been taken seriously because the company offered only point-and-shoot models before the launch of the Alpha 100. Sony's repositioning came about after the company purchased Konica Minolta in 2006.[16]

Reposition the Competition   In many cases, it is better to attempt to reposition the competition rather than change your own position. A direct attack on a competitor's strength may put its products in a less favorable light or even force the competitor to change its positioning strategy. We are all familiar with the dueling campaigns of Coke and Pepsi, Pizza Hut and Papa John's, and McDonald's and Burger King. Napster uses this same strategy when it compares its Napster To Go service to Apple's iTunes. The company describes Napster To Go as a "buffet style" assortment of music where users can access all two million songs on Napster for $14.95 per month. Napster compares this to iTunes' "a la carte" style where songs must be purchased for 99 cents each.[17] This sort of comparison strategy is also used in foreign markets. For example,

Ulker, a large Turkish confectionary and cookie company, hired American actor Chevy Chase to appear in a series of television ads promoting its new soft drink Cola Turka. The ads were designed to reposition Coke and Pepsi as "America" rather than soft drinks. The strategy plays off of the strong anti-American sentiment in Turkey to portray Cola Turka as a true Turkish soft drink.[18]

Managing Products and Brands Over Time

Decisions related to products, product lines, branding, differentiation, and positioning are ongoing strategic issues. So is managing the entire portfolio of products and brands over time. To address this issue, we use the traditional product life cycle—shown in Exhibit 7.8—to discuss product strategy from a product's conception, through its growth and maturity, and to its ultimate death. Our use of the product life cycle is based on its ability to describe the strategic issues and key objectives that should be considered during each phase of a product's life. We note, however, that the product life cycle has many limitations. For one, most new products never get past development, and most successful products never die. Second, the product life cycle really refers to the life of a product/market, industry, sector, or product category—not to specific brands or firms. Hence, if we trace the life cycle of the bricks-and-mortar DVD rental business, we deal with market characteristics for this sector and not single firms like Blockbuster or Movie Gallery. Further, the length of each stage and the time involved in the overall cycle depends heavily on the actions of the firms within the industry. Firms and industries constantly reinvent themselves, which can cause the life cycle to speed up, slow down, or even recycle.

Despite these issues, the product life cycle offers a useful framework for discussing product strategy over time. Exhibit 7.9 summarizes these strategic considerations for

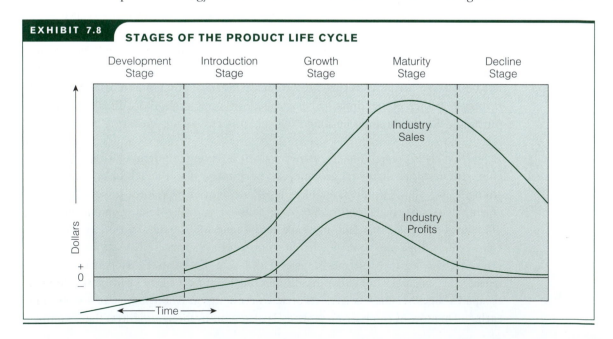

EXHIBIT 7.8   STAGES OF THE PRODUCT LIFE CYCLE

EXHIBIT 7.9	STRATEGIC CONSIDERATIONS DURING THE PRODUCT LIFE CYCLE			
	Life-Cycle Stages			
	Introduction	**Growth**	**Maturity**	**Decline**
Overall Marketing Goals	Stimulate product awareness and trial	Increase market share by acquiring new customers; discover new needs and market segments	Maximize profit by defending market share or stealing it from competitors	Reduce expenses and marketing efforts to maximize the last opportunity for profit
Product Strategy	Introduce limited models with limited features; frequent product changes	Introduce new models with new features; pursue continuous innovation	Full-model line; increase supplemental product offerings to aid in product differentiation	Eliminate unprofitable models and brands
Pricing Strategy	Penetration pricing to establish a market presence or price skimming to recoup development costs	Prices fall due to competition; price to match or beat the competition	Prices continue to fall; price to beat the competition	Prices stabilize at a low level
Distribution Strategy	Gradually roll out product to expand availability; get channel intermediaries on board	Intensify efforts to expand product reach and availability	Extensive product availability; retain shelf space; phase out unprofitable outlets or channels	Maintain a level necessary to keep brand-loyal customers; continue phasing out unprofitable channels
Promotion Strategy	Advertising and personal selling to build awareness; heavy sales promotion to stimulate product trial	Aggressive brand advertising, selling, and sales promotion to encourage brand switching and continued trial	Stress brand differences and benefits; encourage brand switching; keep the brand/product fresh	Reduce to a minimal level or phase out entirely

Source: Adapted from Charles W. Lamb, Jr., Joseph F. Hair, Jr., and Carl McDaniel, *Marketing,* 7th ed. (Mason, OH: South-Western, 2004), 334.

each stage of the life cycle. It is important for product managers to consider the stage of their market's life cycle with respect to planning in the current period as well as planning for the future. Using the product life cycle as a framework has the distinct advantage of forcing managers to consider the future of their industry and their brand. For example, many experts believe that the traditional DVD rental industry is heading rapidly into its decline phase. The advent of DVD distribution via the mail and technological innovations such as video on demand and IPTV (Internet protocol television) offer a dramatic increase in convenience for consumers. Given this fact, it is not surprising that traditional rental houses Blockbuster and Movie Gallery lost a combined $1 billion in fiscal 2006. Conversely, Netflix, the pioneer in through-the-mail DVD rentals, currently enjoys 36 percent annual revenue increases. Despite this success, Netflix is looking to the future by investing in online movie distribution, movie production, and the acquisition of distribution rights of independent films. Netflix's strategy is a hedge against the future of fully digital transmission of movies via ever-improving technology.[19]

Development Stage

As Exhibit 7.8 indicates, a firm has no sales revenue during the product development stage. In fact, the firm experiences a net cash outflow due to the expenses involved in product innovation and development. For most innovations, a substantial investment of financial resources and time are necessary for product development. In addition, the firm assumes a great deal of financial, market, and opportunity risk due to the uncertainty involved in developing new products. For example, the pharmaceutical industry understands the challenges of new product development like no other industry. Firms such as Merck, Pfizer, and AstraZeneca spend millions each year developing new drugs. Upon identifying a new drug, it takes years of testing before earning Federal Drug Administration approval. Then, once the new drug is on the market, the firm has only a few years to recoup its investment before patent protection expires and the market opens to generic competition. In this highly competitive industry, pharmaceutical firms live or die based on the number and quality of drugs that they have in their development pipelines.

The development stage usually begins with a product concept, which has several components: (1) an understanding of the specific uses and benefits that target customers seek in a new product; (2) a description of the product, including its potential uses and benefits; (3) the potential for creating a complete product line that can create synergy in sales, distribution, and promotion; and (4) an analysis of the feasibility of the product concept including such issues as anticipated sales, required return on investment, time of market introduction, and length of time to recoup the investment. Given the odds stacked against most new products, it is not surprising that over 80 percent of all new products fail. This unfortunate fact of life underscores the need to correctly identify target customer needs *before* developing the product strategy. Through effective test marketing, the firm can gauge customer response to a new product before the full-scale launch. New products that closely match customers' needs and have strong advantages over competing products are much easier to market as the new product enters the introduction stage of its life cycle.

Introduction Stage

The introduction stage begins when development is complete and ends when sales indicate that target customers widely accept the product. The marketing strategy devised during the development stage is fully implemented during the introduction stage and should be tightly integrated with the firm's competitive advantages and strategic focus. Marketing strategy goals common to the introduction stage include

- attracting customers by raising awareness of and interest in the product offering through advertising, public relations, and publicity efforts that connect key product benefits to customers' needs and wants.

- inducing customers to try and buy the product through the use of various sales tools and pricing activities. Common examples include free samples of the product and the use of price incentives.

- engaging in customer education activities that teach members of the target market how to use the new product.

- strengthening or expanding channel and supply chain relationships to gain sufficient product distribution to make the product easily accessible by target customers.

- building on the availability and visibility of the product through trade promotion activities that encourage channel intermediaries to stock and support the product.

- setting pricing objectives that will balance the firm's need to recoup investment with the competitive realities of the market.

Although all elements of the marketing program are important during the introduction stage, good promotion and distribution are essential to make customers aware that the new product is available, teach them how to use it correctly, and tell them where to purchase it. Although this is typically a very expensive undertaking, it doesn't have to be. For example, when Mozilla released its open-source Firefox web browser, it garnered 150 million downloads and 10 million permanent users in only 18 months without any marketing staff. The secret to Mozilla's success was a word-of-mouth buzz campaign that centered on its SpreadFirefox.com website. Firefox users were allowed to post ideas on how to market Firefox, while other users volunteered to put these ideas into action.[20]

Growth Stage

The firm should be ready for the growth stage because sustained sales increases may begin quickly. The product's upward sales curve may be steep, and profits should rapidly increase, then decline, toward the end of the growth stage. The length of the growth stage varies according to the nature of the product and competitive reactions. For example, disposable diapers had a long growth stage as they experienced over 30 percent yearly growth for a decade. A short growth stage is typical for new video game consoles, such as Microsoft's Xbox 360 and Nintendo's DS Lite.

Regardless of the length of the growth stage, the firm has two main priorities: (1) establishing a strong, defensible market position and (2) achieving financial objectives that repay investment and earn enough profit to justify a long-term commitment to the product. Within these two priorities, there are a number of pertinent marketing strategy goals:

- Leverage the product's *perceived* differential advantages in terms of branding, quality, price, value, and so on, to secure a strong market position.

- Establish a clear product and brand identity through coordinated promotional campaigns aimed at both customers and the trade.

- Create unique positioning through the use of advertising that stresses the product's benefits for target customers relative to other available solutions or products.

- Maintain control over product quality to ensure customer satisfaction.

- Maximize availability of the product through extensive distribution and promotion activities that capitalize on the product's popularity.

- Maintain or enhance the product's ability to deliver profits to key channel and supply chain partners, especially retailers that control shelf space and product placement.

- Find the ideal balance between price and demand as price elasticity becomes more important as the product moves toward the maturity stage.

- Always keep an eye focused on the competition.

During the growth stage, the overall strategy shifts from acquisition to retention, from stimulating product trial to generating repeat purchases and building brand loyalty. This is true not only for customers but also wholesalers, retailers, and other supply chain members. The key is to develop long-term relationships with customers and partners in order to prepare for the maturity stage. As the market matures, the firm will need loyal customers and good friends in the supply chain in order to remain competitive. Maintaining key relationships is a challenging and expensive proposition. For this reason, the growth stage is the most expensive stage for marketing.

Pricing also becomes more challenging during the growth stage. As more competitors enter the market, the firm must balance its need for cash flow with its need to be competitive. The relationship between price and perceived quality is a complicating factor, as is the increasing price sensitivity of customers. It is not surprising during the growth stage to see competitors stake out market positions based on premium or value-based pricing strategies. Other firms solve the pricing dilemma by offering different products at different price points. You can see this strategy in action in the wireless phone market, where each service provider offers tiered service offerings (that is, minutes and features) at different pricing levels. FedEx implements the same strategy with its tiered service offerings (overnight by 8:30 a.m., overnight by 10:30 a.m., and so on).

Another major challenge during the growth stage is the increasing number of competitors entering the market. There is a tendency for many firms to pay less attention to competitors during the growth stage. After all, the market has grown rapidly, and there is enough business for everyone to have a piece. Why not worry about competitors later? Because growth will eventually end and the market will become mature. To protect itself, the firm must build a defensible market position as it prepares for market maturity. This position may be based on image, price, quality, or perhaps some technological standard. Eventually, the market will go through a shakeout period, and the dominant firms will emerge. This process is now beginning to take shape in the market for digital photography equipment where two dominant firms have emerged (Nikon and Canon control 80 percent of the market), while others have gone out of business (Minolta, Konica, Kyocera, Contax). Industry experts expect that other firms—such as Fuji, Casio, and Olympus—will soon abandon the market. The fate of other firms like Sony and Kodak will depend on their ability to create a defensible market position as the digital photography market enters the maturity stage.[21]

Maturity Stage

After the shakeout occurs at the end of the growth stage, the strategic window of opportunity will all but close for the market, and it will enter the maturity stage. No more firms will enter the market unless they have found some product innovation significant enough to attract large numbers of customers. The window of opportunity often remains open, however, for new product features and variations. A good example is the introduction of light, dry, ice, microbrew, low-alcohol, and low-carbohydrate products in the beer industry. These variations can be important as firms attempt to gain market share. In the face of limited or no growth within the market, one of the few ways for a firm to gain market share is to steal it from a competitor. Such theft often comes only with significant promotional investments or cuts in gross margin because of the lowering of prices. The stakes in this "chess match" are often very high. For example, just a fractional change in market share in the soft-drink industry means millions in additional revenue and profit for the lucky firm.

In the typical product life cycle, we expect maturity to be the longest stage. For the firm that has survived the growth stage, maturity can be a relatively status quo period of time. As long as one maintains sales volume to keep market share constant, a longer-term perspective can be taken due to decreasing market uncertainty. Typically, a firm has four general goals that can be pursued during the maturity stage:

- **Generate Cash Flow** By the time a market reaches maturity, the firm's products should be yielding a very positive cash flow. This is essential to recoup the initial investment and to generate the excess cash necessary for the firm to grow and develop new products.

- **Hold Market Share** Marketing strategy should stress holding market share among the dominant brands in the market. Firms having marginal market share must decide whether they have a reasonable chance of improving their position. If not, they should consider pulling out of the market.

- **Steal Market Share** Any firm in a mature market can pursue this goal; however, it is more likely to be used by firms holding weaker market positions. The key to this strategy is to create incentives that encourage brand switching, even if only temporarily. Even small gains in market share can lead to large increases in profits.

- **Increase Share of Customer** *Share of customer* refers to the percentage of each customer's needs in a particular area met by the firm. This strategy is common in financial services. Likewise, many large grocery chains increase share of customer by adding features ranging from restaurants to video rentals to dry cleaning services in an effort to create one-stop shopping for family needs.

To achieve these goals, the firm has at least four general options for strategy selection throughout the maturity stage: (1) develop a new product image, (2) find and attract new users to the product, (3) discover new applications and uses for the product, or (4) apply new technology to the product. Kraft Foods, for example, launched a massive promotional campaign to create a new product image for Jell-O after a long decline in sales. Today, Jell-O has once again achieved gourmet status with America's children. Similarly, Whirlpool used product innovation to shake itself free from the "sea of white," a phrase that is often used to describe the bland range of offerings in household appliances. Whirlpool's Duet washers and dryers—industry leaders in design, ease of use, and energy efficiency—now command 40 percent of the front-loading market.[22] Finally, as described in Beyond the Pages 7.2, Nintendo used a rebranding strategy to attract new users to its line of puzzle and skill-building games for its DS Lite handheld console.

Stealing customers away from the competition involves creating incentives for noncustomers to try the firm's product. This may entail heavy expenditures in sales promotion activities such as product sampling, couponing, or trade promotion to encourage prominent display of the product on the store's shelves. In some cases, once the brand switch has been accomplished, customers can be locked in through the use of contractual agreements. This is common among wireless phone providers, health clubs, and satellite-television providers. A more common approach is to simply match competitive prices, as is the case among many competing retail firms. For example, most pizza chains will accept competitor's coupons and match their promotional incentives to gain business.

Decline Stage

A product's sales plateau will not last forever, and eventually a persistent decline in revenue begins. A firm has two basic options during the decline stage: (1) attempt to postpone the decline or (2) accept its inevitability. Should the firm attempt to postpone the decline, the product's demand must be renewed through repositioning, developing new uses or features for the product, or applying new technology. For example, despite the decline in sales of muscle cars over two decades, Ford successfully launched a redesigned Mustang in 2005. For 2007, using design cues from the brand's 1960s glory days, Ford introduced the Mustang Shelby GT 500 to eager buyers willing to pay $20,000 over sticker (which itself is around $40,000) to get the first Shelbys produced.[23] Postponing a product's decline in this manner takes a great deal of time and a substantial investment of resources. Many firms, however, do not have the resources or opportunity to renew a product's demand and must accept the inevitability of decline. In such instances, the firm can either harvest profits from the product while demand declines or divest the product, taking steps to abandon it or sell it to another firm.

The *harvesting* approach calls for a gradual reduction in marketing expenditures, and uses a less-resource-intensive marketing mix. A harvesting strategy also allows the firm to funnel its increased cash flow into the development of new products. For example, GM phased out the Oldsmobile brand over several years by offering discounts and other special incentives, such as longer product warranties, to allay customer fears of limited product support. A company using the *divesting* option withdraws all marketing support from the product. It may continue to sell the product until it sustains losses or arrange for the product to be acquired by another firm. For example, P&G dropped its Oxydol laundry detergent and sold it to Redox Brands for $7 million. Though P&G had sold Oxydol for 73 years, the company decided to delete the brand after its sales fell from a high of $64 million in 1950 to only $5.5 million just before the sale. Redox reintroduced the brand as Oxydol Extreme Clean and targeted Generation X consumers with liquid versions and vibrant packaging.[24]

Beyond the Pages 7.2

NINTENDO'S REBRANDING STRATEGY[25]

Admit it. You've always thought of Nintendo's line of game systems as being strictly for kids. You're not alone. Most people associate the Nintendo 64, Gamecube, Wii, GameBoy, and DS with famous characters such as Mario, Luigi, and Princess Peach. However, Nintendo is out to change everyone's opinions about video games and the gamers who enjoy them.

Nintendo's first step was to redesign its DS handheld game system. The new DS Lite is a smaller, lighter, brighter-screened, and distinctly iPod-looking version of the original DS system. It still boasts a touch-sensitive screen, a stylus, long battery life, and the ability to play all DS and GameBoy Advance games. Overall, the new design is much more appealing. Though all ages enjoy the DS Lite, its design is distinctly more upscale than Nintendo's own GameBoy SP or GameBoy Micro, or Sony's popular PlayStation Portable (PSP).

To coincide with the launch of the DS Lite, Nintendo rebranded many of its popular puzzle and skill-building games under the Touch Generations brand. Titles in the series— including *Brain Age, Big Brain Academy, Tetris DS, Nintendogs, Magnetica, Electroplankton, Sudoku Gridmaster,* and *True Swing Golf*— had been available for a while. However, they had not been collectively branded and targeted toward a particular audience. That audience includes 40- and 50-something men and women in the so-called casual gamer market. Unlike younger gamers who enjoy playing for long periods of time, casual gamers prefer to play games in smaller portions: waiting for the kids to finish dance class, riding in mass transit, or as a fun way to fill 10 minutes before a meeting. Nintendo's website for Touch Generations states this market's needs perfectly:

Not a hard-core gamer? That's OK. We've made games for you in mind. Nintendo's Touch Generations series, exclusive to the Nintendo DS handheld game system, allows you simple, engaging interaction with games that promote production over destruction, contemplation over domination.

No complex instructions. No steep learning curve. Play a little. Play a lot. It's up to you.

The website is also filled with photos of consumers in the target market. In one, a middle-aged woman sporting reading glasses is sitting in bed playing a game on the DS Lite. She holds the console sideways, like an open book, rather than opening the console like a notebook computer. Another photo on the Nintendo website features a graying, middle-aged man playing Sudoku on the DS Lite.

Nintendo's Touch Generations strategy takes advantage of emerging trends in the gaming market. The average age of frequent game purchasers is 40, with a full 25 percent of all gamers being over the age of 50. In addition, women account for 47 percent of all gamers who are parents. Nintendo believes that there is large segment of "dormant" gamers in the market who enjoyed playing *Pac-Man* and *Pong* as children or young adults. Many experts agree and point to the huge success of *The Sims* as an example of a game that appeals to this market.

Another key part of the Touch Generations brand is pricing. Most games in the series sell for $19.99. This is in a market where the most popular games sell for $50 or more. Nintendo believes this competitive pricing is important to a market segment that does not want to make a substantial investment in games that are played in smaller portions.

The DS Lite and Touch Generations have been very successful, as has the entire portable gaming market. Portable gaming hardware sales have increased 96 percent in recent years, and portable games surpassed the $1 billion mark for three years in a row, from 2002 to 2005. Although this success is partly the result of the popularity of Sony's PSP, much of it is attributable to Nintendo's ability to bring casual gamers and other non-gamers into the market.

The firm should take several factors into consideration before deciding on an appropriate marketing strategy during the decline stage:

- **Market Segment Potential**   The firm might have loyal-customer segments who will continue to buy the product. If these segments are viable and profitable, the firm should postpone the decline or slowly harvest the product.

- **The Market Position of the Product**   A product in a leading market position with a solid image may be profitable and generate excess cash by attracting customers from competitors' abandoned products.

- **The Firm's Price and Cost Structure**   If the firm is a low-cost producer in the industry and can maintain its selling price, the product can remain viable even in a declining market. The firm's cost structure could also be enhanced by no longer having to invest in the product's marketing program.

- **The Rate of Market Deterioration**   The faster the rate of market deterioration, the sooner the firm should divest the product.

Although the firm should carefully consider these factors, it should not be sentimental about dropping a failing product. On the other hand, the firm should not quickly dismiss a renewal attempt, particularly if the firm does not have a better alternative use for its resources.

Throughout the product life cycle, it is imperative that the firm stays focused on changes in the market, not on the firm's products. Products have life cycles only because markets and customers change. By focusing on changing markets, the firm can attempt to create new and better quality products to match customers' needs. Only in this way can a firm grow, prosper, remain competitive, and continue to be seen as a source of solutions by the target market.

Lessons from Chapter 7

Product strategy

- lies at the heart of every organization in that it defines what the organization does and why it exists.

- involves creating a product offering that is a bundle of physical (tangible), service (intangible), and symbolic (perceptual) attributes designed to satisfy customers' needs and wants.

- strives to overcome commoditization by differentiating product offerings via the service and symbolic elements of the offering.

The product portfolio

- is used in both consumer (convenience, shopping, specialty, and unsought products) and business (raw materials, component parts, process materials, MRO supplies, accessory equipment, installations, and business services) markets.

- is used in most firms due to the advantages of selling a variety of products rather than a single product.

- consists of a group of closely related product items (product lines) and the total group of products offered by the firm (product mix).

- involves strategic decisions such as the number of product lines to offer (variety), as well as the depth of each product line (assortment).

- can create a number of important benefits for firms, including economies of scale, package uniformity, standardization, sales and distribution efficiency, and equivalent quality beliefs.

The challenges of service products

- stem mainly from the fact that services are intangible. Other challenging characteristics of services include simultaneous production and consumption, perishability, heterogeneity, and client-based relationships.

- include the following issues:

  - Service firms experience problems in balancing supply (capacity) with demand.
  - Service demand is time-and-place dependent because customers or their possessions must be present for delivery.
  - Customers have a difficult time evaluating the quality of a service before it is purchased and consumed.
  - Service quality is often inconsistent and very difficult to standardize across many customers.
  - The need for some services is not always apparent to customers. Consequently, service marketers often have trouble tying their offerings directly to customers' needs.

New product development

- is a vital part of a firm's efforts to sustain growth and profits.

- considers six strategic options related to the newness of products:

  - New-to-the-world products (discontinuous innovations) involve a pioneering effort by a firm that leads to the creation of an entirely new market.
  - New product lines represent new offerings by the firm, but they become introduced into established markets.
  - Product line extensions supplement an existing product line with new styles, models, features, or flavors.
  - Improvements or revisions of existing products offer customers improved performance or greater perceived value.
  - Repositioning involves targeting existing products at new markets or segments.
  - Cost reductions involve modifying products to offer performance similar to competing products at a lower price.

- depends on the ability of the firm to create a differential advantage for the new product.

- typically proceeds through five stages: idea generation, screening and evaluation, development, test marketing, and commercialization.

Branding strategy

- involves selecting the right combination of name, symbol, term, or design that identifies a specific product.

- has two parts: the brand name (words, letters, and numbers) and the brand mark (symbols, figures, or a design).

- is not only critical to product identification but also the key factor used by marketers to differentiate a product from its competition.

- to be truly successful should develop a brand that succinctly captures the product offering in a way that answers a question in the customer's mind.

- has many advantages including making it easier for customers to find and buy products.

- involves having a solid understanding of four key issues:

  - Manufacturer versus private-label brands—private-label brands are more profitable than manufacturer brands for the retailers that carry them. However, manufacturer brands have built-in demand, recognition, and product loyalty.

  - Brand loyalty—a positive attitude toward a brand that causes customers to have a consistent preference for that brand over all other competing brands in a product category. Three levels of loyalty include brand recognition, brand preference, and brand insistence.

  - Brand equity—the value of a brand or the marketing and financial value associated with a brand's position in the marketplace.

  - Brand alliances—branding strategies, such as cobranding or brand licensing, that involve developing close relationships with other firms.

- also involves taking steps to protect brand names and brand marks from trademark infringement by other firms.

Packaging and labeling

- are important considerations in branding strategy because packaging often goes hand in hand in developing a product, its benefits, its differentiation, and its image.

- include issues such as color, shape, size, and convenience of the package or the product's container.

- are often used in product modifications or cobranding to reposition the product or give it new and improved features.

- are vital in helping customers make proper product selections.

- can have important environmental and legal consequences.

Differentiation and positioning

- involve creating differences in the firm's product offering that set it apart from competing offerings (product differentiation), as well as the development and maintenance of a relative position for a product in the minds of the target market (product positioning).

- can be monitored through the use of perceptual mapping—a visual, spatial display of customer perceptions on two or more key dimensions.

- are fundamentally based on the brand but is often based on product descriptors, customer support services, and image.

- include the positioning strategies of strengthen the current position, repositioning, or reposition the competition.

Managing products and brands over time

- can be addressed via the traditional product life cycle, which traces the evolution of a product's development and birth, growth and maturity, and decline and death over five stages:

    - Development—a time of no sales revenue, negative cash flow, and high risk
    - Introduction—a time of rising customer awareness, extensive marketing expenditures, and rapidly increasing sales revenue
    - Growth—a time of rapidly increasing sales revenue, rising profits, market expansion, and increasing numbers of competitors
    - Maturity—a time of sales and profit plateaus, a shift from customer acquisition to customer retention, and strategies aimed at holding or stealing market share
    - Decline—a time of persistent sales and profit decreases, attempts to postpone the decline, or strategies aimed at harvesting or divesting the product

- can be influenced by shifts in the market, or by the actions of the firms within the industry as they constantly reinvent themselves.

Questions for Discussion

1. Consider the number of product choices available in the U.S. consumer market. In virtually every product category, consumers have many options to fulfill their needs. Are all these options really necessary? Is having this many choices a good thing for consumers? Why or why not? Is it a good thing for marketers and

retailers that have to support and carry all these product choices? Why or why not?

2. Given the unique characteristics of services, what potential ethical issues could arise in service marketing and delivery? How can a service marketer prevent ethical challenges and convey a sense of trust to customers?

3. Consider the notion that a truly effective brand is one that succinctly captures the product offering in a way that answers a question in the customer's mind. Now, consider these brands (or choose your own): Coca-Cola, Disney, Marlboro, American Express, and Ford. What questions do these brands answer? Why are these effective brands?

Exercises

1. Look back at the list of the Top 25 Brands in Exhibit 7.5. What key attributes do these brands have in common? Which brands seem out of place on the list? Why? Which brands should be on this list but are missing? Why? How do you think this list will look in 5 to 10 years?

2. Do some background research on the following markets: wireless phone service, DVD players, and pizza. Which stage of the product life cycle is each of these markets in currently? What market characteristics lead you to feel this way? Is there evidence that any of these markets are on the verge of moving into the next stage of the life cycle? Explain.

3. Think about the last purchase you made in each of the product categories listed below. What were the features, advantages, and benefits of the specific product or brand that you selected? After completing the table, consider the positioning of the product or brand in the market. Does its positioning match your responses in the table? Explain.

	Features	Advantages	Benefits
Athletic shoes Brand _____			
Sit-down restaurant Name or Franchise_____			
Airline Brand _____			

CHAPTER

8

Pricing Strategy

Introduction

There is no other component of the marketing program that firms become more infatuated with than pricing: "Is our price too high? Is that why our sales are not stronger?" Conversely, managers might ask: "Is our price too low? Our sales are up, but are we leaving money on the table?" These are common concerns that run through the minds of decision makers in all firms. There are at least four reasons for the attention given to pricing. First, the revenue equation is pretty simple: Revenue equals the price times quantity sold. There are only two ways for a firm to grow revenue: increase prices or increase the volume of product sold. Rarely can a firm do both simultaneously. Although there are literally hundreds of ways to increase profit by controlling costs and operating expenses, the revenue side has only two variables—one being price and the other being heavily influenced by price.

A second reason that firms become enamored of pricing is that it is the easiest of all marketing variables to change. Although changing the product and its distribution or promotion can take months or even years, changes in pricing can be executed immediately in real time. Likewise, product, distribution, or promotion changes can also be quite expensive, especially if research and development (R&D) or production must be rescheduled. Conversely, changing prices is a very low-cost option. For example, Kroger can decide that Green Giant whole kernel corn should be $1.29 a can rather than $1.42 and immediately enter this change into the store's point-of-sale system. Similar real-time price changes occur in many other industries, including air travel, hotels, and electronic commerce. As illustrated in Beyond the Pages 8.1, prices for the same product vary around the world to account for differences in currencies, taxes/tariffs, and consumer demand.

The third reason for the importance of pricing is that firms take considerable pains to discover and anticipate the pricing strategies and tactics of other firms. Salespeople learn to read a competitor's price sheet upside down at a buyer's desk. Retailers send "secret shoppers" into competitors' stores to learn what they charge for the same merchandise. In this age of e-commerce, tracking what competitors charge

Beyond the Pages 8.1

PRICING AROUND THE WORLD[1]

If you do much traveling around the world, you'll quickly learn that products are not priced the same in different countries. In fact, despite widespread American sentiment to the contrary, the prices that we pay in the United States are among the lowest in the world. In the latest annual survey done by the Economist Group, New York—the most expensive U.S. city—ranked only twenty-seventh on the list of the most expensive cities in the world. The top-ten cities on the list, shown below, are dominated by European cities due to their strong currencies, high consumer confidence, and low interest rates. Cities at the bottom of this list are mostly from Latin America and the Middle East. For example, Tehran, Iran, is the least expensive city in the survey with an index of 33.

THE WORLD'S TOP-TEN EXPENSIVE CITIES*

Rank	City	Index
1	Oslo, Norway	140
2	Tokyo, Japan	136
3	Osaka/Kobe, Japan	135
4 (tie)	Reykjavik, Iceland	130
4 (tie)	Paris, France	130
6	Copenhagen, Denmark	127
7	London, UK	125
8	Zurich, Switzerland	123
9	Geneva, Switzerland	116
10	Helsinki, Finland	115

*Index is based on New York at 100.

Differences in pricing across national boundaries are also true with respect to so-called global brands. In most cases, the products sold around the world under the same brand name are virtually identical. They are even sold using similar promotional campaigns to the same types of target markets that consume these products in roughly the same manner. Yet, the prices set in different markets can vary dramatically, as the table below shows.

In some cases, there are logical differences in pricing, such as higher costs of transportation or other extra costs associated with bringing a product to market. Other differences are associated with currency valuation. The U.S. dollar is relatively weak compared to other currencies, so it buys less in some cases. Other differences are based on the tax and tariff structures in each country. The United States and Britain, for example, impose very high taxes on tobacco sales. In China, BMW buyers will have to add a 20 percent luxury tax to the manufacturer's suggested retail price (MSRP) before they can take the car home. A final reason for the differences is based on each company's pricing strategy. Firms have a great deal of latitude in setting prices and will often raise prices in some countries simply because consumers are willing to pay the cost to acquire a popular product with few substitutes.

Generally speaking, average prices will be lower in poorer countries than in developed countries. This is especially true in services, which are less expensive to deliver due to lower wage rates. The lower cost of labor in developing countries has spawned a groundswell of activity in outsourcing of services to other countries. The cost savings can be dramatic: Average wage rates in China and India hover around $1.50 per hour including benefits.

PRODUCT PRICES IN DIFFERENT MARKETS*

	New York	Buenos Aires	London	Moscow	Paris	Shanghai	Tokyo
4GB iPod	$249	$592	$287	$299	$296	$300	$249
Coca-Cola Classic (can)	$1	$0.65	$0.77	$1.41	$0.82	$0.44	$1.36
Big Mac	$3.29	$1.58	$3.61	$1.78	$4.09	$1.31	$2.26
Marlboro Red (pack)	$7.30	$1.15	$9.74	$1.08	$5.45	$1.87	$2.73
Motorola Razr Phone	$270	$514	$244	$300	$127	$250	$261
BMW M3 Coupe (MSRP)	$48,900	$99,000	$79,186	$49,700	$49,036	$48,700	$79,682

*All prices shown in U.S. dollars.

for their goods and services has become so daunting that an entire price-tracking industry has emerged. For example, RivalWatch uses a proprietary software program to track the prices, assortment, and promotions of merchants and then sells competitive intelligence reports to subscribing firms.[2]

Finally, pricing is given a great deal of attention because it is considered to be the only real means of differentiation in mature markets plagued by commoditization. When customers see all competing products as offering the same features and benefits, their buying decisions are primarily driven by price. This chapter addresses this and other key issues involved in developing pricing strategy. Having a solid understanding of these issues is important because far too many firms and their managers use a seat-of-the-pants approach to pricing by guessing the best price for their goods and services. Guessing is never a good strategy in marketing; it can be downright deadly when it comes to setting prices.

The Role of Pricing in Marketing Strategy

The fact that prices are easy to change should not be taken to mean that most firms do a good job of setting prices. Many manufacturers, wholesalers, and retailers readily admit that they spend more time worrying about price than they do actually manage pricing strategy. In this section, the role of pricing in marketing strategy will be discussed. First, we look at both the seller's and the buyer's perspectives on pricing. Pricing is often a major source of confrontation between sellers and buyers. Sellers obviously want to sell a product for as much as possible, while buyers would love to get the products they want for free. Somewhere between these two extremes, sellers and buyers must find a way to meet. We also look at the relationship between pricing and revenue, which is an important consideration in pricing strategy.

The Seller's Perspective on Pricing

By their nature, sellers have a tendency to inflate prices because they want to receive as much as possible in an exchange with a buyer. Consider the housing market. Homeowners who list their houses for sale have typically invested a great deal of time, energy, and memories in their homes. So, when they decide to sell, their initial feelings of their home's worth are exaggerated. Because of their emotional attachment, the homeowners may think that their house is worth $250,000. However, the home is only worth that amount if a buyer can be found who will pay that much for the house. If a buyer cannot be found, then the homeowners are guilty of letting sentiment cloud their perceptions of market reality.

This example illustrates that for homeowners or any other seller, price is often more about what the seller will accept in exchange for a product, rather than market reality. Sound pricing strategy should ignore sentimental feelings of worth and instead focus on the market factors that affect the exchange process. From the seller's perspective, four key issues become important in pricing strategy: (1) cost, (2) demand, (3) customer value, and (4) competitors' prices.

Cost is an important consideration in any pricing strategy. A firm that fails to cover both its direct costs (for example, finished goods/components, materials, supplies, sales commission, and transportation) and its indirect costs (for example, administrative expenses, utilities, and rent) will not make a profit. Firms make money either through profit margin, high sales volume, or both. Still, some measure of profit margin, even if rather small, is vital to the viability of the firm. Most smart pricing strategies build in a target profit margin as if it were a cost. Firms that use this approach recognize that a dollar reduction in price is a dollar off the bottom line, whether it comes from a high- or low-margin product.

When the availability of a product is limited, firms must also consider opportunity costs in their pricing strategy. This is particularly appropriate for service firms. For example, if an airline sells a seat from Atlanta to Chicago for $250, then that seat disappears from the inventory. If a different customer would be willing to pay $300 for the same seat and would not want to travel at a different time, then the airline lost $50 worth of profit. Manufacturers of tangible goods who do not sell a product today can sell that same product tomorrow. This is not true for service firms. This is why airlines use complex pricing systems in an attempt to squeeze every dollar out of every seat on every plane. Northwest Airlines, for example, offers deep discounts on remaining seats for flights departing on Saturday and returning on Monday or Tuesday. Northwest offers these "CyberSavers" deals to customers because they realize that an empty seat generates no revenue and that the incremental cost of adding these passengers is negligible.[3]

Market demand is also a key issue in a seller's pricing strategy. The fact that a firm covers its costs does not mean that customers will pay their prices. In this vein, more efficient firms—like low-cost airlines or discount retailers—can cover their costs while offering lower prices to customers. Customer expectations also play a role in market demand. For example, business travelers who will be reimbursed by their firm will pay more for an airline seat or a hotel room than pleasure travelers. Similarly, moviegoers will pay high prices for popcorn and soft drinks because they are a captive audience with few choices. To fully understand the relationship between price and demand, firms must have a good knowledge of the price elasticity associated with their product offering. (We address this topic in greater depth later in the chapter.)

In certain cases, pricing strategy should encompass more than the product and its price. The bottom-line impact or value delivered to the customer is often an issue in setting viable prices. This is particularly true in business markets. For example, if an insurance broker can offer a solution that reduces a client's risk costs by $10 million, what is the solution worth to the client? The same question can be asked about a new piece of production machinery that can increase capacity by 25 percent while using 50 percent less labor. Setting a price for this product may have little to do with

costs but instead focuses on the value associated with the innovation and intellectual capital of the selling firm. Firms in sectors such as marketing research, consulting, information technology, and other professional services increasingly chart the bottom-line impact or value that their services provide to clients.

Finally, a selling organization should be very much aware of what its competitors charge for the same or comparable products. All firms, however, should resist the temptation to blindly meet or beat competitors. Unless the company promotes itself as always having the lowest price, it should think in terms of pricing within an acceptable range of its competitors. Mercedes, for example, does not have to match BMW's pricing. In the case of highly commoditized markets, pricing lower than competitors can be the only viable means of differentiation. Still, rather than beating competitors' prices, a better strategy may be to create real or perceived differentiation for the product offering. This would allow the firm to charge different prices for the same or comparable products.

The Buyer's Perspective on Pricing

In many ways, the buyer's perspective on pricing is the opposite of the seller's perspective. Whereas sellers tend to bid prices up, buyers often see prices as being lower than market reality dictates. In our housing market example, the buyers do not hold an appreciation for the time, energy, and emotion invested in the home by the homeowner. The buyers only see a house and whether its features will fulfill their needs and preferences. Despite the sellers' $250,000 asking price, prospective buyers may think the house is worth only $200,000, given its features, condition, and the prices of other homes in the area.

For buyers, price is about what the buyer will give up in exchange for a product. The key for the selling firm and for the development of pricing strategy is to determine just how much the buyer will give up. Firms must also recognize that buyers give up much more than their money when they buy goods and services. From the buyer's perspective, two key issues determine pricing strategy for most firms: (1) perceived value and (2) price sensitivity.

What buyers will give up in exchange for a product depends to a great extent on their perceived value of the product. *Value* is a difficult term to define because it means different things to different people.[4] Some customers equate good value with high product quality, whereas others see value as nothing more than a low price. The most common definition of *value* relates customer benefits to costs; or to use a more colloquial expression, good value gives "more bang for the buck." For our purposes, we define *value* as a customer's subjective evaluation of benefits relative to costs to determine the worth of a firm's product offering relative to other product offerings. A simple formula for value might look like this:

$$\text{Perceived Value} = \frac{\text{Customer Benefits}}{\text{Customer Costs}}$$

Customer benefits include everything that the customer obtains from the product offering, such as quality, satisfaction, prestige/image, and the solution to a problem.

Customer costs include everything the customer must give up, such as money, time, effort, and all nonselected alternatives (opportunity costs). Although value is a key component in setting a viable pricing strategy, good value depends on much more than pricing. In fact, value is intricately tied to every element in the marketing program. We discuss the strategic implications of value more fully in Chapter 12.

Good pricing strategy is also based on a thorough understanding of the price elasticity associated with a firm's goods and services. On the buyer's side, price elasticity translates into the unique and varying buying situations that cause buyers to be more or less sensitive to price changes. Not only must firms know what customers will pay for a product, but they must also understand their buying behavior in specific situations that lead to price sensitivity. We discuss these buying situations in greater depth later in the chapter.

A Shift in the Balance of Power

Phrases such as "It's a buyer's market" and "It's a seller's market" refer to who holds the power in the exchange relationship. Buyers have increased power over sellers when there are a large number of sellers in the market or when there are many substitutes for the product. Buyers also have power when the economy is weak and fewer customers will part with their money. During a seller's market, prices go up and terms and services become less favorable. Sellers have increased power over buyers when certain products are in short supply or in high demand. Sellers also have increased power during good economic times when customers will spend more money.

For most products and markets, a buyer's market prevails. Of course, there are exceptions such as high-definition DVD players, the Ford Mustang Shelby GT, and the latest iPod design. A buyer's market exists in most markets due to the large number of product choices that are available, increased commoditization among competing products and brands, and a general decline in brand loyalty among customers. This state of affairs is tempered somewhat by sluggish consumer spending and guarded consumer confidence. However, both business and consumer markets have become much more savvy and sophisticated in their buying behavior.

For these reasons, firms must carefully manage price in relation to the entire marketing program. Firms that get greedy in their pricing strategy may find no one standing in line to buy their products.

The Relationship Between Price and Revenue

All marketers understand the relationship between price and revenue. However, firms cannot charge high prices without good reason. In fact, virtually all firms face intense price competition from their rivals, which tends to hold prices down. In the face of this competition, it is natural for firms to see price cutting as a viable means of increasing sales. Price cutting can also move excess inventory and generate short-term cash flow. However, all price cuts affect the firm's bottom line. When setting prices, many firms hold fast to these two general pricing myths:[5]

Myth 1: When business is good, a price cut will capture greater market share.
Myth 2: When business is bad, a price cut will stimulate sales.

Unfortunately, the relationship between price and revenue challenges these assumptions and makes them a risky proposition for most firms. The reality is that any price cut must be offset by an increase in sales volume just to maintain the same level of revenue. Let's look at an example. Assume that a consumer electronics manufacturer sells 1,000 high-end stereo receivers per month at $1,000 per system. The firm's total cost is $500 per system, which leaves a gross margin of $500. When the sales of this high-end system decline, the firm decides to cut the price to increase sales. The firm's strategy is to offer a $100 rebate to anyone who buys a system over the next three months. The rebate is consistent with a 10 percent price cut, but it is in reality a 20 percent reduction in gross margin (from $500 to $400). To compensate for the loss in gross margin, the firm must increase the volume of receivers sold. The question is by how much. We can find the answer using this formula:

$$\text{Percent Change in Unit Volume} = \frac{\text{Gross Margin \%}}{\text{Gross Margin \%} \pm \text{Price Change \%}} - 1$$

$$.25 = \frac{.50}{.50 - .10} - 1$$

As the calculation indicates, the firm would have to increase sales volume by 25 percent to 1,250 units sold in order to maintain the same level of total gross margin. How likely is it that a $100 rebate will increase sales volume by 25 percent? This question is critical to the success of the firm's rebate strategy. In many instances, the needed increase in sales volume is too high. Consequently, the firm's gross margin may actually be lower after the price cut.

Rather than blindly use price cutting to stimulate sales and revenue, it is often better for a firm to find ways to build value into the product and justify the current price or even a higher price rather than cutting the product's price in search of higher sales volume. In the case of the stereo manufacturer, giving customers $100 worth of CDs or DVDs for each purchase is a much better option than a $100 rebate. Video game manufacturers, such as Microsoft (Xbox) and Sony (PlayStation 3), often bundle games and accessories with their system consoles to increase value. The cost of giving customers these free add-ons is low because the marketer buys them in bulk quantities. This added expense is almost always less costly than a price cut. And the increase in value may allow the marketer to charge higher prices for the product bundle.

Key Issues in Pricing Strategy

Given the importance of pricing in marketing strategy, pricing decisions are among the most complex decisions to be made in developing a marketing plan. Decisions regarding price require a tightly integrated balance among a number of important issues. Many of these issues possess some degree of uncertainty regarding the reactions to pricing among customers, competitors, and supply chain partners. Some issues, such as the firm's pricing objectives, supply and demand, and the firm's cost structure, are critically important in establishing initial prices. Other issues become important after the initial price has been set, especially with respect to modifying the pricing strategy over time.

As we review these issues, keep in mind that they are interrelated and must be considered in the context of the firm's entire marketing program. For example, increases in product quality or the addition of new product features often come with an increase in price. This is especially true when the product contains the latest technology such as video messaging and music downloads on wireless telephones. Pricing is also influenced by distribution, especially the image and reputation of the outlets where the good or service is sold. Finally, companies often use price as a tool of promotion. Coupons, for example, represent a combination of price and promotion that can stimulate increased sales in many different product categories. In services, price changes are often used to fill unused capacity (for example, empty airline or theater seats) during nonpeak demand.

Pricing Objectives

Setting specific pricing objectives that are realistic, measurable, and attainable is an important part of pricing strategy. As shown in Exhibit 8.1, there are a number of pricing objectives that firms may pursue. Remember that firms make money on profit margin, volume, or some combination of the two. A firm's pricing objectives will always reflect this market reality.

Pricing objectives are not always about tweaking price to increase profit or volume. Sometimes firms simply want to maintain their prices in an effort to retain their position relative to the competition. This pricing objective is called *status quo pricing*. Although status quo pricing sounds like it involves little or no planning, the decision to maintain prices must be done after a careful analysis of all factors that affect pricing strategy.

Supply and Demand

The basic laws of supply and demand have an obvious influence on pricing strategy. Although the inverse relationship between price and demand is well known and understood (as price goes up, demand goes down), it is essentially a supply-side perspective. That is, the relationship between price and demand is most often seen from the marketer's point of view. However, the demand-side perspective is often quite different. Consider what happens when customer demand increases for a particular product. Does the inverse relationship hold? Do prices fall? Not hardly. In fact, during periods of heavy customer demand, prices tend to stay the same or even increase. Gasoline prices over the summer are a good example, as is a new high-tech product in high demand.

Another important supply-and-demand issue is customer expectations regarding pricing. Customers always hold expectations about price when they purchase products. However, in some situations, customer expectations about price can be the driving force in pricing strategy. For example, moviegoers expect to pay $3 to $4 for a small soft drink or popcorn. Summer vacationers expect to pay more for gasoline.

EXHIBIT 8.1	DESCRIPTION OF COMMON PRICING OBJECTIVES

Pricing Objectives	Description
Profit-Oriented	Designed to maximize price relative to competitors' prices, the product's perceived value, the firm's cost structure, and production efficiency. Profit objectives are typically based on a target return, rather than simple profit maximization.
Volume-Oriented	Sets prices in order to maximize dollar or unit sales volume. This objective sacrifices profit margin in favor of high product turnover.
Market Demand	Sets prices in accordance with customer expectations and specific buying situations. This objective is often known as "charging what the market will bear."
Market Share	Designed to increase or maintain market share regardless of fluctuations in industry sales. Market share objectives are often used in the maturity stage of the product life cycle.
Cash Flow	Designed to maximize the recovery of cash as quickly as possible. This objective is useful when a firm has a cash emergency or when the product life cycle is expected to be quite short.
Competitive Matching	Designed to match or beat competitor's prices. The goal is to maintain the perception of good value relative to the competition.
Prestige	Sets high prices that are consistent with a prestige or high status product. Prices are set with little regard for the firm's cost structure or the competition.
Status Quo	Maintains current prices in an effort to sustain a position relative to the competition.

And college students expect to get roughly half price when they resell their textbooks. Situations such as these allow marketers to set prices in accordance with what the market will pay with little or no regard for their costs, the competition, or other factors that typically affect pricing strategy. However, the flip side is also true. If customers expect to pay 5¢ or less for one minute of long-distance telephone service, then that is all that the firm can charge for the product.

The Firm's Cost Structure

The firm's costs in producing and marketing a product are an important factor in setting prices. After all, costs must be factored out of the revenue equation in order to determine profits and ultimately survival of the firm. Perhaps the most popular way to associate costs and prices is through break-even pricing where the firm's fixed and variable costs are considered:

$$\text{Breakeven in Units} = \frac{\text{Total Fixed Costs}}{\text{Unit Price} - \text{Unit Variable Costs}}$$

To use break-even analysis in setting prices, the firm must look at the feasibility of selling more than the break-even level in order to make a profit. The break-even number is only a point of reference in setting prices because market conditions and customer demand must also be considered.

Another way to use the firm's cost structure in setting prices is to use cost-plus pricing—a strategy that is common in retailing. Here, the firm sets prices based on average unit costs and its planned markup percentage:

$$\text{Selling Price} = \frac{\text{Average Unit Cost}}{1 - \text{Markup Percent (decimal)}}$$

Cost-plus pricing is not only intuitive but also very easy to use. Its weakness, however, lies in determining the correct markup percentage. Industry norms often come into play at this point. For example, average markups in grocery retailing are typically in the 20 percent range, but markups can be several hundred percent or more in furniture or jewelry stores. Customer expectations are also an important consideration in determining the correct markup percentage.

Although break-even analysis and cost-plus pricing are important tools, they should not be the driving force behind pricing strategy. The reason is often ignored: Different firms have different cost structures. By setting prices solely on the basis of costs, firms run a major risk in setting their prices too high or too low. If one firm's costs are relatively higher than other firms, it will have to accept lower margins in order to compete effectively. Conversely, just because a product costs very little to produce and market does not mean that the firm should sell it at a low price (remember the movie theater popcorn example). Cost is best understood as an absolute floor below which prices cannot be set for an extended period of time.

Competition and Industry Structure

Firms that use competitive matching pricing objectives face a constant struggle to monitor and respond to competitors' price changes. This struggle is a way of life in the travel and tourism industry. However, a firm does not always have to match competitors' prices to compete effectively. The competitive market structure of the industry in which a firm operates affects its flexibility in raising or lowering prices. Industry structure also affects how competitors will respond to changes in price. There are four basic competitive market structures:

- **Perfect Competition** This market contains an unlimited number of sellers and buyers who exchange for homogeneous products. Market entry is easy, and no single participant can influence price or supply significantly. For the most part, pure competition does not exist although some agricultural and commodity markets come reasonably close.

- **Monopolistic Competition** This market contains many sellers and buyers who exchange for relatively heterogeneous products. Marketing strategy involves product differentiation and/or niche marketing to overcome the threats imposed by the wide availability of substitute products. The heterogeneous nature of the products gives firms some control over prices. Most markets fall into this category.

- **Oligopoly** This market contains relatively few sellers who control the supply of a dominant portion of the industry's product. However, no one seller controls the market. One firm's prices affect the sales of competing firms, and all firms typically match the price changes of competitors. These firms often turn to nonprice strategies to differentiate their product offerings. Examples of U.S. oligopolies include the automobile, tobacco, oil, steel, aerospace, and music recording industries.

- **Monopoly**   This market is dominated by a single seller who sells a product with no close substitutes. The single seller is the sole source of supply. Essentially, the only monopolies operating in the United States today are regulated utilities.

Monopolies obviously have the most pricing flexibility unless regulated by federal, state, or local governments. Firms operating in oligopolies gain little advantage in pricing due to quick reaction by competitors. The heavy discounting in the automobile industry over the past several years is a good example. Firms facing monopolistic competition must be able to create real or perceived differentiation in order to justify higher prices relative to competitors. Firms also face significant pricing challenges when their industry shifts to a different structure. In the telecommunications industry, for example, decreased regulation and increased merger activity has shifted the industry away from monopolistic competition to an oligopolistic structure.

Stage of the Product Life Cycle

As we noted in Chapter 7, marketing strategy shifts as a product moves through the stages of its life cycle. Pricing changes, like changes in the other elements of the marketing program, occur as demand, competition, customer expectations, and the product itself change over time. Exhibit 8.2 illustrates how pricing changes might occur over the product life cycle.

Pricing strategy in the introduction stage is critical because it sets the standard for pricing changes over time. As price changes over the life cycle, the initial price set during a product's introduction determines whether the firm will make a profit or lose money as time goes on. By the time a product enters the maturity stage, competitive dynamics have established an acceptable and expected range of prices that firms must fall within to remain competitive. As a result, firms must look inward to find ways to cut costs and maintain profits later in the life cycle. Also, very few products enjoy the luxury of raising prices during the decline stage. Vintage items like antique cars, vinyl records, and collectables are among the few to command higher prices at the end of their life cycles.

EXHIBIT 8.2	PRICING STRATEGY OVER THE PRODUCT LIFE CYCLE
Introduction	The price sensitivity of the market determines the initial pricing strategy. When the market is relatively insensitive to price, prices are set high to recoup investment and generate high profits to fuel growth (a price skimming strategy). If the market is sensitive to price, prices are set at, or lower than, the competition to gain a foothold in the market (a price penetration strategy).
Growth	A gradual lowering of prices occurs due to increasing competition and growing economies of scale that reduce production and marketing costs. The product also begins to appeal to a broader base of customers, many of whom are quite price sensitive.
Maturity	Prices continue to decrease as competition intensifies and ineffective firms are eliminated from the market. Most firms focus heavily on cost savings; economies of scale; or synergies in production, promotion, and distribution to maintain profit margins. Specific pricing tactics encourage brand switching in an attempt to steal business away from the competition.
Decline	Prices continue to fall until only one or a few firms remain. At that point, prices begin to stabilize or even increase somewhat as firms squeeze the last bit of profit from a product. Some products can experience sharp increases in price if their popularity and unique appeal remain high.

Pricing Service Products

When it comes to buying services, customers have a difficult time determining quality prior to purchase. Consequently, service pricing is critical because it may be the only quality cue that is available in advance of the purchase experience. If the service provider sets prices too low, customers will have inaccurate perceptions and expectations about quality. If prices are too high, customers may not give the firm a chance. In general, services pricing becomes more important—and more difficult—when

- service quality is hard to detect prior to purchase.

- the costs associated with providing the service are difficult to determine.

- customers are unfamiliar with the service process.

- brand names are not well established.

- customers can perform the service themselves.

- the service has poorly defined units of consumption.

- advertising within a service category is limited.

- the total price of the service experience is difficult to state beforehand.

Most services suffer from the challenges associated with determining costs because intangible expenses such as labor, insurance, and overhead must be taken into account. Poorly defined units of consumption characterize some services. For example, what is the unit of measure for hairstyling services? Is it time, hair length, type of style, or gender of the customer? Many female customers complain that they have to pay more for a cut and style than men, even when a man's hair is longer. When the firm offers services that customers can do for themselves—such as lawn maintenance, oil changes, or house painting—it must be especially mindful of setting the correct price. In these instances, the firm is competing with the customer's evaluation of his or her time and ability, in addition to other competing service providers.

Setting prices for professional services (lawyers, accountants, consultants, doctors, and mechanics) is especially difficult because they suffer from a number of the conditions in the list above. Customers often balk at the high prices of these service providers because they have a limited ability to evaluate the quality or total cost until the service process has been completed. The heterogeneous nature of these services limits standardization; therefore, customer knowledge about pricing is

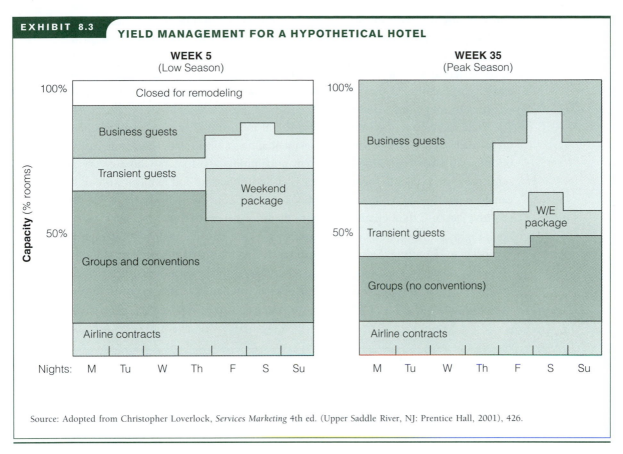

EXHIBIT 8.3   YIELD MANAGEMENT FOR A HYPOTHETICAL HOTEL

WEEK 5 (Low Season)

Capacity (% rooms)

100% — Closed for remodeling

Business guests

Transient guests

Weekend package

50%

Groups and conventions

Airline contracts

Nights: M Tu W Th F S Su

WEEK 35 (Peak Season)

100%

Business guests

W/E package

50% — Transient guests

Groups (no conventions)

Airline contracts

M Tu W Th F S Su

Source: Adopted from Christopher Loverlock, *Services Marketing* 4th ed. (Upper Saddle River, NJ: Prentice Hall, 2001), 426.

limited. Heterogeneity also limits price comparison among competing providers. The key for these firms it to be up front about the expected quality and costs of the service. This is often done through the use of binding estimates and contractual guarantees of quality.

Due to the limited capacity associated with most services, service pricing is also a key issue with respect to balancing supply and demand during peak and off-peak demand times. In these situations, many service firms use yield management systems to balance pricing and revenue considerations with their need to fill unfilled capacity. Exhibit 8.3 depicts an example of yield management for a hotel.

Yield management allows the service firm to simultaneously control capacity and demand in order to maximize revenue and capacity utilization.[6] This is accomplished in two ways. First, the service firm controls capacity by limiting the available capacity at certain price points. In the hotel example in Exhibit 8.3, limited rooms are available to different market segments at different times of the year. In the off-season, many hotels schedule routine maintenance and remodeling and reduce rates for conventions in order to fill unused capacity. Airlines do this by selling a limited number of seats at discount prices three or more weeks prior to a flight's departure. Southwest Airlines, for example, sells limited seats in four categories: Fun Fares (the lowest-priced seats), Advance Purchase, Restricted Fares, and Refundable Anytime (the highest-priced seats).[7]

Second, the service firm controls demand through price changes over time and by overbooking capacity. These activities ensure that service demand will be consistent and that any unused capacity will be minimized. These practices are common in services characterized by high fixed costs and low variable costs, such as airlines, hotels, rental cars, cruises, transportation firms, and hospitals. Because variable costs in these services are quite low, the profit for these firms directly relates to sales and capacity utilization. Consequently, these firms will sell some capacity at reduced prices in order to maximize utilization.

Yield management systems are also useful in their ability to segment markets based on price elasticity. That is, yield management allows a firm to offer the same basic service to different market segments at different price points. Customers who are very price sensitive with respect to travel services—vacation travelers and families with children—can get a good deal on a hotel if they book it early. Conversely, consultants are less price sensitive because their clients reimburse them for expenses. Likewise, business travelers book flights on the spur of the moment, so they are more forgiving of the higher prices just prior to departure. Other firms can reach different market segments with attractive off-peak pricing. Many customers take advantage of the lower prices at theme parks and beach resorts by traveling during the off-season. Similar situations occur in lower-priced movie matinees and lower prices for lunch items at most restaurants.

Price Elasticity of Demand

As we have seen thus far in this chapter, pricing has intricate connections to issues such as demand, competition, and customer expectations. All these issues come together in the concept of price elasticity of demand, which is perhaps the most important overall consideration in setting effective prices. Simply defined, *price elasticity* refers to customers' responsiveness or sensitivity to changes in price. A more precise definition defines *elasticity* as the relative impact on the demand for a product, given specific increases or decreases in the price charged for that product. The following formula is used to calculate price elasticity:

$$\text{Price Elasticity of Demand} = \frac{\text{Percentage Change in Quantity Demanded}}{\text{Percentage Change in Price}}$$

For products where this calculation produces a number less than 1, the product has *inelastic demand*. In this case, an increase or decrease in price does not significantly affect the quantity demanded. When the calculation produces a number greater than 1, the product has *elastic demand*. Here, the quantity demanded is sensitive to price fluctuations, so a change in price will produce a change in demand and total revenue. If the calculation produces a number that equals 1 or is very close to 1, the product has *unitary demand*. In this situation, the changes in price and demand offset, so total revenue remains the same. Exhibit 8.4 displays a graphical illustration of price elasticity.

Firms cannot base prices solely on price elasticity calculations because they will rarely know the elasticity for any product with great precision over time. Further, price elasticity is not uniform over time and place because demand is not uniform

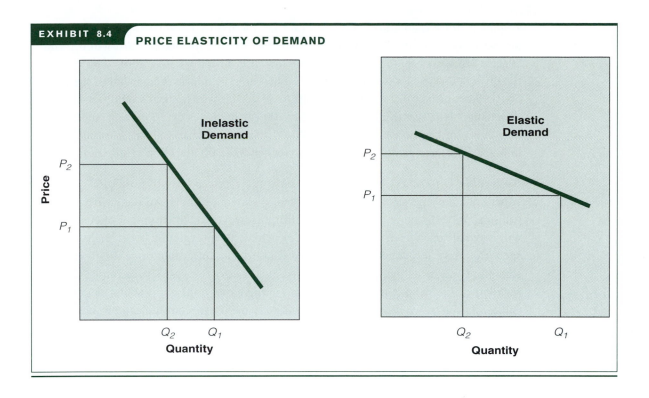

EXHIBIT 8.4   PRICE ELASTICITY OF DEMAND

over time and place. As a result, the same product can have different elasticities in different times, places, and situations. Because the actual price elasticity calculation is difficult to pinpoint precisely, firms often consider price elasticity in regard to differing customer behavior patterns or purchase situations. Understanding when, where, and how customers are more or less sensitive to price is crucial in setting fair and profitable prices. In the sections that follow, we examine many of these behavior patterns and purchase situations that can affect customers' sensitivity to pricing and price changes.

Situations That Increase Price Sensitivity

Generally speaking, customers become much more price sensitive when they have many different choices or options for fulfilling their needs and wants. Price elasticity is higher (more elastic) in the following situations.

Availability of Product Substitutes   When customers can choose among a number of different product substitutes, they will be much more sensitive to price differences. This situation occurs very frequently among brand-name products and in markets where product offerings have become commoditized. Air travel is a perfect example. When AirTran began flying out of Atlanta in the 1990s, travelers saw the carrier as an acceptable alternative to Delta and other existing carriers. As a result, the fare for a flight between Atlanta and other destinations suddenly became more elastic. If Delta had not matched AirTran's lower fare on these routes, their planes would have had more empty seats.

Higher Total Expenditure   As a general rule, the higher the total expenditure to purchase and use a product, the more elastic the demand for that product will be. This effect is actually easier to see if we look at a low-priced product. A 20 percent increase in the price of Q-Tips, for example, would not have a large impact on demand. If the price of a 100-count box increased from $1.00 to $1.20, most customers would not notice the change. However, if the price of a $20,000 car increases by 20 percent, then the impact is a much more noticeable $4,000. At that rate of change, some customers will look for a different car. Others will decide that, at $24,000, they don't really need a car.

Noticeable Differences   Products that have their prices heavily promoted tend to experience more elastic demand. Gasoline is a classic example. An increase in 3¢ per gallon is only 45¢ more on a 15-gallon fill-up. However, a large number of customers will drive all over town to find what they believe is an available lower price (often spending more in gas consumption than they save). Noticeable price differences sometimes occur at specific pricing thresholds. Using the gasoline example, a large segment of the market may not notice price increases until gas reaches $3.00 per gallon. At this price, these customers suddenly move from an inelastic mind-set to an elastic mind-set: "Three dollars! Are you kidding me? I will walk before I spend that much for gas." The move from $2.80 to $2.90 may not have had an impact on these customers, but the jump from $2.90 to $3.00 totally changes their mental framework.

Easy Price Comparisons   Regardless of the product or product category, customers will become more price sensitive if they can easily compare prices among competing products. In industries such as retailing, supermarkets, travel, toys, and books, price has become a dominant purchase consideration because customers can easily compare prices. It should come as no surprise that these industries have also experienced a shift from offline to online sales. Consider how easy it is to compare prices for air travel, hotels, and rental cars on Expedia.com or Travelocity. Likewise, at Fetchbook.info, customers can track down the lowest prices on books across 126 different bookstores. Price comparison has also become a dominant driver behind the success of online retailers such as Amazon.com.

Situations That Decrease Price Sensitivity

In general, customers become much less price sensitive when they have few choices or options for fulfilling their needs and wants. Price elasticity is lower (more inelastic) in the situations discussed here.

Lack of Product Substitutes   When customers have few choices in terms of product substitutes, they will be much less price sensitive. This situation is common in some categories including baking/cooking ingredients, add-on or replacement parts, one-of-a-kind antiques, collectables or memorabilia, and specialized vacation destinations. The more unique or specialized the product, the more customers will pay for it. In 2006, for example, a wealthy collector paid over $3.5 million for a 300-year-old

Stradivarius violin—the most ever paid for any musical instrument at auction.[8] The lack of substitutes also makes customers less sensitive to the time and effort required to obtain products. For example, avid antique collectors often devote every free moment to traveling in search of hidden treasures.

Product Differentiation   The inherent goal of differentiation is to make the demand curve for a product more inelastic. Differentiation reduces the number of perceived substitutes for a product. For example, Coca-Cola's differentiation strategy has worked so well that Coke drinkers will buy the soft drink at $1.25 or $2.25 per six-pack. Product differentiation does not have to be based on real differences in order to make customers less price sensitive. Many times the differences are perceptual. Blindfolded, a person may not know the difference between Coke and Pepsi, but consumers do not buy or consume soft drinks blindfolded. The look of the can, the advertising, and prior experiences all come together to differentiate the product.

The ultimate goal in product differentiation as it relates to price elasticity is brand loyalty. If differentiation can successfully reduce the number of product alternatives to zero, then customers will become brand loyal, and the demand for the product will become very inelastic. Nike, for example, commands extreme brand loyalty because the firm has successfully differentiated its products through technological innovation, effective advertising, and the ubiquitous swoosh. Likewise, Intel has done a great job using real and perceived differentiation to become the dominant supplier of processor chips in the computer industry. Customers who demand a computer with "Intel Inside" do not know the technological differences between a Core Duo, Pentium, or Celeron processor or competing processors such as Athlon, Turion, and Sempron. These customers want an Intel chip because they trust it to be fast, reliable, and compatible with other products.

Real or Perceived Necessities   Many products, such as food, water, medical care, cigarettes, and prescription drugs, have extremely inelastic demand because customers have real or perceived needs for them. If the price of food doubles overnight, we might make some adjustments, but we would still have to eat. Some product categories are price inelastic because customers perceive those products as true necessities. It matters little whether a customer truly has a need for a specific product. If that customer perceives the product as a necessity, then that customer becomes much less sensitive to price increases for that product.

Complementary Products   Complementary products have an effect on the price sensitivity of related products. If the price of one product falls, customers will become less price sensitive with respect to complementary products. For example, when the price of a cruise goes down, the price of shore excursions at each port becomes more inelastic. With more travelers on board and each having more money to spend, excursion operators realize that travelers are less sensitive to the prices they charge. The same is true for strawberries and shortcake, computers and software, or any other set of complementary goods or services.

Perceived Product Benefits   For some customers, certain products are just worth the price. For these purchases, the phrase "expensive but worth it" comes to mind. All of us have certain products that we indulge in from time to time, such as fine wines, gourmet chocolates, imported coffee, or trips to a day spa. Since these products do not comprise the bulk of our purchasing activities, customers rarely notice or simply ignore price increases. Other customers, however, base their entire purchasing patterns on buying the best products in all categories. From Rolex watches to Monte Blanc pens, many customers see high-quality and high-priced products as just being worth it. Customers who embrace this purchasing mentality do not concern themselves with the price of a product or any price increase.

Situational Influences   The circumstances that surround a purchase situation can vastly alter the elasticity of demand for a product. Many of these situational influences occur because time pressures or purchase risk increase to the point that an immediate purchase must be made or the availability of product substitutes falls dramatically. For example, there is a dramatic difference between leisurely shopping for a new set of tires and finding yourself stranded on the highway with a blown tire and no spare tire. The same inelastic demand situation occurs when you need a plumber in the middle of the night or on the weekend. Emergencies like this are one of the more common examples of situational influences that can alter price perceptions.

Other common situational influences revolve around purchase risk, typically the social risk involved in making a bad decision. In a general sense, customers tend to be much less price sensitive when they purchase items for others or for gift giving. Further, customers are less price sensitive when others will notice the purchase. For example, you might be less sensitive to prices when purchasing a new wardrobe for a series of job interviews.

Pricing Strategies

Although prices for individual products are made on a case-by-case basis, most firms have developed a general and consistent approach—or general pricing strategy—to be used in establishing prices. The relationship between price and other elements of the marketing program dictates that pricing decisions cannot be made in isolation. In fact, price changes may result in minor modifications to the product, distribution, or promotion strategies. As we have discussed, it is not so much the actual price being charged that influences buying decisions as the way that members of the target market perceive the price. This reality reminds us that many of the strategic issues involved in pricing have close ties with customer psychology and information processing: What customers think about prices is what those prices are to them.

Base-Pricing Strategies

A firm's base-pricing strategy establishes the initial price and sets the range of possible price movements throughout the product's life cycle. The initial price is critical, not only for initial success but also for maintaining the potential for profit over the long term. There are several different approaches to base pricing, including market intro-duction pricing, prestige pricing, value-based pricing, competitive matching, and nonprice strategies. We have briefly touched on some of these strategies in earlier portions of the chapter. Now let's look more closely at these approaches.

Market Introduction Pricing   Firms often use different pricing strategies when their products are first launched into the market. The two most common intro-duction approaches are called price skimming and penetration pricing. The idea behind *price skimming* is to intentionally set a high price relative to the competi-tion, thereby skimming the profits off the top of the market. Price skimming is designed to recover the high R&D and marketing expenses associated with developing a new product. It may also be used to initially segment the market based on price or to control the initial demand for the product. Virtually all new high-tech products, new computer technology, and new prescription drugs use a price-skimming approach.

For price skimming to work, the product must be perceived as having unique advantages over competing products. When the high price brings unique or new benefits, customers do not mind paying for the product. For example, the $80 per month price for Pfizer's cholesterol-lowering drug Lipitor is worth it to patients who suffer from high cholesterol. The high prices associated with prescription medications like Lipitor are designed to recoup the expenses associated with developing and marketing new drugs. However, in the case of pharmaceuticals, price skimming only works as long as the drug is protected by patent. In Pfizer's case, the patent on Lipitor expires in 2010. However, the patent on Merck's Zocor, a major competitor, expired in 2006, opening the way for generic pricing. Despite its patent protection, Lipitor sales are likely to fall as managed-care companies force patients to switch to lower-priced Zocor clones.[9]

The goal of *penetration pricing* is to maximize sales, gain widespread market acceptance, and capture a large market share quickly by setting a relatively low initial price. This approach works best when customers are price sensitive for the product or product category, R&D and marketing expenses are relatively low, or when new competitors will quickly enter the market. Because of its flexibility, penetration pricing can be used to launch a new product or to introduce new product lines to an established product portfolio. For example, when Motorola introduced its Q smart phone, it did so exclusively through Verizon wireless at a penetration price of $199 after rebate. This relatively low price not only encouraged customers to switch to the Q but also established a presence in the market prior to the onslaught of competition from other smart phone manufacturers.[10]

The benefits of penetration pricing—rapid market acceptance and maximum sales—also have the benefit of discouraging competition from entering the market. This is a powerful advantage that makes a penetration approach appealing. However, the strategy is not for all firms. To use penetration pricing successfully, the firm must have a cost structure and scale economies that can withstand narrow profit margins. As illustrated in Beyond the Pages 8.2, some firms adopt a penetration-pricing strategy

Beyond the Pages 8.2

SELLING AT A LOSS[11]

Sometimes the best pricing strategy involves giving away the product, especially if the firm is looking for rapid adoption among customers. This has long been the case in computer software where manufacturers give away restricted versions of their software to encourage trial. Adobe, for example, gives away its popular Reader to maintain branding of its other software products. McAfee and Norton freely package their antivirus programs with new computer purchases in hopes that buyers will subscribe to their weekly update services. The strategy is also used in consumer products. Procter & Gamble gives away (or sells below cost) its razors in the anticipation that it will sell more blades in the future.

The free or below-cost pricing strategy is common among products that are sold as platforms. A platform product is one that consists of a base product with numerous add-ons or supplemental products. Video gaming systems are a good example. When Microsoft launched the Xbox 360 in 2005, it did so using a "neutral gross margin" strategy. At the core of this strategy is selling each console at a loss. When the cost of parts, cables, and controllers are factored in, Microsoft loses roughly $126 per console. The company makes up that loss through higher profit margins on games, accessories, and brand licensing. Microsoft does not expect to turn any profit on the Xbox 360 until sometime in 2007.

Rival platform maker Sony is expected to lose even more money on each PlayStation 3 (PS3) unit

that it sells. One reason is the cost of two key parts: the cell processor and the high-definition Blu-ray DVD drive. Manufacturing costs for the PS3 range from $500 to $800 per unit. Sony expects to lose as much as $817 million on the PS3 in the first year after launch. While Sony makes up the difference in games and accessories, it will look to quickly reduce the manufacturing costs of the PS3 console.

Toshiba is also using the loss-leader strategy in its battle for supremacy in the high-definition (HD) DVD market. There are two competing technologies in this market: Blu-ray (developed by Sony and included in the PS3) is backed by major movie studios, and HD-DVD (developed by Toshiba) and supported by Microsoft and Intel. Toshiba was first to the market with its $499 HD-A1 player. Samsung introduced the first stand-alone Blu-ray player at a price of $999, exactly twice the price of Toshiba's player.

Analysts have determined that Toshiba spends more than $700 to make and sell the HD-A1 player. However, unlike Microsoft and Sony, Toshiba's losses are only partially tempered through the sale of HD-DVD movies. Instead, Toshiba's loss-leader strategy is designed to maximize product adoption by putting its next generation DVD player in more customers' homes at a faster pace. Many expect the HD-DVD and Blu-ray battle to be significant and bloody—not unlike the battle between VHS and Betamax roughly three decades ago. Toshiba hopes to win the war through high-volume sales and widespread consumer adoption.

---

by selling their products at a loss, hoping to make up the lost revenue via the sale of accessories, add-ons, or subscription services. Although price penetration does not necessarily mean low profit per unit sold, it does require a higher volume of sales to achieve the same total profit that would be achieved using a price-skimming approach. For these reasons, price penetration occurs primarily in situations where the firm has a reasonable expectation of achieving the necessary sales volume to make the product financially viable.

Prestige Pricing   Firms using prestige pricing set their prices at the top end of all competing products in a category. This is done to promote an image of exclusivity and superior quality. Ritz-Carlton Hotels, for example, never wants to compete with other hotels on price. Instead, the company competes only on service and the value of the unique, high-quality experience it they delivers to hotel guests. Prestige pricing is a viable approach in situations where it is hard to objectively judge the true value of a product. In these instances, a higher price may indicate a higher-quality product. Inexperienced wine consumers, for example, might assume that a $40 bottle of wine is better than a $15 bottle. Only a true connoisseur would actually know, but the average wine-buying public would see the $40 bottle as more appropriate for a special occasion or celebration. Consulting and research services are often sold in this fashion as well. Former U.S. presidents and corporate CEOs can command up to $100,000 for a 1-hour speech to a company's employees. The presumption held by the firm is that speaker's message will have a stronger impact than a local professional speaker who earns $5000 for the same amount of time.

Value-Based Pricing   Firms that use a value-based pricing approach set reasonably low prices but still offer high-quality products and adequate customer services. Many different types of firms use value-based pricing; however, retailing has widely embraced this approach, where it is known as everyday low pricing (EDLP). The goal of value-based pricing is to set a reasonable price for the level of quality offered. Prices are not the highest in the market, nor are they the lowest. Instead, value-based pricing sets prices so that they are consistent with the benefits and costs associated with acquiring the product.

Many well-known firms use value-based pricing, including Wal-Mart, Lowe's, The Home Depot, IKEA, Saturn, and Southwest Airlines. Each of these firms exhibits the two major characteristics of the value-based pricing approach. First, these firms have the capacity to offer reasonable prices because they have engineered themselves to be a low-cost provider in their respective industries. Value-based pricing requires that the firm be highly efficient in operations and marketing in order to keep costs and prices low. Second, firms adopting value-based pricing maintain consistent prices over time; they use sales, discounts, and other pricing tactics infrequently. Value-based pricing naturally draws customers because they have confidence in the value of the products that they buy. Customers also like the approach because it requires less effort to find good prices on the products that they want and need.

Competitive Matching   In many industries, particularly oligopolies, pricing strategy focuses on matching competitors' prices and price changes. Although some firms may charge slightly more or slightly less, these firms set prices at what most consider to be the "going rate" for the industry. Two competitive factors largely drive this strategy. First, firms that offer commodity-type products (for example, airlines, oil, and steel) have a very difficult time finding any real or perceived basis for product differentiation. So, when customers see all products as being about the same, the prices have to be about the same as well. Second, some industries are so highly competitive that competitive price matching becomes a means of survival. The automobile industry and its long-running zero-percent financing and generous rebate offers are a good example.

Nonprice Strategies   It may seem odd to discuss nonprice strategies in this chapter, but building a marketing program around factors other than price is an important strategic pricing decision. By downplaying price in the marketing program, the firm must be able to emphasize the product's quality, benefits, and unique features, as well as customer service, promotion, or packaging in order to make the product stand out against competitors—many of whom will offer similar products at lower prices. Nonprice strategies are most effective when (1) the product can be successfully differentiated, (2) customers see the differentiating characteristics as being important, (3) competitors cannot emulate the differentiating characteristics, and (4) the market is generally not price sensitive. For example, theme parks like Disney World, Sea World, and Universal Studios compete on excellent service, unique benefits, and one-of-a-kind experiences rather than price. Customers willingly pay for these experiences because they cannot be found in any other setting.

Adjusting Prices in Consumer Markets

In addition to a base-pricing strategy, firms also use other techniques to adjust or fine-tune prices. These techniques can involve permanent adjustments to a product's price or temporary adjustments used to stimulate sales during a particular time or situation. Although the list of potentially viable pricing techniques is long, we look at four of the most common techniques: promotional discounting, reference pricing, odd–even pricing, and price bundling.

Promotional Discounting   The hallmark of promotional discounting is a sale. All customers love a sale, and that is precisely the main benefit of promotional discounting. Virtually all firms, even those using value-based pricing, will occasionally run special promotions or sales to attract customers and create excitement. Many retailers, particularly department stores, use a type of promotional discounting called high–low pricing. This strategy involves charging higher prices on an everyday basis and then using frequent promotions and sales to increase store traffic. Dillard's, for example, will hold a quick sale early in a selling season and then return prices to their normal levels. Near the end of the season, Dillard's will begin to make these sale prices (or markdowns) permanent as time draws closer to the end-of-season clearance sale. It is interesting to note that the main benefit of promotional discounting is also its main drawback. Customers become so accustomed to sales and promotions that they will postpone purchases until retailers discount prices. Many vacation travelers and car buyers wait until special promotions are offered before making a purchase.

Reference Pricing   Firms use reference pricing when they compare the actual selling price to an internal or external reference price. All customers use internal reference prices, or the internal expectation for what a product should cost. As consumers, our experiences have given us a reasonable expectation of how much to pay for a combo meal at McDonald's, a gallon of gas, or a T-bone steak at a nice restaurant. For these and other common purchases, internal reference prices are critically important. However, customers often have little experience with certain products or product categories. This is especially true in services where the intangibility and heterogeneity of most services make it difficult for customers to judge prices prior to purchase. In these instances, external reference prices become more important.

Typically, the manufacturer or retailer of the good or service in question will provide the external reference price. A common use of reference pricing occurs when sale prices are compared to regular prices. You see this on television when marketers promote their goods as "A $50 value for only $19.99" or in stores such as when Best Buy promotes a television as "Regularly $399, Now $349." To be effective, the reference price—$399 in the case of Best Buy—must be seen as a legitimate, regular price. In other words, the retailer could not inflate the reference price to make the sale price more attractive. Further, the sale price of $349 must be available for a limited time; otherwise, customers will come to see the sale price as the regular price. This is an important legal issue with reference pricing: The reference price must truly be the regular price. Retailers that offer nothing but sale prices essentially mislead customers by comparing the sale price to a higher but never used reference price.

Reference pricing also occurs when firms set prices slightly below most competing products, even the firm's other product offerings. In these cases, the prices of other competing products become the reference price. One natural truth in customer behavior is that some customers will always pick the lowest-priced product. Firms use this to their advantage by creating lines of products that are similar in appearance and functionality but are offered with slightly different features and at different price points. This technique is called price lining. For example, Sony can cut a few features off its top-of-the-line Model A digital camcorder, and Model B can be on the shelf at $799 rather than the original $999. Cut a few more features, and the price can drop to $599 for Model C. Here, each model in the Sony line establishes reference prices for the other models in the line. The same is true for all competing camcorders from other manufacturers.

Odd–Even Pricing   Everyone knows that prices are rarely set at whole, round numbers. The concert tickets are $49.95, the breakfast special is $3.95, and the gallon of gas is $2.859. A couple of factors drive the prevalence of odd prices over even pricing. The first is that demand curves are not straight lines. As we noted earlier, the elasticity of a product's demand will change significantly at various price points. The move from $45.95 to $49.95 may result in very little drop in demand. When the price hits $50.00, just 5¢ more, the drop in demand may be sizable. Many concertgoers see $49.95 as $40, even though with taxes the price would be well over $50. They will tell a friend or a parent that they spent about $40 or that it certainly was not $50 for the ticket. Another reason that odd–even pricing works is that customers perceive that the seller did everything possible to get the price as fine (and thus as low) as he or she possibly could. To say you will cut my grass for $47 sounds like you put a lot more thought into it than if you just said, "Oh, I will do it for about $40," even though the first figure is $7 higher.

Price Bundling   Price bundling is sometimes called solution-based pricing, or all inclusive pricing. This approach brings together two or more complementary products for a single price. At its best, the bundled price is less than if a company sold the products separately. Slow-moving items can be bundled with hot sellers to expand the scope of the product offering, build value, and manage inventory. Some resorts, including Sandals and Club Med, use price bundling because many customers want to simplify their vacations and add budget predictability. The room, food, beverages, and entertainment are all included in a per-person price for a class of room. This allows guests to leave their credit cards and money in their safes and just enjoy themselves. Some packages even include the airfare, purchased in large quantities of seats by the resorts from major departure points. Bundling is an attractive strategy in the banking, travel, insurance, computer, and auto-mobile markets because these customers desire convenience and fewer hassles. Still, many customers dislike bundling because they believe that they can do a better job of creating their own solution and getting better value.

Adjusting Prices in Business Markets

Many of the techniques just discussed are also used in business markets to adjust or fine-tune base prices. However, a number of pricing techniques are unique to business markets, including the following:

- **Trade Discounts**   Manufacturers will reduce prices for certain intermediaries in the supply chain based on the functions that the intermediary performs. In general, discounts are greater for wholesalers than for retailers because the manufacturer wants to compensate wholesalers for the extra functions that they perform, such as selling, storage, transportation, and risk taking. Trade discounts vary widely and have become more complicated due to the growth of large retailers who now perform their own wholesaling functions.

- **Discounts and Allowances**   Business buyers can take advantage of sales just like consumers. However, business buyers also receive other price breaks including discounts for cash, quantity or bulk discounts, seasonal discounts, or trade allowances for participation in advertising or sales support programs.

- **Geographic Pricing**   Selling firms often quote prices in terms of reductions or increases based on transportation costs or the actual physical distance between the seller and the buyer. The most common examples of geographic pricing are *uniform delivered pricing* (same price for all buyers regardless of transportation expenses) and *zone pricing* (different prices based on transportation to predefined geographic zones).

- **Transfer Pricing**   Transfer pricing occurs when one unit in an organization sells products to another unit.

- **Barter and Countertrade**   In business exchanges across national boundaries, companies sometimes use products, rather than cash, for payments. Barter involves the direct exchange of goods or services between two firms or nations. Counter-trade refers to agreements based on partial payments in both cash and products, or to agreements between firms or nations to buy goods and services from each other.

Another important pricing technique used in business markets is price discrimi-nation, which occurs when firms charge different prices to different customers. When this situation occurs, firms set different prices based on actual cost differences in selling products to one customer relative to the costs involved in selling to other customers. Price discrimination is a viable technique because the costs of selling to one firm are often much higher than selling to others. However, price discrimination also has major legal implications, which we discuss later in the chapter.

Fixed Versus Dynamic Pricing

Up to this point in our discussion, we have assumed that once a price is set all buyers will pay the same price. Historically, this has been the case for almost all products in the United States except automobiles, where we expect to haggle and bargain to get the best deal. Sticker prices are only a starting point and usually represent the highest price anyone would have to pay. Interestingly, as cars have moved toward fixed pricing, it seems that almost everything else has become negotiable.

The Internet has played a large role in fostering the dynamic pricing approach to buying everything including airline tickets, hotel rooms, and cars. Firms such as Priceline.com, eBay, and Hotels.com have been major trendsetters in this area. Their approach is simple: Use an online auction strategy to bring buyers and sellers together in a competitive bidding process. Auction strategies, like the ones illustrated in Exhibit 8.5, allow firms to lower marketing and transaction costs, find new buyers or markets, and reduce unwanted inventory. Critics of online auctions contend that they are inconvenient

---

EXHIBIT 8.5   MAJOR ONLINE AUCTION STRATEGIES

Auction Type	Description	Examples
Traditional English auction	This auction system allows individuals and businesses to sell products online using a competitive bidding process where prices increase until the close of the auction. Sellers sometimes use "reserve prices" to ensure that a minimum price is achieved.	eBay, uBid, Yahoo! Auctions
Reverse auction	In this auction system, sellers bid down prices until a lowest price is reached. Business buyers typically use reverse auctions to force suppliers to compete for their business.	Many large firms use reverse auctions to cut their procurement costs.
Dutch auction	In this format, a seller has multiple identical items to sell. The seller specifies the opening bid price, and potential buyers bid at or above that price. At the close of the auction, the highest bidders purchase the items at the lowest successful bid.	eBay and Yahoo! Auctions offer the option of Dutch auctions. OpenIPO uses Dutch auctions to attract individual and institutional investors to an initial stock offering.
Buyer-driven commerce	This system allows customers to specify how much they will pay for a good or service. Different providers then determine whether they will sell at the stated price.	Priceline.com owns the patent on this buyer-driven bidding process, which the company calls "Name Your Own Price."

Source: Adapted from Brad Alan Kleindl, *Strategic Electronic Marketing*, 2nd ed. (Mason, OH: South-Western, 2003), 155.

(haggling takes time and you may end up with an unattractive option), are unfair (the person in the next room may have paid 20 percent less than you did), and promote disloyalty to a company or brand (price is the only thing that matters). Others argue that the online auction process only capitalizes on the underlying nature and structure of these markets. Whatever your opinion, online auction firms have been wildly successful. In fact, eBay Motors is now the world's largest car dealer, doing over $14 billion in online vehicle sales per year.[12]

Although generally new to consumer markets, dynamic pricing has long been a staple of business markets. Salespeople have a great deal of flexibility in terms of the prices that they charge to business buyers, offering big discounts for large-volume purchases. Business buyers go through comprehensive training programs to learn how to squeeze every dime out of every deal. In a dynamic pricing situation, there are three pricing levels that both the buyer and the seller must understand and plan for. The first is the *opening position*. This is the figure that each side will put on the table as a starting point. For example, in a deal for 500 cases of 20-pound paper, a salesperson might open with a price of $23.50 per case. The buyer might counter with his or her opening position of $17.50 per case. It is important to note that neither side expects to get the number that it initially proposes. Rather, these two opening positions establish the negotiation range. If there is to be a deal, it will take place somewhere between $23.50 and $17.50 per case.

Alongside these opening positions, buyers and sellers must know their *aspiration price*, or the number that each side will use to distinguish between a successful negotiation and an unsuccessful negotiation. For the salesperson, this price might be $20.25 per case, while for the buyer it might be $20.00 per case. If the two reach an agreement at a price higher than $20.25, the salesperson will be happy. If they reach an agreement at a price below $20.00, the buyer will be happy. Throughout the negotiation process, each side moves via concessions from their opening position toward their aspiration price in an effort to find common ground. A *concession* is a reduction in the asking price or an increase in the buying price. Some important guidelines for making concessions include the following:

- Avoid being the first side to make a concession.

- Start with modest concessions and make them smaller as you proceed. For the salesperson, a pricing sequence might be $23.50 to $22.50 to $22.10 to $21.85.

- Avoid making concessions early in the negotiation. Instead, the opening position should be supported by additional facts about the exchange. For a salesperson, high quality and good service can support an opening position. For a buyer, high volume and the potential for additional business can back up an opening offer.

- Do not give up anything without getting something in return. For example, a salesperson might drop the price by five percent if the buyer will commit to a longer-term commitment or a larger-volume order.

The third important pricing level is the *limit*, or the least favorable price that either side will agree to during the negotiation. For example, the salesperson's limit might be $18.50, while the buyer's limit might be $20.50. In this example, since the two limits overlap, we know that the two parties will eventually come to an agreement if they continue to negotiate. Unless something changes to alter the conditions of the negotiation, their agreed-on price will lie somewhere between $18.50 and $20.50. Whether the buyer or the seller feels good about the deal depends on the relationship of the final price to each side's aspiration price.

Dynamically negotiating prices can be a long and frustrating process, but it is the most logical and systematic way for two parties who do not initially agree to reach an agreement. Some firms give their salespeople and buyers total authority to negotiate prices within a broad range. Others require management involvement, and some decide they will not negotiate off their published list prices. Increasingly in today's challenging marketplace, the development of good negotiation skills is a prerequisite for survival, much less success.

Legal and Ethical Issues in Pricing

Pricing is one of the most heavily watched and regulated of all marketing activities. Given that a difference in price can create such a significant competitive advantage, any effort to artificially give one company an edge over another is subject to legal or regulatory intervention. We conclude our chapter on pricing by examining four of the most common legal and ethical issues in pricing: price discrimination, price fixing, predatory pricing, and deceptive pricing.

Price Discrimination

As we mentioned previously, *price discrimination* occurs when firms charge different prices to different customers. This is fairly common in consumer markets such as when cable and satellite companies offer lower prices to new customers or when fast-food restaurants offer lower-priced meals for children. Price discrimination is very common in business markets where it typically occurs among different intermediaries in the supply chain. In general, price discrimination is illegal unless the price differential has a basis in actual cost differences in selling products to one customer relative to another. The overriding question in cases of price discrimination is whether the price differential injures competition. The Robinson–Patman Act and the Clayton Act both regulate discriminatory pricing. The intent of these regulations is to provide a level playing field for all competitors.

Essentially, there are two ways to defend price discrimination. One is to base the difference on the lower costs of doing business with one customer compared to another. For example, large-volume orders are generally cheaper per item to deliver than small-volume orders. These cost savings must be documented, and the price reduction cannot exceed the amount of the savings. In the book retailing industry, large players such as Barnes & Noble, Books-A-Million, Borders, and Amazon can obtain lower prices than smaller book retailers due to their bulk buying practices. The second defense of price discrimination occurs when one customer receives a lower-price offer in order to meet the price of a competitor. Again, this lower price must be documented, and the selling organization can only match—but not beat—the lower price.

Price Fixing

Although managers within a firm need to talk about pricing strategies and pricing decisions on a regular basis, they should never discuss pricing with a competitor or in the presence of a competitor. Such collaboration is known as *price fixing,* which is illegal under the Sherman Antitrust Act. Sizable fines and prison terms for those convicted are the norm. Usually, one firm in an industry will be a price leader, and others will be the price followers. The U.S. Department of Justice has determined that, while following a competitor's lead in an upward or downward trend is acceptable, there can be no signaling of prices for particular products in this process. One of the most famous cases of price fixing occurred in the late 1990s when Archer Daniels Midland—a major agribusiness firm—was found guilty of fixing prices in the international lysine (a feed additive) and citric acid markets. ADM was fined $100 million for its role in the price-fixing conspiracy, in addition to the millions of dollars it paid in different civil and antitrust lawsuits filed by many companies. More recently, record gas prices have prompted calls from politicians to pursue price-fixing investigations against oil and gas suppliers.[13]

Predatory Pricing

Predatory pricing occurs when a firm charges very low prices for a product with the intent of driving competition out of business or out of a specific market. Prices then return to normal once the competitors have been eliminated. Predatory pricing is illegal; however, it is extremely difficult to prove in court. The challenge in predatory-pricing cases is to prove that the predatory firm had the willful intent to ruin the competition. The court must also be convinced that the low price charged by the predator is below its average variable cost. The variable-cost definition of predatory pricing is a major reason why very few lawsuits for predatory pricing are successful. The reality is that large firms with lean, efficient cost structures dominate today's competitive landscape. These firms have lower variable costs that allow them to legitimately charge lower prices than the competition in many cases. This is the reason why large retailers such as Wal-Mart, The Home Depot, Lowe's, and Barnes & Noble have been slowly and methodically putting smaller retailers out of business. These large firms are not guilty of predatory pricing—they are only guilty of being more efficient and competitive than other firms.

Deceptive Pricing

Intentionally misleading customers with price promotions is another area that has seen significant court action in recent years. This pricing tactic, known as *deceptive pricing,* is illegal under the Federal Trade Commission Act and the Wheeler–Lea Act. One carefully watched form of deceptive pricing is superficial discounting. This form of deception has ties to reference pricing and occurs when a firm advertises a sale price as a reduction below the normal price when it is not the case. Typically, the firm does not sell the product at the regular price in any meaningful quantities or the sale-price period is excessively long. To avoid this legal violation, a firm should offer a product at the original price, discount the price in a specified dollar amount for a specified period, and then revert to the original price at the end of that period. If the product is a discontinued item, that fact should be noted in the advertisement. Most of the legal activity regarding superficial discounting has taken place at the state attorney general level.

Lessons from Chapter 8

Pricing

- is a key factor in producing revenue for a firm.

- is the easiest of all marketing variables to change.

- is an important consideration in competitive intelligence.

- is considered to be the only real means of differentiation in mature markets plagued by commoditization.

- is among the most complex decisions to be made in developing a marketing plan.

With respect to pricing, sellers

- tend to inflate prices because they want to receive as much as possible in an exchange.

- must consider four key issues in pricing strategy: (1) costs, (2) demand, (3) customer value, and (4) competitors' prices.

- have increased power over buyers when certain products are in short supply, in high demand, or during good economic times.

With respect to pricing, buyers

- often see prices as being lower than market reality dictates.

- must consider two key issues: (1) perceived value and (2) price sensitivity.

- consider value to be the ratio of benefits to costs, expressed colloquially as "more bang for the buck."

- have increased power over sellers when there are a large number of sellers in the market, when the economy is weak, when product information is easy to obtain, or when price comparisons between competing firms or products are easy to make.

In terms of pricing strategy, cutting prices

- can be a viable means of increasing sales, moving excess inventory, or generating short-term cash flow.

- is usually based on two general pricing myths: (1) When business is good, a price cut will capture greater market share, and (2) when business is bad, a price cut will stimulate sales.

- can be a risky proposition for most firms because any price cut must be offset by an increase in sales volume to maintain the same level of gross margin.

- is not always the best strategy. Instead, firms are often better off if they can find ways to build value into the product and justify the current, or a higher, price.

The key issues in pricing strategy include

- the firm's pricing objectives.

- the nature of supply and demand in the industry or market.

- the firm's cost structure.

- the nature of competition and the structure of the industry.

- the stage of the product life cycle.

The firm's cost structure

- is typically associated with pricing through the use of break-even analysis or cost-plus pricing.

- should not be the driving force behind pricing strategy because different firms have different cost structures.

- should be used to establish a floor below which prices cannot be set for an extended period of time.

Pricing strategy in services

- is critical because price may be the only cue to quality that is available in advance of the purchase experience.

- becomes more important—and more difficult—when

    - service quality is hard to detect prior to purchase.
    - the costs associated with providing the service are difficult to determine.
    - customers are unfamiliar with the service process.
    - brand names are not well established.
    - the customer can perform the service him or herself.
    - the service has poorly defined units of consumption.
    - advertising within a service category is limited.
    - the total price of the service experience is difficult to state beforehand.

- is often based on yield management systems that allow a firm to simultaneously control capacity and demand in order to maximize revenue and capacity utilization.

Yield management

- involves knowing when and where to raise prices to increase revenue or to lower prices to increase sales volume.
- is implemented by limiting the available capacity at certain price points, controlling demand through price changes over time, and by overbooking capacity.
- is common in services characterized by high fixed costs and low variable costs such as airlines, hotels, rental cars, cruises, transportation firms, and hospitals.
- allows a firm to offer the same basic product to different market segments at different prices.

Price elasticity of demand

- refers to customers' responsiveness or sensitivity to changes in price.
- can be inelastic in which the quantity demanded does not respond to price changes.
- can be elastic in which the quantity demanded is sensitive to price changes.
- can be unitary in which the changes in price and demand offset, keeping total revenue the same.
- is not uniform over time and place because demand is not uniform over time and place.

Situations that increase price sensitivity include when

- substitute products are widely available.
- the total expenditure is high.
- changes in price are noticeable to customers.
- price comparison among competing products is easy.

Situations that decrease price sensitivity include when

- substitute products are not available
- products are highly differentiated from the competition.
- customers perceive products as being necessities.
- the prices of complementary products go down.
- customers believe that the product is just worth the price.
- customers are in certain situations associated with time pressures or purchase risk.

Major base pricing strategies include

- market introduction pricing—the use of price skimming or penetration pricing when products are first launched into the market.

- prestige pricing—intentionally setting prices at the top end of all competing products in order to promote an image of exclusivity and superior quality.

- value-based pricing, or everyday low pricing (EDLP)—setting reasonably low prices but still offering high-quality products and adequate customer services.

- competitive matching—charging what is considered to be the "going rate" for the industry.

- nonprice strategies—building a marketing program around factors other than price.

Strategies for adjusting or fine-tuning prices in consumer markets include

- promotional discounting—putting products on sale.

- reference pricing—comparing the actual selling price to an internal or external reference price.

- odd–even pricing—setting prices in odd numbers rather than in whole, round numbers.

- price bundling—bringing together two or more complementary products for a single price.

Strategies for adjusting or fine-tuning prices in business markets include

- trade discounts—reducing prices for certain intermediaries in the supply chain based on the functions that the intermediary performs.

- discounts and allowances—giving buyers price breaks including discounts for cash, quantity or bulk discounts, seasonal discounts, or trade allowances for participation in advertising or sales support programs.

- geographic pricing—quoting prices based on transportation costs or the distance between the seller and the buyer.

- transfer pricing—pricing that occurs when one unit in an organization sells products to another unit.

- barter and countertrade—making full or partial payments in goods, services, or buying agreements rather than in cash.

- price discrimination—charging different prices to different customers.

Dynamic pricing

- has started to replace fixed pricing in many different product categories.

- has been growing in importance and popularity due to the growth of online auction firms.

- involves three distinct pricing levels: (1) the opening position, (2) the aspiration price, and (3) the price limit.

- can be a long and frustrating process but is the most logical and systematic way for two parties who do not initially agree to reach an agreement.

Major legal and ethical issues in pricing include

- price discrimination—occurs when firms charge different prices to different customers. The practice is illegal unless the price differential has its basis in the actual cost differences in selling products to one customer relative to another.

- price fixing—occurs when two or more competitors collaborate to set prices at an artificial level.

- predatory pricing—occurs when a firm sets prices for a product below the firm's variable cost with the intent of driving competition out of business or out of a specific market.

- deceptive pricing—occurs when firms intentionally mislead customers with price promotions.

Questions for Discussion

1. One of the key themes stressed throughout this text is the challenge of marketing goods and services in mature markets that are plagued by commoditization. In what ways is pricing strategy related to commoditization? How can a firm offer good value in a mature market where price is the only visible means of differentiation? Are most firms too concerned about their costs to really deliver value in other ways? Explain.

2. Pricing strategy associated with services is typically more complex than the pricing of tangible goods. As a consumer, what pricing issues do you consider when purchasing services? How difficult is it to compare prices among competing services or to determine the complete price of the service before purchase? What could service providers do to solve these issues?

3. Price elasticity often varies for the same product based on the situation. What situational factors might affect the price elasticity of these products: (a) sporting event or concert tickets, (b) staple goods such as milk, eggs, or bread, (c) an electric razor, and (d) eye surgery to correct vision?

Exercises

1. You are in the process of planning a hypothetical airline flight from New York to St. Louis. Visit the websites of three different airlines and compare prices for this trip. Try travel dates that include a Saturday night layover and those that do not. Try dates less than seven days away and compare those prices with flights that are more than 21 days out. How do you explain the similarities and differences you see in these prices?

2. Visit eBay (http://www.ebay.com), choose a product category, and look at some of the current auctions. With respect to everything that you have learned in this chapter, answer these questions:

    a. How might sellers determine the prices that they set for opening bids and reserve prices (the minimum price they will accept for an item)?

    b. For any particular item, how might potential buyers determine internal and external reference prices?

    c. Why do so many sellers use odd pricing?

    d. Does price elasticity play a role in determining the final bid price? If so, how?

3. Visit PriceFarmer (http://www.pricefarmer.com) and search for any book. How do you explain the differences in pricing for that book across different retailers? If you were purchasing this book, which retailer would you select? Why? Is price the most important factor, or are other issues like retailer reputation, product availability, and discount level more important? Explain.

CHAPTER 9

Distribution and Supply Chain Management

Introduction

Distribution and supply chain relationships are among the most important strategic decisions for many marketers. Wal-Mart, Best Buy, and even Starbucks depend on effective and highly efficient supply chains to provide competitive advantage. Throughout most of the twentieth century, distribution was the forgotten element of marketing strategy. After all, most considered marketing to consist of the four "Ps": product, price, promotion, and something most people had a hard time remembering. The fourth "P" really didn't fit. Marketing textbook authors passed it off as "place," but it was really a "D" for distribution. Distribution and supply chain management have remained essentially invisible to customers because the process occurs behind the scenes. Customers rarely appreciate how manufacturers connect to their supply lines, how goods move from the manufacturer to the retailer, or how the retailer's shelves become filled. For example, consider the fact that 20 percent, or $60 billion, of Wal-Mart's sales comes from products manufactured in China. Customers take this and other supply chain issues for granted and only notice when supply lines are interrupted. Although the nature of today's economy has forced customers to notice and appreciate distribution to a much greater extent, most remain naïve about distribution activities and the complex nature of supply chain relationships.

The picture of distribution is drastically different from the firm's perspective. Beginning in the late 1980s and into today, firms have learned the extreme importance of distribution and supply chain management. As described in Beyond the Pages 9.1, these concerns now rank at the top of the list for achieving a sustainable advantage and true differentiation in the marketplace. Prices can be copied easily, even if only for the short term. Products can become obsolete almost overnight. Good promotion and advertising in September can easily be passé when the prime selling season in November and December comes around. The lesson is clear: Distribution is vital to the success and survival of every firm. In fact, firms that neglect the distribution component of marketing strategy face a different kind of "D"—death.

SUPPLY CHAIN MANAGEMENT AT BARNES & NOBLE[1]

In the course of operating more than 799 stores across the United States plus a popular website that features 4 million book titles, Barnes & Noble has become an expert at supply chain management. The largest U.S. bookstore chain made retailing history when it opened the first category-killer bookstore in the late 1980s. At that time, the store was five times the size of a typical bookstore. Today, Barnes & Noble routinely opens massive 100,000-square-foot stores while managing hundreds of smaller mall-based stores, a fast-growing Internet business, and a network of gigantic warehouses. This multipronged distribution strategy has helped the chain boost annual sales to $4.4 billion.

For years, Barnes & Noble managed inventory by having suppliers and wholesalers send orders directly to individual stores. However, as the company opened larger stores, each stocked with up to 200,000 books, it needed a new system to ensure that the right items would be available in the right quantities at the right time and in the right place. To accomplish this, Barnes & Noble built three warehouses totaling one million square feet to receive and store products until they were shipped to the stores. When the website became operational, even this massive amount of warehouse space proved too small to accommodate the amount of merchandise needed to keep up with the surge in sales. Now, after a round of expansion, the warehouses can hold an inventory of 20 million items, ready to go out to Barnes & Noble stores and to online customers in more than 200 countries.

To manage all the intricate details of store and Internet sales, orders, and shipments, Barnes & Noble has forged close relationships with publishers, wholesalers, and other supply chain partners. Sophisticated Internet-based systems help the retailer capture and communicate customer-demand data to improve sales forecasting and help suppliers plan ahead for production. The system also gathers and communicates supplier information about product availability to help Barnes & Noble's

buyers plan ahead for ordering. Finally, the system analyzes location-by-location inventory levels to help managers time shipments to stores and customers. "To live up to our promise to the consumer, we want to have everything that's in print available from our facilities," says William F. Duffy, Barnes & Noble's vice president of operations. "The trick is in the appropriate quantities."

Although costly in both money and time to construct, a solid distribution system will generate profits for years or decades. With great distribution, a firm can overcome some weaknesses in pricing, products, and promotion. However, a poor distribution strategy will certainly kill a firm's efforts to market a superior product, at a good price, using effective marketing communication. Top managers of North American manufacturing firms realize the importance of this; they nearly unanimously rank supply chain management as critical or very important to their firms' successes.

Distribution and Supply Chain Concepts

Distribution and supply chain management are important for many different reasons. Ultimately, however, these reasons all come down to providing time, place, and possession utility for consumer and business buyers. Without good distribution, buyers would not be able to acquire goods and services when and where they need them. However, the expense of distribution requires that firms balance customers' needs with their own need to minimize total costs. Exhibit 9.1 provides a breakdown of total distribution costs across key activities. Note that almost half of these expenses are associated with storing and carrying inventory—a key factor in ensuring product availability for customers. To manage these costs efficiently, distribution strategy must balance the needs of customers with the needs of the firm.

When we think of distribution and supply chain management, we tend to think of two interrelated components:

- **Marketing Channels** This is an organized system of marketing institutions through which products, resources, information, funds, and/or product ownership flow from the point of production to the final user. Some channel members or intermediaries physically take possession or title of products (for example, wholesalers, distributors, and retailers), whereas others simply facilitate the process (for example, agents, brokers, and financial institutions).

- **Physical Distribution** This entails coordinating the flow of information and products among members of the channel to ensure the availability of products in the right places, in the right quantities, at the right times, and in a cost-efficient manner. Physical distribution (or logistics) includes activities such as customer

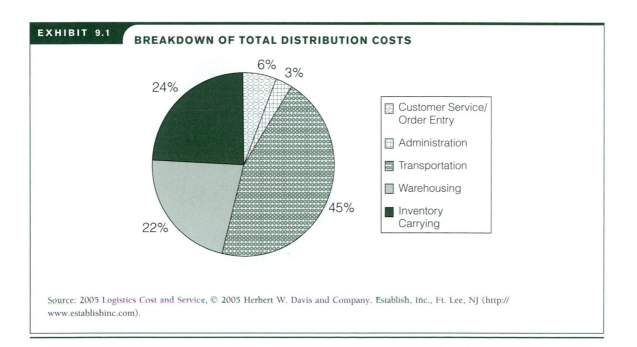

EXHIBIT 9.1

BREAKDOWN OF TOTAL DISTRIBUTION COSTS

6% — Customer Service/Order Entry
3% — Administration
45% — Transportation
22% — Warehousing
24% — Inventory Carrying

Source: 2005 Logistics Cost and Service, © 2005 Herbert W. Davis and Company. Establish, Inc., Ft. Lee, NJ (http://www.establishinc.com).

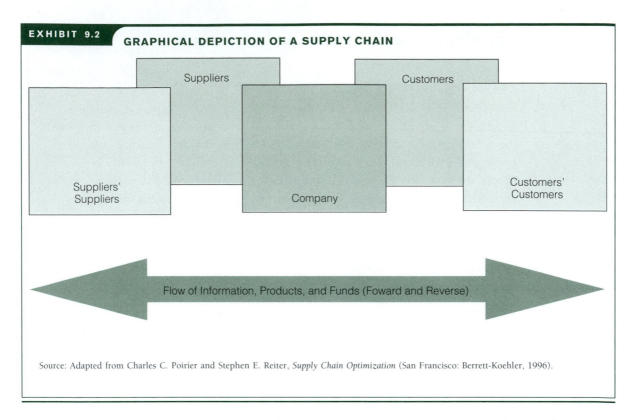

EXHIBIT 9.2   GRAPHICAL DEPICTION OF A SUPPLY CHAIN

Suppliers

Customers

Suppliers' Suppliers

Company

Customers' Customers

Flow of Information, Products, and Funds (Foward and Reverse)

Source: Adapted from Charles C. Poirier and Stephen E. Reiter, *Supply Chain Optimization* (San Francisco: Berrett-Koehler, 1996).

service/order entry, administration, transportation, storage and materials handling (warehousing), inventory carrying, and the systems and equipment necessary for these activities.

The term *supply chain* expresses the connection and integration of all members of the marketing channel. As depicted in Exhibit 9.2, a supply chain integrates firms such as raw material suppliers, manufacturers, resellers, and final customers into a seamless flow of information, products, and funds. Supply chains also include flows that occur forward toward end users and reverse channels where returns and repairs flow away from end users. Velocity, or the need to speed inventory to and from channel members, requires collaborating with technology, transportation, and other outside logistics experts. This supply chain process is designed to increase inventory turns and get the right products to the right place at the right time while maintaining the appropriate service and quality standards.[2] As we will discuss throughout this chapter, the keys to this effective flow through the supply chain are integration and collaboration.

Marketing Channel Functions

Marketing channels make our lives much easier because of the variety of functions performed by channel members. Likewise, channel members, particularly manufacturers, can cut costs by working through channel intermediaries. The most basic benefit of marketing channels is contact efficiency where channels reduce the number of contacts necessary to exchange products. Without contact efficiency, consumers would have to visit a bakery, poultry farm, slaughterhouse, and dairy just to assemble the products necessary for breakfast. Likewise, contact efficiency allows companies such as Del Monte Foods to maximize product distribution by selling to select intermediaries. For Del Monte, Wal-Mart stores represented 29 percent of the company's 2005 sales volume. Del Monte's ten largest customers represented 58 percent of total sales. These percentages will increase if additional consolidation among food retailers and growth of mass merchandisers continues.[3]

Throughout a marketing channel, some firms are good at manufacturing, some are good at transportation or storage, and others are better at selling to consumers. Given the costs involved, it is virtually impossible for a single firm to perform all channel functions well. As a result, channel intermediaries typically attain a level of specialization in one or more of the following functions:

- **Sorting** Manufacturers make one or a few products, but customers need a wide variety and deep assortment of different products. By sorting products in the channel, intermediaries overcome this discrepancy of assortment.

- **Breaking Bulk** Manufacturers produce large quantities of a product to gain the benefits of economies of scale. However, customers typically want only one of a particular item. By breaking bulk in the channel, intermediaries—particularly retailers—overcome this discrepancy of quantity.

- **Maintaining Inventories** Manufacturers cannot make products on demand, so the channel must provide for the storage of products for future purchase and use. By maintaining inventories, intermediaries overcome this temporal (time) discrepancy. Note that this does not apply to services—such as haircuts or airline flights—where the product is produced and consumed simultaneously.

- **Maintaining Convenient Locations** Because manufacturers and customers have a geographic separation, the channel must overcome this spatial discrepancy by making products available in convenient locations.

- **Provide Services** Channels add value to products by offering facilitating services (for example, insurance, storage, and financing) and standardizing the exchange process (for example, payment processing, delivery, and pricing).

With the exception of highly intangible services like consulting, education, or counseling, the fulfillment of these functions occurs in every marketing channel. Also, these functions must be fulfilled in order for the channel to operate effectively. It does not matter which intermediary performs these functions; the fact remains that they must be performed. For example, Sam's Club does not break bulk in the traditional sense. Sam's customers buy in large quantities and actually break bulk after purchase. Further, many emerging trends in distribution and supply chain management have blurred the responsibilities of different intermediaries. Today, large retailers are essentially a one-stop channel of distribution. Due to their immense size and bulk buying ability, these firms now fulfill virtually all traditional channel functions.

Channel Effectiveness and Efficiency

Increasingly, distribution decisions are being evaluated using two criteria: (1) Is the channel effective? (2) Is the channel efficient? For a firm to be competitive, the answer to both questions must be yes. Effectiveness involves meeting the goals and objectives of both the firm and its customers. Today, the key effectiveness issue is whether the channel provides exceptional time, place, and possession utility. With respect to time utility, the new standard is 24/7/365. Business buyers and consumers alike want the ability to access information and purchase products every hour of the day, every day of the week, and every day of the year (including holidays). This requires utilizing a system of technologies and processes that senses and reacts to real-time demand signals across the network of marketing channel members.[4]

Although firms have gotten better in terms of time utility, exceptional place utility remains elusive for many firms. The primary reason is expense. In the past, buyers would often travel great distances to purchase a product. Today, they do not want to leave their home or office. The increasing place demands of customers forces firms to build a distribution infrastructure that puts products in convenient locations. Although the Internet has certainly helped in this regard, many firms cannot leverage the Internet for distribution effectiveness. For these firms, the expense of building multiple outlets in convenient locations is a major challenge.

With respect to possession utility, a key issue in channel effectiveness is the ease of the actual purchase process. Customers want to buy products only in the amounts they need, using the means of payment that they most prefer. These desires increase the need for facilitating services in the channel. For example, the phenomenal growth of PayPal is the result of the increased need to conduct online payments. PayPal (now owned by eBay) facilitates both online and offline transactions by handling online payments for over 100 million members in fifty-five countries around the world.[5] Ease of use is also an issue in reverse channels, especially when tied to recycling and product recalls. For example, when Dell recalled over 4.1 million defective laptop batteries in 2006, it immediately created a website and call center to make the recall process run more efficiently. In the first day alone, Dell received more than 100,000 phone calls, 23 million hits to its website, and roughly 77,000 replacement orders. Many customers received replacement batteries in only one to two days.[6]

To increase channel efficiency, firms must be able to cut costs by eliminating redundancies and waste. Increasing logistical efficiency alone can significantly reduce inventory, transportation, warehousing, and packing costs. For example, General Mills embarked on a 10-year plan to cut $1 billion out of the firm's supply chain. General Mills was able to improve teamwork skills at one plant and cut cereal production costs by 25 percent.[7] Firms that adopt a coordinated supply chain strategy can easily reduce costs by four or five percent. This may not sound like a lot, but given the large sales volume involved, a small reduction in costs can easily result in a $25 to $30 million cost advantage over a less efficient competitor.

Strategic Issues in Distribution and Supply Chain Management

Although the terms often become used interchangeably, there is a key distinction that separates a traditional marketing channel from a true supply chain. With the traditional channel, each channel member has as its main concern how much profit it makes, or the size of its "piece of the pie." In a supply chain, the primary concern is the share of the market the entire channel captures. In this case, there is a clear understanding that the channel is competing against other channels. For firms in the supply chain to achieve their objectives, the entire supply chain must meet its objectives by winning customers' business. In a supply chain, the focus shifts from the size of each individual piece of the pie to the size of the whole pie.

As Exhibit 9.3 shows, any single firm can demand a larger portion of the profit made from the channel's activities, but if the channel's share of the market shrinks, then that firm will earn less profit (outcome #1 in the exhibit). On the other hand, if the channel's share increases, a firm may get a smaller share (outcome #2) or maintain a constant share (outcome #3) yet still earn more profit. Results show clearly that firms involved in supply chains outperform those in traditional marketing channels by a wide margin. Thus, focusing on the size of the channel's market share is good for not only the viability of the channel but also each individual channel member involved.

In this section, we consider three key strategic aspects of any supply chain: the structure of the channel, channel integration, and the means to build value in the supply chain. All of these combine to determine the extent to which the firms involved can advance their relationship from a loosely configured marketing channel to a truly integrated supply chain.

Marketing Channel Structure

There are many strategic options for the structure of a marketing channel; these strategies are often complex and very costly to implement. However, a good distribution strategy is essential for success because, once a firm selects a channel and makes commitments to it, distribution often becomes highly inflexible due to long-term contracts, sizable investments, and commitments among channel members. There are three basic structural options for distribution in terms of the amount of market coverage and level of exclusivity between vendor and retailer: exclusive distribution, selective distribution, and intensive distribution.

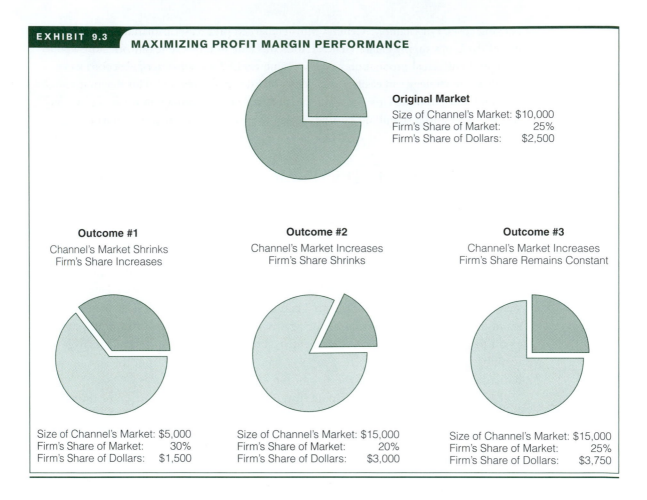

EXHIBIT 9.3

MAXIMIZING PROFIT MARGIN PERFORMANCE

Original Market
Size of Channel's Market: $10,000
Firm's Share of Market: 25%
Firm's Share of Dollars: $2,500

Outcome #1
Channel's Market Shrinks
Firm's Share Increases

Size of Channel's Market: $5,000
Firm's Share of Market: 30%
Firm's Share of Dollars: $1,500

Outcome #2
Channel's Market Increases
Firm's Share Shrinks

Size of Channel's Market: $15,000
Firm's Share of Market: 20%
Firm's Share of Dollars: $3,000

Outcome #3
Channel's Market Increases
Firm's Share Remains Constant

Size of Channel's Market: $15,000
Firm's Share of Market: 25%
Firm's Share of Dollars: $3,750

Exclusive Distribution   Exclusive distribution is the most restrictive type of market coverage. Firms using this strategy give one merchant or outlet the sole right to sell a product within a defined geographic region. This channel structure is most commonly associated with prestige products, major industrial equipment, or with firms that attempt to give their products an exclusive or prestige image. For example, BMW, Jaguar, and Mercedes typically grant exclusive distribution to only one dealer in any given area. Companies sometimes use exclusive distribution for specialty products and can be occasionally seen in shopping goods like furniture or clothing.

Firms that pursue exclusive distribution usually target a single, well-defined market segment. Buyers in this segment must be willing and able to search or travel to buy the product and will typically do so given the prestige or exclusivity of the product or brand. Exclusive distribution is a necessity in cases where the manufacturer demands a significant amount of input regarding the presentation of their products to buyers. This added control also allows the firm to influence pricing to a much greater degree than the other distribution options.

Selective Distribution   Firms using selective distribution give several merchants or outlets the right to sell a product in a defined geographic region. Selective distribution is desirable when customers need the opportunity to comparison shop and after-sale services are important. For example, Kodak digital cameras are available at Circuit City, Best Buy, and Office Depot stores, as well as many online merchants. This broad distribution coverage allows shoppers to collect information on Kodak and competitive products, compare prices, shop at their favorite store, use a variety of means of payment, and get the model they want, even when one location is out of stock on a model. Kodak does not make the cameras available in convenience stores or grocery stores due to the relatively high price of the item, the customer's need for information, and their own desire to maintain some control over prices and the point-of-sale displays for the cameras.

Companies widely use selective distribution across many product categories, including clothing (Tommy Hilfiger), cosmetics (Clinique), electronics (Bose), and premium pet food (Science Diet). McDonald's and most other franchisers also use selective distribution in the allocation of franchises. Such selectivity may be based on population and demographics (for example, one franchise per 250,000 people), dollar volume (for example, when sales reach $5 million in an area, the franchiser awards another franchise), or some other factor. In each case, selective distribution allows the manufacturer to have more control over prices, product display, and selling techniques. Companies carefully screen the image and selling practices of merchants and outlets to ensure that they match those of the manufacturer and its products.

Intensive Distribution   Intensive distribution makes a product available in the maximum number of merchants or outlets in each area to gain as much exposure and as many sales opportunities as possible. This distribution option has close ties with consumer convenience goods, such as candy, soft drinks, over-the-counter drugs, or cigarettes, and with business office supplies like paper and toner cartridges. To gain this visibility and sales volume, the manufacturer must give up a good degree of control over pricing and product display. Given the sheer number of intensively distributed products, manufacturers often have difficulty convincing channel members, particularly retailers, to handle and stock another product that is distributed in the same manner.

Consider the J.M. Smucker Company, the leading manufacturer of fruit spreads and peanut butter in North America. The company's strategy is to own and market leading icon food brands found in the center of the supermarket. Smucker distributes its brands—such as Jif, Smucker's, Crisco, Hungry Jack, and Martha White—through grocery and other retail outlets, food-service establishments, schools, specialty and gourmet shops, health and natural food stores, and consumer direct vehicles such as the Internet and a showcase store in Orrville, Ohio.[8]

Firms that employ a mass-marketing approach to segmentation often opt for an intensive distribution strategy. If customers cannot find one firm's products in a given location, they will simply substitute another brand to fill the need. As products age over the life cycle, they often move toward more intensive distribution.

Channel Integration

The linchpin of effective supply chain management in today's economy is channel integration. Through informational, technological, social, and structural linkages, the goal of channel integration is to create a seamless network of collaborating suppliers, vendors, buyers, and customers. When done correctly, this level of integration results in an extended enterprise that manages value by coordinating the flow of information, goods, and services both upstream and downstream in the supply chain. Creating an extended enterprise requires investments in and commitment to three key factors:[9]

- **Connectivity**   The informational and technological linkages among firms in the supply chain network. Connectivity ensures that firms can access real-time information about the flow in the supply chain network.

- **Community**   The sense of compatible goals and objectives among firms in the supply chain network. All firms must be willing to work together to achieve a common mission and vision.

- **Collaboration**   The recognition of mutual interdependence among members of the supply chain network. Collaboration goes beyond contractual obligations to establish principles, processes, and structures that promote a level of shared understanding. Firms learn to put the needs of the supply chain ahead of their own because they understand that the success of each firm separately has a strong connection to the success of other firms, as well as the entire supply chain.

Channel integration and creating an extended enterprise are extremely challenging goals. In the most seamlessly integrated supply chains, the boundaries among channel members blur to the point where it is difficult to tell where one firm ends and another firm begins. This level of integration creates a tenuous balance of competition and collaboration as well as teamwork and self-serving behaviors.[10] We explore these topics more fully later in the chapter when we discuss power, conflict, and collaboration in the supply chain.

Creating and Enhancing Value in the Supply Chain

Another key consideration in making strategic supply chain decisions is to have a firm grasp on the value components that target customers find attractive. Synergy (the idea that the whole is greater than the sum of the parts) is the driving force behind value creation in the supply chain. By combining and integrating their unique capabilities, channel members can create synergies that enhance communication and sales, improve after-sale service, increase the efficiency of product delivery, add product enhancements, or offer solutions rather than individual products. By combining complementary products, a supply chain can offer solutions to customers' problems that increase overall value. For example, Dell.com customers can create their own solutions by combining products from a number of different vendors. Likewise, combining wine, cheese, crackers, other snacks, plates, flatware, napkins, and a tablecloth all inside a picnic basket results in a combined value much greater that the sum of the individual products in the mix.

Creating value also takes the focus off the price of individual items because both consumers and business buyers tend to put less downward pressure on prices and profit margin when the solution offered meets a genuine need or problem.

For example, the value of an Epson printer will be perceived differently depending upon whether it is a stand-alone item or part of a system and whether it is packaged as part of a solution for the college student, a home office, or for business use. This type of value building can be done at any level of the supply chain. However, the need for rapid delivery, service, or training in close proximity to the customer will tend to push value building downstream in the supply chain to local distributors, merchants, or retailers. Large grocery retailers, for example, are quite good at building value and solutions by offering full-course meal replacements that can be purchased on the way home from work. Separate food manufacturers and distributors could never offer these types of solutions to consumers.

Conflict and Collaboration in the Supply Chain

True supply chain integration requires a fundamental change in how channel members work together. Among these changes is a move from a win-lose competitive attitude to a win-win collaborative approach in which there is a common realization that all firms in the supply chain must prosper. This change shifts the participants from short-term to long-term assessments in evaluating decisions affecting the relationship. The focus has been modified from one of selling to the next level in the channel to one of selling products through the channel to a satisfied, ultimate customer. Information flows move from guarded secrecy to open, honest, and frequent communications. Perhaps most important, the points of contact in the relationship expand from one-on-one at the salesperson–buyer level, to multiple interfaces at all levels and in all functional areas of each firm. The goal of this shift is to create supply chains where all members work together to reduce costs, waste, and unnecessary movement in the entire marketing channel in order to satisfy ultimate customers.

The Basis of Conflict in the Supply Chain

As we mentioned, achieving a high degree of channel integration is a challenging task. The reasons are easy to see. First, each firm in a supply chain has its own mission, goals, objectives, and strategies. Consider the Toro Company that sells turf maintenance equipment, irrigation systems, landscaping equipment, and yard products to both professional and residential markets. This requires many different distributors and dealers as well as supplying products for trademarks owned by retailers such as The Home Depot. Because each firm knows that its survival ultimately depends on its ability to achieve its goals, it is not surprising that firms often assess their own interests before considering others in the supply chain. Self-interest-seeking behavior is natural in both business and everyday life. Second, the recognition and acceptance of mutual interdependence within the supply chain goes against our natural self-interest-seeking tendencies. To work toward mutual interdependence means that each firm must give up some measure of control over its goals, its activities, and even its own destiny. Consequently, putting the needs of the supply chain ahead of the needs of the firm is likely to create tension and conflict as firms collaborate and move toward the creation of the extended enterprise.

Conflict also arises in a supply chain because each firm possesses different resources, skills, and advantages. Thus, each firm will exhibit a different degree of authority or power in managing or controlling the activities within the supply chain. Power can be defined as the influence that one channel member has over others in the supply chain. Powerful channel members have the ability to get other firms to do things that they otherwise would not do. Depending on how the channel member uses its influence, power can create considerable conflict, or it can make the entire supply chain operate more smoothly and effectively. There are five basic sources of power in a supply chain:[11]

- **Legitimate Power**   This power source has to do with the firm's position in the supply chain. Historically, manufacturers have held most of the legitimate power, but this power balance shifted to retailers in the 1990s. In today's economy, retailers still wield a great deal of power. However, the only channel member that can now claim legitimate power with any consistency is the final customer.

- **Reward Power**   The ability to help other parties reach their goals and objectives is the crux of reward power. Rewards may come in terms of higher-volume sales, sales with more favorable margins, or both. Individual salespeople at lower levels in the channel may be rewarded with cash payments, merchandise, or vacations to gain more favorable presentations of a manufacturer's or wholesaler's products. Consumers can be rewarded with free goods or services based upon their purchases of a company's products.

- **Coercive Power**   In contrast to reward power, coercive power is the ability to take positive outcomes away from other channel members or the ability to inflict punishment on other channel members. Legislative and judicial actions have limited coercive power, but it does occur in subtle forms. For example, a manufacturer may slow down deliveries or postpone the availability of some portions of a product line to a wholesaler or retailer. Likewise, a retailer can decide to not carry a product, not promote a product, or to give a product unfavorable placement on its shelves.

- **Information Power**   Having and sharing knowledge is the root of information power. Such knowledge makes channel members more effective and efficient. Information power may stem from knowledge concerning sales forecasts, market trends, competitive intelligence, product uses and usage rates, or other critical pieces of information. In many supply chains, retailers hold the most information power because their close proximity to customers gives them access to data and information that are difficult to obtain from other sources.

- **Referent Power**   Referent power has its basis in personal relationships and the fact that one party likes another party. It has long been said that buyers like to do business with salespeople who they enjoy being around. This is still true, but increasingly referent power has its roots in firms wanting to associate with other firms, as opposed to individual one-on-one relationships. Similar cultures, values, and even information systems can lead to the development of referent power.

The sources of power or influence change as a supply chain moves toward integration and collaboration. Traditional marketing channels have made heavy use of legitimate, reward, and coercive power sources. The use of these types of power is consistent with the high level of conflict that exists in such channels. Firms want to sell a product for as much as possible, provide as few additional services as it can get away with, obtain payment in advance, and deliver the product at its own convenience. By contrast, buyers want to purchase a product for as little as possible, get a large number of additional services both now and in the future, pay months or even years later with no interest, and get immediate delivery. Collaborative supply chains focus on win–win outcomes and work to get past these natural sources of confrontation. Here, reward and referent power become used most frequently, with the most important source of influence being information. Successfully confronting the problems that naturally materialize in a supply chain depends on the effective development, communication, and utilization of information.

Collaborative Supply Chains

Exhibit 9.4 depicts the key factors to successful collaboration in a supply chain. Trust appears at the center of this diagram; it is the glue that holds supply chain relationships together.[12] Without trust, firms will be unwilling to give up control over supply chain activities, unable to put the needs of the supply chain ahead of their own, and prompted to engage in selfish behaviors that will lead to increased conflict and frustration. The presence of trust, however, allows firms to fully cooperate to develop interdependencies that will lead to mutual benefits over the long term. Other keys to supply chain collaboration include top management commitment and investment, clearly stated goals and objectives, complete sharing of data and information, and increased quantity and quality of communication among firms. Finally, firms must also be willing to share in the cost savings realized from collaboration and tighter integration of supply chain activities.[13] By embracing technology solutions, product categories such as apparel, food, health and beauty, and other household items are constructing tight collaborative supply chains, visible and integrated, with all partners reaping the rewards.

One of the best and most widespread collaborative supply chain initiatives is category management, an ongoing and highly successful initiative by innovative members of food product distribution channels. Category management came into being because a group of consumer food product manufacturers and leading supermarket chains had a great deal of dissatisfaction with the traditional, highly competitive channel relationships that existed among their firms. Through their Joint Industry Project on Efficient Consumer Response (ECR), the group developed the concept of category management and defined it as "a supplier process of managing categories (of products) as strategic business units, producing enhanced business results by focusing on delivering continuously enhanced consumer value."[14] Through their combined efforts, the industry task force determined that category management must be all of the following:[15]

- **Customer Driven** Manufacturers and wholesalers should make all decisions with a concern for the challenges faced by retailers in the channel.

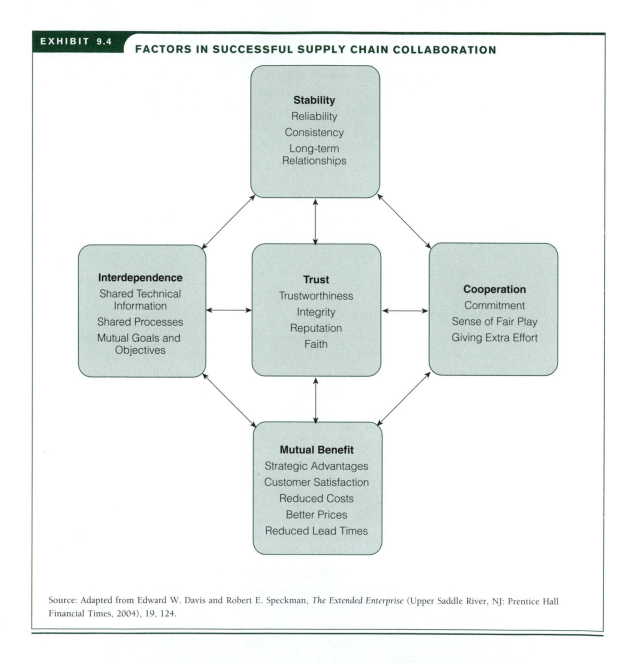

EXHIBIT 9.4   **FACTORS IN SUCCESSFUL SUPPLY CHAIN COLLABORATION**

Stability
Reliability
Consistency
Long-term
Relationships

Interdependence
Shared Technical
Information
Shared Processes
Mutual Goals and
Objectives

Trust
Trustworthiness
Integrity
Reputation
Faith

Cooperation
Commitment
Sense of Fair Play
Giving Extra Effort

Mutual Benefit
Strategic Advantages
Customer Satisfaction
Reduced Costs
Better Prices
Reduced Lead Times

Source: Adapted from Edward W. Davis and Robert E. Speckman, *The Extended Enterprise* (Upper Saddle River, NJ: Prentice Hall Financial Times, 2004), 19, 124.

- **Strategically Driven**   The relationship between the parties should be driven by a strategic plan to advance the relationship and, through this, to advance the outcomes for the parties involved.

- **Multifunctional**   Contact points should go beyond marketing and buying to include areas such as finance, logistics, quality control, and facilities management, in addition to the senior management teams of all firms.

- **Financially Based**   Solid financial targets should be set and met in terms of profitability and the management of both hard and soft costs.

- **Systems Dependent**   Systems (operational and technical) should be designed and put in place to support the activities of the relationship.

- **Focused on Immediate Consumer Response**   Successful channel members implementing category management should be able to give consumers what they want more rapidly than firms operating within traditional marketing channels.

Exhibit 9.5 outlines six components of an ongoing category management process that must be jointly managed by the category manager (retail buyer or merchandising manager) and the channel consultant (manufacturer's or wholesaler's account manager). Each component in the process depends on the quality, planning, and performance of the other five components. Retailers such as Barnes & Noble, Costco, and Wal-Mart are leaders in establishing and coordinating category management with their suppliers. In recent years, firms outside the consumer products industries have begun to adopt components of the ECR category management process to enhance their own supply chain relationships.

EXHIBIT 9.5   **MAJOR COMPONENTS OF CATEGORY MANAGEMENT**

Component	Description
Strategy	This step involves an informed choice by the retailer to move from managing brands or SKUs (stock-keeping units) to managing groups of products that satisfy similar consumer needs. Such groups are known as categories (e.g., deli meats, fresh cut flowers, appearance chemicals, home cleaning products).
The Business Process	An eight-step process that includes: (1) defining categories and subcategories, (2) determining each category's role in meeting retailer goals and objectives, (3) assessing the present performance of each category, (4) setting scorecard targets for measuring performance, (5) jointly developing strategies for achieving scorecard targets, (6) selecting specific tactics to implement selected strategies, (7) implementing plans with calendars and assigned responsibilities, and (8) appraising categories and refining plans.
Scorecard	An ongoing process of setting targets and establishing the means to monitor and improve performance in targeted areas (e.g., profit per square foot of category space, or average dollars purchased per consumer in each category).
Organization Capabilities	Changes in the design and structure of organizations; the required skill bases of the parties to the relationship; and the employee performance measurement, reward, and recognition systems.
Information Technology	Address the acquisition, analysis, and movement of information within and between the organizations involved. It must involve the supplier's marketing information system (MIS), the retailer's MIS, and external syndicated data suppliers (e.g., Nielsen).
Collaborative Trading Partners	The methods used to structure and conduct interactions between members of both the supplier and retailer organizations in a win-win fashion with the open and honest exchange of information for the purpose of identifying and solving problems.

Source: *Category Management Report* © 1995 by the Joint Industry Project on Efficient Consumer Response.

Trends in Marketing Channels

In addition to the trends associated with channel integration discussed to this point in the chapter, a number of other trends have shaped the structure of marketing channels and the ways that supply chains function. In this section, we examine a number of these trends.

Advancing Technology

Significant advancements in information processing and digital communication have created new methods for placing and filling orders for both business buyers and consumers. The growth of the Internet and e-commerce is the most obvious sign of these changes. As business buyers and consumers more fully embrace these technologies, the growth of direct sales from manufacturers to customers will flourish. In one survey, 39 percent of businesses having an online presence stated that they do half or more of their sales online. However, 44 percent responded that they do 25 percent or less of their business online. These statistics show that e-commerce still has a great deal of room to grow in the coming years.[16]

Another promising technology is radio-frequency identification (RFID), which involves the use of tiny computer chips with radio transmitters that can be attached to a product or its packaging. The radio signals emitted from the chip can be used to track inventory levels and product spoilage or prevent theft. They can also be used for instantaneous checkout of an entire shopping cart of items. As addressed in Beyond the Pages 9.2, large retailers and packaged goods manufacturers have funded research to develop RFID, which many expect will replace bar-code technology eventually.[17] Innovations in web-based communication technologies, such as global positioning, are also taking rail and truck equipment to a new level of service in supply chain integration.

Consumer demands for convenience, as well as increased pressures on channel members to cut distribution expenses, have been the primary sparks for the growth in technologies like e-commerce and RFID. Faster, better, *and* cheaper is the demand coming from both business buyers and consumers with a thunderous voice. As the ownership of personal computers and Internet access has literally exploded, the Internet has become a critical channel component for both manufacturers and retailers to consider. Even when the purchase is not made online, the Internet is increasingly viewed as an important source of information in the decision-making process for both consumers and business buyers.

Shifting Power in the Channel

In days gone by, manufacturers had all of the power in the channel of distribution. The scarcity and popularity of many products allowed manufacturers to dictate strategy throughout the supply chain. Further, manufacturers were the best source of information about sales, product trends, and customer preferences. Wholesalers and retailers, who lacked sophisticated inventory management systems at the time, had to

Beyond the Pages 9.2

WAL-MART'S DISTRIBUTION TECHNOLOGY[18]

Wal-Mart Stores Inc.— the world's largest corporation— is possibly the most controversial business in America. With sales over $312.4 billion in 2006 and approximately 1.7 million employees worldwide (of these, 1.3 million are U.S. employees), managing stakeholder relationships is a major challenge. The Wal-Mart that saves the average family an estimated $2,329 per year has its critics. Wal-Mart claims that it is committed to improving the standard of living for its customers throughout the world. Their key strategy is a broad assortment of quality merchandise and services at everyday low prices (EDLP) while fostering a culture that claims to reward and embrace mutual respect, integrity, and diversity. Wal-Mart uses the data it collects about customers as well as radio-frequency identification (RFID) technology throughout its distribution system to maintain its competitive advantage and low costs.

Wal-Mart not only is the world's largest retailer but also operates the world's largest data warehouse, an organization-wide data collection and storage system that gathers data from all the firm's critical operating systems as well as from selected external data sources. Wal-Mart's data warehouse contains more than 460 terabytes (or over 470,000 gigabytes) of data stored on mainframe computers. Amazingly, many experts believe that the entire Internet comprises less than half that amount of data.

Wal-Mart collects reams of data about products and customers primarily from checkout scanners at its Wal-Mart discount and Sam's Club membership stores. Clerks and managers may also use wireless handheld units to gather additional inventory data. The company stores the detailed data and classifies it into categories such as product, individual store, or region. The system also serves as a basis for the Retail Link decision-support system between Wal-Mart and its suppliers. Retail Link permits some vendors, like Kraft, to access data about how well their products are selling at Wal-Mart stores.

The mountain of data that Wal-Mart collects helps boost efficiency dramatically by matching product supplies to demand. This information, for example, helped the firm determine to stock not only flashlights but also extra strawberry Pop-Tarts prior to a hurricane strike (Pop-Tart sales increase as much as seven times their normal rate ahead of a hurricane). The data may also help the company track supplier performance, set ideal prices, and even determine how many cashiers to schedule at a certain store on a certain day. Most important, it helps the retailer avoid carrying too much inventory or not having enough to satisfy demand.

Technology is a driving force in operational efficiency that lowers costs for Wal-Mart. The merchandise-tracking system uses RFID to ensure that a product can be tracked from the time it leaves the supplier's warehouse to the time it enters and leaves a Wal-Mart store. Wal-Mart began the move to RFID in 2004 by insisting that its top 100 suppliers adopt RFID technology. The cost to suppliers was much larger than the cost to Wal-Mart because suppliers needed to continually buy the RFID tags whereas Wal-Mart only needed a system to read the tags. The cost to adopt and implement RFID technology has been estimated to be roughly $9 million per supplier. Smaller Wal-Mart suppliers also have to adopt RFID, but they have a longer lead time to comply.

RFID helps Wal-Mart keep its shelves stocked and curbs the loss of retail products as they travel through the supply chain. RFID at Wal-Mart has directly resulted in a 16 percent reduction in stockouts and a 67 percent drop in replenishment times. As customers go through checkout, the RFID system swiftly combines point-of-sale data on their purchases with RFID-generated data on what is available in the stockroom to produce pick lists that are automatically created in real time. It also ensures that suppliers are notified when products are sold and can ensure that enough of a product is always at a particular store. This strategy also results in time and labor savings because Wal-Mart associates no longer need to scan shelves to determine what is out of stock; nor do they have to scan cartons and cases arriving at the stockroom. The scanners tag incoming pallets and translate the data into supply chain management database forecasting models to address out-of-stock items and reduce stock–restocking mix-ups.

rely on manufacturers for this information. These conditions still exist in many business markets where manufacturers are the chief supply chain strategists. In consumer markets, however, the power of manufacturers eroded as UPC bar-code technology, point-of-sale systems, and inventory management systems converged to give retailers control over information at the point of sale.

Today, the power in most consumer channels is held by discount mass-merchandise retailers—like Wal-Mart, Kmart, and Target—and category-focused retailers (also known as category killers)—such as Toys "R" Us, Lowe's, Office Depot, AutoZone, and Best Buy. These large retailers have gained power in their respective channels for several reasons. First, the sheer size and buying power of these firms allows them to demand price concessions from manufacturers. Second, these firms perform their own wholesaling functions; therefore, they receive trade discounts traditionally reserved for true wholesalers. Third, their control over retail shelf space allows them to dictate when and where new products will be introduced. Manufacturers typically must pay hefty fees, called *slotting allowances,* just to get a single product placed on store shelves. Finally, their closeness to millions of customers allows these large retailers to gather valuable information at the point of sale. As mentioned previously, control over information is a valuable commodity and a source of power in virtually all supply chains.

Outsourcing Channel Functions

Outsourcing—shifting work activities to businesses outside the firm—is a rapidly growing trend across many different industries and supply chains.[19] In the past, outsourcing was used primarily as a way of cutting expenses associated with labor, transportation, or other overhead costs. Today, though cutting expenses is still a main factor, the desire of many firms to focus on core competencies drives outsourcing. By outsourcing noncore activities, firms can improve their focus on what they do best, free resources for other purposes, and enhance product differentiation—all of which lead to greater opportunities to develop and maintain competitive advantages. The hourly labor costs in countries such as China and India are far less than in the United States, Europe, or even Mexico. These developing countries have improved their manufacturing capabilities, infrastructure, and technical and business skills, making them more attractive regions for global sourcing. On the other hand, the cost of outsourcing halfway around the world must be considered in decisions.[20]

As illustrated in Exhibit 9.6, information technology is the primary activity outsourced today. Currently, however, firms are shifting supporting processes to outside businesses. These supporting processes include administrative activities, distribution, human resources, financial analysis, call centers, and even sales and marketing. When a firm has significant needs and insufficient in-house expertise, the importance of outsourcing will increase. For example, an entire industry known as 3PLs (third party logistics providers) has emerged in the United States and Europe as retailers look toward outside expertise as a way to reduce costs and make their products more readily available.[21] These firms manage inventories and handle the physical movement of products in the supply chain to ensure that items are in the right amounts and in the

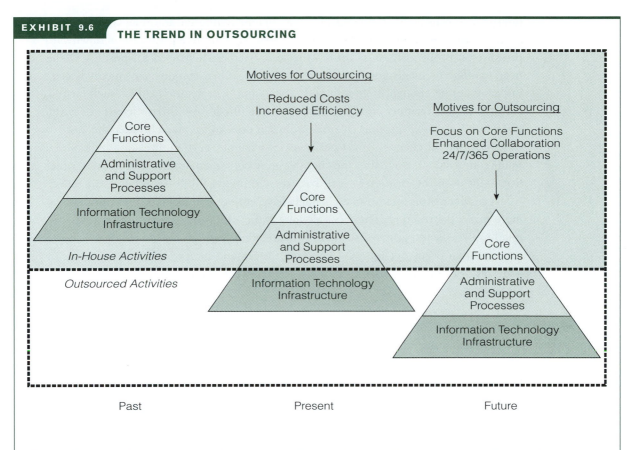

EXHIBIT 9.6   **THE TREND IN OUTSOURCING**

Motives for Outsourcing

Reduced Costs
Increased Efficiency

Core Functions

Administrative and Support Processes

Information Technology Infrastructure

In-House Activities

Outsourced Activities

Core Functions

Administrative and Support Processes

Information Technology Infrastructure

Motives for Outsourcing

Focus on Core Functions
Enhanced Collaboration
24/7/365 Operations

Core Functions

Administrative and Support Processes

Information Technology Infrastructure

Past   Present   Future

Source: Adapted from Edward W. Davis and Robert E. Speckman, *The Extended Enterprise* (Upper Saddle River, NJ: Prentice Hall Financial Times, 2004), 111, based on information from Forrester Research, Inc.

right places when needed. The next-day delivery services offered by FedEx, UPS, and DHL have been a boon to companies practicing just-in-time inventory methods, but some companies are looking for even faster delivery methods for an extra edge. San Francisco–based Ensenda has designed a same-day delivery system that is attracting the attention of shippers who are looking for new ways to cut costs and streamline their delivery fleets. Many of these firms outsource the production of some component parts and need to obtain these supplies just in time for production. To give them what they need, Ensenda developed a business model based on a system of local delivery networks: The company contracts with small, regionally based couriers to provide same-day delivery in markets where there is sufficient demand for such services. Its biggest customers are The Home Depot, Best Buy, Sony, and Crate and Barrel.[22]

The Growth of Direct Distribution and Nonstore Retailing

Used to distribute a wide range of products, the traditional marketing channel of manufacturer to wholesaler to retailer is alive and well today. However, customers' demands for lower prices and greater convenience have put pressure on all channel intermediaries to justify their existence. Every time a different intermediary handles a product, the cost to the final customer increases. This places a great deal of downward pressure on profit margins as firms struggle to balance their need for profit with the need to offer customers good value and fair prices. When margins get squeezed, there just may not be enough to go around for everyone in a channel. Under such circumstances, the channel must evolve into a more direct form or risk its very survival. Keep in mind, however, that channel evolution does not replace or alter the basic functions that all channels must perform (for example, sorting, breaking bulk, and holding inventory). Even after the elimination of certain channel intermediaries, other firms—or even the customer—will have to step in and fulfill these basic functions.

A number of nontraditional channels have emerged to expand opportunities for more direct distribution. The most obvious is the explosive growth of nonstore retailing. The fastest growing segment of the retail industry, nonstore retailing refers to activities that occur outside the traditional "bricks and mortar" of physical stores. In addition to e-commerce channels, there are many other types of nontraditional channels:

- **Catalog and Direct Marketing**   Some of the most popular and successful nonstore merchants, including Lands' End, J. Crew, Cabela's, and GEICO Insurance, are catalog and direct marketers.

- **Direct Selling**   These merchants sell through face-to-face contact with sales associates. Examples include Avon, Tupperware, Discovery Toys, and Pampered Chef. Avon is far and away the largest with over $8 billion in sales each year.

- **Home Shopping Networks**   Networks like QVC and the Home Shopping Network serve millions of satisfied customers every week. QVC, the largest network, sells over $6.5 billion in merchandise each year.

- **Vending**   The advantage of vending is 24/7/365 product availability in virtually any location. Though soft drinks account for over 50 percent of vending sales, products such as flowers, toothpaste, and fishing bait can now be purchased via vending machines.

- **Direct-Response Advertising**   Many companies sell music, toy, and book products via television commercials and 1-800 phone numbers. One of the largest is Time Life, which sells over $350 million in books, CDs, and DVDs each year. Infomercials, a cross between an advertisement, a news program, and a documentary, are also popular programs for products such as exercise equipment and kitchen appliances.

Distribution activities have also changed as manufacturers expand their direct offerings to customers. In some cases, manufacturers have increased direct distribution by opening their own retail outlets. Firms that have done this for some time include Nike (Nike Town stores), Dell, Apple, and Bass Pro Shops, as well as a host of manufacturers that operate stores in factory-outlet centers (for example, Mikasa, Carter's, Black & Decker, Bose, and Zales).

The Growth of Dual Distribution

Supply chain strategy often requires multiple channels to reach various markets. The use of multiple channels may arise out of necessity to meet customer needs or by design. Multiple channels enable a manufacturer to offer two or more lines of the same merchandise through two or more means, thus increasing sales coverage. For example, Hallmark makes extensive use of dual distribution. The company sells its highly respected Hallmark line of greeting cards primarily through selective distribution at Hallmark stores. Hallmark makes its Ambassador line of cards available on an intensive basis through supermarkets, drug stores, and discount retailers. In addition, Hallmark offers both cards and e-cards online.

The use of dual distribution is a strategic decision that manufacturers must consider very carefully. Dual distribution requires considerable resources to implement as it spreads time, effort, and money across two or more channels. Dual distribution also increases the risk of disintermediation, where customers deal directly with manufacturers and bypass traditional channel intermediaries. Consequently, the use of dual channels can create conflict between the manufacturer and its supply chain members. This is particularly true when target market segments do not have clear definitions or distinctions for each channel. For example, the wall covering industry has seen great conflict between traditional decorating centers, 1-800 telephone resellers, and online merchants. Traditional decorating centers resent doing all the presale service to help a customer select the appropriate wall covering, only to have that customer buy from a distributor or online vendor that does not have overhead costs associated with sales associates or a physical store. As a result, many decorating centers boycott the products of manufacturers engaged in aggressive dual distribution.

Legal and Ethical Issues in the Supply Chain

Like every other aspect of marketing strategy, distribution and supply chain decisions must be made with an eye toward ethical and legal considerations. Exhibit 9.7 provides examples of the most common types of misconduct in supply chains. Other examples of ethical issues in supply chain management are discussed in the remaining sections of this chapter.

Dual Distribution

Dual distribution is not necessarily unethical or illegal. However, concerns do arise when a manufacturer uses its own physical or online stores to dominate independent retailers or to drive them out of business. To avoid these issues, manufacturers should not undercut the prices that independent retailers can charge with a reasonable margin. For example, Nike is very careful to protect the retailers who sell its products. Although its Nike Town stores do sell Nike products, the stores are more about brand building than driving sales volume. It is obviously in any firm's best interests to pursue dual distribution in an ethical and legal manner. Those who abuse the strategy may find that they are the only ones who want to retail their products. Because most

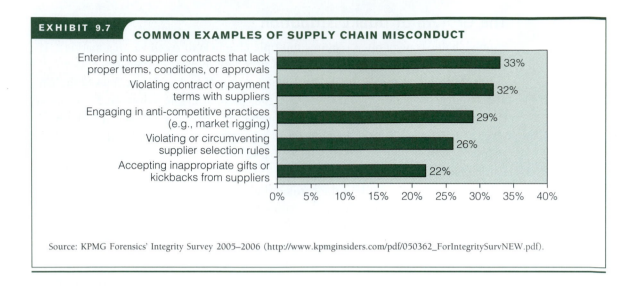

EXHIBIT 9.7

COMMON EXAMPLES OF SUPPLY CHAIN MISCONDUCT

Entering into supplier contracts that lack proper terms, conditions, or approvals — 33%

Violating contract or payment terms with suppliers — 32%

Engaging in anti-competitive practices (e.g., market rigging) — 29%

Violating or circumventing supplier selection rules — 26%

Accepting inappropriate gifts or kickbacks from suppliers — 22%

Source: KPMG Forensics' Integrity Survey 2005–2006 (http://www.kpmginsiders.com/pdf/050362_ForIntegritySurvNEW.pdf).

manufacturers do not want to run a complex retail system, their relationships with retail intermediaries are critical to success.

Exclusive Channel Arrangements

Exclusive channel arrangements benefit a manufacturer by limiting the distribution of its products in one of two ways. First, manufacturers can limit distribution by allowing intermediaries to sell their products in restricted geographic territories. Second, manufacturers can require that wholesalers, brokers, agents, or retailers not carry or represent products from any competing manufacturer. Violations of these exclusive arrangements can cause a manufacturer to cut off supply to the intermediary in question.

Exclusive arrangements give manufacturers control over pricing, distribution, and sales activities. Such arrangements are useful when brand image or quality control are critical to the manufacturer's success. However, not all exclusive channel agreements are legal. There are three tests that determine their validity. First, the arrangement cannot block competitors from ten percent or more of the overall market. Second, the sales revenue involved must not be so sizable that competition could be disrupted. Finally, the manufacturer cannot be much larger (and therefore more intimidating) than the intermediary. Regulators view exclusive arrangements most favorably when consumers and business buyers have access to similar products from other channels or when the exclusivity of a relationship strengthens the otherwise weak market position of the manufacturer.[23]

Tying Arrangements

Tying arrangements occur when a firm conditions the availability of one product (the "tying" product) on the purchase of a different product (the "tied" product). In other words, if a firm wants to buy Product A, it will have to also buy Product B to get it. Tying arrangements, which are considered to be illegal in certain circumstances, can occur at any level in a marketing channel. The legality of tying arrangements depends on several factors. First, the arrangement is more likely to be legal if the tying and tied products are in close relation to each other, required for the proper functioning of the other product, or part of a total package or solution. Franchisors can often successfully argue for tying arrangements when raw materials or components are required for brand image or quality-control reasons. Second, the legality of tying depends on the market power of the firm requiring the arrangement. Powerful firms are less likely to be successful in tying because it gives them an unfair advantage. For example, the U.S. Supreme Court found Kodak guilty of an illegal tying arrangement when the firm would only sell replacement copier parts to customers if they agreed not to use independent service and repair firms.[24] Finally, tying arrangements are illegal if they restrain trade or competition in a meaningful way.

Counterfeit Products

Buyers and sellers alike must make reasonable efforts to be aware of a product's origin. Counterfeit products abound today, particularly in the areas of clothing, audio and video products, and computer software. Any product that can be easily copied is vulnerable to counterfeit activities. Some people argue that only manufacturers become injured when consumers purchase counterfeit products. This is clearly mistaken reasoning. For example, the loss of tax revenues has a huge impact on governments because they can't collect both direct and indirect taxes on the sale of counterfeit products. Likewise, counterfeits leech profits necessary for ongoing product development away from the channel, as well as thousands of jobs at legitimate companies. Customers also feel the impact of counterfeit products because their quality almost never lives up to the quality of the original. For example, faced with increasing risks associated with counterfeit drugs, the FDA launched a pilot study to test the effectiveness of RFID in combating the growing problem and to protect American consumers. The pilot study was prompted by the Federal Drug Administration's (FDA) 2003 discovery of over 150,000 bottles of counterfeit Lipitor (a popular cholesterol-lowering drug). The FDA plans to review the pilot in 2007 with the possibility of mandating RFID throughout the entire U.S. pharmaceutical supply chain.[25]

Lessons from Chapter 9

Distribution and supply chain management

- are among the most important strategic decisions for many marketers.

- were the forgotten elements of marketing strategy throughout most of the twentieth century.

- have remained essentially invisible to customers because the processes occur behind the scenes.

- now rank at the top of the list in achieving a sustainable advantage and true differentiation in the marketplace.

- can overcome some weaknesses in pricing, products, and promotion. However, a poor distribution strategy will kill a firm's efforts to market a product.

- are important to providing time, place, and possession utility for consumer and business buyers.

- are expensive; therefore, distribution strategy must balance the needs of customers with the needs of the firm.

- consist of two interrelated components: marketing channels and physical distribution.

Marketing channels

- are organized systems of marketing institutions through which products, resources, information, funds, and/or product ownership flow from the point of production to the final user.

- depend on logistics strategies to coordinate the flow of information and products among members of the channel to ensure that products are available in the right places, in the right quantities, at the right times, and in a cost-efficient manner.

- can be considered as supply chains when all members of the channel are connected and integrated.

- greatly increase contact efficiency by reducing the number of contacts necessary to exchange products.

- perform a variety of functions: sorting, breaking bulk, maintaining inventories, maintaining convenient locations, and providing services.

- are increasingly evaluated using two criteria: effectiveness and efficiency.

- are distinct from supply chains where the primary concern is the share of the market the entire channel captures.

Marketing channel structures include

- exclusive distribution, where a firm gives one merchant or outlet the sole right to sell a product within a defined geographic region.

- selective distribution, where a firm gives several merchants or outlets the right to sell a product in a defined geographic region.

- intensive distribution, which makes a product available in the maximum number of merchants or outlets in each area to gain as much exposure and as many sales opportunities as possible.

Marketing channel integration

- is the linchpin of effective supply chain management in today's economy.

- has as its goal the creation of a seamless network of collaborating suppliers, vendors, buyers, and customers.

- focuses on connectivity, community, and collaboration to create an extended enterprise that manages value by coordinating the flow of information, goods, and services both upstream and downstream in the supply chain.

- creates a tenuous balance of competition and collaboration, and teamwork and self-serving behaviors.

- strives to create value in the supply chain by developing synergies that enhance communication and sales, improve after-sale service, increase the efficiency of product delivery, add product enhancements, or offer solutions rather than individual products.

Conflict in the supply chain

- stems from each firm attempting to fulfill its mission, goals, objectives, and strategies by putting its own interests ahead of other firms.

- is natural because the notion of mutual interdependence goes against a firm's natural self-interest-seeking tendencies.

- can arise because each firm possesses different resources, skills, and advantages.

- can result as each firm exhibits one of the five different sources of power in the supply chain: legitimate power, reward power, coercive power, information power, and referent power.

Collaborative supply chains

- are characterized by reward and referent power, with the most important source of influence being information.

- depend on trust to hold relationships together.

- can work only if firms will give up some control over supply chain activities, allowing them to fully cooperate to develop interdependencies that will lead to mutual benefits over the long term.

- share in the cost savings realized from collaboration and tighter integration of supply chain activities.

- are exemplified by category management, a highly successful initiative by members of food product distribution channels.

Trends in marketing channels include

- advancing technology, particularly advancement in information processing, digital communication, and the increasing usage of radio-frequency identification (RFID).

- shifting power in the channel, where retailers hold most of the power in consumer channels.

- outsourcing work activities to businesses outside the firm, particularly information technology operations and supporting functions.

- the growth of direct distribution and nonstore retailing. In addition to e-commerce activities, other examples of these nontraditional channels include catalog and direct marketing, direct selling, home shopping networks, vending, and direct-response advertising.

- the growth of dual distribution as firms use multiple channels to reach various markets.

Legal and ethical issues in supply chain management include

- dual distribution if a manufacturer uses its own physical or online stores to dominate independent retailers or to drive them out of business.

- exclusive channel arrangements if (1) a manufacturer's restrictions block competitors from 10 percent or more of the overall market, (2) the sales revenue involved is sizable enough to disrupt competition, and (3) the manufacturer is much larger and more intimidating than the channel intermediary.

- tying arrangements, which occur when a firm conditions the availability of one product (the "tying" product) on the purchase of a different product (the "tied" product).

- counterfeit products, which result in lost profits for legitimate firms, lost tax revenue for governments, and inferior products for customers.

Questions for Discussion

1. What are the major differences that you have experienced in buying a product through a physical retail store, a manufacturer's physical store, a catalog, and an online merchant? What have some retailers in your area done to justify their ongoing presence in the channel?

2. Describe the characteristics of a product that represents something you would go to great lengths to acquire, thus supporting a manufacturer's use of an exclusive distribution strategy. Why is the service better and the salespeople more knowledgeable at an exclusive distribution location versus an intensive distribution location?

3. Some manufacturers and retailers advertise that customers should buy from them because they "eliminate the middleman." Evaluate this comment in light of the functions that must be performed in a marketing channel. Does a channel with

fewer members always deliver products to customers at lower prices? Defend your position.

Exercises

1. Locate a product offered by a manufacturer using a dual-distribution approach. Are there differences between the customers targeted by each channel? How do the purchase experiences differ? In the end, why would a customer buy directly from a manufacturer if the prices were higher?

2. Spend some time looking at what is offered for sale on QVC or the Home Shopping Network. Why do you believe that these direct marketers are so popular? If you have purchased an item from these merchants, why did you do so? If you haven't made a purchase, why not?

3. Visit RFID Journal (http://www.rfidjournal.com) to learn as much as possible about the growth of RFID as a logistics and supply chain tool. What are current the obstacles to widespread adoption of the technology?

10 Integrated Marketing Communications

Introduction

Without a doubt, promotion and marketing communications are the most ubiquitous elements of any firm's marketing strategy. This is not surprising because promotional activities are necessary to communicate the features and benefits of a product to the firm's intended target markets. Marketing communications includes conveying and sharing meaning between buyers and sellers, either as individuals, firms, or between individuals and firms. Integrated marketing communications (IMC) refers to the strategic, *coordinated* use of promotion to create one consistent message across multiple channels to ensure maximum persuasive impact on the firm's current and potential customers. IMC takes a 360-degree view of the customer that considers each and every contact that a customer or potential customer may have in his relationship with the firm. The key to IMC is consistency and uniformity of message across all elements of promotion as shown in Exhibit 10.1.

Due to the many advantages associated with IMC, a full 67 percent of marketers have adopted integrated marketing as the basis for their communication and promotion strategies.[1] By coordinating all communication "touch points," firms using IMC convey an image of truly knowing and caring about their customers that can translate into long-term customer relationships. Likewise, IMC reduces costs and increases efficiency because it can reduce or eliminate redundancies and waste in the overall promotional program. Many firms have embraced IMC because mass-media advertising has become more expensive and less predictable than in the past. As discussed in Beyond the Pages 10.1, target customers are now fragmented across a wide variety of television and cable programs, magazines, newspapers, radio stations, and online communities. Finally, advancing technology allows firms to target customers directly via direct mail, e-mail, or online promotion. This increased focus on individual

Beyond the Pages 10.1

THE END OF TELEVISION ADVERTISING?[2]

The traditional U.S. media business is hanging on for the ride of its life. That ride is called fragmentation, and it's going to forever change the way both media and advertisers do business. The problem is that consumers' attention is being spread across an increasing array of media and entertainment choices. Those choices include the Internet, targeted cable programming, video-on-demand, TiVo (or digital video recorders), iPods, DVDs, video games, and cell phones. Today, mass audiences are dwindling fast as consumers spend less time with traditional media such as television, magazines, and newspapers. Consumers now expect to use media whenever and wherever they want and on any device. They are no longer wed to full-length television programming or to leisurely reading the newspaper.

For advertisers, the trend is alarming because it is their traditional bread-and-butter demographic that is fragmenting the most. For example, the number of 18 to 34 year old men who watch prime-time television declined 5 percent in 2006. Those who watch television increasingly use TiVo or other DVR devices to skip advertising. The news is no better in print media. A full 69 percent of U.S. magazines suffered sales declines in 2006. Due to declining ad revenue, the venerable *New York Times* was forced to cut expenses by trimming the size of its paper, closing a printing plant, and laying off 250 employees.

All these changes are forcing media companies to adapt by fragmenting their content and business models to match their fragmented audiences. One way that companies have addressed the problem is by making their content available on multiple platforms. For example, ESPN makes its content available via cable television, the Internet, satellite radio, and its own wireless phone service,

Mobile ESPN. Major networks distribute their most popular programming on television, online, and via DVD at the completion of a season of episodes. Music is now available on CD, the Internet, and via download on cell phones.

The key to meeting the demands of fragmented audiences is to disaggregate content and make it available *à la carte* style. Consumers can purchase individual songs via iTunes, Urge, or other services. They can access digital RSS (really simple syndication) feeds of newspaper and magazine content to read only parts of a publication. Episodes of popular television shows, such as ABC's *Desperate Housewives,* are available on iTunes for $1.99 per episode. Cable giant Comcast now offers more than 4000 on-demand features. One of its newest features is a deal with CBS that allows viewers to watch popular prime-time shows like *CSI* for 99¢.

Many hail the growth of on-demand television as the beginning of the end for traditional television advertising. One reason is profits. In its deal with iTunes, ABC earns $1.20 for each downloaded episode of *Desperate Housewives*. ABC estimates that even a minimal shift from television to iPod viewing will allow the company to net $1.8 million more per episode than if the show were not available on-demand. The second reason is audience measurement. The science behind traditional broadcast television ratings and audience measurement has always been uncertain. With on-demand services, advertisers are able to precisely measure audience characteristics whether the content is delivered via the Internet, cable, or wireless devices. This one-two punch of profits and precise measurement may mark the death of the traditional 30-second prime-time television spot.

---

customers requires that the overall promotional program be integrated and focused as well.

In this chapter, we examine the role of IMC in marketing strategy. We discuss the strategic use of IMC in informing, persuading, and reminding customers about the firm's products. We also explore the strategic decisions to be made with respect to advertising, public relations, personal selling and sales management, and sales promotion.

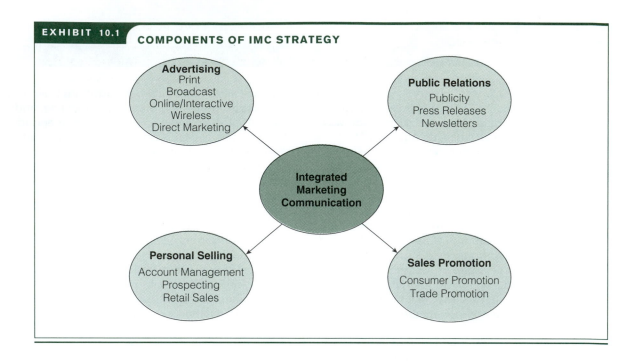

EXHIBIT 10.1   **COMPONENTS OF IMC STRATEGY**

Advertising
Print
Broadcast
Online/Interactive
Wireless
Direct Marketing

Public Relations
Publicity
Press Releases
Newsletters

Integrated Marketing Communication

Personal Selling
Account Management
Prospecting
Retail Sales

Sales Promotion
Consumer Promotion
Trade Promotion

Strategic Issues in Integrated Marketing Communications

When selecting elements to include in the IMC program, it is important to take a holistic perspective that coordinates not only all promotional elements but also the IMC program with the rest of the marketing program (product, price, and supply chain strategy). Taking this approach allows a firm to communicate a consistent message to target customers from every possible angle, thereby maximizing the total impact on those customers. For example, if the advertising campaign stresses quality, the sales force talks about low price, the supply chain pushes intensive distribution, and the website stresses product innovation, then what is the customer to believe? Not readily seeing that a product can deliver all these benefits, the customer is likely to become confused and go to a competitor with a more consistent message.

All too frequently, firms rush to launch an intensive IMC campaign that has no clear

promotional objectives. The vast majority of promotion activities do not create results in the short term, so firms must focus on long-term promotional objectives and have the patience to continue the program long enough to gauge true success. It takes a great deal of time, effort, and resources to build a solid market position. Promotion based on creativity alone, unlinked to the rest of the marketing strategy, can waste limited and valuable marketing resources.

Ultimately, the goals and objectives of any promotional campaign culminate in the purchase of goods or services by the target market. The classic model for outlining promotional goals and achieving this ultimate outcome is the AIDA model—attention, interest, desire, and action:

- **Attention** Firms cannot sell products if the members of the target market do not know they exist. As a result, the first major goal of any promotional campaign is to attract the attention of potential customers.

- **Interest** Attracting attention seldom sells products. Therefore, the firm must spark interest in the product by demonstrating its features, uses, and benefits.

- **Desire** To be successful, firms must move potential customers beyond mere interest in the product. Good promotion will stimulate desire by convincing potential customers of the product's superiority and its ability to satisfy specific needs.

- **Action** After convincing potential customers to buy the product, promotion must then push them toward the actual purchase.

The role and importance of specific promotional elements vary across the steps in the AIDA model. Mass-communication elements, such as advertising and public relations, tend to be used more heavily to stimulate awareness and interest due to their efficiency in reaching large numbers of potential customers. For example, to breathe new life into Sprite's stagnant image, Coca-Cola used a series of television and movie theater ads based on a quirky "sublymonal advertising" theme. The concept is tied to Sprite's roots in the lemon–lime or "lymon" flavored soft-drink market. Coca-Cola spends over $50 million per year in media advertising for Sprite, which is the number-six soft drink in the market with a 5.7 percent market share.[3]

Along with advertising, sales promotion activities, such as product samples or demonstrations, are vital to stimulating interest in the product. The enhanced communication effectiveness of personal selling makes it ideally suited to moving potential customers through internal desire and into action. Other sales promotion activities, such as product displays, coupons, and trial-size packaging, are well suited to pushing customers toward the final act of making a purchase.

Alongside the issue of promotional goals and objectives, the firm must also consider its promotional goals with respect to the supply chain. In essence, the firm must decide whether it will use a pull strategy, a push strategy, or some combination of the two. When firms use a *pull strategy*, they focus their promotional efforts toward stimulating demand among final customers, who then exert pressure on the supply chain to carry the product. The coordinated use of heavy advertising, public relations, and

EXHIBIT 10.2	PROMOTIONAL STRATEGY OVER THE PRODUCT LIFE CYCLE
Introduction	Promotion depends on heavy advertising and public relations to build brand awareness and educate customers on the product's benefits. Personal selling ensures distribution coverage and supply chain cooperation. Consumer sales promotion stimulates product trial, while trade sales promotion facilitates or expedites distribution activities, especially in obtaining favorable shelf space or product display.
Growth	To sustain growth, firms spend heavily on advertising and public relations to build and maintain brand loyalty. Personal selling maintains distribution and supply chain cooperation. Sales promotion activities decline in importance.
Maturity	A firm's use of advertising shifts to emphasize reminding customers of the firm's products. Sales promotion efforts strongly encourage brand switching for both consumers and the trade. Personal selling remains important to ensure supply chain support and distribution coverage.
Decline	Firms begin to drastically reduce their advertising and public relations efforts in an attempt to reduce expenses. Sales promotion and personal selling drop to levels that are just sufficient enough to maintain product support.

consumer sales promotion has the effect of pulling products through the supply chain, hence its name. In a *push strategy*, promotional efforts focus on members of the supply chain, such as wholesalers and retailers, to motivate them to spend extra time and effort on selling the product. This strategy relies heavily on personal selling and trade sales promotion to push products through the supply chain toward final customers.

The role and importance of specific promotional elements also vary depending on the nature of the product. Industrial products, such as heavy equipment, rely more heavily on personal selling; consumer products require greater use of advertising, sales promotion, and public relations. This variability also occurs across stages in a product's life cycle, as shown in Exhibit 10.2. Early in a product's life cycle, even before its introduction, the heavy expenditures on promotional activities are often a significant drain on the firm's resources. At this stage, it is important to consider these expenditures as investments for the long term because the true impact of the promotional program may not be felt for some time. By the time a product has moved into the maturity phase of its life cycle, the firm can reduce promotional expenditures somewhat, thereby enjoying lower costs and higher profits.

Coordinating promotional elements within the context of the entire marketing program requires a complete understanding of the role, function, and benefits of each element. The advantages and disadvantages of each element must be carefully balanced against the promotional budget and the firm's IMC goals and objectives. To ensure a constant and synergistic message to targeted customers, the firm must ultimately decide how to weigh each promotional element in the overall IMC strategy. In the remainder of this chapter, we discuss the important issues associated with advertising, public relations, personal selling, and sales promotion.

Advertising

Advertising is a key component of promotion and is usually one of the most visible elements of an integrated marketing communications program. *Advertising* is paid, nonpersonal communication transmitted through media such as television, radio,

EXHIBIT 10.3

SPENDING ON NATIONAL ADVERTISING

Advertising Media	2006 National Ad Spending ($ billions)	Change (%)
Four TV networks	17.2	+6.5
Spot TV	11.0	+10.0
Cable TV	19.1	+4.5
Syndication TV	4.1	+5.5
Radio	4.3	+1.0
Magazines	13.4	+4.5
Newspapers	7.5	0
Direct mail	59.6	+8.0
Yellow Pages	2.2	+2.0
Internet	9.7	+25.0
Other media	36.9	+6.3

Source: *Bob Coen's Insider's Report,* Universal McCann (http://www.mccann.com/news/pdfs/Insiders6_06.pdf), June 2006.

magazines, newspapers, direct mail, outdoor displays, the Internet, and mobile devices. Exhibit 10.3 outlines the dollars spent on various national advertising media. Note that Internet advertising is far and away the fastest-growing medium, while traditional media such as newspapers, radio, and magazines are struggling with limited or no growth in ad revenues. This spending pattern follows trends in media usage as consumers are spending more time online and less time with traditional media.

Because advertising is so flexible, it can be used to reach an extremely large target audience or a very small, precisely defined market segment. For example, websites and magazines often focus on narrow market segments such as organic gardening, snow skiing, or women's health. One such website is MensHealth.com, which provides information and sells products aimed at men's issues and men's lives. Advertising targeted to market segments such as African Americans, gays, Hispanics, and women has been an accelerating trend among advertisers over the last decade. Regardless of the medium used, targeting potential customers by coordinating the message with their lifestyles is an important strategic consideration. A recent example of this trend is the increased effort of marketers to reach out to the growing Hispanic community by incorporating "Spanglish"—a mix of Spanish and English language—in their advertising. Taco Bell started the trend by using a Chihuahua and the phrase "Yo quiero Taco Bell" in its promotion. Spanglish can now be found in movies and television programming as well as advertising. Likewise, Univision—the country's dominant Spanish-language media company—is growing rapidly and likely to become the fifth traditional network in the United States.[4]

Advertising can be a cost-efficient element of an IMC program when used to reach a large number of people via television, magazines, outdoor displays, or online ads. For example, *Time* magazine reaches a worldwide audience of over 28 million people (22 million in the United States), making the cost to reach 1,000 subscribers (or CPM—an industry cost benchmark) less than $10 for a full-page ad.[5] The recent cost of a 30-second

EXHIBIT 10.4   ONLINE ADVERTISING PLACEMENTS BY INDUSTRY

Industry	Total Monthly Impressions (millions)	Type of Ad Placement				
		Generic Flash* (millions)	Rich Media (millions)	Sponsored Links (millions)	Standard Image (millions)	Standard Image and Text Link (millions)
Financial services	59,466	8,489	321	4,243	10,412	36,001
Web media	45,147	8,380	147	13,547	12,630	10,443
Retail	43,197	7,052	310	12,050	13,416	10,368
Telecommunications	32,294	8,401	140	1,118	18,936	3,699
Public services	15,156	1,495	141	1,618	3,160	8,743
Travel	9,910	4,381	315	2,764	1,830	620
Business-to-Business	7,086	708	45	2,478	2,986	869
Consumer goods	7,012	2,975	368	1,359	2,111	198
Hardware and Electronics	5,968	1,763	69	329	1,731	2,077
Health	4,619	1,932	119	803	1,546	219
Entertainment	3,417	1,282	257	397	1,221	261
Automotive	3,256	1,613	175	294	899	275
Software	2,953	1,040	45	738	1,007	124

Source: Nielsen//NetRatings, June 2006 (http://www.clickz.com/stats/sectors/advertising/article.php/3615576).

*Definition of terms: (1) generic flash: standard interactive flash banners that require a plug-in; (2) rich media: uses animation, sound, video, and/or interactivity; (3) sponsored links: text-based ads that appear as a result of a keyword search: (4) standard image: animated or static image ads; (5) standard image and text link: ads that use both images and text pointing to the same URL.

slot during the Super Bowl is $2.6 million. However, considering that roughly 90 million viewers watch the broadcast worldwide, the CPM of $28 is quite low.[6]

The initial expense for advertising can be quite high, which is obviously a major drawback of advertising in general. However, online advertising provides an opportunity to reach highly specialized markets at a relatively low cost. The most recent estimates point to continued growth in online ad spending, which now tops $8 billion per year. As shown in Exhibit 10.4, most online ads take the form of standard images, images with text links, or generic flash videos. The use of rich media advertising, including animations and audio–video combinations, will continue to grow as broadband Internet access becomes more widely available both in the home and via mobile connections. Over one-half of the top-twenty Internet advertisers shown in Exhibit 10.5 come from the technology and financial services sectors. Although these and other companies enjoy the large number of impressions that can be generated via online advertising, their efforts suffer from the fleeting nature of most online ads. Getting a potential customer to click on a banner ad or look at a message for more than a few seconds can be quite challenging.

Types of Advertising

Advertising promotes all types of products including goods, services, ideas, issues, people, and anything else that marketers want to communicate to potential customers.

EXHIBIT 10.5

TOP-TWENTY INTERNET ADVERTISERS

Rank	Advertiser	Monthly Media Expenditures ($ millions)	Industry Sector
1	Vonage	16.1	Technology
2	Dollar Rent A Car	11.8	Travel/Hospitality
3	University of Phoenix	10.3	Education
4	Netflix	8.9	Entertainment
5	Fidelity Investments	8.8	Financial Services
6	Monster	8.7	Classifieds
7	Scottrade	8.5	Financial Services
8	Classmates.com	8.2	Miscellaneous
9	Forex Capital Markets	7.5	Financial Services
10	Ameritrade	6.5	Financial Services
11	Dell Dimension Computers	5.9	Technology
12	Verizon Wireless	5.8	Technology
13	Victoria's Secret	5.5	Retail
14	Cingular Wireless	5.4	Technology
15	HomePages	5.3	Classifieds
16	Dell VAR Computers	5.3	Technology
17	Discover Card	5.0	Financial Services
18	Hewlett-Packard Printers	4.9	Technology
19	Thrifty Car Rental	4.8	Travel/Hospitality
20	NexTag Services	4.5	Miscellaneous

Source: TNS Media Intelligence, June 2006 (http://www.clickz.com/news/article.php/3618526).

Because the total expenditures for advertising may be great, larger firms with greater market shares tend to advertise the most. Whether used in consumer or business markets, there are two basic types of advertising: institutional and product advertising.

Institutional Advertising   *Institutional advertising* promotes a firm's image, ideas, and culture with the goal of creating or maintaining an overall corporate image. For example, IBM advertises that it provides infrastructure and solutions for e-business. Although the company offers a wide array of products for e-business, many of IBM's advertisements do not name these products or explain how their infrastructure and solutions actually work. Instead, the purpose of the advertisements is to give potential customers the impression that IBM is a company that understands e-business and that has the ability to solve problems.

Aimed at various stakeholders, including shareholders, consumer advocacy groups, government regulators, or the public at large, institutional advertising can create a positive view of the organization. When a firm promotes a position on a public issue, such as tax policy, international trade regulations, or social issues, it uses a type of institutional advertising called *advocacy advertising*. This type of advertising often promotes socially approved behavior such as recycling, the responsible use of alcoholic beverages, support for the arts, or the firm's support for cultural diversity. Some firms are well known for their use of advocacy advertising and their long-standing positions on social issues. Ben & Jerry's Ice Cream, for example, is an ardent participant in many social causes such as global warming and social injustice.

Product Advertising   *Product advertising* promotes the image, features, uses, benefits, and attributes of products. Product advertising comes in many different forms. For example, *pioneer advertising* stimulates demand for a product category rather than any one specific brand. The goal is to increase customer interest and awareness in the product category in order to increase the size of the entire market—an outcome that benefits all firms in the market. The Dairy Board's famous "Got Milk?" campaign is a good example. Another type of product advertising, *competitive advertising*, attempts to stimulate demand for a specific brand by promoting the brand's image, features, uses, and benefits. This is the type of advertising that we see most often in the media. Exhibit 10.6 illustrates

---

EXHIBIT 10.6

RECALL OF ADVERTISING SLOGANS FOR MAJOR BRANDS

Company	Slogan	Correct Recall (%)
Allstate	You're in good hands	87
State Farm	Like a good neighbor	70
Wal-Mart	Always low price. Always.	67
Sprite	Obey your thirst	35
Taco Bell	Think outside the bun	34
McDonald's	I'm Lovin' It	33
Capital One	What's in your wallet?	27
Gatorade	Is it in you?	19
Chevrolet	An American Revolution	17
J.C. Penney	It's all inside	15
Nissan	Shift	12
Toyota	Get the feeling	11
Budweiser	True	10
Hardee's	Where the food's the star	6
Sierra Mist	Yeah, it's kinda like that	6
Coca-Cola	Real	5
Dr. Pepper	Be you	5
GE	Imagination at work	5
Heineken	It's all about the beer	4
Michelob Ultra	Lose the carbs. Not the taste.	4
Sears	Good life. Great price.	4
Chrysler	Inspiration comes standard	3
Corona	Miles away from ordinary	3
Arby's	What are you eating today?	2
Miller	Good call	1
Buick	The spirit of American style	1
Kmart	Right here, right now.	1
Staples	That was easy	0
Wendy's	It's better here	0

Source: David Kiley, "Can You Name That Slogan?" *BusinessWeek Online,* October 14, 2004 (http://www.businessweek.com/bwdaily/dnflash/oct2004/nf20041014_4965_db035.htm).

how recall can vary for the slogans or taglines used in competitive advertising. Typically, the most successful slogans and ad campaigns are those that are combined with other promotional elements in an integrated marketing effort. Other types of product advertising include *reminder advertising* to let customers know that a brand is available and *reinforcement advertising* to assure current customers that they made the right choice in buying and consuming a certain product. Sam Adams Boston Lager and its "Always a Good Decision" campaign is a good example of reinforcement advertising.

Perhaps the most controversial type of advertising is *comparative advertising,* which occurs when one firm compares its product with one or more competing products on specific features or benefits. Comparative advertising is common in product categories such as soft drinks, automobiles, computers, and over-the-counter medications. In some cases, this comparison is direct, as when Zantac launched comparative ads against Prilosec-OTC immediately after its launch. Zantac claimed that it provided immediate relief from heartburn, whereas Prilosec takes several days to reach its full effect. In other cases, the comparison used in the advertisement is indirect or implied. Procter & Gamble uses this tactic when promoting its Mach3 razors as "The Best a Man Can Get." The implied comparison in this case involves all competing razors on the market. Under the provisions of the Trademark Law Revision Act, marketers using comparative advertising must ensure they do not misrepresent the characteristics of competing products. A visit to the Federal Trade Commission website (http://www.ftc.gov) usually provides examples of companies who have crossed the line by misrepresenting their competitors or their products.

Determining the Advertising Budget

The *advertising budget,* or the total amount of money a firm allocates to advertising activities for a specific time period, is difficult to determine because the effects of advertising are difficult to measure. There are many factors that can determine a firm's decision about the appropriate level to fund advertising activities, including the geographic size of the market, the distribution or density of customers, the types of products advertised, sales volume relative to the competition, and the firm's own historical advertising budget. Usually, the advertising budget for business products is small compared to consumer convenience products such as cigarettes, soft drinks, detergents, and cosmetics. There are several different ways to determine an appropriate advertising budget:

- **Objectives and Task Approach**   This approach requires that the firm lay out its goals for the advertising campaign and then list the tasks required to accomplish specific advertising objectives. The firm calculates and sums the costs of each task to determine the total budget. The major drawback of this approach is that the level of effort needed to accomplish advertising objectives is difficult to know with certainty.

- **Percentage of Sales Approach**   This approach is the most widely used method for determining the advertising budget. The approach is simple, straightforward, and based on what the firm traditionally spends on advertising. The obvious flaw of this approach is its implied assumption that sales create advertising. Also, during periods of declining sales, setting the budget as a percentage of sales may be a mistake because reduced advertising is often not the best strategy.

- **Competitive Matching Approach**   This approach involves firms attempting to match major competitor's advertising expenditures in absolute dollars. Many firms review competitive advertising and compare competitor's expenditures across various media in relation to their own spending levels. This competitive tracking can occur at the national and regional levels and at least can provide a benchmark for comparing advertising resources to market share movements. The problem with competitive matching is that all firms are different, so competitors are likely to have different advertising objectives and different resources to devote to advertising.

- **Arbitrary Approach**   Intuition and personal experience set the advertising budget under this approach. The arbitrary approach can lead to mistakes in budgeting because it is not necessarily scientific, objective, or logical. On the other hand, deciding how much to spend on advertising is not an exact science.

Determining the appropriate advertising budget is an important part of any marketing strategy. Setting the budget too high will obviously result in overspending, waste, and lower profits. However, setting the budget too low may be even worse. Firms that do not spend enough on advertising find it very difficult to stand out in an extremely crowded market for customer attention. For example, when the Wrigley Company acquired the Altoids brand from Kraft in 2005, the company discovered that advertising for Altoids had been allowed to wane. Consequently, Altoids' sales had declined rapidly while Hershey's IceBreakers brand of mints was stealing market share. To correct the problem, Wrigley increased the advertising budget for Altoids over 50 percent and introduced new flavors such as Tangerine Sours, Mango Sours, and Liquorice.[7]

Evaluating Advertising Effectiveness

Evaluating the effectiveness of advertising is one of the most challenging tasks facing marketers. Many of the effects and outcomes of advertising take a long time to develop, especially regarding important outcomes such as enhanced brand image, corporate reputation, and positive product attitudes. The effect of advertising on sales is even lagged in some cases, with the effect occurring long after the campaign has ended. The seemingly unending methods that can be used to evaluate advertising effectiveness further complicate the task of measuring advertising results. Some methods include evaluating the achievement of advertising objectives; assessing the effectiveness of advertising copy, illustrations, and layouts; and evaluating the effectiveness of various media. Effectiveness measures can also look at different market segments and their responses to advertising—including brand image; attitudes toward the advertising, the brand, or the firm; and actual customer purchasing behavior. As discussed in Beyond the Pages 10.2, one of the issues facing podcasting as an advertising medium is the

CAN PODCASTING GO MAINSTREAM?[8]

If you don't know what podcasts are, chances are you will soon. Via podcasting, content providers can distribute audio and video files over the Internet using push syndication technology such as RSS (really simple syndication) feeds. These files can be downloaded or streamed to a user's computer for playback on the computer itself or a host of mobile devices. The term *podcast* was coined from a combination of *iPod* and *broadcasting;* however, the name is really a misnomer because an iPod is not needed to play the content. Virtually all podcasts are free and available from many sources, though Apple's iTunes is arguably the most popular provider.

Thousands of podcasts are available today covering topics such as news, technology, comedy, popular television programs, politics, and religion. Most podcasts are created as a series of episodes that are delivered (or pushed out) either periodically or at planned daily or weekly intervals. Interest in podcasts is growing rapidly among both consumers and advertisers. Research estimates that the U.S. podcasting audience will grow from ten million people today to over 50 million by 2010. That pace of growth has advertisers interested in using podcasting as a tool for reaching ever fragmented consumer audiences. Traditional content providers like NPR, CBS, and ABC, which use the technology as a way to repurpose their existing programs, develop many of the most popular podcasts. NPR alone delivers 45 different podcasts on a regular basis. Other made-for-podcast programming is also very popular. One example is the *This Week in Tech,* or *TWIT,* podcast hosted by well-known radio personality Leo Laporte. Each week, panelists discuss tech news, product reviews, and other tech issues in a laid-back 1-hour program. AOL Radio, Dell, Visa, and the $10,000 per month in donations received from its listeners support *TWIT.*

Podcasting is very popular among the highly sought after younger demographic of 18 to 24 year olds. These consumers are more than twice as likely to listen or watch podcasts as are adults aged 45 years and older. The consumption of podcasts is highly correlated with the sales of portable media devices. Podcasting taps into a very appealing young, on-the-go market that advertisers today have a very difficult time reaching with traditional media. By placing ads within a podcast or sponsoring an episode or series, advertisers can match their advertising with targeted programming content. For example, Georgia Pacific—makers of Dixie paper products, Brawny paper towels, and Northern bathroom tissue—sponsors a parent-themed podcast called *The MommyCast*. This sort of product/programming tie-in with a highly interested audience is difficult to do in traditional media advertising.

Despite its roots, the future of podcasting is likely to be tied to wireless phones. The reason is sheer size: There are roughly two billion mobile phones in use around the world compared to roughly 100 million portable media players and 700 million computers. Phone-enabled podcasting is just beginning to take off. Users can dial a number to listen to podcasts or download them for later. Independent music retailer CD Baby spends roughly $1,000 per month to insert 15-second ads into certain podcasts delivered via cell phones. Pod2Mobile has introduced a service that allows advertisers to automatically place ten and 15 second ads into hundreds of podcasts. The service tracks click-through rates for each ad and costs advertisers only $300 for 3,000 downloads. A similar ad-insertion service is also available from Podbridge. Before a user downloads his favorite podcast from a Podbridge-enabled content provider, he is asked three questions: age, gender, and zip code. Podbridge then builds a custom podcast with ad insertions that match the user profile. The content provider is provided with the responses to the three questions, along with the time of day the user downloaded the podcast. Many believe that podcasting's move into the advertising mainstream will depend on the ability of firms like Podbridge to provide information on who is actually listening to and watching podcasts.

difficulty associated with tracking listeners and measuring the effectiveness of podcast sponsorships.

Advertising effectiveness can be evaluated before, during, or after the campaign. A pretest attempts to evaluate the potential effectiveness of one or more elements of the advertising program. To pretest advertisements, firms often use a panel of actual or potential buyers who then judge one or more aspects of an advertisement. A pretest has as its foundation the belief that customers are more likely to know what type of advertising will influence them. During an ad campaign, the company typically measures effectiveness by looking at actual customer behavior patterns such as purchases, their responses to toll-free telephone numbers, the rate of coupon redemption, page visits to the firm's website, or even personal communications. The firm may record the number of inquiries or communication contacts and judge advertising effectiveness based on industry norms or the firm's own internal benchmarks. Firms may even peruse online web logs for evidence of the effectiveness of their promotional campaigns.

The evaluation of advertising effectiveness after a campaign is a *posttest*. The nature of the firm's advertising objectives will determine what kind of posttest is most appropriate. For example, if a campaign's objective is to increase brand awareness or create a more favorable attitude toward the firm, then the posttest will measure changes in these variables. Customer surveys, panels, or experiments may be used to evaluate a campaign based on communication objectives. Firms will also use performance outcomes such as sales or market share changes to determine campaign effectiveness. Unfortunately, the connection between advertising and these types of outcomes is not always clear. A study of the top-100 advertisers determined that 20 percent of ad spending is not efficient in generating sales volume.[9] The difficulty in linking advertising to sales becomes compounded by the fact that many factors can affect sales. Furthermore, most of these factors are beyond the control of the firm. For instance, competitors' actions, regulatory decisions, changes in economic conditions, and even the weather might influence or diminish a firm's sales or market share during a specific time period when advertising effectiveness is under scrutiny.

Public Relations

In Beyond the Pages 4.2, we discussed corporate affairs as a collection of strategic activities aimed at marketing an organization, its issues, and its ideals to potential stakeholders (consumers, general public, shareholders, media, government, and so on). Public relations is one component of a firm's corporate affairs activities. The goal of public relations is to track public attitudes, identify issues that may elicit public concern, and develop programs to create and maintain positive relationships between a firm and its stakeholders. A firm uses public relations to communicate with its stakeholders for the same reasons that it develops advertisements. Public relations can be used to promote the firm, its people, its ideas, and its image and can even create an internal shared understanding among employees. Because various stakeholders' attitudes toward the firm affect their decisions relative to the firm, it is very important to maintain positive public opinion.

Public relations can improve the public's general awareness of a company and can create specific images such as quality, innovativeness, value, or concern for social issues. For example, New Belgium Brewery in Fort Collins, Colorado, has a strong reputation for its stance on environmental efficiency and conservation. The brewery takes an aggressive stance toward recycling and uses windmills to generate electricity.[10] Likewise, Starbucks has gained international awareness through its fair treatment of employees. The company was also the first coffee retailer to establish a global code of conduct for fair treatment of agricultural suppliers—the small farmers who supply the coffee beans for its products. Ben & Jerry's has a global reputation for being socially responsible, especially with respect to environmental concerns. The company has partnered with SaveOurEnvironment.org and the Dave Matthews Band to promote environmental awareness and fight global warming through its Lick Global Warming website (http://www.lickglobalwarming.org).[11]

Public Relations Methods

Firms use a number of public relations methods to convey messages and to create the right attitudes, images, and opinions. An in-house staff often executes the public relations program; however, many firms use public relations professionals to prepare materials such as brochures, newsletters, annual reports, and news releases that reach and influence desired stakeholders. Public relations often becomes confused with publicity. Although publicity is one part of public relations, it is more narrowly defined to include the firm's activities designed to gain media attention through articles, editorials, or news stories. By encouraging the media to report on a firm's accomplishments, publicity helps maintain positive public awareness, visibility, and a desired image. Publicity can be used for a single purpose, such as to launch a new product or diminish the public's opinion regarding a negative event, or it can be used for multiple purposes to enhance many aspects of the firm's activities. Having a good publicity strategy is important because publicity can have the same effect as advertising, though typically with greater credibility. There are a number of different methods used in public relations and publicity efforts:

- **News (or Press) Releases** A news release is a few pages of typewritten copy—typically fewer than 300 words—used to draw attention to a company event, product, or person affiliated with the firm. News releases can be submitted to newspapers, magazines, television contacts, suppliers, key customers, or even the firm's employees.

- **Feature Articles** A feature article is a manuscript of up to 3,000 words prepared for a specific purpose or target audience. For example, a firm building a new production facility in northeast Georgia might supply a feature article to regional and local media outlets, chambers of commerce, local governments, and major firms in the area. Feature articles typically focus on the implications or economic impact of a firm's actions. They are also very useful when responding to negative events or publicity.

- **White Papers**   White papers are similar to feature articles; however, they are more technical and focus on very specific topics of interest to the firm's stakeholders. White papers promote a firm's stance on important product or market issues and can be used to promote the firm's own products and solutions. White papers have been used extensively in the information technology field where firms continually work to establish standards and keep up with technological innovation.

- **Press Conferences**   A press conference is a meeting with news media called to announce or respond to major events. Media personnel receive invitations to a specific location, with written materials, photographs, exhibits, and even products given to them. Multimedia materials may be distributed to broadcast stations in hopes that they will air some of the activities that occurred at the press conference. Firms typically hold press conferences when announcing new products, patents, mergers or acquisitions, philanthropic efforts, or internal administrative changes.

- **Event Sponsorship**   Corporate sponsorship of major events has become an entire industry in itself. Sponsorships can range from local events, such as high school athletics and local charities, to international events such as the Tour de France or NASCAR racing. A growing trend in sponsorship involves the naming of sports stadiums and venues.

- **Product Placement**   Product placement in movies and television programs is a rapidly growing practice, especially among highly identifiable brands like beverages, computers, clothing, and automobiles. These firms have a strong interest in placing their products in the hands of movie and television characters that consumers see as enjoying the product or using the product as a part of the action.

- **Employee Relations**   Employee relations are every bit as important as public and investor relations. Employee relations' activities provide organizational support for employees with respect to their jobs and lives. Employee relations can encompass many different activities including internal newsletters, training programs, employee assistance programs, and human resource programs.

When these methods generate publicity in the media, the public perceives the message as having more credibility due to the implied endorsement of the media that carries the story. The public will typically consider news coverage more truthful and credible than advertising because the firm has not paid for the media time. One major drawback of public relations activities is that the firm has much less control over how the message will be delivered. For example, many media personnel have a reputation for inserting their own opinions and biases when communicating a news story. Another drawback involves the risk of spending a great deal of time and effort in developing public relations messages that fail to attract media attention.

Negative Public Relations

One of the most important aspects of public relations deals with the unexpected and often unfavorable public reactions resulting from an ethical or legal inquiry, unsafe products, accidents, or the controversial actions of employees and executives. For example, all airlines have carefully planned procedures and personnel in place to respond to an aviation accident; however, they always face a very difficult and distressing situation when these accidents occur. Likewise, the news has been filled with ethical and legal scandals involving many firms. For example, past charges of deceptive pricing against Columbia HCA—the nation's largest hospital organization—resulted in negative publicity and a total restructuring of the company. Microsoft (anticompetitive activities) and Ford Motor Company (the Explorer tire recall) have also dealt with negative publicity in recent years.

Negative coverage of a company's problems can have quick, dramatic, and long-lasting effects. Negative publicity is critically important when its effects reduce the degree of trust that customers have in a specific industry or firm. Exhibit 10.7 lists U.S. firms having some of the strongest and weakest public reputations. Note that firms with lower reputation scores, such as Enron, WorldCom, Halliburton, and Martha Stewart Living Omnimedia, have experienced a number of scandals and legal problems in recent years.

The range of reputation scores in Exhibit 10.7 is also quite telling of the effects that negative publicity can have on a firm. Exxon's response to the *Valdez* accident in 1989 is one of the classic examples of how *not* to respond to negative publicity. When faced with the massive oil spill in Alaska, Exxon failed to communicate effectively with the press and various stakeholders. It took several days before top executives communicated clearly how Exxon was going to deal with the environmental disaster. As shown in the exhibit, Exxon still struggles with a relatively weak corporate reputation. Conversely, Johnson & Johnson's response to the Tylenol cyanide-tampering scare in 1982 is the classic example of effective crisis management. When faced with tremendous negative publicity, Johnson & Johnson immediately recalled all Tylenol products that were on store shelves. The company's quick action and honesty in dealing with the situation was a tremendous boost to the company's image and Tylenol's market share. Today, Johnson & Johnson and Tylenol enjoy a high degree of customer trust.

A single negative event, especially one that is potentially dangerous to customers, can wipe out a company's image and negate the goodwill generated over decades of expensive advertising campaigns. Today, the media can report incidents through television and the Internet faster than ever before. As a result, negative stories receive more attention now than in the past. To avoid negative publicity, it is vital to avoid negative incidents and events that can create problems. Firms can achieve this goal through effective ethical and legal compliance programs, safety programs, quality-control procedures, and programs designed to enhance employee integrity. However, no matter how hard a firm tries to avoid negative events, the potential for negative incidents and publicity is always present. Therefore, all firms should have plans and procedures in place to respond to negative events when they occur. In particular, specific policies and procedures for handling the media and their coverage of the event are absolutely necessary. One of the great public relations lessons learned over time is that firms must expedite news coverage of negative events rather than try to block the news or cover up facts about the incident.

EXHIBIT 10.7

CORPORATE REPUTATION: THE STRONGEST AND WEAKEST U.S. CORPORATIONS

Rank	Company	Reputation Quotient[SM]
The Strongest Reputations		
1	Johnson & Johnson	80.56
2	The Coca-Cola Company	79.69
3	Google	79.52
4	United Parcel Service (UPS)	79.37
5	3M Company	78.78
6	Sony Corporation	78.75
7	Microsoft Corporation	78.11
8	General Mills	78.03
9	FedEx Corporation	77.79
10	Intel Corporation	77.27
11	Toyota Motor Corporation	77.27
12	Home Depot	76.50
13	The Procter & Gamble Company	75.91
14	The Walt Disney Company	75.88
15	Dell Computer Corporation	75.73
The Weakest Reputations		
46	Time Warner Inc.	63.85
47	ChevronTexaco Corporation	62.46
48	AT&T Corporation	62.37
49	Comcast Corporation	62.08
50	Altria Group	61.62
51	Sprint Corporation	61.01
52	Martha Stewart Living Omnimedia	60.99
53	ExxonMobil Corporation	59.57
54	Royal Dutch/Shell	59.45
55	Tyco International, Ltd.	58.39
56	United Airlines/UAL Corporation	53.09
57	Halliburton Company	52.22
58	Adelphia Communications Corporation	49.75
59	MCI (formerly WorldCom)	46.80
60	Enron	30.05

Source: Harris Interactive, Annual Reputation Quotient Survey. © 2005 (http://www.harrisinteractive.com/services/reputation.asp).

Personal Selling and Sales Management

Personal selling is paid personal communication that attempts to inform customers about products and persuade them to purchase those products. Personal selling takes place in many forms. For example, a Circuit City salesperson who describes the benefits of a Sony television to a customer engages in personal selling. So is the salesperson who attempts to convince a large industrial organization to purchase photocopy machines. Some types of personal selling are highly complex and relational in nature. For example, the vice president of business development at Parsons, Inc.

(a large engineering and construction firm) will hold many meetings with government officials in planning major highway or bridge construction projects. The complexity of these types of purchases requires a long-term relationship between Parsons and the governmental agency.

Compared to other types of promotion, personal selling is the most precise form of communication because it assures companies that they are in direct contact with an excellent prospect. Though one-on-one contact is highly advantageous, it does not come without disadvantages. The most serious drawback of personal selling is the cost per contact. In business markets, a single sales presentation can take many months and thousands of dollars to prepare. For instance, to give government officials a real feel for the design and scope of a bridge construction project, Parsons must invest thousands of dollars in detailed scale models of several different bridge designs. Personal selling is also expensive due to the costs associated with recruiting, selecting, training, and motivating salespeople. Despite the high costs, personal selling plays an increasingly important role in IMC and overall marketing strategy.

The goals of personal selling vary tremendously based on its role in a long-run approach to integrated communications. These goals typically involve finding prospects, informing prospects, persuading prospects to buy, and keeping customers satisfied through follow-up service after the sale. To effectively deliver on these goals, salespeople have to be not only competent in selling skills but also thoroughly trained in technical product characteristics. For example, pharmaceutical salespeople (drug reps) who sell to physicians and hospitals must have detailed training in the technical medical applications of the drugs and medical devices that they sell. In fact, it is not unusual for salespeople who sell medical implants such as knee or hip replacements to have as much technical training about the product as the physicians who actually implant these devices during surgery. Obviously, when the products and buyers are less sophisticated, salespeople will require much less training.

Very few businesses can survive on the profits generated from purely transactional marketing (one-time purchases). For long-term survival, most firms depend on repeat sales and the development of ongoing relationships with customers. For this reason, personal selling has evolved to take on elements of customer service and marketing research. More than any other part of the firm, salespeople are closer to the customer and have many more opportunities for communication with them. Every contact with a customer gives the sales force a chance to deliver exceptional service and learn more about the customer's needs. Salespeople also have the opportunity to learn about competing products and the customer's reaction toward them. These relational aspects are important—whether the salesperson makes a sale or not. In today's highly competitive markets, this frontline knowledge held by the sales force is one of the most important assets of the firm. In fact, the knowledge held by the sales force is often an important strength that can be leveraged in developing marketing strategy.

The Sales Management Process

Because the sales force has a direct bearing on sales revenue and customer satisfaction, the effective management of the sales force is vital to a firm's marketing strategy.

In addition to generating performance outcomes, the sales force often creates the firm's reputation, and the conduct of individual salespeople determines the perceived ethicalness of the entire firm. The strategic implementation of effective sales management requires a number of activities, discussed in the following sections.

Developing Sales Force Objectives   Sales force objectives are vital to the overall IMC strategy and must be fully integrated with the objectives and activities of other promotional elements. Sales objectives will determine the type of salespeople that the firm needs to hire. For example, salespeople may be needed to find new customers through *prospecting*—the identification of potential customers most likely to buy the firm's products. The selling skills required for prospecting differ from those associated with generating repeat sales from current customers. Furthermore, a different skill set must be developed to provide product support, educate customers, and provide service after the sale. The connection between selling skills and sales force objectives reinforces the importance of having a fully integrated sales management process.

The technical aspects of establishing sales force objectives involve desired sales dollars, sales volume, or market share. These sales objectives can be translated into sales quotas for individual salespeople. Further, individual sales objectives might be based on order size, the number of sales calls, or the ratio of orders to calls. Ultimately, sales objectives help evaluate and control sales force activities, as well as compensate individual salespeople.

Determining Sales Force Size   The size of the sales force is a function of many variables including the type of salespeople used, specific sales objectives, and the importance of personal selling within the overall IMC program. The size of the sales force is important because the firm must find a balance between sales expenses and revenue generation. Having a sales force that is too large or too small can lead to inflated expenses, lost sales, and lost profit. Achieving this balance in practice is challenging because the sales force is one of the first targets for cost cutting when a firm must find ways to reduce expenses. Although trimming the sales force is a quick and easy way to cut costs, doing so often gives competitors an opportunity to improve their market position with valued customers.

Although there is no exact analytical method for determining the optimum size of the sales force, there are several general approaches. Determining the specific objectives and tasks that are required to fulfill sales and IMC goals is one approach. For example, this method might focus on the number of sales calls per year necessary to effectively serve a market. This number can be divided by the average number of sales calls that a salesperson can make in 1 year to derive an estimate of sales force size. Another method involves marginal analysis, where additional salespeople join the sales force until the cost of adding an additional salesperson equals the potential sales that can be generated by that salesperson. Though firms can develop sophisticated, quantifiable models to determine the size of the sales force, most companies make these decisions subjectively based on the experience of sales managers.

Recruiting and Training Salespeople   Recruiting the right types of salespeople should be closely tied to the personal selling and IMC strategies. Firms usually recruit potential salespeople from a number of sources including within the firm, competing firms, employment agencies, educational institutions, and direct-response advertisements placed on the Internet, in magazines, or in newspapers. Salesperson recruitment should be a continuous activity because firms must ensure that new salespeople are consistently available to sustain the sales program. Contrary to popular belief, the best applicant these days may be male or female. In a study of gender differences in sales organizations, results indicated that there are few differences among men and women salespeople in areas such as expectations, job satisfaction, compensation, or performance.[12]

The cost of hiring and training a salesperson can be expensive. For example, A.G. Edwards spends roughly $75,000 over 5 years to train each financial consultant.[13] In recent years, successful salespeople have had many opportunities to leave their current firms and earn higher salaries at competing firms. This situation creates a serious problem with sales force turnover, a considerable cost of doing business in highly technical fields. In an effort to reduce turnover, many firms have instituted very restrictive recruitment and selection procedures. For example, State Farm Insurance strives for low sales force turnover by forcing applicants for agent positions to undergo a yearlong series of interviews, tests, and visits with agents before finding out whether they will be hired.

Sales training has moved toward formal programs in recent years although some companies still depend on less formal methods like on-the-job training. Formal training methods have moved toward self-directed, online training modules and away from classroom training. Although the majority of training continues to be in the classroom, projections indicate that within a few years the majority of sales training will be done online or via wireless delivery to handheld devices. The worldwide online sales training market is expected to grow from $6.6 billion to $23.7 billion, mainly because it is much more cost effective than traditional training.[14]

Controlling and Evaluating the Sales Force   Controlling and evaluating the sales force requires a comparison of sales objectives with actual sales performance. This analysis can be made at the individual salesperson level or for the entire sales force. To effectively evaluate a salesperson, predetermined performance standards must be in place. These standards also determine the compensation plan for the sales force.

EXHIBIT 10.8

COMPARISON OF SALES FORCE COMPENSATION METHODS

Method	Most Useful When:	Advantages	Disadvantages
Straight Salary	Salespeople are new Salespeople move into new territories Products require intense presale and postsale service	Easy to administer Gives salespeople more security Allows for greater control over salespeople More predictable selling expenses	Gives salespeople little or no incentive Requires close supervision of salespeople
Straight Commission	Aggressive selling is required Nonselling tasks can be minimized The firm outsources some selling functions	Gives sales people maximum incentive Selling expenses are tied directly to sales volume Differential commissions on some products can increase sales for those products	Gives sales people little security Gives managers less control over salespeople May result in less service for smaller accounts
Combination	Sales territories have similar sales potential The firm wants to provide incentive and still have some control	Good balance of incentive and security for salespeople	Selling expenses are less predictable May be difficult to administer

Source: Adapted from William M. Pride and O. C. Ferrell, *Foundations of Marketing* (Boston: Houghton Mifflin Company, 2004), 409.

Exhibit 10.8 provides a comparison of various sales force compensation systems. Systems using a combination of salary and commission are the most commonly used because they offer the best balance of the benefits offered by salary- and commission-only programs.

Without a formal evaluation and control system, the firm will not be able to determine whether its performance targets have been met. Well-designed evaluation and control systems have built-in mechanisms for corrective action when personnel do not achieve sales targets. To improve sales performance, the firm can increase incentives to better motivate the sales force, provide additional training to salespeople, or perhaps even change the performance standards if they are inconsistent with market realities. It is also possible that the entire IMC program will require corrective action if the sales strategy is inconsistent with the overall promotional program.

The Impact of Technology on Personal Selling

Across many different industries, sales forces have shrunk due to advances in communications technology and mobile computing. The development of integrated supply chains and the procurement of standardized products over the Internet have reduced the need for salespeople in many industries. Although these developments reduce selling costs, they create a major management challenge for most firms: How can firms use new technology to reduce costs and increase productivity while maintaining personalized, one-to-one client relationships?

One of the keys to using sales technology effectively is to seamlessly integrate it with customer relationship management systems, competitive intelligence activities, and internal customer databases. By automating many repetitive selling tasks, like filling repeat orders, sales technology can actually increase sales, productivity, and one-to-one client relationships at the same time. Although many firms develop and maintain their own sales automation systems, others who lack the resources to do so can turn to third-party providers like Salesforce.com—an on-demand, web-based provider of integrated CRM and sales automation solutions.[15] Whether in-house or third-party, the key to these solutions is integration. By pushing integrated customer, competitive, and product information toward the salesperson, technology can increase salesperson productivity and sales revenue by allowing the sales force to serve customers' needs more effectively.

Sales Promotion

Despite the attention paid to advertising, sales promotion activities account for the bulk of promotional spending in many firms. This is especially true for firms selling consumer products in grocery stores and mass-merchandise retailers where sales promotion can account for up to 70 percent of the firm's promotional budget.[16] Sales promotion involves activities that create buyer incentives to purchase a product or that add value for the buyer or the trade. Sales promotion can be targeted toward consumers, channel intermediaries, or the sales force. Exhibit 10.9 breaks down total spending for various sales promotion activities. As can be seen in the exhibit, sales

---

EXHIBIT 10.9   **SPENDING ON VARIOUS SALES PROMOTION ACTIVITIES**

Promotional Activities	Spending ($ millions)	Yearly Change (%)
Couponing	9,980	8
POP displays	18,009	6
In-store promotions	891	−2
Sampling	1,800	18
Premiums	31,564	5
Ad specialties	17,745	5
Promotional licensing	6,161	1
Specialty print	6,656	4
Sponsorships	11,027	8
Interactive	3,500	25
Direct mail	56,800	8
Business-to-business promotions	45,675	5
Trade shows	24,880	6
Contests and sweepstakes	1,840	0
Trade promotion	110,214	−3

Source: Promotion Marketing Association, "State of the Promotion Industry Report," © 2005 Promotion Marketing Association (http://www.pmalink.org/resources/pma2005report.pdf).

promotion includes a broad assortment of promotional elements because it encompasses activities other than advertising, public relations, and personal selling. Regardless of the activity and toward whom it is directed, sales promotion has one universal goal: to induce product trial and purchase.

Most firms use sales promotion in support of advertising, public relations, or personal selling activities rather than as a stand-alone promotional element. Advertising frequently becomes coordinated with sales promotion activities to provide free product samples, premiums, or value-added incentives. For example, a computer company such as Compaq might offer free Internet service for 1 year with the purchase of a new computer. Furthermore, a manufacturer might offer free merchandise to channel intermediaries who purchase a stated quantity of product within a specified time frame. A 7-Up bottler, for example, might offer a free case of 7-Up for every ten cases purchased by a retailer.

Sales Promotion in Consumer Markets

Any member of the supply chain can initiate consumer sales promotions, but manufacturers and retailers typically offer them. For manufacturers, sales promotion activities represent an effective way to introduce new products or promote established brands. Coupons and product sampling are frequently used during new product launches to stimulate interest and trial. Retailers typically offer sales promotions to stimulate customer traffic or increase sales at specific locations. Coupons and free products are common examples, as are in-store product demonstrations. Many retailers are known for their sales promotions such as the free toys that come with kid's meals at McDonald's, Burger King, and other fast food establishments.

A potentially limitless variety of sales promotion methods can be used in consumer markets. Truthfully, developing and using these methods is limited only by the creativity of the firm offering the promotion. However, firms will typically offer one or more of the following types of sales promotions to consumers:

- **Coupons**   Coupons reduce the price of a product and encourage customers to try new or established brands. Coupons can be used to increase sales volume quickly, to attract repeat purchasers, or even to introduce new product sizes or models. To be most effective, coupons need to be accessible, easy to recognize, and easy to use. For the most part, this requires that coupons be distributed on packages (the highest redemption rates), through inserts in print advertising, through direct mail, or through in-store displays.

- **Rebates**   Rebates are very similar to coupons except that they require much more effort on the consumer's part to obtain the price reduction. Although consumers prefer coupons because of the ease of use, most firms prefer rebates for several reasons. First, firms have more control over rebates because they can be launched and ended very quickly. Second, a rebate program allows the firm to collect important consumer information that can be used to build customer databases. The best reason is that most consumers never bother to redeem rebate offers. This allows a firm to entice customers to purchase a product with only a minimal loss of profit.

- **Samples**   Free samples are one of the most widely used consumer sales promotion methods. Samples stimulate trial of a product, increase volume in the early stages of the product's life cycle, and encourage consumers to actively search for a product. Samples can be distributed through the mail, attached to other products, and given out through personal selling efforts or in-store displays. Samples can also be distributed via less direct methods. For example, free samples of soap, shampoo, coffee, or sunscreen might be placed in hotel rooms to create consumer awareness of new products.

- **Loyalty Programs**   Loyalty programs, or frequent-buyer programs, reward loyal customers who engage in repeat purchases. These programs are popular in many industries due to their potential to dramatically increase profits over the long term. We are all familiar with the frequent-flier programs offered by major airlines. Other companies, such as hotels, auto rental agencies, and credit card companies, offer free goods or services for repeat purchases. For instance, the Discover Card provides a one percent cash-back bonus to each cardholder at the end of the year.

- **Point-of-Purchase Promotion**   Point-of-purchase (POP) promotion includes displays, counter pieces, display racks, or self-service cartons that are designed to build traffic, advertise a product, or induce impulse purchases. POP promotions are highly effective because they are used in a store where consumers make roughly 70 to 80 percent of all purchase decisions. Another type of POP promotion is an in-store product demonstration. Examples of these demonstrations include fashion shows, food preparation demonstrations in grocery stores, and free makeovers in the cosmetics departments of department stores and specialty stores. Clinique, for instance, offers potential customers free makeovers to demonstrate the features of their cosmetics and to teach customers proper application techniques.

- **Premiums**   Premiums are items offered free or at a minimum cost as a bonus for purchasing a product. Examples of premiums include a free car wash with a gasoline fill-up, a free toothbrush with a purchase of a tube of toothpaste, and the toys offered inside a McDonald's Happy Meal. Premiums are good at increasing consumption and persuading consumers to switch brands.

- **Contests and Sweepstakes**   Consumer contests, games, and sweepstakes encourage potential consumers to compete for prizes or try their luck by submitting their names in a drawing for prizes. In addition to being valuable information collection tools, contests and sweepstakes are good at attracting a large number of participants and generating widespread interest in a product. Because they require no skill to enter, sweepstakes are an effective way to increase sales or market share in the short term.

- **Direct Mail**   Direct mail, which includes catalog marketing and other printed material mailed to individual consumers, is a unique category because it incorporates elements of advertising, sales promotion, and distribution into a coordinated effort to induce customers to buy. The use of direct mail has grown tremendously in recent years due to consumer time constraints, relatively low cost, and the advent of sophisticated database management tools.

Firms can use any one or all of these consumer promotion methods in their overall IMC program. However, the choice of one or more methods must be made in consideration of the firm's IMC objectives. Furthermore, the choice must also consider the use of sales promotions by competitors and whether a particular method involves ethical or legal dimensions. Consumer sweepstakes, in particular, have specific legal requirements to ensure that each entrant has an equally likely chance of winning.

Sales Promotion in Business Markets

Sales promotion in business markets is also known as trade promotion. By targeting channel intermediaries with promotional activities, manufacturers hope to push their products through the channel by increasing sales and encouraging increased effort among their channel partners. Manufacturers use many of the same promotional methods that target consumers; however, a number of sales promotion methods are unique to business markets:

- **Trade Allowances** Manufacturers offer a number of different trade allowances, or price reductions, to their channel intermediaries. Buying allowances are price reductions for purchasing specified quantities of a product at a single time (the equivalent of a bulk discount). Related to this is a buy-back allowance where the reduction is proportional to the total amount of product purchased during the time frame of the promotional offer. Finally, a merchandise allowance is a manufacturer's agreement to pay intermediaries a specific sum of money in exchange for specific promotional efforts such as special displays or advertising. In each case, the goal of the allowance is to induce intermediaries to perform specific actions.

- **Free Merchandise** Manufacturers sometimes offer free merchandise to intermediaries instead of quantity discounts. Typically, they provide the free merchandise to reduce invoice costs as a way of compensating the intermediary for other activities that assist the manufacturer.

- **Training Assistance** In some cases, a manufacturer can offer free training to an intermediary's employees. This typically occurs when the products involved are rather complex.

- **Cooperative Advertising** Cooperative advertising is an arrangement whereby a manufacturer agrees to pay a certain amount of an intermediary's media cost for advertising the manufacturer's products. This is a very popular sales promotion method among retailers.

- **Selling Incentives** Selling incentives come in two general forms: push money and sales contests. Intermediaries, particularly their salespeople, receive push money in the form of additional compensation to encourage a more aggressive selling effort for a particular product. Push money is appropriate when personal selling is an important part of the marketing effort and it is necessary to gain commitment from an intermediary's sale force. This method is expensive and should be used carefully to avoid any ethical or legal issues. Sales contests encourage outstanding performance within an intermediary's sales force. Sales personnel can be recognized for outstanding achievements by receiving money, vacations, computers, or even cars for meeting or exceeding certain sales targets.

Trade sales promotion encompasses a wide variety of activities and is often one of the largest expenditures in the overall promotional budget. Trade promotion is vital when a manufacturer needs the cooperation and support of the channel to fulfill its own sales and marketing objectives. This is particularly true when a manufacturer must obtain support for a new product launch or a new consumer sales promotion. Given the importance of integrated supply chains that we discussed in Chapter 9, it should not be surprising that effective trade promotion is also vital to fulfilling a firm's distribution strategy.

Lessons from Chapter 10

Integrated marketing communications

- includes conveying and sharing meaning between buyers and sellers, either as individuals, firms, or between individuals and firms.

- includes the traditional elements of the promotion mix: advertising, public relations, personal selling, and sales promotion.

- refers to the strategic, *coordinated* use of promotion to create one consistent message across multiple channels to ensure maximum persuasive impact on the firm's current and potential customers.

- takes a 360-degree view of the customer that considers every contact that a customer or potential customer may have in his relationship with the firm.

- can reduce or eliminate redundancies and waste in the overall promotional program.

- has become widely embraced as firms struggle to adapt to fragmented audiences across a wide variety of traditional media outlets.

- typically sets goals and objectives for the promotional campaign using the AIDA model—attention, interest, desire, and action.

- can change depending on whether the firm uses a pull or push strategy with respect to its supply chain.

- varies in its emphasis on specific promotional elements depending on the nature of the product and its stage in the product life cycle.

Advertising

- is one of the most visible and key components of promotion.

- is identified as paid, nonpersonal communication transmitted through the media such as television, radio, magazines, newspapers, direct mail, outdoor displays, the Internet, and mobile devices.

- is rapidly expanding online as consumers spend less time with traditional media.

- offers many benefits because it is extremely cost efficient when it reaches a large number of people. On the other hand, the initial outlay for advertising can be expensive.

- is hard to measure in terms of its effectiveness in increasing sales.

- comes in two general forms: institutional advertising—used to promote a firm's image, ideas and culture—or product advertising—used to promote the image, features, uses, benefits, and attributes of products.

- budgets can be set using one of several approaches including the objectives and task approach, the percentage of sales approach, the competitive matching approach, and the arbitrary approach.

- effectiveness can be measured before, during, or after the campaign has been executed. Consumer panels, surveys, or experimental designs may be used to evaluate a campaign based on communication objectives.

Public relations

- is one component of a firm's corporate affairs activities.

- is the element of an IMC program that tracks public attitudes, identifies issues that may elicit public concern, and develops programs to create and maintain positive relationships between a firm and its stakeholders.

- can be used to promote the firm, its people, its ideas, and its image and even to create an internal shared understanding among employees.

- can improve the public's general awareness of a company and can create specific images such as quality, innovativeness, value, or concern for social issues.

- is often confused with publicity; however, publicity is more narrowly defined to include the firm's activities designed to gain media attention through articles, editorials, or news stories.

- can involve the use of a wide variety of methods, including news or press releases, feature articles, white papers, press conferences, event sponsorship, product placement, and employee relations.

- includes the management of unexpected and unfavorable public relations resulting from an ethical or legal inquiry, unsafe products, accidents, or the controversial actions of employees and executives.

Personal selling

- is paid, personal communication that attempts to inform customers about products and persuade them to purchase those products.

- is the most precise form of communication because it assures companies that they are in direct contact with an excellent prospect.

- does not come without disadvantages. The most serious drawback of personal selling is the cost per contact.

- goals are typically associated with finding prospects, informing prospects, persuading prospects to buy, and keeping customers satisfied through follow-up service after the sale.

- has evolved to take on elements of customer service and marketing research in order to generate repeat sales and develop ongoing relationships with customers.

- and sales management activities include the development of sales force objectives, determining the size of the sales force, recruiting and training salespeople, and controlling and evaluating the sales force.

- has been greatly impacted by technological advances, especially online sales training and sales automation systems that push integrated customer, competitive, and product information toward the salesperson.

Sales promotion

- involves activities that create buyer incentives to purchase a product or that add value for the buyer or the trade.

- can be targeted toward consumers, channel intermediaries, or the sales force.

- has one universal goal: to induce product trial and purchase.

- is typically used in support of advertising, public relations, or personal selling activities rather than as a stand-alone promotional element.

- directed toward consumers:
    - Can be initiated by any member of the supply chain, but manufacturers or retailers typically offer them.
    - Represents an effective way to introduce new products or promote established brands.
    - Can include such activities as coupons, rebates, samples, loyalty programs, point-of-purchase promotion, premiums, contests and sweepstakes, and direct mail.

- directed toward the trade (business markets):
    - Is undertaken to push products through the channel by increasing sales and encouraging increased effort among channel partners.

– Uses many of the same promotional methods that are targeted toward consumers; however, it involves a number of unique methods including trade allowances, free merchandise, training assistance, cooperative advertising, and selling incentives offered to an intermediary's sales force.

Questions for Discussion

1. Review the steps in the AIDA model. In what ways has promotion affected you in various stages of this model? Does promotion affect you differently based on the type of product in question? Does the price of the product (low versus high) make a difference in how promotion can affect your choices? Explain.

2. What does the future hold for traditional mass-media advertising? If you were the CEO of a major television network, magazine publisher, or newspaper company, what would you be doing now to ensure the livelihood of your company in 10 to 20 years?

3. What would happen if a company suddenly stopped using sales promotion activities after having used them for a long period of time? Is it possible for a company to become dependent on the use of sales promotion activities? Explain.

Exercises

1. Go to *BusinessWeek*'s cover story podcasts (http://www.businessweek.com/mediacenter/podcasts/cover_stories/current.html) and listen to one or more of the podcasts that are available. What advertising is inserted into each podcast? Do you believe that podcast advertising has a mainstream future, or will advertising be limited to products that match tech- and Internet-oriented audiences?

2. Shadow a salesperson for a day and talk about how his or her activities integrate with other promotional elements used by their firm. How does the salesperson set objectives? How is he or she made aware of the firm's overall IMC strategy? Does the sales force participate in planning marketing or promotional activities?

3. Visit the Cents Off website (http://www.centsoff.com) and browse the available coupons and read the FAQs. What are the benefits of the Cents Off service for advertisers and consumers? If you were a manufacturer that issues coupons, what factors would favor using the Cents Off website for distribution rather than the traditional Sunday newspaper insert?

11

Marketing Implementation and Control

Introduction

Throughout the history of business, many firms and their top executives have emphasized strategic planning at the expense of strategic implementation. Historically, and even today, this emphasis on planning occurs because many executives believe that strategic planning by itself is the key to marketing success. This belief is logical because a firm must have a plan before it can determine where it is going. Many firms are quite good at devising strategic marketing plans; however, they are often unprepared to cope with the realities of implementation.

Marketing implementation is the process of executing the marketing strategy by creating and performing specific actions that will ensure the achievement of the firm's marketing objectives. Strategic planning without effective implementation can produce unintended consequences that result in customer dissatisfaction and feelings of frustration within the firm. Likewise, poor implementation will most likely result in the firm's failure to reach its organizational and marketing objectives. Unfortunately, many firms repeatedly experience failures in marketing implementation. Out-of-stock items, overly aggressive salespeople, long checkout lines, and unfriendly or inattentive employees are examples of implementation failure that occur all too frequently today. These and other examples illustrate that even the best-planned marketing strategies are a waste of time without effective implementation to ensure their success.

To track the implementation process, firms must have ways of evaluating and controlling marketing activities, as well as monitoring performance to determine whether marketing goals and objectives have been achieved. As illustrated in Beyond the Pages 11.1, implementation, evaluation, and control go hand-in-hand in determining the success or failure of the marketing strategy, and ultimately the entire firm. One of the most important considerations in implementing and controlling marketing activities involves gaining the support of employees. Because a marketing strategy cannot implement itself, all firms depend on employees to carry out marketing activities. As a result, the firm must devise a plan for implementation, just as it devises a plan for marketing strategy.

Beyond the Pages 11.1

GREEN MOUNTAIN COFFEE GETS IT DONE[1]

Green Mountain Coffee Roasters, Inc. is a leader in the specialty-coffee industry. The Waterbury, Vermont, company uses a coordinated multichannel distribution network that is designed to maximize brand recognition and product availability. Green Mountain roasts high-quality Arabica beans and offers over 100 coffee selections including single origins, estates, certified organics, Fair Trade Certified™, proprietary blends, and flavored coffees sold under the Green Mountain Coffee Roasters® and Newman's Own® Organics brands. Its products come in a variety of packages including whole bean, fractional packages, premium one-cup coffee pods, and Keurig® K-Cup® single-serving coffee cartridges. The company also operates an active e-commerce business at www.GreenMountain Coffee.com.

Most of Green Mountain's revenue is derived from over 8000 wholesale customer accounts located primarily in the eastern United States. Green Mountain's customers include supermarkets, specialty-food stores, convenience stores, food service companies, hotels, restaurants, universities, and office coffee services. One of the company's signature accounts is McDonald's, which sells Green Mountain's organic coffee under the Newman's Own label at 658 restaurants across the Northeast. Roughly 30 percent of Green Mountain's business comes from the convenience store sector, where the company counts ExxonMobil and its 1000 stores as one of its largest customers.

Green Mountain has an ambitious goal to increase sales at an annual rate of 20 to 25 percent. To achieve this goal, the company pursues three key strategies: boosting market share, expanding into new markets, and making key acquisitions. To increase market share and expand, the company relies on direct relationships with farms, coffee estates, cooperatives, and other parties to ensure a consistent supply and price of seventy-five different varieties of high-quality coffee beans. This, combined with a custom-roasting process, allows Green Mountain to differentiate its coffee offerings. One of Green Mountain's key acquisitions was a 41 percent stake in Keurig—the company that makes its K-Cup coffee cartridges. Keurig is a dominant player in the office coffee service segment with plans to move into the home market as well.

One of the major reasons for Green Mountain's success is its overall focus on implementation. The company employs 676 people but has a very flat organizational structure. This promotes open communication, passion, and commitment among employees, who have open access to all levels of the organization including the CEO Bob Stiller. As a part of the company's evaluation and control system, Green Mountain uses a process called the after-action review—a process adapted from the U.S. Army. The goal of the review is to answer four key questions: What did we set out to do? What happened? Why did it happen? What are we going to do about it? Most of the effort is spent on this last question to ensure that the company learns from both its successes and failures. Employees are empowered to apply these lessons and encouraged to share their views in a "constellation of communication" that ensures a collaborative style of getting things done.

Green Mountain Coffee has consistently appeared on *Forbes*'s list of the "200 Best Small Companies in America," and *Fortune*'s list of the "100 Fastest-Growing Small Companies in America." The company was also ranked as number one on *Business Ethics* magazine's list of the "100 Best Corporate Citizens." In addition, the Society of Human Resource Management has recognized Green Mountain for its socially responsible business practices.

In this chapter, we examine the critical role of marketing implementation and control in the strategic planning process. First, we discuss a number of important strategic issues involved in implementation, including the major components of implementation that must work together for a strategy to be executed successfully. Then, we examine the advantages and disadvantages of major marketing implementation approaches. This discussion also describes how internal marketing can be used to motivate employees to implement marketing strategy. Finally, we look at the marketing evaluation and control process.

Strategic Issues in Marketing Implementation

Marketing implementation is critical to the success of any firm because it is responsible for putting the marketing strategy into action. Simply put, *implementation* refers to the "how" part of the marketing plan. Marketing implementation is a very broad concept, and for that reason it is often misunderstood. Some of this misunderstanding stems from the fact that marketing strategies almost always turn out differently than expected. In fact, all firms have two strategies: their intended strategy and a realized strategy.[2] Intended marketing strategy is what the firm wants to happen—it is the firm's planned strategic choices that appear in the marketing plan itself. The realized marketing strategy, on the other hand, is the strategy that actually takes place. More often than not, the difference between the intended and the realized strategy is a matter of the implementation of the intended strategy. This is not to say that a firm's realized marketing strategy is necessarily better or worse than the intended marketing strategy, just that it is different in execution and results. Such differences are often the result of internal or external environmental factors that change during implementation.

In the sections that follow, we discuss a number of important strategic issues in planning for the implementation phase of the marketing plan. First, we examine the relationship between implementation and strategic planning. As we will see, planning and implementation are really two sides of the same coin that must be integrated to achieve maximum effectiveness in the marketing plan. Then we explore the major elements of marketing implementation and discuss how these elements must work together to fully execute the marketing plan.

The Link Between Planning and Implementation

One of the most interesting aspects of marketing implementation is its relationship to the strategic planning process. Many firms assume that planning and implementation are interdependent but separate issues. In reality, planning and implementation intertwine within the marketing planning process. Many of the problems of marketing implementation occur because of its relationship to strategic planning. The three most common issues in this relationship are interdependency, evolution, and separation.

EXHIBIT 11.1   **THE SYMBIOTIC RELATIONSHIP BETWEEN MARKETING STRATEGY AND MARKETING IMPLEMENTATION**

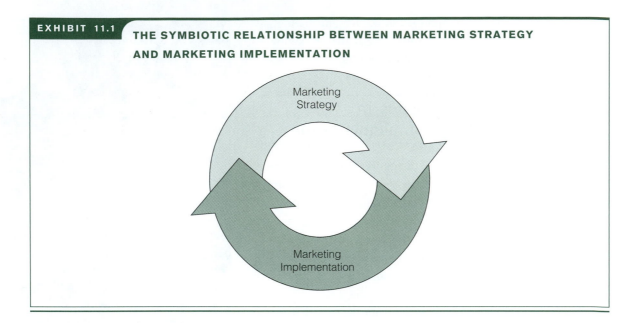

Interdependency   Many firms assume that the planning and implementation process is a one-way street; that is, strategic planning comes first, followed by implementation. Although it is true that the content of the marketing plan determines how it will be implemented, it is also true that how the marketing strategy is to be implemented determines the content of the marketing plan. Exhibit 11.1 depicts this symbiotic relationship between marketing strategy and marketing implementation.

Certain marketing strategies will define their implementation by default. For example, a firm such as Southwest Airlines with a strategy of improving customer service may turn to employee-training programs as an important part of that strategy's implementation. Through profit sharing, many Southwest employees are also stockholders with a vested interest in the firm's success. Employee-training and profit-sharing programs are common in firms that depend on their employees' commitment and enthusiasm to ensure quality customer service. However, employee training, as a tool of implementation, can also dictate the content of the firm's strategy. Perhaps a competitor of Southwest, who is in the process of implementing its own customer service strategy, may realize that it does not possess adequate resources to offer profit sharing and extensive training to its employees. Perhaps the company simply lacks the financial resources or the staff required to implement these activities. Consequently, the company will be forced to go back to the planning stage and adjust its customer service strategy. These continual changes in marketing strategy make implementation more difficult. Clearly, a SWOT (strengths, weaknesses, opportunities, and threats) analysis conducted with an eye toward what the company can reasonably implement can reduce but not completely eliminate this problem.

Evolution   All firms face a simple truth in planning and implementation: Important environmental factors constantly change. As the needs and wants of customers change, as competitors devise new marketing strategies, and as the firm's own internal environment changes, the firm must constantly adapt. In some cases, these changes occur so rapidly that once the firm decides on a marketing strategy it quickly becomes out of date. Because planning and implementation are intertwined, both must constantly evolve to fit the other. The process is never static because environmental changes require shifts in strategy, which require changes in implementation, which require shifts in strategy, and so on.

A related problem is that firms often assume that there is only one correct way to implement a given strategy. This is simply not true. Just as strategy often results from trial and error, so does marketing implementation. Firms that are truly customer oriented must be flexible enough to alter their implementation on the fly to fully embrace customer intimacy and respond to changes in customers' preferences. Firms that operate in oligopolistic markets face the evolution of strategy and implementation every day. In the airline industry, for example, all competitors quickly alter their pricing strategies when one firm announces a reduction in fares on certain routes. These rapid changes require that firms be flexible in both marketing strategy and implementation.

Separation   The ineffective implementation of marketing strategy is often a self-generated problem that stems from the way that planning and implementation are carried out in most firms. Middle- or upper-level managers often do strategic planning; however, the responsibility for implementation almost always falls on lower-level managers and frontline employees. Exhibit 11.2 depicts this separation of planning and implementation. Top executives often fall into a trap of believing that a good marketing strategy will implement itself. Because there is distance between executives and the day-to-day activities at the frontline of the firm, they often do not understand the unique problems associated with implementing marketing strategy. Conversely, frontline employees—who do understand the challenges and hurdles of implementation—usually have a limited voice in planning the strategy.

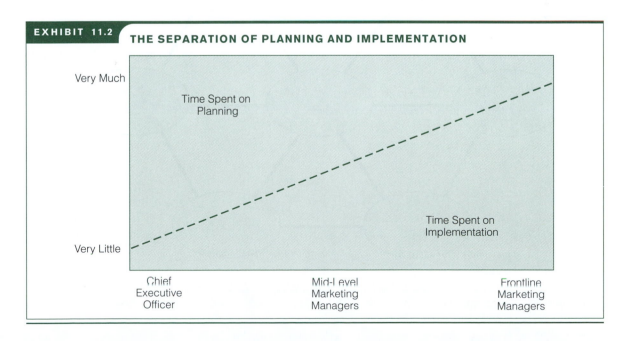

EXHIBIT 11.2   **THE SEPARATION OF PLANNING AND IMPLEMENTATION**

Another trap that top executives often fall into is believing that frontline managers and employees will be excited about the marketing strategy and motivated to implement it. However, because they are separated from the planning process, these managers and employees often fail to identify with the firm's goals and objectives and thus fail to fully understand the marketing strategy.[3] It is unrealistic for top executives to expect frontline managers and employees to be committed to a strategy that they had no voice in developing or to a strategy that they do not understand or feel is inappropriate.[4]

The Elements of Marketing Implementation

Marketing implementation involves a number of interrelated elements and activities, as shown in Exhibit 11.3. These elements must work together for strategy to be implemented effectively. Because we examined marketing strategy issues in previous chapters, we now look briefly at the remaining elements of marketing implementation.

Shared Goals and Values   Shared goals and values among all employees within the firm are the "glue" of successful implementation because they bind the entire organization together as a single, functioning unit. When all employees share the firm's goals and values, all actions will be more closely aligned and directed toward the betterment of the organization. Without a common direction to hold the organization together, different areas of the firm may work toward different outcomes, thus limiting the success

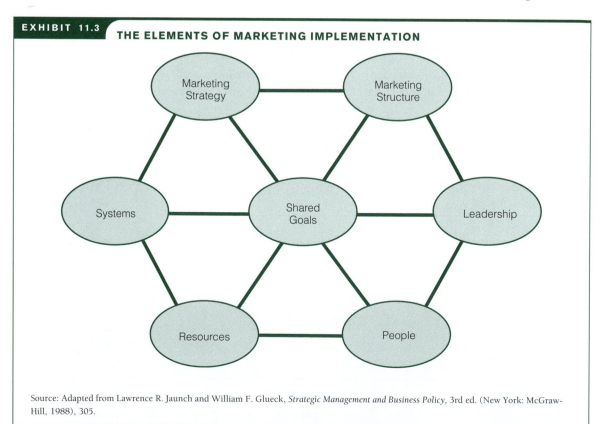

EXHIBIT 11.3   **THE ELEMENTS OF MARKETING IMPLEMENTATION**

Source: Adapted from Lawrence R. Jaunch and William F. Glueck, *Strategic Management and Business Policy,* 3rd ed. (New York: McGraw-Hill, 1988), 305.

of the entire organization. For example, one of the reasons for the tremendous success of the New Belgium Brewery is the fact that all employees have a commitment to make excellent craft beer in ways that conserve environmental resources.[5] Other firms, such as Federal Express (FedEx), Saturn, and ESPN, are well known for their efforts to ensure that employees share and are committed to corporate goals and values.

Institutionalizing shared goals and values within a firm's culture is a long-term process. The primary means of creating shared goals and values is through employee training and socialization programs.[6] Although creating shared goals and values is a difficult process, the rewards are worth the effort. Some experts have argued that creating shared goals and values is the single most important element of implementation because it stimulates organizational commitment where employees become more motivated to implement the marketing strategy, to achieve the firm's goals and objectives, and to serve more fully the needs of the firm's customers.[7]

Marketing Structure   Marketing structure refers to the methods of organizing a firm's marketing activities. Marketing structure establishes formal lines of authority, as well as the division of labor within the marketing function. One of the most important decisions that firms make is how to divide and integrate marketing responsibilities. This decision typically comes down to the question of centralization versus decentralization. In a centralized marketing structure, the top of the marketing hierarchy coordinates and manages all marketing activities and decisions. Conversely, in a decentralized marketing structure, the frontline of the firm coordinates and manages marketing activities and decisions. Typically, decentralization means that frontline marketing managers have the responsibility of making day-to-day marketing decisions.

Both centralized and decentralized marketing structures have advantages. Centralized structures are very cost efficient and effective in ensuring standardization within the marketing program. These advantages can be particularly critical to firms whose competitiveness depends upon maintaining a tight control over marketing activities and expenses.[8] For example, firms employing a strategy of operational excellence, such as Wal-Mart or Dell Computer, may find a centralized structure beneficial to ensuring operational efficiency and consistency. Decentralized marketing structures have the important advantage of placing marketing decisions closer to the frontline where serving customers is the number-one priority. By decentralizing marketing decisions, frontline managers can be creative and flexible, allowing them to adapt to changing market conditions.[9] For this reason, firms that employ a strategy of customer intimacy, such as the Ritz-Carlton Hotels or Nordstrom's, may decentralize to ensure that they can respond to customers' needs in a timely manner. The decision to centralize or decentralize marketing activities is a trade-off between reduced costs and enhanced flexibility. However, there is no one correct way to organize the marketing function. The right marketing structure will depend on the specific firm, the nature of its internal and external environments, and its chosen marketing strategy.[10]

Systems and Processes   Organizational systems and processes are collections of work activities that absorb a variety of inputs to create information and communication outputs that ensure the consistent day-to-day operation of the firm.[11] Examples include information systems, strategic planning, capital budgeting, procurement, order fulfillment, manufacturing, quality control, and performance measurement. At IBM, for example, research engineers are evaluated on one- and three-year time frames. Employees receive bonuses based on the one-year evaluation but are awarded rank and salary based on the three-year time frame. This unique system is designed to encourage innovation by minimizing the risk of failure in any single yearly evaluation.[12]

Resources   A firm's resources can include a wide variety of assets that can be brought together during marketing implementation. These assets may be tangible or intangible. Tangible resources include financial resources, manufacturing capacity, facilities, and equipment. Although not quite as obvious, intangible resources such as marketing expertise, customer loyalty, brand equity, corporate goodwill, and external relationships/strategic alliances are equally important.

Regardless of the type of resource, the amount of resources available can make or break a marketing strategy. However, a critical and honest evaluation of available resources during the planning phase can help ensure that the marketing strategy and marketing implementation are within the realm of possibility. Upon completion of the marketing plan, the analyst or planner must seek the approval of needed resources from top executives. This makes the communication aspects of the actual marketing plan document critical to the success of the strategy. Top executives allocate scarce resources based on the ability of the plan to help the firm reach its goals and objectives.

People (Human Resources)   The quality, diversity, and skill of a firm's human resources can also make or break the implementation of the marketing strategy. Consequently, human resource issues have become more important to the marketing function, especially in the areas of employee selection and training, evaluation and compensation policies, and employee motivation, satisfaction, and commitment. In fact, the marketing departments of many firms have taken over the human resources function to ensure that employees have a correct match to required marketing activities.[13] A number of human resource activities are vitally important to marketing implementation:

- **Employee Selection and Training**   One of the most critical aspects of marketing implementation is matching employees' skills and abilities to the marketing tasks to be performed.[14] It is no secret that some people are better at some jobs than others. We all know individuals who are natural salespeople. Some individuals are better at working with people, and others are better at working with tools or computers. The key is to match these employee skills to marketing tasks. Corporate downsizing and tight job markets in recent years have forced firms to become more demanding in finding the right employee skills to match their required marketing activities.

Employee diversity is an increasingly important aspect of selection and training practices. As the U.S. population becomes more ethnically diverse, many firms take steps to ensure that the diversity of their employees matches the diversity of their customers. Many firms also face challenges with generational diversity in that most middle and upper managers are baby boomers (born 1946–1964), whereas most entry-level positions consist of members of Generation X (born 1965–1976) or Generation Y (born after 1976). In many cases, these younger employees have better training, more technological sophistication, and fewer political inclinations than their baby-boomer bosses. Managers must recognize these issues and adapt selection and training practices accordingly.

- **Employee Evaluation and Compensation** Employee evaluation and compensation are also important to successful marketing implementation. An important decision to be made in this area is the choice between outcome- and behavior-based systems.[15] An outcome-based system evaluates and compensates employees based on measurable, quantitative standards such as sales volume or gross margin. This type of system is fairly easy to use, requires less supervision, and works well when market demand is fairly constant, the selling cycle is relatively short, and all efforts directly affect sales or profits. Conversely, behavior-based systems evaluate and compensate employees based on subjective, qualitative standards such as effort, motivation, teamwork, and friendliness toward customers. This type of system ties directly to customer satisfaction and rewards employees for factors that they can control. However, behavior-based systems are expensive and difficult to manage because of their subjective nature and the amount of supervision required. The choice between outcome- and behavior-based systems depends on the firm and its products, markets, and customers' needs. The important point is to match the employee evaluation and compensation system to the activities that employees must perform in order to implement the marketing strategy.

- **Employee Motivation, Satisfaction, and Commitment** Other important factors in the implementation of marketing strategy are the extent to which employees have the motivation to implement the strategy, their overall feelings of job satisfaction, and the commitment they feel toward the organization and its goals.[16] For example, one contributor to the highly successful implementation at FedEx is the motivation and commitment of FedEx employees. These employees are so dedicated to FedEx that they are often said to have purple blood—one of the company's official colors.[17]

   Though factors such as employee motivation, satisfaction, and commitment are critical to successful implementation, they highly depend on other elements of implementation, especially training, evaluation/compensation systems, and leadership. Marketing structure and processes can also have an impact on employee behaviors and attitudes. The key is to recognize the importance of these factors to successful marketing implementation and to manage them accordingly.

Leadership The leadership provided by a firm's managers and the behaviors of employees go hand in hand in the implementation process. Leadership—often called the art of managing people—includes how managers communicate with employees, as well as how they motivate their people to implement the marketing strategy. As

Beyond the Pages 11.2

THE NEW RULES OF CEO LEADERSHIP[18]

As we have discussed throughout this text, the rules of the road in marketing have changed in today's economy. Customers now hold most of the power due to increasing access to information, massive product selection and its associated competition, and increasingly mature markets characterized by commoditization. The dynamic nature of today's marketplace has touched all sectors of the global economy. Nowhere is this truer than in the executive suite of today's corporations. Many CEOs struggle with managing their monolithic organizations in an increasingly fast-paced environment.

According to *Fortune* magazine, there is a good reason for the challenges facing today's CEOs: Many of them operate using a set of rules developed in the 1980s and 1990s glory days of corporate expansion and global domination. Many of those rules were developed by the celebrity CEOs of the day such as Jack Welch (General Electric), Lou Gerstner (IBM), Al Dunlap (Sunbeam), and Roberto Goizueta (Coca-Cola). Of these, Jack Welch was the iconic leader. Most major corporations adopted his rules for business during the 1980s and 1990s. Welch's rules focused on corporate growth, maximizing market share, and the

preeminence of quarterly earnings. However, *Fortune* argues that Welch's corporate playbook is ill suited for today's market because the rapid pace of change and increasingly relentless competition force CEOs to take a long-term view of competitiveness. That view is less about market share and stock price and more about making decisions that ensure the viability and long-term survival of the corporation. Today's problems are different than those of 10 to 25 years ago. Consequently, old solutions no longer work.

As a way to provoke discussion of the issue, *Fortune* published a set of seven new rules for business that contradict virtually all of the old-school rules advocated by CEOs both past and present. These new rules argue for a dramatic shift away from short-term results in favor of long-term survival (see chart on next page).

Of these new rules, the sixth (hiring a courageous CEO) may be the most critical. CEOs who adopt *Fortune*'s new rules for business must be willing to make investments that will not pay off for years— when that CEO is no longer in charge. The old ways of doing business— such as driving down costs through efficiency, growth through mergers and acquisitions, and careful manipulation

(continued)

discussed in Beyond the Pages 11.2, today's business leaders must be courageous enough to take a long-term view of corporate success—one that often sacrifices short-term gains for the sake of the future.

Leaders have responsibility for establishing the corporate culture necessary for implementation success.[19] A good deal of research has shown that marketing implementation is more successful when leaders create an organizational culture characterized by open communication between employees and managers. In this way, employees are free to discuss their opinions and ideas about the marketing strategy and implementation activities. This type of leadership also creates a climate where managers and employees have full confidence and trust in each other.

Approaches to Marketing Implementation

Whether good or bad, all leaders possess a leadership style, or way of approaching a given task. Managers can use a variety of approaches in implementing marketing strategies and motivating employees to perform implementation activities. In this section, we examine four of these approaches: implementation by command, of financial and accounting decisions— are solutions that simply do not work any longer. Anne Mulcahy, CEO of Xerox, puts it this way: "You have to change when you're at the top of your game in terms of profit. If you're not nimble, there's no advantage to size. It's like a rock."

Unfortunately, Wall Street gives today's CEOs little incentive to change. A study by Booz Allen found that CEOs become vulnerable to being fired if their company's stock price falls below the S&P 500 by an average of two percent. To be courageous in the face of this obstacle, today's CEOs must be willing to take risks and stand up for what they believe is in the long-term interest of their firm. "You have to have the courage of your convictions," argues John Chambers, CEO of Cisco Systems.

Old Rules	New Rules	Examples
Big dogs own the street.	Agile is best; being big can bite you.	Big pharmaceutical companies are losing to smaller biotech firms; the decline of major U.S. automakers such as General Motors; Samsung's rise above Sony.
Be number one or two in the market.	Find a niche; create something new.	Energy drinks are more profitable than traditional soft drinks; the growth of Starbucks from a niche player to a coffee powerhouse.
Shareholders rule.	The customer is king.	Businesses are better at managing earnings rather than the goods and services that produce those earnings; major scandals at firms like Enron and WorldCom.
Be lean and mean.	Look outside, not inside.	Innovation drives today's success (e.g., Apple's iPod); the drive for quality and efficiency only improves current processes—it does not promote innovation.
Rank your players; go with the A's.	Hire passionate people.	Employees want purpose and meaning in their work; the growth in hiring employees with passion (Apple, ESPN, Genentech).
Hire a charismatic CEO.	Hire a courageous CEO.	Today's CEOs must have the fortitude to make decisions that have long-term payoffs, not the quick fixes that are rewarded by Wall Street investors.
Admire my might.	Admire my soul.	Powerful corporations are increasingly targeted by activists on a number of fronts; it is better to be company with a long-term vision that legitimizes its role in society.

implementation through change, implementation through consensus, and implementation as organizational cultural.[20]

Implementation by Command

Under this approach, the firm's top executives develop and select the marketing strategies, which are transmitted to lower levels where frontline managers and employees implement them. Implementation by command has two advantages: (1) It makes decision making much easier, and (2) it reduces uncertainty as to what is to be done to implement the marketing strategy. Unfortunately, this approach suffers from several disadvantages. The approach places less emphasis on the feasibility of implementing the marketing strategy. It also divides the firm into strategists and implementers: Executives who develop the marketing strategy are often far removed from the targeted customers it is intended to attract. For these reasons, implementation by command often creates employee motivation problems. Many employees do not have motivation to implement strategies in which they have little confidence.

Implementation by command is common in franchise systems. For example, McDonald's use of this approach creates a great deal of ongoing tension between the corporate office and its franchisees around the globe. In some cases, the tensions have become so hostile that franchisees have flatly refused to implement some corporate strategies, including service guarantees and some specific promotions. The latest battle is over the refurbishment of aging McDonald's restaurants, which now sport a design that is 30 years old. McDonald's wants to update its restaurants with a clean, simple design that incorporates a sloping curved roof, warm colors, more brick and wood, softer lighting, and plush chairs. Many franchisees are completely against the change citing the high cost of renovation ($300,000 to $400,000 per outlet—all paid by the franchisee) and the loss of 30 years of branding inherent in the current design. Franchisees typically lease their locations from McDonald's, hence their reluctance to refurbish stores that they do not own. However, they have little choice because McDonald's can refuse to renew their contracts if they do not comply.[21]

Implementation Through Change

Implementation through change is similar to the command approach except that it focuses explicitly on implementation. The basic goal of implementation through change is to modify the firm in ways that will ensure the successful implementation of the chosen marketing strategy. For example, the firm's structure can be altered; employees can be transferred, hired, or fired; new technology can be adopted; the employee compensation plan can be changed; or the firm can merge with another firm. Mergers and acquisitions are common today in many industries, particularly in pharmaceuticals. Given the enormous expense of developing new drugs, many pharmaceutical firms have decided that it is easier and less expensive to offer new products or enter new markets by acquiring firms that already possess those capabilities.

The manager who implements through change is more of an architect and politician, skillfully crafting the organization to fit the requirements of the marketing strategy. There are many good historical examples of implementation through change. For example, during Lee Iacocca's tenure as CEO of the Chrysler Corporation, the firm's purchase of AMC and Jeep/Eagle were crucial steps in the slow process of rebuilding Chrysler. Similarly, FedEx Chairman Fred Smith has guided his company through numerous changes in its history—including several acquisitions and corporate restructurings—to build the company into a global logistics and distribution powerhouse. One of today's emerging stories is Samsung and CEO Yun Jong Yong's passion for marketing. Once recognized as a cheap, high-volume supplier of computer chips, circuit boards, and electronic components, Samsung has emerged as a serious threat in the consumer electronics market. Samsung changed by dropping its 50-plus low-budget brands in favor of a single master Samsung brand. The shift has been so successful that Interbrand, a brand consulting firm, has ranked Samsung as the world's fastest-growing brand since 2000—up over 186 percent in value. By shifting Samsung's operational focus from production to marketing, Yong has guided the company past Sony and Nokia in many product categories.[22]

Because many business executives are reluctant to give up even a small portion of their control (as is the case with the next two implementation approaches), they often favor implementation through change. The approach achieves a good balance between command and consensus, and its successes are evident in business today. However, despite these advantages, implementation through change still suffers from the separation of planning and implementation. By clinging to this power-at-the-top philosophy, employee motivation often remains an issue. Likewise, the changes called for in this approach often take a great deal of time to design and implement. This can create a situation in which the firm becomes frozen while waiting on the strategy to take hold. As a result, the firm can become vulnerable to changes in the marketing environment.

Implementation Through Consensus

Upper- and lower-level managers work together to evaluate and develop marketing strategies in the consensus approach to implementation. The underlying premise of this approach is that managers from different areas and levels in the firm come together as a team to "brainstorm" and develop the strategy. Each participant has different opinions as well as different perceptions of the marketing environment. The role of the top manager is that of a coordinator, pulling different opinions together to ensure the development of the best overall marketing strategy. Through this collective decision-making process, the firm agrees on marketing strategy and reaches a consensus as to the overall direction of the firm.

Implementation through consensus is more advantageous than the first two approaches in that it moves some of the decision-making authority closer to the frontline of the firm. Lower-level managers who participate in the strategy-formulation process have a unique perspective on the marketing activities necessary to implement the strategy. These managers are also more sensitive to the needs and wants of the firm's customers. In addition, because they have more involvement in developing the marketing strategy, lower-level managers often have a stronger motivation and commitment to the strategy to see that it is properly implemented. The inclusion of managers from other functional areas within the firm also ensures the coordination of the strategy across the entire firm. This, too, helps make the implementation process run more smoothly.

Implementation through consensus tends to work best in complex, uncertain, and highly unstable environments. The collective strategy–making approach works well in this environment because it brings multiple viewpoints to the table. However, implementation through consensus often retains the barrier between strategists and implementers. The end result of this barrier is that the full potential of the firm's human resources is not realized. Thus, for implementation through consensus to be truly effective, managers at all levels must communicate openly about strategy on an ongoing rather than an occasional basis.

Implementation as Organizational Culture

Under this approach, marketing strategy and its implementation become extensions of the firm's mission, vision, and organizational culture. In some ways, this approach is similar to implementation through consensus, except that the barrier between strategists and implementers completely dissolves. When personnel see implementation as an extension of the firm's culture, employees at all levels have permission to participate in making decisions that help the firm reach its mission, goals, and objectives.

With a strong organizational culture and an overriding corporate vision, the task of implementing marketing strategy is about 90 percent complete.[23] This occurs because all employees adopt the firm's culture so completely that they instinctively know what their role is in implementing the marketing strategy. Employees can design their own work procedures as long as they are consistent with the organizational mission, goals, and objectives. This extreme form of decentralization is often called *empowerment*. Empowering employees means allowing them to make decisions on how to best perform their jobs. The strong organizational culture and a shared corporate vision ensure that empowered employees make the right decisions.

Although creating a strong culture does not happen overnight, it is absolutely necessary before employees can be empowered to make decisions. Employees must be trained and socialized to accept the firm's mission and to become a part of the firm's culture.[24] Despite the enormous amount of time involved in developing and using this approach to implementation, its rewards of increased effectiveness, efficiency, and increased employee commitment and morale are often well worth the investment. Notable firms that incorporate implementation within their cultures include ESPN, Google, and General Electric.

To summarize, firms and their managers can use any one of these four approaches to implement marketing strategy. Each approach has advantages and disadvantages as outlined in Exhibit 11.4. The choice of an approach will depend heavily on the firm's resources, its current culture, and the manager's own personal preferences. Many managers don't want to give up control over decision making. For these managers, connecting implementation and culture may be out of the question. Regardless of the approach taken, one of the most important issues that a manager must face is how to deal with the people who have responsibility for implementing the marketing strategy. To examine this issue, we now turn our attention to internal marketing—an increasingly popular approach to marketing implementation.

Internal Marketing and Marketing Implementation

As more firms come to appreciate the importance of employees to marketing implementation, they have become disenchanted with traditional implementation approaches. Several factors have caused these forces for change: U.S. businesses losing out to foreign competitors, high rates of employee turnover and its associated costs, and continuing problems in the implementation of marketing strategy. These problems have led many firms to adopt an internal marketing approach to marketing implementation.

The practice of internal marketing comes from service industries where it was first used as a means of making all employees aware of the need for customer satisfaction. *Internal marketing* refers to the use of a marketing-like approach to motivate, coordinate, and integrate employees toward the implementation of the firm's marketing strategy. The goals of internal marketing are to (1) help all employees understand and accept their roles in implementing the marketing strategy, (2) create motivated and customer-oriented employees, and (3) deliver external customer satisfaction.[25] Note

EXHIBIT 11.4

ADVANTAGES AND DISADVANTAGES OF IMPLEMENTATION APPROACHES

Implementation by Command

Basic Premise: Marketing strategies are developed at the top of the organizational hierarchy and forced downward to lower levels where frontline managers and employees must implement them.

Advantages: Makes decision making easier
Reduces uncertainty
Good when a powerful leader heads the firm
Good when the strategy is simple to implement

Disadvantages: Does not consider the feasibility of implementing the strategy
Divides the firm into strategists and implementers
Does not consider how strategy and implementation affect each other
Can create employee motivation problems

Implementation through Change

Basic Premise: The firm is modified in ways that will ensure the successful implementation of the chosen marketing strategy.

Advantages: Specifically considers how the strategy will be implemented
Considers how strategy and implementation affect each other
Used successfully by a large number of U.S. businesses

Disadvantages: Still clings to a "power-at-the-top" mentality
Requires a skilled leader who can be both an architect and a politician
Changes often take a great deal of time to design and implement
The firm can become unresponsive while waiting on the strategy to "take"
The time required for changes to occur can make the firm vulnerable to changes in the marketing environment

Implementation through Consensus

Basic Premise: Managers from different areas of the firm come together to "brainstorm" and develop the marketing strategy. Through collective agreement, a consensus is reached as to the overall direction of the firm.

Advantages: Incorporates multiple opinions and viewpoints into the marketing strategy
The leader coordinates by pulling different opinions together
Firm-wide commitment to the strategy makes implementation easier
Upper- and lower-level managers work together, thus moving some of the decision making closer to the frontline of the firm
Perhaps the best choice in complex, uncertain, and unstable environments

Disadvantages: Many upper-level managers will not give up their authority
The approach can lead to groupthink
Slows tremendously the overall strategy development and implementation process
Requires ongoing and open horizontal and vertical communication throughout the firm

Implementation as Organizational Culture

Basic Premise: The marketing strategy is a part of the overall mission and vision of the firm; therefore, the strategy is embedded in the firm's culture. Top executives continually manage the firm's culture to ensure that all employees are well-versed in the firm's strategy.

continued

EXHIBIT 11.4   *Continued*

Advantages:	Completely eliminates the barrier between strategists and implementers
	Increases employee commitment to a single organizational goal
	The participative style leads to an overriding corporate vision
	If done correctly, this approach makes marketing implementation much easier to accomplish
	Allows for the empowerment of employees
Disadvantages:	Must spend more money on employee selection and training
	Creating the required culture can be a painful, time-consuming process
	The quick adoption of this approach as a shift from a different approach typically causes many internal problems

that internal marketing explicitly recognizes that external customer satisfaction depends on the actions of the firm's internal customers—its employees.

The Internal Marketing Approach

In the internal marketing approach, every employee has two customers: external and internal. For retail store managers, for example, the people who shop at the store are external customers, whereas the employees who work in the store are the manager's internal customers. For implementation to be successful, the store manager must serve the needs of both customer groups. If the internal customers do not receive proper information and training about the strategy and are not motivated to implement it, then it is unlikely that the external customers will be satisfied completely.

This same pattern of internal and external customers takes place throughout all levels of the firm. Even the CEO is responsible for serving the needs of his or her internal and external customers. Thus, unlike traditional implementation approaches where the responsibility for implementation rests with the frontline of the firm, the internal marketing approach places this responsibility on all employees regardless of their level within the firm. In the end, successful marketing implementation comes from an accumulation of individual actions whereby all employees have responsibility for implementing the marketing strategy. Wal-Mart founder Sam Walton was keenly aware of the importance of internal marketing. He visited Wal-Mart stores on a regular basis, talking with customers and employees about how he could better serve their needs. He felt so strongly about the importance of his associates (his term for store personnel) that he always allowed them the opportunity to voice their concerns about changes in marketing activities. Sam had strong convictions that if he took good care of his associates, they would take good care of Wal-Mart's customers.

The Internal Marketing Process

The process of internal marketing is straightforward and rests on many of the same principles used in traditional external marketing. As shown in Exhibit 11.5, internal marketing is an output of and input to both marketing implementation and the external marketing program. That is, neither the marketing strategy nor its implementation can be designed without a consideration for the internal marketing program.

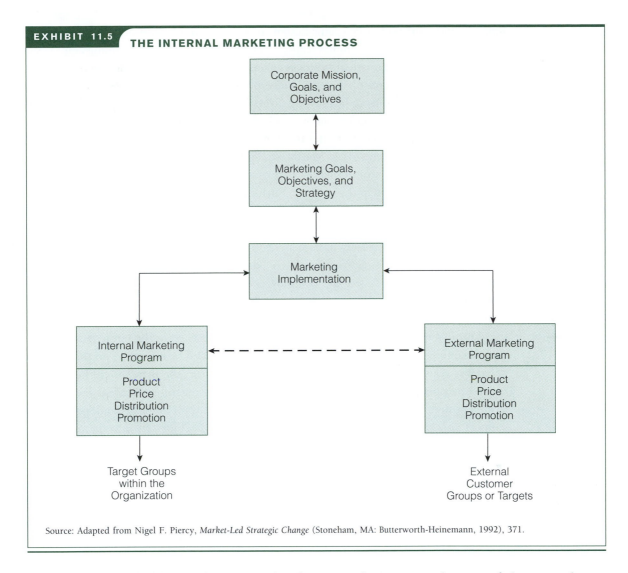

EXHIBIT 11.5 **THE INTERNAL MARKETING PROCESS**

Corporate Mission, Goals, and Objectives

Marketing Goals, Objectives, and Strategy

Marketing Implementation

Internal Marketing Program
Product
Price
Distribution
Promotion

External Marketing Program
Product
Price
Distribution
Promotion

Target Groups within the Organization

External Customer Groups or Targets

Source: Adapted from Nigel F. Piercy, *Market-Led Strategic Change* (Stoneham, MA: Butterworth-Heinemann, 1992), 371.

The product, price, distribution, and promotion elements of the internal marketing program are similar to the elements in the external marketing program. Internal products refer generally to marketing strategies that must be "sold" internally. More specifically, however, internal products refer to any employee tasks, behaviors, attitudes, or values necessary to ensure implementation of the marketing strategy.[26] Implementation of a marketing strategy, particularly a new strategy, typically requires changes on the part of employees. They may have to work harder, change job assignments, or even change their attitudes and expand their abilities. The increased effort and changes that employees must exhibit in implementing the strategy are equivalent to internal prices. Employees pay these prices through what they must do, change, or give up when implementing the marketing strategy.

Internal distribution refers to the internal communication of the marketing strategy. Planning sessions, workshops, formal reports, and personal conversations are all examples of internal distribution. Internal distribution also includes employee education, training, and socialization programs designed to assist in the transition to a new marketing strategy. Finally, all communication aimed at informing and persuading employees about the merits of the marketing strategy comprise internal promotion. Internal promotion can take the form of speeches, video presentations, audiotapes, and/or internal company newsletters. Given the growing diversity of today's employees, it is unlikely that any one medium will communicate with all employees successfully. Firms must realize that telling employees important information once in a single format is not good communication. Until the employees "get the strategy," communication has not taken place.

Successfully using an internal marketing approach requires an integration of many factors already discussed in this chapter. First, the recruitment, selection, and training of employees must be considered an important element of marketing implementation, with marketing having input to these human resource and personnel activities as necessary.[27] This ensures that employees will be matched to the marketing tasks to be performed. Second, top executives must be completely committed to the strategy and the overall marketing plan. It is naïve to expect employees to be committed when top executives are not. Simply put, the best-planned strategy in the world cannot succeed if the employees responsible for its implementation do not believe in it or have a commitment to it.[28]

Third, employee compensation programs must be linked to the implementation of the marketing strategy. This means that employees should be rewarded on the basis of behaviors consistent with the marketing strategy. Fourth, the firm should be characterized by open communication among all employees, regardless of their level in the firm. Through open, interactive communication, employees come to understand the support and commitment of top executives and how their jobs fit into the overall marketing implementation process. Finally, the firm's structure, policies, and processes should match the marketing strategy to ensure that the strategy can be implemented in the first place. On some occasions, the firm's structure and policies constrain the ability of employees to implement the strategy effectively. Although eliminating these constraints may mean that employees should be empowered to creatively fine-tune the strategy or its implementation, empowerment should be used only if the firm's culture can support it. However, if a company uses empowerment correctly as a part of the internal marketing approach, the firm can experience more motivated, satisfied, and committed employees as well as enhanced customer satisfaction and improved marketing performance.[29]

Evaluating and Controlling Marketing Activities

A marketing strategy can achieve its desired results only if implemented properly. *Properly* is the key word. It is important to remember that a firm's intended marketing strategy often differs from the realized strategy (the one that actually takes place). This also means that actual performance is often different from expectations. Typically, there are four possible causes for this difference:

1. The marketing strategy was inappropriate or unrealistic.

2. The implementation was inappropriate for the strategy.

3. The implementation process was mismanaged.

4. The internal and/or external environments changed substantially between the development of the marketing strategy and its implementation.

To reduce the difference between what actually happened and what the company expected—and to correct any of these four problems—marketing activities must be evaluated and controlled on an ongoing basis. Although the best way to handle implementation problems is to recognize them in advance, no manager can successfully recognize all the subtle and unpredictable warning signs of implementation failure.

With that in mind, it is important that the potential for implementation failures be managed strategically by having a system of marketing controls in place that allows the firm to spot potential problems before they cause real trouble. Exhibit 11.6 outlines a framework for marketing control that includes two major types of control: formal controls and informal controls.[30] Although we discuss each type of marketing control separately, most firms use combinations of these control types to monitor strategy implementation.

Formal Marketing Controls

Formal marketing controls are activities, mechanisms, or processes designed by the firm to help ensure the successful implementation of the marketing strategy. The elements of formal control influence the behaviors of employees before and during implementation and are used to assess performance outcomes at the completion of the implementation process. These elements are referred to as input, process, and output controls, respectively.

Input Controls   Actions taken prior to the implementation of the marketing strategy are input controls. The premise of input control is that the marketing strategy cannot be implemented correctly unless the proper tools and resources are in place for it to succeed. Among the most important input controls are recruiting, selecting, and training employees. Another critical input control deals with financial resources. These control activities include resource allocation decisions (manpower and financial), capital outlays for needed facilities and equipment, and increased expenditures on research and development. Financial resources can make or break a marketing strategy or its implementation. For example, General Motors has only recently started infusing more capital into its Saturn division. For years, Saturn has been unable to compete effectively due to constrained resources that limited its ability to develop and market new vehicles. Consequently, Saturn did not enter the highly profitable SUV market until 2002. With $18 billion in renewed support from GM, Saturn is now in a position to launch a series of new products and promotional campaigns. Among the most exciting for Saturn is the launch of the Sky roadster under the new "Like Always. Like Never Before." campaign.[31]

Process Controls   Process controls include activities that occur during implementation, designed to influence employee behavior so that they will support the strategy and its objectives. Although the number of process controls is potentially limitless and will vary from one firm to the next, Exhibit 11.6 provides some examples of universal process controls that all firms must employ and manage well.

The process control that stands out above all others is management commitment to the strategy. Several research studies have confirmed that management commitment to the marketing strategy is the single most important determinant of whether the strategy will succeed or fail.[32] This commitment is critical because employees learn to model the behavior of their managers. If management has commitment to the marketing strategy, it is more likely that employees will be committed to it as well. Commitment to the

---

EXHIBIT 11.6   **A FRAMEWORK FOR MARKETING CONTROL**

Formal Controls: Control Activities Initiated by Management

Input controls—actions taken prior to implementation of the strategy

- Employee recruitment and selection procedures
- Employee-training programs
- Human resource allocations
- Allocation of financial resources
- Capital outlays
- Research and development expenditures

Process controls—actions taken during implementation of the strategy

- Employee evaluation and compensation systems
- Employee authority and empowerment
- Internal communication programs
- Lines of authority/structure (organizational chart)
- Management commitment to the marketing plan
- Management commitment to employees

Output controls—evaluated after implementation of the strategy

- Formal performance standards (for example, sales, market share, and profitability)
- Marketing audits

Informal Controls: Unwritten Control Activities Initiated by Employees

Employee self-control—control based on personal expectations and goals
- Job satisfaction
- Organizational commitment
- Commitment to the marketing plan

Social control—small-group control based on group norms and expectations
- Shared organizational values
- Social and behavioral norms in workgroups

Cultural control—cultural control based on organizational norms and expectations
- Organizational culture
- Organizational stories, rituals, and legends
- Cultural change

Source: Adapted from Bernard J. Jaworski, "Toward a Theory of Marketing Control: Environmental Context, Control Types, and Consequences", *Journal of Marketing* 52 (July 1988): 23–39.

marketing strategy also means that managers must be committed to employees and support them in their efforts to implement the strategy.

Another important process control is the system used to evaluate and compensate employees. In general, employees should be evaluated and compensated based on criteria relevant to the marketing strategy.[33] For example, if the strategy requires that salespeople increase their efforts at customer service, they should be rewarded on the basis of this effort, not on other criteria such as sales volume or the number of new accounts created. Further, the degree of authority and empowerment granted to employees is another important process control. Although some degree of empowerment can lead to increased performance, employees given too much authority often become confused and dissatisfied with their jobs.[34] Having good internal communication programs—another type of process control—can help alleviate these problems.

Output Controls   Output controls ensure that marketing outcomes are in line with anticipated results. The primary means of output control involves setting performance standards against which actual performance can be compared. To ensure an accurate assessment of marketing activities, all performance standards should be based on the firm's marketing objectives. Some performance standards are broad, such as those based on sales, profits, or expenses. We say these are broad standards because many different marketing activities can affect them. Other performance standards are specific, such as many customer service standards (for example, number of customer complaints, repair service within 24 hours, overnight delivery by 10:00 a.m., or on-time airline arrivals). In most cases, how the firm performs relative to these specific standards will determine how well it performs relative to broader standards.

But how specific should performance standards be? Standards should reflect the uniqueness of the firm and its resources as well as the critical activities needed to implement the marketing strategy. In setting performance standards, it is important to remember that employees are always responsible for implementing marketing activities and ultimately the marketing strategy. For example, if an important part of increasing customer service requires that employees answer the telephone by the second ring, then a performance standard should be set for this activity. Standards for the performance of marketing personnel are typically the most difficult to establish and enforce.

One of the best methods of evaluating whether performance standards have been achieved is to use a marketing audit to examine systematically the firm's marketing

EXHIBIT 11.7   **A SAMPLE MARKETING AUDIT**

Identification of Marketing Activities

1. In what specific marketing activities is the company currently engaged?

   - Product activities: for example, research, concept testing, test marketing, and quality control
   - Customer service activities: for example, installation, training, maintenance, technical support, and complaint handling
   - Pricing activities: for example, financing, billing, cost control, and discounting
   - Distribution activities: for example, availability, channels used, and customer convenience
   - Promotion activities: for example, media, sales promotion, personal selling, and public relations

2. Are these activities conducted or provided solely by the company, or are some conducted or provided by outside contractors? If outside contractors are used, how are they performing? Should any of these outside activities be brought in-house?
3. What additional marketing activities do customers want, need, and/or expect?

Review of Standard Procedures for Each Marketing Activity

1. Do written procedures (manuals) exist for each marketing activity? If so, are these procedures (manuals) up to date? Do employees follow these procedures (manuals)?
2. What oral or unwritten procedures exist for each marketing activity? Should these procedures be formally included in the written procedures, or should they be eliminated?
3. Do marketing personnel regularly interact with other functional areas to establish standard procedures for each activity?

Identification of Performance Standards for Each Marketing Activity

1. What specific quantitative standards exist for each activity?
2. What qualitative standards exist for each activity?
3. How does each activity contribute to customer satisfaction within each marketing program element (that is, product, pricing, distribution, and promotion)?
4. How does each activity contribute to marketing goals and objectives?
5. How does each activity contribute to the goals and objectives of the company?

(continued)

---

objectives, strategy, and performance.[35] The primary purpose of a marketing audit is to identify problems in ongoing marketing activities and to plan the necessary steps to correct these problems. A marketing audit can be long and elaborate, or it can be short and simple. Exhibit 11.7 displays a sample marketing audit. In practice, the elements of the audit must match the elements of the marketing strategy. The marketing audit should also be used to gauge the success of ongoing implementation activities—not just when problems arise.

Regardless of the organization of the marketing audit, it should aid the firm in evaluating marketing activities by

- describing current marketing activities and their performance outcomes.

- gathering information about changes in the external or internal environments that may affect ongoing marketing activities.

- exploring different alternatives for improving the ongoing implementation of marketing activities.

Identification of Performance Measures for Each Marketing Activity

1. What are the internal, profit-based measures for each marketing activity?
2. What are the internal, time-based measures for each marketing activity?
3. How is performance monitored and evaluated internally by management?
4. How is performance monitored and evaluated externally by customers?

Review and Evaluation of Marketing Personnel

1. Are the company's current recruiting, selection, and retention efforts consistent (matched) with the requirements of the marketing activities?
2. What is the nature and content of employee-training activities? Are these activities consistent with the requirements of the marketing activities?
3. How are customer-contact personnel supervised, evaluated, and rewarded? Are these procedures consistent with customer requirements?
4. What effect do employee evaluation and reward policies have on employee attitudes, satisfaction, and motivation?
5. Are current levels of employee attitudes, satisfaction, and motivation adequate?

Identification and Evaluation of Customer Support Systems

1. Are the quality and accuracy of customer service materials (for example, instruction manuals, brochures, and form letters) consistent with the image of the company and its products?
2. Are the quality and appearance of physical facilities (for example, offices, furnishings, layout, and store decor) consistent with the image of the company and its products?
3. Are the quality and appearance of customer service equipment (for example, repair tools, telephones, computers, and delivery vehicles) consistent with the image of the company and its products?
4. Is the record-keeping system accurate? Is the information always readily available when it is needed? What technology could be acquired to enhance record keeping abilities (for example, bar-code scanners, RFID, portable computers, wireless telephones, or PDAs)?

Source: Adapted from Christopher H. Lovelock, *Services Marketing*, 3rd ed. (Upper Saddle River, NJ: Prentice Hall, 1996), 504.

- providing a framework to evaluate the attainment of performance standards as well as marketing goals and objectives.

The information in a marketing audit often has its basis in a series of questionnaires that are given to employees, managers, customers, and/or suppliers. In some cases, outside consultants perform this ongoing evaluation. Using outside auditors has the advantages of being more objective and less time consuming for the firm. However, outside auditors are typically expensive. A marketing audit can also be very disruptive, especially if employees are fearful of the scrutiny.

Despite their drawbacks, marketing audits are usually beneficial for the firms that use them. They are flexible in that the scope of the audit can be broad (to evaluate the entire marketing strategy) or narrow (to evaluate only a specific element of the marketing program). The results of the audit can be used to reallocate marketing efforts, correct implementation problems, or even to identify new opportunities. The end results of a well-executed marketing audit are usually better marketing performance and increased customer satisfaction.

Informal Marketing Controls

Formal marketing controls are overt in their attempt to influence employee behavior and marketing performance. Informal controls, on the other hand, are subtler. Informal marketing controls are unwritten, employee-based mechanisms that subtly affect the behaviors of employees, both as individuals and in groups.[36] Here, we deal with personal objectives and behaviors as well as group-based norms and expectations. There are three types of informal control: employee self-control, social control, and cultural control. As you read the descriptions of each type, note that the formal controls employed by the firm affect, to a great extent, the elements of informal control. However, the premise of informal control is that some aspects of employee behavior cannot be influenced by formal mechanisms and therefore must be controlled informally through individual and group actions.

Employee Self-Control   Through employee self-control, employees manage their own behaviors (and thus the implementation of the marketing strategy) by establishing personal objectives and monitoring their results. The type of personal objectives that employees set depends on how they feel about their jobs. If they have high job satisfaction and a strong commitment to the firm, they are more likely to establish personal objectives that are consistent with the aims of the firm, the marketing strategy, and the firm's goals and objectives. Employee self-control also depends on the rewards that employees receive. Some employees prefer the intrinsic rewards of doing a good job rather than the extrinsic rewards of pay and recognition. Intrinsically rewarded employees are likely to exhibit more self-control by managing their behaviors in ways consistent with the marketing strategy.

Social Control   Social, or small-group, control deals with the standards, norms, and ethics found in work groups within the firm.[37] The social interaction that occurs within these work groups can be a powerful motivator of employee behavior. The social and behavioral norms of work groups provide the "peer pressure" that causes employees to conform to expected standards of performance. If employees fall short of these standards, the group will pressure them to align with group norms. This pressure can be both positive and negative. Positive group influence can encourage employees to increase their effort and performance in ways consistent with the firm's goals and objectives. However, the opposite is also true. If the work group's norms encourage slacking or shirking of job responsibilities, employees will feel pressured to conform or risk being ostracized for good work.

Cultural Control   Cultural control is very similar to social control, only on a much broader scale. Here, we concern ourselves with the behavioral and social norms of the entire firm. One of the most important outcomes of cultural control is the establishment of shared values among all members of the firm. Marketing implementation is most effective and efficient when every employee, guided by the same organizational values or beliefs, has a commitment to the same organizational goals.[38] Companies such as Lockheed Martin and Lexmark have strong organizational cultures that guide employee behavior. Unfortunately, cultural control is very difficult to master, in that it takes a great deal of time to create the appropriate organizational culture to ensure implementation success.

Scheduling Marketing Activities

Through good planning and organization, marketing managers can provide purpose, direction, and structure to all marketing activities. However, the manager must understand the problems associated with implementation, understand the coordination of the various components of implementation, and select an overall approach to implementation before actually executing marketing activities. Upon taking these steps, the marketing manager with the responsibility for executing the plan must establish a timetable for the completion of each marketing activity.

Successful implementation requires that employees know the specific activities for which they are responsible and the timetable for completing each activity. Creating a master schedule of marketing activities can be a challenging task because of the wide variety of activities required to execute the plan, the sequential nature of many activities (some take precedence over others and must be performed first), and the fact that time is of the essence in implementing the plan.[39] The basic steps involved in creating a schedule and timeline for implementation include the following:

1. *Identify the specific activities to be performed.* These activities include all product, pricing, distribution, and promotion activities contained within the marketing plan. Specific implementation activities, such as employee training, structural changes, or the acquisition of financial resources, should be included as well.

2. *Determine the time required to complete each activity.* Some activities require planning and time before they can come to fruition. Others can occur rather quickly after the initiation of the plan.

3. *Determine which activities must precede others.* Many marketing activities must be performed in a predetermined sequence (such as creating an advertising campaign from copywriting, to production, to delivery). These activities must be identified and separated from any activities that can be performed concurrently with other activities.

4. *Arrange the proper sequence and timing of all activities.* In this step, the manager plans the master schedule by sequencing all activities and determining when each activity must occur.

5. *Assign responsibility.* The manager must assign one or more employees, teams, managers, or departments to each activity and charge them with the responsibility of executing the activity.

A simple but effective way to create a master implementation schedule is to incorporate all marketing activities into a spreadsheet, like the one shown in Exhibit 11.8. A master schedule such as this can be simple or complex depending on the level of detail included within each activity. The master schedule will also be unique to the

EXHIBIT 11.8   A HYPOTHETICAL 3-MONTH MARKETING IMPLEMENTATION SCHEDULE

Month		March				April				May			
Activities													
Week		1	2	3	4	1	2	3	4	1	2	3	4
Product Activities													
Finalize package changes		X											
Production runs		X	X			X	X			X	X		
Pricing Activities													
Hold 10% off sale at retail							X						
Hold 25% off sale at retail												X	
Distribution Activities													
Shipments to warehouses		X		X		X		X		X		X	
Shipments to retail stores			X		X		X		X		X		X
10% quantity discount to the trade		X	X	X	X	X	X	X	X	X	X	X	X
Promotion Activities													
Informational website operational		X											
Television advertising			X	X			X	X			X	X	
Newspaper advertising			X		X	X	X		X	X	X		X
Coupon in newspaper insert					X					X			
In-store point-of-purchase displays			X	X	X	X							
In-store signage					X	X	X	X				X	X

specific marketing plan tied to it. As a result, a universal template for creating a master schedule does not truly exist.

Although some activities must be performed before others, other activities can be performed concurrently with other activities or later in the implementation process. This requires tight coordination between departments—marketing, production, advertising, sales, and so on—to ensure the completion of all marketing activities on schedule. Pinpointing those activities that can be performed concurrently can greatly reduce the total amount of time needed to execute a given marketing plan. Because scheduling can be a complicated task, most firms use sophisticated project management techniques, such as PERT (program evaluation and review technique), CPM (critical path method), or computerized planning programs to schedule the timing of marketing activities.

Lessons from Chapter 11

Marketing implementation

- is critical to the success of any firm because it is responsible for putting the marketing strategy into action.

- has been somewhat ignored throughout the history of business because most firms have emphasized strategic planning rather than strategic implementation.

- is the process of executing the marketing strategy by creating and performing specific actions that will ensure the achievement of the firm's marketing objectives.

- goes hand-in-hand with evaluation and control in determining the success or failure of the marketing strategy and ultimately for the entire firm.

- is usually the cause for the difference between intended marketing strategy—what the firm wants to happen—and realized marketing strategy—the strategy that actually takes place.

- maintains a relationship with strategic planning that causes three major problems: interdependency, evolution, and separation.

The elements of marketing implementation include

- marketing strategy—the firm's planned product, pricing, distribution, and promotion activities.

- shared goals and values—the glue of implementation that holds the entire firm together as a single, functioning unit.

- marketing structure—how the firm's marketing activities are organized.

- systems and processes—collections of work activities that absorb a variety of inputs to create information and communication outputs that ensure the consistent day-to-day operation of the firm.

- resources—include a wide variety of tangible and intangible assets that can be brought together during marketing implementation.

- people—the quality, diversity, and skill of a firm's human resources. The people element also includes employee selection and training, evaluation and compensation, motivation, satisfaction, and commitment.

- leadership—how managers communicate with employees, as well as how they motivate their employees to implement the marketing strategy.

Approaches to implementing marketing strategy include

- implementation by command—marketing strategies developed and selected by the firm's top executives and then transmitted to lower levels where frontline managers and employees are expected to implement them.

- implementation through change—explicit focus on implementation by modifying the firm in ways that will ensure the successful implementation of the chosen marketing strategy.

- implementation through consensus—upper- and lower-level managers from different areas of the firm working together to evaluate and develop marketing strategies.

- implementation as organizational culture—marketing strategy and implementation seen as extensions of the firm's mission, vision, and organizational culture. Employees at all levels can participate in making decisions that help the firm reach its mission, goals, and objectives.

Internal marketing

- refers to the use of a marketing-like approach to motivate, coordinate, and integrate employees toward the implementation of the firm's marketing strategy.

- explicitly recognizes that external customer satisfaction depends on the actions of the firm's internal customers—its employees. If the internal customers are not properly educated about the strategy and motivated to implement it, then it is unlikely that the external customers will be satisfied completely.

- places the responsibility for implementation on all employees regardless of their level within the firm.

- is based on many of the same principles used in traditional external marketing. The product, price, distribution, and promotion elements of the internal marketing program are similar to the elements in the external marketing program.

In evaluating and controlling marketing activities,

- the firm's intended marketing strategy often differs from the realized strategy for four potential reasons: (1) The marketing strategy was inappropriate or unrealistic, (2) the implementation was inappropriate for the strategy, (3) the implementation process was mismanaged, or (4) the internal and/or external environments changed substantially between the development of the marketing strategy and its implementation.

- it is important that the potential for implementation failures be managed strategically by having a system of marketing controls in place.

- firms design and use formal input, process, and output controls to help ensure the successful implementation of the marketing strategy.

- firms use output controls, or performance standards, extensively to ensure that marketing outcomes are in line with anticipated results.

- employees individually (self-control), in work groups (social control), and throughout the firm (cultural control) use personal objectives and group-based norms and expectations to informally control their behaviors.

Scheduling marketing activities

- requires that employees know the specific activities for which they are responsible and the timetable for completing each activity.

- can be a challenging task because of the wide variety of activities required to execute the plan, the sequential nature of many marketing activities, and the fact that time is of the essence in implementing the plan.

- involves five basic steps: (1) identifying the specific activities to be performed, (2) determining the time required to complete each activity, (3) determining which activities must precede others, (4) arranging the proper sequence and timing of all activities, and (5) assigning responsibility to employees, managers, teams, or departments.

Questions for Discussion

1. Forget for a moment that planning the marketing strategy is equally as important as implementing the marketing strategy. What arguments can you make for one being more important than the other? Explain your answers.

2. If you were personally responsible for implementing a particular marketing strategy, which implementation approach would you be most comfortable using, given your personality and personal preferences? Why? Would your chosen approach be universally applicable to any given situation? If not, what would cause you to change or adapt your approach? Remember, adapting your basic approach means stepping out of your personal comfort zone to match the situation at hand.

3. What do you see as the major stumbling blocks to the successful use of the internal marketing approach? Given the hierarchical structure of employees in most organizations (for example, CEO, middle management, and staff employees), is internal marketing a viable approach for most organizations? Why or why not?

Exercises

1. Find a recent news article about an organization that changed its marketing strategy. What were the reasons for the change? How did the organization approach the development and implementation of the new strategy?

2.   One of the best sources for shared goals and values to guide implementation is the firm's own mission or values statement. Find the mission or values statement for the organization that you identified in Exercise 1. Do you see evidence of the mission or values in the way the organization handled its change in marketing strategy? Explain.

3.   Think about the unwritten, informal controls in your life. Develop a list of the controls that exist at work, at home, or at school (or substitute another context such as church, social gatherings, or public activities). Are these controls similar or different? Why?

	Controls at Work	Controls at Home	Controls at School
Self-Control (personal norms and expectations for behavior)			
Social Control (norms and expectations in small groups)			
Cultural Control (norms and expectations in the entire organization)			

CHAPTER 12

Developing and Maintaining Long-Term Customer Relationships

Introduction

To this point in the text, we have examined the process of strategic planning from its initial stages through the implementation of the marketing plan. At this point, however, we take the opportunity to step back from the process to look at it holistically. Firms often lose sight of the big picture as they rush to complete product development and test marketing or put the finishing touches on a media campaign. All the activities involved in developing and implementing the marketing program have one key purpose: to develop and maintain long-term customer relationships. However, as we have seen, implementing a marketing strategy that can effectively satisfy customers' needs and wants has proven difficult in today's rapidly changing business environment. The simple fact is that thorough research, strong competitive advantages, and a well-implemented marketing program are often not enough to guarantee success.

In times past, developing and implementing the "right" marketing strategy was all about creating a large number of transactions with customers in order to maximize the firm's market share. Companies paid scant attention to discovering customers' needs and finding better ways to solve customers' problems. In today's economy, however, that emphasis has shifted to developing strategies that attract and retain customers over the long term. As illustrated in Beyond the Pages 12.1, 1-800-Flowers.com does this effectively through a comprehensive understanding of its customers, including their expectations, motivations, and behaviors. With this knowledge in hand, firms like 1-800-Flowers.com can then offer the right marketing program to increase customer satisfaction and retain customers over the long term.

In this chapter, we examine how the marketing program can be leveraged as a whole to deliver quality, value, and satisfaction to customers. We begin by reviewing the strategic issues associated with the customer relationship management process. Developing long-term customer relationships is one of the best ways to insulate the firm against competitive inroads and the rapid pace of environmental change. Next, we address the critical topics of quality and value as we concern ourselves with how the entire marketing program is tied to these issues. Finally, we explore key issues

Customer service. Trust. One-to-one customer interactions. Customer loyalty. These are the foundations of the steady growth of 1-800-Flowers.com over the past decade. Since the company's founding in 1995, CEO Jim McCann has used a laserlike focus on customers to make 1-800-Flowers the number-one floral retailer in the United States. McCann's company earned $671 million in 2005 and adds roughly three million new customers every year.

1-800-Flowers.com uses the Internet as a means of connecting to customers by putting a lot of effort into creating a 360-degree, holistic view of each customer. The company collects customer information at every point where it contacts a customer—sales, loyalty programs, surveys, direct mail advertising, sales promotions (contests and sweepstakes), and affiliate programs (with florists, credit card companies, and airlines)—and uses it to create customized communications and product offerings for each of the 25 million customers in its database. 1-800-Flowers.com uses a sophisticated segmentation system that analyzes transactional behaviors (recency, frequency, and monetary) and combines it with gift-buying behaviors. This information is then tied to each customer's psychographic profile to create targeted messages for each customer segment. The company then uses a variety of different metrics—financial, customer retention and acquisition, brand awareness, purchase intentions, and customer recommendations—to measure performance.

To increase customer loyalty, 1-800-Flowers.com launched Fresh Rewards, a point-based loyalty program. Customers earn 1 point for every dollar they spend and then receive a Fresh Reward pass via email when they have accumulated 200 points. There are also higher-tiered programs for customers who spend $400 or $800 per year. The program is somewhat unique in that it offers only 1-800-Flowers.com merchandise as rewards. In addition to increasing customer loyalty, the Fresh Rewards program also allows the company to collect more in-depth information from customers.

For 1-800-Flowers.com, the key to success has been its ability to integrate and leverage the massive amount of data that it collects from its customers. However, CEO McCann also favors the old-school approach to understanding customers. McCann states that his training as a social worker helps him understand the importance of solid relationships. True to his background, McCann regularly goes into the field to talk with customers. On key occasions such as Mother's Day and Valentine's Day, McCann and other executives answer the phones, deliver products, and work in the company's retail stores. McCann puts it this way: "Our competitors are all about the sales, we're about relationships. We are helping our customers connect with the important people in their lives through flowers and gifts created and designed for specific relationships, occasions, and sentiments. That's the difference."

with respect to customer satisfaction, including customer expectations and metrics for tracking customer satisfaction over time.

Managing Customer Relationships

As we briefly mentioned in Chapter 1, creating and maintaining long-term customer relationships requires that organizations see beyond the transactions that occur today to look at the long-term potential of a customer. To do this, the organization must strive to develop a relationship with each customer rather than generate a large number of discrete transactions. Before a relationship can be mutually beneficial to both the firm and the customer, it must provide value to both parties. This is one of the basic requirements of exchange noted in Chapter 1. Creating this value is the goal of *customer relationship management* (CRM), which is defined as a business philosophy aimed at defining and increasing customer value in ways that motivate customers to remain loyal.[2] In essence, CRM is about retaining the right customers. It is important to note that CRM does not focus solely on end customers. Rather, CRM involves a number of different groups:[3]

- **Customers**   These are the end users of a product, whether they be businesses or individual consumers.

- **Employees**   Firms must manage relationships with their employees if they are to have any hope of fully serving customers' needs. This is especially true in service firms where employees *are* the service in the eyes of customers. Retaining key employees is a vital part of CRM.

- **Supply Chain Partners**   Virtually all firms buy and sell products upstream and/or downstream in the supply chain. This involves the procurement of materials or the sale of finished products to other firms. Either way, maintaining relationships with key supply chain partners is critical to satisfying customers.

- **External Stakeholders**   Relationships with key stakeholders must also be managed effectively. These include government agencies, nonprofit organizations, or facilitating firms that provide goods or services that help a firm achieve its goals.

Delivering good value to customers requires that firms use CRM strategies to effectively manage relationships with each of these groups. This effort includes finding ways to integrate all these relationships toward the ultimate goal of customer satisfaction.

To fully appreciate the concepts behind CRM, organizations must develop a new perspective on the customer—one that shifts the emphasis from "acquiring customers" to "maintaining clients," as shown in Exhibit 12.1. Although this strategic shift has been under way for some time in business markets, technological advancements allow CRM to be fully embraced in consumer markets as well. Firms that are exceptionally good at developing customer relationships possess "relationship capital" that stems from the value generated by the trust, commitment, cooperation, and interdependence among relationship partners. With respect to competitive advantages, many see relationship capital as the most important resource or asset that an organization can possess because it represents a powerful advantage that can be leveraged to make the most of marketing opportunities.[4]

Developing Relationships in Consumer Markets

Developing long-term customer relationships can be an arduous process. Over the life of the relationship, the firm's goal is to move the customer through a progression of stages, as shown in Exhibit 12.2. The objective of CRM is to move customers from having a simple awareness of the firm and its product offering, through levels of increasing relationship intensity, to the point where the customer becomes a true

EXHIBIT 12.1	STRATEGIC SHIFT FROM ACQUIRING CUSTOMERS TO MAINTAINING CLIENTS	
Acquiring Customers	**Maintaining Clients**	
Customers are "customers."	Customers are "clients."	
Mass marketing	One-to-one marketing	
Acquire new customers.	Build relationships with current customers.	
Discrete transactions	Continuous transactions	
Increase market share.	Increase share of customer.	
Differentiation based on groups	Differentiation based on individual customers	
Segmentation based on homogeneous needs	Segmentation based on heterogeneous needs	
Short-term strategic focus	Long-term strategic focus	
Standardized products	Mass customization	
Lowest-cost provider	Value-based pricing strategy	
One-way mass communication	Two-way individualized communication	
Competition	Collaboration	

advocate for the firm and/or its products. Note that true CRM attempts to go beyond the creation of satisfied and loyal customers. Ultimately, the firm will possess the highest level of relationship capital when its customers become true believers or sponsors for the company and its products. For example, Harley-Davidson, which is now over 100 years old, is a great example of a firm that enjoys the highest levels of customer advocacy. Harley owners exhibit a cultlike love for the brand that most other companies do not possess. Other firms, such as Apple, Coca-Cola, and eBay also enjoy a high degree of customer advocacy.

In consumer markets, one of the most viable strategies to build customer relationships is to increase the firm's *share of customer* rather than its market share. This strategy involves abandoning the old notions of acquiring new customers and increasing transactions to focus on more fully serving the needs of current customers. Financial services are a great example of this strategy in action. Most consumers purchase financial services from different firms. They bank at one institution, purchase insurance from a different institution, and handle their investments through another. To counter this fact of life, many companies now offer all these services under one roof. For example, Regions Financial Corporation offers retail and commercial banking, trust, securities brokerage, mortgage and insurance products to customers in a network of over 1,300 offices in sixteen states. Regions' commitment to relationships is evident in its product offerings such as "personal banking" and "relationship money market accounts."[5] Rather than focus exclusively on the acquisition of new customers, Regions tries to more fully serve the financial needs of its current customers, thereby acquiring a larger share of each customer's financial business. By creating these types of relationships, customers

EXHIBIT 12.2	STAGES OF CUSTOMER RELATIONSHIP DEVELOPMENT	
Relationship Stage	**CRM Goals**	**Examples**
Awareness	Promote customer knowledge and education about the product or company. Prospect for new customers.	Product advertising Personal selling (cold calls) Word of mouth
Initial purchase	Get product or company into customers' evoked set of alternatives. Stimulate interest in the product. Stimulate product trial.	Advertising Product sampling Personal selling
Repeat customer	Fully satisfy customers' needs and wants. Completely meet or exceed customers' expectations or product specifications. Offer incentives to encourage repeat purchase.	Good product quality and value-based pricing Good service before, during, and after the sale Frequent reminders and incentives
Client	Create financial bonds that limit the customer's ability to switch products or suppliers. Acquire more of each individual customer's business. Personalize products to meet evolving customer needs and wants.	Frequent customer cards Frequent-flier programs Broad product offering
Community	Create social bonds that prevent product or supplier switching. Create opportunities for customers to interact with each other in a sense of community.	Membership programs Affinity programs Ongoing personal communication
Advocacy	Create customization or structural bonds that encourage the highest degree of loyalty. Become such a part of the customer's life that he or she is not willing to end the relationship. Think of customers as partners.	Customer events and reunions Long-term contracts Brand-related memorabilia

have little incentive to seek out competitive firms to fulfill their financial services needs. This relationship capital gives Regions an important strategic asset that can be leveraged as it competes with rival banks and financial institutions, both locally and online.

Focusing on share of customer requires an understanding that all customers have different needs; therefore, not all customers have equal value to a firm. The most basic application of this idea is the 80/20 rule: 20 percent of customers provide 80 percent of business profits. Although this idea is not new, advances in technology and data collection techniques now allow firms to profile customers in real time. In fact, the ability to track customers in detail can allow the firm to increase sales and loyalty among the bottom 80 percent of customers. The goal is to rank the profitability of individual customers to express their lifetime value (LTV) to the firm. Some customers—those who require considerable handholding or that frequently return products—are simply too expensive to keep given the low level of profits that they generate. These bottom-tier customers can be "fired" or required to pay very high fees for additional service. Banks and brokerages, for example, slap hefty maintenance fees on small accounts. This allows the firm to spend its resources to more fully develop relationships with its profitable customers.

The firm's top-tier customers (those that fall into the top 20 percent) are the most obvious candidates for retention strategies. These customers are the most loyal and the most profitable, so the firm should take the necessary steps to ensure their continuing satisfaction. Customers that fall just outside of this tier, or second-tier customers, can be encouraged to be better customers or even loyal customers with the right incentives. Exhibit 12.3 outlines strategies that can be used to enhance and maintain customer relationships. The most basic of these strategies is based on financial incentives that encourage increased sales and loyalty. However, financial incentives are easily copied by competitors and are not typically good for retaining customers in the long run. To achieve this ultimate goal, the firm must turn to strategies aimed at closely tying the customer to the firm. These structural connections are the most resilient to competitive action and the most important for maintaining long-term customer relationships.

Developing Relationships in Business Markets

Relationship management in business markets is much like that in consumer markets. The goal is to move business buyers through a sequence of stages where each stage represents an increasing level of relationship intensity. Although business relationships may not approach the cultlike, emotional involvement found in some consumer markets, businesses can nonetheless become structurally bound to their supply chain partners. These relationships can give both parties an advantage with respect to relationship capital: One firm maintains a loyal and committed customer; the other maintains a loyal and committed supplier. Both parties may also consider each other to be strong partners or advocates within the entire supply chain.

Although our discussion certainly involves generalizations (for example, some consumer marketers are better at building relationships than many business marketers), relationship development in business markets can be more involving, more complex, and much riskier than relationships in consumer markets. This occurs because business buyers typically have fewer options to choose from and the financial risks are typically higher. For example, chip maker AMD's decision to purchase ATI (a respected maker of graphics chips) will change the buying and partnering options for AMD, Intel, and other firms in the computer industry. Intel is likely to work more closely with Nvidia (ATI's major competitor) in the future.[6] The tight integration of firms in the business market is due to the nature of business buying, the presence of long-term contractual obligations, and the sheer dollars involved in many business purchases. Further, business relationships are built on win–win strategies that focus on cooperation and improving the value of the exchange for both parties, not on strict negotiation strategies where one side "wins" and the other side "loses."

Business relationships have become increasingly complex because decisions must be made with an eye toward the entire supply chain, not just the two parties involved. In these cases, the relationships that are developed enhance the ability of the entire

EXHIBIT 12.3   STRATEGIES FOR ENHANCING AND MAINTAINING CUSTOMER RELATIONSHIPS

→ Increasing Relationship Intensity

	Financial Incentives	Social Bonding	Enhanced Customization	Structural Bonding
Strategy	Using financial incentives to increase customer loyalty	Using social and psychological bonds to maintain a clientele	Using intimate customer knowledge to provide one-to-one solutions or mass customization	Creating customized product offerings that create a unique delivery system for each client
Examples	Volume discounts Coupons Frequent-customer programs	Membership programs Customer-only events Community outreach programs	Customer reminder notifications Electronic recommendation engines Personal shopping programs	Structured, lock-step programs Automated electronic transactions Contractual relationships
Used by	Airlines Grocery retailers Music clubs	Health clubs Churches Country clubs	Auto service centers Electronic retailers Professional services	Colleges and universities Banks Bundled telecom services
Advantages	Effective in the short term Easy to use	Difficult for competitors to copy Reduces brand switching	Promotes strong loyalty and greatly reduces brand switching Very difficult for competitors to copy customer knowledge	Ultimate reduction in brand switching Products become intertwined in customers' lifestyles
Disadvantages	Easily imitated Hard to end incentives once started Can promote continual brand switching	Social bonds take time to develop Customer trust is critical and must be maintained at all times	Can be expensive to deliver Takes time to develop	Customer resistance Time consuming and costly to develop

Source: Adapted from Leonard L. Berry and A. Parasuraman, *Marketing Services* (New York: Free Press, 1991), Ch. 8.

supply chain to better meet the needs of final customers. Over the past several years, a number of changes have occurred in business relationships, including:

- **A Change in Buyers' and Sellers' Roles**   To build stronger relationships, buyers and sellers have shifted away from competitive negotiation (trying to drive prices up or down) to focus on true collaboration. This represents a major change for many companies.

- **An Increase in Sole Sourcing**   Supplier firms will continue to sell directly to large customers or move to selling through systems suppliers that put together a set of products from various suppliers to deliver a comprehensive solution. The continuing growth in online e-procurement systems is one result of this trend.

- **An Increase in Global Sourcing**   More than ever, buyers and sellers scan the globe in search of suppliers or buyers that represent the best match with their specific needs and requirements. The relationship-building process is so costly and complex that only the best potential partners will be pursued.

- **An Increase in Team-Based Buying Decisions**   Increasingly, teams from both buying and supplying firms make purchase decisions. These teams consist of employees from different areas of expertise that are central to the success of both firms. Increasingly, senior management of both firms will be represented on these teams as economic buyers for both sides play a major role in setting goals and objectives.

- **An Increase in Productivity through Better Integration**   Firms that closely align their buying and selling operations have the capacity to identify and remove any inefficiency in the process. This increased productivity leads to a reduction in both hard and soft costs, thereby enhancing the profitability of both firms. This integration can be extended throughout the supply chain. In the future, only the most efficient supply chains will survive, particularly as more procurement moves into the electronic arena.

These fundamental changes in the structure of most business relationships will lead to dramatic changes in the way that organizations work together. Only those firms willing to make strategic, as opposed to cosmetic, changes in the way they deal with their customers or suppliers are likely to prosper as we move forward in this century.

Quality and Value: The Keys to Developing Customer Relationships

To build relationship capital, a firm must be able to fulfill the needs of its customers better than its competitors. It must also be able to fulfill those needs by offering high-quality goods and services that are a good value relative to the sacrifices that customers must make to acquire them. When it comes to developing and maintaining customer relationships, quality is a double-edged sword. If the quality of a good or service is poor, the organization obviously has little chance of satisfying customers or maintaining relationships with them. The adage of "trying something at least once" applies here. A firm may be successful in generating first-time transactions with customers, but poor quality guarantees that repeat purchases will not occur. On the other hand, good quality is not an automatic guarantee of success. Think of it as a necessary but insufficient condition of CRM. It is at this point where value becomes critical to maintaining long-term customer relationships.

Understanding the Role of Quality

Quality is a relative term that refers to the degree of superiority of a firm's goods or services. We say that quality is relative because it can only be judged in comparison to competing products or when compared to an internal standard of excellence. The concept of quality also applies to many different aspects of a firm's product offering. The total product offering of any firm consists of at least three interdependent components, as illustrated in Exhibit 12.4: the core product, supplemental products, and symbolic and experiential attributes.

The Core Product   The heart of the offering, the core product, is the firm's *raison d'être*, or justification for existence. As shown in Exhibit 12.4, the core can be a tangible good—such as a Chevy Silverado—or an intangible service—such as the Verizon wireless communication network. Virtually every element of the marketing program has an effect on the quality (or perceived quality) of the core product; however, the firm's product and branding strategies are of utmost importance. Because the core product is the part of the offering that delivers the benefits desired by customers, the form utility offered by the core product is vital to maintaining its quality. For example, the quality of an entrée in a restaurant depends on the form utility

---

EXHIBIT 12.4   COMPONENTS OF THE TOTAL PRODUCT OFFERING

	Core Product	Supplemental Products	Symbolic and Experiential Attributes
Chevrolet Silverado	The truck itself Transportation Hauling/towing	Accessories GMAC financing Replacement parts Service department	"Like a Rock" Combination of work and fun
Verizon Wireless communication network	Communication	Phone options Rate plan options Free long distance VCAST music and video	"IN Calling" Leather slipcase Changeable faceplates
John Deere lawn tractor	The tractor itself Lawn and garden maintenance	Accessories Financing Delivery	John Deere "Green" "Nothing Runs Like a Deere"
Michelin tires	Tires Safety	Broad availability Installation Financing	Security—"Because a lot is riding on your tires" "A Better Way Forward" The Michelin Man
Waldorf Astoria, New York City	Bed/room	Mid-Manhattan location Restaurants Room service Executive lounge	Extraordinary hospitality The first "Grand Hotel" Art Deco styling

created through the combination of quality raw ingredients and expert preparation. In service offerings, the core product is typically composed of three interrelated dimensions:[7]

- **People**   The interaction among the customer, the firm's employees, and other customers present during service delivery.

- **Processes**   The operational flow of activities or steps in the service delivery process. Processes can be done through technology or face-to-face interaction.

- **Physical Evidence**   Any tangible evidence of the service including written materials, the service facility, people, or equipment.

As a whole, service firms struggle daily with maintaining the quality of their core service offerings. Because services are so people intensive, effective implementation of the marketing strategy (that is, shared goals, employee motivation, and employee skills) is key to ensuring consistency and quality. The quality of service also depends more on issues such as responsiveness to customer requests, consistent and reliable service over time, and the friendliness and helpfulness of the firm's employees. The quality of tangible goods depends more on issues such as durability, style, ease of use, comfort, or suitability for a specific need.

Whether a good or a service, the firm has little chance of success if its core product is of inferior quality. However, even providing a high-quality core product is not enough to ensure customer satisfaction and long-term customer relationships. This occurs because customers expect the core product to be of high quality or at least at a level necessary to meet their needs. When the core product meets this level of expected quality, the customer begins to take it for granted. For example, customers take their telephone service for granted because they expect it to work every time. They only take notice when clarity becomes an issue or when the service is unavailable. The same thing can be said for a grocery retailer who consistently delivers high-quality food and service. Over time, the core product no longer stands out at a level that can maintain the customer relationship in the long term. It is at this point where supplemental products become critical.

Supplemental Products   Supplemental products are goods or services that add value to the core product, thereby differentiating the core product from competing product offerings. In most cases, supplemental products are extra features or benefits that enhance the total product experience; however, they are not necessary for the core product to function correctly. In many product categories, the true difference between competing products lies in the supplemental products provided by the firm. For example, every hotel is capable of delivering the core product—a room with a bed in which to spend the night. Although the quality of the core product varies among hotels, the important differences lie in the supplemental products. Upscale hotels such as Hyatt or Hilton offer many amenities—such as spas, restaurants, health clubs, valet parking, and room service—that budget hotels like Motel 6 or Econolodge do not. Wireless phone service is another example. All wireless firms can fulfill their customers' communication needs; however, customers use supplemental products—such as different phone options, rate plans, and "freebies" like rollover minutes, free roaming, and free long distance—to differentiate one product offering from another. In business markets, supplemental services are often the most important factor in developing long-term relationships. Services such as financing, training, installation, and maintenance must be of top quality to ensure that business customers will continue to maintain a relationship with the supplier firm.

It is interesting to note that companies do not market many products with the core product in mind. When was the last time an automaker touted a car or truck on its ability to fulfill your transportation needs (that is, getting you from Point A to Point B)? Rather, they focus on supplemental product attributes such as special financing, roadside assistance, and warranties. Supplemental products such as these depend heavily on the product, pricing, and distribution elements of the marketing program. For example, in addition to selling a wide range of brand-name products, Amazon.com also offers its own credit card and free "super saver" shipping on many orders of $25 or more. These supplemental services, along with 24/7 access and competitive pricing, make Amazon.com a formidable competitor in many different product categories.

Symbolic and Experiential Attributes   Marketers also use symbolic and experiential differences—such as image, prestige, and brand—to differentiate their products. These features are created primarily through the product and promotional elements of the marketing program. Without a doubt, the most powerful symbolic and experiential attributes are based on branding. In fact, many brands—like Mercedes, iPod, Ritz-Carlton, Coca-Cola, Rolex, Disney World, and Ruth's Chris Steak House—only need their names to get the message across. These brands have immense power in differentiating their products because they can project the entire product offering (core, supplemental, and symbolic/experiential) with one word or phrase. Other types of products don't necessarily rely on branding but on their uniqueness to convey their symbolic and experiential nature. Major sporting events, such as the Super Bowl, the NCAA Final Four, or the Tour de France, are certainly good examples of this. Even local athletic events, such as high school football games, can reach a symbolic and experiential quality if the rivalry is intense.

Delivering Superior Quality

Delivering superior quality day in and day out is one of the most difficult things that any organization can do with regularity. In essence, it is difficult to get everything right all or even most of the time. During the 1980s and 1990s, strategic initiatives such as total quality management, ISO 9000, and the advent of the Baldrige Award were successful in changing the way businesses thought about quality. As a result, virtually every industry saw dramatic improvements in product quality during that time.

Today, however, most businesses struggle with improving the quality of their products, whether they are the core product or supplemental products. As we discussed in Chapter 1, this has happened because (1) customers have very high

Beyond the Pages 12.2

INTERNAL EFFICIENCY VERSUS CUSTOMER SERVICE[8]

As consumers, we are supposed to be living the good life. After all, we have access to an unprecedented variety and assortment of goods and services from around the globe. Everything we need is practically at arm's length and available 24/7. If things are so great, then why do we still suffer from poor service, long wait times, ignored complaints, and the feeling that we are just another number to most firms? In other words, why is customer service so bad? Are we just spoiled, or do companies not care anymore?

While we may be spoiled and some companies might not care about service, the truth is that our own demands for convenient, fast, and low-priced products are at odds with our demands for better customer service. As firms look to drive down costs and increase speed, they focus more on internal efficiency benchmarks based on costs and time-based measures of performance. This means they focus less on customer-driven benchmarks like customer service performance. This tendency is also driven by human nature: It is much easier to measure costs and time than something as subjective as customer satisfaction. As a result, more and more firms must continuously walk a fine line between service and operational efficiency.

Some companies successful walk this line (Southwest Airlines is a good example). Others, however, have damaged their customer relationships in a shortsighted attempt to reduce costs.

Three recent examples include The Home Depot, Dell, and Northwest Airlines.

The Home Depot

After years of record growth and profits, The Home Depot shifted its strategy to focus on expanding its contractor supply business and increasing efficiency through cost cutting and streamlined operations. Along the way, customer service slipped on the company's list of priorities. Full-time employees were replaced by part timers (now 40 percent of store staff). Employee incentives for good service were cut. And, the employee profit-sharing pool declined from $90 million to $44 million in one year. The end result: The Home Depot slipped to dead last in customer satisfaction among major U.S. retailers. More important, the company found itself 11 percentage points behind Lowe's, which had pursued a strategy that promoted more customer-friendly stores. The Home Depot argues that delivering perfect service is impossible because it processes 1.3 billion transactions per year. However, the company plans to launch a major customer service program that will provide millions of dollars in employee incentives to deliver top-quality service.

Dell

Dell's strategy and its success have long been tied to internal efficiency. Its business model of selling via phone and Internet is a textbook example of supply

(continued)

expectations about quality, (2) most products today compete in mature markets, and (3) many businesses compete in markets with very little real differentiation among product offerings. As products become further commoditized, it becomes very difficult for marketers to make their products stand out among a crowd of competitors. A great deal of research has been conducted to determine how businesses can improve the quality of their products. These four issues stand out:[9]

- **Understand customers' expectations**   It is not surprising that the basis of improving quality is also the starting point for effective CRM. The delivery of superior quality begins with a solid understanding of customers' expectations. This means that marketers must stay in touch with customers by conducting research to better identify their needs and wants. Although this research can include large-scale efforts such as surveys or focus groups, it can also include simple and chain integration and operational excellence. In recent years, however, Dell has pursued cost cutting with a vengeance. The reason is competition. Virtually all of Dell's competitors now match the company on pricing and product availability. Unfortunately, Dell's recent moves have alienated its customers, especially in the company's call center operations. For example, Dell staffed some customer call centers with fewer than 500 employees— a recipe that virtually guaranteed problems. The issue came to a head in November 2005 when 3,000 callers per week to the company's help line had to wait for at least 30 minutes before reaching a representative (rep). Things got so bad that Dell removed the toll-free service number from its website. Not surprising, Dell's customer satisfaction rating fell 6.3 percent, the largest decline in the industry. In the first quarter of 2006, Dell's market share fell from 31 percent to 28 percent, partly due to its damaged service reputation.

To turn things around, Dell initiated a $100 million program to improve customer service. The company began by appointing Richard Hunter as its new director of customer service. Hunter, who was previously responsible for managing Dell's highly efficient assembly plants, immediately expanded the size of Dell's call centers to 1,000 to 3,000 reps and began an aggressive cross-training program. Before the training, 45 percent of customer service calls required at least one transfer to an appropriate specialist. By cross-training reps to handle more issues, Hunter hopes to create a situation where a caller's problem can be handled by the rep that answers the phone. So far, the program appears to be working. During a recent week, only eighty customers waited more than 30 minutes to speak with a customer service rep.

Northwest Airlines

It's difficult to paint a rosy picture for Northwest Airlines. The airline filed for Chapter 11 bankruptcy in September 2005. And, after forcing major concessions from its pilots and union employees, the airline is expected to lose over $900 million in 2006— its sixth consecutive year of losses. To combat this bleak situation, Northwest drastically cut its customer service. The company stopped offering magazines, pillows, movies, and pretzels on domestic flights. Northwest began charging passengers $1 for a snack of raisins and nuts and $15 for a roomier aisle or exit row seat. When this scenario is combined with higher fares and a drastically reduced flight schedule, it is not surprising that Northwest came in dead last in J.D. Power & Associates customer satisfaction poll of the airline industry.

Northwest's only saving grace has been that it dominates the midwestern skies with respect to routes and scheduling. As a result, many dissatisfied customers have few alternatives and no choice but to fly with Northwest. However, low-cost carriers are beginning to appear along Northwest's routes. One example is Spirit Airlines, which recently began round-trip service between Detroit and Boston for $109 compared to $330 for Northwest. Although Northwest dropped its price in response, many customers are so angry at Northwest that they spurn the carrier at all costs.

---

inexpensive efforts such as customer comment cards or having managers that will interact in a positive fashion with customers. Advances in technology have greatly improved our ability to collect and analyze information from individual customers. New tools such as data warehousing and data mining hold great promise in enabling firms to better understand customers' expectations and needs.

- **Translate expectations into quality standards**   Firms that can successfully convert customer information into quality standards ensure that they hear the voice of the customer. If customers want better ingredients, friendlier employees, or faster delivery, then standards should be set to match these desires. It is often the case, however, that managers set standards that meet organizational objectives with no consideration for customer expectations. As discussed in Beyond the Pages 12.2, this commonly occurs when managers set standards based on productivity or efficiency rather than quality or customer service. In these cases, the temptation is to focus on internal benchmarks such as cost control or speed rather than customer benchmarks such as quality and satisfaction.

- **Uphold quality standards**   The best quality standards are of little use if they are not delivered accurately and consistently. At issue is the ability of managers and employees to deliver quality that is consistent with established standards. Greeting customers by name, answering the phone on the second ring, and delivering a hot pizza within 30 minutes are all examples of quality standards that may, or may not, be achieved. Successfully achieving these standards depends mostly on how well the strategy is implemented. However, it also depends on the ability of the firm to fully fund the quality effort. For example, many retailers—including Wal-Mart—at one time had standards for opening additional checkout lanes when there were more than three people in line. However, these retailers failed to deliver on this standard due to the expense of staffing additional employees to operate the registers.

- **Don't overpromise**   It goes without saying that customers will be disappointed if an organization fails to deliver on its promises. The key is to create realistic customer expectations for what can and cannot be delivered. All communication to customers must be honest and realistic with respect to the degree of quality that can be delivered. Intentionally misleading customers by making promises that cannot be kept is a guaranteed recipe for disaster.

Of these four issues, having a thorough understanding of customer expectations is the most critical because it sets the stage for the entire quality improvement effort. Customer expectations are also vital to ensuring customer satisfaction. We look more closely at customer expectations later in this chapter.

Understanding the Role of Value

Earlier, we stated that quality is a necessary but insufficient condition of effective CRM. By this we mean that exceptionally high product quality is of little use to the firm or its customers if the customers cannot afford to pay for it or if the product is too difficult to obtain. In the context of utility (want satisfaction), sacrificing time, place, possession, and psychological utility for the sake of form utility may win product design awards, but it will not always win customers.

Value is critical to maintaining long-term customer relationships because it allows for the necessary balance among the five types of utility and the elements of the marketing program. As a guiding principle of marketing strategy, value is useful because it includes the concept of quality but is broader in scope. It takes into account every marketing program element and can be used to consider explicitly customer perceptions of the marketing program in the strategy development process. Value can also be used as a means of organizing the internal aspects of marketing strategy development.

In Chapter 8, we defined value as a customer's subjective evaluation of benefits relative to costs to determine the worth of a firm's product offering relative to other product offerings. To see how each marketing program element is related to value, we

EXHIBIT 12.5	CONNECTIONS BETWEEN VALUE AND THE MARKETING PROGRAM			
	Marketing Program Elements			
Value Components	**Product Strategy**	**Pricing Strategy**	**Distribution Strategy**	**IMC Strategy**
Core product quality	Product features Brand name Product design Durability Reliability Ease of use Warranties Guarantees	Image Prestige	Product availability Exclusivity	Image Prestige Reputation Personal selling
Supplemental product quality	Supplemental features Accessories Replacement parts Repair services Training Customer service Friendliness of employees	Financing Layaway Image Prestige	Product availability Exclusivity Delivery services Installation services On-site training	Friendliness of employees Personal selling
Experiential quality	Entertainment Uniqueness Psychological benefits	Image Prestige	Convenience Retail atmosphere Retail décor 24/7 availability Overnight delivery	Image Prestige Reputation Personal selling
Monetary transactional costs	Product quality Exclusive features	Selling price Delivery charges Installation charges Taxes Licensing fees Registration fees	Delivery charges Installation charges Taxes	Image Prestige Reputation Personal selling
Monetary life-cycle costs	Product quality Product design	Maintenance costs Cost of consumables Repair costs Costs of replacement parts	Availability of consumables Availability of replacement parts Speed of repairs	Reputation Personal selling
Nonmonetary costs	Product quality Minimize opportunity costs	Guarantees Return policy	Convenience Wide availability 24/7 access	Reputation Reinforce purchase decision

need to break down customer benefits and costs into their component parts, as shown below and in Exhibit 12.5:

$$\text{Perceived Value} = \frac{\text{Core Product Quality} + \text{Supplemental Product Quality} + \text{Experiential Quality}}{\text{Monetary Costs} + \text{Nonmonetary Costs}}$$

Different buyers and target markets have varying perspectives on value. Although monetary cost is certainly a key issue, some buyers place greater importance on other elements of the value equation. To some, good value is about product quality. To these customers, the product element of the marketing program is the most crucial to achieving good value. To others, value hinges on the availability and quality of supplemental products. Here, the firm's product, customer service, pricing, and distribution strategies come together to create value. For other buyers, good value is all about convenience. These customers place greater emphasis on distribution issues such as wide product availability, multiple locations, 24/7 access, or even home delivery to achieve good value. The relationships among marketing program elements must constantly be managed to deliver good value to customers. It is important for managers to remember that any change in one program element will have repercussions for value throughout the entire marketing program.

Core Product, Supplemental Product, and Experiential Quality   The relationship between quality and value is most apparent in the quality of the customer benefits depicted in the top portion of the value equation. Here, good value depends on a holistic assessment of the quality of the core product, supplemental products, and experiential attributes. Although each can be judged independently, most customers look at the collective benefits provided by the firm in their assessments of value. Consequently, firms can create unique combinations of core, supplemental, and experiential benefits that help drive value perceptions. Consider a meal at the Waffle House versus a meal at the Rainforest Café. Despite their obvious differences, both meals can deliver the same value to different customers at different times. The overall perception of value is driven by customer needs, expectations, and the sacrifices required in obtaining the benefits provided by each firm.

Monetary and Nonmonetary Costs   Customer costs include anything that the customer must give up to obtain the benefits provided by the firm. The most obvious cost is the monetary cost of the product, which comes in two forms: transactional costs and life-cycle costs. *Transactional costs* include the immediate financial outlay or commitment that must be made to purchase the product. Other than the purchase price of the product, examples of these costs include sales taxes, usage taxes, licensing fees, registration fees, and delivery or installation charges. *Life-cycle costs* include any additional costs that customers will incur over the life of the product. The costs of maintenance and repairs are good examples. Firms that have the capability to reduce one or more of these costs can often provide a better value than their competitors. For example, appliance or furniture retailers can increase value by offering free delivery or installation when their competitors charge for these services. Hyundai and Kia offer long-term warranties on their cars, vans, and SUVs that significantly reduce life cycle costs for their customers. Likewise, manufacturers of durable goods can charge higher prices if customers perceive their life-cycle costs as being lower. Product quality, warranties, and the availability of repair services all play into the equation when customers judge monetary costs.

Nonmonetary costs are not quite as obvious as monetary costs, and customers sometimes ignore them. Two such costs include the time and effort customers expend to find and purchase goods and services. These costs are closely related to a firm's distribution activities. To reduce time and effort, the firm must increase product availability, thereby making it more convenient for customers to purchase the firm's products. The growth in nonstore and e-retailing is a direct result of firms taking steps to reduce the time and effort required to purchase their products, thereby reducing customers' nonmonetary costs. The sheer number of products that customers can have delivered directly to their homes is a testament to the growing importance of customers' time.

Offering good basic warranties or extended warranties for an additional charge can reduce risk, another nonmonetary cost. Retailers reduce risk by maintaining liberal return and exchange policies. Personal safety and security risks come into play when customers purchase products that are potentially dangerous. Common examples include tobacco products, alcohol, firearms, and exotic products like skydiving, bungee jumping, and dangerous pets. The final nonmonetary cost, opportunity costs, is harder for the firm to control. Customers incur opportunity costs because they forgo alternative products in making a purchase. Some firms attempt to reduce opportunity costs by promoting their products as being the best or by promising good service after the sale. To anticipate opportunity costs, marketers must consider all potential competitors, including total budget competitors that offer customers alternatives for spending their money.

Competing on Value

After breaking down value into its component parts, we can better understand how a firm's marketing strategy can be designed to optimize customer value. By altering each element of the marketing program, the firm can enhance value by increasing core, supplemental, or experiential quality and/or reducing monetary or nonmonetary costs. This effort must be based on a thorough understanding of customers' needs and wants, as well as an appreciation for how the firm's customers define value.

In consumer markets, retailers offer good examples of how value can be delivered by altering one or more parts of the value equation. Convenience stores offer value to customers by reducing nonmonetary costs (time and effort) and increasing monetary prices. These high-priced (in dollars) stores stay in business because customers value their time and effort more than money in many situations. Online retailers offer a similar mix of value by reducing time and effort costs and, in some cases, by reducing monetary costs through free shipping or by not collecting sales taxes. Customers who want the best quality may be willing to spend large sums of money and/or spend more time searching because they consider their nonmonetary costs to be less important. These consumers are likely to shop at retailers such as Macy's, Nordstrom, or Saks rather than discount chains. Finally, specialty stores, like Victoria's Secret or Banana Republic, offer an attractive mix of value in terms of quality clothing, fashionable styling, excellent service, and attractive décor, albeit at higher monetary prices.

Those in business markets often define value in terms of product specifications, availability, and conformity to a delivery schedule rather than in terms of price or convenience. Business customers must ensure that the products purchased will work right the first time, with minimal disruption to ongoing operations. In some cases, products have value not only because of their features or quality but also because the buying firm has a long-standing relationship with the supplying firm. Business buyers tend to become loyal to suppliers that consistently meet their expectations, solve their problems, and cause them no headaches. All of this is not to say that monetary considerations are not important. In fact, unlike most consumers, business buyers are keenly aware of total transactional and life-cycle costs as they seek to reduce the total lifetime expenditure associated with a particular purchase. Business customers will often pay more in up-front costs if the total lifetime cost can be reduced.

Obviously, different market segments will have different perceptions of good value. The key is for the marketer to understand the different value requirements of each segment and adapt the marketing program accordingly. From a strategic perspective, it is important to remember that each marketing program element is vital to delivering value. Strategic decisions about one element alone can change perceived value for better or worse. If a decision lowers overall value, the firm should consider modifying other marketing program elements to offset this decrease. For example, an increase in price may have to be offset by an increase in customer benefits to maintain the value ratio.

Customer Satisfaction: The Key to Customer Retention

In the final part of this chapter, we look at customer satisfaction and the role that it plays in maintaining long-term customer relationships. To maintain and manage customer satisfaction from a strategic point of view, managers must understand customer expectations and the differences between satisfaction, quality, and value. They must also make customer satisfaction measurement a long-term, continuous commitment of the entire organization.

Understanding Customer Expectations

Although customer satisfaction can be conceived in a number of ways, it is typically defined as the degree to which a product meets or exceeds the customer's expectations about that product. Obviously, the key to this definition lies in understanding customer expectations and how they are formed. Marketing researchers have discovered that customers can hold many different types of expectations, as shown in Exhibit 12.6. Customer expectations can vary based on the situation. For example, expectations are likely to be very high (that is, closer to the ideal end of the range) in situations where personal needs are very high. In highly involving situations such as weddings, birthdays, or funerals, customers will demand a great deal from the firm. Expectations also tend to be higher when customers have many alternatives for meeting their needs. This connection between expectations and alternatives is one reason that serving customers in highly commoditized markets is so challenging. Other situations can cause expectations to be lower. Customers may have lower expectations (that is, closer to the tolerable end of the range) when the purchase is not involving or when it is low in monetary and nonmonetary price. Customers can also

EXHIBIT 12.6	RANGE OF CUSTOMER EXPECTATIONS		
Type of Expectation	**Descriptive Example**	**Typical Situations**	**Expectation Range**
Ideal expectations	"Everyone says this is the best MP3 player on the market. I want to get my sister something special for her birthday."	Highly involving purchases Special occasions Unique events	**High (Desired)**
Normative expectations	"As expensive as this MP3 player is, it ought to hold a lot of music and come with several included accessories."	Shopping comparisons Value judgments	
Experience-based expectations	"I bought this brand of MP3 player last time, and it served me very well."	Frequent purchase situations Brand loyalty	
Minimum tolerable expectations	"I know it's not the best MP3 player out there. I only bought it because it was inexpensive."	Price-driven purchases Low involvement purchases	**Low (Adequate)**

Source: Adapted from James H. Myers, *Measuring Customer Satisfaction* (Chicago: American Marketing Association, 1999); and Valarie A. Zeithaml, Leonard L. Berry, and A. Parasuraman, "The Nature and Determinants of Customer Expectations of Service," *Journal of the Academy of Marketing Science* 21 (January 1993):1–12.

become more tolerable of weak or poor performance when they have fewer product alternatives or when the poor performance is beyond the control of the firm (for example, bad weather, excessively high demand, or natural disasters).

The Zone of Tolerance The difference between the upper and lower end of the range of possible customer expectations is an important strategic consideration in managing customer satisfaction. Marketers often refer to the upper end of expectations as desired performance expectations (what customers want) and the lower end of the range as adequate performance expectations (what customers are willing to accept). As shown in Exhibit 12.7, the extent of the difference between desired and adequate performance is called the zone of tolerance.[10] The width of the zone of tolerance represents the degree to which customers recognize and are willing to accept variability in performance (that is, quality, value, or some other measurable aspect of the marketing program). Performance can fall above the zone of tolerance, within the zone of tolerance, or below it:

- *Customer delight* occurs when actual performance exceeds the desired performance expectation. This level of performance is rare and surprising when it occurs. Therefore, customers find it to be memorable.

- *Customer satisfaction* occurs when actual performance falls within the zone of tolerance. Satisfaction levels vary based on where performance falls within the zone (high or low).

- *Customer dissatisfaction* occurs when actual performance falls below the adequate performance expectation. Depending on the severity of the performance level,

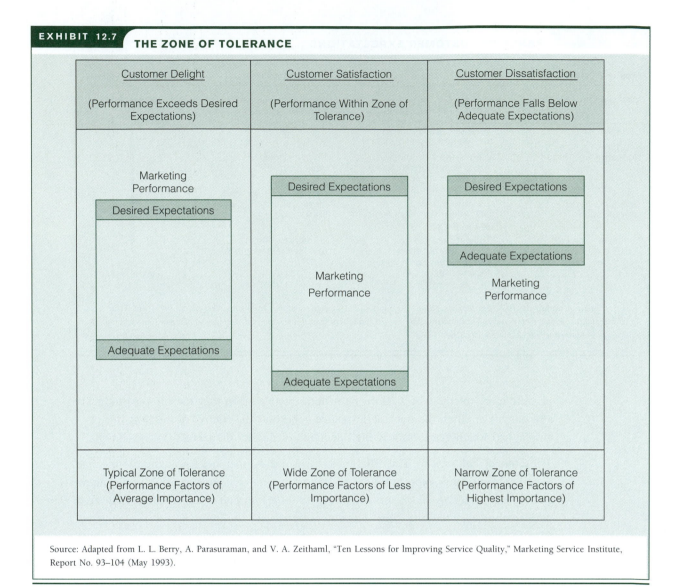

EXHIBIT 12.7 **THE ZONE OF TOLERANCE**

Source: Adapted from L. L. Berry, A. Parasuraman, and V. A. Zeithaml, "Ten Lessons for Improving Service Quality," Marketing Service Institute, Report No. 93–104 (May 1993).

customers may go beyond dissatisfaction to become frustrated or even angry. This too can be very memorable for customers.

We addressed these three issues in Chapter 6 as being a consequence of the buying process. Now, with the marketing plan developed and implemented, we can think of these issues in a strategic sense by considering the zone of tolerance as a moving target. If the zone is narrow, the difference between what customers want and what they are willing to accept is also narrow. This means that the marketer will have a relatively more difficult time matching performance to customer expectations. Hence, customer satisfaction is harder to achieve when the zone of tolerance is narrow. Conversely, customer satisfaction is relatively easier to achieve when the zone of tolerance is wide. In these instances, the marketer's hurdle is lower and the satisfaction targets are easier to hit. Delighting the customer by exceeding desired expectations is an exceedingly

difficult task for any marketer. Causing customer dissatisfaction by failing to meet even adequate expectations is a situation that should be avoided at all times.

Customers will typically hold different expectation levels and zones of tolerance for different factors of performance. In a restaurant, for example, customers might have a narrow zone of tolerance for food quality, an even narrower zone of tolerance for service quality, an average zone of tolerance for wait time, and a relatively wide zone of tolerance for cleanliness. From the marketer's point of view, two issues are important. First, the firm must clearly understand the salient performance factors about which customers will hold performance expectations. Customers can have expectations for just about anything, though there are typically only a few factors that are critical for most customers. Many firms look first at factors dealing with product strategy; however, critical performance factors can cut across the entire marketing program. Second, the firm must track expectations and performance over time. Tracking performance levels vis-à-vis expectations and the zone of tolerance is a useful diagnostic tool for both strategic planning and the management of customer satisfaction. The approach is also useful for tracking the effectiveness of performance improvements and in assessing the performance of new goods or services. In the end, tracking both expectations and performance is an important way to ensure that customer satisfaction remains stable or improves over time. Declining customer satisfaction suggests a need for immediate corrective action.

Managing Customer Expectations   As they work toward managing customer expectations, many marketers ask two key questions: (1) Why are customer expectations unrealistic? (2) Should we strive to delight our customers by consistently exceeding their desired expectations? Although it is true that customers are more demanding today than ever (especially American consumers), their expectations are typically not that unrealistic. Most customers are looking for the basics of performance—things that a firm is supposed to do or has promised to do.[11] For example, flights should take off and land on time, meals in a restaurant should taste good and be prepared as ordered, new cars should be hassle free throughout the warranty period, and your soft drink should be cold and fresh. On these and other basic factors of performance, it is essentially impossible for the firm to exceed customer expectations. These basic factors represent the bare minimum: If the firm wants to exceed expectations, it has to go above and beyond the call of duty.

The second question about delighting the customer is a bit more controversial. Firms should always strive to exceed adequate expectations. After all, this is the basic delineation between satisfaction and dissatisfaction. The tougher question is whether the firm should try to exceed desired expectations. The answer depends on several issues. One is the time and expense involved in delighting customers. If delighting a customer does not translate into stronger customer loyalty or long-term customer retention, then it is not likely to be worth the effort. It may also not be a good investment if delighting one customer lowers performance for other customers. Another issue is whether continually delighting customers raises their expectations over time. To be effective, customer delight should be both surprising and rare, not a daily event. Firms should look for small ways to delight customers without elevating expectations beyond what can reasonably be delivered. Finally, the firm must be aware

of whether competitors can copy the initiatives involved in delighting the customer. If customer delight is easily copied, it ceases to be a key means of differentiation for the firm.

Satisfaction Versus Quality Versus Value

Now that we better understand customer expectations, let's look at how satisfaction differs from quality and value. The answer is not so obvious because the definition of each term closely overlaps the others. Because customer satisfaction is defined relative to customer expectations, it becomes difficult to separate satisfaction from quality and value because customers can hold expectations about quality or value or both. In fact, customers can hold expectations about any part of the product offering, including seemingly minor issues such as parking availability, crowding, or room temperature in addition to major issues like quality and value.

To solve this dilemma, think of each concept not in terms of what it is but in terms of its size. The most narrowly defined concept is quality, which customers judge on an attribute-by-attribute basis. Consider a meal at a restaurant. The quality of that meal stems from specific attributes: the quality of the food, the drink, the atmosphere, and the service are each important. We could even go so far as to judge the quality of the ingredients in the food. In fact, many restaurants, like Ruth's Chris Steakhouse, promote themselves based on the quality of their ingredients. When the customer considers the broader issue of value, he or she begins to include things other than quality: the price of the meal, the time and effort required getting to the restaurant, parking availability, and opportunity costs. In this case, even the best meal in a great restaurant can be viewed as a poor value if the price is too high in terms of monetary or nonmonetary costs.

When a customer considers satisfaction, he or she will typically respond based on his or her expectations of the item in question. If the quality of the food is not what the customer expected, then the customer will be dissatisfied with the food. Similarly, if the value of the meal is not what the customer expected, the customer will be dissatisfied with the value. Note that these are independent judgments. It is entirely possible for a customer to be satisfied with the quality of the meal but dissatisfied with its value. The opposite is also true.

However, most customers do not make independent judgments about satisfaction. Instead, customers think of satisfaction based on the totality of their experience without overtly considering issues like quality or value. We are not saying that customers do not judge quality or value. Rather, we are saying that customers think of satisfaction in more abstract terms than they do quality or value. This happens because customers' expectations—hence their satisfaction—can be based on any number of factors, *even factors that have nothing to do with quality or value.* Continuing with our restaurant example, it is entirely possible for a customer to receive the absolute best quality and value yet still be dissatisfied with the experience. The weather, other customers, a bad date, and a bad mood are just a few examples of nonquality and nonvalue factors that can affect customers' expectations and cloud their judgments of satisfaction.

Customer Satisfaction and Customer Retention

Customer satisfaction is the key to customer retention. Fully satisfied customers are more likely to become loyal customers, even advocates for the firm and its products. Satisfied customers are less likely to explore alternative suppliers, and they are less price sensitive. Therefore, satisfied customers are less likely to switch to competitors. Satisfied customers are also more likely to spread positive the word about the firm and its products. However, the way that customers think about satisfaction creates some interesting challenges for marketers. It is one thing to strive for the best in terms of quality and value, but how can a firm control the uncontrollable factors that affect customer satisfaction? Certainly, marketers cannot control the weather or the fact that their customers are in a bad mood. However, there are several things that marketers can to manage customer satisfaction and leverage it in their marketing efforts:

- **Understand what can go wrong**   Managers, particularly those on the frontline, must understand that an endless number of things can and will go wrong in meeting customers' expectations. Even the best strategies will not work in the face of customers who are in a bad mood. Although some factors are simply uncontrollable, managers should be aware of these factors and be ready to respond if possible.

- **Focus on controllable issues**   The key is to keep an eye on the uncontrollable factors, but focus more on things that can be controlled. Core product quality, customer service, atmosphere, experiences, pricing, convenience, distribution, and promotion must all be managed in an effort to increase share of customer and maintain loyal relationships. It is especially important that the core product be of high quality. Without that, the firm stands little chance of creating customer satisfaction or long-term customer relationships.

- **Manage customer expectations**   As we have seen already, managing customer expectations is more than promising only what you can deliver. To manage expectations well, the marketer must educate customers on how to be satisfied by the firm and its products. These efforts can include in-depth product training, educating customers on how to get the best service from the company, telling customers about product availability and delivery schedules, and giving customers tips and hints for improving quality and service. For example, the U.S. Postal Service routinely reminds customers to mail early during the busy holiday season in November and December. This simple reminder is valuable in managing customers' expectations regarding mail delivery times.

- **Offer satisfaction guarantees**   Companies that care about customer satisfaction back up their offerings by guaranteeing customer satisfaction or product quality. Exhibit 12.8 provides several examples of customer satisfaction guarantees. Guarantees offer a number of benefits. For the firm, a guarantee can serve as a corporate vision, creed, or goal that all employees can strive to meet. A good guarantee is also a viable marketing tool that can be used to differentiate the firm's product offering. For customers, guarantees reduce the risk of buying from the firm and give the customer a point of leverage if they have a complaint.

EXHIBIT 12.8   EXAMPLES OF CUSTOMER SATISFACTION GUARANTEES

Hampton Inn

Our friendly service and complimentary amenities are all backed by our 100% Hampton Guarantee™. If you're not 100% satisfied, we don't expect you to pay. That's our promise and your guarantee. That's 100% Hampton™.

L. L. Bean

Our products are guaranteed to give 100% satisfaction in every way. Return anything purchased from us at any time if it proves otherwise. We do not want you to have anything from L.L. Bean that is not completely satisfactory.

Xerox

At Xerox we are committed to the highest quality in the design, manufacture and service of all we sell. We measure our success by one standard: Total Customer Satisfaction. Our winning of the Malcolm Baldrige National Quality Award testifies to this principle. Taking this commitment one step further, we now offer this exclusive Xerox Total Satisfaction Guarantee:

> If you are not satisfied with the performance of your Xerox equipment, at your request Xerox will repair it or will replace it without charge to you with an identical model or a machine with comparable features and capabilities. The term of the Xerox Total Satisfaction Guarantee is three years from initial equipment delivery. If the newly delivered equipment is financed by Xerox for more than three years, the Guarantee to repair it or replace it will apply during the entire term of your Xerox financing. This Xerox Total Satisfaction Guarantee applies to Xerox equipment acquired by you from Xerox or Xerox resellers/dealers, and continuously maintained by Xerox or its authorized representatives under our manufacturers warranty or a Xerox Service Agreement. This guarantee is subject to all limitations set forth in the warranty and service agreement for this equipment.

Midas

We believe that auto care should be a hassle-free experience. For almost 50 years, we have built trusted customer relationships based on Midas reliability and professional service. And because we know that quality parts and services are important to you, we stand behind them with our guarantees. In fact, we guarantee *all* our work. And, we're known for our lifetime-guaranteed brakes, mufflers and shocks and struts. Our lifetime guarantee is valid for as long as you own your car.

Eddie Bauer

Every item we sell will give you complete satisfaction or you may return it for a full refund.

Publix Supermarkets

We will never knowingly disappoint you. If for any reason your purchase does not give you complete satisfaction, the full purchase price will be cheerfully refunded immediately upon request.

Source: www.hamptoninn.hilton.com, www.llbean.com, www.xerox.com, www.midas.com, www.eddiebauer.com, www.publix.com

- **Make it easy for customers to complain**   Over 90 percent of dissatisfied customers never complain—they just go elsewhere to meet their needs. To counter this customer defection, marketers must make it easy for customers to complain. Whether by mail, phone, e-mail, or in person, firms that care about customer satisfaction will make customer complaints an important part of their ongoing research efforts. However, tracking complaints is not enough. The firm must also be willing to listen and act to rectify customers' problems. Complaining customers are much more likely to buy again if the firm handles their complaints effectively and swiftly.

- **Create relationship programs**   As we discussed earlier in the chapter, firms can use relationship strategies to increase customer loyalty. Today, loyalty or membership programs are everywhere: banks, restaurants, supermarkets, and even bookstores. The idea behind all of these programs is to create financial, social, customization, and/or structural bonds that link customers to the firm.

- **Make customer satisfaction measurement an ongoing priority**   If you don't know what customers want, need, or expect, everything else is a waste of time. A permanent, ongoing program to measure customer satisfaction is one of the most important foundations of CRM.

Customer Satisfaction Measurement

A number of different methods are available for measuring customer satisfaction. The simplest method involves the direct measurement of performance across various factors using simple rating scales. For example, a customer might be asked to rate the quality of housekeeping services in a hotel using a ten-point scale ranging from poor to excellent. Although this method is simple and allows the firm to track satisfaction, it is not diagnostic in the sense that it permits the firm to determine *how* satisfaction varies over time. To do this, the firm can measure both expectations and performance at the same time. Exhibit 12.9 illustrates how this might be done for a hypothetical health club.

The ongoing measurement of customer satisfaction has changed dramatically over the last decade or so. Although most firms track their customer satisfaction ratings over time, firms that are serious about CRM have adopted more robust means of tracking satisfaction based on actual customer behavior. Advances in technology, which allow firms to track the behaviors of individual customers over time, provide the basis for these new metrics. Some of these new metrics include the following:[12]

- **Lifetime Value of a Customer (LTV)**   LTV is the net present value of the revenue stream generated by a specific customer over a period of time. LTV recognizes that some customers are worth more than others. Companies can better leverage their customer satisfaction programs by focusing on valuable customers and giving poor service or charging hefty fees to customers with low LTV profiles to encourage them to leave.

EXHIBIT 12.9	MEASURING EXPECTATIONS AND PERFORMANCE FOR A HYPOTHETICAL HEALTH CLUB		
When it comes to . . .	The Lowest Adequate Level of Service That I Expect Is: Low High	The Highest Desired Level of Service That I Expect Is: Low High	The Actual Performance of this Health Club Is: Low High
The quality and variety of exercise equipment provided	1 2 3 4 5	1 2 3 4 5	1 2 3 4 5
The amount of time that I have to wait for a specific piece of exercise equipment	1 2 3 4 5	1 2 3 4 5	1 2 3 4 5
The quality and variety of exercise classes offered	1 2 3 4 5	1 2 3 4 5	1 2 3 4 5
The availability of specific exercise classes	1 2 3 4 5	1 2 3 4 5	1 2 3 4 5
The availability of such facilities as racquetball or basketball courts, the running track, or the pool	1 2 3 4 5	1 2 3 4 5	1 2 3 4 5
Having a clean, attractive, and inviting facility	1 2 3 4 5	1 2 3 4 5	1 2 3 4 5
Having a comfortable atmosphere (temperature, lighting, music)	1 2 3 4 5	1 2 3 4 5	1 2 3 4 5
The overall helpfulness and friendliness of the staff	1 2 3 4 5	1 2 3 4 5	1 2 3 4 5
Having convenient hours of operation	1 2 3 4 5	1 2 3 4 5	1 2 3 4 5
Having plenty of available parking	1 2 3 4 5	1 2 3 4 5	1 2 3 4 5

- **Average Order Value (AOV)**   AOV is a customer's purchase dollars divided by the number of orders over a period of time. The AOV will increase over time as customer satisfaction increases and customers become more loyal. E-commerce companies often use AOV to pinpoint customers that need extra incentives or reminders to stimulate purchases.

- **Customer Acquisition/Retention Costs**   It is typically less expensive to retain current customers than to acquire new customers. As long as this holds true, a company is better off keeping its current customers satisfied.

- **Customer Conversion Rate**   This is the percentage of visitors or potential customers that actually buy. Low conversion rates are not necessarily a cause for concern if the number of prospects is high.

- **Customer Retention Rate**   This is the percentage of customers who are repeat purchasers. This number should remain stable or increase over time. A declining retention rate is a cause for immediate concern.

- **Customer Attrition Rate**   This is the percentage of customers who do not repurchase (sometimes called the churn rate). This number should remain stable or decline over time. An increasing attrition rate is a cause for immediate concern.

- **Customer Recovery Rate**   This is the percentage of customers who leave the firm (through attrition) who can be lured back using various offers or incentives. Record and movie clubs, such as Columbia House and BMG Music Service, frequently offer special incentives to lure former customers back to their services.

- **Referrals**   These are dollars generated from customers referred to the firm by current customers. A declining referral rate is a cause for concern.

- **Viral Marketing**   This is an electronic form of word-of-mouth communication. The number of Internet newsgroups and chat rooms where customers praise and complain about companies is staggering. Companies can track customer satisfaction by closely monitoring this online commentary.

Firms also have another research method at their disposal: the focus group. Long used as a means of understanding customer requirements during product development, companies use focus groups more often to measure customer satisfaction. Recent research in customer satisfaction measurement indicates that satisfaction is a more holistic concept than previously thought.[13] Focus groups allow firms to more fully explore the subtleties of satisfaction, including its emotional and psychological underpinnings. By better understanding the roots of customer satisfaction, marketers should be better able to develop marketing strategies that can meet customers' needs.

Lessons from Chapter 12

Developing and implementing the marketing program

- must be looked at holistically to avoid getting caught up in the details.

- has one key purpose: to develop and maintain long-term customer relationships.

- is often not enough to guarantee success in today's rapidly changing economy.

The "right" marketing strategy

- is not necessarily about creating a large number of customer transactions in order to maximize market share.

- is one that attracts and retains customers over the long term.

- considers customers' needs, wants, and expectations to ensure customer satisfaction and customer retention.

- develops long-term customer relationships to insulate the firm against competitive inroads and the rapid pace of environmental change.

Customer relationship management (CRM)

- requires that firms look beyond current transactions to examine the long-term potential of a customer.

- is based on creating mutually beneficial relationships where each party provides value to the other party.

- is a business philosophy aimed at defining and increasing customer value in ways that motivate customers to remain loyal to the firm.

- at its core is about retaining the right customers.

- involves a number of stakeholders in addition to customers including employees, supply chain partners, and external stakeholders such as government agencies, nonprofits, and facilitating firms.

- shifts the firm's marketing emphasis from "acquiring customers" to "maintaining clients."

- involves the creation of relationship capital—the ability to build and maintain relationships with customers, suppliers, and partners based on trust, commitment, cooperation, and interdependence.

CRM in consumer markets

- is a long-term process with the goal of moving consumers through a series of stages ranging from simple awareness, through levels of increasing relationship intensity, to the point where consumers become true advocates for the firm and its products.

- attempts to go beyond the creation of satisfied and loyal customers to create true believers and sponsors for the company.

- is usually based on strategies that increase share of customer rather than market share.

- abandons old notions of acquiring new customers and increasing transactions to focus more on fully serving the needs of current customers.

- is based on the precept that all customers have different needs; therefore, not all customers have equal value to the firm.

- involves estimating the worth of individual customers to express their lifetime value (LTV) to the firm. Some customers are simply too expensive to keep given the low level of profits that they generate.

- involves not only strategies to retain top-tier customers but also finding ways to encourage second-tier customers to be even better customers.

- involves the use of four types of relationship strategies: financial incentives, social bonding, enhanced customization, and structural bonding.

CRM in business markets

- also involves moving buyers through a sequence of stages where each stage represents an increasing level of relationship intensity.

- is based more on creating structural bonds with customers or supply-chain partners.

- creates win–win scenarios where both parties build relationship capital; one firm maintains a loyal and committed customer, and the other maintains a loyal and committed supplier.

- is typically more involving, more complex, and much riskier due to the nature of business buying, the presence of long-term contractual obligations, and the sheer dollars involved in many business purchases.

- leads to many changes in the way that companies conduct business, including a change in buyers' and sellers' roles, as well as increases in sole sourcing, global sourcing, team-based buying decisions, and productivity through better integration of operations.

As one of the keys to customer relationship management, quality

- is a relative term that refers to the degree of superiority of a firm's goods or services.

- is a double-edged sword: Good quality can successfully generate first-time transactions, but poor quality guarantees that repeat purchases will not occur.

- is not an automatic guarantee of success—it is a necessary but insufficient condition of customer relationship management.

- is affected by every element in the marketing program. However, the firm's product and branding strategies are of utmost importance.

- depends heavily on the form utility offered by the core product. In service offerings, the core product is typically based on a combination of people, processes, and physical evidence.

- is often taken for granted in the core product because customers expect the core product to be of high quality or at least at a level necessary to meet their needs.

- is critical in supplemental products that add value to the core product. In most cases, these supplemental products, not the core product, are responsible for product differentiation.

- is often found in the symbolic and experiential attributes of a product. Characteristics such as image, prestige, or brand have immense power in differentiating product offerings.

- is hard to maintain with regularity because (1) customers have very high expectations about quality, (2) most products today compete in mature markets, and (3) many businesses compete in markets with very little real differentiation among product offerings.

- is difficult to continuously improve over time. Delivering superior quality involves understanding customers' expectations, translating expectations into quality standards, upholding quality standards, and avoiding the tendency to overpromise.

As one of the keys to customer relationship management, value

- is critical to maintaining long-term customer relationships because it allows for the necessary balance among the five types of utility and the elements of the marketing program.

- is a useful guiding principle of marketing strategy because it takes into account every marketing program element and can be used to consider explicitly customer perceptions of the marketing program in the strategy development process.

- is defined as a customer's subjective evaluation of benefits relative to costs to determine the worth of a firm's product offering relative to other product offerings.

- breaks down into customer benefits (for example, core product quality, supplemental product quality, and experiential quality) and customer costs (monetary and nonmonetary costs).

- can vary across different situations or times, depending on a customer's expectations and needs.

- depends on much more than the selling price of a product. Value perceptions are also affected by transaction costs (taxes, fees, and other charges), life-cycle costs (maintenance, repairs, and consumables), and nonmonetary costs (time, effort, risk, and opportunity costs).

- can be altered by changing one or more parts of the marketing program. If a change lowers overall value, the firm should consider modifying other marketing program elements to offset this decrease.

Customer expectations

- are at the core of customer satisfaction.

- can be described as ideal (essentially perfect performance), normative ("should be" or "ought to be" performance), experience based (based on past experiences), or minimum tolerable (lowest acceptable performance).

- can be examined strategically by considering the zone of tolerance between desired performance expectations and adequate performance expectations. The zone of tolerance represents the degree to which customers recognize and are willing to accept variability in performance.

- as measured against the zone of tolerance can lead to three outcomes:
  - Customer delight: Actual performance exceeds desired expectations.
  - Customer satisfaction: Actual performance falls within the zone of tolerance.
  - Customer dissatisfaction: Actual performance falls below adequate expectations.

- are typically not unrealistic. Customers are looking for the basics of performance—things that the firm is supposed to do or has promised to do.

- can be increased over time if the firm is not mindful of its initiatives aimed at delighting customers on a continuous basis.

Customer satisfaction

- is defined as the degree to which a product meets or exceeds the customer's expectations about that product.

- is typically judged by customers within the context of the total experience, not just with respect to quality and value. Customer satisfaction can also include any number of factors that have nothing to do with quality or value.

- is the key to customer retention. Fully satisfied customers are

    - more likely to become loyal customers, even advocates for the firm.
    - less likely to explore alternative suppliers.
    - less price sensitive.
    - less likely to switch to competitors.
    - more likely to spread good word-of-mouth about the firm and its products.

- creates some interesting challenges for marketers. Some of the steps that marketers can take to manage customer satisfaction include:

    - Understand what can go wrong.
    - Focus on controllable issues.
    - Manage customer expectations.
    - Offer satisfaction guarantees.
    - Make it easy for customers to complain.
    - Create relationship programs.
    - Make customer satisfaction measurement an ongoing priority.

- can be measured using simple rating scales to directly measure performance across various factors in the marketing program.

- can be tracked diagnostically by measuring both expectations and performance at the same time.

- is now tracked using a number of new metrics based on actual customer behavior, including lifetime value of a customer; average order value; customer acquisition/ retention costs; customer conversion, retention, attrition, and recovery rates; referrals; and viral marketing.

Questions for Discussion

1. One of the common uses of customer relationship management (CRM) in consumer markets is to rank customers on profitability or lifetime value measures. Highly profitable customers get special attention, while unprofitable customers

get poor service or are often "fired." What are the ethical and social issues involved in these practices? Could CRM be misused? How and why?

2. Given the commoditized nature of many markets today, does CRM—and its associated focus on quality, value, and satisfaction—make sense? If price is the only true means of differentiation in a commoditized market, why should a firm care about quality? Explain.

3. Of the two types of customer expectations, adequate performance expectations fluctuate the most. Describe situations that might cause adequate expectations to increase, thereby narrowing the width of the zone of tolerance. What might a firm do in these situations to achieve its satisfaction targets?

Exercises

1. Visit *1-to-1 Magazine* at http://www.1to1media.com to learn more about customer relationship management. You can register for free access to useful tools, articles, and discussions of CRM and its use in a number of different industries.

2. Think about all of the organizations with which you maintain an ongoing relationship (banks, doctors, schools, accountants, mechanics, and so on). Would you consider yourself to be unprofitable for any of these organizations? Why? How might each of these organizations fire you as a customer? What would you do if they did?

3. J.D. Power and Associates is a well-known research company specializing in the measurement of product quality and customer satisfaction. Explore its website at http://www.jdpower.com to look at their customer satisfaction ratings for a number of industries. What role will third-party firms like J.D. Power play in the future, given the increasing use of internal customer satisfaction metrics?

Napster
The Cat Fights On

The History of Napster

S hawn Fanning—a 17-year-old Northeastern University freshman who left college to develop a technology to trade music over the Internet—launched Napster on June 1, 1999. Napster allowed computer users to share high-quality digital copies (MP3s) of music recordings via the Internet using its proprietary MusicShare software. Napster didn't actually store the recordings on its own computers but instead provided an index of all the songs available on the computers of members who were logged onto the service. Napster functioned as a sort of clearinghouse where members could search by artist or song title and identify MP3s of interest so that they could be downloaded from another member's hard drive. Napster became one of the most popular sites on the Internet, claiming some 15 million users in little more than a year. Indeed, so many college students were downloading songs from Napster that many universities were forced to block the site from their systems in order to regain bandwidth.

From the beginning, Napster's service was as controversial as it was popular. Barely a year after its launch, Napster was sued by the Recording Industry Association of America (RIAA), which represents major recording companies such as Universal Music, BMG, Sony Music, Warner Music Group, and EMI. The RIAA claimed that Napster's service violated copyright laws by allowing users to swap music recordings for free. The RIAA also sought an injunction to stop the downloading of copyrighted songs, as well as damages for lost revenue. The RIAA argued that song swapping via Napster and similar firms had cost the music industry more than $300 million in lost sales. A few months after the RIAA lawsuit was filed, Metallica, a heavy metal band, and rap star Dr. Dre filed separate lawsuits accusing Napster of copyright infringement and racketeering. Lars Ulrich, Metallica's drummer, told a Senate committee that Napster users are basically stealing from the band every time they download one of its songs.

On July 26, 2000, U.S. District Judge Marilyn Patel granted the RIAA's request for an injunction and ordered Napster to stop making copyrighted recordings available

Michael D. Hartline, Florida State University, prepared this case for classroom discussion rather than to illustrate effective or ineffective handling of an administrative, legal, or ethical situation. Research support for the marketing plan that appears in this case was provided by Brian Cooper, Treva Gorman, Margaret Jarvis, Matt Lake, Matt Long, Danny O'Connor, Rebecca Payne, Kaleem Sultan, and Viktoria Szilagyi (Florida State University MBA Class of 2005 and 2007). The marketing plan portion of this case is intended for classroom discussion rather than to illustrate effective or ineffective marketing planning.

for download, which would have effectively shut down the service by pulling the plug on its most popular feature. However, on July 28, 2000, just nine hours before Napster would have shut down, the Ninth Circuit Court of Appeals stayed that order, granting Napster a last-minute reprieve until the lawsuits could be tried in court.

In its battle with the RIAA, Napster turned to three past rulings on copyright infringement to support its defense: Sony Betamax, the 1992 Audio Home Recording Act, and the 1998 Digital Millennium Copyright Act. In the Sony Betamax case, the Motion Picture Association of America (MPAA) filed suit against Sony out of fears that its new video recording technology would unlock the door for widespread film production. Although a lower court found Sony guilty of copyright infringement, the U.S. Supreme Court overturned the decision, stating that a new technology must be "merely capable of substantial non-infringing uses in order to be protected by law." Because Napster's MP3 technology had legitimate uses, Napster argued that it should have the same protections as Sony.

Napster also sought to apply the 1992 Audio Home Recording Act (AHRA), which permits people to copy music for personal use. The law, enacted in response to the development of digital audiotape recorders, was passed before the Internet revolution. Napster supporters contended that the law applies to music downloads because the music being copied is for personal use, not redistribution for profit. Many others, however, including the U.S. Department of Justice, disagreed because this act was based on digital audiotapes, not web-distributed music files. The 1998 Digital Millennium Copyright Act (DMCA) granted immunity to Internet service providers for the actions of their customers. Napster attorneys argued that the company had broad protection from copyright claims because it functions like a search engine rather than having direct involvement with music swapping. However, according to the legal community, "Napster does not take the legal steps required of search engines in dealing with copyright violations."

Despite its claims, Napster was found guilty of direct infringement of the RIAA's musical recordings, and the ruling was upheld on appeal on February 12, 2001. The District Court of Appeals refuted all of Napster's defense tactics and ordered the company to stop allowing its millions of users to download and share copyrighted material without properly compensating the owners of the material. The court determined the Audio Home Recording Act was irrelevant because it did not address the downloading of MP3 files or digital audio recording devices. The court also rejected Napster's reliance on the Digital Millennium Copyright Act, stating simply that it does not include contributory infringers.

In response to the ruling, Hank Barry, CEO of Napster and Shawn Fanning, Napster's founder, released statements to the public. They claimed that they remained committed to finding an industry-supported solution to the controversy, such as a membership-based service. They also acknowledged negotiations with Bertelsmann AG to expand and improve Napster with the goal of prohibiting pirated music transfers and counting the number of song downloads in order to properly reimburse their artists.

A few days later, Napster offered $1 billion to the recording industry to settle the lawsuit. Under the proposal, $150 million would be paid annually for the first five years to Sony, Warner, BMG, EMI, and Universal, with $50 million allotted annually for independent labels. However, record industry executives refused to accept Napster's proposal, saying they were not willing to settle for anything less than shutting down Napster. The service was not shut down at that point, however, because doing so could have violated the rights of artists who had given Napster permission to trade their music. But, the company was required to block all songs on a list of 5,000 provided by the RIAA.

In late September 2001, Napster agreed to pay $26 million for past distribution of unauthorized music and made a proposal that would let songwriters and musicians distribute their music on Napster for a fee. This agreement would have covered as many as 700,000 songs, but Napster still needed an agreement before the company could legally distribute the music.

However, with failed attempts to reach a suitable compromise with the recording industry and litigation expenses mounting, the company filed for Chapter 11 reorganization in June 2002 as a last grasp effort to try and reach a deal with Bertelsmann AG, Napster's strategic partner.

The final "nail in the coffin" for Napster came on September 3, 2002, when a Delaware bankruptcy judge blocked the sale of the company to Bertelsmann, ruling that negotiations with the German media company had not been made at arm's length and in good faith. Bertelsmann had agreed to pay creditors $8 million for Napster's assets. According to the bankruptcy petition, the company had assets of $7.9 million and debts of $101 million as of April 30, 2002. Shortly after the judge's ruling, Napster laid off nearly its entire staff of 42 people and proceeded to convert its Chapter 11 reorganization into a Chapter 7 liquidation. At the time, this seemed like the ultimate end of Napster as most thought the company was closing its doors forever.

The Emergence of the Online Music Market

Napster's problems were not so much about Napster as they were about the inability of the recording industry to adapt to changing technology and shifting consumer preferences. Each of the major music labels had been dabbling in online distribution, but Napster had beaten them all to the punch and had done it with striking efficiency. Research conducted on the effects of online music distribution had revealed some interesting findings:

- A study by Jupiter Research concluded that people who downloaded music from the Internet were 15 percent more likely to buy music through regular channels.

- Another survey by the Digital Media Association and Yankelovich Partners showed that of the respondents who had downloaded music from an online source, 66 percent said listening to a song online had prompted them to later buy a CD featuring that song.

- A survey by the Wharton School of Business concluded that 70 percent of Napster members reported using the service to sample music before buying it.

- Many music-store owners actually saw an increase in sales during the Napster controversy. As one owner stated, "Our sales are up 19% over last year because of all the publicity . . . you can't open a newspaper or magazine and not see a Napster headline. We've never got so much free advertising. Music is exciting again."

- Some studies indicated that college students were not the thieves that everyone thought—a full 27 percent had never used Napster or similar services.

- Contrary to popular belief, college students were not the only fans of online music sites. In fact, Media Metrix found that adults over 50 years old comprised 17% of the visitors to music sites—a number that had increased 92 percent in one year.

On both sides of the controversy, it was clear that online music distribution was here to stay. It was only a matter of time until a compromise could be reached among the recording studios, the artists, and Napster-like music providers. Some thorny issues remained, however. First, even pay-for-download services are not immune to piracy. As a result, the recording industry wanted to develop technology that would prevent downloaders from swapping files on their own even after making a legitimate purchase. To protect the artists, the industry also wanted to limit the number of times that a song could be downloaded and copied. Suggestions included using the MD5 hash—a digital fingerprint—or software that monitors sound patterns to detect illegal copies. A second issue was the development of a revenue model. Should MP3 files be available individually, as one file in a complete album, or both? Should pricing be based on a per-download basis or on an unlimited basis for a monthly subscription fee?

In late 2002, Roxio, a company that was widely known for its CD-burning software, purchased Napster's name and assets. Shortly after, Roxio announced its intentions to relaunch Napster as a fee-based service in late 2003. In the meantime, other content providers were rapidly getting their houses in order. One of the first was AOL, who in February 2003 launched MusicNet offering twenty music streams and twenty downloads for $3.95 per month. By far the most newsworthy foray into online music was Apple's launch of iTunes in April 2003:

> *Apple today announced the launch of its iTunes Music Store, a new online store that lets customers quickly find, purchase and download the music they want for 99 cents per song, without subscription fees. The iTunes Music Store, which is integrated with iTunes 4 (also released today), offers "groundbreaking" personal use rights, including burning songs onto an unlimited number of CDs for personal use, listening to songs on an unlimited number of iPods, playing songs on up to three Macs, and using songs in any application on the Mac, including iPhoto, iMovie and iDVD. The iTunes Music Store features over 200,000 songs from music companies including BMG, EMI, Sony Music Entertainment, Universal and Warner.*

Apple's launch of iTunes hailed the beginning of the online music frenzy that followed. The following music services launched in mid- to late 2003:

- Rhapsody (www.listen.com), a division of Real Networks, whose RealPlayer is ubiquitous on millions of PCs. Rhapsody now offers over one million songs for download.

- MusicMatch (www.musicmatch.com), which was later acquired by Yahoo!, now offers over 900,000 songs for download.

- BuyMusic.com (www.buymusic.com), a subsidiary of Buy.com, now offers over one million songs, some as low as 79¢ per download.

- Apple's release of iTunes for Windows. Since 2003, the iTunes Music Store has been upgraded several times and now offers over three million songs, as well as videos and podcasts for download.

The Launch of Napster 2.0

After much fanfare and excitement, Roxio revived Napster as Napster 2.0 on October 29, 2003. Later in 2004, Roxio sold its consumer software division and changed its corporate name to Napster. This cemented a single identity for the company, allowing it to focus on the task of gaining users in the face of daunting competition. Since its relaunch, Napster has successfully navigated the pay-for-play market though it pales in comparison to the success of Apple's iTunes and its extremely popular iPod. Although estimates are sketchy, Apple holds roughly 70 to 80 percent of the online music market. Second-place Rhapsody controls 10 to 15 percent of the market, and Napster is third with roughly 5 to 10 percent. The remaining portion of the market is divided among several different companies.

Napster's strategy has been focused more on a subscription-based revenue model rather than the download-to-own model favored by Apple. The company's Napster-to-Go service—its primary offering—allows users to download as much music as they want from Napster's library of over two million songs for a flat $14.95 per month fee. Napster also offers Free Napster, which allows any computer user to listen to all two million songs up to three times each before they are required to buy the song for 99¢ or subscribe to Napster to Go. Urge.com (a joint effort between MTV and Microsoft), Rhapsody, and Yahoo! Music offer similar services. Napster has also worked hard to establish corporate partnerships with BellSouth, Ericsson, and XM Satellite Radio as a way to enter untapped markets.

In October 2006, Napster launched Napster Japan in partnership with Tower Records Japan. The service features 1.9 million songs, 10 percent of which are comprised of music by Japanese artists. The service launched 14 months after Apple scored a resounding success with its launch of iTunes Japan. However, Napster has also partnered with NTT DoCoMo, Japan's largest and most popular mobile phone company, to create handsets that can download and play songs from Napster. This partnership is significant because a full 90 percent of music downloads in Japan occur through wireless phones. Napster hopes that its "all-you-can-eat" subscription model and its partnership with NTT DoCoMo will push it past Apple in Japan.

Napster has also sent signals that it is interested in being acquired by another firm. The first signs of this began in mid-2006 when Napster started partnership conversations with Google. More recently, Napster has hired UBS Investment Bank to help it with a possible sale. Companies rumored to be interested in acquiring Napster include Creative (makers of a line of popular MP3 players), Amazon.com, Samsung, and Motorola.

A Shift in Music Distribution

Since the launch of Napster 2.0, the growth in the online music market has been remarkable and is expected to explode over the next several years. Revenue from downloaded music topped revenue from physical media (for example, CDs) for the first time in 2007. Worldwide, online music sales are expected to grow from $1.5 billion to roughly $11 billion by 2010 (Case Exhibit 1.1). A full 20 percent of all Americans own at least one portable music player. Among teens, however, ownership tops 54 percent.

Despite the phenomenal potential of the online music market, two major statistics are troubling for Napster. First, half of all music downloaders use CDs (from their own collections or from a friend) as the primary source of content for their MP3 players. These users simply move their current music collection onto a portable player rather than acquire a new collection from online sources (Case Exhibit 1.2). Further, only 25 percent fill their portable players with songs downloaded over the Internet. Even more alarming for Napster: A full 67 percent of portable-player owners prefer to download music on a per-song basis rather than use a subscription-based service.

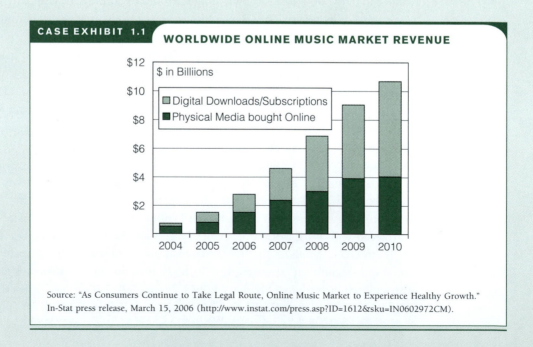

CASE EXHIBIT 1.1   WORLDWIDE ONLINE MUSIC MARKET REVENUE

$ in Billiions

■ Digital Downloads/Subscriptions
■ Physical Media bought Online

Source: "As Consumers Continue to Take Legal Route, Online Music Market to Experience Healthy Growth." In-Stat press release, March 15, 2006 (http://www.instat.com/press.asp?ID=1612&sku=IN0602972CM).

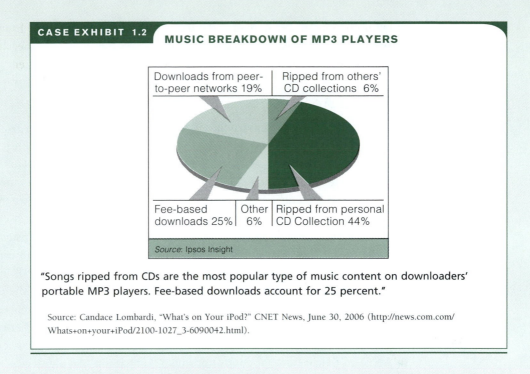

CASE EXHIBIT 1.2 **MUSIC BREAKDOWN OF MP3 PLAYERS**

Downloads from peer-to-peer networks 19%

Ripped from others' CD collections 6%

Fee-based downloads 25%

Other 6%

Ripped from personal CD Collection 44%

Source: Ipsos Insight

"Songs ripped from CDs are the most popular type of music content on downloaders' portable MP3 players. Fee-based downloads account for 25 percent."

Source: Candace Lombardi, "What's on Your iPod?" CNET News, June 30, 2006 (http://news.com.com/ Whats+on+your+iPod/2100-1027_3-6090042.html).

A sizable number still acquire music via illegal peer-to-peer networks—the very sector pioneered by Napster.

Your Challenge

Although no one knows what the future will hold for Napster or other online music providers, the ability to purchase music free of physical media is here to stay. Your task is to develop a marketing plan for Napster that leverages its advantages in an effort to increase users and revenue within the online music industry. To assist you in this effort, the first half of a potential marketing plan for Napster is provided in the following sections. Your assignment is to update the Napster case, add to and refine the marketing plan sections that exist here, and develop the remaining portions of the marketing plan. You will have to develop goals and objectives for Napster, develop a marketing strategy, and discuss how your strategy will be implemented, evaluated, and controlled. This marketing plan follows the marketing planning worksheets in Appendix A. Use these worksheets to complete the remaining portions of the marketing plan.

Marketing Plan for Napster

Executive Summary

This marketing plan is designed to expand Napster's customer base and revenue stream and make Napster the market leader in the online music industry. This plan discusses the goals and objectives that can be implemented to reach our ultimate goal of being the best in the industry. We have developed a marketing strategy that will increase Napster's value to consumers. Napster has the potential to become the best and most popular online music provider in the industry.

Situation Analysis

Analysis of the Internal Environment   Our goal is to bring Napster back to where it once was in the online music industry. Napster should be the destination of choice for music lovers to purchase all types of music at a competitive price. This goal is consistent with Napster's mission to provide "great music experiences more accessible to all music fans." Our current objectives focus on broadening our reach among current and potential customers, primarily focusing on increasing subscriptions to Napster to Go. Through Napster.com and other tie-ins including Napster on Campus, we strive to increase awareness of all that Napster can offer to the music lover.

Currently, Napster is third in the industry with respect to overall market share. Though we compete with Apple, its iTunes Store focuses solely on the download-to-own sector of the industry. Though we offer downloads, Napster focuses on the subscription-based model. Our service is compatible with a number of popular MP3 players and other portable music devices. However, we are somewhat at a disadvantage to Apple in that we do not control our own companion playing device.

Analysis of the Customer Environment   With so many ways to access the Internet, it is difficult to define our customer base. Further, because music spans so many generations, pinpointing the demographics and lifestyles of our customers is a challenging task. However, the typical music downloader does possess certain defining demographic characteristics, as shown in Case Exhibit 1.3. Our service can be accessed anywhere in the world, any time of day. Given the worldwide interest in music, our customers come from all walks of life. Without parameters such as mandatory membership length, anyone with access to the Internet is a possible customer.

Napster also has the potential to convert illegal peer-to-peer users into paying customers. Recent research indicates that the use of peer-to-peer networks is declining: Roughly 41 percent of music downloaders admit to pulling music from peer-to-peer networks; down from 58 percent two years ago.

Our customers choose Napster because of convenience and a wide selection of music titles. Many customers choose Napster because they do not like Apple and its insistence on tying its music library to the iPod. We allow customers to choose from a wide selection of seventy-five different MP3 players and smart phones. However, there are several reasons that potential customers do not purchase our services. One reason is competition. Many music downloaders still prefer peer-to-peer networks rather than pay-for-play services. Others love the style and chic of the iPod, so they are loyal users of the iTunes Store. A second reason is the lack of a broadband Internet connection. Broadband is now available in over 50 percent of U.S. households. However, music lovers who are stuck with their dial-up accounts are hesitant to use our services due to the time involved in downloading music. These users are more likely to fill their portable players with music from their own CD collection. A third reason is cost.

CASE EXHIBIT 1.3

DEMOGRAPHIC CHARACTERISTICS OF MUSIC DOWNLOADERS

	March 2003 (%)	March 2005 (%)
All Adults	29	22
Men	32	25
Women	26	19
Age Cohorts		
18–29	52	40
30–49	27	18
50+	12	13

The percentage of each group of Internet users who download music:

Source: Pew Internet and American Life Project Surveys, March 2003 and March 2005. Margin of error is ±3%.

Although our price of $14.95 for Napster to Go is competitive, it is more expensive than Yahoo! Music Unlimited. However, their $11.99 per month fee only gets users access to a library of one million songs. Napster's music library is twice as large.

Analysis of the External Environment

Competition   Our major competitors in the pay-for-play market include iTunes, Urge, Yahoo! Music Unlimited, AOL's Music Now, and Rhapsody (Case Exhibit 1.4). These services are all brand competitors because they offer the same basic service offered by Napster. Our product competitors consist of the many peer-to-peer file-sharing services, such as Limewire and BitTorrent, which offer free downloads of pirated music. Other competitors include the thousands of offline and online music record stores that offer CDs and other merchandise. However, given the movement in the industry toward online downloading of music, these competitors may soon become less worrisome.

We consider our biggest competitors to be iTunes and Urge. The iTunes library of three million songs is easily the largest in the industry. Plus, the popularity of the iPod gives Apple a distinct advantage. The iTunes software application is easy to use, works for both Macintosh and Windows operating systems, and boasts fewer

CASE EXHIBIT 1.4

MAJOR COMPETITORS IN THE ONLINE MUSIC MARKET

Music Service	Monthly Cost for PC Access Only ($)	Monthly Cost for "To Go" Service ($)	Price per Song Download ($)	Price per Album ($)	Songs Available ($)
Napster	9.95	14.95	0.99	9.95	2 million
iTunes	—	—	0.99	9.99	3 million
Urge	9.95	14.95	0.99	9.99	2 million
AOL Music Now	9.95	14.95	0.99	10.00	2 million
Rhapsody	9.99	14.95	0.89	9.00	2 million
Yahoo! Music Unlimited	6.99	11.99	0.79	9.99	1 million

restrictions than other competitors. The services offered by Urge are very similar to our own. We consider Urge to be a major competitor because MTV and Microsoft back it. MTV adds a unique brand identity, while Microsoft adds the ability to create the ultimate software and hardware integration with the Urge service.

Economic Growth and Stability   The United States is considered to have the largest music market in the world. According to statistical measures, 40 percent of all annual global sales and almost 33 percent of all unit sales are made in the United States. Per-capita spending on music in the United States averages roughly $50 per year. According to the RIAA, more than $10.5 billion in CDs were sold in the United States in 2005, an 8.1 percent decline. However, during the same time period, U.S. sales of downloaded music singles topped $363 million, an increase of 163 percent. U.S. sales of downloaded albums exceeded $135 million, an increase of 199 percent. Worldwide, sales of downloaded music totaled $790 million, an increase of more than 350 percent.

Though online sales pale in comparison to CD sales, all the growth is in online music. The RIAA predicts that traditional U.S music sales (mostly CDs) will continue to fall five to eight percent per year. The main reason for the decline is the low value added by traditional physical media. Although consumers value CDs because they provide "long-term" entertainment, when asked by a survey conducted by the RIAA, many stated that CDs cost too much. According to the RIAA's research, a significant number of consumers do not fully understand the variables that play a role in the overall pricing of a CD. Consumers counter that they resent paying $13 to $18 for a CD to get only one or two popular songs. This is precisely why downloading music appeals to so many.

Political, Legal, and Regulatory Issues   The RIAA is an organization that represents the U.S. recording industry. The mission of the trade group is to facilitate a business and legal environment that ensures and encourages its members' creativity and sound financial existence. Its members include well-known national record companies. The responsibilities of the RIAA members include the creation, manufacturing, and distribution of approximately 90 percent of all recordings made and marketed in the United States.

The RIAA is also in charge of protecting intellectual-property rights worldwide, ensuring the First Amendment Rights of performers, engaging in consumer and technical research, and overseeing and enforcing state as well as federal rules and regulations regarding music industry policies. The RIAA also certifies several sales awards, such as the Gold®, Platinum®, Multi-Platinum®, Diamond® and Los Premios De Oro y Platino™.

In addition to regulation by the RIAA, the music industry is affected by a number of laws and regulations, including the following:

- **U.S. Copyright Law**   The U.S. Copyright Law protects owners of copyright from the illegal reproduction, adaptation, performance, display, and/or distribution of copyrighted material. Depending on the nature of the offense, whether it is criminal or civil, penalties may differ.

- **The Federal Anti-Bootleg Statute**   This statute was established to disallow illegal recording, manufacturing, distribution, or trafficking in audio or visual recordings of artists' performances. Offenders may be penalized for fines up to $250,000 and up to five years in prison.

- **Fair Use Doctrine** The Fair Use Doctrine is a federal law that controls the use of copyrighted material. The "fair use" of a copyrighted work includes instances when it is used as a comment, teaching material, or criticism.

- **The Sonny Bono Copyright Term Extension Act** The Sonny Bono Copyright Term Extension Act extended the U.S. copyright term from the artist's life and 50 years, to the artist's life and 70 years. This act was enacted to protect U.S. artists' work abroad.

- **The Audio Home Recording Act of 1992 (AHRA)** The AHRA was enacted to protect consumers against lawsuits for copyright infringement. According to this act, it is legal to record music for personal use/entertainment. Commercial use of copied material is prohibited under this act. This act also facilitates easier access to advanced digital audio-recording technologies and ensures royalties for artists and music related organizations. Recording devices, such as CD and cassette players, are covered under the AHRA with the conditions that the manufacturer of the covered device registers with the Copyright Office, pays a royalty on each device sold, and adds the serial copyright management technology to each device.

- **The Digital Performance Right in Sound Recordings Act of 1995 (DPRA)** DPRA was the first to protect public performance rights in sound recordings. Sound-recording copyright holders have the discretion "to perform the copyrighted work publicly by means of a digital audio transmission." This enables the record companies who hold the sound-recording rights to collect a royalty on digital "performances" of the sound recording.

- **The Digital Millennium Copyright Act (DMCA)** The DMCA was established as a result of the 1996 World Intellectual Property Organization's Diplomatic conference in Geneva. The act was passed in 1998 to strengthen copyright protections. The DMCA prohibits the manufacturing and distribution of devices that are used to "challenge" technology used to protect copyrighted materials. The DMCA also streamlined the activities and responsibilities of Internet service providers attempting to decrease the number of online copyright cases.

- **No Electronic Theft Law (NET Act)** The NET Act was enacted in December 1997 as an effort to lessen computer-based piracy by implementing criminal penalties for copyright infringement. Copyright violations may result in criminal prosecution even though there may not be a profit gain from the illegal activity. Fines can be as high as $250,000 along with up to three years in prison. The NET Act also altered the definition of "commercial advantage or private financial gain" by adding the need of a receipt of any copyrighted material.

- **Piracy Deterrence and Education Act of 2003** The Piracy Deterrence and Education Act of 2003 was enacted in order for the Federal Bureau of Investigation

(FBI) to develop methods to deter copyright violation and for the Department of Justice to obtain authority to educate the public about copyright violations and its consequences.

- **Author, Consumer, and Computer Owner Protection and Security Act** This act proposed $15 million to the Department of Justice to enhance the enforcement of copyright laws both domestically and internationally. The act also covers copyright violation penalties of up to five years in prison.

Technological Advancements In 1999 Shawn Fanning combined three key functions to create new technology. He combined a search engine, which was dedicated to finding MP3 files; file-sharing technology, which gave users the ability to trade without a centralized server; and Internet Relay Chat, which created a peer-to-peer file-sharing network. This technological advancement revolutionized the way that consumers listened to music. Consumers no longer needed to go to a music store to purchase a CD, a record, or a cassette tape to listen to their favorite songs. Consumers could opt to download just the song they liked instead of being forced to purchase the entire CD. The fact that a consumer could download a song and play it immediately added to the attractiveness of the original Napster service.

Despite the obvious threat to the music industry represented in this technology, the ability to download music online also creates a number of benefits for traditional record companies. First, companies no longer have to manufacturer as many CDs to sell in music stores. Second, distribution costs are lowered tremendously because distribution through a physical store is no longer needed. Third, music download sites can use tracking technology to better understand their customers' music preferences. These data, combined with demographic information, can be valuable in promoting artists and record sales.

Though technological trends are often difficult to predict, the next "big thing" in digital music distribution is likely to be wireless or satellite technology. Makers of wireless devices are working on technology that will allow music to be downloaded to smart phones, PDAs, and other handheld devices. In fact, Microsoft has launched an "iPod Killer" called Zune that will allow users to purchase music via integrated wireless access. This will probably be the next step in the evolution of portable music devices because it will allow users to purchase music without the need to be tethered to a computer. In the future, music will likely be available on demand via wireless players and satellite-based systems for both home and car.

Sociocultural Trends Customers flock to online music services due to their ease of use and convenience. Customers value our services because they purchase only the songs that they want instead of wasting money on an entire CD. Our service provides customers with a convenient way to purchase the music they love. In today's culture, people spend less time in front of the television and more time in front of a computer. Our service is poised to take advantage of this trend and the growing opportunity in online music.

Of course, our business must be operated with ethical and social responsibilities in mind. Today's parents are concerned with what their children do on the Internet.

There is a growing concern for more parental controls on children's Internet browsing capabilities. In addition to these concerns, the late 1980s and early 1990s brought about parental advisory warnings for CDs. It is our responsibility to include these controls in our software to prevent children from coming into contact with explicit songs that are not age appropriate.

SWOT Analysis

Case Exhibit 1.5 summarizes the SWOT (strengths, weaknesses, opportunities, and threats) analysis for Napster. Each point is briefly discussed in the following sections.

Napster's Strengths

- **Strong Brand Name and Reputation**   Napster pioneered the concept of downloading and sharing music over the Internet. Napster's parent company, Roxio, officially changed its name to Napster to capitalize on this strong reputation. As an industry leader, Napster is one of the first names associated with digital music.

- **Large Music Library**   Napster's agreements with all major recording labels gives them access to a very large library of digital music.

- **Partnerships with Other Industry Leaders**   Napster's partnership with Samsung (one of the world's most innovative companies) has led to the creation of several innovative MP3 players carrying the Napster brand. Napster also has a partnership with XM radio that takes advantage of the growing satellite-radio market. Napster also maintains partnerships with Best Buy and several leading universities throughout the United States. Napster's partnership with Tower Records Japan and NTT DoCoMo gives it a significant advantage in the Japanese music market.

- **Convenient and Easy to Use**   Napster offers its entire music library via an innovative format that does not require downloading any bulky software packages.

CASE EXHIBIT 1.5   **THE SWOT MATRIX**

Strengths	Opportunities
• Strong brand name and reputation	• Young and rapidly growing market
• Large music library	• Decline in illegal file sharing
• Partnerships with other industry leaders	• Emerging technologies
• Convenient and easy to use	

Weaknesses	Threats
• Limited avenues for differentiation	• Powerful competition
• Lack of compatibility	• Potential for disintermediation
• Pricing structure	• Emerging technologies

Napster allows consumers to listen to music directly through its website for free by registering an email address.

Napster's Weaknesses

- **Limited Avenues for Differentiation**   Increasing our customer base is difficult because our service is essentially the same as other competitors. We offer a large, but not the largest, online music library. Our services are competitively priced but are not the least expensive in the industry. Therefore, standing out in such a highly competitive market is difficult.

- **Lack of Compatibility**   Napster is not compatible with all MP3 players, especially the market-leading iPod. Potential customers who already own an incompatible player will not be inclined to purchase our services.

- **Pricing Structure**   Because Napster pioneered free file sharing, many customers are not interested in a pay-for-play service. For these users, a number of free peer-to-peer suppliers are still in existence. Further, other competitors—like iTunes, Urge, and Yahoo!—are backed by powerful firms with very efficient cost structures. Consequently, Napster has a limited ability to cut prices should a price war ensue.

Napster's Opportunities

- **Young and Rapidly Growing Market**   Music lovers obviously have a preference for downloading music from the Internet. The explosive growth in the digital music market attests to this fact. Our service will give these customers a vehicle for fulfilling their needs and preferences.

- **Decline in Illegal File Sharing**   The declining use of peer-to-peer networks, along with the continued efforts of the RIAA, indicates that customers need a source whereby music can be obtained legally. Users of peer-to-peer networks are becoming more concerned about the legality of downloading music for free. Consequently, these individuals are potential customers for our service.

- **Emerging Technologies**   A number of emerging and improving technologies will allow music lovers to access music more conveniently in the future. Wireless and satellite technologies hold the most promise in the short term. The continued integration of handheld devices like phones, PDAs, and MP3 players will continue unabated in the future.

Napster's Threats

- **Powerful Competition**   In addition to the continuing popularity of peer-to-peer networks, Napster faces very stiff competition from very powerful firms. The sheer dominance of Apple's iTunes and iPod prevents Napster from making significant gains in the industry. Also, other large firms (for example, Wal-Mart, Google, and Amazon) are making progress toward their online music services. Finally, a large number of music lovers consider themselves to be audiophiles who prefer the highest-quality recordings possible. These consumers will always prefer CDs until technology evolves to a point where online music no longer has to be compressed to facilitate online distribution.

- **Potential for Disintermediation** One reason for the early rift between Napster and recording labels was that Napster beat them to the online market. The major record labels still depend on intermediaries such as Napster and iTunes to electronically distribute their music. As these firms wean their revenues off of the traditional CD-based business model, they have the potential to electronically distribute their own music. When this happens, Napster and other music services will lose out because they do not control the content that customers seek.

- **Emerging Technologies** As new technology allows customers to access music via their phones or other wireless/satellite-based devices, these customers will no longer be tied to a computer or even the Internet. Wireless phone providers, such as Verizon and Cingular, already allow their customers to purchase music over their networks. As these trends continue, the potential exists for Napster to be marginalized as a means for obtaining digital music.

Sources

The facts of this case are from the Napster website (http://www.napster.com); Apple website (http://www.apple.com/pr/library/2003/apr/28musicstore.html); "As Consumers Continue to Take Legal Route, Online Music Market to Experience Healthy Growth." In-Stat press release, March 15, 2006 (http://www.instat.com/press.asp?ID=1612&sku=IN0602972CM); "The Legitimate Digital Music Market Takes Off," IFPI press release, April 4, 2006 (http://www.ifpi.org/site-content/PRESS/20060404g.html); Recording Industry Association of America, *2005 Year-End Statistics,* RIAA website (http://www.riaa.com/news/newsletter/pdf/2005yrEndStats.pdf); Hans Greimel, "Napster Launches Japanese Service," *BusinessWeek Online,* October 3, 2006 (http://www.businessweek.com/ap/financialnews/D8KH0UH80.htm); Arik Hesseldahl, "A Needy Napster Searches for Takers," *BusinessWeek Online,* September 19, 2006 (http://www.businessweek.com/technology/content/sep2006/tc20060919_053475.htm); Candace Lombardi, "What's On Your iPod?" CNET News, June 30, 2006 (http://news.com.com/Whats+on+your+ iPod/2100-1027_3-6090042.html); Tony Smith, "Microsoft Confirms Zune Software, Hardware Family," *The Register Online,* July 24, 2006 (http://www.reghardware.co.uk/2006/07/24/ms_confirms_zune/); Eric Bangeman, "Legal Music Downloads Soar as CD Sales Fall," arstechnica.com, October 3, 2005 (http://arstechnica.com/news.ars/post/20051003-5381.html); John Borland, "Newsmaker: Betting It All on Napster," CNET News, September 1, 2004 (http://news.com.com/Betting+it+all+on+Napster/2008-1027_3-5331890.html); "Napster, but in Name Only," *Associated Press,* July 28, 2003 (http://www.wired.com/news/digiwood/0,1412,59798,00.html); "U.S. Electronic Media and Entertainment," Infoshop.com (http://www.theinfoshop.com/study/fi13558_electronic_media.html); Michael Pastore, "The Online Music Debate Rambles On," Cyberatlas (http://cyberatlas.internet.com/markets/retailing/article/0,6061_

420571,00.html); Stephen Hinkle, "RIAA, Surrender Now!" Dmusic.com (http://news.dmusic.com/print/5026); "GartnerG2 Says 'Big 5' Record Labels Must Standardize Digital Music Delivery to Profit from the Market Opportunity," Gartner Group (http://gartner.com/5_about/press_releases/2001/pr20010829c.html); Martin Peers, "Survey Studies Napster's Spread on Campuses," *Wall Street Journal,* May 5, 2000, B8; Anna Wilde Mathews, "Web Music Isn't Just for Kids," *Wall Street Journal,* September 26, 2000, B1; "Stats Speak Kindly of Napster," *The Standard Online,* July 21, 2000 (http://www.thestandard.com); "Napster: Downloading Music for Free Is Legal," CNET News, July 3, 2000 (http://news.cnet.com/news); Martin Peers and Lee Gomes, "Music CD Sales Suffer in Stores Near 'Wired' Colleges, Study Says," *Wall Street Journal,* June 13, 2000, A4; Amy Doan, "MP3.com Loses Big in Copyright Case," *Forbes Online,* September 7, 2000 (http://www.forbes.com); Lee Gomes, "Napster Ruling May Be Just the Overture," *Wall Street Journal,* July 28, 2000; Anna Wilde Mathews, "Sampling Free Music over the Internet Often Leads to Sale," *Wall Street Journal,* June 15, 2000, A3, A12; Lee Gomes, "Napster, Fighting for Survival, to Make Case Before Appeals Panel," *Wall Street Journal,* October 2, 2000, B24; Lee Gomes, "Think Music Moguls Don't Like Sharing? Try Copying Software," *Wall Street Journal,* August 14, 2000, B1; Don Clark and Martin Peers, "Can the Record Industry Beat Free Web Music?" *Wall Street Journal,* June 20, 2000, B1; Lee Gomes, "When Its Own Assets Are Involved, Napster Is No Fan of Sharing," *Wall Street Journal,* July 26, 2000, A1, A10; and Jack Ewing, "A New Net Powerhouse?" *BusinessWeek,* November 13, 2000, 46–52.

USA Today and the Future of Information Distribution

*U*SA *Today,* subtitled "The Nation's Newspaper," debuted in 1982 as America's first national general-interest daily newspaper. The paper was the brainchild of Allen H. Neuharth, who until 1989 was Chairman of Gannett Co., Inc.—a diversified international $7.6 billion news, information, and communications company. Gannett is a global information juggernaut that publishes 100 daily and 1,000 nondaily newspapers, operates 20 broadcast television stations and roughly 130 websites, and is engaged in marketing, commercial printing, newswire services, data services, and news programming. Gannett is currently the largest U.S. newspaper group in terms of circulation—its 100 daily newspapers have a combined circulation of 7.3 million.

When *USA Today* debuted in 1982, it achieved rapid success due to its innovative format. No other media source had considered a national newspaper written in shorter pieces than a traditional paper and sprinkled with eye-catching, colorful photos, graphs, and charts. Designed to address the needs of a sound-byte generation, readers found *USA Today*'s content refreshing and more engaging than other papers. Circulation grew rapidly from roughly 350,000 in 1982 to approximately 2.3 million today. *USA Today,* the nation's largest-selling daily newspaper, easily outsells second-place *Wall Street Journal* and its 1.7-million circulation. *USA Today*'s website, www. usatoday.com, is one of the Internet's top sites for news and information.

The History and Growth of *USA Today*

In February 1980, Allen Neuharth met with "Project NN" task-force members to discuss his vision for producing and marketing a unique nationally distributed daily newspaper. Satellite technology had recently solved the problem of limited geographic distribution. Neuharth was also ready to take advantage of two trends in the reading public: (1) an increasingly short attention span among a generation nurtured on television and (2) a growing hunger for more information. Neuharth believed that readers face a time crunch in a world where so much information is available but so little time to absorb it. His vision for *USA Today* positioned the paper as an information source that would provide more news about more subjects in less time.

Geoffrey Lantos, Stonehill College, prepared this case with significant research support from Casey Brossett, David Davenport, Kelly Mitchell, and Sherry Thompson (Florida State University MBA Class of 2006–2007). This case is intended for classroom discussion rather than to illustrate effective or ineffective handling of an administrative situation.

Research suggested that *USA Today* should target achievement-oriented men in professional and managerial positions who were heavy newspaper readers and frequent travelers. Whereas the *New York Times* targeted the nation's intellectual elite, thinkers, and policy makers and the *Wall Street Journal* targeted business leaders, *USA Today* was to be targeted at Middle America—young, well-educated Americans who were on the move and cared about current events.

By early 1982, a team of news, advertising, and production personnel from the staffs of Gannett's daily newspapers developed, edited, published, and tested several different prototypes. Gannett sent three different 40-page prototype versions of *USA Today* to almost 5,000 professional people. Along with each prototype, they sent readers a response card that asked what they liked best and least about the proposed paper and whether they would buy it. Although the content of each prototype was similar, the layout and graphics presentations differed. For example, one prototype included a section called "Agenda" that included comics and a calendar of meetings to be held by various professional organizations. According to marketplace feedback, readers liked the prototypes. The Gannett board of directors unanimously approved the paper's launch. On April 20, 1982, Gannett announced that the first copies of *USA Today* would be available in the Washington, DC, and Baltimore areas.

USA Today Launches

On September 15, 1982, 155,000 copies of the newspaper's first edition hit the newsstands. On page 1, founder Neuharth wrote a short summary of *USA Today*'s mission statement, explaining that he wanted to make *USA Today* enlightening and enjoyable to the public, informative to national leaders, and attractive to advertisers. The first issue sold out. A little over a month following its debut, *USA Today*'s circulation hit 362,879—double the original year-end projection. In April 1983, just seven months after its introduction, the newspaper's circulation topped the one-million mark. The typical reader turned out to be a professional, usually a manager, about 40 years old, well educated, with an income of about $60,000 a year. The typical reader was also a news or sports junkie.

For a newspaper, *USA Today* was truly unique. Designed for the TV generation, the paper was laid out for easy access and quick comprehension by time-pressed readers. Examples of this formatting included extensive use of briefs, columns, secondary headlines, subheads, breakouts, at-a-glance boxes, and informational graphics. These techniques capture the most salient points of a story and present them in a format that readers appreciate. Gannett's research had shown that readers get most of their information from such snippets and that they were just as interested in sports, movie reviews, and health information as they were in traditional news. Each issue presented four sections: News, Money, Life, and Sports. The paper's motto fit its design: "An economy of words. A wealth of information."

Because *USA Today* was nontraditional, the critics were numerous and fierce. In their view, the paper was loaded with gimmicks—tight, short stories; no jumps from page to page, except for the cover story (stories that jump to another page are one of newspaper readers' major complaints); splashy, colorful graphics everywhere; a distinctive, casual writing style; a colorful national weather map; a round-up of news items from each state, one paragraph each; summary boxes; little charts and statistics-laden sports coverage; and a focus on celebrity and sports, with more detailed sports stories than almost any other paper in the nation. There was no foreign staff and little interest in the world outside the United States. It was quickly derided for its shallowness by journalists and labeled "McPaper"—junk-food journalism or the fast food of the newspaper business—due to its terse, brash writing style and its short coverage of complex issues. It was not considered serious. Even within Gannett, Neuharth met with bitter resistance from certain senior executives. Nevertheless, readers admired the paper for its focus on brevity and clarity—short sentences and short words.

Clearly, the paper filled a gap in the market, satisfying several unmet needs and wants. *USA Today*'s success came from listening to its readers and giving them what they wanted. The paper communicates with readers on a personal level very quickly (many of the short, fact-filled stories are under 250 words), clearly, and directly, in an upbeat and positive way. The color is riveting and gives the paper a contemporary look, as do the space-defying number of stories, factoids, larger-than-usual pictures, bar graphs, and charts, all squeezed onto each page without seeming too crowded. Instead of confusion, readers get neatness and order. The paper's dependably consistent organization enables readers to go directly to any one of *USA Today*'s major sections. As a result, it takes an average of only 25 minutes for a reader to peruse the paper.

Marketing Program Adjustments

Despite its critics, *USA Today*'s circulation surpassed 1.4 million by late 1985 as the paper expanded to 56 pages in length. The cover price had also increased to 50¢, double its original price of 25¢ per issue. By this time, *USA Today* had become the second largest paper in the country, with a circulation topped only by the *Wall Street Journal*. Although Neuharth had predicted that *USA Today* would turn a profit within a few years, his prediction proved to be overly optimistic. It took about five years to move into profitability, with *USA Today* losing an estimated $600 million during its first decade as it slowly built a national reputation. By 1993, however, profits were approximately $5 million. One year later, profits doubled to about $10 million.

During its early growth, the paper unearthed a class of newspaper reader few others had stumbled upon: the business traveler. Airline deregulation had led to a large general price decline for airline tickets, inducing a swell in business travel. On-the-road business travelers wished to keep abreast of both world and national news as well as what was going on in their home state and how their local sports teams were doing. *USA Today* rushed in to fill the void but in doing so quickly entered direct competition with the *Wall Street Journal*. By this time, hard-line newspapers, including the *New York Times,* began adding color; shorter, more tightly written stories; and beefed-up circulation campaigns to compete with "The Nation's Newspaper." The *Wall Street Journal* followed suit by introducing two new sections—Money & Investing and Marketplace—to broaden the paper's coverage of media, marketing, technology, and personal investing. In the face of this competition, as well as an awareness of changing reader needs, *USA Today* responded through innovation of its own.

Product Innovation   To stay ahead of the imitative competition, *USA Today* decided to become a more serious newspaper with improved journalism. The shift from primarily soft news to hard news began with the space shuttle *Challenger* disaster in 1986. By 1991 editors began focusing much more sharply on hard news rather than soft features, and by 1994 under president and publisher Tom Curley, there was a massive drive to upgrade the paper to be a more serious, more responsible news-oriented product.

Gannett also incorporated less traditional value-added features to keep readers interested. The paper added 1-800 and 1-900 "hot-line" numbers that readers could call for expert information on financial planning, college admissions, minority business development, taxes, and other subjects. Thousands of readers responded to reader-opinion polls and write-in surveys on political and current event issues. Editorial pages were also redesigned to provide more room for guest columnists and to encourage debate. Gannett also initiated a high school "Academic All Star" program that it later expanded to include colleges and universities. The increasing ubiquity of the Internet in the late 1990s also resulted in some changes in content. For instance, the Money section began to focus more on technology issues and to look at business through an e-commerce perspective.

The first major redesign in *USA Today*'s history occurred in 2000 as the paper moved from a 54-inch to a 50-inch width. The goal of the redesign was to make the paper easier to read and cleaner in design. The pages were slimmer and hence easier to handle, especially in tight spaces like airplanes, trains, buses, and subways, and the paper fit more readily into briefcases as Gannett had learned from focus groups.

Promotional Innovation   *USA Today* also innovated in its promotional activities. Historically, the paper had limited its promotion to outdoor advertising and television. However, in the late 1980s Neuharth undertook a "BusCapade" promotion tour; traveling to all fifty states to talk with people about *USA Today*. Neuharth succeeded in raising public awareness of his paper, which was credited for the *USA Today* move into profitability. Encouraged by his success, Neuharth forged ahead with a "JetCapade" campaign where he and a small news team traveled to thirty countries in seven months, stimulating global demand for the paper. During a visit to the troops of Operation Desert Storm in the Persian Gulf in 1991, General Norman Schwarzkopf expressed a need for news from home. *USA Today* arranged for delivery of 18,000 copies per day. The overseas success of *USA Today* led to the publication of *USA Today International,* which is now available in more than ninety countries in Western Europe, the Middle East, North Africa, and Asia.

Early on, *USA Today* faced a challenge in selling ad space to advertisers because they were not convinced that it would pay to advertise in the paper. Gannett's first strategy for enlisting advertisers was the Partnership Plan, which provided six months of free space to those who purchased six months of paid advertising. *USA Today* also began to accept regional advertising across a wide variety of categories such as travel, retail, tourism, and economic development. Color advertisements could arrive as late as 6:00 p.m. the day before publication, giving local advertisers increased flexibility. The paper also moved aggressively into "blue-chip circulation," where bulk quantities of *USA Today* are sold at discounted prices to hotels, airlines, and restaurants, and are provided free of charge to customers. Today, over 500,000 copies of *USA Today* are distributed daily through blue-chip circulation.

USA Today pulled off another promotional first in 1999 when it broke one of the most sacred practices of daily newspapers and began offering advertising space on the front page (one-inch strips across the entire width of the bottom of the page). This highly sought after front-page position was sold through one-year contracts for $1 to $1.2 million each, with each advertiser taking one day a week. As *USA Today* continued to prosper, advertisers became quite attracted to the paper's large volume of readers. To help cope with advertiser demand, the paper implemented the necessary technology to allow advertisers to transmit copy electronically 24 hours per day.

Distribution Innovation   Fast delivery has always been important to *USA Today*. By the late 1990s, the paper was earning kudos for its ability to deliver timely news, thanks to its late deadlines. For instance, in many parts of the country, *USA Today* could print later sports scores than local or regional papers. In hard news, *USA Today* was able to offer more up-to-date coverage by rolling the presses over four hours earlier than the *Wall Street Journal* and almost three hours later than the *New York Times*. The paper added print sites around the world in a move to further speed up distribution. An innovative readership program was also added that brought *USA Today* to more than 160 college campuses around the nation. Likewise, technological advances allowed the paper's production to be totally digital. A new computer-to-plate technology was implemented to give newsrooms later deadlines and readers earlier delivery times.

The Launch of *USA Today Online*

A decade after *USA Today*'s launch, Gannett found itself in the enviable position of owning one of America's most successful newspapers. *USA Today* was the most widely read newspaper in the country, with a daily readership of over 6.5 million. In an era when nearly all major national media were suffering declines in readership or viewing audience, *USA Today* continued to grow. Rising distribution and promotion costs, however, were beginning to make the newspaper slightly unprofitable. To reverse this trend, *USA Today* created several spin-offs, including its first special-interest publication, *Baseball Weekly*. During its first month of operation, *Baseball Weekly*'s circulation reached 250,000 copies. Venturing into news media, *USA Today* joined with CNN to produce a football TV program and launched SkyRadio to provide live radio on commercial airline flights.

The major spin-off, however, was *USA Today Online*, which the company introduced on April 17, 1995. The online version was seen as a natural companion to the print version of *USA Today*, given the paper's worldwide distribution. The first version was available through CompuServe's Mosaic browser and required special software, a CompuServe Network connection, and a monthly subscription of $14.95 plus $3.95 per hour. By June 1995, *USA Today Online* converted to a free service that worked with any web browser and Internet service provider. The *Online* was later dropped in favor of USAToday.com.

Like its print sister, USAToday.com is bright, upbeat, and full of nugget-sized news stories. The online version allows readers to receive up-to-the-moment news that incorporates colorful visuals and crisp audio. It provides one of the most extensive sites on the web, featuring thousands of pages of up-to-the-minute news, sports, business and technology news; four-day weather forecasts; and travel information available 24/7.

Another revenue generator, launched in 1998 in response to frequent reader requests for archived material, was the pay-per-view archives service (http://archives.usatoday.com). The *USA Today* Archives section allows readers to do a free, unlimited search of the paper's articles that have appeared since April 1987. Articles may be downloaded for $3.95 per story or as a part of the site's monthly and yearly service plans.

USA Today is not an operation that rests on its laurels, so the website has also been updated several times. A number of partnerships have been added to the site in the areas of online classifieds and a marketplace where users can purchase a variety of goods and services. The company added a companion travel site in 2002.

USA Today—Today

In looking at the total national newspaper market, *USA Today* is successful. It has seen over 20 years of continuous growth and now boasts over 2.3 million readers. Gannett's newspaper revenues consist primarily of advertising sales (75 percent) and circulation sales (19 percent). Total newspaper publishing revenues for the first quarter in 2006 were $1.7 billion. Advertising sales accounted for $1.3 billion, and circulation sales accounted for $324 million. Overall revenues are up six percent compared to the first quarter of 2005. The increase is due to Gannett's acquisition of some of Knight-Ridder's properties. Had Gannett not acquired part of Knight-Ridder, its revenues would have declined 1.6 percent.

Newsprint costs have risen lately for all newspapers. At Gannett they have increased a little more than 12 percent in the second quarter of 2006. The company is currently testing cheaper newsprint from China, in hopes of reducing this cost.

The *USA Today* website receives roughly 55 million visits per month, with 10.5 million unique visitors per month. It is interesting that this success has occurred during a time when overall newspaper readership is declining. In the United States, weekly newspaper readership declined from 58.6 percent of adults in 1998 to 51.6 percent in 2005. At the beginning of the twenty-first century, only *USA Today,* the *Los Angeles Times,* and the *Denver Post* were experiencing large gains in circulation among all national, daily papers in the United States. Partly due to rising newsprint costs, *USA Today* raised its single-copy price to 75 cents in 2004. This represented a significant jump in revenue for the company because single-copy sales comprise 65 percent of the its paid circulation. The move had no effect on overall paid circulation, which grew by 0.1 percent in the six-month period ending March 2006.

Newsprint costs are a key challenge for the newspaper industry as a whole. In fact, rising costs have forced virtually all newspaper firms to add online news as a means to increase readership and cut distribution expenses. However, the move to free online news is a double-edged sword: Some experts suggest that approximately 14 percent of readers will switch from newspaper to online news, effectively cannibalizing the readership of printed news. Whether online news poses a major threat to *USA Today* is debatable.

However, recent changes in Gannett leadership, in the industry, and in the way that the company approaches business are meant to prepare the company for the twenty-first century. New CEO Craig Dubow comes from the company's Broadcast Division and is committed to getting news and information into the hands of consumers faster than ever before. To aid the company in doing this, Gannett created a new position, president of Gannett Digital, responsible for the web-based and innovative technological components of the business. USAToday.com has added blogs, RSS (really simple syndication), and podcasting to ensure that its news stays relevant to busy and mobile readers. Perhaps Gannett's most important recent decision was to purchase interest in a company with unique technology that aggregates news on the Internet and categorizes the news into 300,000 topics. The technology also has the ability to sort information by zip code. Another technology gained through acquisition, PointRoll, is a service that allows Internet advertisers to expand their online space. One innovative way Gannett has leveraged this service is to provide local advertisers with a means to direct consumers to local merchants. As a web user rolls the cursor over an ad, the ad expands, revealing information about the closest retailer. Finally, *USA Today* has moved quickly to establish partnerships that can prepare the company for the future. The company's partnerships with Cingular, Sprint, and Verizon allow it to provide news content specifically formatted for small-screen devices.

The Future of *USA Today*

Despite its success, *USA Today* will never be able to rest on its laurels. Competition in print and online information distribution is fierce. Internet-based companies, like Yahoo! and Google, have now moved into the advertising market. The multitude of choices for both consumers and advertisers means that *USA Today* will have to work harder at innovation, finding a way to differentiate its products from the sea of competition. This will be a challenging task given the continuing decline in newspaper readership and the growing consumer demand for free online news.

As *USA Today* looks toward its future, a number of issues must be considered. The following sections describe the current situation of *USA Today* as well as the key issues that the company must face as it plans for its future.

Customer Environment

The overwhelming majority of *USA Today*'s circulation is within the United States. The readers of the newspaper are 64 percent male and 36 percent female with an average age of 46 and an average income of $91,210. The readers of the online site are 53 percent male and 47 percent female with an average age of 45. Most *USA Today* readers work in middle- to upper-management positions and are often purchasing decision makers for their offices and households, technological junkies, and sports fans. They also participate in a wide range of leisure activities. Eighty-six percent of print and online readers combined own a computer, and most of those have Internet access. Seventy-five percent of readers participate in sports and are active sports fans. Seventy-five percent of *USA Today* readers have active lives that include attending movies and domestic and foreign travel.

Important players in the purchase process are subscribers, single-copy buyers, and third-party sponsors, often referred to as blue-chip buyers. Eighty percent of *USA Today*'s purchasers are also users, and they bear the financial responsibility for the product. These consumers also share their papers with family and friends, which increases readership. Twenty percent of paid copies are purchased by third parties, which distribute complimentary copies to the end user to add value to their own goods or services. For example, hotel guests often enjoy a copy of *USA Today* during breakfast or while waiting in the lobby. Newspapers purchased at coin-operated vending machines do not always have associated complimentary products.

Paid editions of *USA Today* are currently distributed via newsstand retailers, large grocery store chains, bookstores, coin-operated vending machines, and directly to the consumer through home delivery. Home-delivery customers are the newspaper's most loyal customers and are most likely to buy daily delivery at 13- to 52-week intervals. Single-copy buyers tend to purchase the paper out of daily routine (heavy users) or on occasion based on specific newsworthy events (light users). Complimentary distribution of *USA Today* occurs primarily in hotels, airport terminals, and restaurants and at college campuses across the United States. *USA Today* content is also available in e-formats from USAToday.com, mobile phone access, and e-mail updates. The availability of *USA Today* via e-distribution is a deterrent for some consumers to purchasing the print product. Currently, however, customers cannot receive updated news in real time unless they have access to an RSS-enabled mobile device.

Competition

Gannett has competitors from several fields including other national newspapers such as the *Wall Street Journal* and the *New York Times*; cable networks; nationally syndicated terrestrial and satellite radio such as XM and Sirius; and Internet information portals such as Yahoo!, Google, and AOL.

The Wall Street Journal   One of *USA Today*'s biggest newspaper competitors is the *Wall Street Journal,* owned by Dow Jones & Co. Inc. The company's product lines include newspapers, newswires, magazines, websites, indexes, television, and radio. The *Journal*'s website, www.wsj.com, adds over 1,000 news stories per day and includes price information on over 30,000 stocks and funds worldwide. The *Wall Street Journal* has strategic alliances with other information companies including CNBC, Reuters, and SmartMoney.

Circulation for the *Wall Street Journal* print version is two million, and wsj.com receives 175,000 unique visitors per day and has 768,000 paid subscriptions. The *Wall Street Journal* targets influential business readers as its primary audience. Sixty percent of the print newspaper's readers and 54 percent of its online readers are employed as top management. The average household income is $191,000, and net worth is $2.1 million. Net worth for online readers is $1.6 million. The company charges a subscription fee of $99 per year for both the print and online versions. The paper also offers a bundled package with both print and online content for $125 per year. Single copies of the weekday print version cost $1, and the weekend print version costs $1.50.

Dow Jones has been making improvements to the *Journal* in an attempt to make it more competitive. It added a Weekend Edition in 2005, designed to help advertisers reach the paper's audience at home on the weekends. Some new plans for improvement include reformatting the paper to a 48-inch width and changing the navigational format and content of the print version. The change is expected to reduce operating expenses by $18 million per year. The *Wall Street Journal* has already launched changes in its international version. The international print edition has become more compact and includes stronger links to the website. These changes are expected to improve profits by $17 million per year. The *Wall Street Journal* is also planning to add advertisements to its front page. *USA Today* was criticized for doing this in the past, but this practice is becoming more common as newspapers look for ways to increase revenue.

The New York Times   In addition to the *New York Times,* the New York Times Co. owns other newspapers and related websites, two New York City radio stations, nine television stations serving seven states, and the search engine About.com, which they acquired in 2005 for $410 million. The *New York Times* is available at 60,000 newsstands and retailers and 4,000 Starbucks coffee shops.

Circulation for the *New York Times* is 1.7 million; the website, www.nytimes.com, enjoys 1.3 million unique visitors per day and 10.8 million registered users. The newspaper's target market is the intellectual elite. As explained in its press kit, "The New York Times—Influential people read it because influential people read it." The average household income is $88,523. The *New York Times* costs $252.20 per year for the seven-day paper in New York and $130 per year for either the weekday paper or the weekend paper in New York. Outside of New York, the paper costs $309.40 per year for the seven-day paper and $153.40 per year for the weekday paper and $187.20 per year for the weekend paper. The *New York Times*' online content is free although it requires a registration. Online users can also acquire extra content, including access to the archives, through its TimesSelect site, which is $49.95 per year. The price of a single copy of the print version is $1.

The company has recently made some changes in an attempt to be more profitable. The *New York Times* raised its home-delivery rates by four percent, which the company expects will raise circulation revenues by $7 or $8 million in 2006. The *Times* also reduced the number of pages in its stock section, which is expected to reduce expenses by $4 million per year. Additionally, the paper has also begun to implement cost-saving policies, including staff reductions, which is expected to reduce costs by $45 million per year. They have decided to also follow the examples of other newspapers by making plans to reduce the width of its print version.

Other Competitors   *USA Today* also faces competition for audience attention and advertising dollars from companies outside its industry, including television, radio, and Internet providers. When compared to other media options, newspapers fare poorly in terms of daily media consumption:

	Percentage of Adults Reached (aged 18 and over)	Percentage of Daily Media Consumption	Percentage Citing as Primary News Source
Television	89.9	58.3	70.1
Radio	74.2	22.8	9.3
Newspapers	62.6	4.4	11.2
Internet	59.8	12.4	9.4

In 2005 the major television networks started taking advantage of new distribution technologies. NBC entered into a partnership with DIRECTV to offer a day-after service, and its NBC News division is the first to distribute its news through iTunes. ABC partnered with Apple to offer some of its programs to iPod users for $1.99 per download. ABC also offers a $4.95 per month subscription to its ABC News Now service, which is targeted at young adults. CBS partnered with Comcast Cable to offer its programming on Comcast's video-on-demand service. CBS also offered content from its local news, weather, and sports programs available to Sprint users for $4.99 per month. Overall, the television industry has started a consolidation trend with many cable and network channels joining together under one parent company. The industry faces a 2009 deadline to fully convert to digital programming. Currently, however, only one percent of consumers have purchased the necessary equipment to receive digital programming.

Radio has always been a strong competitor for newspapers. However, the growth of satellite radio has made the medium more attractive to advertisers. Both satellite providers, XM and Sirius, offer a comparable mix of music, news, sports, and talk programming for a flat fee of $12.95 per month. XM, the larger network, offers 170 channels to its over seven million subscribers. Sirius offers 125 channels to its 4.5 million subscribers. Both services are extremely popular, with impressive annual revenue growth of 128 percent (XM) and 262 percent (Sirius).

Internet information providers are another source of competition for *USA Today*. One billion people globally have access to the Internet either at home or at work. Most Internet information providers make their money through subscriptions, advertising, or both. It is important to note that the Internet as a communications and advertising medium is no longer tied to desktop computers. Virtually all major Internet providers and content developers are working to push information to handheld devices. Cingular and Sprint have led the way by offering multimedia content to their users via Internet-enabled cell phones. CBS Radio and Clear Channel Radio provide sports radio to Sprint customers through the Mspot service for $5.95 per month. MSNBC.com has recently launched a new mobile service that provides sports, local, and national news content.

Economic Issues

Higher newsprint costs, a shaky advertising environment, and declining circulation have been plaguing the newspaper industry. The high cost of newsprint is a constant problem for newspapers; however, the industry has been able to cut costs through the increased use of recycled fiber. Between 1989 and 2004, the amount of recycled fiber in newspapers rose from 10 percent to 32 percent. With respect to advertising, newspapers have been struggling in the midst of a soft ad market, particularly in the automotive, retail, and employment sectors. National newspaper advertising in the first quarter of 2006 fell 4.8 percent. However, Internet advertising rose 19.4 percent during this same period. Total advertising expenditures in the United States through all media are expected to grow by 5.6 percent during 2006.

The roughly 1,500 daily newspapers in the United States have a combined circulation of 54 million daily and 58 million for Sunday. In the first quarter of 2006, daily circulation fell 2.5 percent while Sunday circulation declined by 3.1 percent. Newspaper website visits, however, increased during the same time period. More than one-third of web users visit a newspaper website at least once per month.

Technological Advancements

Technology is central to the future of the newspaper industry because of the changes it has brought in the way that consumers can seek out timely and relevant news and information. Technological advancements offer interested consumers more options than ever to access news and news coverage, and this has led to a marked decline in newspaper circulation as people use the Internet and other means to get timely news and information. Technology has not only given consumers more options but it has also allowed them the ability to customize the news that they receive at a level they were never able to do before.

Delivering news via the latest wireless devices is perhaps the most threatening alternative to newsprint. However, these devices are also an opportunity for *USA Today* to maintain its readership. Wireless handheld devices, such as the Blackberry and a growing list of smart phones, are increasingly being used to deliver news coverage in specific content areas such as stock reports and sports scores. For example, ESPN and Sprint at one time partnered to offer Mobile ESPN using mobile virtual network operator (MVNO) technology, giving sports fans the ability to receive almost continuous scores and stats for their favorite teams and players. Similarly, *USA Today* and Gannett have developed partnerships with such companies as MobileVoiceControl, Inc. to allow those who have Blackberries to enjoy natural voice access to *USA Today*'s news content. The partnership allows *USA Today* to give Blackberry users the ability to search and receive continuously updated and customizable coverage in news, finances, sports, and even weather by merely pressing a button and speaking a command. Thus, *USA Today* has already recognized a need to transition from print to wireless, and the company has begun to do just that in partnering with companies on the leading edge of wireless technology.

Other information-distribution technologies are on the horizon. One of the most promising is electronic paper, or e-paper. E-papers are flexible digital screens that are similar to newsprint with respect to thickness, rolling/curling ability, and portability. Unlike newspapers, however, e-papers are reusable in that users can download up-to-date information to them via wireless technology. The technology is already being used for e-poster advertisements in stores. A typical e-paper is expected to cost $300 to $400 and is expected be available beginning in 2007.

Overall, advancing technology may have initiated the decline of the newspaper industry. However, technology is also likely to be the industry's savior. Technology allows *USA Today* and other newspapers to deliver news in more cost-efficient, customizable, and useful ways than will ever be possible using newsprint.

Sociocultural Trends

As many in the industry are aware, newspaper readership stands to lose a great deal due to changing demographics. The Newspaper Association of America notes that newspaper readership is strongest among adults aged 65 and older because 70 percent of this group reads a newspaper daily. Within other mature-age groups, specifically those constituting baby boomers (adults aged 40–59), only 50 to 60 percent read a newspaper daily. These figures support the contention that newspapers will lose readers at an alarming rate as this segment of the population ages over the next 10 to 30 years. To offset this trend, newspapers are attempting to attract and cater to new and younger readers. The transition is a difficult one, however, because there is a significant difference between the interests of current newspaper readers and the younger demographic that newspapers hope to gain. Baby boomers are most interested in major news stories and local news coverage. Younger readers, however, are more interested in sports (mainly males) and entertainment coverage, along with comics.

Addressing this concern and hoping to boost readership among younger generations, *USA Today* now includes in its online version a blog entitled "Pop Candy" where readers can exchange information and opinions about aspects of pop culture such as music and celebrities. Also, in 2006 *USA Today* planned to include excerpts from its "On Deadline" blog in the print edition. One part of the blog, "Looking Ahead," will serve in print as a guide to upcoming events, while another will round up other outlets' news coverage in true blog fashion.

Looking Ahead

Although increasing digital options for news and information have some industry observers bemoaning the death of newspapers, the majority seems to feel that newspapers do have a bright future and will thrive if they develop a healthy online presence and adapt to evolving media-consumption patterns. A 2006 survey conducted by the Pew Research Center for the People and the Press found that 79 percent of newspaper readers read the printed paper only, 12 percent read a paper's website only, and 9 percent read both. Another 2006 Pew Center study reported that, although the Internet has grown significantly over the past decade, it is supplementing rather than replacing traditional media outlets like newspapers and television. The study found that one-third of Americans go online for news, mainly to read the headlines. Nonetheless, online readers still spend more time getting news from traditional sources than they do getting it online. Further research suggests that the online editions of newspapers are actually driving readers to their print editions, thereby helping prevent further readership losses.

In the face of continual competition in both offline and online markets, *USA Today* continues to push the envelope of innovation and marketing strategy. To remain successful, *USA Today* must continue to use a value-added strategy that can further enhance distribution of its proprietary content and ensure continued differentiation with respect to the competition.

Questions for Discussion

1. What opportunities in the marketing environment did Gannett seize in launching *USA Today*? How did the company learn about and respond to these opportunities? Answer these same questions for USAToday.com.

2. How has a continuous strategy of marketing innovation proved successful for *USA Today* and USAToday.com? Do you believe that *USA Today* is well positioned for the future? Explain.

3. What are the SWOT implications for *USA Today* as it looks toward its future? What strengths and opportunities can *USA Today* leverage as it looks for a competitive advantage in the distribution of news and information?

4. Based on *USA Today*'s experiences with print and online news, evaluate the long-term potential of printed news and the newspaper publishing industry. Do you believe that printed newspapers will continue to survive despite digital competition?

Sources

The facts of this case are from Steven Anderson, Director of Communications, *USA Today,* personal interview, August 5, 2003; "Broadcast Television Industry Profile," Yahoo! Finance (http://biz.yahoo.com/ic/profile/723_1469.html), accessed September 1, 2006; *Bob Coen's Insider's Report,* Universal McCann (http://www.mccann.com/news/pdfs/Insiders6_06.pdf), June 2006; R. Curtis, "Introducing your new *USA Today*," *USA Today,* April 3, 2000, 27A; "Deadline," *Fortune,* July 8, 2002, 78–86; Dow Jones, Inc. Fact Sheet (http://www.dj.com/Pressroom/FactSheets.htm); Dow Jones, Inc. Profile, Yahoo! Finance (http://finance.yahoo.com/q/pr?s=dj); "Electronic Paper," *Wikipedia* (http://en.wikipedia.org/wiki/Electronic_paper), accessed September 1, 2006; Gannett Company, Inc., 2005 Annual Report; Gannett Company Profile (http://gannett.com/map/gan007.htm), accessed September 1, 2006; "Gannett Hits Heights in Print but Fall Short of TV Stardom," *Campaign,* January 17, 1997, 24; "Internet Information Providers Industry Profile," Yahoo! Finance (http://biz.yahoo.com/ic/profile/851_1457.html), accessed September 1, 2006; Peter Johnson, "Internet News Supplements Papers, TV," *USA Today,* July 31, 2006, 5D; K. Jurgensen, "Quick Response; Paper Chase: *USA Today* Editor Sees Shifts in How Information Is Generated and Delivered to Readers,"

Advertising Age, February 14, 2000, 1A S6; K. Jurgensen, "*USA Today*'s New Look Designed for Readers," *USA Today,* April 3, 2000, 1A; Kenneth Li, "E-Newspapers Just Around the Corner. Really," *Newswatch India,* June 12, 2006 (http://www.newswatch.in/ ?p=5032); P. Long, "After Long Career, *USA Today* Founder Al Neuharth Is Ready for More," *Knight-Ridder/Tribune Business News,* April 28, 1999; "Media Trends Track," Television Bureau of Advertising http://www.tvb.org/mediacomparisons/02_A_ Consumers_Continue.asp?mod=R), accessed September 1, 2006; J. McCartney, "*USA Today* Grows Up," *American Journalism Review,* September 1997, 19; B. Miller, "*USA Today,* Gannett to Launch *USA Today Live,*" *Television & Cable,* February 8, 2000; New York Times, Inc. Media Kits (http://www.nytco.com/press-kits.html); New York Times, Inc. Profile, Yahoo! Finance (http://finance.yahoo.com/q/pr?s=NYT), accessed September 1, 2006; Sirius Satellite Radio, Inc. Profile, Yahoo! Finance (http://finance. yahoo.com/q/pr?s=SIRI), accessed September 1, 2006; M. L. Stein, "Don't Sweat the Internet Says *USA Today*'s Curley," *Editor & Publisher,* August 22, 1998, 40; M. Stone, "*USA Today Online* Listens to Its Logs," *Editor & Publisher,* August 7, 1999, 66; J. Strupp, "*USA Today* Ads Go Page One," *Editor & Publisher,* May 8, 1999, 40; "*USA Today* and Gannett Partner with MobileVoiceControl to Bring Voice-Driven Mobile Search to Blackberry," TMCnet, May 23, 2006 (http://www.tmcnet.com/usubmit/2006/05/23/ 1658295.htm); "*USA Today*'s Circulation Lead Grows with 1.8% Rise," *USA Today,* May 6, 2003, 2B; "*USA Today* Launches New Life Section Friday Format," *PR Newswire,* March 16, 1998, 316; "*USA Today* Launches Online Classifieds Area and 17 New Marketplace Partnerships," *Business Wire,* April 15, 1997; "*USA Today* Launches Pay- per-View Archives Service," *Business Wire,* January 5, 1998; "*USA Today* No Longer a Newspaper," *Advertising Age,* September 9, 2002, 18; *USA Today* Media Kit (http:// www.usatoday.com/media_kit/usatoday/ut_usatoday_home.htm), accessed September 1, 2006; "*USA Today Online* Launches Real Time Survey System," *Business Wire,* February 18, 1998; "*USA Today* Sells Page One Advertising Space," *PR Newswire,* May 5, 1999, 351; *USA Today,* "Snaphot," August 22, 2006, 1; I. Wada, "*USA Today* Marketplace sSgns Up Six for On-line Services," *Travel Weekly,* April 28, 1997, 44; and XM Satellite Radio Holdings, Inc. Profile, Yahoo! Finance (http://finance.yahoo.com/q/pr?s=XMSR), accessed September 1, 2006.

Saturn

At a Crossroads

I n 1990, after seven years of incubation, Saturn, a division of General Motors (GM), debuted in the crowded market of compact cars. Since 1985, GM's share of the U.S. passenger car market had fallen 11 points to 33 percent. Moreover, a J.D. Power & Associates study revealed that 42 percent of all new car shoppers didn't even consider buying a GM car. Saturn's mission, then, was to sell 80 percent of its cars to drivers who would not otherwise have bought a GM product.

GM established Saturn as a separate and independent subsidiary in 1985 with an investment of $5 billion. Former GM Chairman Robert B. Smith envisioned Saturn as a "laboratory" to find better ways to manufacture and market cars. GM believed that Saturn was the key to its long-term competitiveness and survival. Saturn managers spent years developing the new company from scratch. They viewed partnerships as a key element of Saturn's future relationships between management and labor and between company and supplier, with everyone sharing the risks and rewards. To truly separate Saturn from the traditional Detroit auto-building mentality, GM decided to build Saturn in Spring Hill, Tennessee. GM lent its financial support to Saturn by providing the latest technology, manufacturing methods, pace-setting labor relations, and participatory management ideas. Saturn represents the largest single construction project in the history of GM. Whereas other GM plants merely assembled parts, Saturn manufactured almost everything at its facility, including power trains, moldings, and instrument panels.

Saturn's Initial Success

At first, management expected to totally automate the Saturn assembly line. However, GM learned many costly lessons about robotics, including the fact that robots do not always perform as expected. A joint venture with Toyota in California taught GM and Saturn that good labor–management relations could do more for productivity and quality. Consequently, Saturn adopted the outlook that technology should take a backseat to people.

The United Auto Workers Union (UAW) and GM management both wanted Saturn to succeed from the start, and in a partnership unprecedented in the auto

---

Don Roy, Middle Tennessee State University, prepared this case for classroom discussion rather than to illustrate effective or ineffective handling of an administrative situation.

industry, the two entities joined hands and decided to work side by side. All decisions at Saturn were reached by consensus. UAW members, for example, helped select Saturn "partners" such as suppliers, Saturn's advertising agency, and dealers. All employees, blue collar and white collar, had to be approved by both union members and management. New employees at Saturn's Tennessee plant also faced extensive training to teach them how to work in teams and how to keep track of costs.

Even the plant's design reflected thought for cost efficiency and people. For example, there were many entrances to the plant instead of one main entrance, and each was designed to be no more than a five-minute walk to an employee's station. Parking was designed so that no one had to dodge delivery trucks. Street names around the plant—Handshake Road and Greater Glory Road—also reflected a people-oriented philosophy. Inside, cars on the assembly line could be raised or lowered to make the workers' jobs easier. Another first in North America was that the assembly line was made of wood, which was easier on employees' feet.

Early Marketing Strategy

Promotion   The story of Saturn is inseparable from its promotion history because Saturn involved all marketing entities, from the advertising agency to the dealers, in all decisions from the very beginning. In 1987 Saturn began looking for an advertising agency to handle what would become a more than $100 million account, searching for an agency that could understand the importance of partnership. After reviewing applications from more than fifty agencies, Saturn decided to widen its search. San Francisco's Hal Riney & Partners had already attracted attention in the car industry with its work for Austin Rover Cars of North America, with an ad for the Sterling that showed only brief glimpses of the car itself. In May 1988, after a review by a panel of company executives, two dealers, and a UAW representative, Saturn named Riney as its advertising agency, 29 months before the first car went on sale.

Riney immediately became involved with many aspects of the company's innovative start-up. Unlike other ad agencies handling automotive accounts, Riney did not open a satellite office in Detroit because it wanted to remain free of Detroit's limited worldview, where 80 percent of the cars were domestic. Riney understood that Saturn had to cater to baby boomers who preferred Japanese automobiles for their perceived higher quality and value.

Riney, along with a panel of sixteen Saturn dealers, contributed to many Saturn decisions. Keeping in mind the target market of college-educated men and women aged 25–49, they decided to adopt a "straight-talk" philosophy, which became applied to many aspects of the Saturn brand. For example, all Saturn retail stores would be called "Saturn of (Geographic Location)" to stress the Saturn name rather than the dealer's. Car color descriptions are also simple, using names like "red" rather than "raspberry red."

Riney's first real promotion task was internal communication. When members of his agency interviewed Saturn employees for this task, they found the Saturn employees enthusiastic and emotionally involved with their new company, a fact that

Riney would use to advantage in both internal and external promotions. In April 1989, Riney produced a 26-minute documentary film called *Spring in Spring Hill,* which chronicled the start-up of a new company dedicated to building cars "in a brand new way." The film was used to help explain Saturn to new employees and suppliers and for training; dealers used it to make presentations; and the film was aired on some cable television networks. The film featured employees explaining, often quite emotionally, just what Saturn was all about and what it meant to them.

Riney applied the straight-talk, people-oriented philosophy in consumer advertising, stressing the company over individual models. The theme line was "A different kind of company, A different kind of car." The first commercials told stories about the Spring Hill heartland and about Saturn employees. All Saturn ads had a down-home feeling and featured ordinary people talking about the cars and the Saturn concept. They told the story of how employees took a risk and left Detroit for something new and exciting-to start from the drawing board and "build cars again . . . but in a brand new way." The ads stressed that, by recapturing the United States' can-do spirit, Saturn knew how to make cars.

Later ads featured the stories of Saturn customers, focusing on Saturn buyers' lifestyles and playing up product themes that baby boomers held dear, such as safety, utility, and value. One commercial, for example, highlighted a recall order that Saturn issued to fix a seat problem and showed a Saturn representative traveling to Alaska to fix the Saturn owned by Robin Millage, an actual customer who had ordered her car, sight unseen, from a dealer in the continental United States. The result of Riney's folksy, straight-talk campaign was a sharply focused brand image for Saturn.

Most Saturn dealers had salespeople working in teams to avoid high-pressure sales techniques. Salespeople typically split commissions and cooperated in providing a relaxed, inviting showroom environment, allowing customers to browse and offering service and advice only as customers sought it.

The Product Offering   Initially, Saturn offered only four products: the Saturn SC1 and SC2 coupes and the Saturn SL1 and SL2 sedans. An SW1 and SW2 station wagon and entry-level coupe (SL) were introduced in 1993. The EV1 (a limited-production electric car) was introduced in late 1996. An innovative three-door version of the SC1 and SC2 appeared on the market in 1998. The long-awaited introduction of a midsize sedan and station wagon known as the L-Series took place in mid-1999. Saturn's products were not the most stylish but were innovative in many respects. For example, body panels were made of dent-resistant polymer. Many potential customers visited Saturn dealerships just to kick a Saturn and watch the body panel pop back into place. Cars could also be fitted with the latest amenities and were a good value for the money. Still, Saturn was better known for its branding and advertising than for the street appeal of its products.

Distribution   With marketing and distribution of new cars accounting for 30 to 35 percent of a car's cost, Saturn planned its distribution very carefully. Dealers were given large territories so that each competed with rival brands rather than with one another. Saturn generally had only one dealership in a metropolitan area. The first dealerships were set up in areas where import car sales were high, and most were located on the East and West Coasts to avoid cannibalizing sales of other GM cars. In addition, Saturn chose dealers who knew how to appeal to import car buyers.

Pricing   The revolutionary ideas employed at Saturn continued with its pricing strategy. Saturn pioneered the "no-haggle" pricing policy where customer paid the price shown on the window sticker. No negotiating or discounts were allowed. If the sticker stated $15,960 as the price, that was what the customer paid. Saturn's cars were competitively priced in the $14,000 to $18,000 range. The SL1 and SL2 sedans offered amenities comparable to the Camry and Accord but at prices that were $2,000 to $3,000 less. Dealers found the one-price policy very desirable because of tight profit margins and the high-integrity sales approach that supported it.

The Buying Experience   One of the most unique elements of Saturn's marketing strategy was captured in the overall buying experience. Customers were free to shop at their leisure and were not approached by pushy salespeople. Because prices were nonnegotiable, buyers were confident in the prices that they would be paying. Once customers decided to buy a Saturn, they were immediately treated like members of the family. The staff took photographs of the customers with their new Saturns and posted them in a conspicuous spot in the dealership. Customers were contacted by phone the next day, and again a few days later, to answer questions and reassure them. As a result, most Saturn customers suffered little in the way of buyer's remorse. It was not surprising that Saturn had one of the highest customer satisfaction ratings in the automotive industry.

Early Growing Pains

Saturn's marketing mix was a resounding success in the first half of the 1990s. Initial sales of Saturn cars were tremendous. One Memphis dealership sold all nine of its Saturns on the first day, with a backlog of orders. Similar success stories occurred all over the country. However, the company experienced great difficulty meeting demand, with many customers waiting more than 6 weeks to receive their automobiles. For example, in late 1992, the Plymouth, Michigan, dealer had only four Saturns on hand instead of the usual 200, and she had sold the nine demonstration models that her sales staff had been driving. Saturn officials stated that part of the problem with shortages was that they were unwilling to compromise on quality.

　　With serious troubles of its own, GM wanted Saturn to stand on its own and was reluctant to invest more money in the project. Specifically, GM wanted the Spring Hill plant to be more productive, saying there was room for improvement. However, Saturn employees said quality suffered when personnel and equipment were pushed too hard. Because their pay was tied to quality targets, they were especially concerned about the quality of Saturn cars. In October 1991 they held a slow-down during a visit by then GM Chairman Robert C. Stempel to protest a production increase that resulted in high defect rates. Saturn president Richard G. "Skip" LaFauve tried to increase production without harming quality, partly by adding a third shift to the Spring Hill plant. Saturn's future was further threatened by the fact that GM had yet to commit money to fund new Saturn models beyond 1995. This was a real problem due to the length of time required to develop a new car. However, GM pinned hopes on Saturn buyers and the expectation that they would graduate to larger, more expensive GM models in future years.

Despite production restraints and other problems, Saturn sold 170,495 cars in the 1992 model year, a 236 percent increase over its first-year sales in 1991. That gave Saturn a 2.1 percent share of the U.S. auto market, helping it leapfrog over Hyundai, Subaru, Volkswagen, and Mitsubishi. More significantly, Saturn ranked third in J.D. Power & Associates' measurement of new-car buyer satisfaction, behind only Lexus and Infiniti.

May 1993 was the first profitable month for the Saturn Corporation since its first car was produced. Saturn expected to sell 300,000 cars in the 1993 calendar year but failed to reach this objective. A third production shift was added to cut overtime costs. With 20 hours of production, six days a week, quality was still the company's main concern. Saturn employees stopped the assembly line if a car was not up to standards.

Until 1996 Saturn was able to maintain its sales momentum by developing a cultlike following with its down-home advertisements and customer picnics, where all Saturn owners were invited to Spring Hill, Tennessee, to celebrate the joy of Saturn ownership. After 1996, however, even creative advertising and high-profile customer events were not enough to overcome a slowdown in the subcompact market. Fewer people wanted to buy small, fuel-efficient cars. Another factor was the 1997 Asian currency crisis that helped foreign small-car makers drop prices.

Saturn's Challenges Mount

In the late 1990s and into the early twenty-first century, Saturn's challenges began to replace its successes. Unit sales peaked during 1994 at approximately 286,000 units. Over the next few years, unit sales declined while the industry experienced record sales. Sales decreased 7.7 percent in 1998, followed by a modest 0.3 percent increase in 1999. Introduction of the L-Series helped spark a 16.8 percent increase in 2000, but a weakened economy led to a 4.1 percent sales decrease in 2001. Saturn's rather narrow product line was cited as one reason for the sales decline. The company's focus on small cars left it vulnerable to the shift in demand toward bigger vehicles, including minivans and sport utility vehicles (SUVs). At the time, many believed that Saturn had missed a golden opportunity to build on its early success. Even Saturn employees had suggested that the company make a small SUV. Then they watched as Honda (CR-V) and Toyota (RAV4) sold all they could make.

Keeping with GM's vision of Saturn as a laboratory for new product development, GM selected the Saturn unit to market the company's first electric vehicle, named EV1. This two-seat coupe, which went from 0 to 60 miles per hour in 8.5 seconds, was introduced at select Saturn dealers in Arizona and California in late 1996 and was supported by a $25 million marketing campaign. The development of the EV1 was in response to mandates passed in California, Massachusetts, and New York that required a certain percentage of vehicles sold in any given year be "zero-emissions vehicles." GM was the first company to have an electric vehicle on the market, but other manufacturers—including Chrysler, Honda, and Nissan—quickly followed with their own products. True to Saturn's reputation for customer service, the company employed EV specialists, who worked with customers throughout the leasing process. EV specialists assisted customers by explaining how to install the battery charger, how to charge batteries, how to arrange a lease agreement, and how to obtain tax credits.

Although many believe that electric vehicles hold promise for the future, their impact on Saturn was minimal. Many consumers were just not ready to switch to electric vehicles. A survey by J.D. Power & Associates found that only 23 percent of consumers would consider buying or leasing an electric vehicle. Pricing was another reason that electric vehicles did not enjoy widespread acceptance. Monthly lease payments for the EVI ranged from $424 to $574, depending on the type of lease agreement signed. The number of dealers participating in the EV1 program represented a small percentage of Saturn's 400 dealers. Despite a number of passionate EV1 drivers and the potential benefits of electric cars, GM phased out the EV1 by the end of 2003. As customer leases expired, Saturn took possession of the vehicles. In the end, all EV1s were destroyed, creating a cloud of skepticism among some industry experts.

Saturn also struggled with its attempt to become established in the Japanese market. Saturn began selling right-side-drive cars in Japan in 1997 and began working to build a network of exclusive Saturn dealers in that country. The entry into Japan was complicated by a strong dollar versus all Asian currencies, thus hurting Japanese consumers' purchasing power. Saturn's small cars also faced intense competition in Japan from domestic producers Toyota, Honda, and Nissan.

Saturn's struggles could not be blamed solely on leadership within the division. Although GM's vast resources were a huge strength for Saturn, GM was hesitant to support Saturn. Instead, GM executives decided to make heavy investments in the Oldsmobile brand in an attempt to revive it. Another GM decision allowed Cadillac to develop a near-luxury sedan, the Catera, when Saturn could have benefited from the addition of a midsize sedan to its product line. Saturn was not included in GM's plans for development of SUVs. First, GM produced an SUV for Cadillac, the Escalade. Then it created a new category with the Pontiac Aztek: sports recreation vehicles (SRVs). When Saturn's VUE was introduced in late 2001, it was several years behind in the SUV market.

Saturn in the New Millennium

With Saturn appearing to be at a crossroads at the beginning of the twenty-first century, GM faced a difficult decision about what to do with its once-prized brand. In April 2000, GM announced that it would invest $1.5 billion in its Saturn unit for development of new products. About $1 billion of the investment went to develop and produce the VUE and the ION. Another $500 million was invested in the Spring Hill plant. Also, increased distribution became a focal point of Saturn's strategy. The company decided to grow from 433 dealerships in 2002 to 750 by 2012. As Saturn moved into its second decade, it faced the challenge of using the resources of its parent company while maintaining the distinct brand image it had developed during its first decade.

In an effort to expand its limited product line, Saturn rolled out several new models. The L-Series sedans and station wagons were introduced in the summer of 1999 with a $116 million advertising campaign. A midsize car, the L-Series represented Saturn's first models outside of its core subcompact line. The design of the L-Series sedan was based on the Opel Vectra, a GM Europe model. GM executives chose this route for developing an L-Series design rather than commissioning its domestic designers to create a unique design for Saturn. For the first time, production of Saturn models took place outside of Spring Hill—a former Chevrolet factory in Wilmington, Delaware, was selected as the site for L-Series production. GM's executives expected the L-Series to compete with popular import sedans such as the Honda Accord and the Toyota Camry. One advantage the L-Series held was price: The LS sedan was priced a couple of thousand dollars less than both Accord and Camry.

Unfortunately, the first year for the L-Series was filled with problems. Clashes between GM designers in Europe and the United States led to production delays at the Delaware plant. Thus, Saturn dealers did not have enough of the new models to sell when the ad campaign began. As production was accelerated to increase inventory levels, demand for the new models decreased. The resulting inventory buildup forced GM to shut down the Delaware plant for several days. Another factor contributing to the L-Series' slow start was an unsuccessful advertising campaign. The "Next Big Thing" campaign failed to show consumers that the L-series models were larger than the Saturn compact. GM scaled back its annual production forecast to 150,000 units from the more than 200,000 units that it had originally planned. Styling of the L-Series was also cited as a reason for its unspectacular splash in the market. Although some industry experts called the L-Series styling practical, many consumers saw the L-Series as plain and uninspired compared to such rivals as the Volkswagen Passat.

Saturn's long awaited entrance into the SUV market came with the introduction of the VUE in late 2001. With a base price of just over $17,000, the VUE was less expensive than comparable models such as Honda CR-V, Jeep Liberty, Ford Escape, and Hyundai Santa Fe. The VUE's design was consistent with Saturn's reputation for quality. Saturn positioned the VUE as an entry-level SUV for drivers 18–45 years old. The VUE's transmission uses a unique system of pulleys instead of gears. As a result, gas mileage is increased approximately 10 percent to 24 miles per gallon. The initial target market for the VUE was current Saturn owners. Next, former Saturn owners, many of whom switched from Saturn because of its limited product line, were targeted. Potential customers were targeted through event marketing. Saturn offered test drives of the VUE and L-Series at minor league baseball games in twenty-eight cities in 2002.

The reliable but conservatively styled S-Series was replaced with the ION in 2002. In addition to the quality focus for which Saturn was known, the ION had a considerably more modern look than the S-Series. Also, the ION had more interior room and a longer wheelbase than its predecessor. The ION was manufactured in a single four-door sedan and two quad coupe models featuring suicide doors. ION models were priced at $12,000 to $16,000, making them competitively priced with competing models such as the Ford Focus and Toyota Echo.

The design emphasis given to the ION was a deliberate attempt by Saturn to reach the 18- to 34-year-old market. Although many perceive Saturn as a car for younger consumers, the average age of a Saturn buyer is about 43. Promotion efforts for the ION targeted the younger demographic that Saturn desired to reach. In 2002 the ION was the title sponsor of a national tour by the rock band, Goo Goo Dolls. The thirty-three-city tour featured an ION display and interactive exhibits at the concerts. Young consumers were also targeted through Saturn's sponsorship of *Cram*, a television game show. In one episode, contestants were given an ION owner's manual and told to stay awake all night studying it to learn about the car. Then, if the contestants could correctly answer questions about the ION, they would win the car. College students were targeted through a traveling display that visited 65 colleges and interactive games on websites such as http://www.collegesports.com and http://www.collegeclub. com. Saturn was also battling a perception that it was a "chick's car." Over half of all Saturn owners are female, and there is a belief that some male buyers do not consider Saturn an option because they favor a sportier alternative.

Saturn at a Crossroads

Introduction of the VUE and the ION did little to reverse the trend of declining sales for Saturn. Sales in 2002 approached an all-time high for Saturn at approximately 280,000 units. However, the short-term boost provided by the VUE and ION quickly disappeared. Over the next three years, sales declined sharply, with 2005 sales down 24 percent from 2002 levels at just under 214,000 units (Case Exhibit 3.1). The favorable initial response to the VUE was overshadowed somewhat in 2004 when Saturn was forced to recall every VUE produced since its introduction—nearly 250,000 vehicles. A potential suspension failure caused the left rear wheel to buckle during government rollover tests. Even after Saturn replaced the suspension system, the VUE tipped up on two wheels during rollover tests. This created negative publicity about the VUE's safety.

Sales of the L-Series continued to be a major disappointment. Despite its price advantage and potential to appeal to present and former Saturn owners who desired a larger sedan, the L-Series never gained traction in the marketplace. With little prospect of increased sales for the L-Series, GM dropped it from the Saturn line in 2004. At the same time, sales of the ION coupe and sedan were not meeting expectations. At one point in early 2004, Saturn had a 108-day supply of IONs on hand, well over the normal level of 60 days. Numerous engineering and design changes were made to the ION for the 2005 model year in an attempt to correct problems that led to customer complaints. Despite all attempts to improve the ION, slow sales led GM to phase out the ION by the end of 2006. This decision left Saturn without a low-priced coupe or sedan, which was one of its key selling points during its early days.

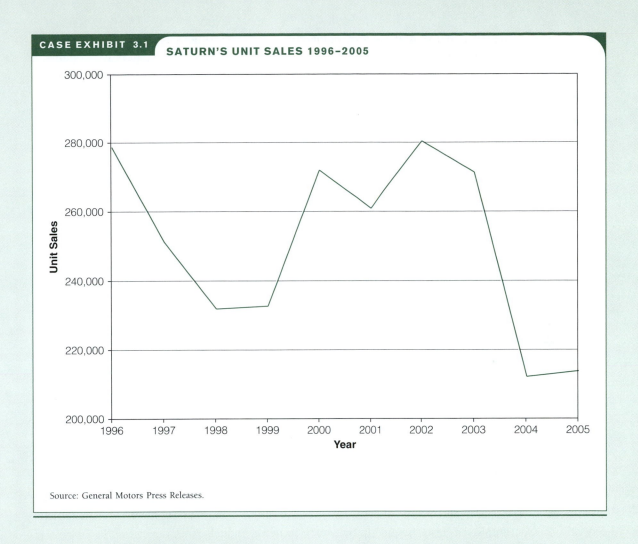

CASE EXHIBIT 3.1   SATURN'S UNIT SALES 1996–2005

Source: General Motors Press Releases.

In addition to product problems, Saturn's advertising strategy seemed to lack the clear direction of earlier years. Saturn parted ways with its original ad agency in 2002. A change in promotion strategy accompanied the change in ad agencies. The brand has had three different campaign slogans since the original "A different kind of company. A different kind of car." slogan was replaced in 2002. In a span of four years, the theme has changed from "It's different in a Saturn" (2002–2004) to "People first" (2004–2006), to "Like always. Like never before." (2006–). The most recent tagline is an attempt to return the brand to its roots in the hopes of recapturing the magic of the early years of Saturn.

Saturn's recent problems can be partially attributed to the nature of its relationship with GM. The lack of attention Saturn received from GM in the late 1990s had set back the company in its attempts to respond to shifting customer preferences. Many GM insiders disliked the autonomy that Saturn was given and thought the resources used to develop the Saturn brand should have been used on long-time GM brands such as Chevrolet and Oldsmobile. The autonomy of Saturn has diminished greatly in recent years, as more of the engineering and design functions have been centralized within GM. One distinct feature of Saturn vehicles, the dent-resistant polymer doors, is being switched to sheet-metal doors as used on other GM models. Also, the days of all Saturn models being built in Spring Hill are gone. Now several existing GM plants have begun producing Saturn models. Some GM executives and auto industry experts, in an effort to help GM manage its sizable portfolio of brands, have suggested the possibility of dropping the Saturn brand.

However, the elimination of Saturn does not appear to be the path that GM will take. In 2004 top management committed $3 billion to rejuvenate Saturn. Still, the problems at Saturn may be difficult to overcome as GM struggles with similar problems at the corporate level. The company has lost market share and been criticized for boring designs and slow reaction to changes in customer preferences. GM also struggles with many internal issues such as its overwhelmingly expensive employee retirement program. It remains to be seen whether GM can turn around the fortunes of the corporate brand as well as the Saturn nameplate.

Going Forward

The current emphasis at Saturn is on new products. Long criticized for lacking variety in its product line, Saturn is responding by introducing five new models during the 2004–2007 time period. The first new product in this period was the RELAY, a minivan introduced in 2004. It was the first Saturn model made without polymer fenders or door panels. The decision to stop using polymer panels was made in part because the plastic shrinks in cold temperatures, thereby increasing the gap between the panels (an obvious sign of poor fit and finish used in the auto industry). Polymer panels also take longer to produce than sheet-metal panels. The RELAY shares components with three different GM minivan models, another engineering characteristic employed more frequently by Saturn in newer models.

The second new model was the SKY, a two-seat roadster built on the same platform as the Pontiac Solstice but with a price tag $2,000 to $3,000 more. Introduced in 2006, the SKY emphasizes a sporty design that was developed by a collaboration of GM designers from Detroit, California, and the United Kingdom. A turbocharged model known as SKY Red Line was introduced at the end of 2006. In terms of image, the SKY represents GM's attempt to move Saturn away from a reputation of developing dependable but uninspiring cars. Rather than aiming at Japanese imports, Saturn is seeking to develop affordably priced cars with a European-design influence, sharing design and engineering resources with GM's Opel brand in Germany.

Three additional product introductions also appeared during this time frame. A hybrid VUE, known as the VUE Green Line, was introduced in the 2007 model year. Although it is not the first hybrid SUV on the market, the VUE Green Line has a pricing advantage over other hybrid models. Its price differential over the traditional VUE is $2,000, whereas the average differential in competing hybrids is over $3,000. The AURA sedan was introduced in late 2006 and has a distinctively European-design influence. The AURA gives Saturn a viable competitor to popular sedans such as the Camry and Accord. The final new product during this period was the OUTLOOK, a model that fits into the crossover category. Crossover vehicles provide benefits to consumers who want SUV-like capability but a carlike drive. The OUTLOOK is a seven-passenger vehicle with second-row seats that slide forward to allow easier access to third-row seating in the rear. It is expected that the next product introduction for Saturn will be a small crossover vehicle called the PREVUE. As of 2006, the PREVUE exists only as a concept vehicle. When launched, the PREVUE will represent Saturn's return to the small-car category. Although sales have slowed for Saturn in this category, record gas prices make its reentry into this market very appealing.

The emphasis on new product development fits with Saturn's strategy of moving toward selling higher-priced cars. Saturn has long held a reputation as an entry-level brand, and the move toward differentiating the brand through design and engineering improvements is an effort to expand beyond the lower-priced market. Some auto industry observers question Saturn's wisdom as its expanded product line makes it look more like other GM divisions rather than the unique company it set out to be. It has been noted that if Saturn had taken advantage of its early success in the small-car market and focused marketing efforts there, it would be firmly entrenched in that market today and not experiencing declining sales. For example, Saturn's S-Series outsold Honda's Civic by seven percent in 1994. Just 10 years later, Civic outsold Saturn's ION (the S-Series replacement) by 197 percent. Saturn's product line expansion is consistent with GM's strategy of expanding offerings within each nameplate. The company has moved away from designating certain brands to reach specific target markets. Instead, each brand has a mix of models that are intended to appeal to different customer segments.

Despite Saturn's challenges, the company has many positives on which to build. Customer satisfaction with Saturn vehicles remains very high. In 2002 Saturn ranked first in a J.D. Power & Associates survey of satisfaction with dealer service departments. This marked the first time a nonluxury brand took top honors. Saturn's new ad agency, Goodby, Silverstein & Partners, won a prestigious Golden Lion Award at the 2003 International Advertising Festival for "Sheet Metal," a commercial in which people are shown in car-related situations without their cars. Saturn dealers credited the ad campaign with increasing customer traffic in showrooms. In 2006 the VUE was the best small SUV according to the Total Quality Index, an annual survey of automobile owners' satisfaction with all aspects of the car ownership experience. Accomplishments such as these give Saturn a foundation for its future development.

Questions for Discussion

1. Analyze strategic market planning throughout Saturn's history. Has Saturn been successful in its planning efforts?

2. What do you make of Saturn's inconsistent performance since its early successes? What were the major causes of Saturn's challenges?

3. Is Saturn's recent focus on more stylish products such as the SKY and AURA inconsistent with its brand image? Is this a strength or a weakness for Saturn as it moves forward?

4. Would you purchase a Saturn? Why or why not? Do your reasons match Saturn's positioning?

Sources

These facts are from the General Motors website (http://www.gm.com) accessed April 22, 1998; Saturn website (http://www.saturn.com) accessed October 7, 2003; Marty Bernstein, "Auto Ads Create a Buzz at Cannes Festival," *Automotive News,* July 21, 2003, 18; Kristine Breese, "First Saturn Day: Diary of a Dealer," *Advertising Age,* October 29, 1990, 68; Julie Cantwell, "Saturn Works to Shed Small-Car Label," *Automotive News,* October 28, 2002, 1; Julie Cantwell, "Saturn's VUE: Attract Owners, Current and Past," *Automotive News,* January 22, 2001, 20; Sharon Silke Carty, "Saturn Puts Its Models Where Its Mouth Is," *USA Today,* April 19, 2006, 3B; Rich Ceppos, "Saturn—Finally, It's Here, But Is It Good Enough?" *Car and Driver,* November 1990, 132–138; Brian Corbett, "Saturn's Mission: Lassoing Those Young 'Uns," *Ward's Dealer Business,* January 1, 2003; Stuart Elliott, "Campaign Takes Aim at Heartstrings," *USA Today,* November 1, 1990, 1B, 2B; Jerry Flint, "Saturn: The Forgotten Promise," *Forbes Online,* (http://www.forbes.com/2004/08/17/cz_jf_0817flint_print.html) accessed August 17, 2004; "GM Again Earns Most Quality Awards, Says Strategic Vision," StrategicVison.com http://www.strategicvision.com/press_release.php?pr=15) accessed June 19, 2006; "GM Recalls All Saturn VUE SUVs for Suspension Failure," *Consumer Reports,* October 2004, 10; Bob Garfield, "Down-to-Earth Ads Give Saturn an Underrated Liftoff," *Advertising Age,* October 29, 1990, 68; Karl Greenberg, "Saturn Eyes Its Loyalists in VUE Debut," *Brandweek,* March 5, 2001, 6; Dave Guilford, "Slow-Selling Saturn ION Gets Mid-Course Correction, *Automotive News,* May 31, 2004, 4; Jean Halliday, "Saturn Revamps Strategy: New Advertising Tack Moves Beyond Customer Service, Focuses on Safety, Style," *Advertising Age,* October 28, 2002, 4; James R. Healey, "Saturn Demand Delivers Excitement to Dealers," *USA Today,* November 5, 1990, 1B; James R. Healey, "Saturn, Day One: Business is Brisk," *USA Today,* October 26, 1990, 1B, 2B; Rick Kranz, "Saturn Takes Plastic Off Its New Minivan, *Automotive News,* October 6, 2003, 1; Barbara Lippert, "It's a Saturn Morning in America," *Adweek,* October 15, 1990, 67; Michelle Maynard, "Fulfilling Buyers' Wishes, Saturn's Well Runs Dry," *USA Today,* August 18, 1992, 1B; Michelle Maynard, "Sales Slump Forces Saturn to Cut Production," *USA Today,* January 21, 1998, 1B; Robyn Meredith, "As Sales Fall, Saturn Workers to Vote on Ditching Contract," *Commercial Appeal [Memphis, TN],* March 8, 1998, C1, C3; Steve Miller, "Saturn Shoots for the Moon with Updated Slogan," *Brandweek Online,* (http://www.brandweek.com/bw/news/recent/_display.jsp?vnu_content_id=1002315190) accessed April 11, 2006; Ian P. Murphy, "Charged Up: Electric Cars Get Jolt of Marketing," *Marketing News,* August 18, 1997, 1, 7; Matt Nauman, "Saturn's VUE Worthy of Consideration,"

Knight-Ridder/Tribune News Service, May 10, 2002; Rick Popely, "Non-Luxury Saturn Auto Tops Customer Service Survey,"*Knight-Ridder/Tribune Business News,* July 15, 2002; Al Ries, "The Sad and Unnecessary Decline of Saturn," *Advertising Age Online,* (http://adage.com/news.cms?newsid=46020) accessed September 12, 2005; "Saturn's Next Frontier," *Automotive Industries,* December 2004, 21–23; "Saturn Tries to Change 'Chick Car' Image," *Marketing to Women: Addressing Women and Women's Sensibilities,* March 2003, 9; Amy Schatz, "GM Saturn's SUV Still Tips Up in Rollover Test Despite New Parts," *Wall Street Journal,* August 24, 2004, D4; Raymond Serafin, "Saturn's Goal: To Be Worthy," *Advertising Age,* November 5, 1990, 21; Raymond Serafin, "The Saturn Story," *Advertising Age,* November 16, 1992, 1, 13, 16; Raymond Serafin and Patricia Strand, "Saturn People Star in First Campaign," *Advertising Age,* August 27, 1990, 1, 38; Neal Templin and Joseph B. White, "GM's Saturn, in Early Orbit, Intrigues Buyers," *Wall Street Journal,* October 25, 1990, B1, B6; James B. Treece, "Here Comes GM's Saturn," *BusinessWeek,* April 9, 1990, 56–62; "23 More Dealers Open Doors to Saturn Buyers," *USA Today,* November 15, 1990, 6B; Gary S. Vasilash, "Saturn Turns Green," *Automotive Design & Production,* April 2006, 42; Phil West, "Saturn Corp. Rings Up First Profitable Month," *Commercial Appeal [Memphis, TN],* June 11, 1993, B2; David Welch, "Will These Rockets Rescue Saturn?" *BusinessWeek,* January 17, 2005, 78; David Welch, "Can Saturn Get Off the Ground Again?" *BusinessWeek,* October 14, 2002, 79–80; Joseph B. White and Melinda Grenier Guiles, "Rough Launch," *Wall Street Journal,* July 9, 1990, A1, A12; G. Chamber Williams III, "ION Recharges Saturn's Entry-Level Lineup," *Seattle Post-Intelligencer,* January 17, 2003, F1; Cindy Wolff, "First Saturn Here Runs Jag Off Road," *Commercial Appeal [Memphis, TN],* October 26, 1990, A1, A12; Gary Witzenburg, "GM's New Minivans," *Automotive Industries,* December 2004, 35; and David Woodruff, James B. Treece, Sunita Wadekar Bhargava, and Karen Lowry Miller, "Saturn: GM Finally Has a Real Winner. But Success Is Bringing a Fresh Batch of Problems," *BusinessWeek,* August 17, 1992, 86–91.

Champ Car World Series

Champ Car World Series LLC originally began as Championship Auto Racing Teams (CART) in 1978. Several team owners created CART as a sanctioning body for open-wheel racing in the United States. Open-wheel racing refers to cars whose wheels are located outside the body of the car rather than underneath the body or fenders as found on street cars. Also, they have an open cockpit, also called a pod, with the engine housed at the rear of the vehicle. The United States Auto Club (USAC) originally sanctioned the sport in the mid-1950s, but many racing teams were dissatisfied with USAC's administration and promotion of open-wheel racing. Consequently, CART was founded when 18 of the 21 team owners left USAC. Among the founders of CART were Roger Penske, Dan Gurney, and Pat Patrick, all of whom were highly respected figures in American motor sports. CART held fourteen races in its 1979 inaugural season, including the prestigious Indianapolis 500. The next season, the CART racing series signed PPG Industries as a title sponsor—a relationship that continued until 1997.

Growth and Division of Open-Wheel Racing in the United States

For the first 17 years of its existence, CART dominated auto racing in the United States, and open-wheel racing enjoyed greater notoriety than other forms of racing, including stock-car racing. One of the reasons was the excitement factor: Open-wheel cars regularly exceeded 230 miles per hour. In the 1980s, CART attracted legendary driver Mario Andretti to participate in its series after he had spent several seasons splitting time between U.S. open-wheel racing and Europe's premier open-wheel racing series, Formula 1. Also, CART attracted Paul Newman, a famous actor with a passion for auto racing, to become involved with the series as a team co-owner. During this time, a board of directors composed of team owners managed and promoted CART.

Don Roy, Middle Tennessee State University, prepared this case for classroom discussion rather than to illustrate effective or ineffective handling of an administrative situation.

The CART series continued to enjoy increasing popularity at the beginning of the 1990s. In 1990, prizes of over $1 million were offered for six of CART's events. CART went international at the beginning of the 1991 season. That year, the season opening race was held in Surfer's Paradise, Australia. Further interest in CART in foreign countries developed when Formula 1 champion Nigel Mansell became a teammate of Mario Andretti in 1993. Mansell's participation in the CART series drew considerable media coverage from foreign media at CART events. The success of another foreign driver, Brazil's Emerson Fittipaldi, provided CART with even more international exposure.

Everyone associated with open-wheel racing in the United States did not welcome the success enjoyed by CART in the early 1990s. One person with major concerns about the direction of CART was Anton H. "Tony" George, president of the Indianapolis Motor Speedway. George's family had founded the Indianapolis 500 and developed it into the premier American auto race and an event of worldwide significance. George was concerned that CART was beginning to lose sight of the interests of American open-wheel racing by holding events in foreign countries, putting too much emphasis on racing at road courses instead of oval tracks, and focusing too much on promoting top foreign drivers as CART stars. CART responded to George's concerns by reorganizing the board of directors into a seven-member body with nonvoting seats for CART's CEO and the president of the Indianapolis Motor Speedway (Tony George).

The move to include Tony George on CART's board of directors failed to appease him. In 1994 George announced that he was creating a new open-wheel league that would compete with CART beginning in 1996. The proposed Indy Racing League (IRL) was divisive to open-wheel racing in the United States because team owners were forced to decide whether to remain with CART or move to the new IRL. Only IRL members would be allowed to race in the Indianapolis 500. George deepened the rift further when he proposed a "25/8" rule for the 1996 Indianapolis 500: The first twenty-five positions in the thirty-three-car field would go to IRL members, while only eight positions would be available for CART members. CART teams responded to this tactic by planning its own event on the same day as the Indianapolis 500. CART held the U.S. 500 at the Michigan International Speedway on Memorial Day weekend, 1996, and drew over 100,000 spectators to the event. The rift between CART and the IRL moved to the courts when lawsuits were filed over use of the terms "IndyCar" and "Indy car," which CART had licensed from the Indianapolis Motor Speedway for several years. The result of the lawsuit was that neither party could use the terms until December 31, 2002.

CART continued to be a dominant force in American open-wheel racing after the split with the IRL. The seven-member board was scrapped, and the board membership structure returned solely to the team owners. Although CART teams continued to be excluded from the Indianapolis 500, its stable of corporate sponsors remained strong. Both Honda and Toyota remained as engine suppliers for CART. In 1998 Federal Express (FedEx) became the title sponsor of the CART Racing Series, replacing PPG Industries, and the series was renamed the CART-FedEx Championship Series.

The single most significant move following the CART/IRL split was the incorporation of CART as a publicly traded company in 1998. CART was listed on the New York Stock Exchange, and the initial public offering yielded over $100 million for CART to employ in its battle against IRL.

CART's success immediately following the split with IRL was replaced by disappointment at the turn of the century. After four years away from the Indianapolis 500, a CART team entered the race in 2000. Two cars owned by Chip Ganassi Racing entered the race, and one of Ganassi's cars won. CART races in Brazil and Texas were canceled during the 2001 season, resulting in public relations embarrassments for CART. Toyota and Honda discontinued their association with CART and forged new partnerships with the rival IRL. Top management turmoil was evident, too, as CART went through four CEOs during 2000 and 2001: Andrew Craig, Bobby Rahal, Joseph Heitzler, and Chris Pook. Pook had been successful as the promoter of the CART Long Beach Grand Prix event. Pook's challenge was to bring stability to an organization that had been so embroiled in a battle with the IRL that fan interest shifted to NASCAR in the United States and Formula 1 in Europe.

CART's Troubled Times

CART's feud with the IRL distracted both leagues and stock-car racing solidified its standing as the favorite motor sport in the United States. A 2001 ESPN Sports Poll survey found that 56 percent of American auto-racing fans said stock-car racing was their favorite type of racing, with open-wheel racing third at nine percent (drag racing was second at 12 percent). Worse yet for CART was that open-wheel racing fans said that IRL was their favorite type of open-wheel racing, with 42 percent preferring IRL versus 32 percent for CART. Television broadcasts of CART races could be instrumental in expanding the league's following, but CART was mired in an unfavorable television rights deal. CART had to pay to have its races broadcast, whereas IRL was paid by ABC for the rights to broadcast its races on ABC and ESPN. For the 2003 season, television contracts with CBS and Fox called for seven CART races to be broadcast on CBS, with CART paying for air time and production costs. CART sold advertising inventory to generate revenues. Speed TV carried the remaining CART races under the same arrangement as with CBS. Although Speed TV is a cable television outlet that targets auto-racing enthusiasts, its reach of about 75 percent of U.S. households is not as great as a broadcast network such as CBS.

The diminished appeal of CART may have contributed to additional problems with sponsor relationships. Three major partners left CART in recent seasons. Two partners, Honda and Toyota, provided engines and technical support to CART and its teams. The departure of these engine suppliers forced CART to scramble and line up support from Ford's Cosworth engines. Ford's participation was timely because another need arose when FedEx discontinued its title-sponsor relationship with CART after the 2002 season. The loss of FedEx was significant for two reasons. First, FedEx had renewed its sponsorship after the 2001 season for another four years, but it exercised an exit clause in its contract after only one year of the renewal period. Second, FedEx was valuable to CART because it shipped a great deal of cargo to CART racing sites in foreign markets. For the 2003 season, CART had two major series sponsors, Ford and the Bridgestone Tire Company. CART's Champ Car series was now known as "Bridgestone Presents Champ Car World Series Powered by Ford."

CART's viability as a major racing league was negatively impacted by the defection of key racing teams to IRL. The major loss was when Roger Penske, one of CART's founders, moved his racing team to IRL following the 2001 season. Also, Michael Andretti, one of CART's most successful drivers, assumed a new role as a team owner in IRL after the 2002 season. Another key owner leaving for the IRL was Chip Ganassi, whose teams had been very successful in CART. The defection of teams to IRL left CART in a position that it might not be able to field the eighteen cars needed to hold races. CART responded by offering financial incentives to team owners to ensure enough cars would participate in its races. Also, CART was forced to become the promoter of its own races after losing promoters in some markets. Further, selling sponsorships at the league and individual race levels was complicated by a weak economy. The combined result of an unfavorable television deal, sponsor and team owner defections, and increased costs of holding races forced CART into a dangerous financial position.

The financial stability brought about by the initial public offering of CART stock in 1998 was gone, and questions arose about CART's ability to survive. During 2003 the company reported that increased operating costs and sluggish advertising and sponsorship revenue created uncertainty about CART's ability to complete the 2004 season. CART retained investment banking firm Bear, Stearns & Company to explore strategic options for CART, including a possible sale. Three options were mentioned by auto-racing industry observers as possible solutions to CART's problems:

1. CART could merge with Formula 1 and become a feeder series to the Formula 1 circuit.

2. CART could focus solely on road courses and position itself as a road course circuit.

3. CART could merge with IRL.

A New Beginning: Champ Car World Series

CART's financial position continued to deteriorate during 2003. The low point for CART occurred in late 2003 when the company's stock was delisted by the New York Stock Exchange after it traded below $1 per share for 30 consecutive days. Ultimately, CART filed for Chapter 11 bankruptcy organization. About the same time, a group of three CART team owners, Gerald Forsythe, Paul Gentilozzi, and Kevin Kalkhoven, announced that they were making an offer to purchase the embattled company. The group formed Open Wheel Racing Series LLC (now known as Champ Car World Series LLC) and purchased CART's assets for 56¢ per share. The group took CART private once again and announced that it would continue to operate under the name "Champ Car World Series." The decision was made not to merge with another racing league and attempt to return the circuit to the prominence it enjoyed prior to the formation of the IRL.

Despite the skepticism of many racing observers whether Champ Car could survive, it has done just that in its first three seasons since going private. A distinctive strategy emerged as the series worked to gain traction in the auto-racing market. A key part of the strategy Champ Car implemented pertained to the number of races held and mix of venues. The season schedule was reduced from 19 races to 14, with the geographic scope of races focused primarily on North America. Champ Car's 2006 schedule included eight U.S. races, as well as races in Canada (three), Mexico (two), and Australia (one). Champ Car continued CART's focus of racing on road courses. Road courses are either permanent racetrack facilities or temporary courses that run through the streets of an urban area. For example, Champ Car runs races on temporary courses through the streets of Denver and on the grounds of the Burke Lakefront Airport in Cleveland. In 2006, only one of Champ Car's fourteen scheduled races took place on an oval track. The other 13 races were basically split between road courses (seven races) and temporary street courses (six races).

Another key component of Champ Car's differentiation strategy is the positioning of individual race events. Champ Car has coined the phrase "Festival of Speed" to position its events, where the race itself is only one piece of Champ Car's product offering. In addition to the race, fans can often partake in such activities as kids' zones, beach volleyball, wine tasting, or live concerts. Champ Car President Steve Johnson gave the best description of Champ Car's strategy when he said, "We throw a party and a race breaks out." He adds that "we don't want people to come out and sit in metal grandstands for three hours and get sweaty and get sunburned and go home. We want stuff going on everywhere." The festival concept appears to be a success so far. The 2006 street race at Long Beach, California, attracted an estimated 200,000 people during the three-day event, including more than 80,000 people on race day. Champ Car is optimistic that the festival concept will deliver similar success stories in other markets.

Champ Car's drivers represent North America, South America, Europe, and Australia. Champ Car leverages the geographic diversity of its drivers by placing emphasis on geographic allegiances. In 1995, CART created the Nations Cup, an award that recognizes the country whose drivers score the best overall finish during the season. France won the Nations Cup for the first time in 2005 after two consecutive wins for Canada (2003–2004), four consecutive wins for Brazil (1999–2002), and four consecutive wins for the United States (1995–1998). As a result of Champ Car's international focus, it enjoys greater television exposure outside of the United States than the IRL because televised Champ Car races reach auto-racing fans in more than 200 countries each year.

While Champ Car enjoys substantial global television exposure, its U.S. television coverage has been a concern for several years. A priority for the new ownership was to land a television deal that did not require Champ Car to pay to air its races. In 2004 Champ Car races were aired on cable television channel Spike TV. This deal gave

Champ Car coverage on a male-targeted channel, but low ratings (audiences of less than one percent of U.S. television households) left Champ Car longing to have a broadcast partner with greater impact. In 2006 all 14 races were televised, with a mix of seven races broadcast by Speed TV, three races by NBC, and four races by CBS. Sponsor interest in Champ Car appears to be on the upswing, too. In addition to series sponsors Bridgestone and Ford, Champ Car has signed McDonald's and Sherwin-Williams as official sponsors. In individual race markets, high-profile brands such as Coca-Cola, Wal-Mart, FedEx, Red Bull, and Samsung have been signed as event sponsors. Champ Car officials attribute the increased sponsor interest in the festival concept and its potential for sponsors to have a presence among 150,000 or more people in a three-day period.

The Motor Sports Market

Many forms of motor sports exist, but competition for Champ Car can be narrowed to three properties: the IRL, Formula 1, and NASCAR. Each competitor is discussed next.

IRL

Champ Car's primary competitor is the Indy Racing League. When CART and IRL split before the 1996 season, it did more than split the racing teams. Fans tended to follow the league in which their favorite drivers participated instead of following both leagues. More important, sponsorship support was split between the two open-wheel leagues. IRL had the Indianapolis 500 to offer corporate sponsors but little else. CART's value as a sponsorship property decreased considerably without the Indy 500 on its schedule. In an effort to distinguish one league from the other, both IRL and CART attempted to brand their leagues. IRL now calls its cars "Indy Cars," a term it can finally use after its use was restricted in the CART/IRL legal dispute. Champ Car has branded its cars "Champ Cars" although the name has not gained widespread acceptance among motor sports fans.

Despite the apparent duplication of open-wheel racing by Champ Car and IRL, two major differences exist between the two leagues. First, the leagues differ with respect to the types of racecourses employed. IRL races are held primarily on oval tracks whereas the majority of Champ Car races are held on road courses. Only three of fourteen IRL races in 2006 were held on road courses. A major difference between road courses and oval tracks is that it is more difficult for cars to pass on road courses, which places a premium on drivers' skills to successfully navigate a track. On the other hand, oval-track racing is influenced more by the horsepower and aerodynamics of the racecars, placing a premium on engineering and technical expertise to gain an edge over competitors. Second, Champ Car and IRL differ in terms of the geographic scope of their leagues. Champ Car holds races throughout North America and a single race in Australia, and the IRL is almost exclusively an American circuit. Only one of fourteen IRL races in 2006 was held outside the United States, in Motegi, Japan. IRL's focus on U.S. venues is consistent with Tony George's concerns in the early 1990s that CART had lost its American roots. The IRL is not only U.S. oriented but also can be defined further as midwestern focused. Of the thirteen races in 2006, only one race was held farther west than Texas. Its marquee event continues to be the Indianapolis 500 although interest in the event as measured by television ratings has declined substantially since the CART/IRL split.

Like CART/Champ Car, the IRL has experienced ups and downs in the years following the split. Interest in IRL as measured by television ratings took a noticeable dip between 2002 and 2004, with 25 percent fewer viewers tuning in 2004 than just two years earlier. The declining television audience has been a factor in the IRL's inability to sell naming rights for its series. The IRL last had a title sponsor for the series in 2001, Internet search engine Northern Light. In contrast, NASCAR signed a blockbuster deal with Nextel that called for more $700 million over ten years beginning in 2004. Industry experts believe that the most the IRL could command for its title sponsorship currently is about $50 million over ten years.

In response to declining interest in the IRL, marketing initiatives were taken to reverse the trend. First, the IRL beefed up its marketing staff. The league did not even have a dedicated marketing staff until 2001. Prior to 2001, IRL marketing was handled by marketing personnel at the Indianapolis Motor Speedway. In 2005, the IRL launched a new ad campaign that targeted 18- to 34-year-old males. The focus of the ads was different, too. Instead of focusing on the cutting-edge technology found in IRL cars, as had been done in previous ad campaigns, the focus shifted to drivers and the drama created on the track. The campaign was part of a broader strategy to expand the association of IRL beyond a sport for middle-aged midwestern males. The idea is to position the brand as hip and young.

In support of this effort, two developments can be noted. First, the IRL has followed a trend observed in NASCAR and has gotten several celebrities involved in the sport through team ownership. Among the celebrities involved with IRL teams are talk show host David Letterman, NBA star Carmelo Anthony, former NFL quarterback Jim Harbaugh, and actor Patrick Dempsey. Another celebrity involved with the IRL is rock star Gene Simmons, a partner in Simmons Abramson Marketing, who was hired to help the IRL devise new marketing strategies. The firm's entertainment marketing savvy is being tapped to help the IRL connect with fans on an emotional level through its drivers, whom Simmons referred to as "rock stars in rocket ships." Second, the emergence of Danica Patrick as a star in the IRL has broadened appeal of the league and assists the efforts to reach young males. Patrick was a 23-year-old IRL rookie in 2005 who finished fourth in the Indianapolis 500. The combination of the novelty of a female driver and her captivating looks and personality made Patrick the darling of American sports in 2005. Patrick's effect on the IRL was very noticeable; the IRL reported gains in event attendance, merchandise sales, website traffic, and television ratings during Patrick's rookie season. Patrick has drawn the interest of many companies that have sought to hire her as a product endorser.

Formula 1

Formula 1 is an open-wheel series that has the greatest global reach in terms of race venues and races exclusively on road courses. Formula 1's eighteen-race 2006 schedule included ten races in Europe as well as races in Australia, Bahrain, Brazil, Canada, China, Japan, Malaysia, and the United States. A Formula 1 race is known as a Grand Prix, with each race taking on the name of the country hosting a particular race (for example, Grand Prix of Spain). Formula 1 was the first racing league in the Western Hemisphere to stage an event in the lucrative Chinese market. Formula 1 drivers have the same international flavor as Champ Car: Most hail from European countries although there are also drivers from Canada, Columbia, and Japan. The winner of the Formula 1 season series is referred to as the "World F1 Driving Champion," further reinforcing Formula 1 as a global racing league.

NASCAR

The auto-racing leader in the U.S. motor sports market is NASCAR (National Association of Stock Car Auto Racing). It was founded in the early 1950s, approximately the same time period when USAC was founded. NASCAR fields three racing circuits in the United States: The Nextel Cup Series, the Busch Grand National Series, and the Craftsman Truck Series. The Nextel Cup Series is NASCAR's premier circuit. Its thirty-six races are held primarily on oval tracks and exclusively in U.S. markets. Like the IRL, NASCAR has a strong regional following, with the southeastern United States being a long-time hotbed for the league. NASCAR was predominantly a southern U.S. sport until the 1990s as exposure provided by cable television and the emergence of strong driver personalities such as Dale Earnhart and Jeff Gordon led to an explosion in NASCAR's popularity. The league has become even more popular as it has focused on promoting its drivers, especially young drivers often referred to as NASCAR's "Young Guns." League and sponsor promotion of drivers such as Dale Earnhart, Jr., Jimmie Johnson, Ryan Newman, and Kasey Kahne has vaulted NASCAR to a level of popularity in the United States second only to the National Football League.

Today, NASCAR towers over Champ Car and IRL in the United States in terms of sponsor support and audiences. NASCAR has sought to expand to become a truly national sport, adding races in Chicago, southern California, and Texas while eliminating races in smaller markets such as Rockingham, North Carolina. Future expansion plans include adding events in the Pacific Northwest and the New York City area. The average television audience for NASCAR races in 2006 averaged approximately 6 percent of U.S. households, compared to less than 2 percent for IRL and less than 1 percent for Champ Car. As a result of NASCAR's popularity growth, it was able to negotiate a lucrative, multibillion dollar contract with Fox and ESPN, while Champ Car has struggled to secure a favorable television deal.

A Look to the Future

Many racing observers believe that open-wheel racing could have been as popular as NASCAR is today. In the 1980s and early 1990s, it was CART that enjoyed greater popularity and television ratings. The split in open-wheel racing that led to the formation of the IRL was a setback to open-wheel racing in general. The split resulted in a dilution of competition quality, sponsor dollars, and fan support. Many experts believe a reunification of open-wheel racing is the only way to compete against NASCAR. The animosity that existed in the mid-1990s appears to have subsided somewhat as many owners and drivers in both leagues have come to the same conclusion. While reunification has been rumored occasionally in recent years, no indication of such a move has been evident. However, hopes for reunification were raised in 2006 when the IRL's Tony George and Champ Car's Kevin Kalkhoven held talks about merging the two bodies.

Great optimism that IRL and Champ Car might finally resolve their differences and once again form a single open-wheel racing league circulated in 2006. Media reports indicated that George and Kalkhoven had agreed on many points about a unified league. Speculation circulated about the makeup of the merged league's schedule. The marquee event of the league would be the Indianapolis 500, with about fifteen other events that included the most popular races from both leagues' schedules. The schedule would likely be more of a blend of road courses and oval tracks than each league has had on its own schedule. Also, the schedule would likely include events from Champ Car's schedule in Canada and Mexico, markets that the IRL has not visited. Engine and tire suppliers for both leagues have given positive feedback to reunification and appear to be willing to work with a merged IRL/Champ Car. Finally, a merger would positively impact the quality and quantity of competition. For most races, IRL and Champ Car have about eighteen to twenty entries. A combined open-wheel league would create a larger pool of drivers and bring the most talented drivers together. However, with the pace of progress toward reunification slow to nonexistent, it appears that Champ Car should prepare for the near future as an independent entity.

Kevin Kalkhoven and other top management at Champ Car have much to consider when it comes to a proposed merger with the IRL. Although many drivers, owners, and sponsors in both Champ Car and the IRL are in favor of a merger, Champ Car might not be in need of help to survive as it was just a few years ago. The festival concept has been very successful, and the league has stabilized in terms of the markets in which it races as well as its overall health. Outside of the Indianapolis 500, Champ Car races packaged around three-day festivals have much higher attendance than IRL races. It has differentiated itself from IRL through a focus on road courses. For the 2007 racing season, Champ Car plans races in new venues such as Las Vegas, Phoenix, St. Jovite, Canada, and Zhuhai, China. Also, it has a series title sponsor, and the IRL does not. It is possible that Champ Car could continue its growth and eclipse the IRL as the preferred open-wheel racing league in the United States.

Conclusion

Auto racing is the fastest-growing spectator sport in the United States. Unfortunately, open-wheel racing has experienced a period of decline while other forms of auto racing have grown. Champ Car's new owners have repositioned the league and allowed it to survive at a time when its survival was uncertain. However, Champ Car is still second to the IRL in terms of popularity, and both leagues are far behind

NASCAR. Champ Car must strengthen its standing, either by overtaking the IRL in the marketplace or joining forces with it in a merger. That sentiment was shared by many sports industry executives in a 2006 survey, which indicated that 75 percent of industry executives polled believe that there are not enough fans in the United States to support both the IRL and Champ Car.

Questions for Discussion

1. Identify the external factors that have impacted and continue to impact Champ Car and its marketing efforts. Which factors appear to be Champ Car's greatest threats?

2. What are Champ Car's greatest strengths? Which weaknesses would you recommend that Champ Car attempt to convert into strengths? How might these weaknesses be converted?

3. What advantages does Champ Car possess over the IRL? How should these advantages be used by Champ Car to compete with the IRL?

4. How should Champ Car be positioned to differentiate it from other racing leagues, both in the United States and abroad?

5. What can Champ Car learn from NASCAR's success? Are there elements of NASCAR's marketing strategy that Champ Car could adopt?

Sources

The facts of this case are from Debbie Arrington, "Racing Factions Talking Merger: Champ Car and the IRL Could Be on the Verge Mending a Decade-Old Rift," *Knight-Ridder/Tribune Business News*, April 14, 2006, 1; Debbie Arrington, "IRL Preview: IRL Tweaks Tune, Vies for New Dance Partners," *Knight-Ridder/Tribune Business News,* March 24, 2006, 1; Steve Ballard, "Championship Auto Racing Teams' Board Votes to Accept Buyout," *Knight-Ridder/Tribune Business News,* December 16, 2003, 1; Terry Blount, "Reuniting IRL, Champ Car Is an Uphill Climb," *Knight-Ridder/Tribune Business News,* June 4, 2006, 1; Theresa Bradley, "Racing League Gears Hip Events at Youth," *Knight-Ridder/Tribune Business News,* March 23, 2006, 1; "Celebrities Who Are Revved Up Over Racing," *Street & Smith's Sports Business Journal,* May 22, 2006, 27; "Championship Auto Racing Teams Announces Its Plan to Explore Strategic Alternatives and Outlines 2003 Financial Guidance," Shareholder.com, June 16, 2003 (http://www/shareholder.com/cart/news/20030616-111383.cfm); "Champ Car World Series Announces 15-Race Schedule for 2007," Champ Car World Series press release, September 27, 2006 (http://www.champcarworldseries.com/News/Article.asp?ID=10945); "Corporate and Sponsor Support Continues to Grow for Champ Car World Series," Champ Car World Series website, June 30, 2006 (http://www.champcarworldseries.com/News/Article.asp?ID=10487&print=true); Robin Miller, "New Owners Could Focus on Streets," ESPN.com, August 10, 2003 (http://espn.go.com/rpm/cart/2003/0810/159430.html); Neil Hohlfeld, "Champ Car Has Its Strong Points," *Knight-Ridder/Tribune Business News,* July 22, 2006, 1; Neil Hohlfeld, "Champ Car Hoping to Use Houston to Gain Momentum," *Knight-Ridder/Tribune Business News,* May 12, 2006, 1; Bill McGuire, "From Survival to Success?" *Autoweek,* February 21, 2005, 32–33; Jennifer Pendleton, "Danica Patrick," *Advertising Age,* November 7, 2005, S4; "Say It's So: Champ Car and IRL to End War?" *Autoweek,* February 27, 2006, 37–38; Anthony Schoettle, "Merger Talks Near Finish?" *Indianapolis Business Journal,* May 8, 2006, 1; Anthony Schoettle, "IRL Ratings Continue Their Skid," *Indianapolis Business Journal,* November 1, 2004, 3; Anthony Schoettle, "IRL Shops for Title Sponsor," *Indianapolis Business Journal,* August 18, 2003, 3; Alan Snel, "Kiss Rocker Lends Voice to Indy Races," *Knight-Ridder/Tribune Business News,* April 1, 2006, 1; "Turnkey Sports Poll," *Street & Smith's Sports Business Journal,* May 22, 2006, 24; J. P. Vettraino, "Champ Car: Midseason Update," *Autoweek,* July 26, 2004, 48; J. P. Vettraino, "Television Rating: The Peaks and Valleys of CART's New Package," *Autoweek,* August 21, 2001; J. K. Wall, "Indy Racing League Sets Sights on Marketing Dollars," *Knight-Ridder/Tribune Business News,* May 27, 2004, 1; Scott Warfield, "IRL Marketing Chief Aims for Consistency," *Street & Smith's Sports Business Journal,* February 20, 2006, 9; Scott Warfield, "Danica Patrick Provides Sizzle to IRL," *Street & Smith's Sports Business Journal,* May 23, 2005, 1; and Scott Warfield, "IRL in Line to Court Young Males," *Street & Smith's Sports Business Journal,* November 29, 2004, 4.

Blockbuster
Movie Rentals in the Digital Era

In 2005 Blockbuster, Inc. sat at the top of the global home video-rental industry. However, Blockbuster's success, its future beyond 2006, was uncertain. At the close of 2005, Blockbuster owned or franchised over 9,000 stores in 25 countries. A majority (62 percent) of its stores and revenues were within the United States. Looking into the future, the success of the company would depend upon its ability to adapt to and adopt new technology and marketing practices. From its meager beginnings, Blockbuster has consistently faced competitive challenges. However, changing technology and shifting customer preferences with respect to movie distribution are likely to be Blockbuster's biggest challenge to date.

Blockbuster's History

Blockbuster started in 1985 as a small entrepreneurial venture. David Cook sold his computing services business and started a handful of computerized video-rental stores. Then in 1986, he transformed his company into Blockbuster Entertainment. As the company showed strong growth and potential, investors began eyeing the company as a potential investment opportunity. In stepped entrepreneur Wayne Huizenga, who in 1987 brought to the company a large financial boost ($18 million) and a vision to expand the company into the largest video-rental company in the United States. By the end of 1987, Huizenga bought full interest in the company. In three years, Huizenga took the company from 130 stores to 1,500 stores. The growth included the acquisition of Major Video (175 stores) and Erol's, which was the third largest U.S. video-rental chain at the time.

Early Expansion

In the 1990s, the company maintained a very aggressive expansion and acquisition program. Blockbuster expanded into the music industry when it acquired Sound Warehouse and Music Plus in 1992. These acquisitions allowed the company to develop the Blockbuster Music component of its overall business. While this was taking place, the company also expanded internationally. One of the largest international

Keith C. Jones, North Carolina A&T State University, prepared this case for classroom discussion rather than to illustrate effective or ineffective handling of an administrative situation.

moves was the purchase of Cityvision, which provided Blockbuster with 875 stores throughout the United Kingdom. Then in 1993, Blockbuster made its next expansion move with the acquisition of the Spelling Entertainment group. This provided Blockbuster with key industry access. Huizenga's final visionary action before moving on to other entrepreneurial ventures was the handing off of Blockbuster to Viacom, which created the Blockbuster Entertainment Group.

The mid-1990s was a tumultuous era for Blockbuster. From 1994 to 1997, Blockbuster experienced frequent turnover in upper management and a repositioning—changes that almost proved fatal to the company. When Huizenga stepped down as CEO, Steven Berrard filled the vacancy. Berrard stayed on as CEO until 1996 when he left the company and joined forces with Huizenga. Then Bill Fields stepped in from an executive position at Wal-Mart. Fields brought with him the Wal-Mart persona and immediately started repositioning Blockbuster from a rental format to a retail sales format. During this repositioning, Fields closed 50 of the music stores and moved the corporate headquarters from Florida to Dallas, Texas. Some members of the upper management group opted not to follow the company to Texas, creating critical vacancies in the company. Fields resigned from his position in 1997.

Back to Basics

In a lifesaving move, Blockbuster's board brought in John Antioco as the next CEO. After a review of the company, Antioco immediately repositioned the company back to its traditional competitive advantage in home entertainment rental. In doing so, Antioco reformatted the stores as rental facilities for movies and games. He retained a minimal retail sales component but focused all promotional efforts on the rental industry. To improve the competitive advantage of the company, Antioco renegotiated contracts with movie studios. Traditionally, movie rental companies were required to pay large sums of money per copy of a movie (as much as $120). Antioco developed a revenue-sharing approach that allowed Blockbuster to obtain more copies of a movie (paying a smaller fee) but sharing with the movie studio a royalty per rental. This provided Blockbuster with the ability to develop an availability guarantee for new releases through a larger inventory holding.

The next major strategic change that Antioco instituted was the harvesting of the Blockbuster Music component of the company in 1998. This finalized the transformation of Blockbuster back to a focus on the movie- and game-rental industry. When Viacom spun off a partial interest in Blockbuster in 1999, Antioco restructured the company into three operating units: retail, e-commerce, and database and brand marketing. This new operating structure allowed Blockbuster to be at the forefront of innovation as DVDs began to replace VHS rentals in 2001.

Not all of Antioco's changes during this time were successful. In 2001, Blockbuster attempted to partner with Radio Shack by providing store space to sell necessary equipment to renters. This was a short-lived relationship when Radio Shack pulled out in 2002, accusing Blockbuster of limiting access to customer information. This was a mutual dissolution as Blockbuster accused Radio Shack of selling unnecessary items to customers and thus negatively impacting the image of Blockbuster in the eyes of the consumer.

Blockbuster Evolves

By 2002, customers' demands for home entertainment had evolved beyond traditional movie rentals. In a letter to Blockbuster shareholders, Antioco stated: "In 2002, we again began to change the way we do business to capitalize on the changes in the home entertainment marketplace brought about by DVD and introduction of the next-generation game platforms." The mission for Blockbuster was to become the complete source for movies and games. This led to the purchase of Game Station (a retail format specializing in electronic games) and an expansion of the gaming section of the stores to include equipment sales and rentals. To stay competitive, Blockbuster also purchased a chain of movie-trading stores and an online company called Film Caddy. Antioco also recognized the threat posed by the growing popularity of rent-by-mail formats such as Netflix. And, not forgetting the international component of the company, Blockbuster began testing a nonsubscription online rental with postal delivery approach in the United Kingdom.

By 2003, Blockbuster had launched its rental subscription program, which allowed subscribers to rent an unlimited number of movies during the subscription period (there were limitations within the program). Through this program, subscribers no longer had to worry about the extended viewing fees to which renters were subject. The company also continued to expand and improve on its store-in-store concepts, especially in the DVD and electronic game sections. Finally, Antioco continued to emphasize the importance of the e-commerce component and the Blockbuster.com website. During this time, the main function of the website was to provide potential renters with movie, promotions, and feedback information. While contemplating entering the online rental market in the United States, Blockbuster did not make the jump during 2003.

Blockbuster was able to capitalize on the home entertainment–growth trends during this time. Game software sales in the United States grew from $5.8 billion to $6.2 billion. The movie-rental sector was growing at seven percent annually and was expected to be a $1.1 billion industry by 2008. While Blockbuster continued to improve its rental subscription programs and the movie- and game-trading components, the company's critical move was the launch of its online movie rental program in 2004. This strategic move was a reaction to the burgeoning level of competition in alternative movie-rental options. However, Blockbuster did not want to abandon its flagship in-store offerings, so the company gave online subscribers two free in-store rentals (movies or games) each month. This program was designed to overcome customer complaints about having to wait for online movies to arrive. It was also seen as a competitive advantage against Netflix.

Competition Heats Up

Many companies have danced in and out of the movie-rental industry since the 1980s. When Blockbuster was first formed, the competitive market consisted of many small local and regional entrepreneurial businesses. Major players such as Wal-Mart dabbled in the industry but didn't stay long. By 2005, Blockbuster was facing increasing competition, primarily from Movie Gallery and Netflix. To remain competitive, Blockbuster fine-tuned its rental program and introduced a no-late-fee policy. This strategy became a legal nightmare for Blockbuster when a barrage of lawsuits followed over the language and the fine print of the rental contract.

To further promote its online service and create a more efficient service, Blockbuster began online rental order fulfillment through 1,000 of its local stores. This change in fulfillment process allowed the company to get to customers in remote locations in an expedited nature. By the end of 2005, Blockbuster had approximately 1.2 million online subscribers with a goal of reaching two million subscribers within the next year. To further entice new subscribers, Blockbuster changed its tactics by giving new subscribers a free movie or game rental each week (rather than two per month). Through these changes, Blockbuster was attempting to integrate "click and brick" to create an image and level of service that Netflix could not duplicate.

Today, there are at least twenty-one major competitors in the sales and rental industry that compete with Blockbuster. These include major retail firms such as Wal-Mart, Target, Best Buy, Amazon.com, and Time Warner. In the rental sector, Blockbuster faces intense competition from Movie Gallery, Netflix, and Hastings Entertainment.

Movie Gallery

It is ironic that Movie Gallery—the number-two company in the movie-rental industry—was also founded in 1985 in a manner similar to Blockbuster. Through the acquisition of Hollywood Video, Video Update, and Game Crazy, Movie Gallery now operates over 4800 stores in the United States, Canada, and Mexico. Before its international expansion, Movie Gallery focused on small communities with little or no competition. However, Movie Gallery's growth has forced the company into very intense competition with Blockbuster. This rivalry came to a head in 2004 when Movie Gallery successfully outbid Blockbuster in its $1.2 billion acquisition of Hollywood Entertainment (that is, Hollywood Video). Movie Gallery moved into online rentals via its acquisition of VHQ Entertainment of Canada in 2005. Today, Movie Gallery earns 95 percent of its revenues within the United States, four percent within Canada, and 1 percent within Mexico. Eighty-two percent of the company's revenues are from rentals.

Netflix

Netflix is one of the fastest-growing U.S. companies—capturing the twenty-ninth position on *BusinessWeek*'s Hot Growth List for 2006. Intense competition from Netflix was a main reason why Blockbuster dropped its late-fee program in 2005 (a shift that led to a $400 million loss in revenue for Blockbuster). Netflix, with its five million subscribers, touts itself as the largest online entertainment subscription service. CEO Reed Hastings has set a goal of reaching 20 million subscribers by 2012—a number that would equate to roughly 20 percent of all U.S. households. This goal far exceeds analysts' growth projections of 13 million subscribers.

Netflix built its success around the online rental of movies with next-day delivery (in most cases). Netflix subscribers can rent as many movies as they want within a month for one flat fee. Once they return a movie, the next movie on their list is shipped to their home. Shipping is free both directions. Netflix achieves this fast turnaround time because it ships from forty different locations around the United States.

Netflix's strategy differs somewhat from those of Blockbuster and Movie Gallery. Within its catalog of 65,000 movie titles, only 30 percent of Netflix rentals are new releases. This compares to 70 percent for Blockbuster. During the summer of 2006, Netflix created an advertising campaign that focused on its niche of renting non-new release movies. Netflix arrived in Dyersville, Iowa, to provide a free screening of the movie *Field of Dreams* (released in 1989). Netflix convinced Kevin Costner (the star of the movie) to return to the field where the movie was filmed to play ball with the over 5,000 fans in attendance. This was just one stop in a ten-city tour developed by Netflix to promote several of its classic film offerings. The tour stops were at each movie's filming location.

Looking forward, CEO Hastings is cognizant of the new technology entering the home entertainment industry. However, he is confident that the traditional formats will be the mainstay of the rental industry for at least the next decade. With that said, however, Netflix has explored the viability of online movie downloads. The company has also explored moving away from the mainstay movie studios into investment in small film production products. This strategy of content creation and ownership is similar to HBO's strategy of releasing its own content for distribution via DVD.

Hastings Entertainment

Compared to Blockbuster, Movie Gallery, and Netflix, Hastings Entertainment is a small player in the industry. Founded in 1968 as a part of Western Merchandisers, Hastings is primarily a regional company with more than 150 stores in twenty western and midwestern states. Its stores, which are rarely larger than 20,000 square feet, are located in small communities with a population base ranging between 33,000 and 150,000 people. Some of Hastings' larger stores offer unique amenities including coffee bars, reading chairs, listening stations, and play areas for children. Roughly 35 percent of the company's sales are generated through the sale and rental of movies and video games. Another 25 percent comes from sales of new and used CDs; the remainder is generated by books, magazines, and related electronics. Hastings' growth is slow and methodical, with only one or two store openings per year. The company has felt the impact of mail-order rental houses and video-on-demand competitors and has experienced a drop in the movie-rental component of its business.

Changing Movie Distribution Technology

Since the creation of home entertainment systems, technology has played a leading role in the evolution of the movie industry. For example, the growth of home theaters has created a change in the competitive environment. A study by the Pew Research Center reported that 75 percent of adults prefer to watch movies at home rather than go to a theater. The study also reported that half of adults watch at least one movie per week via DVD rental or pay-per-view. This increase in home movie watching was largely a result of vastly improved and less expensive home theater electronics and the readily available access to movies through movie-rental chains or pay-per-view cable and satellite services. The result has been challenging for the traditional movie theater business, where ticket sales have declined seven percent in recent years.

Now, evidence is mounting that a similar fate is awaiting the traditional movie-rental industry. Several of the major movie production companies have now opted to bypass the theater experience and instead promote a selection of their movies directly to the home-viewing audience. Consequently, movie distribution is slowing moving more toward a direct model where customers can access movies via on-demand services or via broadband downloads. This trend creates an interesting relationship between the movie studios and the movie distribution channel. Through increasing disintermediation (bypassing theaters and rental chains), movie studios stand to increase profit margins dramatically. Of the various movie distribution methods, many experts believe that broadband distribution stands to gain the most traction with customers. Broadband technology did not really gain steam until 2000 with the widespread access to high-speed Internet services in over 40 million U.S. households. Now, as broadband speeds have improved, customers have the ability to download full-length feature films in less than one hour. The practice is very popular in other countries. In South Korea, for example, 58 percent of broadband users have downloaded movies. That number stands at 24 percent in the United States.

The increasing capabilities of ever-improving broadband technology have caught the attention of the movie industry. In 2002 five major Hollywood studios (MGM, Paramount, Sony Pictures, Universal, and Warner Bros.) created Movielink, LLC—an online service that offers both sales and rentals of movies from their vast libraries, plus movies from Disney, Miramax, Artisan, and others. Movielink customers can rent movies by downloading them to their hard drive. Movies remain on the hard drive for 30 days or until they are activated (rented movies cannot be burned to a DVD). Once activated, a movie can be watched as many times as possible within 24 hours. Rental prices start at 99¢, but most new releases rent for $4.99. Customers may also purchase movies for playback on a computer. Users are allowed to make backup copies to DVD but cannot play the copies in a standard DVD player. Prices start at $8.99, but new releases are typically priced at $19.99. A similar company, CinemaNow, actually launched before Movielink, has grown more slowly. CinemaNow's offerings are very similar to Movielink's. However, CinemaNow's rental prices are somewhat lower. Plus, CinemaNow recently added a Burn-to-DVD feature on select movie titles that allows the user to play their purchased movie using a standard DVD player.

Looking Ahead

As Blockbuster looks to its future, one key challenge is on the horizon. Many experts believe that the traditional DVD-rental industry is heading rapidly into its decline phase. The continued growth of Netflix, video-on-demand, Movielink, and CinemaNow, as well as the coming move to IPTV (Internet Protocol Television), offer dramatic increases in moving-renting convenience for consumers. Given this level of increasing competition, it is not surprising that Blockbuster and Movie Gallery lost a combined $1 billion in fiscal 2006. As Blockbuster decides on its strategic initiatives for the coming years, the company must find ways to competing with advancing technology—especially electronic distribution via the Internet. The heart of this challenge is simple in concept but difficult to execute in practice: How can Blockbuster increase the value-added components of its product offering in order to offset the inconveniences associated with its traditional brick-and-mortar movie rental business?

Questions for Discussion

1. What role has Netflix played in the development of Blockbuster's strategic planning? How important is Netflix to Blockbuster's future strategic plans?

2. As an advisor to Antioco, what strategic options would you recommend for Blockbuster as the company moves forward? In particular, how would you approach the technology issues facing the company?

3. What value-added components could Blockbuster offer to the movie studios that might entice them to more closely align with Blockbuster as a distribution channel?

4. In the long term, how can Blockbuster increase the value-added components of its product offering in order to offset the inconveniences associated with its traditional brick-and-mortar movie rental business? Will Blockbuster survive as we know it today? Explain.

Sources

The facts of this case are from Blockbuster, Inc. Annual Reports for 2005, 2004, 2003 and 2002 (http://www.b2i.us/profiles/investor/fullpage.asp?f=1&BzID=553&to=cp&Nav=0&LangID=1&s=0&ID=1442); Catherine Colbert, *Blockbuster, Inc.,* Hoover's Company Capsules (http://cobrands.hoovers.com/global/cobrands/proquest/factsheet.xhtml?COID=10218), accessed August 3, 2006; Catherine Colbert, *Hastings Entertainment, Inc.,* Hoover's Company Capsules (http://cobrands.hoovers.com/global/cobrands/proquest/factsheet.xhtml?ID=42256), accessed August 3, 2006; Catherine Colbert, *History of Blockbuster, Inc.,* Hoover's Company Capsules (http://cobrands.hoovers.com/global/cobrands/proquest/history.xhtml?ID=10218), accessed August 3, 2006; "'Dreams' Field Still an Inspiration: Tourism at Movie Site Has Been Steady of the Years," *Winston-Salem [NC] Journal,* August 14, 2006, A2; Peter Grant, "Telecommunications; Outside the Box: As Broadband Connections Proliferate, So Do the Opportunities for Niche Video-Content Providers," *Wall Street Journal,* December 19, 2005, R11; Ronald Grover, "Will *Bubble* Burst a Hollywood Dogma?" *BusinessWeek Online,* January 24, 2006 (http://www.businessweek.com/bwdaily/dnflash/jan2006/nf20060124_4959_db011.htm); Richard Hull, "Content Goes

Hollywood: How the Film Industry Is Struggling with Digital Content," *EContent,* October 2004, 22; Unmesh Kher, "A Bid for Bigger," *Time,* December 6, 2004, A3; Anna Wilde Mathews, "E-Commerce (A Special Report): Selling Strategies—Stop, Thief! Movie Studios Hope to Slow Widespread Online Piracy Before It Takes Off; They're Convinced They Can," *Wall Street Journal,* April 28, 2003, R6; Timothy J. Mullaney, "Netflix," *BusinessWeek Online,* May 25, 2006 (http://www.businessweek.com/smallbiz/content/may2006/sb20060525_268860.htm); Timothy J. Mullaney, "The Mail-Order Movie House That Clobbered Blockbuster," *Business Week,* June 5, 2006, 56–57; Netflix, Inc. Annual Reports for 2002 and 2005 (http://ir.netflix.com/annuals.cfm); and Netflix, Inc. Overview (http://ir.netflix.com).

Mobile ESPN

The Sports Fan's MVP?

As brands go, ESPN is a high-performance machine. In fulfilling its mission to provide 24-hour sports programming and information to sports fans anytime, anywhere, ESPN has extended its brand across multiple platforms. Its popular *SportsCenter* program on the ESPN cable network is every fan's daily bible on sports news. Fans can tune in to edgy, competitive debates on *Pardon the Interruption.* On ESPN and ESPN2, the running ticker at the bottom of the screen on most programs keeps viewers up to date on the latest scores and news. ESPN has dabbled in reality television. Online, ESPN.com draws more visitors than SI.com (*Sports Illustrated*) and Yahoo! Sports. In print, *ESPN the Magazine* has increased its subscription base and now surpasses *Sports Illustrated*—all without the help of an annual swimsuit issue.

With all of its marketing and branding prowess, it was only natural for ESPN to extend the brand in other directions. However, ESPN was not able to leverage its clout in the launch of Mobile ESPN—a joint venture with Sprint Nextel. Launched on Super Bowl Sunday 2006, Mobile ESPN was an ESPN-branded wireless phone service that delivered 24-hour sports information without the need for a television or computer. Mobile ESPN was the first product that offered fans fully customizable sports information through wireless delivery. The service included standard features found on all wireless phone plans: unlimited minutes on nights and weekends, voice mail, call waiting, three-way calling, call forwarding, downloadable ring tones, screensavers, games, wireless Internet access, and text messaging. ESPN leased network time from Sprint Nextel and outsourced their billing, messaging, and customer service operations. The big difference was the phone's "E" button, which users pressed to gain access to the ESPN "experience" including real-time scores, alerts, news, video, fantasy games, and the ability to participate in opinion polls. Users also received a one-year subscription to *ESPN the Magazine* and the *ESPN Insider* as a part of their Mobile ESPN subscription.

Despite the fanfare and the "cool" factor, ESPN pulled the plug on Mobile ESPN on December 31, 2006 after only eleven months of operation. When Mobile ESPN was launched, many skeptics felt that the company's entry into wireless phone service was going too far. The service did face many challenges. One key issue was strategic in

This case was prepared by Christin Copeland, Florida State University MBA Class of 2006, for classroom discussion rather than to illustrate effective or ineffective handling of an administrative situation. Brandon Burg, Charles Dettmann, Ashley Jantzen, Lindsey St. Romain, and Bobby Tate (Florida State University MBA Class of 2007) provided additional research support.

nature. Although ESPN is known as a leader in sports, wireless phone service is not one of the company's core competencies. The fact that all technological and customer service operations were not directly under ESPN's control was potentially problematic. However, the key issue, and the one that led to Mobile ESPN's downfall, was convincing current users of wireless phone services to switch to Mobile ESPN. At the time the company announced its decision in late September 2006, it had managed to attract only 50,000 subscribers—far short of the projected 240,000 in the first year.

The demise of Mobile ESPN left the company in an interesting position. No one blamed the company for failing; after all experimentation and innovation are often necessary to open new markets. In addition, ESPN is still the king of sports information. Plus, the ESPN brand has a lot of power in the market. Given its key strengths and its experience with Mobile ESPN, the question remained as to how ESPN should plan its next move.

A Branding Empire

The 24-hour Entertainment and Sports Network (ESPN) was founded by father and son Bill and Scott Rasmussen, broadcasting primarily out of studios in Bristol, Connecticut. The Rasmussen family created ESPN out of their frustration in not getting local ball games on television. The studios were located in Connecticut because of low land prices. Prior to the launch of ESPN in 1979, many skeptics felt as though there were not enough sports to fill a 24-hour cable network. Today, ESPN has nine domestic networks.

The company's small initial operations forced it to broadcast smaller-audience sporting events such as tractor pulls and Australian-rules football. In 1987, ESPN landed a contract to televise National Football League (NFL) games on Sunday evenings. This was the milestone event that allowed ESPN to cross over from a small cable network to become a leader in the enthusiastic "sports culture" that it helped to establish. ESPN was once owned by a joint venture between Getty Oil Company and Nabisco. Since 1984 the American Broadcasting Company (ABC) has owned the entire family of ESPN Networks and franchises, which is now 80 percent owned by the Walt Disney Company and 20 percent by the Hearst Corporation.

Once its growth began, ESPN extended its reach through not only television but also radio and Internet. It launched *ESPN Radio Network* on New Year's Day 1992 and its own website *ESPN SportsZone* (espn.com) in 1995. Launched October 1, 1993, to 10 million households, ESPN2 reached 70 million households faster than any cable network in history, hitting the milestone in only 80 months. The company moved into print with *ESPN the Magazine* and later added ESPN Zone—a franchise of restaurant and entertainment complexes. The company also offers ESPN-branded toys, games, BMX bikes, and other retail items.

The ESPN network now reaches more than 90 million homes with more than 5,100 hours of live, original programming covering sixty-five sports. This represents more than 78 percent of American homes with a television. ESPN2 offers 4,800 hours of similar programming to almost as many homes. Other brands in the ESPN network include ESPN Classic, ESPN-U, ESPN-HD, ESPN2-HD, ESPN Deportes, and ESPN News.

ESPN: The Company

ESPN's mission is to serve sports fans anytime, anywhere. Given the rate of technological change over the past decade, ESPN's mission is consistent with finding new ways to reach sports fans on the go. Currently, television and Internet news are the most popular ways of receiving sports information. With convenience and cutting edge being at the core of their product development, ESPN is adamant about creating new ways to keep sports fans entertained and informed.

ESPN's culture of being free and fun fuels the creative energy that is needed to bring new products to sports fans. ESPN executives are given a large degree of autonomy in deciding programming and service offerings. The most prosperous period for ESPN occurred in the 1990s under the leadership of then-president, Steve Bornstein. During Bornstein's tenure, ESPN was extended to television, print, and the Internet. The current president of ESPN, George Bodenheimer, was appointed to that position in 1998. Upon becoming president, Bodenheimer maintained the ESPN culture and continues to use it to the company's advantage. For example, Bodenheimer leaves arena skyboxes at games to walk around and study the crowds, thus giving him a direct link to what consumers need and want from sports and potentially ESPN. Bodenheimer also made a key change by unifying ESPN's sales and marketing divisions into one team. Combining these departments creates a coalescence of focus on serving sports fan anytime, anywhere. This organizational restructuring had to be executed perfectly not to damage the source of ESPN's creative energy because ESPN's brand strategy relies heavily on marketing tactics. Employees have responded well to this change and are working together to launch new product and brand extensions.

A big financial loser at the start, ESPN is now worth $19 billion and continues to grow. Furthermore, with Disney being able to fund ESPN's initiatives, it is not likely that the financial resources will become limited anytime soon. Disney admits that ESPN is very profitable. For example, in the aftermath of September 11, 2001, Disney lost a great deal of revenue due to reduced theme park attendance and lost viewership of popular television programs. ESPN was able to help Disney make up some of the difference by generating $5 billion of Disney's $30.7 billion revenue for the fiscal year. In addition to its profitability, ESPN is a good complement to other Disney product offerings.

ESPN's Customers

ESPN's current and potential customers come from all walks of life but are primarily men ages 18 to 34. These sports fans want real-time scores, breaking news, commentary, and analysis; fantasy sports information and team management; and audio and video programming. Almost one-fourth (24 percent) of ESPN's out-of-home viewership comes from colleges and universities. In addition, over one-third (34 percent) of viewers are in bars, restaurants, and similar locales. The majority of these on-the-go fans already have wireless phone service through one of the nation's major suppliers: Cingular, Verizon, T-Mobile, Sprint Nextel, and Alltel.

ESPN's Competitors

ESPN has competitors on many fronts; however, television programming and the Internet are the most profitable venues for ESPN. Regarding programming, CNN, NBC, MTV, and other news reporting networks are considered competitors of ESPN. Online, the main competitors to ESPN.com are SI.com (*Sports Illustrated*), Yahoo! Sports, MSN.com, *USA Today* Sports, and NFL.com. However, the reach of these competitors does not approach that of ESPN's. ESPN.com alone has lured more viewers from ages 18 to 34 than any of its competitors and enjoys over 17 million unique visitors per month. Of its main online rivals, MSN.com and NFL.com have roughly 13 million unique visitors per month. Yahoo! Sports has 12 million, and SI.com has only five million.

The cable network industry has undergone some consolidation of late as many firms look to cut costs. UPN, for example, merged with Time Warner due to UPN's general lack of viewers. Sustainability and scale are key in this industry as traditional distribution avenues are being threatened by digital distribution. Many television networks, including ABC and Disney, have begun experimenting with online digital distribution of programming. There is potential here for ESPN as well because games and other sporting programming can be repackaged for digital distribution. During March Madness 2006, CBS allowed games to be viewed online after the live broadcast had ended. The nature of live programming throughout the sports industry ensures that fresh content will always be available.

The Wireless Market

Within the wireless industry, Mobile ESPN was one of a growing number of mobile virtual network operators (MVNOs). A MVNO conducts business as a mobile operator, but it does not own a wireless spectrum or its own network infrastructure. Instead, MVNOs partner with traditional network operators and buy minutes to sell to their own customers. MVNOs are attractive to traditional carriers because they add brand appeal that draws a different customer base. This added revenue is important because it helps traditional operators offset the expenses associated with developing and maintaining their wireless networks.

Mobile ESPN operated a bit differently than other MVNOs. First, Mobile ESPN used a postpayment plan just like a traditional wireless provider. Plan prices ranged from $39.99 to $199.99 per month. Most MVNOs use prepaid accounts. Second, Mobile ESPN targeted a much higher-income bracket: sports fanatics that earn a median of $77,000 per year. In contrast, Virgin Mobile—the industry leading MNVO—targets a younger demographic that is willing to spend $10 to $15 per month for service. Virgin Mobile has over two million customers but is not as profitable as had been expected. Disney (owner of ESPN) also operates a MVNO called "Disney Mobile" that is targeted toward young consumers. It too has not been as successful as expected. Finally, while most MVNOs focus on voice services, Mobile ESPN placed much more emphasis on data services. In fact, ESPN expected customers to be so involved in game highlights and sports content that they would overlook the fact that they could also make phone calls.

Competition in the wireless phone market is increasing as competitors race to launch content services similar to Mobile ESPN. Sprint Nextel recently signed a deal with Major League Baseball (MLB) to carry its Gameday audio programming on Sprint phones. Fans will be able to listen to live radio broadcasts of every MLB game for only $5.99 per month. Verizon Wireless has started negotiations with many professional football teams. They intend to offer services like text messages with up-to-the-minute news about NFL teams, players, and coaches. As more deals like these are completed, there is a potential for fragmentation of sports information. For example, Sprint will carry MLB programming, Verizon could carry NFL programming, and other carriers could sign deals with the NBA and NHL (National Hockey League).

SWOT Analysis

Strengths

Decentralized Structure   The decentralized structure of ESPN has been the fuel for ESPN's creative energy. The employees are given tremendous amounts of autonomy to come up with ways of fulfilling the mission of delivering sports to fans "anytime, anywhere." This autonomy initiates innovation and creative thinking among different departments. Bodenheimer upholds this structure because of the various ideas that are needed to create products that will be delivered over different platforms.

Free But Fun Culture   ESPN acts as a sports team itself. The individuals are considered aggressive, creative, risk takers who are willing to create and act "out of the box." ESPN considers its employees to be the true "highlights" of their company. These sports-minded employees are flourishing in a culture where they are not monitored continuously on results. Current and past CEOs agree that this sports culture has to be stimulated by free and fun employees who enjoy being collectively competitive yet supportive.

Brand Leader in the Industry   ESPN is the brand leader in its industry and will soon become the first cable network to achieve 70 percent worldwide penetration. With ESPN extending across so many media outlets, this leaves a wide array of products to be used by consumers. This vast number of products increases customer exposure to ESPN and its quality and works to increase the value of the brand.

Extensive Reach Across Many Platforms   Currently, ESPN has nine U.S. cable channels, a radio network, a popular website, *ESPN the Magazine*, and eight ESPN Zone restaurants. Despite the failure of Mobile ESPN, the company remains committed to reaching sports fan "anytime, anywhere," bringing the access of sports news to the pockets of these sports fanatics.

Weaknesses

Mark Shapiro, Lead Programming Developer, Has Left ESPN   Shapiro was a large part of the creative energy that propelled ESPN through many of its successes. Shapiro was the brainchild behind adding edgy twists to ESPN's programming lineup, including *Pardon the Interruption* and *NBA Nation*.

Small Target Market   Despite its success, ESPN caters to a relatively small target market of men ages 18–34. Compared to other news and information networks, this market is fairly small.

ESPN's "Boy's Club" Image   Most consumers hold the opinion that ESPN is for men only. ESPN's target has worked well for branding and advertising efficiency. However, the image limits ESPN's potential market.

Opportunities

Digital Revolution   The increasing pace of technological change has hastened the digital revolution. This revolution gives companies the chance to capitalize upon what these new technologies can bring to consumers. Of particular importance is the increasing speed and reliability of high-speed wireless networks used by cell phone providers.

Demand for Convenient, 24-Hour Information   Partly due to the live coverage of the Gulf War in the early 1990s, today's consumers demand convenient access to 24-hour news and information. The growth of live 24-hour news programs on cable networks is a result of this trend. Consumers increasingly want access to this information on the go when they are away from home.

High-Tech Culture   Consumers increasingly embrace high-tech products such as wireless handheld devices that offer communication and entertainment in one package. The growing popularity of smart phones is a result of this trend.

Demand for Personalization   The demand for personalized products is growing rapidly. Today's wireless phones have caught onto this trend by offering personalized services, ring tones, wallpaper, e-mail capability, cameras, and MP3 players. Wireless phones, along with other personal technology, are now seen as an extension of an individual's image and personality.

Audience Fragmentation   The introduction of digital video recorders (like TiVo), a growing number of media options, on-demand services, and increasing usage of the Internet have fragmented audiences across a wide variety of media. As a result, advertisers are rushing to find new ways of targeting consumers, especially while they are on the go. Advertising over wireless networks is growing rapidly to fill this need.

Threats

The "On-Demand" Revolution   As more television programming becomes available on-demand, the value of any network will depend on its branded programming. As more programming is delivered on-demand, traditional channels will not mean much to the viewer.

Strong Competitors   Some competitors within the industry have yet to explore their wireless transmission options (*USA Today* and CBS, for example). Most of these networks have the ability to deliver more than sports. This broadens their reach to different target markets of consumers.

Sports League Networks   As sports leagues develop their own distribution networks (such as the NFL Network and NFL.com), they maintain copyright control over content such as games and video clips. Moreover, powerful professional sports leagues such as NASCAR, the NFL, the NBA (National Basketball Association), and MLB have the ability to deliver their own content to consumers.

Customer Loyalty   Wireless providers make it difficult for their users to switch to competing services. All providers charge hefty penalties for canceling an existing contract. Further, these companies continuously add new services in an effort to retain their customers. Examples include free in-network calling and family plans that allow users to share minutes across multiple lines.

Has ESPN Struckout with Mobile ESPN?

ESPN's brand is phenomenally successful compared to others within its industry. The company has made all the right moves to ensure that its brand is recognizable and valuable to a large number of consumers. ESPN has successfully extended its brand into a multitude of product categories and content-delivery platforms. Mobile ESPN seemed like the logical next step in the company's brand evolution. However, a number of key issues stood in the way of its success:

- Wireless phone customers are locked into a contract with their current provider. Consequently, most users did not want to pay a termination fee to switch to a new carrier.

- Mobile ESPN did not provide a sustainable competitive advantage for the company. Other wireless providers, most noticeably Verizon, use similar high-speed networks with comparable or better coverage areas. There is absolutely nothing to stop a competitor—such as MSN, Yahoo!, *Sports Illustrated*, CBS, or NBC—from offering a competing service. Some of these providers could offer access to non-sports programming in addition to real-time sports news.

- ESPN failed to understand that its true advantage lies in branded content, not technology. As such, the company needed to find a better, more effective way of distributing its content to a wider audience of on-the-go sports fans.

- Internal management shakeups at Sprint Nextel may have led to a loss of focus on the MVNO sector. In addition, Sprint's deal with MLB in effect created an in-house competitor for Mobile ESPN.

ESPN seems to understand these issues as it plans to move forward. By all indications, the company expects to revive Mobile ESPN in the future. The company's website states it this way:

> *The good news is the Mobile ESPN content you have come to enjoy and expect will soon be available through the service of another nationwide wireless provider. Before the end of the year, Mobile ESPN will contact you with details about future service options to assist your transition to the new home of Mobile ESPN, including information about any valuable offers we can provide.*

Other sources suggest that ESPN will reinvent Mobile ESPN as a content provider for many different wireless carriers, similar to the Sprint/MLB deal. In the future, millions of wireless customers may be able to access Mobile ESPN content as an add-on to their current service.

Questions for Discussion

1. Evaluate ESPN's launch of Mobile ESPN. Was this the right move at the wrong time? Was the failure caused by ESPN's lack of experience in the wireless phone market, or was it caused by factors beyond its control? Explain.

2. In launching Mobile ESPN, what could ESPN have done differently to attract a mass of initial users? What should ESPN do now to maximize the number of customers who can access its branded content?

3. Evaluate the launch of Mobile ESPN as a branding initiative. Did Mobile ESPN add to the equity inherent in the ESPN brand? Does its failure somewhat dilute the company's brand image? Explain.

4. Put yourself in the place of one of ESPN's major competitors (such as *Sports Illustrated, USA Today*, MSN, or any major television network). How would you have responded to ESPN's launch of Mobile ESPN?

Sources

These facts are from Anthony Crupi, "Merrill Lynch: Time to Pull Plug on Mobile ESPN," *MediaWeek,* July 19, 2006 (http://www.mediaweek.com/mw/news/recent_display.jsp?vnu_content_id=1002876073); "Disney Teams with Sprint to Offer National Wireless Service for Families," Disney press release, July 6, 2005 (http://corporate.disney.go.com/wdig/press_releases/2005/2005_0706_disney.html); "ESPN Rebrands Wireless Service," ESPN press release, September 27, 2005 (http://sports.espn.go.com/espn/mobile/release?id=2173856); "Mobile ESPN Hits Stores

Super Bowl Sunday," MobileTracker.com, February 3, 2006 (http://www.mobiletracker.net/archives/2006/02/03/mobile-espn); Mobile ESPN website (http://mobile.espn.go.com/the-service.html); Om Malik, "Mobile ESPN, UnMobile Soon?" GigaOm, September 27, 2006 (http://mobile.gigaom.com/2006/09/27/mobile-espn-unmobile-soon/); "Visage Enables Mobile ESPN," RedHerring.com, February 3, 2006 (http://www.redherring.com/PrintArticle.aspx?a=15584&sector=Industries); Stephen Baker, "ESPN: Leading Mobile News Service," *BusinessWeek Online,* January 30, 2006 (http://www.businessweek.com/the_thread/blogspotting/archives/2006/01/espn_ leading_mo.html); Enid Burns, "ESPN Signs Six Sponsors for its Mobile Service," Clickz.com, December 16, 2005 (http://www.clickz.com/news/print.php/3571651); Andrew Grossman, "ESPN Extends Brand into Retail," ChiefMarketer.com (http://chiefmarketer.com/media360/broadcast_cable/espn_09132005/); Rod Kurtz, "Online Extra: Why Mark Shapiro Left ESPN," *BusinessWeek Online,* October 17, 2005 (http://www.businessweek.com/print/magazine/content/05_42/b3955016.htm); Greg Levine, "Sprint Scores with MLB Gameday Deal," *Forbes Online,* August 11, 2006 (http://www.forbes.com/2006/08/11/sprint-baseball-0811markets04.html); Amol Sharma and Merissa Marr, "Mobile ESPN to End Venture, Seek New Strategy," *Wall Street Journal,* September 28, 2006, B2; and Frank Rose, "ESPN Thinks Outside the Box," Wired.com (http://www.wired.com/wired/archive/13.09/espn_pr.html).

Gillette
The Razor Wars Continue

Since its inception in 1901, Gillette has always prided itself on providing the best shaving care products for men and women. In fact, the company was so visionary that it didn't have any serious competition until 1962 when Wilkinson Sword introduced its stainless-steel blade. Since that time, the Wilkinson Sword-Schick Company has evolved into Gillette's primary competitor. Through the years, Gillette has strived to stay on the cutting edge of shaving technology in a market that thrives on innovation. This focus has led to a game of one-upmanship with Schick as each company introduced three-bladed (Gillette's Mach3), four-bladed (Schick's Quattro), and five-bladed (Gillette's Fusion) razors in rapid succession. Now, under the ownership and guidance of Procter & Gamble (P&G), Gillette faces a saturated U.S. market that fluctuates only when newer, more innovative products are introduced. However, many analysts believe that Gillette and Schick have reached the end of meaningful product innovation. Given this, Gillette faces the challenge of further expanding its already dominant market share around the world. And, in a market that thrives on innovation, Gillette must continue to dedicate significant resources to research and development in order to create "the next big thing" in the global shaving market.

History of Gillette

Founded in 1901 by King C. Gillette, the Gillette Company was one of the first great multinational organizations and a marvel of marketing effectiveness. Only four years after founding the firm in Boston, King Gillette opened a branch office in London and rapidly obtained sales and profits throughout Western Europe. About 20 years later, he said this of his safety razor:

> There is no other article for individual use so universally known or widely distributed. In my travels, I have found it in the most northern town in Norway and in the heart of the Sahara Desert.

Michael D. Hartline, Florida State University, prepared this case for classroom discussion rather than to illustrate effective or ineffective handling of an administrative situation. Chondi Bell Imani, John Gilligan, Chris Logan, Chase Razabdouski, and Melanie Yeager (Florida State University MBA Class of 2007) provided significant research support. This is a revised version of an earlier case developed by Don Roy, Middle Tennessee State University.

Gillette set this goal for his company: to offer consumers high-quality shaving products that would satisfy basic grooming needs at a fair price. Having gained more than half of the entire razor and blades market, Gillette's manufacturing efficiency allowed it to implement marketing programs on a large scale, which propelled Gillette forward in profits and in market leadership. Riding this tide of good fortune, the company was able to weather the storm brought on by World War II and emerged in a very healthy condition. In 1948, Gillette set its all-time performance record with profits per share of $6.80. Gillette has not approached this level of success since that time.

In 1955, Gillette decided to tread new waters and undertook two unrelated acquisitions. The first acquisition was the Toni Company, maker of do-it-yourself home permanent-wave kits. Although this was a profitable venture initially, sales and profits soon faded. The second major acquisition was the Paper Mate pen company, which at that time made only retractable, refillable ballpoint pens. It, too, was profitable, but soon Bic's low-priced, disposable (nonrefillable) pens came over from France. Partly due to these two acquisitions, Gillette slowly began to lose its edge, and net profit slumped to $1.33 per share in 1964.

In 1962 Gillette's U.S. market share hovered around 70 percent, and its success abroad was even better. Around this time, the English firm Wilkinson Sword introduced a stainless-steel blade in the United States and began taking a substantial portion of Gillette's market share. Partly due to the time devoted to experimenting with the home permanent-wave and pen businesses and partly due to the small size of the Wilkinson Sword Company, Gillette underestimated the potential impact on its core business. Also, Gillette executives were unsure how to react. Should they introduce their own stainless-steel blade or ignore the rival and hope that its market niche would remain small?

Gillette was lucky. Although it eventually introduced its own stainless-steel blade, the real break came when Wilkinson could not exploit the niche it had created. Due to its lack of resources, Wilkinson Sword could not compete with the powerful Gillette machine and eventually sold much of its blade business to Gillette. However, the impact of this dilemma had already been felt. In 1965, Gillette's market share hit an all-time low of 49 percent. The lessons learned from this challenging time are still with Gillette today and guide many of its decisions and actions.

Attempting to resolve the crises of the early 1960s was Gillette's new CEO, Vincent Ziegler. Ziegler was aggressive, marketing oriented, and ambitious for the company, believing in diversification through the acquisition of companies in other business segments. Within the next few years, Ziegler spearheaded the acquisition of the following companies:

Braun AG (German manufacturer of small appliances)

S.T. Dupont (French maker of luxury lighters)

Eve of Roma (high-fashion perfume)

Buxton Leather goods

Welcome Wagon, Inc.

Sterilon hospital razors

Jafra Cosmetics (home sales)

Four of these acquisitions proved to be unprofitable or unsuitable and were divested, and the other three yielded low profits by Gillette's standards. Other troubles came from the French manufacturer Bic, which excelled in disposable products. Its 19¢ disposable stick pens particularly affected the Paper Mate line of refillable pens and drove Paper Mate's share of the retail ballpoint pen market from over 50 percent down to 13 percent. Gillette had retaliated quickly with its new Write Brothers line of disposable pens, which failed on the first introduction in 1972 but succeeded in building market share when reintroduced to the market in 1975 with heavy price promotions. Bic was also threatening Gillette's strengths with two other products—its disposable razors and lighters—which were being marketed very successfully in Europe and elsewhere.

The Ziegler era had its successes. Cricket disposable lighters were introduced in 1974 and did well. Soft & Dri antiperspirant joined Right Guard, expanding Gillette's position in the deodorant market. However, the belief that aerosols destroy the ozone layer caused sales of spray versions of these products (along with all other brands of spray) to plummet suddenly, creating a crisis in these segments. Meanwhile, Gillette's Trac II razor was a great success, and the razor segment continued its dominance. Earnings per share rose to $2.83 in 1974, but slipped again the next year.

At this juncture, Ziegler retired from active direction of the company and sought to hire a successor. The first-choice candidate did not remain in the position very long, and Colman Mockler was then asked to step into this position, which he accepted in 1976. Under Mockler, Gillette's strategy was to cut costs dramatically and pour the money saved into ad and product development budgets. The Mockler era was one of the most successful in Gillette history, producing such memorable innovations as the Atra razor, the Good News! disposable razor, and the Daisy razor for women. With such product additions, Gillette held held a majority of the U.S. shaving market (including the leading shaving cream) but also up to 75 percent of the global market share. By the end of 1980, Gillette sales topped the $2 billion mark for the first time in the company's history.

The introduction of new products that were developed in the Gillette laboratories helped boost sales in the razor and blades, personal care, and writing instruments segments. First, in the razor and blades segment, Gillette introduced the Atra-Plus shaving system, which featured a refillable Atra cartridge with a lubricating strip. This overtook the Trac II as the number-one selling razor. Also, Gillette updated the Good News! line to include a disposable razor with a lubricating strip. In the personal care segment, Gillette made several introductions including Aapri facial care products, Dry Idea deodorant, Bare Elegance body lotion, Mink Difference hair spray, White Rain hair care products, and Silkience shampoo and moisturizers. These additions had mixed results and left Gillette still searching for the keys to success in this business segment. In the writing instruments segment, Gillette achieved moderate success with the development of Eraser Mate erasable, disposable pens. Also, the steady sales of Paper Mate pens and Liquid Paper correction fluids helped maintain company performance.

Despite its ability to post above-average performance during the 1980s, many analysts saw Gillette as a stagnant, lazy, sleeping giant, with earnings potential far above current realizations. These analysts based their evaluation on Gillette's considerable name recognition and market power and its well-established marketing and production channels worldwide. Though the company was successful, Gillette just could not seem to leverage its core strengths to become dominant in each of its markets. Part of the problem was that Gillette was still growing and changing. The Oral B Company was acquired in 1984, and the Cricket division was divested in 1986. In fact, Gillette's attractiveness led to an unsuccessful takeover attempt by the Revlon Group in 1986.

Corporate activities during the late 1980s and early 1990s included additional acquisitions, product innovations, and promotional campaigns that defined Gillette until its acquisition by P&G. Gillette's stationery market was growing with the acquisition of the Waterman Pen Company in 1987 and Parker Pen Holdings in 1993. However, by 2000 stiff competition and corporate restructuring led to the divestment of the stationary unit to Newell Rubbermaid. In 1996, Gillette acquired Duracell International and the rights to the famous "coppertop" battery positioning. Batteries were a natural addition to the Gillette product mix due to synergies in distribution. Finally, in the late 1990s, Gillette created its "The Best a Man Can Get" campaign— arguably one of the most successful marketing campaigns in history. The campaign coincided with the launch of the Mach3 shaving system in 1998.

The Razor Wars Begin

The razor wars began unassumingly in 1990 with Gillette's launch of the original Sensor razor. The Sensor was wildly popular and quickly rose to a dominant sales position around the world. Gillette followed the Sensor with the Sensor Excel in 1993. Gillette leveraged both the Sensor and Sensor Excel brands by developing versions of these products targeted at women. The Sensor for Women system, launched in 1992, established a major hold on the market for female razor products in the United States. The follow up with the Sensor Excel for Women in 1996 was also very successful. The continued success of the Sensor family of shaving systems led to the gradual decline of the Atra and Trac II twin-blade shaving systems. Despite this decline, both systems continued to hold sizable share positions worldwide. The company's disposable twin-blade razors' moderate increases in sales enabled it to maintain its position as the number-one seller in this product category worldwide. Gillette's Good News! brand had been the best-selling disposable razor in the United States each year since 1976.

In 1998, Gillette introduced the Mach3, a razor with three thin blades designed to provide a closer shave in fewer strokes with less irritation. To develop the Mach3, Gillette invested heavily in research and development and made a strong marketing commitment to gain market share. The Mach3, with its blades mounted on tiny springs like the Sensor Excel, became Gillette's most successful new product ever as sales of the Mach3 hit $1 billion in only 18 months. The Mach3 was named winner of the American Marketing Association's Grand Edison Award as the best new product of 1998. Mach3 technology was further enhanced in the Mach3Turbo for men and the Venus system for women. Further efforts to build market share for women's shaving products included targeting teen shavers with a line of Sensor razors in a variety of colors in an attempt to develop lifelong customers at a young age.

The razor wars turned ugly in 2003 with Schick's introduction of the Quattro—the world's first four-bladed razor. Prior to the launch, Gillette had sued Energizer Holdings and its Schick division over patent infringement of its Mach3 technology. Gillette argued that the Quattro illegally used the same "progressive geometry" technology as the Mach3. Although Gillette asked for injunctive relief and monetary damages, Schick was allowed to launch the Quattro pending the resolution of the lawsuit. Shortly after the launch, Schick sued Gillette for misleading claims of technological superiority in its advertising. Schick argued that Gillette's advertisements for the Mach3 used misleading statements such as "the world's best shave" and "the best a man can get."

Many industry analysts saw the dueling lawsuits as a sign that Gillette was threatened by Schick's reemergence as a player in the razor and blades market. Schick's Intuition razor for women was selling very well and beginning to affect Gillette's share of the women's market. Schick's total share of the U.S. market had risen 2.9 percent to 17 percent, while Gillette's total share of the razor and blades market had fallen 4.3 percent to about 63 percent. Increasing competition within the U.S. market was one of the major reasons that Gillette began moving aggressively to strengthen its global blade and razor position. A major thrust in this effort involved converting consumers from single- and twin-blade razors to the more profitable Sensor, Sensor Excel, and Mach3 lines. A second thrust involved continued geographic expansion into countries such as Romania and the former Yugoslavia, as well as the acquisition of blade firms in the former Soviet Union and the Czech Republic.

The culmination of Gillette's aggressive focus was the launch of the Fusion razor in 2005. The Fusion uses a unique five-blade design with a single blade on the back of the cartridge for use in trimming moustaches and sideburns. The launch was backed by a $200 million advertising campaign. Initial sales were brisk as over four billion razors sold within the first two months—a full 20 percent more than when the Mach3 launched in 1998.

Despite its initial success, the Fusion faced a great deal of skepticism. First, it is considerably more expensive than the Mach3 (each Fusion cartridge costs 75¢ to $1 more than the Mach3). The Fusion's five-blade design was also the butt of many jokes, including a popular skit on *Saturday Night Live*. Critics wondered why five blades were needed to get the best shave when Gillette had touted its three-bladed Mach3 as "The Best a Man Can Get" since the late 1990s. Further, a *Consumer Reports* study concluded that the Fusion was no better than other razors, particularly the Mach3. Another troubling sign was that later sales figures indicated that the razors were outselling the cartridge refills. It is well known that razor manufacturers earn most of their profits from refills, not the initial razor purchase. Despite these issues, P&G has stated that the Fusion is on track to top $1 billion in sales by 2008.

Situation Analysis for the Fusion

Under P&G's leadership, Gillette intends to make the Fusion its flagship brand, eventually overtaking the Mach3. Some issues that Gillette and P&G must consider as they move forward are addressed in the following sections.

The Customer Environment

Approximately 1.3 billion men worldwide shave with a razor blade. Within the United States, 94 million men aged 15 years and older remove hair in some fashion. Of these, 72.3 percent prefer to wet shave with a razor blade. The average American male begins to shave between the ages of 14 and 16 and continues to shave for the majority of his life. In addition, 100 million women in the United States aged 13 years and older remove hair in some fashion. Of these women, 94 percent prefer to shave with a razor blade.

On average, men in the United States shave 5.33 times per week, or 24 times a month. Men in the United States spend approximately $22 a year for razors, blades, and shave preparations. On average, women in the United States shave 11 times a month and spend approximately $11 a year for razors, blades, and shave preparations. There are a variety of methods used throughout the world to remove body hair. In addition to wet shaving, other methods of temporary hair removal include dry shaving (electric), depilatories, tweezing, waxing, sugaring, and rotary epilators. Methods of permanent hair removal include electrolysis, laser hair removal, and flash-lamp hair removal. Within the United States, roughly 26 million men and six million women use something other than a razor blade to remove hair.

Internationally, 15 percent of the world's male population does not shave due to discomfort from shaving; seven percent do not shave for religious reasons, and three percent simply does not care to shave. In addition, culture plays a large role in whether people choose to shave. For example, many German women do not remove body hair because it is traditionally viewed as a sign of adulthood. However, there is still an opportunity for further market penetration, particularly in emerging markets that increasingly embrace Western lifestyles. According to Gillette estimates, only about one-third of European women wet shave. This varies by market; for example, only one-fifth of German women regularly remove hair. If European women embraced hair elimination at the same pace as American women, total blade sales would increase by hundreds of millions each year. Younger generations of European women are being influenced by American movies and television that depict women with sleek underarms and legs. European women who do remove hair choose different methods depending on where they live. In France and the United Kingdom, women choose to shave, but Spanish and Italian women are more likely to go to waxing salons.

Competition

Gillette has consistently dominated the shaving market since the company was founded in 1901. Currently, Gillette controls about 70 percent of the wet-shaving market. Schick claims roughly 18 percent, Societe BIC holds about five percent, and the remainder of the market is controlled by generics and store brands. The major products offered by each firm and their typical prices are provided in Case Exhibit 7.1.

Legal and Political Issues

Gillette has been embroiled with Energizer Holdings in a number of lawsuits since 1998. The first court battle surfaced when Energizer protested Gillette's mass mailing of samples in Germany. The German court rejected the claim, saying that Gillette hadn't crossed an improper threshold of 100,000 samples. The District Court of Massachusetts denied Gillette's patent infringement suit against Energizer. A similar patent dispute was turned down by the District Court in Düsseldorf, Germany. The latter judge decided that Quattro's fourth blade was indeed different enough from

---

CASE EXHIBIT 7.1   WET-SHAVING PRODUCTS AND PRICES

	Brand	Initial Price of Razor	Price of Replacement Cartridges
Men's Products			
Gillette	Fusion Power	$11.99	4 for $14.29 8 for $28.99
	Fusion	$9.99	4 for $12.99 8 for $23.99
	M3 Power Nitro	$11.99	4 for $10.99 8 for $19.99
	Mach3 Turbo	$8.99	4 for $9.49 8 for $17.99
	Mach3	$8.29	4 for $8.49 8 for $15.99
Schick	Quattro Power	$11.99	4 for $10.49 8 for $19.99
	Quattro Titanium	$8.99	4 for $10.99
	Quattro	$8.99	4 for $9.29 8 for $16.99
Bic	Comfort 3	$4.29 for 4	
	Comfort Twin Sensitive	$5.29 for 10	
	Sensitive	$3.29 for 12	
Women's Products			
Gillette	Venus Vibrance	$8.29	4 for $8.49 8 for $19.99
	Venus Divine	$8.99	4 for $9.49 8 for $17.99
	Venus Disposable	$7.99 for 3	
Schick	Quattro for Women	$8.99	4 for $9.29 8 for $16.99
	Intuition Plus	$8.99	3 for $9.49
	Intuition	$8.49	3 for $8.29 6 for $14.99
Bic	Comfort Twin Sensitive	$5.29 for 10	

Source: Drugstore.com (http://www.drugstore.com) and CVS.com (http://www.cvs.com).

Gillette's Mach3 system. When Gillette released the first battery-operated shaver in 2004, Energizer challenged its advertising campaign that boasted a closer shave than any other wet shaver. A German court agreed, saying any difference was too minimal to support such a claim of superior shaving. Gillette fired back with a similar suit against Energizer in the Netherlands for its Quattro advertising. That judge allowed both ads, saying that consumers are practically immune to advertising claims: "By a good legal tradition, some exaggeration is permissible, as long as it is not misleading in nature, because it will be skeptically received by the average consumer."

Gillette has also come under fire from consumer advocacy groups, particularly Consumers Against Supermarket Privacy Invasion and Numbering (CASPIAN), which objects to the company using radio-frequency identification (RFID). RFID tags, seen as the successors to bar codes, have been called "spy chips" by critics, who see the technology as nothing short of a Big Brother technique. These and other critics fear that consumer purchases can be tracked when the RFID tags embedded in products are read by strategically placed RFID readers. CASPIAN launched a boycott of Gillette goods because of its planned retail trials of RFID-based smart-shelf technology. Gillette and its biggest retailer, Wal-Mart, eventually canceled the planned trials. CASPIAN has fought similar Gillette moves in Europe and Australia.

Technological Advancements

Razor manufacturers have also experimented with a number of technological advancements in addition to the number of blades contained in the cartridge. Gillette and Schick offer powered versions of their razors that contain tiny electric motors in the handle. These motors create a vibration in the blades that cause hair to stand more erect—thus giving a closer and smoother shave. These powered razors also help promote each company's batteries.

In addition to advancing razor technology, manufacturers have also devoted resources to advancing supplemental products to offer complete shaving solutions. For example, the chemistry of shaving creams, gels, and aftershaves has been reformulated to reduce friction and soothe the skin. These preparations are also designed to work in conjunction with powered razor technology to create a smoother shave than with traditional methods.

Sociocultural Trends

As an increasing number of world cultures begin to adopt the grooming practices of English-speaking cultures, demand for personal grooming products will grow. Interestingly, the shaving culture in Western countries is also changing to one that is increasingly including the removal of hair from other parts of the body. These trends include men who remove hair from their chests and backs, hair removal beyond the bikini line (so-called intimate hair removal), to full-body hair removal. This trend is not new but dates back several thousand years to Greece and Rome where hairless female statues were regarded as the epitome of beauty. Razor manufacturers have begun offering products that tie into these trends.

Gillette's Marketing Activities

To promote the Fusion, Gillette has undertaken a massive advertising and sponsorship campaign. In particular, Gillette has leaned heavily on sports-related promotion and sponsorship. Among its most visible promotions is Gillette Stadium, which is home to the NFL's New England Patriots and soccer's New England Revolution. In addition, the facility—which seats nearly 70,000 fans—hosted the 2002 MLS Cup, 2003 AFC Championship Game, and four games of the 2003 FIFA Women's World Cup. Gillette Stadium will also host the NCAA Men's Lacrosse Championship in 2008. Gillette also enjoyed a major coup in 2004 when it signed soccer superstar David Beckham as its worldwide spokesman. Gillette's sponsorships reach a broad spectrum of fans with its involvement in football, soccer, lacrosse, and car racing.

Gillette has also taken steps to reach other markets. For example, the company has attempted to reach the gay and lesbian market with an extension of its Gillette Complete line. Gillette has placed ads in the United Kingdom's *Gay Times* and plans to put more ads in newsprint geared toward gay and lesbian audiences. Gillette officials are convinced, however, that it doesn't need to use gay or lesbian themes in its ads because it considers the needs of male and female customers to be universal. Gillette spokeswoman Kara Salzillo has said, "We don't market specifically to any one group: ethnic, religious, or otherwise. Our goal is to share our message with our target audience . . . as effectively as possible and through a variety of channels that will reach this audience."

Gillette also makes extensive use of its 1-800 phone number and views its call center operations as a key component in the company's marketing strategy. By leveraging its call center as a customer interaction center, Gillette links its consumer input directly into its quality assurance system. Gillette uses the information gathered for marketing and product development purposes.

Gillette generates the majority of its sales in the global market. More than 60 percent of its sales are generated outside the United States. Gillette practices aggressive advertising in other countries as is evidenced by its recent support of the World Cup—an event that is wildly popular outside the United States. Gillette does not market its products the same worldwide. The M3Power razor, for example, is still Gillette's focus in European markets.

Looking Ahead

In many ways, Gillette and P&G are in an enviable position. Gillette's products dominate the world wet-shaving market. The company continues to grow, although slowly, in every worldwide market. Still, many industry analysts wonder if Gillette has reached the end of its historical innovation in wet-shaving technology. The market waits in anticipation of Schick's response to the Fusion, though most doubt that a six-bladed razor will be introduced. Given that the wet-shaving market is mature, Gillette must depend on innovation to perpetuate its dominance—whether than innovation is in product design or marketing remains to be seen.

If product innovation has come to an end, however, Gillette will need to find new ways to stay on top. The challenge for Gillette is to push the envelope without creating innovations that are seen as trivial. For now, customers still welcome advances in shaving technology as they continue to search for the perfect shave.

Questions for Discussion

1. Evaluate product innovation at Gillette throughout its history. Has Gillette been a victim of its own success? Has product innovation in the wet-shaving market come to an end? Explain.

2. What do you make of the battle between Gillette and Schick? Is the battle of one-upmanship good for either company?

3. What actions would you recommend over the next five years that would help Gillette maintain its worldwide dominance in the shaving market? What specific marketing program decisions would you recommend? Should Gillette be worried about Schick? Explain.

Sources

These facts of this case are from Julia Boorstin, "Can Fusion Become a Billion-Dollar Razor?" MSN Money, July 7, 2006 (http://articles.moneycentral.msn.com/Investing/CNBC/TVReports/AfterHypedStartFusionHitsLull.aspx); "The Power of Fusion?" *Consumer Reports Online,* July 2006 (http://www.consumerreports.org/cro/health-fitness/beauty-personal-care/gillette-fusion-razor-7-06/overview/0607_fusion-razor_ov.htm?resultPageIndex=1&resultIndex=6&searchTerm=fusion) (subscription required for access); Molly Prior, "Fighting for the Edge in Shaving—Blade Wars: Shaving Report," March 8, 2004, FindArticles.com (http://www.findarticles.com/p/articles/mi_m0FNP/is_5_43/ai_114404714); Catherine Colbert, "Global Gillette," Hoovers.com, July 6, 2006 (http://www.hoovers.com/gillette/–ID_10655–/free-co-factsheet.xhtml); Michael Wilke, "L'Oreal, Gillette and SC Johnson Crowd onto Gay Shelves," *TheCommercial Closet,* March 17, 2005; Slaven Marinovich, "A Competitive Edge in a Cutthroat Market," BrandChannel.com, November 21, 2005 (http://brandchannel.com/features_effect.asp?pf_id=290); "Anti-RFID Campaigners Launch Gillette," *Frontline Solutions* (Pan-European edition), 12, no. 7 (2003): 8; Steve Ulfelder, "Raising an RFID Ruckus," *Network World,* September 29, 2003, 73; "Cutting Edge: Moore's Law for Razor Blades," *The Economist,* March 16, 2006, 8; Afrooz Family, "Vibrating Gillette Razors," MadPhysics.com, April 2, 2006 (http://www.madphysics.com/ask/vibrating_gillette_razors.htm); Elayne Saltzberg and Joan C. Chrisler, "Beauty Is the Beast: Psychological Effects of the Pursuit of the Perfect Female Body," in *Women: A Feminist Perspective,* ed. Jo Freeman (Mountain View, CA: Mayfield Publishing, 1995), 306–315; "Battle of the Blades Draws Corporate Blood," DataMonitor.com, October 8, 2003 (http://www.datamonitor.com/~eb69fbdf57f24f129c0c4f3f3ac1ccbd~/consumer/news/product.asp?pid=4D673D8B-

F3F4-4A53-9BE9-BB5D806FCD14); "Gillette Sues Schick Over Razor Launch," *Promo Online,* November 20, 2003 (http://www.promomagazine.com/ar/marketing_gillette_sues_schick/); Mercedes M. Cardona, "Gillette's Mach3 Captures Top Prize at Edison Awards," *Advertising Age,* March 22, 1999, 54; Jeremy Kahn, "Gillette Loses Face," *Fortune,* November 8, 1999, 147–152; Mark Maremount, "Gillette to Unveil Women's Version of Mach3 Razor," *Wall Street Journal,* December 2, 1999, B14; Mark Maremont, "Gillette to Shut 14 of Its Plants, Lay Off 4,700," *Wall Street Journal,* September 29, 1998, A3; Mark Maremount, "Gillette's New Strategy Is to Sharpen Pitch to Women," *Wall Street Journal,* May 11, 1998, B1; Wes Conard, "3-Blade Razor a Cut Above, Gillette Says," *Commercial Appeal [Memphis, TN],* April 15, 1998; "Gillette's Edge," *BusinessWeek,* January 19, 1998, 70–77; "How Gillette Is Honing Its Edge," *BusinessWeek,* September 28, 1992, 60; Lawrence Ingrassia, "Gillette Ties New Toiletries to Hot Razor," *Wall Street Journal,* September 18, 1992, B1, B6; Lawrence Ingrassia, "Keeping Sharp," *Wall Street Journal,* December 10, 1992, A1, A6; and Seema Nayyar, "Gillette Jumps into Men's Toiletries," *Brandweek,* July 20, 1992, 6.

Best Buy

Best Buy Co., Inc. is a Minneapolis-based specialty retailer of consumer electronics, home-office products, entertainment software, appliances, and related services. It is an innovative *Fortune* 100 growth company continually striving to create superior customer experiences. Best Buy operates as a "clicks-and-mortar" company with over 940 retail stores across the United States and Canada. Its operations include Best Buy (BestBuy.com and BestBuyCanada.ca), Future Shop (FutureShop.ca—Canada's largest national consumer electronics retailer), Geek Squad (GeekSquad.com—a 24-hour computer support task force), Magnolia Audio Video (Magnoliaav.com—a high-end consumer electronics retail store), and an outlet store on eBay. The company has been categorized as a *Fortune* Blue Ribbon Company based on its being ranked on *Fortune*'s Fortune 500, Global 500, Most Admired, and Global Most Admired lists.

Best Buy's vision is to make life fun and easy for consumers. Its business strategy is to bring technology and consumers together in a retail environment focused on educating consumers on the features and benefits of technology and entertainment products while maximizing overall profitability. Best Buy believes that its stores offer consumers meaningful advantages in store atmosphere, product value, product selection, and customer service—all of which advance the company's objectives. Best Buy has four strategic initiatives: (1) customer centricity, (2) efficient enterprise, (3) win with service, and (4) win in entertainment. Historically, Best Buy was a product-focused company. In switching its focus to customers, Best Buy aims to create better experiences for its customers, thereby creating greater customer loyalty. Best Buy is also looking to streamline its company operations. By fine-tuning the company and focusing on customers, Best Buy hopes to rank as "best in class" with respect to customer service and the creation of the ultimate entertainment experience.

The Company's Growth

Best Buy plans to grow its business in four ways. First, the company is converting more stores to the customer-centric operating model and intends to have all U.S. stores converted by the end of fiscal 2007. Second, it is constantly adding new stores

---

Melanie Drever and Alexi Sherrill, University of Wyoming, prepared this case under the direction of Dr. O. C. Ferrell for classroom discussion rather than to illustrate effective or ineffective handling of an administrative, ethical, or legal situation.

to better serve existing and new markets. Third, Best Buy is expanding and strengthening service offerings including services such as Geek Squad and home-theater installation. Fourth, the company is boosting employee retention in order to deliver better customer experiences while increasing productivity. Best Buy is also adding individualized marketing capabilities to its skills in mass marketing and simplifying its internal processes so that it responds better to changing customer needs.

Best Buy operates in the highly competitive consumer electronics retail industry and must compete against other electronics retailers (such as Circuit City), mass merchants (such as Wal-Mart and Target), home-improvement superstores (such as Lowe's and The Home Depot), and a growing number of direct-to-consumer alternatives (such as Crutchfield, Sony Style, and J&R). Best Buy also competes against independent dealers, regional chain discount stores, wholesale clubs, video rental stores, and other specialty retail stores. There is also increasing pressure from online sites that offer downloadable entertainment (such as Cinema Now) and on-demand services from cable companies. Although Best Buy ranked number 19 on the *BusinessWeek* 50 list, Circuit City and Wal-Mart are looking to cut into the company's market. To stay on top, Best Buy has been working hard to stock more products and offer quantitatively and uniquely more services than the competition. In a coup of sorts, the Samsung Group awarded its business to Best Buy rather than Wal-Mart due to its somewhat more sophisticated and appealing selling environment. Thus far, Best Buy has made notable gains in market share: from 15 percent in 2003 to 18 percent in 2005. This 20 percent gain in market share in two years is at least partially attributable to Best Buy's new customer-centric focus.

Focusing on Customers

Part of Best Buy's strategy is to operate with an old-fashioned corner store feel within the giant technical abundance of its stores—a difficult task requiring a great deal of research and preparation. Since 1996, Best Buy has collected data on nearly every transaction that it makes, rain check that it issues, and call center problem that it solves for over 75 million customers. The company decided that no one knew the data on its customers as well as the company itself and that it would have to leverage this core capability to ensure that it discovered what its customers want and need. Best Buy developed a database that incorporated information from nineteen customer touch points and then used Experian's INSOURCE^{SM} consumer marketing data to enhanced this database. The end result was a 360-degree perspective on Best Buy customers. The company developed insight by using purchase histories to develop a more complete picture of its customers and their current as well as future needs through segmentation analysis. This allowed Best Buy to develop and identify new customer segments, better understand existing customers, more precisely target promotions, and identify key locations for expansion.

By this point, Best Buy was armed with transactional data, demographic information from local census statistics, survey responses of customers, and insight from targeted focus groups. Then, in 2004 the company launched Reward Zone—a customer loyalty program that quickly grew to six million members. Additional customer information was culled from the program to give the company even more valuable insights regarding its core customers. Best Buy retained Larry Selden, a professor at Columbia University's Graduate School of Business, as a consultant. As part of his approach to helping businesses see greater success, Selden argues that losses produced by what he calls "devil" customers can wipe out profits generated by what he refers to as "angels." Best Buy analyzed its data and discovered that 20 percent of its customers generated a large portion of its revenue and profits. Through its consultation with Selden and its data analysis with Experian, Best Buy identified five angel customer segments as well as its devil customer segments. Angels were customers who bought high-definition TVs, portable electronics, and newly released DVDs without waiting for markdowns or rebates. Devils were customers who bought products, applied for rebates, returned the products, and then bought them back again at returned merchandise discounts. The company was able to categorize its angel customers into five groups:

- **Small Businesses Customers**　This group uses Best Buy's goods and services to enhance the profitability of their businesses.

- **Young Entertainment Enthusiasts (aka "Buzz")**　Active younger men who want the latest technology and entertainment, these customers are early adopters interested in buying and showing off the latest gadgets.

- **Affluent Professionals (aka "Barry")**　These customers want the best technology and entertainment experiences, do not mind spending money to get the best product, and are enthusiasts of action movies and cameras.

- **Busy Suburban Moms (aka "Jill")**　These customers look to enrich their children's lives with technology and entertainment. These customers are busy but willing to talk about helping their families. They are smart and affluent but usually avoid electronics stores because the products intimidate them. These women are typically the main shoppers for their families and will make purchases based on staff recommendations.

- **Tech-Savvy Family Men (aka "Ray")**　Family men who want technology to improve their lives, these customers are practical adopters of technology and entertainment.

The New Customer-Centric Business Model

Best Buy's customer-centric business model focuses on these five key customer segments. Best Buy launched its strategy by having an initial 67 stores analyze the demographics of their local markets and focus on one or two of these customer segments. Each store would then stock merchandise according to its focus and include elements designed to appeal to its key customer segments. Best Buy believes that this model offers customers a richer in-store experience, including better shopping assistance as well as more of the products that these customers want. The model also empowers employees to recognize unique sets of customers and to build offerings and experiences to meet their needs. Employees are trained in how to differentiate between the customers and how to help them based on the categories into which they fit.

Targeting Angels and Devils   To encourage its angels—in other words, lure the high-spenders—Best Buy has created a number of category-specific enticements. Company associates toting pink umbrellas will escort Jills to and from their cars on rainy days. Personal shopping assistants have been provided to help Jills from the moment they enter the store until they leave via Express Check Out. These assistants help Jills shop efficiently and practically. They are also there to help Jills understand how products work and to determine the best products for Jills' needs. Stores that have personal shopping assistants tend to offer a wider variety of products in the digital imaging, kitchen, laundry, gaming, home-theater, and mobile video areas.

For Barrys, the stores sport leather couches for watching big-screen TVs connected to high-end sound systems. Popcorn is even included to add to the atmosphere. Magnolia Home Theater specialists are available to provide Barrys with personalized expert advice on premium audio/video products. They also provide home-theater consultations, in-home system design, and custom installation. For Buzzes, Best Buy established video-game areas called "Test Drive" with leather chairs and game consoles connected to big-screen high-definition TVs. Buzzes are encouraged to sample games and components and associates are on hand to provide advice on gaming skills. These Test Drive stores include interactive gaming, surround sound, and wireless technology displays and much more interactive displays. The full assortment of TVs and games are located just a short walk from the Test Drive area. To reach Rays, Best Buy focuses on pricing and special offers on name-brand products. Rays are not necessarily wealthy, so their desire for the latest technology must be balanced with the realities of raising a family on a budget.

To discourage its devils—or to deter the undesirable customers—Best Buy has reduced the promotions and sales tactics that tend to draw these customers to the stores. They also removed many of these individuals from its mailing lists. Best Buy also enforces a 15 percent restocking fee on returned merchandise in an attempt to discourage customers from returning items with the intention of repurchasing them at "open-box" discounts. The company is also experimenting with reselling returned merchandise over the Internet so that returned products do not reappear in the stores where they were originally purchased.

Another component of the new strategy is the launch of concept stores that may later become new chains under the Best Buy umbrella. For example, the company has opened the concept store "studio d" in Naperville, Illinois, to cater specifically to soccer moms. The store sells much of the latest technology and also provides its shoppers with classes on how to use the items they purchase. Another concept store is Best Buy's "eq-life" where customers can take part in Pilates, massage, and shop for health-related technical products.

Customer-Centricity Works   Best Buy began the switch to the customer-centric model by converting a small number of stores into test labs. It did not take long for the company to see positive results such as higher comparable store sales gains and a more rounded mix of products in these stores. The company also saw greater customer loyalty, employee retention, and higher market share in these stores. Once the test was completed, Best Buy converted 85 stores to the new customer-centric model in early 2005. By 2006 Best Buy had converted a total of 300 stores, or 40 percent of its U.S. locations.

On average, converted stores report comparable store sales increases of 8.2 percent, whereas the figure is only 1.9 percent for unconverted stores. A major reason for the difference is the more profitable product mixes in converted stores. Consumer electronics account for 43 percent of the revenue mix in converted stores, up from 39 percent before the shift. The remaining revenue comes from home-office products (32 percent), entertainment and software products (19 percent), and appliances (six percent). In addition to product changes, Best Buy also improved services. Between 2005 and 2006, the company increased its number of Geek Squad agents by 5,000 and created an in-house home-theater installation service—both aimed at better serving the customer. Membership in the Reward Zone program grew 20 percent and now tops 7.2 million customers. Further, Best Buy boasts one of the highest customer satisfaction and retention rates in the industry. A full 36 percent of its customers give Best Buy perfect marks on performance.

Continuing Innovation   Best Buy has also been working to increase its speed in providing customers with the latest technology ahead of the competition. Best Buy's approach to this has been to develop new products under its own brand rather than to wait for big name brands to bring new products to the market. For instance, the Geek Squad team created an external hard drive for PCs. It took Best Buy only 120 days from idea to delivery to the customer. The company has other house brands in the works. Best Buy also began courting startup companies. A recent example is Sling Media Inc., the creator of the Slingbox—a $250 product that allows owners to send TV programming from their cable or satellite connections to their PCs. Users can then be anywhere in the world with an Internet-connected PC and still have access to their television programming. When Slingbox was introduced in 2005, Best Buy had a three-month lead on launching the product.

The Challenges of Change

Although Best Buy has done much to increase its focus on the customer, it has faced a number of challenges. The company has found that in addition to the one-time conversion costs, the selling, general, and administrative expenses for converted stores are higher than for unconverted stores. As a result, the operating income for converted stores is less than for unconverted stores. Best Buy also struggled through organizational issues in that its traditional product focus could not handle the changes required by customer centricity. Looking back, Bradbury Anderson, vice chairman and CEO, admitted that the company may have overestimated its capacity for change and moved a bit too quickly to get its new model up and running. The company had asked a lot from the stores targeted for conversion. Although most stores had great success in implementing a few of the required changes, none had success in all areas. Still, buoyed by the success, Anderson decided to slow the pace of conversion. Best Buy finished the 2006 fiscal year with revenue growth of 12 percent and earnings growth of 22 percent.

Best Buy continues to support conversion to the customer-centric model. As many companies are concluding, customer service is only as good as the employees who deliver it. Given this fact, Best Buy announced in 2006 that it was doing away with the traditional workday by encouraging much of its corporate staff to work their own hours and in the locations of their choice. The company claims productivity is soaring as a result. Best Buy has also been working hard to increase employee retention at all levels within the organization. To this end, the company strives to do a better job of listening to its employees and their needs. Among other things, the company has created an incentive system for store employees. With happier employees, the company knows that it can better create satisfying customer experiences.

In another effort to further its customer-centric model, Best Buy is focusing some of its energy on small-business customers. The company recently entered into partnership with Microsoft to make it easier for customers to access the best technology for their businesses. Best Buy now gives its small-business customers access to Best Buy For Business specialists, associates who can quickly understand the needs of small-business owners and easily direct these customers to the Microsoft technology and/or advice that will best enhance their businesses. Best Buy has also become a Microsoft Gold Certified Partner and is currently the only national retailer to reach this status in its relationship with Microsoft.

Looking Toward the Future

Best Buy is completely convinced that the profitability of stores operating under the customer-centric platform will improve over time and cites its historical experience with new-store openings as encouraging evidence to support this belief. To this end, the company has set new goals for the 2007 fiscal year. First, the company plans to convert all remaining U.S. stores to the customer-centric model. Best Buy also plans to open about ninety new North American stores and to capitalize on customer interest in flat-panel TVs by adding 200 Magnolia Home Theater locations to its Best Buy stores. The company plans to double its Best Buy For Business locations and to train over 900 new Microsoft-certified professionals. It would like to increase its services business as well by improving computer services and home-theater installation. The company plans to focus on offering customers one-stop solutions by offering digital music subscriptions, digital cable, and voice-over-Internet telephony at the same locations where customers buy companion products. Finally, Best Buy plans to grow its international business, beginning with increased operations in Canada and China.

The company estimates its will earn $34 to $35 billion for the 2007 fiscal year; which would be an increase of 10 to 13 percent over fiscal 2006. Best Buy expects revenue growth from new store openings and comparable store sales gains to average three to five percent. Although the company is aware that its industry is highly competitive, it is highly optimistic about the potential of the customer-centric model and what it can do for both customers and the company. It only remains to keep an eye on Best Buy to see if the company's predictions and hopes come to pass.

Questions for Discussion

1. Comment on Best Buy's customer-centric strategy. Is this a viable approach for breaking out of the commodity status associated with electronics retailing?

2. Buzz, Barry, Jill, or Ray: Which Best Buy customer segment do you fall into? Would Best Buy's customer-centric focus on your segment induce you to shop and buy more often at a Best Buy store?

3. How can Best Buy's customer segmentation scheme be leveraged online at BestBuy.com?

4. Do you believe that Best Buy's approach to its devil customers is the correct approach? Should the company be more aggressive in dealing with these bad customers?

Sources

The facts of this case are from the Best Buy website (http://www.BestBuy.com), accessed October 5, 2006; "Fast Forward," *Best Buy's Fiscal 2005 Annual Report,* MediaCorporate.net (http://media.corporate-ir.net/media_files/IROL/83/83192/ 2005AR/html/index.htm) accessed October 5, 2006; "Wired," *Best Buy's Fiscal 2006 Annual Report,* MediaCorporate.net (http://media.corporate-ir.net/media_files/irol/83/ 83192/BestBuyARCode/bb06ar_home.htm) accessed October 5, 2006; "Geek Squad," *Best Buy News Center,* MediaCorporate.net (http://bestbuymedia.tekgroup.com/news/ section_news.cfm?news_section=1327) accessed October 5, 2006; "Future Shop," (http://bestbuymedia.tekgroup.com/news/section_news.cfm?news_section=1328) accessed October 5, 2006; "Magnolia Audio Video," (http://bestbuymedia.tekgroup.com/ news/section_news.cfm?news_section=1324) accessed October 5, 2006; "Best Buy Enriches Customer Experience in Stores Across the U.S.," Best Buy press release, August 26, 2005 (http://bestbuymedia.tekgroup.com/article_display.cfm?article_id= 232); "Fact Sheet," *Fiscal 2006,* (http://www.bbycommunications.com/newscenter/ FY05_Fact_Sheet_Q4.pdf), accessed October 5, 2006; Stacey Collett, "Turning Data into Dollars," *Computerworld Online,* September 24, 2004 (www.Computerworld.com/ action/article.do?command=viewArticleBasic&articleId=95954); "Experian Partners with Best Buy: INSOURCE Data Contributes to Best Buy's Successful Customer Relationship Management (CRM) Strategy," Experian.com (http://www.experian.com/ case_studies/best_buy.pdf); Ariana Eunjung Cha, "In Retail, Profiling for Profit: Best Buy Stores Cater to Specific Customer Types," *Washington Post Online,* August 17, 2005 (http://www.washingtonpost.com/wp-dyn/content/article/2005/08/16/ AR2005081601906.html); Gary McWilliams, "Minding the Store: Analyzing Customers, Best Buy Decides Not All Are Welcome. Retailer Aims to Outsmart

Dogged Bargain Hunters and Coddle Big Spenders—Looking for 'Barrys' and 'Jills,'" *Wall Street Journal Online,* August 11, 2004 (http://online.wsj.com/article/ SB109986994931767086.html); "The *BusinessWeek* 50 Rankings," *BusinessWeek Online,* July 27, 2006 (www.businessweek.com/bw50/2006/19.htm); "The Best Performers 2006," *BusinessWeek Online,* April 3, 2006 (http://www.businessweek.com/ print/magazine/content/06_14/b3978401.htm); Wendy Kaufman, "Best Buy Cuts Workers Loose from Clocks, Desks," *NPR, Morning Edition Online,* July 19, 2006 (www.npr.org/templates/story/story.php?storyId=5567202); "Microsoft Expands Small-Business Alliance with Best Buy," Microsoft press release, Microsoft website, March 14, 2006 (http://www.microsoft.com/presspass/press/2006/mar06/03-14BestBuyPartnershipPR.mspx); and "Best Buy: How To Break Out of Commodity Hell," *BusinessWeek Online,* March 27, 2006 (http://www.businessweek.com/magazine/ content/06_13/b3977007.htm).

New Belgium Brewing Company (A)

Ethical and Environmental Responsibility

Although most of the companies frequently cited as examples of ethical and socially responsible firms are large corporations, it is the social responsibility initiatives of small businesses that often have the greatest impact on local communities and neighborhoods. These businesses create jobs and provide goods and services for customers in smaller markets that larger corporations often are not interested in serving. Moreover, they also contribute money, resources, and volunteer time to local causes. Their owners often serve as community and neighborhood leaders, and many choose to apply their skills and some of the fruits of their success to tackling local problems and issues that benefit everyone in the community. Managers and employees become role models for ethical and socially responsible actions. One such small business is the New Belgium Brewing Company, Inc., based in Fort Collins, Colorado.

History of the New Belgium Brewing Company

The idea for the New Belgium Brewing Company began with a bicycling trip through Belgium. Belgium is arguably the home of some of the world's finest ales, some of which have been brewed for centuries in that country's monasteries. As Jeff Lebesch, an American electrical engineer, cruised around that country on his fat-tired mountain bike, he wondered if he could produce such high-quality beers back home in Colorado. After acquiring the special strain of yeast used to brew Belgian-style ales, Lebesch returned home and began to experiment in his Colorado basement. When his beers earned thumbs up from friends, Lebesch decided to market them.

The New Belgium Brewing Company (NBB) opened for business in 1991 as a tiny basement operation in Lebesch's home in Fort Collins. Lebesch's wife, Kim Jordan, became the firm's marketing director. They named their first brew Fat Tire Amber Ale in honor of Lebesch's bike ride through Belgium. NBB beers quickly developed a small but devoted customer base, first in Fort Collins and then throughout Colorado. The brewery soon outgrew the couple's basement and moved into an old railroad depot before settling into its present custom-built facility in 1995. The brewery includes an

© O. C. Ferrell 2006. This case was prepared for classroom discussion rather than to illustrate effective or ineffective handling of an administrative, ethical, or legal decision by management. We appreciate the assistance of Nikole Haiar in drafting the previous edition of this case and Melanie Drever who assisted in this edition.

automated brew house, two quality-assurance labs, and numerous technological innovations for which NBB has become nationally recognized as a "paradigm of environmental efficiencies."

Today, the New Belgium Brewing Company offers a variety of permanent and seasonal ales and pilsners. The company's standard line includes Sunshine Wheat, Blue Paddle Pilsner, Abbey Ale, Trippel Ale, 1554 Black Ale, and the original Fat Tire Amber Ale—still the firm's bestseller. Some customers even refer to the company as the Fat Tire Brewery. The brewery also markets two types of specialty beers on a seasonal basis. Seasonal ales include Frambozen and Abbey Grand Cru, which are released at Thanksgiving and Christmas, and Farmhouse Ale, which are sold during the early fall months. The firm occasionally offers one-time-only brews, such as LaFolie, a wood-aged beer, which are sold only until the batch runs out.

Until 2005 NBB's most effective form of advertising has been its customers' word of mouth. Indeed, before NBB beers were widely distributed throughout Colorado, one liquor-store owner in Telluride is purported to have offered people gas money if they would stop by and pick up NBB beer on their way through Fort Collins. Although NBB beers are distributed in just one-third of the United States, the brewery receives numerous e-mails and phone calls every day inquiring when its beers will be available elsewhere.

With expanding distribution, however, the brewery recognized a need to increase its opportunities for reaching its far-flung customers. It consulted with David Holt, an Oxford professor and branding expert. After studying the young company, Holt, together with Marketing Director Greg Owsley, drafted a 70-page "manifesto" describing the brand's attributes, character, cultural relevancy, and promise. In particular, Holt identified in NBB an ethos of pursuing creative activities simply for the joy of doing them well and in harmony with the natural environment. With the brand thus defined, NBB went in search of an advertising agency to help communicate that brand identity; it soon found Amalgamated, an equally young, independent New York advertising agency. Amalgamated created a $10 million advertising campaign for NBB that targets high-end beer drinkers, men aged 25 to 44, and highlights the brewery's image as being down to earth. The grainy ads focus on a man rebuilding a cruiser bike out of used parts and then riding it along pastoral country roads. The product appears in just five seconds of each ad between the tag lines, "Follow Your Folly . . . Ours Is Beer." The ads helped position the growing brand as whimsical, thoughtful, and reflective. In addition to the ad campaign, the company maintained its strategy of promotion through event sponsorships.

New Belgium's Ethical Culture

According to Owsley, beyond a desire for advertising and promotion ethics, NBB also has a fundamental focus on the ethical culture of the brand. Although consumer suspicion of business is at an all-time high, a new paradigm has emerged in which businesses that fully embrace citizenship in the community can forge enduring bonds with customers. Meanwhile, these are precarious times for businesses that choose to ignore consumer's looking at brands from an ethical perspective. More than ever before, what the brand says and what the company does must be synchronized.

NBB believes that the mandate for corporate social responsibility gains momentum beyond the courtroom to the far more powerful marketplace. Any current and future manager of business must realize that business ethics are not so much about the installation of compliance codes and standards as they are about the spirit in which they are integrated. Thus, the modern-day brand steward (usually the most externally focused member of the business management team) must prepare to be the internal champion of the bottom line necessity for ethical, values-driven company behavior.

At NBB, a synergy of brand and values occurred naturally and was in place long before the firm had a marketing department. Back in early 1991 when NBB was just a home-brewed business plan, Lebesch and Jordan took a hike into Rocky Mountain National Park. Armed with a pen and a notebook, they took their first stab at what the fledgling company's core purpose would be. If they were going forward with this venture, what were their aspirations beyond profitability? What was the real root cause of their dream? What they wrote down that spring day has evolved into the values and beliefs that you can read on the NBB website today. More important, ask any NBB employee, and he or she can list for you many, if not all, of these shared values and can inform you which are the most personally poignant. For NBB, branding strategies are as rooted in the company values as in other business practices.

New Belgium's Purpose and Core Beliefs

NBB's dedication to quality, the environment, and its employees and customers is expressed in its mission statement: "To operate a profitable brewery which makes our love and talent manifest." The company's stated core values and beliefs about its role as an environmentally concerned and socially responsible brewer include the following:

- Producing world-class beers
- Promoting beer culture and the responsible enjoyment of beer
- Continuous, innovative quality and efficiency improvements
- Transcending customers' expectations
- Environmental stewardship: minimizing resource consumption, maximizing energy efficiency, and recycling
- Kindling social, environmental, and cultural change as a business role model
- Cultivating potential: through learning, participative management, and the pursuit of opportunities
- Balancing the myriad needs of the company, staff, and their families
- Committing ourselves to authentic relationships, communications, and promises
- Having fun

Employees believe that these statements help communicate to customers and other stakeholders what NBB is about. These simple values developed over 15 years ago are just as meaningful to the company and its customers today despite NBB's phenomenal growth.

Employee Concerns

Recognizing employees' role in the company's success, NBB provides many generous benefits. In addition to the usual paid health and dental insurance and retirement plans, employees get a free lunch every other week as well as a free massage once a year, and they can bring their children and dogs to work. Employees who stay with the company for five years earn an all-expenses paid trip to Belgium to "study beer culture." Perhaps most important, employees can also earn stock in the privately held corporation, which grants them a vote in company decisions. NBB's employees now own one-third of the growing brewery. Open-book management lets employees see the financial costs and performance.

Environmental Concerns

NBB's marketing strategy involves linking the quality of its products, as well as their brand, with the company's philosophy toward affecting the planet. From leading-edge environmental gadgets and high-tech industry advancements to employee-ownership programs and a strong belief in giving back to the community, NBB demonstrates its desire to create a living, learning community.

NBB strives for cost-efficient, energy-saving alternatives to conducting its business and reducing its impact on the environment. In staying true to the company's core values and beliefs, the brewery's employee-owners unanimously agreed to invest in a wind turbine, making NBB the first fully wind-powered brewery in the United States. Since the switch from coal power, NBB has been able to reduce its carbon dioxide emissions by 1,800 metric tons per year. The company further reduces its energy use by employing a steam condenser that captures and reuses the hot water that boils the barley and hops in the production process to start the next brew. The steam is redirected to heat the floor tiles and de-ice the loading docks in cold weather. Another way that NBB conserves energy is by using "sun tubes," which provide natural daytime lighting throughout the brew house all year long.

NBB also takes pride in reducing waste through recycling and creative reuse strategies. The company strives to recycle as many supplies as possible, including cardboard boxes, keg caps, office materials, and the amber glass used in bottling. The brewery also stores spent barley and hop grains in an on-premise silo and invites local farmers to pick up the grains, free of charge, to feed their pigs. NBB even encourages its employees to reduce air pollution by using alternative transportation. As an incentive, NBB gives its employees "cruiser bikes"—like the one pictured on its Fat Tire Amber Ale label—after one year of employment and encourages them to ride to work.

NBB has been a long-time participant in "green" building techniques. With each expansion of the facility, they have incorporated new technologies and learned a few lessons along the way. In 2002 NBB agreed to participate in the U.S. Green Building

Council's Leadership in Energy and Environment Design for Existing Buildings (LEED-EB) pilot program. From sun tubes and day lighting throughout the facility to reusing heat in the brew house, they continue to search for new ways to close loops and conserve resources.

NBB believes strongly in the three "Rs" of environmental stewardship: reduce, reuse, and recycle. The reuse program includes heat for the brewing process, cleaning chemicals, water, and much more. Recycling at NBB takes on many forms, from turning "waste" products into something new and useful (like spent grain to livestock feed) to supporting the recycling market in creative ways (like turning their keg caps into table surfaces). They also buy recycled whenever they can, from paper to office furniture. Reduction surrounds them—from motion sensors on the lights throughout the building to induction fans that pull in cool winter air to chill their beer—and offsetting their energy needs is the cornerstone to being environmentally efficient.

Social Concerns

Beyond its use of environment-friendly technologies and innovations, NBB strives to improve communities and enhance people's lives through corporate giving, event sponsorship, and philanthropic involvement. Since its inception, NBB has donated more than $1.6 million to organizations in the communities in which they do business. For every barrel of beer sold the prior year, NBB donates $1 to philanthropic causes within their distribution territory. The donations are divided between states in proportion to their percentage of overall sales. This is their way of staying local and giving back to the communities that support and purchase NBB products. Thus far, Arkansas, Arizona, California, Colorado, Idaho, Kansas, Missouri, Montana, Nebraska, Nevada, New Mexico, Oregon, Texas, Washington, and Wyoming have received funding.

Funding decisions are made by the NBB Philanthropy Committee, which is composed of employees throughout the brewery and includes owners, employee-owners, area leaders, and production workers. NBB looks for nonprofit organizations that demonstrate creativity, diversity, and an innovative approach to their mission and objectives. The Philanthropy Committee also looks for groups that involve the community to reach their goals.

NBB also maintains a community bulletin board in its facility where it posts an array of community involvement activities and proposals. This community board allows tourists and employees to see the different ways that they can help out the community, and it gives nonprofit organizations a chance to make their needs known. Organizations can even apply for grants through the NBB website, which has a link designated for this purpose.

NBB also sponsors a number of events, with a special focus on those that involve "human-powered" sports that cause minimal damage to the natural environment. Through event sponsorships, such as the Tour de Fat, NBB supports various environmental, social, and cycling nonprofit organizations. NBB also sponsors the MS 150 "Best Damn Bike Tour," a 2-day, fully catered bike tour, from which all proceeds go to benefit more than 5,000 local residents with multiple sclerosis. NBB also sponsors the

Ride the Rockies bike tour and donates the proceeds from beer sales to local nonprofit groups. The money raised from this annual event funds such local projects as improving parks and bike trails. In the course of 1 year, NBB can be found at anywhere from 150 to 200 festivals and events, across all fifteen western states.

NBB also combines its social and environmental missions. In 2003 the company began using corn-based plastic cups at its various events to encourage recycling and waste reduction. When it travels to each event, NBB uses a fuel called B20, which is composed of 20 percent bio-diesel and 80 percent diesel. The use of B20 reduces carbon monoxide and particulate matter by 12 percent.

Organizational Success

NBB's efforts to live up to its own high standards have paid off with numerous awards and a very loyal following. It was one of three winners of *Business Ethics* magazine's Business Ethics Awards for its "dedication to environmental excellence in every part of its innovative brewing process." It also won an honorable mention in the Better Business Bureau's 2002 Torch Award for Outstanding Marketplace Ethics competition. Kim Jordan and Jeff Lebesch were named the recipients of the Rocky Mountain Region Entrepreneur of the Year Award for manufacturing. The company also captured the award for best midsized brewing company of the year and best midsized brew master at the Great American Beer Festival. In addition, NBB took home medals for three different brews, Abbey Belgian Style Ale, Blue Paddle Pilsner, and LaFolie specialty ale.

According to David Edgar, director of the Institute for Brewing Studies, "They've created a very positive image for their company in the beer-consuming public with smart decision-making." Although some members of society do not believe that a company whose major product is alcohol can be socially responsible, NBB has set out to prove that for those who make a choice to drink responsibly, the company can do everything possible to contribute to society. Its efforts to promote beer culture and the connoisseurship of beer has even led it to design a special "Worthy Glass," the shape of which is intended to retain foam, show off color, enhance the visual presentation, and release aroma. NBB also promotes the responsible appreciation of beer through its participation in and support of the culinary arts. For instance, it frequently hosts New Belgium Beer Dinners, in which every course of the meal is served with a complementary culinary treat.

According to Owsley, the Fat Tire brand has a bloodline straight from the enterprise's ethical beliefs and practices; the firm's work is not done. They must continually reexamine ethical, social, and environmental responsibilities. In 2004 NBB received the Environmental Protection Agency's regional Environmental Achievement Award. NBB saw the award as both an honor and a motivator to not rest on its laurels. There are still many ways for NBB to improve as a corporate citizen. For example, the company still doesn't offer an organic beer. Its manufacturing process is far from being zero waste or emission free. And, NBB believes that there will always be a need for more public dialogue on avoiding alcohol abuse. Practically speaking, NBB has a never-ending to-do list.

NBB management acknowledges that as its annual sales increase, so do the challenges of keeping the brand both humane and culturally authentic. It has always been a challenge for NBB to grow while keeping true to its core beliefs. For example, NBB brewed roughly 400,000 barrels in 2006, up from 300,000 in 2005. A $21 million plant expansion is underway that will increase NBB's production capacity to 800,000 barrels per year. NBB is also growing geographically. After adding West Coast states in recent years, NBB now distributes to sixteen states: Colorado, Wyoming, Kansas, Missouri, Nebraska, New Mexico, Arizona, Texas, Montana, Idaho, Washington, Oregon, Nevada, Arkansas, California, and Illinois. In 2006 NBB began distribution of Fat Tire Ale for the first time in the Chicago area and has not ruled out expanding to other states.

Every six-pack of NBB displays the phrase, "In this box is our labor of love, we feel incredibly lucky to be creating something fine that enhances people's lives." Although Jeff Lebesch has "semiretired" from the company to focus on other interests, the founders of NBB hope that this statement captures the spirit of the company. According to employee Dave Kemp, NBB's environmental concern and social responsibility give it a competitive advantage because consumers want to believe in and feel good about the products they purchase. NBB's most important asset is its image—a corporate brand that stands for quality, responsibility, and concern for society. Defining itself as more than just a beer company, the brewer also sees itself as a caring organization that is concerned with all stakeholders, including the community, the environment, and employees.

Questions for Discussion

1. What environmental issues does the New Belgium Brewing Company work to address? How has NBB taken a strategic approach to addressing these issues? Why do you think that the company has chosen to focus on environmental issues?

2. What else could NBB do to foster ethical and responsible conduct?

3. What are the challenges associated with combining the need for growth with the need to maintain customer intimacy and environmental responsibility? Does NBB risk losing focus on its core beliefs if it grows too quickly? Explain.

4. Should NBB even worry about growth? If NBB's customers, employees, and owners are happy, should growth even be a priority for the company? Explain.

5. Some segments of society vigorously contend that companies that sell alcoholic beverages and tobacco products cannot be socially responsible organizations because of the nature of their products. Do you believe that NBB's actions and initiatives are indicative of an ethical and socially responsible corporation? Why or why not?

Sources

The facts of this case are from Greg Owsley, "The Necessity for Aligning Brand with Corporate Ethics," in *Fulfilling Our Obligation, Perspectives on Teaching Business Ethics,* ed. Sheb L. True, Linda Ferrell, and O. C. Ferrell (GA: Kennesaw State University Press Kennesaw, 2005), 128–132; New Belgium website (http://www.newbelgium.com /sustainability.php) and (http://www.newbelgium.com/philanthropy.php), accessed October 5, 2006; "New Belgium Planning Big Expansion, New Plant," CBS4Denver. com, May 25, 2006 (http://cbs4denver.com/business/local_story_145115039.html); Peter Asmus, "Goodbye Coal, Hello Wind," *Business Ethics,* 13 (July/August 1999): 10–11; Robert Baun, "What's in a Name? Ask the Makers of Fat Tire," *[Fort Collins] Coloradoan,* October 8, 2000, E1, E3; Rachel Brand, "Colorado Breweries Bring Home 12 Medals in Festival," *Rocky Mountain News,* November 6, 2000 (http:// www.insidedenver.com/news/1008beer6.shtml); Stevi Deter, "Fat Tire Amber Ale," The Net Net, April 29, 2003 (http://www.thenetnet.com/reviews/fat.html); DirtWorld.com, November 6, 2000 (http://www.dirtworld.com/races/Colorado_ race745.htm); Robert F. Dwyer and John F. Tanner, Jr., *Business Marketing* (Columbus, OH: Irwin/McGraw-Hill, 1999), 104; "Four Businesses Honored with Prestigious International Award for Outstanding Marketplace Ethics," Better Business Bureau press release, September 23, 2002, Better Business Bureau website (http:// www.bbb.org/alerts/2002torchwinners.asp); Del I. Hawkins, Roger J. Best, and Kenneth A. Coney, *Consumer Behavior: Building Marketing Strategy,* 8th ed. (Columbus, OH: Irwin McGraw-Hill, 2001); David Kemp, Tour Connoisseur, New Belgium Brewing Company, personal interview by Nikole Haiar, November 21, 2000; Julie Gordon, "Lebesch Balances Interests in Business, Community," *[Fort Collins] Coloradoan,* February 26, 2003; New Belgium Brewing Company Tour by Nikole Haiar, November 20, 2000; "New Belgium Brewing Wins Ethics Award," *Denver Business Journal Online,* January 2, 2003 (http://denver.bizjournals.com/denver/ stories/2002/12/30/daily21.html); and Dan Rabin, "New Belgium Pours It on for Bike Riders," *Celebrator Beer News Online,* August/September 1998 (http://www.celebrator. com/9808/rabin.html).

New Belgium Brewing (B)

Developing a Brand Personality

The idea for the New Belgium Brewing Company began with a bicycling trip through Belgium. Belgium is arguably the home to many of the world's finest ales, some of which have been brewed for centuries in that country's monasteries and small artisan breweries. As Jeff Lebesch, an American electrical engineer by trade and a home brewer by hobby, cruised around that country on his fat-tired mountain bike, he wondered if he could produce such high-quality beers back home in Colorado. After acquiring the special strain of yeast used to brew Belgian-style ales, Lebesch returned home and began to experiment in his Colorado basement. When his beers earned thumbs up from friends, Lebesch decided to market them.

The New Belgium Brewing Company (NBB) opened for business in 1991 as a tiny basement operation in Lebesch's home in Fort Collins. Lebesch's wife, Kim Jordan, handled all the marketing, sales, and deliveries from her station wagon. NBB beers quickly developed a small but devoted customer base, first in Fort Collins and then throughout Colorado. The brewery soon outgrew the couple's basement and moved into an old railroad depot before settling into its present custom-built facility in 1995. The company's standard line has grown to include Sunshine Wheat, Blue Paddle Pilsner, Abbey Ale, Trippel Ale, 1554 Black Ale, and the original Fat Tire Amber Ale, still the firm's bestseller. Today, NBB is America's third largest craft brewer, with Sam Adams number one and Sierra Nevada number two. The craft beer market is just under four percent of the total U.S. beer market. However, it is the fastest growing segment of the U.S. alcoholic beverage market. Craft brew sales jumped 11 percent in 2006 after increases of nine percent in 2005 and seven percent in 2004.

New Belgium's Marketing Strategy

When a company has grown as rapidly as NBB, the tendency is not to mess with a good thing. This applies to the beer portfolio, the culture, and the marketing process. For many years, the brewer, best known for Fat Tire Amber Ale, thrived on word-of-mouth communication to sell the brand. In fact, for the first four years of its existence, NBB's marketing consisted of traveling to beer festivals and handing out free samples.

Relational marketing, done barstool to barstool, launched the advent of its Ranger Team—a sales staff who acts as brand stewards throughout territories of distribution.

When Greg Owsley was hired as marketing director in 1996, NBB became more focused and proactive in its marketing efforts. Festivals and sponsorships, coupled with print media in alternative weeklies, increased brand sales to over 100,000 barrels annually by 1998 (After NBB's plant expansion is completed, the company will be able to produce 800,000 barrels per year.) Owsley and his team introduced such signature NBB events as the multicity philanthropic bike festival, Tour de Fat. They launched an educational "Beerstream" in the form of a traveling slide show and beer tasting in an old Airstream trailer. NBB developed engaging contests like "What's Your Folly?" which invites consumers to pitch their Beerdream (an adventure enhanced by NBB beers) to win immortal fame on an NBB postcoaster (mailable postcard and coaster). "The Worthy Endeavor" is a web-based contest in which applicants can win a trip to the Crested Butte Al Johnson Uphill Downhill. All events, sponsorships, and inter-active games have been bolstered by strategic purchase of print media advertising.

In 2003 as NBB expanded into northern California, it became evident that new avenues would have to be considered to effectively reach the increasingly far-flung consumer base. For the first time, NBB looked to a more formalized and systematic approach to analyzing its audience. A consulting firm conducted research in Colorado and in other markets and suggested a mind-share approach to branding. However, Owsley rejected the consulting firm's suggestion and continued researching branding's foremost progressive thinkers, eventually coming across the works of Douglas Holt.

Developing a Brand Manifesto

Holt, then of Harvard Business School and currently with Oxford, is the leading proponent of "cultural branding"—a philosophy of branding that tries to speak to tensions within society. Owsley contacted Holt after reading some of his published work online. The two agreed to meet, and Holt was hired as a consultant to NBB in September 2003. Holt came to NBB on several occasions to study the brand and immerse himself in the brewery's unique culture. This process led to the creation of a brand manifesto—a 70-page document coauthored over many months by Owsley and Holt describing the brand's attributes, character, cultural relevancy, and potential. This opened the door to a relationship with Amalgamated Inc., a young upstart ad-vertising agency in New York. In discussing the brand with the agency, NBB's creative team collaborated with Amalgamated to flesh out the brand's cultural contributions and what should be communicated.

Selecting Media

Working with the manifesto as a guide, Amalgamated explored a wide breadth of possibilities within a somewhat restrictive budget. Underwriting of National Public Radio, production of radio shorts, television, and theatrical screenings were all thrown into the mix. Television, with its low cost per viewer and wide reach, quickly rose as the preferred option. It also seemed more authentic to embrace the medium where consumers expected to see advertising interwoven with entertainment.

Creating a television campaign for a craft brewer provided a litany of challenges and opportunities. The "Big Three" brewers—Anheuser-Bush, Coors, and Miller—have long dominated mainstream televised beer advertising in the United States. Boston Brewing's foray into television several years back presented an interesting case study. The makers of Sam Adams started a campaign with founder Jim Koch delivering a folksy voice-over that positioned Sam Adams as a beer of the highest quality. Over time, this morphed into televised spots that looked more and more like the positioning of America's Big Three.

Message Development

NBB understood at the inception that the power of television could work to bolster or undermine the brand with equal efficacy. If the spots did not ring true to the NBB character, there was a potential to alienate the core consumers who had helped build the company to this point. Within the ethos of NBB, Holt unearthed a mind-set where a highly creative activity or avocation is pursued for the intrinsic value of doing it, as well as performed in a balanced manner with nature. It is the cultural counterpoint to the Urban Professional. The mind-set personified is the mountain local who eschews a high-dollar job in Denver to pursue a simpler existence. It is the unsigned musician who writes songs just to entertain her friends. It is the amateur bread maker who bakes experimental breads and then hand-delivers them on his bike. It is the juxtaposition of traditional American values that often compels workers into a position of compromising their true selves in order to exist within a modern technopoly—those people who live their lives in a way that emphasizes experience for the sake of experience rather than for the sake of profit.

With these shared attributes in mind, the audience for NBB's commercials would likely be the professional who follows the traditional route of existing within a capitalist economy but still has artistic leanings and desires. These are the executives, lawyers, and accountants who live in Kansas or Missouri but come to Colorado for a ski week every year to indulge in the mountain lifestyle. These are folks who look at the mountain local and envy his dedication but could never fathom making that career sacrifice. The cultural tension then can be seen as the compromise between living the life one wants with balancing the economic needs of existing within a technopoly. NBB beers could be positioned as a manifestation of that lifestyle. It would be possible to pop a cap off a Fat Tire in Springfield, Missouri, and travel metaphorically to the Colorado mountains and the mountain local's life.

With this understanding, Amalgamated's creative director, Jason Gaboriau, developed a series of storyboards for the commercials featuring the "Tinkerer," a character who discovers an old cruiser bike that has been customized, modernized, and ultimately left for scrap. The Tinkerer then proceeds to strip the cruiser bike back down to its bare elements. The original boards featured three complete narratives with a potential fourth when Amalgamated flew to NBB to present its material at the company's monthly all-staff meeting. True to a culture based on employee ownership and ownership mentality, the entire crew was offered the opportunity to weigh in on the storyboards.

The NBB team reacted positively to the presentation with the exception of Amalgamated's suggested tag line: "Follow Your Folly . . . Ours Is Beer." Several people suggested that *folly* had too negative a connotation or undermined the science and technology it took to produce such consistently high-quality beers. The debate built steam over several weeks with the creative team suggesting that a word like *folly* had fallen so far from the vernacular that it was ripe for reinterpretation and a fresh new definition. Following one's folly also aptly alluded to the ideal of offbeat endeavors versus the traditional "follow the money" thinking that created the social tensions inherent to potential consumers' lives. After a healthy volley of e-mails from nearly every NBB department, the creative team won out and "Follow Your Folly" became the campaign's tagline.

At this stage in the process, a search for the right director for the commercials ensued. Amalgamated reviewed dozens of highlight reels and passed the most likely fits along to NBB. Much of the work represented had great visual power with big-budget, 70-millimeter sheen. The look and feel of such glossy and cinematic work was tempting, but in the end NBB went with Jake Scott, who suggested shooting the spots on grittier 16-millimeter film stock and giving the work a timeless feel influenced by the photography of the 1960s documentarian William Eggelston. Scott flew to the brewery to learn about NBB and then jumped into a car and scouted locations throughout Colorado. He sent still photos from a variety of locales, and ultimately the group committed to shooting in and around Hotchkiss and Paonia. After reviewing a tape of locals for potential casting shot outside bike shops in Fort Collins and Boulder, Colorado, Scott decided on Boulder craftsman Charles Srbecky to play the Tinkerer. Srbecky, formerly of the Czech Republic, was an atypical choice with tousled hair, weathered features, and a maturity not seen in contemporary U.S. beer advertising.

In September 2004, members of NBB, Amalgamated, and the production company RSA out of Los Angeles met in Hotchkiss and commenced shooting over a three-day period. Much of the talent and crew came from surrounding Colorado communities. The production quickly took on a collaborative and improvisational feel reflective of NBB's culture. While great attention was paid to fulfilling the promise of Gaboriau's boards, spontaneous opportunities were embraced as they arose. This led to no fewer than nine potential spots coming out of the three-day shoot.

Amalgamated returned to New York to begin postproduction of the spots with NBB's input. Choosing a musical bed quickly developed into the next creative challenge. Editors at Whitehouse Post in New York tried a variety of genres, from progressive to country alternative, and landed on an artist in the category of "Freak Folk" by the name of Devendra Banhart. Banhart's tunes added a haunting sense of cheerful nostalgia to the works. With the 16-millimeter film stock giving a mid-1970s feel buoyed by Banhart's acoustic tunes, the campaign took a far more muted and poignant tone than the ubiquitous mainstream beer advertising seen elsewhere. The NBB product appeared only in the final five seconds of film between the tag lines, "Follow Your Folly . . . Ours Is Beer." Quick to embrace the latent talents of their own crew, NBB allowed brewery employees to compose a reggaelike score for one of the 15-second spots—a playful little film called "Joust."

Even as NBB decided to speak to a wider audience through a new medium, the roots-style marketing that launched the company could not be abandoned. It became even more important to speak to the insiders who helped build the brand in the same authentic and personal tone they had come to know and embrace. Rather than redirect energies from event sponsorship to media, events became an even greater opportunity to maintain that vital dialogue. Rather than test the spots on focus groups, NBB turned to insiders in the bike community and friends of the brewery with some personal history and knowledge of the brand. The theory was that the medium of television would reach those faraway outposts where Ranger sales staff penetration was difficult and not cost effective. In mature markets, the personal touch would be redoubled. The spots first aired in Arizona in January 2005 with a summer campaign to follow throughout the rest of the western United States. After viewing the NBB spots at a brewing industry conference in March 2005, Miller SAB vice president of marketing, Bob Mikulay, had this to say:

> *At its heart, the basic proposition of beer has to be about fun. The small brewers have always done this well . . . often with great irreverence, quirkiness or just plain silliness . . . but always with a strong, instinctive understanding of the unique personality of their brands. And we need them to keep it coming . . . and even step it up a bit. In fact, I was encouraged to see New Belgium actually taking their brand of fun into a television spot.*
>
> *Now humility will probably prevent Kim [Kim Jordan, CEO of New Belgium] from saying this later . . . but I believe that's a truly great piece of advertising. Is there anybody who doesn't now have a very good idea about what Fat Tire is all about? So the specialty and other small brewers are showing every sign that they are ready to fulfill their role in the industry better than ever.*

In the end, NBB's first television-based advertising campaign—approached with a great deal of inner reflection—mirrored well the craft brewer's personality. In a sea of loud, flashy beer advertising aimed seemingly at a youthful demographic, NBB positioned itself as whimsical, thoughtful, and reflective. The bicycling imagery shot in Colorado gave a palpable sense of place to the brand among viewers on the coasts and in the plains. The iconic cruiser bike itself harkened the idea of creative play. The act of rescuing the bike from bad technology and neglect can be read as metaphor for NBB's efforts to recycle and reuse materials to the point of 98 percent diversion of their waste stream. The Tinkerer himself pays homage to the bicycle tour that NBB's founder Jeff Lebesch took through Belgium that inspired his home-brewing shift toward Belgian-based beers. Even the texture of the film and the musical tone capture the ideals of whimsy and joy inherent to NBB's philosophy of brewing and quality of life. At a time when marketers are seeking ever-more insidious means to cut through the clutter, NBB chose to redefine a category in a very traditional medium where ads are acceptable and the rare good ones can still be groundbreaking, thoughtful, and effective.

To see New Belgium's television spots, go to http://www.newbelgium.com.

Questions for Discussion

1. Rather than testing its television spots using focus groups, New Belgium Brewing Company instead tested these spots using insiders in the bike community and brewery friends who had a personal history and knowledge of the brand. Evaluate NBB's decision not to use focus groups.

2. How does the use of 16-millimeter film and Freak Folk music relate to NBB's advertising objectives?

3. What are some of the benefits of NBB's decision to redouble its roots-based, personal touch marketing efforts aimed at its mature markets?

4. What roles did the advertising agency, NBB's leadership, and NBB's employees play in the development of the advertising campaign?

5. NBB seemed to agonize over the use of the word *folly* in its advertising campaign. What do you make of the company's struggle with this decision? Also, how do you personally feel about their use of the word?

Sources

The facts of this case are from Jeremy Mullman, "Craft Beer Steps into Wine Country," *Advertising Age,* June 19, 2006; New Belgium Brewing Company website (http://www.newbelgium.com/story.php), accessed October 6, 2006; "New Belgium New Expansion," Probrewer.com, May 30, 2006 (http://www.probrewer.com/news/news-002935.php); Janet Forgrieve, "Sales of Craft Beer Make Biggest Jump in Decade," *Rocky Mountain News Online,* August 22, 2006 (http://www.rockymountainnews.com/drmn/other_business/article/0,2777,DRMN_23916_4936608,00.html); "New Belgium Expansion On Tap," *Rocky Mountain News Online,* May 25, 2006 (http://www.rockymountainnews.com/drmn/other_business/article/0,2777,DRMN_23916_4725068,00.html); and Greg Owsley, "The Necessity for Aligning Brand with Corporate Ethics," in *Fulfilling Our Obligation,* ed. Sheb True, Linda Ferrell, and O. C. Ferrell (Kennesaw, GA: Kennesaw State University Press, 2005).

Mattel, Inc.

M attel, Inc., with $5.2 billion in annual revenues, is one of the world's leaders in the design, manufacture, and marketing of children's toys. The company's major toy brands include Barbie (with more than 120 different Barbie dolls), Fisher-Price, Disney entertainment lines, Hot Wheels and Matchbox cars, Tyco Toys, American Girl, and games such as UNO. In addition, Mattel promotes international sales by tailoring toys for specific international markets instead of simply modifying favorites from the United States. The company's headquarters is in El Segundo, California, but Mattel also has offices in 36 countries. In fact, Mattel markets its products in more than 155 nations throughout the world.

History of Mattel

In 1945, a garage workshop housed the beginnings of Mattel. Harold Matson and Elliot Handler combined their names and their ideas to form Mattel. Although picture frames were the first Mattel product, Handler soon began making dollhouse furniture out of picture frame scraps. Shortly thereafter, Matson sold out to Handler, who, along with his wife, Ruth, expanded the Mattel product line.

The company's emphasis switched to toys due to the success of the dollhouse furniture. Child-sized ukuleles, a patented music box, and variations on these products were Mattel's "staple" business and the primary revenue generators in the 1950s and 1960s. The Burp Gun, an automatic cap gun, was introduced in 1955, along with a "Mouseguitar." For the first time, a company had bought advertising to market toys year-round, and this advertising was for 52 weeks on *The Mickey Mouse Club*.

Replica rifles and guns that were prevalent on television during the 1950s followed the musical toy success. This move capitalized on the popularity of the numerous Western-themed television shows of the time, such as *Gunsmoke* and *Bonanza*. At the end of the 1950s, Mattel made the move that would establish it at the forefront of the toy industry. After seeing her daughter's fascination with cutout paper dolls, Ruth suggested that a three-dimensional doll should be produced so that young girls could

---

Debbie M. Thorne, Texas State University–San Marcos, prepared this case for classroom discussion rather than to illustrate effective or ineffective handling of an administrative situation. Laura Leigh Saenz and Kevin Sample provided research support on previous versions of this case.

live out their dreams and fantasies. This doll was named "Barbie," the nickname of Ruth and Elliot Handler's daughter.

Mattel went public in 1960 and within five years was ranked in *Fortune*'s list of the 500 largest U.S. industrial companies. Mattel also went global during the 1960s. Favorable responses to test marketing prompted the company to grant licensing agreements in England, France, Germany, South Africa, Italy, and Mexico. Mattel's first international sales office was opened in Switzerland in 1964 as headquarters for the worldwide marketing program.

Chatty Cathy, See 'N Say, and the Thingmaker were some of Mattel's stronger innovations in the 1960s. In 1968 Hot Wheels was introduced, and boys' imaginations were captured in the same way that Barbie captured girls' imaginations. At the onset of the 1970s, Mattel generated revenues of $300 million annually. The company was not only very profitable but also diversifying via acquisitions. These acquisitions consisted of non-toy companies, such as Barnum and Bailey Circus, Circus World, Turco, Metaframe, and even a motion picture company, Radnitz/Mattel Productions.

The Handlers left the Mattel organization in the mid-1970s, and the new management expanded into electronics. Handheld electronic games and "Intellivision," a gaming platform, were soon released. However, Intellivision was not as successful as hoped because pirates of the technology produced a plethora of cheap imitation software. This forced retailers to drop the price and become disenchanted with Intellivision and Mattel. The failure of Intellivision caused significant change at the company as manufacturing plants, headquarters staff, and overhead spending were all reduced.

In 1984 there was another shift in Mattel's strategy based on trends in revenues. Executives and analysts acknowledged that Mattel's expansion into nontoy areas was continually lowering revenues while the toy lines of Mattel were constantly increasing revenues. As a consequence, Mattel sold off or closed all nontoy parts of the company and focused on its core revenue producer—toys. Thus, Mattel aligned its business with the core competency of toy manufacturing and marketing. The company focused on the maximization of core brands while identifying new brands with excellent potential. Many new accessory lines and add-ons were developed to accompany the Hot Wheels and Barbie core brands.

In 1988 Mattel revived its association with The Walt Disney Company and began to make baby products and toys based on famous Disney characters. Mattel began to see more and more success due to this strategy, and a merger with Fisher-Price in 1993 further strengthened the strategy. The acquisition of UNO, Skip-Bo, Power Wheels, and Scrabble continued to support the core brand strategy. In 1997 Mattel merged with Tyco Toys, makers of Matchbox cars, Tyco R/C, View-Master, and Magna-Doodle. This merger also gave Mattel the toy license for *Sesame Street,* the popular children's educational program. Other multiyear agreements granted Mattel the master toy licenses for Looney Tunes, Baby Looney Tunes, Batman, and Justice League.

Although most of these mergers and acquisitions positively supported Mattel's marketing strategy, not all were successful. For example, the company's merger with

The Learning Company in 1999 made Mattel the second-largest consumer software company in the world. The merger seemed to make strategic sense because The Learning Company produced interactive software for computer games and activities that could be tied to Mattel's brands. At the peak of the technology stock excitement, executives touted a desire to evolve Mattel from a children's toys producer to a family products company. The attempt to broaden the corporate scope led to huge losses for Mattel. "Mattel should never have tried to get into the multimedia world," said Kevin G. Grant, comanager of Oakmark Fund. "Buying The Learning Company was like falling off a cliff." By late 2000, Mattel obviously agreed with critics and divested The Learning Company.

Despite Mattel's troubles with electronic toys, the company's marketing prowess and reach have been generally successful. For example, in a 1997 poll conducted by the annual J. D. Power Brands study, Mattel had strong popularity among consumers. As many as four out of ten people said that if they were shopping for toys, Mattel would be the brand that they most prefer. Retailers also singled out Mattel as a solid performer. This survey clearly proved that both children and adults are enthused about Mattel and its line of products. In 2002 the Mattel and Fisher-Price names were tops in a survey of consumers asked about their brand preferences when buying toys in discount stores or superstores. Barbie and Hot Wheels were also mentioned many times by these same consumers. Mattel owns all of the leaders in this survey's report of top toy brands.

Leadership at Mattel

From 1997 until early 2000, Mattel was under the managerial control of CEO Jill Barad. For several years, Barad was the subject of many news stories because she was one of only four female CEOs leading Fortune 500 firms. She usually resisted being depicted as a "female executive" and preferred to focus on merit alone. However, by 1999 she was hinting that gender might have played a role in the negative publicity and scrutiny she was beginning to receive in the press. Barad's management style was characterized as strict, businesslike, and people oriented. In addition, Barad was known for her personal preferences, including brightly colored suits and a lively presentation style that reportedly put off some of the conservative Wall Street establishment.

When Barad was named CEO in January 1997, Mattel's stock was trading for less than $30 per share. However, by March 1997, it had risen to more than $46. Before she was CEO, Barad was in charge of the Barbie product line and played a crucial role in building sales of Barbie from $200 million in 1982 to $1.9 billion in 1997. The challenges that Barad faced increased throughout 1998 and 1999. Mattel announced in October 1998 that earnings growth for the year would be between nine and 12 percent rather than the 18 percent that Wall Street had anticipated. This meager performance was due to the decline of sales to Toys "R" Us, the retail chain that accounted for 18 percent of Mattel's revenue in 1997. Barad stated in an interview that if performance continued to deteriorate sharply, the generous rewards given to employees might have to be cut back. In other words, holiday time and overtime would be shortened. However, throughout 1999, some industry analysts said that Mattel's overall strategy was sound and that the company should rebound to outperform most stock market indexes. Other analysts and investors publicly called for her departure. While Mattel did have net sales of $5.5 billion and earnings of $182.1 million in 1999, its acquisition of The Learning Company brought more problems than anticipated.

A pretax loss of $183 million occurred due to the sales slump of Mattel's CD-ROM software, inventory problems, and discounting on products. This, along with the 1999 fourth-quarter net loss of $18.4 million, led to the resignation of Jill Barad. Even amidst the problems in 1998 and 1999, many analysts believed that she would stay on as CEO for another year, partly because she was very close to the firm's board of directors. The fourth-quarter performances of Barbie, Fisher-Price, and Mattel Entertainment were all strong, but The Learning Company problems overshadowed these achievements. In total, Mattel's stock had dropped 60 percent during Barad's three-year reign as CEO. The board appointed Ronald M. Loeb as acting CEO, but the debate on the correct person to lead Mattel through this problem loomed large.

By March 2000, Mattel's stock price was below $10 a share, representing an eight-year low for a stock that once traded above $45. One frustrated analyst commented, "I'm done with Mattel." The company soon installed Robert Eckert as chairman and CEO. Eckert joined Mattel after a 23-year career at Kraft where he started in marketing and rose to president and CEO. During Eckert's first three years on the job, the company's stock price increased to over $20 per share, and Mattel was ranked fortieth on *Business Week*'s list of top-performing companies. Implementing techniques used by consumer-product companies, Eckert adopted a mission to bring stability and predictability to Mattel. After selling The Learning Company, Eckert turned his attention to such other issues as improving inventory control, developing more toys in-house instead of overseas, and depending less on costly licensed properties. This huge transformation was driven by the need to revamp supply chain management at Mattel. Eckert increased the use of focus groups and used the data to determine the demand for products at an earlier stage during production. For example, high-volume buyers like Wal-Mart and Toys "R" Us received products earlier in the year to ensure that the most popular toys were on store shelves in ample supply.

Mattel also adopted new packaging practices. In the past, packages were printed in many languages and tailored to each country's particular tastes. Now, there are only three versions of packaging, each of which includes information in several languages. This allows Mattel to ship products from country to country midseason in the event the toy is not as popular in, for example, France as it is in Italy.

Finally, Eckert's restructuring plan included improving relations with retailers. Prior to these changes, Mattel's service rate was at 50 percent, meaning that stores received only about half of the products on time. In a collaborative effort, members of the manufacturing, logistics, sales, operations, and marketing departments spent months studying key accounts with retailers. The teams visited various warehouses and implemented such improvements as new pallet patterns and box shapes and better information flow. Because of these efforts, the service level increased to 90 percent.

Today, Eckert continues to focus on excellent service rates, following in the footsteps of some of the best consumer-products companies.

Currently, stockholders and financial analysts are content with Eckert's performance as CEO. Eckert and his leadership team make every effort to ensure that the company is becoming "The World's Premier Toy Brand—Today and Tomorrow." Mattel's leadership team strives to guide the 26,000 employees worldwide toward that vision. Every Tuesday morning, all function and division heads get together to share information and determine the priority of various projects and opportunities. These priorities are based on annual corporate goals, so there is synergy between daily activities and longer-term plans.

Mattel's Core Brands

Barbie

Barbie is Mattel's flagship brand and its number-one seller—routinely accounting for more than 50 percent of Mattel's sales revenue. The first Barbie doll sported open-toed shoes, a ponytail, sunglasses, earrings, and a zebra-striped bathing suit. Fashions and accessories were also available for the doll. Although buyers at the annual Toy Fair in New York took no interest in the Barbie doll, little girls of the time certainly did. The intense demand seen at the retail stores was insufficiently met for several years. Mattel just could not produce the Barbie dolls fast enough.

Although Barbie was introduced as a teenage fashion model, she has taken on almost every possible profession. She has also acquired numerous male and female friends and family over the years. Ken, Midge, Skipper, Christie, and others were introduced from the mid-1960s on. The Barbie line has even seen a disabled friend in a wheelchair: Share a Smile Becky. Barbie's popularity has even broken stereotypes. Retrofitted versions of Barbie dolls, on sale in select San Francisco stores, feature "Hooker" Barbie, "Trailer Trash" Barbie, and "Drag Queen" Barbie. There are also numerous "alternative" Barbies, such as "Big Dyke" Barbie, but Mattel does not want the Barbie name to be used in these sales. Redressed and accessorized Barbies are okay with Mattel as long as no one practices trademark infringement. Altogether the Barbie line has sold more than 1 billion dolls in four decades. This makes Barbie the best-selling fashion doll in most global markets, which involves about $2 billion in worldwide sales annually. According to Associated Press, the more than 100 different Barbie dolls are sold on the average of two per second.

March 1999 marked the 40th anniversary of Barbie. It also marked a new campaign, "Be Anything," which focused on girls being anything from athletes to computer experts to dreamers. A Barbie doll was barely visible in the ads, and not one of Barbie's accessories appeared. The whole effort was an attempt to retain the interest of girls for another two years after the usual post-Barbie age of seven years old and to make things more "real" with these older girls.

Barbie has also expanded into the realm of young girls' clothing. Barbie clothes are now available for children, and Barbie herself received a makeover. In response to criticism and the need to keep the brand strong, the company developed a more modern version of Barbie, with a smaller chest, larger waist, and softer hairstyle, which more accurately reflect a natural female body. More in-style clothes are available for the doll, and a bellybutton is now found on the doll. The Barbie line is even being expanded into computers, which are designed with a Barbie theme and include a digital camera. This is all being done in an effort to recapture more of a customer base and even to expand the market by attracting older girls to the Barbie product line.

By August 2002, Barbie's popularity slipped and the stalwart brand failed to make the top-five-selling dolls. This decline is due to new and innovative competition, including the Bratz doll line that has gained significant market share. In an attempt to recover, Mattel introduced the new line of My Scene dolls aimed at "tweens." These dolls are trendier, look younger, and are considered to be more hip for this age group who is on the cusp of outgrowing playing with dolls. A website (http://www.myscene.com) engages girls in a variety of fun, engaging, and promotional activities. Other efforts targeted at "tweens" include the Mystery Squad, a crime-solving crew, and the Barbie Doll as Elle Woods, which is a tribute to the blonde character in the MGM Pictures film *Legally Blond 2: Red, White and Blonde.*

American Girl

In 1998 Mattel acquired Pleasant Company, maker of the American Girl collection—a well-known line of historical dolls, books, and accessories. Originally, American Girl products were sold exclusively through catalogs. Mattel extended that base by selling American Girl accessories (not the dolls) in major chain stores like Wal-Mart and Target. More recent efforts to increase brand awareness include the opening of American Girl Place shops New York, Chicago, and Los Angeles. The New York store features three floors of dolls, accessories, and books in the heart of the 5th Avenue shopping district. The store also offers a café where girls can dine with their dolls, and a stage production where young actresses bring American Girl stories to life.

The American Girl collection is wildly popular with girls in the seven- to 12-year-old demographic. The dolls have a wholesome and educational image—the antithesis to Barbie. This move by Mattel represented a long-term strategy to reduce reliance on traditional products and to take away the stigma surrounding the "perfect image" of Barbie. Each American Girl doll lives during a specific time in American history, and all have stories that describe the hardships they face while maturing into young adults. For example, Felicity's stories describe life in 1774 just prior to the Revolutionary War. Likewise, Josephina lives in New Mexico in 1824 during the rapid growth of the American West. Other dolls include Kaya (a Native American girl growing up in 1764), Elizabeth (Colonial Virginia), Kirsten (pioneer life in 1854), Addy (1864 during the Civil War), Samantha and Nellie (1904 New York), Kit (1934 during the Great Depression), Molly (1944 during World War II), and Emily (a British girl who comes to America during World War II).

Hot Wheels

With over 15 million boys ages five to 15 years old collecting Hot Wheels cars, this line of small die-cast vehicles is now involved with almost every racing circuit in the world including NASCAR (National Association for Stock Car Auto Racing), Formula One, NHRA (National Hot Rod Association), Champ Car World Series, AMA (American Motorcycle Association), and many others. This immense popularity has created a group of collectors with the average boy collector owning more than forty-one Hot Wheels cars. Mattel continues its strategy of focusing on basic toys with fresh, innovative products relevant to the market. Hot Wheels vehicles have even extended into other X-treme wheeled sports lines, including skateboard products and motocross products endorsed by Jeremy McGrath.

Hot Wheels celebrated its thirty-fifth anniversary in 2003 with a massive marketing campaign called the Hot Wheels Highway 35 World Race. Mattel created story- and character-based packaging that included collectible cars, racetracks, comic books, home videos, a video game, a television network special, and an online race. The idea was to appeal to the many age groups of collectors whom Mattel had acquired in more recent years. The vehicles have features that are popular with young boys, including California-inspired designs and edgy-urban racers. Other promotions include peel- and-win stickers with a chance to win one of 50,000 prizes, a free Ultimate Track Set for collecting all thirty-five World Race Cars, and a World Race Team starter kit that includes an official World Race driver's license and ID badge. Mattel has gone to great lengths to provide boys with imaginative role-playing possibilities that offer the Hot Wheels experience not only as toys but also as entertainment.

Fisher-Price

Acquired in 1993 as a wholly owned subsidiary, Fisher-Price is the umbrella brand for all of Mattel's infant and preschool lines. The brand is trusted by parents around the world and appears on everything from children's software to eyewear and books to bicycles. Some of the more classic products include the Rock-a-Stack and Little People play sets. New favorites include Power Wheels vehicles and Rescue Heroes, a line of firefighter action figures that has been in great demand since September 11, 2001. Through licensing agreements, the brand also develops character-based toys such as *Sesame Street*'s Elmo and Big Bird and Disney's Winnie the Pooh and Mickey Mouse.

Fisher-Price has built a trust with parents by creating products that are educational, safe, and useful. For example, during recent years, the brand has earned high regard for innovative car seats and nursery monitors. One project includes collaboration with Microsoft to develop an activity table that teaches infants through pre- schoolers with "smart technology." Fisher-Price keeps pace with the interests of today's families through innovative learning toys and award-winning baby gear.

International Sales

Although Mattel was already the world's largest toy company, former CEO Barad planned to double Mattel's international sales throughout the late 1990s and early 2000 as part of a strategy aimed at worldwide growth. Under current CEO Eckert's leadership, Mattel has maintained the strategy of strong expansion overseas with a goal of raising international sales to 50 percent of Mattel's sales, from 34 percent in 2002. Of international sales, two-thirds are in Europe, one-third in Latin America, and a small percentage are in the Asia–Pacific region. International sales increased 13 percent from 2000 to 2001 and another 11 percent from 2001 to 2002. In 2005, domestic sales decreased by approximately two percent while international sales expanded by five percent. Fisher-Price has been especially successful in international markets while Barbie sales have tumbled. The international segment has benefited from Mattel's strategic focus on globalization of brands, including improved product availability, better alignment of worldwide marketing and sales plans, and strong product launches.

In 1999, Mattel entered in a global marketing alliance with Bandai Company, the world's third-largest toy maker with offices in eighteen countries and headquarters in Tokyo. Under the terms of the agreement, Mattel has been selling Bandai products, such as Power Ranger and Digimon toys, in Latin America. For its part, Bandai has been responsible for Japanese sales of Mattel products, including Barbie, Hot Wheels, and Fisher-Price products. Bandai has also been involved with adjusting Mattel's brands to match the Japanese market more carefully, such as the targeting of young women with miscellaneous Barbie-related goods unique to the Japanese market and the opening of stores dedicated to these kinds of products. Expanding the initial agreement, Bandai and Mattel released ROBO WHEELS, a minicar series designed by Bandai to complement Mattel's Hot Wheels line in the United States and Europe. This was the first time that the two companies used their business relationship to release products in countries other than Japan and Latin America.

Worldwide the most recognized product for Mattel continues to be Barbie. In a study conducted by Interbrand and published in *BusinessWeek,* Barbie was the only Mattel brand that made the list of the 2002 "The 100 Best Global Brands." However, the traditional Barbie doll does not receive a warm welcome in some international markets. The Malaysian Consumers' Association of Penanghas tried to ban Barbie because of her non-Asian appearance and the lack of creativity needed to play with her. The public and media outcry soon retaliated against this ban. But government agencies in other countries, such as Iran, have carried out similar practices. In May 2002, Iranian police confiscated Barbie from toy stores because of the doll's non-Islamic characteristics. Western influences, such as makeup and revealing clothes, are not wanted in a society where women must wear head scarves in public and men and women are not allowed to go to the pool or beach together.

The same might occur in Russia where the Russian Ministry of Education has included Barbie and other toys and games, such as Pokémon, on a list of items to be banned. The ministry's reasoning for the ban is the supposedly harmful effects that these toys and games have on the minds of young children. Barbie, in particular, is under fire because the doll is thought to awaken sexual impulses in the minds of the very young and encourage consumerism among Russian infants. The move will be seen as part of the government's attempts to control the sense of identity of young Russians and foster ideals of family and patriotism. Regardless, Barbie continues to sell relatively well, despite her appearance, all over the world.

Customer Orientation at Mattel

Mattel's management philosophy focuses on satisfying customer's needs and wants. Today, this philosophy, commonly known as customer orientation, has been widely adopted by consumer goods manufacturers like Mattel. For example, Mattel redesigned Barbie to more naturally reflect a normal athletic woman in an attempt to meet the demands for a more realistic doll. Barbie has also taken on many different professions so as to reach a wider audience. These product modifications and extensions are designed to meet consumer and social demands while still accomplishing company objectives. Likewise, Hot Wheels now feature NASCAR logos in an attempt to meet consumer demand for more merchandise related to this popular televised sport. Mattel's pursuit of interactive multimedia is an attempt to adapt to the shorter span of time that young girls want Barbie and other dolls and toys. Children are turning to more interactive toys sooner than was the case in years past, and Mattel's acquisition of The Learning Company was designed to meet this demand and capitalize on it.

As another indicator of its commitment to customers, Mattel employs market research so that its strategy and tactics meet customer needs and wants. This is combined with research and development in an effort to release new products yearly, based on consumer input. A recent edition to the Mattel product line includes the new construction and activity set called Ello. The product is meant to compete with Lego and draw girls to building toys, which have traditionally been geared almost exclusively to boys. Mattel research teams watched girls play with pipe cleaners, scissors, glue, paper, and cardboard and learned that girls wanted to make panels and tell stories about the space. The idea behind Ello is to build a house or figures using interconnecting plastic shapes allowing girls to build and create while engaging in social play. Mattel hopes Ello will be a globally recognized brand with a unique name that does not require translation.

Social Responsibility at Mattel

Like any other organization, Mattel has recognized the different responsibilities that it has to various stakeholders including customers, employees, investors, suppliers, and the community. These stakeholders have some claim, or stake, in Mattel's products, markets, and business outcomes. Mattel demonstrates a commitment to economic, legal, ethical, and philanthropic responsibilities. For example, because the company's products are designed primarily for children, it must be sensitive to societal concerns about children's rights. In addition, the international environment often complicates business transactions, especially in the area of employee rights and safety in manufacturing facilities. Different legal systems and cultural expectations about business can create ethical conflict. Finally, the use of technology may present ethical dilemmas, especially with regard to consumer privacy. Mattel has recognized these potential issues and has taken steps to strengthen its commitment to business ethics and social responsibility. The company recently published its first "Corporate Social

Responsibility" report, including this strong statement about Mattel's commitment to economic, legal, ethical and philanthropic responsibilities:

> *Being a responsible corporate citizen permeates everything we do at Mattel.*
> *Our employees make it a reality every single day around the world, whether*
> *ensuring a product's safety, volunteering in a community, developing a*
> *best practice or even treating colleagues with respect and dignity.*
>
> *Through these efforts, and countless others, Mattel works hard to be a leader*
> *in making our communities—and the lives of children—better.*
>
> *And we will continue to lead the way with the hope that others will follow.*

Privacy and Marketing Technology

Advances in technology have created special issues for Mattel's marketing efforts. Mattel has recognized that, because it markets to children, it has the responsibility to communicate with parents about its corporate marketing strategy. The company has taken special steps to inform both children and adults about its philosophy regarding Internet-based marketing tools. For example, at the Barbie.com website, parents are encouraged to read and follow suggestions on Internet safety. The company provides a full explanation of how it collects information, precautions it takes to protect information, and other issues relevant to parents and children. It takes a similar approach at other brand-specific websites. For example, the following statement appears on the Hot Wheels website:

> *Mattel, Inc. and its family of companies ("Mattel") are committed to protecting*
> *your online privacy when visiting a website operated by us. We do not collect*
> *and keep any personal information online from you unless you volunteer it*
> *and you are 13 or older. We also do not collect and keep personal information*
> *online from children under the age of 13 without consent of a parent or*
> *legal guardian, except in limited circumstances authorized by law and described*
> *in this policy. Please review the information below to familiarize yourself with*
> *our policies on website privacy, so that you can take full advantage of all the*
> *fun activities available at our sites for you and your family. Please remember that*
> *this site and the servers that make this site available are located in the U.S.*
> *By using this site you agree to the transfer, collection, processing and use of*
> *data by this site.*
>
> *A Special Note For Parents And Legal Guardians: Mattel adheres to*
> *the Children's Online Privacy Protection Act of 1998 and the guidelines of*
> *the Children's Advertising Review Unit (CARU) of the Council of Better Business*
> *Bureaus, Inc. in each of our websites for children. You can help by spending*
> *time online with your children and monitoring your children's online use. Please*
> *help us protect your child's privacy by instructing them never to provide personal*
> *information on this site or any other without your permission.*
>
> *If you are under 18, please be sure to read this policy with your parents or legal*
> *guardians and ask questions about things you do not understand. Children under 13*

should get your parent's or legal guardian's permission before giving out your e-mail address or any personal information to Mattel or to anyone else on the Internet.

Global Manufacturing Principles

Beyond concerns about marketing to children, Mattel takes its commitment to business ethics very seriously. In late 1997, the company completed its first full ethics audit of each of its manufacturing sites and those facilities of primary contractors. The audit indicated that the company was not using any child labor or forced labor, a problem that plagued other overseas consumer products manufacturers (for example, Nike). However, several contractors were found in violation of Mattel's standards and were forced to change their operations or lose Mattel's significant business. In an effort to continue its strong record on human rights–related ethical standards, Mattel instituted a code of conduct called "Global Manufacturing Principles" (GMP). These principles, as audited by the Mattel Independent Monitoring Council (MIMCO), require all Mattel-owned and contracted manufacturing facilities to, among other things, favor business partners who are committed to ethical standards that are comparable with Mattel's. Other principles relate to safety, wages, and adherence to local laws. Mattel also uses the International Center for Corporate Accountability for audit purposes.

Mattel has not designed its auditing effort and subsequent code of conduct to be a punitive force. Rather, the company is dedicated to creating and encouraging responsible business practices. As one company consultant noted, "Mattel is committed to improving the skill level of workers . . . [so] in turn [they] will experience increased opportunities and productivity." This statement reflects Mattel's concern for relationships with employees and business partners that extend beyond pure profit considerations. Although the company will surely benefit from its code's principles, Mattel has formally acknowledged its willingness to consider multiple stakeholders' interests and benefits in its business philosophy. The company's code is a signal to potential partners, customers, and other stakeholders that Mattel is making a serious commitment to ethical values and is willing to base business decisions on them.

For example, contracts with business partners are based on how well they meet all of Mattel's manufacturing principles. If Mattel determines that any one of its partners' manufacturing facilities or any vendor has violated these principles, it can either terminate their business relationship or require the facility to implement a corrective action plan. If corrective action is advised but not taken, Mattel will immediately terminate current production and suspend placement of future orders. Thus, a key challenge for Mattel is the certification of business partners and potential partners with respect to its manufacturing principles.

In November 2002, Mattel published MIMCO's findings of the audits conducted at the manufacturing facilities in Indonesia, Malaysia, and Thailand. The results revealed satisfactory and, on occasion, exemplary findings such as addressing employee health needs and providing job-related skill-enhancement programs. Some recommendations included increased lunch schedules to accommodate meals and prayers and addressing employee feelings of discrimination in hiring and promotion practices. Mattel is committed to the compliance of its GMP to set an example of responsible conduct for manufacturing facilities worldwide. The results of a recent audit in 2006 were very complimentary. One expert noted that "Mattel's GMP continues to play an important role in leading contractor manufacturing facilities to achieve or even surpass compliance standards."

The Mattel Foundation

In another effort to demonstrate a strong commitment to its stakeholders, Mattel established the Mattel Foundation, which promotes philanthropy and community involvement among Mattel's employees and makes charitable investments to help children in need. Mattel views philanthropy as an investment and has therefore sought out nonprofits that hold and demonstrate the same beliefs of compassionate outreach to children and financial accountability.

The work of the Mattel Foundation is funded primarily through a percentage of Mattel's pretax corporate profits. The limited resources and numerous needs have made the Foundation focus primarily on national Foundation-sponsored initiatives that address relevant children's issues. For example, the Foundation was able to provide for construction of the Mattel Children's Hospital at the University of California, Los Angeles. The Foundation also supports annual fundraising events such as the Children Affected by Aids Foundation (established by an HIV-positive Mattel executive), the Mattel Family Learning Program, and the annual giving campaign targeted toward Mattel employees.

Many of Mattel's philanthropic endeavors are tied to the company's subsidiaries and brands. For example, Wisconsin-based Pleasant Company—makers of the American Girl collection—provided $449,500 in grants to support children's programming throughout Dane County. One- and two-year grants were awarded to such projects as environmental education for elementary school children, various cultural programs, and a performing arts series for children. Funding is made possible through the Madison Children's Museum annual benefit sale of second and returned American Girl products.

The Barbie brand debuted a worldwide cause-related program called "Barbie Cares: Supporting Children in the Arts" dedicated to supporting arts education for children. This program, made possible by a $2 million donation to the Entertainment Industry Foundation, includes a celebrity public-service announcement campaign, an Arts Teacher of the Year Search, and the creation of innovative, relevant products that expose girls to the world of arts education and creative exploration.

Mattel's Employee Volunteer Program, established in 1991, provides all members of the Mattel family with opportunities to give back to their communities. Every year, Mattel employees contribute many hours of volunteer service to the lives of needy children. The Mattel Foundation also offers a generous Employee Matching Gifts Program, matching dollar for dollar the charitable gifts made by employees to qualified nonprofit organizations. Mattel's combination of responsibility and personal involvement is the basis for the company's philanthropic vision and its deeply held commitment to helping children.

Moving Forward

As this case has shown, while the beginning of the twenty-first century continues to challenge Mattel's executive leadership and financial standing, the company has also made strong strides. Today, Mattel faces many market opportunities and threats including the rate at which children are growing up and leaving toys, the role of technology in consumer products, and purchasing power and consumer needs in global markets. The continuing lifestyle shift of American youth is of particular concern for Mattel. Today, many children, tweens, and teens prefer to spend time with music, movies, or the Internet. The phenomenal success of the iPod and social networking sites like MySpace.com are a testament to this shift. Children and teens are also more active in extracurricular activities (for example, sports, music, and volunteerism) than ever before. Consequently, these young consumers have less time to spend with traditional toys. This shift has created challenges for all toy makers. For example, sales growth in Mattel's key brands has been relatively flat for some time (Case Exhibit 11.1). Barbie's worldwide sales, in particular, have been declining over the past several years due to changes in the youth market and intense competition from the Bratz line. As a whole, Mattel has also underperformed competitors Hasbro (best known for G.I. Joe, Play-Doh, and Tonka) and JAKKS Pacific (best known for its wrestling action figures and games) over the past five years.

Despite these concerns, Mattel has a lot to offer both children and investors. Barbie remains the number-one doll in the United States and worldwide. And Barbie.com, the number-one website for girls, routinely gets over 50 million visits per month. Furthermore, all of Mattel's core brands are instantly recognizable around the world. Hence, the ability to leverage one or all of these brands is high. A few remaining issues include Mattel's reliance on Wal-Mart and Target (which lessens Mattel's pricing power), volatile oil prices (oil is used to make plastics), and increasing competition on a global scale. However, analysts believe Mattel has a great growth potential, especially in international markets, with technology-based toys and in light of changing demographic and socioeconomic trends. For a company that began with two friends making picture frames, Mattel has demonstrated marketing dexterity and

CASE EXHIBIT 11.1	SALES GROWTH AMONG MATTEL'S CORE BRANDS					
	2005 (%)	2004 (%)	2003 (%)	2002 (%)	2001 (%)	2000 (%)
Barbie	−13	−8	0	17	−2	5
American Girl	15	10	−2	−1	4	7
Hot Wheels	−1	7	3	5	2	2
Fisher-Price	1	9	5	8	−1	26
Total	1	3	2	7	2	2

Source: Philip Durell, "Barbies Gone Wild," The Motley Fool, February 21, 2006 (http://www.fool.com/news/commentary/2006/commentary06022106.htm), based on Mattel company filings.

longevity. The next few years, however, will test the firm's resolve and strategy within the highly competitive yet lucrative toy market.

Questions for Discussion

1. Do manufacturers of products for children have special responsibilities to consumers and society? What are these responsibilities, and how well has Mattel met them? Provide evidence of Mattel's strengths and weaknesses in this area.

2. Comment on the strengths and weaknesses of Mattel's core brands. In looking at Barbie specifically, has Mattel's success with the American Girl collection cannibalized sales from Barbie? Explain.

3. What are the opportunities and threats that Mattel faces as it looks ahead?

4. If you could make only one recommendation to Mattel, what would it be?

5. How can Mattel reverse the decline in Barbie's sales? Should Mattel give up on Barbie and accept the fact that the brand will never regain its former sales status? Explain.

Sources

These facts of this case are from "Corporate Social Responsibility Report," Mattel website (http://www.mattel.com/about_us/Corp_Responsibility/csr_final.pdf), accessed September 10, 2006; "Leadership," Mattel website (http://mattel.com/about_us/default.asp), accessed July 5, 2006; "Global Manufacturing Principles," Mattel website (http://www.mattel.com/about_us/Corp_Responsibility/cr_global.asp), accessed September 13, 2006; "Barbie Ban," Samizdata.net (http://www.samizdata.net/blog/archives/004492.html), accessed July 7, 2006; Deborah Adamson, "Trouble in Toyland," CBS MarketWatch, March 8, 2000 (http://cbs.marketwatch.com/); American Girl website (http://www.americangirl.com), accessed May 27, 2003; Anonymous, "Barbie Is Banned from Russia, Without Love," *Observer [UK] Online,* November 24, 2002 (http://www.observer.co.uk/), accessed May 27, 2003; Anonymous, "Iran Enforces Barbie Ban," *Associated Press,* May 23, 2002; Anonymous, "Mattel, Inc. Launches Global Code of Conduct Intended to Improve Workplace, Worker's Standard of Living," *Canada NewsWire,* November 21, 1997; Anonymous, "Mattel Lands WB Master Toy Licenses," *Home Textiles Today,* September 2002, 14; Anonymous, "Mattel Combines Girls, Boys Divisions, Cuts Management," *Associated Press,* February 28, 2003; Bandai website (http://www.bandai.com), accessed May 27, 2003; Lisa Bannon, "Let's Play Makeover Barbie," *Wall Street Journal,* February 17, 2000, B2; Lisa Bannon and Joann S. Lublin, "Jill Barad Abruptly Quits the Top Job at Mattel," *Wall Street Journal,* February 4, 2000, A1; Lisa Bannon, "Mattel Sees Untapped Market for Blocks: Little Girls," *Wall Street Journal,* June 6, 2002, B1; Lisa Bannon, "New Playbook: Taking Cues from GE, Mattel's CEO Wants Toy Maker to Grow Up," *Wall Street Journal,* November 14, 2001, A1; Adam Bryant, "Mattel CEO Jill Barad and a Toyshop That Doesn't Forget to Play," *New York Times,* October 11, 1998, C8; Sherri Day, "As It Remakes Itself, Mattel Does Same for Barbie," *New York Times,* November 9, 2002, C1; Philip Durell, "Barbies Gone Wild," The Motley Fool, February 21, 2006 (http://www.fool.com/news/commentary/2006/commentary 06022106.htm); Bill Duryea, "Barbie-holics: They're Devoted to the Doll," *St. Petersburg [FL] Times,* August 7, 1998, B1; Fisher-Price website (http://www. fisherprice.com/us/), accessed September 14, 2006; Hot Wheels website (http:// www.hotwheels.com/), accessed September 14, 2006; Debbie Howell, "Top Brands 2002: A Longing for Labels Returns," *DSN Retailing Today,* October 28, 2002, 24–27; Interbrand, "The 100 Best Brands," *BusinessWeek Online,* (http://www.businessweek. com), accessed May 27, 2003; Stephanie Kang, "Mattel Profit Falls Slightly on Barbie Weakness," *Wall Street Journal,* January 31, 2006, B5; Nancy J. Kim, "Barbie Gets an Image Makeover," *Puget Sound Business Journal,* March 15, 1999, 17; Mattel website (http://www.mattel.com), accessed September 14, 2006; Marla Matzer, "Deals on Hot Wheels," *Los Angeles Times,* July 22, 1998, D18; My Scene Barbie website (http:// www.myscene.com), accessed August 15, 2006; Christopher Palmeri, "Mattel's New Toy Story," *BusinessWeek,* November 18, 2002, 72–74; Reuters, "Mattel Swings to Better Than Expected Profit," *Reuters News & Financial Intelligence Online,* April 13, 2003 (http://www.reuters.com/); Patricia Sellers, "The 50 Most Powerful Women in American Business," *Fortune,* October 12, 1998, 32–36; Pamela Sherrid, "Troubles in BarbieLand," *U.S. News & World Report,* January 17, 2000, 47–48; J. Alex Tarquino, "Barbie & Co. Reviving Mattel," *New York Times,* March 9, 2003, sec. 3, 7; "The Glass Ceiling: The CEO Still Wears Wingtips," *BusinessWeek,* November 22, 1999, 62–63; "Toymaker Mattel Bans Child Labor," *Denver Post,* November 21, 1998, A8; and Michael White, "Barbie Will Lose Some Curves When Mattel Modernizes Icon," *Detroit News,* November 18, 1997, E32.

PETCO Develops Successful Stakeholder Relationships

Walter Evans founded PETCO in 1965 as a mail-order veterinary-supplies store. The original name was UPCO, United Pharmacal Co. In 1976 they opened their first retail store in La Mesa, California, buying quality pet and veterinary supplies and selling them directly to animal professionals and the public at discount prices. In 1979, UPCO became PETCO with a vision to promote the highest level of well-being for companion animals and to support the human–animal bond. Their aim is to provide a broad array of premium products, companion animals, and services and a fun and exciting shopping experience. Their value proposition to the "pet-parent" customer is provided through friendly, knowledgeable associates (employees) in convenient, community-based locations.

PETCO Animal Supplies, Inc. is now the nation's number-two pet supply specialty retailer of premium pet food, supplies, and services with over 780 stores in 49 states and the District of Columbia. Their pet-related products include pet food, pet supplies, grooming products, toys, novelty items, vitamins, veterinary supplies, and small pets such as fish, birds, other small animals (excluding cats and dogs). In fiscal 2005, PETCO generated sales of $2 billion—an increase of 10.2 percent over 2004. By mid-2006, PETCO's sales had grown by another 10 percent to $1.05 billion for the half year. The company plans a net increase of 75 new stores over a two-year period.

PETCO's strategy is to offer their customers a complete assortment of pet-related products and services at competitive prices, with superior levels of customer service at convenient locations. The company also operates a successful e-commerce business at www.petco.com. PETCO believes that this combination differentiates their stores and provides them with a competitive advantage. Their principal format is a 12,000 to 15,000 square-foot store, conveniently located near local neighborhood shopping destinations, including supermarkets, bookstores, coffee shops, dry cleaners, and video stores, where their target pet-parent customer makes regular weekly shopping trips. PETCO believes that their stores are well positioned, both in terms of product offerings and location, to benefit from favorable long-term demographic trends: a growing pet population and an increasing willingness of pet owners to spend on their pets.

Since mid-2001, all new stores have been opened in their new formats, which incorporate a more dramatic presentation of their companion animals and emphasize higher-margin supply categories. Each store has approximately 10,000 pet-related items including premium cat and dog foods, collars, leashes, grooming products, toys, and animal habitats. The stores also offer grooming, obedience training, and veterinary services, and they sponsor pet adoption for cats and dogs with local animal-welfare organizations. PETCO has 17,900 employees, 9,000 of which are full time.

The Pet Industry

The pet food, supplies, and services industry is benefiting from a number of favorable demographic trends that are continuing to support a steadily growing pet population. The U.S. pet population has now reached 378 million companion animals, including 143 million cats and dogs, with an estimated 62 percent of all U.S. households owning at least one pet, and three-quarters of those households owning two or more pets. It is widely believed that the trend for more pets and for more pet-owning households will continue, driven by an increasing number of children under 18 years of age and a growing number of empty nesters whose pets have become their new "children." Estimates have suggested that U.S. retail sales of pet food, supplies, small animals (excluding cats and dogs), and services increased to approximately $34 billion in 2004. PETCO believes that it is well positioned to benefit from several key growth trends within the industry.

The growth of the pet industry has been so phenomenal that many pet-related products have gone decidedly upscale: Harley Davidson offers a line of leather dog jackets; Paul Mitchell now offers a line of pet shampoos; many hotels offer pet-friendly rooms; and Japanese pet-toy company Takara has introduced Bow-Lingual—a device that translates dog barks. Most pet owners treat their animals as a part of their families, often lavishing as much care and attention on the pet as they do on other family members. Consequently, pet owners, now more than ever, are prepared to spend considerable sums of money on pet products.

Given the rate of growth, it is not surprising that PETCO competes in a highly competitive industry against such names as PetSmart and Wal-Mart. Industry competition can be categorized into three different segments: (1) supermarkets, warehouse clubs, and mass merchants; (2) specialty pet store chains; and (3) traditional pet stores and independent service providers. The principal competitive factors influencing PETCO are product selection and quality, convenient store locations, customer service, and price. PETCO believes that it competes effectively within its various geographic areas. However, some of its competitors are much larger in terms of sales volume and have access to greater capital and management resources than PETCO does.

The Risks of Competing in the Pet Industry

All industries have some degree of operating risk. Industries and firms are concerned about public- or special-interest groups that might uncover some activity that can immediately be used by critics and the mass media, competitors, or simply skeptical stakeholders to undermine their reputations. Therefore, most companies make on-going risk assessment an important aspect of their strategic planning initiatives. A single negative incident can influence perceptions of a firm's image and reputation instantly and possibly continue for years afterwards.

Because pets have such a strong emotional attachment for most individuals, the pet industry is subject to many allegations of wrongdoing and unethical behaviors. For all firms in the pet industry, the question is not whether accusations will occur but when they will occur. Therefore, pet industry firms must have plans in place to respond rapidly when accusations are made that can threaten their image and reputation.

PETCO is committed to pets and animals in general. However, selling animals has inherent risks. Between 2000 and 2005, PETA (People for the Ethical Treatment of Animals) made several allegations against PETCO over questionable animal conditions. PETA, a special-interest group whose views are not always supported by the general public, is highly critical of most organizations that sell or use animals for commercial purposes.

One of the most notable incidents occurred in May 2004 when PETCO paid nearly $1 million in precedent-setting settlements involving the mistreatment of animals in PETCO stores in five California counties. After PETA released undercover footage of extreme neglect at North American Pet Distributor, Inc. (NAPD), which supplied at least 55 PETCO stores, PETCO halted its business with NAPD.

Another notable incident occurred when PETA filed a complaint with the Securities and Exchange Commission (SEC) alleging cruelty and neglect to animals in PETCO's care. In particular, PETA was concerned about the sale of large birds. When kept as companions, large birds need plenty of space to move around and exercise. They also need a great deal of socialization and attention—at least eight hours a day. Most parrots die from diseases caused by the same conditions that adversely affect humans (for example, obesity, high-stress environments, or too-little exercise). Adding to the problem is that roughly 70 percent of parrots suffer from "miner's lung" disease (pneumoconiosis) due to living in dry, stuffy, indoor environments. All of these problems are exacerbated by the 40- to 70-year lifespan of most large birds. These animals easily outlive their owners; hence, they typically live with several families during their lives.

On April 12, 2005, PETA and PETCO announced an agreement that would advance animal welfare across the country. PETA agreed to end its campaign against PETCO, to take down all references to "PETNO," and dismantle its "PETCOCruelty" website. PETCO agreed to end the sale of large birds in its stores upon completion of the sale of the limited number of birds they had in stock. PETCO also agreed to continue working with shelter partners in its "Think Adoption First" program to help promote the adoption of homeless birds and other pets. PETCO also agreed to make changes to benefit rats and mice, including separating the animals by gender to prevent breeding. Although not required to answer to PETA, PETCO decided to respond as an indication of its desire to cooperate, resolve issues and misunderstandings, and improve operations.

Other non-PETA problems have also plagued PETCO. In 2002 inspectors and customers found sick finches, a moldy dead turtle, dead birds, and a toad "cooked to death" at two San Francisco PETCO stores that were also overcharging customers on sale items. PETCO settled this case in 2004, agreeing to pay more than $900,000—most of which was spent on new scanners in its stores. PETCO also agreed to increase training for its managers and employees in regard to caring for animals. Again, this demonstrated the desire to do the right thing and respond to mistakes made by employees.

In 2004, PETCO agreed to settle a Federal Trade Commission charge that it did not take reasonable or appropriate measures to prevent commonly known attacks by hackers to obtain customer information. The settlement required PETCO to implement a comprehensive information security program for its website.

Managing risk is an important aspect of any business but especially for companies that sell animals. PETCO has tried to limit its risk by selling only a few types of animals and avoiding the sale of dogs and cats. Consequently, animal sales make up only 5 percent of PETCO's revenues (the rest comes from pet supplies and services). By avoiding this risk, PETCO ensures that it not only keeps its customers, investors, and animal rights activists happy but also the animals in its care.

The PETCO Ethics Program

PETCO was founded on the principle of "connecting with the community." In that regard, one of PETCO's most important missions is to promote the health, well-being, and humane treatment of animals. The company does this through its vendor selection programs, pet adoption programs, and its partnerships with animal-welfare organizations. Consider this excerpt from PETCO's Code of Ethics:

> *PETCO's vision is to best promote, through our people, the highest level of well-being for companion animals and to support the human-animal bond.*
>
> *At PETCO, we believe it is better to hire animal lovers and train them to work in a retail environment than to hire retailers and hope they like animals. This belief stems from PETCO's commitment to making sure that Animals Always Come First and recognizes that Our People Make It Happen! Whether you're caring for animals, educating prospective pet parents, or promoting PETCO's Think Adoption First philosophy, your everyday decisions make all the difference in achieving PETCO's high ethical standards regarding animal care.*

In addition to its "Animals First" philosophy, PETCO's twenty-eight-page "Code of Ethics" takes a comprehensive view of company operations. Customer relationships and marketing practices are a key part of the code:

Customer Privacy

PETCO's customers trust us to handle their personal information with the utmost care and respect and to protect it from misuse or unauthorized disclosure.

At PETCO we take this responsibility seriously and expect associates to comply with all administrative, technical and physical safeguards PETCO has implemented to protect customer information.

Selling Practices

PETCO maintains its reputation as a pet loving company by providing guidance to our customers that is in the best interest of the animals. We interact honestly with each customer and clearly explain the purpose and benefits of our products and services. Each associate should be knowledgeable about the products and services to help customers make sound decisions that best fit their needs.

Advertising Practices

PETCO's advertising practices show the ways that our products and services strengthen the bonds between people and animals. Advertising practices may include packaging, product press releases, brochures, and most other forms of product communication in addition to television, print, and radio advertising. All statements of fact included in advertisements must be true and must be substantiated. Advertisements must be clear and cannot be misleading, even if literally true. Any additional information that may be required to ensure that an advertisement is not misleading (e.g., disclaimer) must be communicated clearly and conspicuously.

Pricing Practices

PETCO makes its own pricing decisions without influence from vendors, contractors, or competitors. To do otherwise may violate federal and state antitrust laws and is strictly forbidden.

Buying Practices

Associates who make the decisions to buy products and supplies, or who contract services for PETCO, must make informed decisions. We are obligated to contract with vendors who supply products and services that are high quality, safe, and conform to all applicable laws.

The Code of Ethics also addresses the courtesy, dignity, and respect among associates. The code addresses concerns about sexual and other types of harassment that could occur in the workplace. If any employee makes a complaint about harassment, it will be treated with confidentiality and appropriate corrective action. Discipline will be directed at offending parties, which may include dismissal. Drug abuse, asset protection, and violence in the workplace are also concerns for PETCO and are addressed in the code. PETCO has implemented measures that aim to increase associate, vendor, and customer protection with the goal of providing a safe working environment.

PETCO associates are to avoid conflicts of interest or what appear to be conflicts of interest. This means that PETCO associates must not place themselves in situations that might force them to choose between their own personal or financial interests and the interests of PETCO. For example, PETCO associates are prohibited from accepting gifts or gratuities from vendors or potential vendors, whether it is money, merchandise, services, lavish entertainment, travel, or any other form. Employment with suppliers, vendors, or others doing business with PETCO is expected to be done at the discretion of associates, and their supervisors are expected to be contacted. Investments in vendors made by associates or their immediate families are not permitted without prior approval from the Ethics Committee. PETCO discourages workplace romances when there is a direct or indirect reporting relationship because undue pressure can occur. Outside interests are allowed; however, they should not be endorsed, funded, or sponsored by PETCO. It is considered inappropriate for associates to publicly make negative remarks about PETCO. If associates have a grievance or concern, they are asked to work with the company to obtain a mutually satisfactory resolution.

Associates must also agree not to interfere with PETCO's business by directly or indirectly soliciting the business of any persons or entities who were the customers of PETCO or soliciting an associate of PETCO for a period of 6 months immediately after the termination of her or his employment. Trade secrets and other proprietary information must also be kept in strict confidence both during employment and forever following separation.

The Code of Ethics also addresses other concerns such as workplace safety, wage and hour laws, and reporting time worked. Political contributions from PETCO funds are not allowed, as are payments to government personnel. PETCO also respects the environment and strives to conserve natural resources as much as possible.

A section concerning managers and supervisors encourages them to be role models when dealing with employment decisions. When dealing with the media, managers and supervisors are asked to discuss any situations with all parties to determine an appropriate media response if necessary. An associate may also at no time submit or knowingly accept false or misleading information, documents, or proposals. When in doubt, associates are encouraged to phone the Code of Ethics hot line or ask a supervisor on the appropriate course of action to take.

The Code of Ethics also presents a chain of command to follow in case an employee is faced with an ethical dilemma. There is an anonymous 24-hour hot line for associates to call if they do not feel that their immediate supervisor is being responsive or if it involves their immediate supervisor. The Code of Ethics is reviewed on an annual basis. The company also has an internal Ethics Committee, which oversees compliance with the code and continually monitors related best practices.

The PETCO Foundation

In 1999, PETCO established the PETCO Foundation to help promote charitable, educational, and other philanthropic activities for the betterment of animals everywhere. The PETCO Foundation is dedicated to serving the "Four Rs": reduce, rescue, rehabilitate, rejoice. Since its inception, the foundation has raised more than $28 million for animal-welfare groups and to promote pet adoption. Through a combination of programs and fundraisers—"Round Up," "Think Adoption First," "Spring a

Pet," "Tree of Hope," "National Pet Adoption Days," and "Kind News"—more than 3300 nonprofit animal-welfare organizations have received support. PETCO is also responsible for the donation of in-kind goods and services to worthwhile organizations with the same mission of strengthening the bond between people and pets. With an exclusive long-term agreement with Petfinder.com, they also support over 7,000 additional animal welfare agencies.

The "Round Up" Program

Every year between five and 10 million pets are euthanized in the United States. PETCO launched an annual "Spay Today" initiative in 2000 to address the significant problem of pet overpopulation—a growing problem that sends millions of animals to animal shelters each year. The "Spay Today" funds come from customer donations at PETCO stores where customers are encouraged to round up their purchases (hence the name of the program) to the nearest dollar or more. Each PETCO store selects one or more spay/neuter–focused charitable partners to which the funds are donated. In addition, 10 percent of all funds raised are donated to the Petfinder.com Foundation to assist with their spay/neuter efforts. In 2000, PETCO allowed pet owners to purchase a voucher at PETCO stores to have a cat spayed or neutered for $10 and a dog spayed or neutered for $20 (compared to the regular price of more than $100). In 2004, this program raised $817,000 for local animal-welfare organizations across the country.

The "Think Adoption First" Program

"Think Adoption First," launched in 2005, supports and promotes the person–animal bond. It is a program that sets the standard for responsibility and community involvement for the industry. Each year, eight to 12 million pets are relinquished to shelters and rescue groups. PETCO, the PETCO Foundation, and Petfinder.com offer a second chance for those orphaned companion animals. "Think Adoption First" recommends the adoption of companion animals beyond dogs and cats as an alternative first choice to consider. The program works in conjunction with PETCO's "National Pet Adoption Days" program—an annual event that finds homes for 12,000 to 14,000 rescued animals. Access to rescued animals is provided through PETCO's partnership network of rescue groups. They have strengthened their relationship with Petfinder.com, and together they have found homes for over two million animals.

The "Spring a Pet" Program

The "Spring a Pet" fundraiser encourages pet lovers to donate $1, $5, $10, or $20 to animal-welfare causes. Donors receive a personalized cutout bunny to display in their neighborhood store or take home as a reminder of their generosity. Each PETCO store selects an animal-welfare organization to be the recipient of the money raised at its location. In the past, the money has provided veterinary care for homeless and abused animals and outreach programs to help handicapped and disadvantaged individuals adequately care for their companion animals. In 2005, this program raised $1.51 million.

The "Tree of Hope" Program

Customers visiting one of PETCO's stores during the Christmas season can purchase card ornaments for $1, $5, $10, or $20. They can also choose from red or blue "Making a Difference" wristbands or a 2007 PETCO Foundation calendar loaded with coupons. All funds go toward the "Tree of Hope." Anyone donating $20 or more receives a PETCO Foundation hand-painted globe ornament. In 2005, this program raised $2.1 million.

The "Kind News" Program

"Kind News" is a humane education program that educates children about the humane treatment of companion animals and fellow human beings. It features stories about responsible pet environmental concerns and issues as well as information on all types of animals. It contains many learning tools to reinforce the concept of compassion and concern for all living things.

PETCO's Stakeholder Orientation

Most companies focus on customers to help establish their reputation and success, but PETCO has adopted a stakeholder orientation and is concerned about its impact on society. Although PETCO seeks long-term customer relationships, the company's concerns go beyond customers to address important issues related to the existence and role of animals in our society. Through the various programs sponsored by the PETCO Foundation, the company makes animal husbandry a key part of its mission and vision. In addition, PETCO's "Kind News" program is vital in ensuring that the next generation of adults carries on the tradition of humane treatment of animals. Finally, PETCO's comprehensive Code of Ethics ties all these issues together in a proactive manner. This is not only good business but also a key method of managing PETCO's operating risk. It is also a vital part of ongoing stakeholder relationship management.

All large organizations know that misconduct can and will occur somewhere in the organization. Therefore, it is important to take a proactive stance so that the firm can discover, expose, and address any event before it can damage the firm's reputation. For PETCO, the desire to do the right thing and to train all organizational members to make ethical decisions assures success in the marketplace and a significant contribution to society.

Questions for Discussion

1. What are the ethical risks associated with selling pets and pet products in a retail environment?

2. How has PETCO managed the various ethical concerns that have been expressed by its stakeholders? How do you evaluate the company's response to PETA?

3. What do you make of PETCO's Code of Ethics? How might the code influence the company's ethical culture? Explain.

Sources

The facts of this case are from "Animal Abuse Case Details. PETCO Lawsuit—Mistreating Animals San Diego, CA," Pet-Abuse.com, May 28, 2004 (http://www.pet-abuse.com/cases/2373/CA/US); Catherine Colbert, "PETCO Animal Supplies, Inc.," Hoovers.com (http://www.hoovers.com/petco-(holding)/ID_17256–/free-co-factsheet.xhtml), accessed September 7, 2006; Michelle Higgins, "When the Dog's Hotel Is Better Than Yours," *Wall Street Journal,* June 30, 2004, D1; "Just Say No! PETCO—The Place Where Pets Die," Kindplanet.org (http://www.kindplanet.org/petno.html), accessed July 5, 2006; Ilene Lelchuk, "San Francisco Alleges Cruelty at 2 PETCOs," *San Francisco Chronicle,* June 19, 2002 (http://www.anapsid.org/pettrade/petcocit2.html); "Lifestyle Trends Affect Pet Markets," *Pet Age,* January 2006 (http://www.petage.com/News010607.asp); Robert McMillan, "PETCO Settles Charge It Left Customer Data Exposed," IDG News Service, November 17, 2004 (http://www.networkworld.com/news/2004/1117petcosettl.html); Chris Penttila, "Magic Markets," *Entrepreneur's Start Ups,* September 2004 (http://www.entrepreneur.com/article/0,4621,316866-2,00.html); "PETA and PETCO Announce Agreement," PETA website, April 2005 (http://www.peta.org/feat/PETCOAgreement/default.asp); PETCO 10-Q Report, PETCO website, August 24, 2006 (http://ir.petco.com), accessed September 7, 2006; PETCO 2005 Annual Report to Shareholders (http://media.corporate-ir.net/media_files/irol/93/93935/AnnualReport/2005_Petco_AnnualReport.pdf), accessed September 7, 2006; "PETCO Animal Supplies, Inc.," Yahoo! Finance (http://finance.yahoo.com/q?s=PETC); accessed September 7, 2006; "PETCO's Bad Business Is Bad for Animals," PETA website, Spring 2003 (http://www.peta.org/living/at-spring2003/comp2.html); PETCO Code of Ethics (http://media.corporate-ir.net/media_files/irol/93/93935/corpgov/COE.pdf), accessed September 7, 2006; "PETCO Foundation to 'Round-Up' Support for Spay/Neuter Programs," *Forbes Online,* July 13, 2005 (http://www.forbes.com/prnewswire/feeds/prnewswire/2005/07/13/prnewswire200507131335PR_NEWS_B_WES_LA_LAW067.html); PETCO Foundation website (http://www.petco.com/Content/Content.aspx?PC=petcofoundationhome&Nav=11); "PETCO Looks to the Web to Enhance Multi-Channel Marketing," *Internet Retailer,* January 16, 2006; "PETCO pays fine to settle lawsuit," PETA Annual Review 2004, PETA website (http://www.peta.org/feat/annual_review04/notToAbuse.asp); "PETCO Settles FTC Charges," Federal Trade Commission, November 17, 2004 (http://www.ftc.gov/opa/2004/11/petco.htm); "PETCO 'Spring a Pet' Campaign Blossoms for Animals Nationwide," Corporate Social Responsibility press release, Citizenship at Boston College, May 11, 2005 (http://www.csrwire.com/ccc/article.cgi/3910.html); "Pet Portion Control," *Prevention,* February 2006, 201; "Pet Store Secrets: PETA Uncovers Shocking Back-Room Secrets," PETA website, Summer 2000 (http://www.peta.org/living/at-summer2000/petco.html); "Say No to PETCO," PETA website, Spring 2002 (http://www.peta.org/living/at-spring 2002/specialrep/); Julie Schmit, "Pet Bird Buyers Asking Sellers

About Avian Flu," *USA Today*, November 27, 2005 (http://www.usatoday.com/money/industries/health/2005-11-27-bird-questions-usat_x.htm); Jessica Stannard-Freil, "Corporate Philanthropy: PR or Legitimate News?" *On Philanthropy Online,* May 5, 2005 (http://www.onphilanthropy.com/tren_comm/tc2005-05-20.html); and "The Pet Market- Market Assessment 2005," Research and Key Note Publications Ltd., April 2005 (http://www.researchandmarkets.com/reports/c26485/).

FedEx Corporation

Frederick W. Smith founded the Federal Express Corporation in 1973 with part of an $8 million inheritance. At the time, the U.S. Postal Service and United Parcel Service (UPS) provided the only means of delivering letters and packages, and they often took several days or more to get packages to their destinations. While a student at Yale in 1965, Smith wrote a paper proposing an independent, overnight delivery service. Although he received a C on the paper, Smith never lost sight of his vision. He recognized that time is money and believed that many businesses would be willing to pay more to get letters, documents, and packages delivered overnight. He was right.

Federal Express began shipping packages overnight from Memphis, Tennessee, on April 17, 1973. On the first night of operations, the company handled six packages—one of which was a birthday present sent by Smith himself. Today, FedEx Corporation, as the company is now called, handles over six million shipments per day around the world. Though most people are familiar with FedEx's overnight delivery services, the company is actually divided into eight operating companies:

FedEx Express   The world's largest express transportation company, serves over 220 countries and every address in the United States.

FedEx Ground   Provides cost-effective, small-package delivery from business to business or to residential addresses.

FedEx Kinko's   The world's leading provider of document solutions and business services.

FedEx Freight   The leading U.S. regional less-than-truckload (LTL) freight company, provides next-day and second-day delivery of heavyweight freight in both the United States and international markets.

FedEx Custom Critical   Provides 24/7 nonstop, door-to-door delivery of urgent freight, valuable shipments, and hazardous materials in the United States, Canada, and Europe.

Michael D. Hartline, Florida State University, prepared this case for classroom discussion rather than to illustrate effective or ineffective handling of an administrative situation. Melanie Drever, University of Wyoming, provided research assistance.

CASE EXHIBIT 13.1

FINANCIAL INFORMATION BY BUSINESS SEGMENT

	FedEx Express ($ millions)	FedEx Ground ($ millions)	FedEx Freight ($ millions)	FedEx Kinko's ($ millions)	Total ($ millions)
2006					
Total Revenue	21,446	5,306	3,645	2,088	32,294
Operating Income	1,767	705	485	57	3,014
2005					
Total Revenue	19,485	4,680	3,217	2,066	29,363
Operating Income	1,414	604	354	100	2,471
2004					
Total Revenue	17,497	3,910	2,689	521	24,710
Operating Income	629	522	244	39	1,440

Source: FedEx Corporation 2006, 2005, and 2004 Annual Reports, FedEx website (http://fedex.com/us/investorrelations/financialinfo/2006annualreport/?link=4), accessed October 6, 2006.

FedEx Trade Networks   One of the largest-volume customs entry filers in North America, facilitates international trade, customs brokerage, and freight forwarding.

FedEx Supply Chain   Offers a portfolio of modular and scalable solutions to firms wishing to outsource their supply chain operations.

FedEx Services   Coordinates sales, marketing, and information technology support for all FedEx brands. Provides FedEx customers with a convenient, single point of access to the entire FedEx family of services.

FedEx Express and FedEx Ground provide the bulk of the company's business, offering valuable services to anyone who needs to deliver letters, documents, and packages. FedEx controls more than 50 percent of the express delivery market and roughly 16 percent of the ground delivery market (UPS dominates the ground sector with over 69 percent of the market). In 2006, FedEx registered over $3 billion in operating income and an astounding $32.3 billion in total revenue (Case Exhibit 13.1). According to the company, FedEx is not in the package and document transport business; rather, it delivers "certainty" by connecting the global economy with a wide range of transportation, information, and supply chain services. Whether dropped-off at one of over 41,000 drop boxes, over 700 world service centers, over 1,400 FedEx Kinko's Office and Print centers, picked up by FedEx courier, packages are taken to a local FedEx office where they are trucked to the nearest airport. The package is flown to one of the company's distribution hubs for sorting and then flown to the airport nearest its destination. The package is then trucked to another FedEx office where a courier picks it up and hand delivers it to the correct recipient. All of this takes place overnight, with many packages being delivered before 8:00 a.m.

CASE EXHIBIT 13.2   **FEDEX EXPRESS 1-POUND PACKAGE RATES**

FedEx Express Services	Delivered By	Zone Rates ($)
First Overnight Service	8:00 or 8:30 a.m. next day	42.00 to 58.30
Priority Overnight Service	10:30 a.m. next day	17.00 to 34.45
Standard Overnight Service	3:00 p.m. next day	14.00 to 29.60
2-Day Delivery	4:30 p.m. second day	8.50 to 26.15
Express Saver	4:30 p.m. third day	8.15 to 10.60

Source: FedEx Express Zone Rates, FedEx website (http://www.fedex.com/ratetools/RateToolsMain.do), accessed October 6, 2006.

---

the next day. FedEx confirms that roughly 99 percent of its deliveries are made on time.

To accomplish this amazingly high delivery rate, FedEx maintains an impressive infrastructure of equipment and processes. The company owns over 70,000 vehicles and its 671 aircraft fly over 500,000 miles every day. FedEx operates its own weather-forecasting service, ensuring that most of its flights arrive within 15 minutes of schedule. Most packages shipped within the United States are sorted at the Memphis super hub, where FedEx takes over control of the Memphis International Airport at roughly 11 p.m. each night. FedEx planes land side by side on parallel runways every minute or so for well over one hour each night. After the sorting of packages, all FedEx planes take off in time to reach their destinations. Not all packages are shipped via air. When possible, FedEx uses ground transportation to save on expenses. For international deliveries, FedEx uses a combination of direct services and independent contractors.

FedEx services are priced using a zone system where the distance a package must travel to reach its final destination determines the price. Case Exhibit 13.2 illustrates typical rates for a one-pound package using various FedEx Express services. FedEx also offers FedEx SameDay Delivery for $173 for packages up to 25 pounds. FedEx Ground rates vary widely by package weight and shipping zone. For an extra $4, customers can have a courier pick up their packages rather than dropping them off at a drop box. Saturday pickup and delivery is also available for an additional $12.50 each. Prices vary for larger packages and international shipments.

FedEx Express garnered a major coup in January 2001 when it announced two seven-year service agreements with the U.S. Postal Service. In the first agreement, FedEx Express provided air transportation for certain postal services, including Priority Mail. The second agreement gave FedEx Express the option to place a drop box in every U.S. post office. FedEx did not get the exclusive rights to drop boxes, which left open the potential for UPS to negotiate its own agreement with the postal service. In 2006, FedEx renewed its domestic air transportation contract with the U.S. Postal Service—this contract served to replace the years remaining on the 2001 contract. The new contract, which runs through 2013, is predicted to produce about $8 billion in revenue for FedEx over time. Both FedEx and the Postal Service operate competitively and maintain separate services in all other categories.

The Growth of FedEx into a Global Distribution Powerhouse

Despite its tremendous successes, FedEx has faced some difficult times in its efforts to grow and compete against strong rival firms. The overnight delivery market matured very rapidly as intense competition from the U.S. Postal Service, UPS, Emery, DHL, RPS, and electronic-document delivery (that is, fax machines and e-mail) forced FedEx to search for viable means of expansion. In 1984, facing a growing threat from e-document delivery, FedEx introduced its ZapMail service for customers who could not afford expensive fax machines. For $35, FedEx would fax up to ten pages of text to any FedEx site around the world. The document was then hand delivered to its recipient. Soon after the service was introduced, the price of fax machines plummeted, ultimately forcing FedEx to drop ZapMail after losing over $190 million. Many analysts still argue that the overnight delivery market could eventually lose as much as 30 percent of its letter business to e-document delivery, especially e-mail.

After its experience with ZapMail, FedEx began to focus its resources on expanding its overseas operations, the most rapidly growing area of the overnight market. In an increasingly global economy, businesses must be able to communicate quickly with employees around the world, with partners in other nations, with other businesses, and with customers. Though FedEx had been shipping packages from the United States to Canada since 1975, its acquisition of Gelco International in 1984 enabled FedEx to expand its operations to Europe and the Far East. Political changes in foreign markets—such as the establishment of the European Union and the dismantling of once-closed Eastern European markets—allowed FedEx to gain entry into large, untapped markets.

Global Expansion

FedEx's most important strategic move into international markets was its 1988 purchase of Tiger International Inc., owner of the Flying Tiger Line airfreight service. The $880 million purchase gave FedEx valuable routes, airport facilities, and expertise in European and Asian markets that it had been struggling to enter. Such valuable assets would have taken the company years to develop alone. The purchase also gave the company valuable landing slots in Sydney, Singapore, Bangkok, Hong Kong, Seoul, Paris, Brussels, and Tokyo. However, the purchase of Flying Tiger created some problems for FedEx. The purchase left the company with a debt of $2.1 billion. It also thrust FedEx into the heavy-freight distribution market, which was more cyclical and capital intensive than small-package distribution. In addition, many of Tiger's key customers, including UPS, were competitors of FedEx. Finally, FedEx had trouble integrating Tiger's 6,500 union employees into its own nonunion workforce. Despite the difficulties in merging the two companies, the merger was a key ingredient in making FedEx a powerful global delivery service.

By 1991, the company had taken advantage of its opportunities and was offering international service to more than 100 countries. By 1992, next-morning service was available to and from major markets including Paris, London, Frankfurt, Milan, Brussels, Geneva, Zurich, Antwerp, Amsterdam, Hong Kong, Tokyo, Singapore, and Seoul. FedEx's Canadian operations remained strong, and the company's operations in Latin America were growing. Despite this success, however, FedEx's international operations were troublesome. This was particularly true in Europe, where the total volume of express shipments between European countries was only 150,000 packages per day. Deciding that the intra-European market lacked potential, FedEx abandoned it and closed some domestic businesses in Italy, Germany, France, and the United Kingdom. The company took a $254 million restructuring charge in the third quarter of its 1992 fiscal year to cover the closures. FedEx then restricted its European focus to shipments to and from Europe, rather than within Europe. By the end of 1992, FedEx experienced a total loss of $113 million and negative earnings per share of $2.11. Company officials pointed to several reasons for the losses. First, the company was still recovering from its purchase of Flying Tiger, which increased its fixed costs in international operations. Second, FedEx had difficulty building a global infrastructure to support its operations. Negotiating for landing rights, dealing with foreign customs regulations, and establishing information networks all proved to be very costly.

Despite the problems in Europe, FedEx was doing very well in Asia. The Asian economy was growing rapidly—seven of the top-ten growth economies at the time were in Asia. Additionally, Asia's manufactured product exports were increasing at a rate of 28 percent per year. To capitalize on this growth, FedEx introduced its "AsiaOne" network in 1995 and began offering effective "late-day" pick ups and "next-day" deliveries not only across Asia but also between Asia and North America. AsiaOne grew quickly, in part to FedEx's unparalleled capability to gain Asian air-route authority. For instance, FedEx was the only U.S. all-cargo airline with aviation rights to the Chinese trade centers of Shenzhen, Shanghai, and Beijing. The AsiaOne network provided quick, reliable package delivery to, from, and within Asia—all backed up by a money-back guarantee.

In 1997, FedEx became the only cargo carrier allowed to fly its own aircraft and use its own warehousing facilities in Moscow. This was a breakthrough for FedEx because the Moscow and overall Russian market was growing rapidly. This exclusive capability allowed FedEx customers to receive reliable next-business-day service (by 10:30 a.m.) from Moscow to North America and Western Europe. Likewise, FedEx offered two- to three-day service between Moscow and many Asian cities. At the same time, FedEx instituted a similar service from the United States to Argentina, as projections indicated that the South American market would also grow substantially. To maintain its impressive growth, FedEx introduced several new international services during this time. FedEx introduced International First service offering one- to two-day, 8:00 a.m. delivery to and from 20 European countries. They also introduced International Priority service (one- to three-day, 10:30 a.m. delivery to 210 countries) and International Economy service (four- to five-day delivery to 29 countries).

Today, FedEx's international operations remain strong. The company was the first to offer express services in India with direct international air routes—connecting 4,348 Indian cities and towns with the rest of the world. The company started the first overnight express flight from India to China and doubled its capacity from Europe to Asia through an eastbound around-the-world flight. FedEx's Asian operations are also strong. The company runs 120 weekly flights to and from Asia, 26 of which fly in and out of China. In 2006, FedEx bought out its Chinese 50/50 delivery partner, Datian Group, which gives FedEx complete control over Datian's fleet and hubs. In 2008, FedEx plans to close its Asian hub located in the Philippines and open a $150 million superhub in Guangzhou, China.

Emergence of the FedEx Family of Services

Despite the importance of global expansion, FedEx did not become a complete transportation delivery network until its 1998 acquisition of Caliber System, a trucking company whose RPS subsidiary was second only to UPS in ground shipments. The $2.7 billion merger created a new holding company, called FDX Corporation, which owned both Federal Express and Caliber System. Caliber's subsidiaries included RPS (a ground service), Roberts Express (an expedited delivery service), Viking Freight (a regional, LTL freight carrier), Caribbean Transportation Services (airfreight forwarding between the United States and Caribbean nations), and Caliber Logistics and Caliber Technology (integrated logistics services).

Though Caliber had many attractive assets, RPS was the crown jewel in the deal. RPS's fleet of delivery trucks and its customer base helped FedEx grow and compete more effectively with UPS in the nonexpress, ground-delivery business. The acquisition of RPS, along with the 1997 UPS strike, allowed FedEx to steal business from UPS and increase its market share. The purchase of RPS made FedEx not only more profitable but also more attractive to current and potential customers. Suddenly, FedEx had the ability to fulfill any customer's needs by providing one-stop shopping for express and nonexpress shipping and delivery.

To better leverage and integrate the Caliber assets, Federal Express made a number of internal structural changes between 1998 and 2001. First, the FDX Corporation was renamed FedEx Corporation in order to better leverage the FedEx brand. In a similar fashion, Federal Express was renamed FedEx Express, RPS was renamed FedEx Ground, and Roberts Express was renamed FedEx Custom Critical. FedEx also combined Caliber Logistics and Caliber Technology to establish FedEx Global Logistics as a world leader in transportation management and integrated logistics. A new subsidiary, FedEx Services, was also created to centralize all sales, marketing, customer service, and information technology (IT) operations. Also during this time, FedEx acquired Tower Group International—a firm specializing in international logistics and trade information—and WorldTariff—a customs duty and tax information firm. These firms were combined with Caribbean Transportation Services and FedEx Global Logistics to create FedEx Trade Networks. FedEx also acquired American Freightways, a leading LTL freight carrier, and merged the company with Viking Freight to create FedEx Freight. FedEx's transformation was completed when it acquired Kinko's in February 2004. Shortly thereafter, Kinko's was rebranded as FedEx Kinko's Office and Print Services. With over 1,500 locations in over eleven countries, Kinko's was a natural addition to the FedEx family. Kinko's allowed FedEx to offer not only new services to its customers but also another venue for promoting its shipping services.

Today, FedEx has successfully transformed into a global distribution and logistics powerhouse that offers virtually all transportation services that any customer might need. FedEx summarizes the FedEx family this way:

Together, we are FedEx—a worldwide network of companies providing customers and businesses with the same "absolutely, positively" zeal for service you've come to expect. Independently, each company offers flexible, specialized services that represent the broadest array of supply chain, transportation, business and related information services.

The unique FedEx operating strategy works seamlessly—and simultaneously— on three levels.

- *Operate independently by focusing on our independent networks to meet distinct customer needs.*
- *Compete collectively by standing as one brand worldwide and speaking with one voice.*
- *Manage collaboratively by working together to sustain loyal relationships with our workforce, customers and investors.*

Current Challenges

Although FedEx continues to expand and succeed, the company currently faces some difficult internal challenges. Its most publicized issue has been the increasing number of lawsuits filed by its FedEx Ground/Home Delivery drivers over the past few years. As of 2006, hundreds of drivers across thirty states have sued FedEx for misclassification. FedEx classifies each of these employees as an independent contractor. However, the drivers argue that, based on the demands placed on them by FedEx, they should be classified as employees and are entitled to company benefits. According to the drivers, FedEx strictly dictates working hours and routes, requires them to wear FedEx uniforms and purchase company scanners, and enforces all company rules upon them. The drivers also claim they are prohibited from working for other companies. Although the company claims that these contractors have the potential to earn $80,000 to $120,000 annually before paying for trucks and gasoline (an earning potential that FedEx says should equal roughly $50,000 per year), the drivers cite low wages as another issue. One of the plaintiffs, Gerold Pelkey, states that he actually earned $20,000 per year for each of the three years that he worked for FedEx Ground.

In June 2006, a federal judge rejected FedEx's request to dismiss the claims. According to a website devoted to the lawsuits (www.fedexdriverslawsuit.com), the class-action lawsuit is now in the discovery stage in which each side is allowed time to gather facts. In its 2006 Annual Report, FedEx addressed the issue by saying that the company strongly believes its drivers to be correctly classified as independent contractors and that the company intends to prevail. It does acknowledge that, should it have to convert its FedEx Ground/Home Delivery drivers to employee status, it will dramatically increase the company's costs.

Also in June 2006, FedEx paid $61 million to two Lebanese drivers who alleged racial harassment from their manager for over two years. Although the drivers say they had their complaints to senior management ignored and are supported by testimony from fellow workers, FedEx argues that the settlement is excessive and plans to appeal.

In August 2006, FedEx finally reached a tentative agreement with its 4,700 FedEx Express pilots after two full years of negotiation. The agreement was reached after a stalemate was declared in 2005 when FedEx requested the assistance of the National Mediation Board. This issue is an ongoing challenge for both FedEx and the Airline Pilots Association.

Looking Ahead

FedEx continuously strives to improve its services by enhancing its distribution networks, transportation infrastructure, IT, and employee performance. FedEx also continues to invest heavily in IT by installing computer terminals at customers' offices and giving away its proprietary tracking software. Today, the vast majority of FedEx customers electronically generate their own pickup and delivery requests. FedEx has also moved more aggressively into e-commerce with respect to order fulfillment for business-to-business and business-to-consumer merchants. For example, FedEx's Home Delivery network has grown rapidly and now reaches virtually every U.S. residential address.

An interesting competitive development emerged in 2003 when German-based DHL acquired U.S.-based Airborne Express. Although Airborne was the third-largest overnight service in the United States, DHL led the market for international express services in all countries outside of the U.S. market. Both FedEx and UPS raised questions about the merger because DHL is owned by the German postal service. U.S. law prohibits foreign ownership of domestic airlines. However, after being legally challenged by both FedEx and UPS, DHL won this battle in 2004. Although DHL is competing to catch up to FedEx and UPS in the United States (it controls only 3.1 percent of the U.S. market), in many international markets, DHL is the company with which FedEx and UPS have to compete. For example, DHL has been delivering packages in the Korean market since 1977 while FedEx has only been fully operational in Korea since 2000. In an age where the outsourcing of logistics operations is at its height, FedEx, UPS, and DHL are all major players in a high-profile game.

As FedEx moves ahead, the company has a lot going for it. No other carrier can match FedEx's global capabilities or one-stop shopping—at least not yet. To increase its competitiveness, FedEx is focusing on increasing revenue and reducing costs through tighter integration and consolidation, improved productivity, and reduced capital expenditures. Six themes frame FedEx's efforts to fully leverage the strong franchise of the FedEx brand:

- *People*   We value our people and promote diversity in our workplace and in our thinking.

- *Service*   Our absolutely, positively spirit puts our customers at the heart of everything we do.

- *Innovation*   We invent and inspire the services and technologies that improve the way we work and live.

- *Integrity*   We manage our operations, finances and services with honesty, efficiency and reliability.

- *Responsibility*   We champion safe and healthy environments for the communities in which we live and work.

- *Loyalty*   We earn the respect and confidence of our FedEx people, customers and investors every day, in everything we do.

Why has FedEx been so successful? A major reason is the company's enviable corporate culture and workforce. Because employees are critical to the company's success, FedEx strives to hire the best people and offers them the best training and compensation in the industry. FedEx employees are loyal, highly efficient, and extremely effective in delivering good service. In fact, FedEx employees claim to have "purple blood" to match the company's official color. It is not surprising that FedEx has been named as one of the "100 Best Companies to Work For" nine consecutive years. FedEx is also recognized as one of the most diverse in the United States. It is also the number-one company in the United States in terms of creating new jobs.

Another reason for FedEx's success is well-planned expansion through strategic acquisitions. The company's focus on "delivering certainty" has allowed it to hone in on opportunities that give FedEx added capabilities in virtually all transportation and logistics services. A final reason for success is good marketing—FedEx is a master at recognizing untapped customer needs and filling them well. FedEx is also never content to sit on its laurels, and it constantly strives to improve service and offer more options to its customers. After 30-plus years of success, there is little doubt that Fred Smith's "C" paper has become an indispensable part of the business world.

Questions for Discussion

1.   Evaluate the methods used by FedEx to grow, both domestically and internationally. Why do you think that the company initially had problems in its global operations?

2.   What are the major SWOT considerations in FedEx's attempt to continue its growth and dominance in the domestic and global express delivery markets?

3. Picture a world without FedEx. How would business be different? How would your life be different?

4. Comment on the competitive landscape among FedEx, UPS, and DHL. How can FedEx make inroads into UPS's dominance in the ground delivery market?

Sources

The facts of this case are from Peter Bradley, "Express Service," DCVelocity.com, April 2005 (http://dcvelocity.com/articles/20050401/enroute.cfm), accessed August 29, 2006; "DHL/Airborne Deal Could Shake Up U.S. Express Market," *Logistics Management Online,* April 1, 2003 (http://www.manufacturing.net/lm/index.asp?layout=article&articleid=CA290554); "DHL's American Adventure," *BusinessWeek Online,* November 29, 2004 (http://www.businessweek.com/magazine/content/04_48/b3910115_mz017.htm), accessed August 29, 2006; FedEx Corporation 2004, 2005, and 2006 Annual Reports, FedEx website (http://fedex.com/us/investorrelations/financialinfo/2006annualreport/?link=4), accessed October 6, 2006; FedEx Drivers Lawsuit, Background (http://www.zimmreed.com/FedEx_Drivers_Lawsuit.htm), accessed August 29, 2006; "FedEx Ground Opens 'Super Hub,'" *Transportation & Distribution,* November 2000, 12–13; "FedEx Loses Ruling over Contractor Status," *Pittsburgh Tribune-Review Online,* August 22, 2006 (http://www.pittsburghlive.com/x/pittsburghtrib/search/print_467079.html), accessed August 29, 2006; "FedEx Pilots Reach a Tentative Contract, *New York Times Online,* August 28, 2006 (http://www.nytimes.com/2006/08/28/business/28fedex.html?_r=1&oref=slogin), accessed August 29, 2006; "FedEx, Postal Service Renew Contract," *BusinessWeek Online,* August 1, 2006 (http://www.businessweek.com/ap/financialnews/D8J7M52O2.htm), accessed August 29, 2006; "FedEx Shows Gains in Market Share," *Logistics Today Online,* March 21, 2005 (http://www.logisticstoday.com/sNO/7030/LT/displayStory.asp), accessed September 10, 2006; "FedEx: Taking Off like 'aRrocket Ship,'" *BusinessWeek Online,* April 3, 2006 (http://www.businessweek.com/magazine/content/06_14/b3978412.htm), accessed August 29, 2006; "FedEx to Create Shanghai Hub Office," *AirWise News Online,* October 24, 2003 (http://news.airwise.com/stories/2003/10/1066964235.html); Julie Forester, "FedEx drivers Sue for Worker Status," *Pioneer Press,* April 5, 2005 (http://www.zimmreed.com/Includes/pdf/FedEx_PioneerPress_4.05.05.pdf), accessed August 29, 2006; Linda Grant, "Why FedEx Is Flying High," *Fortune,* November 10, 1997, 155 ; "The Ground War at FedEx," *BusinessWeek Online,* November 28, 2005 (http://www.buinessweek. com/magazine/content/05_48/b3961086.htm), accessed August 29, 2006; Nicole Harris, "Flying into a Rage?" *Business Week,* April 27, 1998, 119; "Jury Awards $61 Million to Two FedEx Drivers," MSNBC.com, June 4, 2006 (http://www.msnbc.msn.com/id/13132754), accessed August 29, 2006; Michele Kayal, "FedEx Launches Sunday Service Amid Skepticism," *Journal of Commerce and Commercial,* March 11, 1998, 1A; Kristin S. Krause, "Handling the Holiday Crush," *Traffic World,* December 4, 2000, 33; Park Kyong-ki, "FedEx, DHL Set Up

Battle in Korea," *Korea Times Online* (http://times.hankooki.com/lpage/200608/
kt2006081717530510220.htm), accessed August 29, 2006; "Major Victory in Pre-
Trial Stage of FedEx Ground/Home Delivery Drivers Lawsuit," FedEx news release
(http://www.fedexdriverslawsuit.com), accessed August 29, 2006; Theo Mullen,
"Delivery Wars Go High-Tech—FedEx Ground Sends Message with $80M Investment
to Improve Package Tracking," *Internetweek,* October 23, 2000, 18; Jayne O'Donnell,
"FedEx-Postal Service Alliance Delivers Goods," *USA Today Online,* January 11, 2001
(http://www.usatoday.com/money); Deborah Orr, "Delivering America," *Forbes Online,*
September 20, 2004 (http://www.forbes.com/global/2004/0920/064_print.html),
accessed August 29, 2006; "Philadelphia Inquirer: FedEx, Workers Battle Over Vote to
Organize First Drivers Union," FedEx Watch, December 18, 2005 (http://www.
teamster.org/fedex/news/news_051218_4.htm), accessed August 29, 2006; "Post
Office, FedEx to Work Together," *USA Today Online,* January 10, 2001 (http://
www.usatoday.com/money); Monica Roman, "FedEx Hitches Up a New Trucker,"
BusinessWeek, November 27, 2000, 66; Marc L. Songini, "FedEx Expects CRM System
to Deliver," *Computerworld,* November 6, 2000, 10; "Stand Your Ground: The Official
Website of the FedEx Ground/Home Delivery Drivers Nationwide Class-Action
Lawsuit, Status of Class Action," FedEx website (http://www.fedexdriverslawsuit.com/
status.htm), accessed August 29, 2006; Richard Tomkins, "The Bear and the Alligator
Enter Into a Race to Deliver," *Financial Times,* March 13, 1998, 30; "UPS Wants Fed
Probe into DHL-Airborne Deal," *San Francisco Business Times,* March 27, 2003 (http://
www.bizjournals.com/sanfrancisco/stories/2003/03/24/daily40.html); and Michael
Weingarten and Bart Stuck, "No Substitutions?" *Telephony*, February 2, 1998, 26.

IKEA

The name IKEA is a combination of its founder's initials, Ingvar Kamprad, with the first letters of the farm and village where he grew up. At the time of IKEA's founding in 1943, Kamprad could not have guessed that his company would become one of the most popular and iconic brands in the world. From the beginning, IKEA was founded on different principles—namely, frugality and low cost. Most furniture companies offer service and advice in settings where salespeople compete for sales commissions. Kamprad recognized that customers were willing to trade off typical amenities to save money. Today, the no-frills frugality is the cornerstone of the IKEA cachet and the reason for its immense popularity.

The IKEA concept works to build customer relationships. IKEA's positioning statement reflects this philosophy: "Your partner in better living. We do our part, you do yours. Together we save money." For IKEA's part, the company provides stylish, functional, low-cost home furnishings that customers must assemble themselves. This enables IKEA to save money on manufacturing and distribution, which they then pass on to customers in the form of lower prices at retail. To compensate for the customer having to do-it-themselves, IKEA offers other services that make this proposition a little more attractive. These extra services include in-store child-care and play areas, restaurants, and longer hours of operations. To help visitors prepare for this experience, IKEA provides its customers with pencils, paper, tape measures, store guides, catalogs, strollers, and shopping bags. IKEA even offers delivery for the bulky items that customers cannot carry themselves. For those who want to carry their own bulky furniture home, IKEA rents carracks for convenience. IKEA stores are designed as a circle so that everything is seen, no matter what direction the customer is headed. The aisles are wide to reduce traffic that may occur while stopping to look at different showrooms and displays.

IKEA is owned by the IKEA Group, which includes IKEA of Sweden (which designs and develops all IKEA products), Swedwood (which makes all IKEA furniture), the sales companies that operate IKEA stores, and all purchasing and supply chain functions. The IKEA Group is owned by INGKA Holding BV, which itself is owned by the Stichting INGKA Foundation of the Netherlands. Many estimates peg

Christin Copeland, Florida State University MBA Class of 2006, prepared this case for classroom discussion rather than to illustrate effective or ineffective handling of an administrative situation.

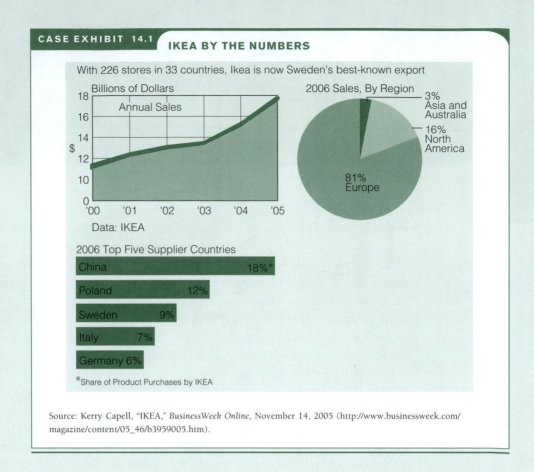

CASE EXHIBIT 14.1   IKEA BY THE NUMBERS

With 226 stores in 33 countries, Ikea is now Sweden's best-known export

Billions of Dollars — Annual Sales

Data: IKEA

2006 Sales, By Region
- 3% Asia and Australia
- 16% North America
- 81% Europe

2006 Top Five Supplier Countries
- China 18%*
- Poland 12%
- Sweden 9%
- Italy 7%
- Germany 6%

*Share of Product Purchases by IKEA

Source: Kerry Capell, "IKEA," *BusinessWeek Online,* November 14, 2005 (http://www.businessweek.com/magazine/content/05_46/b3959005.htm).

the foundation as one of the world's wealthiest charities—worth an estimated $36 billion. This type of ownership is unique in that the foundation is a nonprofit organization designed to promote innovation in architectural and interior design. Some criticize IKEA's ownership as an arrangement that leverages the uniqueness of Dutch law to avoid taxes and prevent a hostile takeover attempt.

IKEA is now Sweden's best-known export. This privately-owned company had 2005 sales totaling $18.1 billion and an enviable yearly growth rate of 17.3 percent. There are more than 226 IKEA stores in 33 countries, with 200 of these stores belonging to the IKEA Group (Case Exhibit 14.1). The remaining stores are owned and operated by franchisees. There are currently 28 U.S. stores with plans to have fifty stores open by 2010. With all of its growth and success, IKEA has a manufacturing challenge: On its current growth trajectory, IKEA will soon have to supply twice the amount of products that it does today.

IKEA's Functional Divisions

Production

IKEA's key objective regarding production is to establish and maintain long-term supplier relationships. IKEA works with more than 1,600 suppliers in more than

Clean lines are the hallmark of IKEA's furniture designs.

fifty-five countries. Its oldest suppliers are Swedish; however, other major suppliers are located in China, Poland, Italy, and Germany. IKEA accounts for five to ten percent of the furniture market in each country where its products are manufactured.

One strategy that IKEA has implemented is to place trading offices around the world to localize its operations. This gives IKEA leverage to increase production capacity (that is, labor hours and purchasing materials) when needed. The strategy also allows IKEA to closely monitor manufacturing performance. Producing high-quality products at the lowest possible cost drives IKEA's production mentality. In addition to local trading offices, IKEA also manages production through long-term contractual relationships based on bulk buying. Committing to high-volume purchases over a longer time frame allows IKEA to dramatically cut costs. Additionally, IKEA is in a position to offer its suppliers financial assistance if necessary. This optimization is key to achieving the low-cost business model that IKEA wants to maintain.

Cost consciousness dominates all aspects of IKEA's operations. In land acquisition, IKEA locates stores on property just outside of target cities. In production, the remnants of fabric and wood used for products are used to create more products. IKEA uses natural colors to cut production costs and increase social responsibility to the environment through the manufacturing process. In distribution, flat packages are used to efficiently transport the large bulk of products from suppliers to IKEA stores. The use of flat packages lowers warehousing and distribution costs and the environmental impact throughout the supply chain.

Marketing

IKEA's marketing program has four focal areas: product design, catalogs, advertising, and public relations/sales promotions. IKEA's product designs are arguably the most important part of its brand image. Customers love the clean lines, frugal styling, and cachet that ownership affords. IKEA admits that creating stylish and inexpensive products is a challenging task. To fulfill its vision, the company's twelve full-time designers and 80 freelancers work closely with in-house production teams to pair the appropriate materials with the least costly suppliers. Though the work is tedious, IKEA is well known for its innovation.

IKEA's main marketing focus is its printed catalog where the company spends 70 percent of its annual marketing budget. The catalog is produced in 38 different editions in 17 languages for 28 different countries. In 2006, 110 million copies were put into circulation. In addition to the catalog, IKEA also uses television, radio, and Internet-based communication to reach its target customers. The company's advertising is intended to increase both brand awareness and store traffic. Some of the company's advertising is controversial, especially ads that portray gay customers shopping for IKEA products. Advertising, however, is not a major focus of IKEA's promotional efforts. The company prefers to rely on word-of-mouth communication.

IKEA does use promotional stunts and games to attract customers into its stores. For instance, IKEA managers invited Atlanta locals to apply for the post of Ambassador of Kul (Swedish for "fun"). The five winners of an essay contest received $2,000 in vouchers, had to live in the store for three days, sleep in the bedding department, and participate in contests. Prior to the opening of the Atlanta store, IKEA offered $4,000 in gift certificates to the first person in line. By the time the store opened, there were more than 2,000 customers waiting. IKEA also holds "Antibureaucracy Weeks" on a regular basis. These are times when executives work on the shop floor or stockroom, operate cash registers, and even load trucks and cars for IKEA customers. This simple step goes a long way in upholding the IKEA culture and maintaining employee morale.

IKEA's marketing program is designed to be thrifty but still effective. In fact, all of IKEA's operations are designed to maintain a downward pressure on operating expenses. For example, in most stores, IKEA does not accept checks—only cash or credit cards. This reduces IKEA's accounts receivable and minimizes losses. It also eliminates the need to maintain an expensive collections operation. With policies like these, it is not surprising that IKEA's pretax operating profit for 2005 was an estimated $1.7 billion. The company's operating margin of ten percent is among the best in the home-furnishings industry. And, despite its low cost and price model, IKEA aims to cut prices by an average of two to three percent every year.

SWOT Analysis

Strengths

Low-Cost Structure   IKEA's low-cost structure has been the very essence of its success. Being that low-cost measures are ingrained into IKEA's corporate DNA, the company does not have a hard time tailoring its operations around this business model. This model also pairs nicely with customers who appreciate IKEA's operating style.

Antibureaucracy   IKEA treats all of its employees the same. The company's anti-bureaucracy weeks help maintain a strong corporate culture and its low-cost business model.

Do-It-Yourself Approach   IKEA can maintain its low-cost business model by creating a different furniture-shopping experience. IKEA supplies customers with all possible materials needed to complete their furniture shopping when they enter the store (that is, measuring tape, paper, and pencils). The floor has showrooms displaying IKEA furniture with multiple accessories that will accentuate the style. With this approach, customers do not have to be bothered with salespeople who work on commission. Customers can pick and choose among the different options of accessories that they would like to use with furniture.

Added Amenities   Although IKEA is not set up as a traditional furniture store, IKEA does provide delivery for customers who cannot fit all their items into their vehicles. If the item can be carried on top of the customer's car, IKEA rents carracks that the customer can use to get the items home. IKEA also provides child-care services to give parents time to shop. Once the children are in a safe place, parents will delegate more time to browsing and purchasing IKEA furniture and accessories. As another amenity, IKEA places restaurants in its stores to urge consumers to stay a little longer. At this point, customers can choose to have lunch or dinner with their children or another shopping partner. IKEA wants the customer to feel as if there is not a rush to leave the store and customers can do more than just shop for furniture.

Weaknesses

Do-It-Yourself Approach   Some customers may not appreciate the do-it-yourself approach. IKEA targets young, cost-conscious customers who want stylish furniture. High salary–earning individuals may not want to indulge in shopping and picking out their furniture from a warehouselike environment. Some individuals may actually enjoy having a conversation with a salesperson and getting individual ideas and input from an employee. These same customers may not have the time to wrestle with assembly of their furniture once they get it home. Customers who feel that this is an unnecessary step may continue to buy furniture from traditional retailers.

Service Trade-offs   IKEA's business model trades service for cost. This trade-off may not be appealing to some customers who are accustomed to traditional furniture shopping and may feel that IKEA does not care about its customers and what they buy. With IKEA operating as numerous franchises, this lack of customer service may begin to taint the IKEA brand. This trade-off could present a future brand-loyalty problem for IKEA.

Limited Promotional Expenditures   IKEA does not spend an enormous amount of money on promotion. Instead, the company depends on word of mouth and catalogs to generate a buzz among customers. Most of IKEA's television commercials are unknown outside of the United Kingdom. Further, many of the company's ads are controversial. Overall, this is a weakness in the United States where consumers watch much more television than in any other nation. As a result, IKEA may be missing out on a larger potential customer base.

Opportunities

Urban Sprawl   In most major metropolitan areas, residents continue to move away from the city center into outlying areas. Many of these residents are young, educated, and value conscious. IKEA's strategy ties well into this geographic/demographic trend.

Value-Dominant Buying Logic   Most American consumers still ascribe to a value-dominant logic when it comes to purchasing goods and services. However, these customers want not only high quality at a good price but also convenient access and time-saving services. IKEA can play into this buying logic but may have to expand its service offerings to increase customer convenience.

Growing Popularity of Swedish Design   In many ways, Swedish design has always been highly regarded. However, the trend is accelerating. Target Stores has contracted with Swedish designer Todd Oldham to design furniture for its stores. The growing popularity of Swedish design is a positive sign for IKEA.

Threats

Copycat Competitors   IKEA has found its competitive advantage in the home-furnishings industry and has gained the first-mover advantage. However, this leaves IKEA susceptible to other companies attempting to imitate this business model.

Changing Customer Needs   Customer demand constantly changes. At some point, customer interest in Swedish design and do-it-yourself furniture will wane. In addition, furniture needs and preferences change as customers age. Overall, there are relatively fewer younger customers when compared to baby boomers. The end result could be a decline in demand for trendy low-cost furniture.

The Future of IKEA's U.S. Expansion

IKEA has solidified the United States as a key to its expansion. The standard of living is higher than most countries; however, most American consumers actively buy into the cost-conscious mentality. The value of the U.S. dollar is stable and not prone to wide exchange rate fluctuations. Another factor that makes the United States favorable to IKEA is its melting pot of cultures. There are different lifestyles and ways of life that IKEA would like to appeal to.

However, an important issue for IKEA to address is the overwhelming individuality of U.S. consumers. American consumers are very demanding and tend to reward marketers that go out of their way to address individual tastes and needs. Expansion into the U.S. market will require IKEA to adapt its offerings and stores to local tastes—a marketing strategy that is much more expensive to deliver and contrary to IKEA's cost-conscious design. IKEA's franchised structure is well suited to this task. This allows IKEA to get closer to customers by hiring local employees that represent the same values, cultures, and lifestyles of the local area.

IKEA's U.S. expansion is expected to move fairly slowly. The company does not have the financial resources and marketing experience to roll out a large number of products and stores simultaneously. In addition, IKEA will slowly adapt its promotional strategy to U.S. standards. For example, most of IKEA's current commercials are considered too "edgy" for American television. Despite any adaptations it might make in its marketing program, the IKEA vision is consistent throughout the world.

Questions for Discussion

1. Why are the styling and design of IKEA products so popular (for additional photographs, go to http://www.ikea.com)? Does IKEA's blend of style and pricing have appeal to mainstream U.S. consumers?

2. How do you account for IKEA's growth and popularity: value or image? What can IKEA do to sustain growth after it loses some cachet?

3. Speculate on what will happen at IKEA stores as they are tailored to fit local tastes. Is the company's trade-off of service for low cost sustainable in the long term?

Sources

The facts of this case are from the IKEA website (http://www.ikea.com); IKEA marketing strategy (http://www.ikea.com/ms/en_GB/about_ikea/press_room/student_info.html), accessed October 6, 2006; "25 Innovators, 6 Industries," *BusinessWeek Online,* April 13, 2006 (http://www.businessweek.com/print/innovate/content/apr2006/id20060413_268232.htm); "Business: Flat-Pack Accounting; IKEA," *The Economist,* May 13, 2006, 76; Kerry Capell, "IKEA," *BusinessWeek Online,* November 14, 2005 (http://www.businessweek.com/magazine/content/05_46/b3959005.htm); Kerry Capell, "Online Extra: Sweden's Answer to Sam Walton," *BusinessWeek Online,* November 14, 2005 (http://www.businessweek.com/print/magazine/content/05_46/b3959011.htm); Cora Daniels, "Create IKEA, Make Billions, Take Bus," *Fortune,* via CNNMoney.com, May 3, 2004 (http://money.cnn.com/magazines/fortune/fortune_archive/2004/05/03/368549/index.htm); and Gianfranco Zaccai, "What IKEA Could Teach Alitalia," *BusinessWeek Online,* January 19, 2006 (http://www.businessweek.com/print/innovate/content/jan2006/id20060119_361779.htm).

Mistine

"Mistine was born in 1988 when Avon was already in the market for ten years. If Mistine hides in the corner, we will never be able to fly high."

Dr. Amornthep Deerojanawong in "We Are Number One"

Company Background

Founded in 1988 by Thailand's king of direct selling, Amornthep Deerojanawong, in partnership with Boonyakiat Chokwatana, Better Way (Thailand) Company was established. In 1991, the company launched its Mistine brand and began its rapid ascent as a key player in Thailand's direct-selling cosmetics industry. At the time, Thai people were not very familiar with cosmetics direct selling. Today, direct selling accounts for over 52 percent of the market and is the preferred method of selling and distributing cosmetics in Thailand. Mistine and Better Way quickly became the leader in the Thai direct-selling cosmetics market—a position it has held since 1997 (Case Exhibit 15.1).

Mistine started with fewer than ten employees and fewer than 100 products. Today, its warehouse is considered the largest cosmetics depot in Southeast Asia with 1,170 regular employees. With the principle and commitment of Better Way to "create the better way of life" for Thai people, there are approximately 600,000 Mistine salespersons nationwide and more than 4,000 products sold under the Mistine brand.

Products under the Mistine brand are divided into five categories and target markets:

- **Makeup**   Confident, smart, stylish, and trendy women who are sociable and love meeting people

- **Skin Care**   Confident and stylish women with sensitive skin who are looking for good product quality at an inexpensive price

- **Fragrance**   Cute, sweet, charming, and confident women, as well as bright, energetic, freedom-loving, and confident men

© O. C. Ferrell and Linda Ferrell, University of New Mexico, 2006. Ekachai Wangprapa, Nuntiya Ittiwattanakorn, Rawadee Mekwichai, and Supishsha Sajjamanochai (Thammasat University) prepared this case under the direction of Dr. O. C. Ferrell and Dr. Linda Ferrell for classroom discussion rather than to illustrate effective or ineffective handling of an administrative situation.

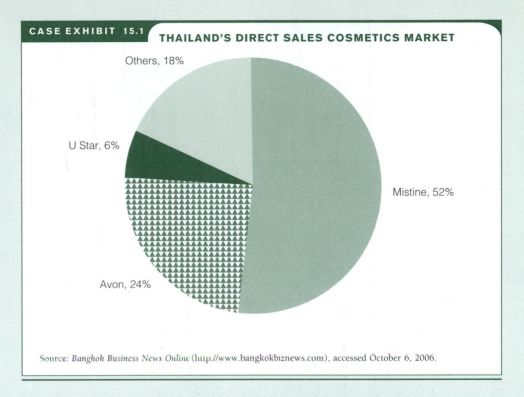

CASE EXHIBIT 15.1 **THAILAND'S DIRECT SALES COSMETICS MARKET**

Others, 18%

U Star, 6%

Mistine, 52%

Avon, 24%

Source: *Bangkok Business News Online* (http://www.bangkokbiznews.com), accessed October 6, 2006.

- **Personal Care** Women and men who are concerned about quality and are health conscious

- **Friday** Single and married people with children who want good-quality products and brand names at a lower price

   Mistine products offer a wide variety that serves the needs of customers at an economical price. Mistine's main focus is its cosmetic portfolio (every category except Friday), which is sold via catalogs. The number of pages allocated per product within the catalog depends on the sales of the product. The Friday category consists of products such as clothes, home décor, electronic appliances, ladies' and men's accessories, sports gear, stationery, toys, gifts, and souvenirs. The 120-page Friday catalog generates an average of $10,000 (U.S.) per page per selling period. The Friday product category alone generates an average of $12.5 million (U.S.) in annual revenue for Better Way.

   For the cosmetics portfolio, the best-quality cosmetics manufacturers in the world manufacture Mistine products. Kolmar Laboratories, the largest and most experienced cosmetics manufacturer in the United States, provides additional support. An experienced production team develops hundreds of new and unique products each year. At least two to three new products are launched each month. Kalaya Pattanasemakul is in charge of Mistine's production. Her previous experience was in the area of research and development for Sahapattanapibul Plc. (Thailand's retail giant) for more than ten years. She became one of the driving forces of Better Way from the beginning of her tenure with the company.

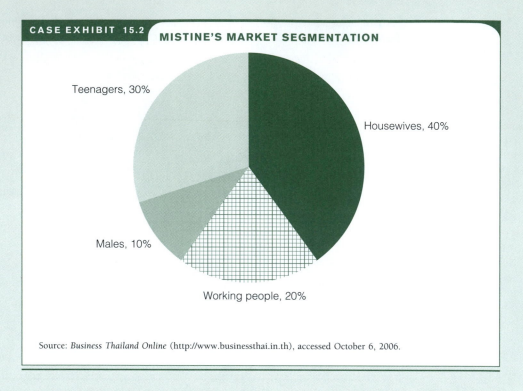

CASE EXHIBIT 15.2   MISTINE'S MARKET SEGMENTATION

Teenagers, 30%

Housewives, 40%

Males, 10%

Working people, 20%

Source: *Business Thailand Online* (http://www.businessthai.in.th), accessed October 6, 2006.

Every Mistine product is thoroughly inspected and tested before being delivered to the warehouse. Customers can be assured that they will receive only the highest quality, "value-for-money" products. In addition, every Mistine product comes with a satisfaction guarantee that if, for any reason, a customer is unsatisfied with his or her purchase, Mistine will replace the product or offer a full refund without condition. Mistine's slogan—"Our customer's satisfaction is what we care about the most"— allows it to maintain leadership in a competitive market.

Mistine's core target market, which accounts for 70 to 80 percent of sales, includes housewives with a high school, occupational certificate level, or high occupational certificate level of education and a monthly income of about $125 to $200 (U.S.). The company also targets professional women who earn $200 to $300 (U.S.) per month. In 2004, the company increased its customer base of working people, males, and vocational school students, especially working people who have high purchasing power (Case Exhibit 15.2). There are now more than 420,000 customers nationwide.

Mistine's Marketing Operations

Cosmetics are the number-one product sold through direct-selling channels in Thailand. The total direct-selling market is roughly $675 million (U.S.) per year and growing at a rate of 15 percent annually. Of that amount, the cosmetics market accounts just over 55 percent, or $375 million (U.S.). In terms of market share, the top-five direct-selling cosmetics companies are Mistine, Avon, U*Star, Giffarine, and

Cute Press (see Case Exhibit 15.1). Prospects for continued growth in the industry are excellent: Only 24 percent of Thailand's population has bought products via direct-selling channels. Price, quality, and attractive packages are the three most important criteria for Thai consumers when buying cosmetics.

Mistine's Key Competitors

Avon   Founded in 1978, AVON Cosmetics (Thailand) Co., Ltd. is the twenty-second branch of AVON Products Inc., USA. It was the first company in Thailand at that time to use a single-level marketing direct-selling approach to Thai consumers. With the company's motto—The Company for Women—Avon targets teenagers and working women.

Customer service is offered through distributors called Avon Members. The company has a team of representatives from the headquarters in Bangkok who visit all the customers in their areas of responsibility. Not only do they sell products, but these Avon Members also provide beauty tips for customers and ensure that they are all satisfied with the products.

To strengthen its position in the market, Avon Thailand launched "Avon Beauty Boutique," which was an additional distribution channel. The idea was to sell the beauty boutique as a franchise to any interested entrepreneur. The main promotional campaign focuses on women and feminine appreciation in addition to sponsoring beauty pageants such as Miss Thailand World.

Avon cosmetics are truly high-quality products for which the brand is recognized throughout the world. As such, it is not difficult for Avon Thailand to sell its products and gain the confidence of consumers. Currently, Avon Thailand has more than 500 full-time employees with 140 sales districts and more than 200,000 Avon Members throughout Thailand.

U*Star   GMM Grammy PLC launched U*Star in early 2003 as the newest player in Thailand's cosmetics direct-selling business. Grammy, the market leader in Thailand's growing market for Western music, is a diversified company with interests in television, radio, film, concerts, education and publishing, and retail stores. The idea for U*Star was the brainchild of Paiboon Dumrongchaitam, one of Grammy's board members, who realized that the firm employed a large number of makeup artists. His idea was to produce cosmetics for these professionals and for people who wanted to look like famous musicians, actors/actresses, and television stars.

U*Star also uses a single-level marketing approach that targets females aged 18 to 25 years old who have an interest in fashion, movie stars, singers, costumes, and makeup. In only a year, U*Star had more than 600 products and revenues exceeding $15 million (U.S.). U*Star's current direct-selling sales force is roughly 100,000 members. The company expanded its distribution channels by opening U*Star shops in big cities throughout the country. These shops use mobile technology and e-mail in their ordering process.

U*Star's products are high-quality, innovative cosmetic products using ingredients such as white tea or deep-sea water. Its products, which come in slick packaging, are sold using a "semi-catalog magazine" that covers not only products but also members' news and updates, beauty trends and tips, health information, and articles on selling techniques. Based on a strong entertainment business in Thailand, U*Star claims to have a brand awareness of 90 percent. U*Star's, phenomenal annual growth of 30 percent may put it in a position to be the number-one firm in the market within five years.

Amway   Established in May 1988, Amway (Thailand) Co., Ltd. sells various consumer products in addition to cosmetics using a multilevel-marketing approach. Amway's sales are roughly $232 million (U.S.) with an annual growth rate of 15 percent. The company's catalog offers more than 100 different products and 500 stock-keeping units. Its most popular products include health products, herbal products, air purifiers, and water purifiers. Amway offers nutritional supplements under the Nutrilite brand and cosmetics products under the Artistry brand.

Amway Thailand recently invested more than $2 million (U.S.) to renovate its offices, expand its warehouses, and move into upcountry areas by opening new Pick-n-Pay shops. The company expects to have Pick-n-Pay shops in every Thai province within five years. Amway has also invested in technology. Amazingly, three percent of Amway Thailand's revenue comes from e-commerce transactions.

Mistine's Competitive Response   Right after U*Star launched in 2003 and quickly moved to number three in the direct-selling market, Mistine launched a TV campaign to emphasize its leading position. The campaign presented the outstanding beauty of a popular actress who chose Mistine's New Star cosmetic collection. The message: "New Star from Mistine, the best selling cosmetics in Thailand."

In addition, Mistine positions itself as an Asian company that produces products that are developed and formulated especially for Asian woman. Mistine products are created to blend well with Asian complexions and skin tones. They are also made to better suit the warmer and more humid climate of the Asian region so that the product stays on longer and looks fresher throughout the day.

Mistine's Direct-Selling Operations

In the direct-selling business, the length of a selling period is critical and shapes the operation of the business. A selling period starts when the product catalog is sent to the sales force. The selling period ends when the sales force submits purchase orders to the company. Normally, direct-selling companies use a three-week selling period, totaling eighteen periods within a year. Although Mistine used this approach, the company found that most salespeople did not begin selling products to customers until the last week of the selling period. As such, most of the customers' purchase orders were generated from sales during the third week of the selling period. Accordingly, Mistine's management decided to reduce the selling period to two weeks, resulting in 26 selling periods per year.

The change was a challenge for Mistine's operations. Because as many as 20,000 purchase orders were submitted to the company each day, the company was forced to implement an efficient mail traffic–management plan to control and balance the workload. Within a two-week selling period, personnel had only ten days to work. If order processing were not completed each day, salespersons would not be able to deliver the products as promised. After some time, the new operating plan worked smoothly and was a resounding success. Sales increased by 80 percent compared to the previous year, and salespeople became more active in selling products. Impressive sales were not only a result of reducing the distribution cycle but also due to the positive attitude created throughout the company. The company's pledge—"We will make Mistine No. 1"—was successful in motivating salespeople and personnel to adapt to the changes and cooperate with the company's direction.

Mistine's single-level marketing approach to its direct sales operations is simple and efficient. It is also suitable to the Thai culture and lifestyle. The company recruits district managers who in turn recruit as many salespeople as he or she can handle. Each day, the new recruits make their rounds to meet customers and prospective customers. Once a sale is confirmed, the salesperson submits a purchase order. Each salesperson earns full commission without having to share his or her earnings with others. The more sales that a salesperson makes, the more income that he or she receives. Each district manager earns a fixed salary plus commission based on sales generated by the salespersons under his or her responsibility. In addition, as a means to increase morale, mobility, and efficiency, the company provides a car to each of its district managers. The district manager's fuel expenses are borne by the company.

In terms of recruiting, the company welcomes anyone, man or woman, with free time on their hands who would like to earn money, make new friends, and develop self-confidence. Salespeople can plan their own schedule and movement in order to reach target sales and obtain rewards. Generally, the turnover rate for salespeople is 200 percent per year because most salespeople sell Mistine products as a second job. Although they receive 25 to 30 percent commission, only the most determined and committed remain with the company.

With the belief that the salespeople can live without Mistine but Mistine cannot live without its salespeople, Mistine has launched several programs to maximize employee loyalty. Internal relationship programs such as the "Mistine Thank You Concert" were organized in nine Thai provinces to gather Mistine salespeople together as a family and demonstrate the company's concern for its employees. The company also provides life insurance with coverage of $50,000 (U.S.) to each salesperson. Nonmonetary rewards and recognition incentives for salespeople include crystal trophies and photos in the Hall of Fame.

Mistine's Advertising

Direct-selling companies normally depend on word of mouth to develop brand awareness, recruit salespeople, and encourage product purchases. Better Way decided to do things differently by being the first direct-selling company in the world to use mass-media advertising. Continuous advertising campaigns have been executed to build brand image and positioning in the customers' minds. Many advertising campaigns have been developed to recruit additional salespeople.

When the company first started, Deerojanawong used his credibility to advertise Mistine during interviews with the media and at seminars with educational institutions. People applied as district managers with the company mainly because of his reputation. He was certain that the district managers would be able to establish a large network of salespeople.

"Mistine is here!" was launched as the company's very first television campaign with the objectives to communicate to the public that Mistine is a direct-selling cosmetics business and to create a brand character of beauty for Mistine's products. Using the message "Mistine is here!" was an effective way for the public to envision a salesperson coming to visit them with Mistine products. After only two months, the campaign generated an incredible buzz as it increased brand awareness from 10 percent to roughly 70 percent.

Mistine's second campaign was designed to assist district managers in their efforts to recruit new salespeople. This campaign consisted of two advertisements. The message of the first ad was that it was possible to buy a car by becoming a Mistine salesperson. Within three months, a total of 30,000 people applied and were recruited. Sales rose by 100 percent. The message of the second ad was that it was possible to buy a house by becoming a Mistine salesperson. Again, the company succeeded in creating stronger brand awareness through this campaign.

Based on this success, the company decided that it needed to increase its customers' confidence in Mistine products as well as generate more product trial. As such, "If you're not satisfied, we will give you your money back" was the concept for the third campaign. This campaign was not only successful in stimulating product trial but also created a great deal of brand switching from competitors' products to Mistine products. In the end, there were very few cases of product dissatisfaction or customers requesting for their money back.

The company's fourth campaign was a series of six 30-second television spots—each spot was shown for two to three weeks over a four-month run for the campaign. The spots were like short scenes of a mini–soap opera. The campaign, the most expensive in the history of the Thai cosmetics direct-selling industry, firmly cemented Mistine in the number-one position. The campaign, which was produced by a small agency called Fameline, also proved that good advertising didn't have to be created by a well-known advertising agency. Together, the two companies succeeded in positioning Mistine products and in creating a unique selling proposition for Better Way.

Mistine has remained a first mover in the direct-selling market as it has launched advertising campaigns using popular actresses, actors, and music bands that match with Mistine's brand personality. Such advertising campaigns have had much impact and have been designed to capture specific target groups:

- One advertisement, targeting housewives, used a very popular Thai actress as the presenter for Mistine's Neo Bright products. As a result of this advertisement, Better Way successfully expanded its network of salespeople to cover upcountry provinces.

- Another advertisement, using another very popular Thai actress who was voted by the public as the sexiest girl in Thailand, targeted working women. This advertisement imparted a sexier, more modern and confident image to Mistine's products.

- Another advertisement, targeting teenagers, used a very popular boy band called D2B to promote Mistine's Pink Magic lipstick. As a result of this advertisement, Mistine increased its share of the teen market by ten percent. The total breakdown of Mistine's sales also shifted to a point where teens generated 30 percent of the company's sales.

- To acquire new salespeople, Mistine launched an ad using a very popular Thai actor as the presenter. Mistine was also interested in building brand image among men.

Growth and Expansion

Despite Deerojanawong's passion for the company that he founded, he was forced to transition out of day-to-day operations when he developed liver cancer in 1999 (he died in 2000). Better Way and Mistine are now under the control of his son, Danai Deerojanawong. Under new leadership, Mistine plans to respond to its ever-increasing competition as follows:

- Increase the number of Mistine salespeople by ten percent.

- Increase sales by instituting a five percent discount on all product items.

- Expand from 550 service areas to 600 service areas.

- Increase the promotion budget by 50 percent.

- Introduce 400 new product items (especially men's products).

The company has formed a strategic alliance with DTAC, a major Thai tele-communications service provider, under the name Mistine Corporate Solution. This system enables Mistine salespeople to call the 24-hour Mistine Call Center for free when using the DTAC cellular network system. This innovative direct-selling tactic will facilitate the salespeople in ordering products, requesting product information, and asking about promotions. This strategic alliance will help the company cut phone expenses by $25,000 (U.S.) per month.

Aligned with its strategies in stronger targeting of teens, Mistine has signed RS Promotions as a long-term partner. Mistine learned a great deal when it used D2B (the boy band managed by RS Promotions) in its campaign for Pink Magic lipstick. The company plans to use other popular artists managed by RS Promotions in its future campaigns as it attempts to capture an increasing share of the teen market.

Mistine has begun an aggressive strategy of marketing its products in foreign markets. Considering the relationship of Thailand with neighboring countries, its geographic proximity, and Thailand's position in Asia, foreign markets are extremely interesting for Mistine. The company opened manufacturing sites in the Philippines and Vietnam and has successfully offered products for sale in Cambodia, Laos, and Myanmar. The success is due to Mistine's affordable prices that match the income of the people in these countries. Moreover, Mistine's advertising campaigns use popular actresses who are also well known to people in these countries. Mistine will soon export cosmetic products to distributors in Taiwan and China. Hungary and Russia are potential markets for the future.

Looking Ahead

Mistine successfully conquered the cosmetics direct-selling market in Thailand within a very short period of time. The company's success is not a miracle. Instead, Deerojanawong's vision and determination made the company what it is today. Now his son, Danai, is poised to take Mistine into the modern era of Thailand's direct-selling business. His aim is to bring Mistine into the global market.

Danai Deerojanawong knows that there will be many bumps on the road ahead with strong competitors such as U*Star and Avon at Mistine's doorstep. In looking ahead to the next ten years, he is considering the best way to take Mistine successfully into the global arena. How can Better Way and Mistine leverage its current strengths to take advantage of global opportunities? How can Mistine maintain its number-one position in Thailand while it simultaneously looks outside its borders? As Deerojanawong considered these issues, his father's words—"Face what you fear!"—echo in his mind.

Questions for Discussion

1. What are the major SWOT considerations in Mistine's attempt to continue its growth and dominance in the Thai market?

2. How can Better Way stay on top in Thailand while it looks to expand internationally?

3. What specific marketing program actions would you recommend over the next five years?

Sources

The facts of this case are from the Better Way (Thailand) Company website (http://www.mistine.co.th/main.html), accessed October 6, 2006; "Big Five Direct Sellers," *Business Thailand Online,* October 12, 2001 (http://www.businessthai.in.th); "Branding for Direct Selling," *Business Thailand Online,* December 12, 2003 (http://www.businessthai.in.th); Anuwat Dharamadhaj, "How Direct Selling Is Regulated and Managed in Different Markets in Thailand," Asian Symposium on Direct Selling, 2003; "Direct Selling," *Marketeer* 43 (September 2003):62 ; "Direct Selling War," *Bangkok Business News Online,* March 24, 2003 (http://www.bangkokbiznews.com); The Grammy Entertainment Company website (http://www.grammy.co.th), accessed

October 6, 2006; Jaturong Kobkaew, *King of Direct Sales* (Bangkok: Thai Public Relations and Publishing, 2002); The RS Promotion Company website (http://www.rs-promotion.com), accessed October 6, 2006; "Thailand Direct Selling," Competitive Strategies in Marketing, Thammasat University, Thailand, 2004; The Total Access Communication Company website (http://www.dtac.co.th/en/default.aspx), accessed October 6, 2006; "U*Star and GMM Grammy Artists," *Bangkok Business News Online,* October 2, 2004 (http://www.bangkokbiznews.com); "U*Star to the Market," *Go To Manager Online,* September 13, 2003 (http://www.gotomanager.com); and Ara Wilson, "The Empire of Direct Sales and the Making of Thai Entrepreneurs," *Critiques of Anthropology* 19 (1999): 402–422.

Museum of Fine Arts Boston

A full day before the latest exhibition at the Museum of Fine Arts (MFA) opened, the front page of *The Boston Globe* proclaimed, "Furor Ahoy; MFA Exhibit of Koch's Collections Stirs Questions over Choices, Motives."[1] Entitled "Things I Love: The Many Collections of William I. Koch," the exhibition featured the private collection of William Koch, a resident of Massachusetts and Florida, who, as the article acknowledged, had "assembled a collection renowned for its range and quality." What made the exhibition somewhat unusual was not the rare works of European masters such as Monet and Picasso, or American paintings and sculptures by Remington, but other remarkable pieces such as the firearm that killed the infamous outlaw of the American West, Jesse James, and the two large racing yachts on the lawn of the MFA. That same article reproduced others' criticisms of the MFA for having Koch underwrite a significant portion of the costs of staging the exhibition and publishing the associated catalog, and still others charged that this exhibition was more to do with "glamorizing the collector than fulfilling the museum's educational mission," obliquely suggesting that the exhibition was a means of enticing a prodigal patron back into the fold.

The MFA's director, Malcolm Rogers, quite used to such criticisms, asserted that this was but another step in his mission to bring new visitors to the MFA. "It is as simple and straightforward as that," offered Rogers.

In 2005, Rogers had been working actively toward achieving that goal. Just months before the Koch exhibition, another exhibition, "Speed, Style, and Beauty: Cars from the Ralph Lauren Collection," had caused its own fury with some traditionalists in the art world deriding the exhibition as overly populist and commercial. Yet, while some were questioning the exhibition's artistic merit, male visitors (a scarce demographic for the MFA and all art museums) were flooding through its doors. Many were avid collectors themselves who did not typically attend the MFA, including an owner of the Boston Celtics (Boston's professional basketball team), who noted, "When this invitation landed on my desk . . . my assistant put it right on the top.

Professor V. Kasturi Rangan and Research Associate Marie Bell prepared this case. HBS cases are developed solely as the basis for class discussion. Cases are not intended to serve as endorsements, sources of primary data, or illustrations of effective or ineffective management.

Normally, the MFA invitations wouldn't be right at the top."[2] Ultimately, the car exhibition attracted 197,000 patrons, far exceeding initial projections of 140,000 visitors.

The MFA had been alert to its audience's tastes in other ways as well. In an opening-day tribute to the Boston Red Sox (who had won the Baseball World Series in 2005 after an 86-year drought), the MFA presented a special exhibition entitled "Rockwell and the Red Sox." The exhibition featured a Norman Rockwell painting that depicted the 1956 Red Sox locker room and also included a special selection of Red Sox memorabilia.

Rogers's motivations for bringing new visitors to the MFA were twofold. The first was mission—the MFA was dedicated to bringing art and people together to enrich lives. Without appealing to a broader base of patrons, Rogers felt that the MFA would be compromising its mission, and indeed, most of the MFA Board of Tustees felt likewise. To a great extent the MFA had continued to fulfill that mission. The second reason for bringing in a wider audience was fiscal. As seen in Figure A below, since 1998, base attendance (defined as purchasing a ticket to see the core collection) had slowly declined, and special-exhibit attendance (defined as purchasing a ticket to a special exhibition that also included access to the core collection) was volatile. Declining attendance had an immediate impact and was an important fiscal priority for Rogers and his team, especially as the museum's trustees urged the museum to maintain a balanced budget.

In September 2005, the MFA announced that it had raised more than $302 million of the $500 million needed to reorganize existing gallery space and commence work on a new wing of the museum devoted to its American collection. While more than halfway to its objective, it was now moving into the challenging "public" phase of fund-raising, which

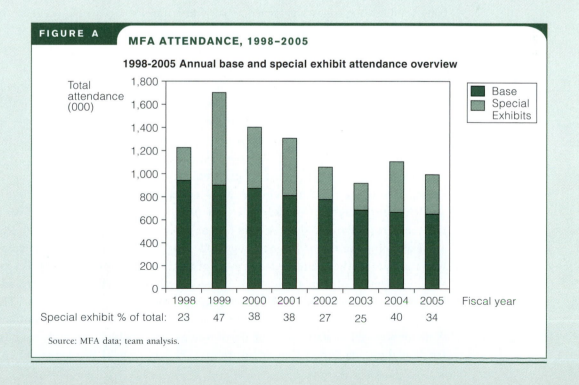

FIGURE A

MFA ATTENDANCE, 1998–2005

1998-2005 Annual base and special exhibit attendance overview

Total attendance (000)

Legend: Base, Special Exhibits

Fiscal year	1998	1999	2000	2001	2002	2003	2004	2005
Special exhibit % of total:	23	47	38	38	27	25	40	34

Source: MFA data; team analysis.

required targeting and soliciting support from a broader audience. Adding to the challenge, a number of high-profile companies that would have been potential supporters of the MFA had been merged or acquired, moving corporate headquarters outside the Boston area (for example, Gillette was acquired by Procter & Gamble; Fleet Bank was acquired by Bank of America; and the local department store, Filene's, was acquired by Federated Stores) and making continued and future corporate support uncertain.

"All the more reason to connect and expand one's base of patrons," commented Rogers.

The American system of funding the arts differed from those of other nations. For example, some European art institutions received as much as 90% of their funding from government agencies.[3] In contrast, most U.S. art institutions relied on private donations to support half of their annual operating budget, with the other half raised through admissions and other revenue-generating activities. The National Endowment for the Arts, established in 1965, with its $140 million annual budget, was the largest annual funder for the arts in the U.S. While there was limited direct governmental support for the arts, arts organizations did benefit from certain tax benefits. Indeed, although the MFA generally received less than 1% of its operating revenue from public funding, as a 501(c)3 organization, the MFA enjoyed tax-exempt status; donations to the museum were a tax-free benefit to the donors.

Traditionally, philanthropy, especially as it related to the arts, was primarily based on the generosity of individuals with a devotion to the arts. Secondary contributions came from local corporations, often when corporate leaders either participated in or believed in the importance of the arts. Beginning in 2000, news reports and editorials began to note three significant trends in the rarified world of philanthropy. First, with the aging of the baby boomers, the largest intergenerational wealth transfer ever would occur by the middle of the twenty-first century. One study suggested that $6 trillion would be donated to nonprofits through bequests from 1998 to 2052. Second, the new pool of prospective donors, especially the younger highly successful entrepreneurs, had different attitudes toward giving. Specifically, they were more likely to donate to social (e.g., public health and medicine) and educational causes and sought a direct connection between their donations and concrete actions. The third change was in the behavior of corporate donors. Corporate donors were becoming more strategic in their support and sought to tie their gifts more closely to their company's business objectives.[4]

Patricia Jacoby, deputy director of external relations, remarked on the reasons people gave to the museum: "One group of our donors is simply devoted to art, another group feels that it is their civic responsibility, and a third group believes that it is a social requirement. Many donors devote much of their personal time to learning and expanding their knowledge through collecting." She also noted that New England was a unique market: "Unlike many areas of the country where donors revel in the acknowledgment of their donations or gifts of a collection, many New Englanders don't want to be acknowledged. It is a quiet and dignified kind of support." The external relations group competed with other New England cultural institutions for donations as well as with educational institutions (such as Harvard) and area hospitals (such as the Dana-Farber Cancer Institute). "The bad news is that we are often targeting the same people as Harvard; the good news is that Harvard is so effective at fund-raising that donors become used to considering multimillion gifts," noted Jacoby.

The MFA

In the words of its founders in 1870, the museum and its collection were to be "a means of culture to the public, of education to artists and artisans, and of elevated enjoyment to all."[5] Over the next 135 years, the MFA had attempted to live up to that mission and by and large succeeded with only modest drift, according to Rogers. (see Exhibit 1 for the MFA's current mission statement.) "There is a perception that art museums belong to the visually literate elite," noted Rogers, "but I believe that this is wrong. Two truths have motivated me as a museum curator and then later as a museum administrator and director. The first: that great works of art embody much of what is best and most enduring in the human spirit. The second: that great art institutions are crucial components of a civilized society, resources for every member of the community and indeed for citizens of the world."[6]

EXHIBIT 1   **MFA MISSION STATEMENT (ADOPTED 1991)**

The Museum of Fine Arts houses and preserves preeminent collections and aspires to serve a wide variety of people through direct encounters with works of art.

The Museum aims for the highest standards of quality in all its endeavors. It serves as a resource for both those who are already familiar with art and those for whom art is a new experience. Through exhibitions, programs, research and publications, the Museum documents and interprets its own collections. It provides information and perspectives on art through time and throughout the world.

The Museum holds its collections in trust for future generations. It assumes conservation as a primary responsibility which requires constant attention to providing a proper environment for works of art and artifacts. Committed to its vast holding, the Museum nonetheless recognizes the need to identify and explore new and neglected areas of art. It seeks to acquire art of the past and present which is visually significant and educationally meaningful.

The Museum has obligations to the people of Boston and New England, across the nation and abroad. It celebrates diverse cultures and welcomes new and broader constituencies. The Museum is a place in which to see and to learn. It stimulates in its visitors a sense of pleasure, pride and discovery which provides aesthetic challenge and leads to a greater cultural awareness and discernment.

The Museum creates educational opportunities for visitors and accommodates a wide range of experiences and learning styles. The Museum educates artists of the future through its School. The creative efforts of the students and faculty provide the Museum and its public with insights into emerging art and art forms.

The Museum's ultimate aim is to encourage and to heighten public understanding and appreciation of the visual world.

Source: Museum of Fine Arts Boston.

The MFA was the leading cultural institution in Boston and one of the leading art museums in the world.[7] The museum's expansive collection of over 400,000 works was organized into eight major departments:

- Art of Asia, Oceania, and Africa

- Art of Europe

- Art of the Americas

- Art of the Ancient World

- Contemporary Art

- Musical Instruments

- Prints, Drawings, and Photographs

- Textile and Fashion Arts

The background and taste of the museum's benefactors influenced the composition of the MFA's collection. For example, the museum included 1,600 masterpiece paintings of Dutch, English, French, and Spanish art. The MFA was particularly strong in impressionist and post-impressionist paintings; the museum had one of the largest collections of Monet outside of Paris. The Art of the Ancient World included objects from the Near East, Egypt, Greece, Nubia, and Rome. The MFA, in conjunction with Harvard University, had excavated for 37 years at Giza, resulting in one of the best collections of art from the Old Kingdom (the age of the great pyramids) outside of Egypt. Boston's place in U.S. history, at the heart of the American Revolution, also resulted in an exceptional collection of American works including the paintings of Winslow Homer, John Singer Sargent, and Mary Cassatt and the silverware of American patriot Paul Revere. The MFA also had an exceptional Asian collection; notable were its Japanese prints and postcards.

The MFA originally opened in 1876 in Copley Square in Boston's Back Bay area. By the turn of the century, it was clear that the museum needed additional space to house its burgeoning collection, and in 1909 the first section of the MFA opened about one mile away in its present location on Huntington Avenue, a major thoroughfare that was also home to Symphony Hall. That first section, with a 500-foot granite façade that faced Huntington Avenue, included the grand rotunda (with murals by John Singer Sargent) and exhibition galleries. Led by its trustees, the expansion of the MFA was financed entirely by private donations. Two years later a donation from a single patron funded the next phase of the master plan, building a wing along the Fenway to house painting galleries. (The Fenway was a major street running parallel to Huntington Avenue. See Exhibit 2.)

Over the next 80 years, the MFA went through several phases of expansion. A decorative arts wing was built in 1928 and subsequently was enlarged in 1968. In 1970, the White wing, with space for a research laboratory, library, dining facilities, education facilities, and administrative offices, opened on the west side of the

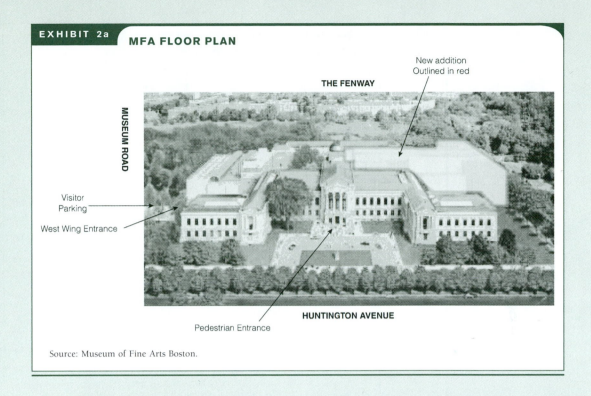

EXHIBIT 2a   MFA FLOOR PLAN

New addition
Outlined in red

THE FENWAY

MUSEUM ROAD

Visitor
Parking

West Wing Entrance

Pedestrian Entrance

HUNTINGTON AVENUE

Source: Museum of Fine Arts Boston.

building. In the late 1970s, the MFA commissioned the renowned architect I. M. Pei to design the west wing, which would surround and enhance the White wing and create space for special exhibitions, a large auditorium, and enhanced dining and retail facilities. Entry to the west wing was from Museum Road (a small one-way street that connected Huntington Avenue and the Fenway).

In 2005, the MFA's footprint was about 531,000 square feet., with 34% of space devoted to exhibitions (permanent and temporary), 13% to visitor amenities (dining, retail, and lobby areas), 2% to educational space, and the remaining 51% to administrative, conservation, support, and storage space. The museum's collections were housed in galleries spread over two floors of display space (as indicated in Exhibit 2). Many visitors entered the museum via the west wing entrance, as it was adjacent to the visitor parking lots on Museum Road and provided easy access to the main information desk and the Gund Gallery, which housed special exhibitions. Those taking public transportation were also more likely to enter via the west wing entrance, as buses and the "T" (rapid transit service) stopped nearest that entrance. Additionally, as the Huntington entrance had been closed for a period in the 1990s, many visitors expected to enter the museum via the west wing. Those that entered via the Huntington Avenue entrance, then, were primarily new visitors drawn to the MFA's impressive façade. For those entering from Huntington Avenue, there was a smaller satellite ticket booth and information desk.

Generally speaking, the galleries of the MFA were ringed around two courtyards—the Calderwood Courtyard and the Garden Court. In addition to the galleries, the MFA offered three restaurants: cafeteria-style dining in the Courtyard

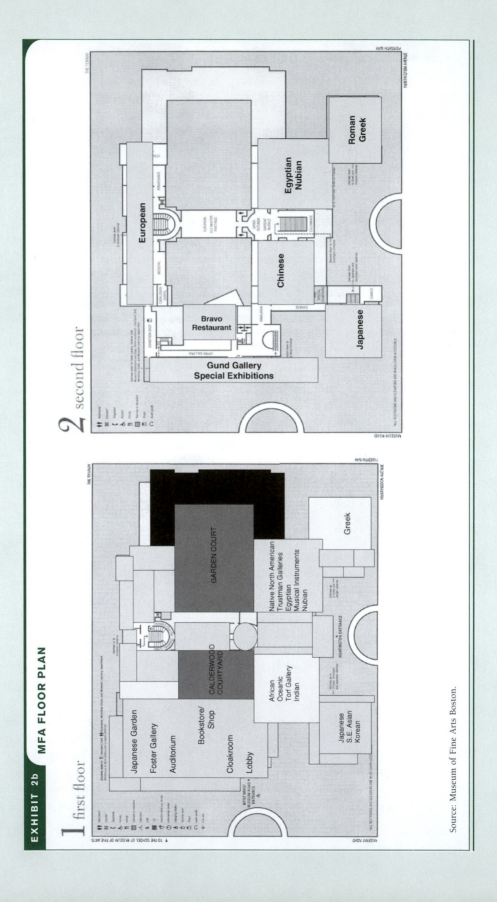

Source: Museum of Fine Arts Boston.

Café, lighter fare in the Galleria Café, and fine dining in Bravo. There were two major retail spaces, the museum bookstore and shop on the first floor and an exhibition shop on the second floor that primarily sold merchandise related to the special exhibition on display. The Remis Auditorium on the first floor in the west wing was a venue for films and lecture series. The MFA's largest temporary exhibitions were displayed in the 10,000-square-foot Gund Gallery; the smaller Trustman Galleries and Torf Gallery also had changing exhibitions on view. The Gund Gallery was located on the second floor above the Remis Auditorium, up the escalator adjacent to the first-floor ticket counter.

Organization

The MFA was organized into five major divisions: curatorial, the Museum School, external relations, programs and services, and communications. (See Exhibit 3 for an organization chart.)

In business terms, the curatorial staff was focused on product development. These professionals were responsible for the museum's reputation for product quality and integrity. Specifically, the curators were responsible for the conservation and display of the current collection and the enhancement of the collection with strategic acquisitions. The MFA enlarged its collection through strategic acquisitions and donations to the museum, often based on the serendipitous nature of the art market. In the volatile fine art market, curatorial expertise was critical. For example, the head curator of the Art of Europe was a key player in the MFA's decision to sell several meaningful impressionist works in order to acquire an even more significant Degas painting (a transaction estimated at $18 million). The curatorial staff published scholarly papers in journals, furthering the art community's knowledge and enhancing the reputation of the museum. The curatorial staff also played a critical role in special exhibitions. As Rogers noted, "One of our curators has to embrace the idea of the special exhibition because it requires rigorous planning and scholarship to bring it to fruition."

The School of the Museum of Fine Arts (SMFA), established in 1876, was devoted to the education of future artists. The school, with about 1,000 students, offered eight programs of study that included a diploma program as well as undergraduate and graduate degree programs. The SMFA was affiliated with Tufts University. The external relations group was responsible for planning, constructing, and funding improvements to the MFA. Most recently, the group had focused on raising the funds required to build the new east wing. There were about 35 people on the development staff, 15 frontline fund-raisers and 15–20 noncampaign staff.

The programs and services division executed the operations of the MFA. Led by John Stanley, the museum's COO, programs and services comprised 10 departments ranging from finance and human resources to education and visitor and member services. The museum's three restaurants were contracted out to Restaurant Associates. The learning and public programs department had a significant outreach effort to both adults and children, offering courses and seminars that leveraged off the assets of the MFA. The program for schools offered free admissions to Boston schools

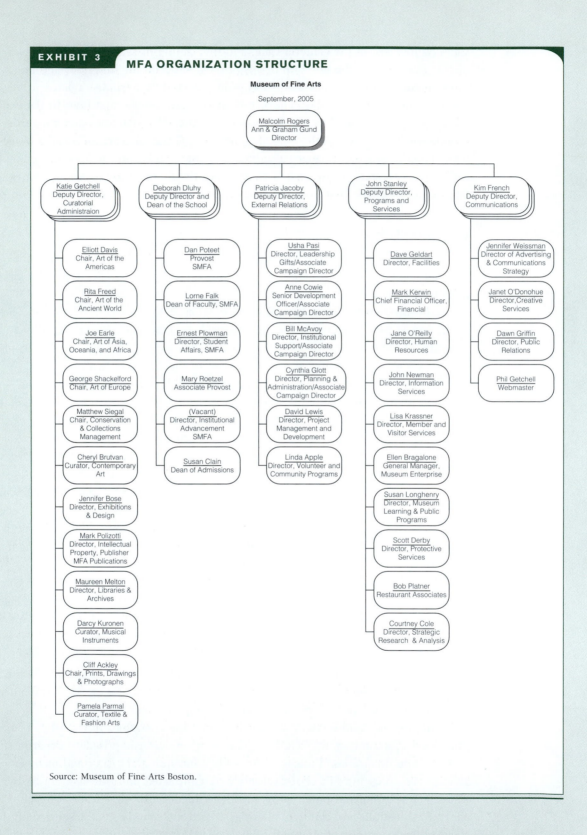

EXHIBIT 3

MFA ORGANIZATION STRUCTURE

Source: Museum of Fine Arts Boston.

and a modest $5–$7 fee per student for its guided or self-guided tours. Prior to bringing students to the museum, teachers were encouraged to attend classes that could be used to meet their professional development requirements.

A marketing effort had been started in 1996 based on the initiative of Jacoby, the MFA's current deputy director of external relations, to inculcate a marketing mind-set into the MFA. "The 1990s were a boom period for the arts in general. The Boston-area economy was rapidly expanding. Both our donations and our audience were growing, too. Marketing then was intuitive, nothing fancy," noted Jacoby. Starting with the basics, the MFA created logos and established marketing standards. The following year and for several years thereafter, the MFA invested in advertising, and riding a wave of growing interest in art, high-profile donations to museums generally, and blockbuster exhibitions, the MFA flourished. That period was followed by decreased marketing expenditures as operating expenditures rose. Beginning in 2002, Stanley, deputy director, programs and services, took over the effort and recognized a need for a return to a greater focus on understanding the museum's market and its audience. This refocus included a considerable investment in market research and the creation of the post of manager of research. In 2004, the marketing and public relations efforts were joined to create the stand-alone communications division under the direction of Kimberly French, deputy director of communications, who had joined the MFA from Fidelity Investments.

Leadership

In September 1994, Rogers, who was then the deputy director of The National Portrait Gallery in London, was appointed the Ann and Graham Gund Director of the MFA. In 1997, the MFA began a long-term planning effort that resulted in a three-phased strategic plan: One Museum-New Museum-Great Museum. The first phase, One Museum, focused on creating a team of colleagues that made decisions based on the return to the entire museum rather than a specific department. The New Museum phase addressed the MFA's programs and practices to create an organization willing to experiment and innovate, while the Great Museum phase sought to fulfill the MFA's potential as one of the world's greatest art museums. It was an ambitious strategic plan. When Rogers arrived, the museum faced financial crisis—five months after his arrival he cut 20% of the workforce in what would be the most serious downsizing in his tenure. Additionally, Rogers re-organized the museum's departments, in several cases combining painting and decorative arts (to create the Art of Europe, for example) that resulted in the departure of two senior curators.[8] "We are a world-class museum but without all of the world-class appreciation we deserve," commented Rogers, who had set for himself the goal of raising the profile of the MFA.

Access was the focal point of Rogers's leadership. Over the course of his 11 years, Rogers's emphasis on creating access had drawn both praise and criticism. In 1995, Rogers reopened the museum's main doors on Huntington Avenue as a welcoming gesture to the community (five years earlier they had been closed for financial reasons). In the following year, Rogers eliminated admission fees for children under 17 and then extended the MFA's hours of operation so that the museum was available to the public seven days a week and more than 60 hours per week. Under Rogers's guidance the MFA reached out to the community with three free open houses each year, expansion of the education program, and, in conjunction with Boston's mayor, the renaming of Huntington Avenue as Avenue of the Arts. A noted scholar, Rogers worked extensively with curatorial staff to enhance and expand the MFA's collection. Indeed, from 2000 to 2004, investment in curatorial services expanded by over 50%.

Yet Rogers was also a self-described risk taker, and it was primarily in the area of exhibitions that he drew fire. While traditional exhibitions such as Monet, van Gogh, and Pharaohs of the Sun drew praise, others, such as a 1996 exhibit of popular photographs of subjects such as Madonna and Richard Gere by fashion photographer Herb Ritts, "Herb Ritts: Work"; "Dangerous Curves: the Art of the Guitar," in 2000; and, as indicated earlier, most recently an exhibition of classic cars, "Speed, Style, and Beauty: Cars from the Ralph Lauren Collection," in July 2005, drew criticism. While certain critics questioned whether the works within these exhibitions were indeed art, Rogers countered, "Our work is to bring art into people's lives. It is not just to preach to the converted but to make conversions."[9] Notably, the Ritts show, with more than 250,000 visitors, ranked as one of the top five in attendance at the MFA's Gund Gallery.

In 2004, the MFA loaned 21 paintings from its Monet collection, some of Monet's most celebrated works (and several not permanently displayed), to Paper Ball, a subsidiary of the New York art dealership PaceWildenstein, a firm that operated the Bellagio Gallery of Fine Art in Las Vegas, for a show entitled "Claude Monet: Masterworks from the Museum of Fine Arts, Boston." In 2005, the museum announced that it was loaning 27 works for "The Impressionist Landscape from Corot to Van Gogh," the exhibition that replaced the Monet exhibition. It was reported that the MFA received a fee of $1 million for the loan of its Monet paintings.[10] An estimated 450,000 people went to the Las Vegas exhibit, paying the $15 entry fee. Rogers's decision to loan the paintings to the Bellagio created a stir among the art community. Traditionally, art museums had lent out their collections to other art museums without a fee. Generally, the receiving museum only paid for the transportation of the pieces and incurred the on-site costs necessary to exhibit the paintings. Several were concerned that the MFA's actions were the beginning of a transition to "renting" rather than "sharing" art works, leaving poorer nonprofit art museums to compete with richer, private, for-profit corporations for access to rare works of art. However, there had been a long history of museums renting out their collections to commercial concerns like Japanese department stores. Others charged that as a tax-exempt nonprofit organization, the MFA should not be engaged in commercial enterprise. Despite controversy, the MFA's trustees supported Rogers. One trustee noted, "I don't recall an instance in 10 years where trustees have second-guessed his exhibition ideas. I don't see what he has done as risk-taking. I see it as audience building."[11]

Rogers was responsible to the MFA's 135-person board of overseers. The MFA had a two-part governance structure—the board of overseers and the board of trustees. The board of trustees, with 76 elected, appointed, and honorary members, governed the museum's executive operations and oversaw its operations and programs. The board of overseers assured that the board of trustees was functioning and amended or repealed amendments to the museum's bylaws recommended by the board of trustees. Members of the board were initially drawn to the MFA based on their own interest in collecting or their interest in art. There were several subcommittees with assigned roles and responsibilities, but collectively the board took on a governance role and was active in fund-raising for the museum. In addition, the MFA had developed a museum council of younger people interested in the arts. It was hoped that these individuals would represent a part of the future board.

Toward the end of 2004, the museum formally revisited its strategic plan, creating a new plan entitled New Museum-Great Museum-Your Museum. The new strategic plan established three core components (collections, audience, and exhibitions) and three supporting platforms (facilities, financial, and organization) that made the achievement of the core components possible.

- Collections established a continued need to improve the quality of the collection, improve its management and care, and provide electronic access to the collection.

- Audience (defined as audience development and visitor experience) included the need to engage, educate, and delight visitors as well as retain and expand the audience by better understanding its needs.

- Special exhibitions entailed the creation of an exhibition schedule that met a variety of goals including an intellectual contribution, the attraction of visitors, and revenue generation.

- Facilities focused specifically on the execution of the master plan to enlarge and improve the physical plant of the MFA.

- Financial reiterated the need for fiscal stability and fund-raising that would support facility expansion as well as other strategic needs.

- Organization focused on the adoption of an "audience-aware, results-oriented, experimental attitude and realignment of the organization as needed to support these strategies."

Performance

In the 2004 annual report, the departing treasurer and chairman of the MFA's Budget and Finance Committee remarked on the museum's financial complexity, noting, "The MFA is a business made up of many businesses. We are a museum, a school, a publisher, a retailer, a restaurateur, a film theater, and more, each financially demanding in its own right." (Exhibits 4 and 5 detail the MFA's financial performance.) The MFA's expenditures in 2004 were approximately $81 million. With revenues from program and support of approximately $83 million, the MFA enjoyed a profit of about $2 million. Approximately 44% of the museum's revenues came from operations including membership, admissions, sales of merchandise, and restaurant food sales. Another 24% of revenues were received as school tuition (though slightly more than that figure was spent on the administration of the school). Of the

EXHIBIT 4

MFA BALANCE SHEET ($000s)

Year ended June 30	2000	2001	2002	2003	2004
Assets					
Cash and cash equivalents	9,285	8,603	5,731	10,739	12,181
Short-term investments	6,798	8,433	11,617	23,454	26,741
Net accounts receivable	3,448	1,972	1,828	1,049	1,797
Interest and dividends receivable	711	777	139	22	43
Inventories net of reserve	7,615	7,565	5,531	3,187	1,844
Prepaid expenses	1,769	2,014	1,813	2,316	2,441
Pledges receivable	2,866	9,128	9,605	9,107	20,683
Total current assets	32,492	38,492	36,264	49,874	65,730
Pledges receivable net	10,495	7,303	18,731	23,065	38,914
Investments at market	445,503	414,135	380,104	362,007	408,534
Property, plant and equipment net	84,048	84,300	86,074	91,098	98,289
Assets held for debt service	3,341	4,051	3,977	3,802	3,706
Beneficial interest in perpetual trusts	24,746	24,446	21,800	21,125	22,383
Assets of split-interest agreements	19,189	8,393	8,395	8,693	9,725
Bond issuance costs, net	322	234	146	59	–
Collections	–	–	–	–	–
Other Assets	–	–	–	–	168
Total Assets	620,136	581,354	555,491	559,723	647,449
Liabilities and Net Assets					
Line-of-credit	5,300	7,000	8,400	11,555	2,038
Current portion of long-term debt	2,890	3,025	3,150	3,300	3,475
Interest payable	578	506	445	380	296
Accounts payable	7,011	4,739	4,512	4,020	4,653
Accrued expenses	7,011	7,360	10,923	11,460	7,378
Income taxes payable	–	–	14	13	–
Accrued restructuring costs	5,047	3,724	1,138	750	–
Accrued cost-reduction in force	–	–	–	–	445
Deferred income	3,073	1,034	1,401	1,363	1,780
Total Current Liabilities	30,910	27,388	29,983	32,841	20,065
Liability under split-interest agreements	7,000	2,195	2,970	3,555	4,826
Note payable	–	–	–	500	500
Long-term debt	20,485	17,460	14,310	11,010	7,535
Other Liabilities	–	–	–	–	18
Total Liabilities	58,395	47,043	47,263	47,906	32,944
Commitments and contingencies					
Paid-in capital	–	–	88	37	37
Net assets and accumulated deficit	561,741	534,311	508,140	511,780	614,780
Total net assets and shareholders equity	620,136	581,354	508,228	511,817	614,505
Total Liabilities and net assets	620,136	581,354	555,491	559,723	647,449
Details of net assets and accumulated deficit					
Undesignated	184	(1,028)	(1,204)	(5,871)	(3,608)
Endowment	112,390	119,952	118,264	121,725	176,270
Other funds and functioning as endowment	395,677	357,610	333,274	335,068	368,011
Net investment in plant	53,490	57,777	61,580	66,817	79,754
Accumulated deficient	–	–	(3,774)	(5,959)	(5,959)
Total net assets and accumulated deficit	561,741	534,311	508,140	511,780	614,468

Source: Museum of Fine Arts Boston.

EXHIBIT 5

MFA INCOME STATEMENT ($000s)

Year ended June 30	2000	2001	2002	2003	2004
Support:					
Gifts to annual appeal	4,508	4,639	4,546	4,559	4,958
Contributions, gifts, and grants	237	26	322	423	340
Total Support	4,745	4,665	4,868	4,982	5,298
Program Revenue					
Membership Corporate	925	997	950	934	985
Membership General	8,203	7,431	7,236	6,917	7,719
Tuition—School	16,529	16,669	18,420	20,657	19,855
Admissions	6,455	6,630	4,388	4,069	5,610
Exhibitions	4,218	3,389	3,271	2,167	3,224
Education programs	1,782	1,310	1,366	1,593	1,488
Sales from merchandise operations	38,712	41,224	30,989	17,551	9,706
Beneficial investment in perpetual trust income	771	1,029	953	1,139	1,063
Short-term investment income	605	743	450	368	399
Investment return designated for current operations	8,978	9,554	8,788	9,044	10,380
Funds released from restriction	2,955	7,170	10,632	11,187	9,235
Parking operations	2,654	2,584	2,463	2,599	2,994
Restaurant food service	4,291	5,628	4,922	3,460	2,021
Other ancillary services	2,655	3,468	3,649	3,310	3,644
Total Program revenue	99,733	107,826	98,477	84,995	78,323
Total Support and revenue	104,478	112,491	103,345	89,977	83,621
Expenses					
Program services:					
Exhibitions	6,114	3,948	4,160	4,141	4,179
Collections and curatorial	5,953	6,881	7,736	8,566	9,030
Educational programs	1,504	1,408	1,560	1,724	1,870
Educational services	736	716	773	633	517
Program support	2,110	2,884	2,565	1,681	1,781
Membership activities	1,456	1,479	1,408	1,820	1,782
School program expenses	16,153	17,664	19,332	21,339	20,854
Parking operations	1,378	1,302	1,278	850	841
Restaurant food service	3,309	4,353	4,068	2,612	660
Merchandising operations	42,229	42,545	33,887	20,585	9,030
Other	–	–	1,587	1,124	2,026
Total program services expenses	80,942	83,180	78,354	65,075	52,570
Supporting services:					
Administration	6,692	6,717	7,208	7,514	7,685
Development	3,810	4,172	5,151	5,288	5,706
Public information	4,574	4,233	4,067	3,896	4,325
Facilities	3,600	4,111	4,376	4,086	3,496
Utilities costs	1,447	1,464	1,514	1,436	1,936
Protective services	4,610	3,298	3,736	3,983	4,027
Interest on debt	1,210	1,084	951	826	676
Other	353	438	14	131	156
Total supporting services	26,296	25,517	27,017	27,160	28,007
Total expenses	107,238	108,697	105,371	92,235	80,577
Change in net assets before restructuring and other costs, and provision for income taxes	(2,760)	3,794	(2,026)	(2,258)	3,044
Restructuring, reduction in force and other costs	(6,259)	–	2,198	–	(691)
Provision for income taxes	–	–	(14)	(13)	–
Change in net assets after restructuring costs, other costs and provision for income taxes	(9,019)	3,794	158	(2,271)	2,353

Source: Museum of Fine Arts Boston.

remaining 32% of revenues, 20% came from the support to the MFA through its annual appeal and contributions, gifts, and grants, and 80% from the MFA's investments (short-term investment income, investment return on the endowment that had been designated for current operations, etc.). Following several years of deficit in the 1980s, the board stressed the need for a balanced budget; while not a board policy per se, it was viewed as a directional imperative.

The MFA relied almost exclusively on private funding, receiving only limited funding from government. As Rogers noted, "The MFA is almost certainly the largest privately funded museum in the world, for unlike the other great museums of America, we receive no generous dollars from our city and less than half a percent of our annual income from public sources all told. True, and a great tribute to Bostonian and New England philanthropy." One report found that in 2001–2002, Boston's Office of Cultural Affairs contributed $870,000 to the arts, compared with $5 million given by Dallas's, $14 million by Charlotte's, $28.5 million by Pittsburgh's, and $37 million by San Francisco's.[12]

Over the past five years, there had been significant changes in the way the MFA approached its merchandise sales. In 2001, the museum had established a separate for-profit company, Museum Enterprises Partners (MEP), to replace the in-house museum enterprises division. The museum had run its in-house gift shops since the 1950s and since 1970 produced a gift catalog but by 2001 also had two retail stores (Copley Place and Faneuil Hall), an outlet on Cape Cod, and a 100,000-square-foot warehouse in Avon, Massachusetts, that included a call center. Sales were approximately $40 million—$18 million from the catalog, $18 million from the stores, $2 million from online sales, and $2 million through a wholesale unit.[13] In 2003, having lost $6 million in two years, the MFA bought out the company's managers and eliminated the catalog, the website, and the wholesale business. The enterprise division returned to its origins—offering merchandise for sale at the MFA's on-site gift shops. Based on these changes, the enterprise division earned a profit of $800,000 in 2004 and $1.2 million in 2005.

Under Rogers's guidance, the museum's fiscal responsibilities were well under control; the one pressing issue was the decline in revenue from general admittance. Taken together, the revenue from general and corporate memberships, admissions, and exhibits had declined 15% from 2000 to 2004. This decline had occurred in the context of a "perfect storm" (9/11, a recession, a stock market collapse in 2001, and a large fall-off in tourism), and while the MFA was not the only museum facing this problem, it remained a disturbing trend. From an operating perspective, membership and attendance drove the profitability of other revenue-generating departments such as parking, food service, and merchandise sales. But more importantly, if fewer people were visiting the museum, it raised the question of whether the MFA could achieve the museum's ultimate aim as stated in its mission statement: to encourage and to heighten public understanding and appreciation of the visual world. "Attendance is a key priority for us," said Stanley. "We need to understand if the decline is structural or cyclical. If it is cyclical, time heals economic cycles, but if it is a structural problem we need to make investments to reverse the trend." This was especially important in light of plans to break ground for the "New Museum" with the American wing in November 2005 and open it in 2010.

The Customer Environment

Many perceived Boston as one of the most culturally oriented cities in the U.S. The Greater Boston area had over a dozen significant art museums including urban institutions such as the MFA and the Isabella Stewart Gardner Museum, suburban museums such as the Peabody Essex Museum in Salem and the DeCordova sculpture museum in Lincoln, and university museums such as the Fogg at Harvard and the Davis at Wellesley College. The MFA was the clear market share leader among art museums with a 53% share (of those in the Boston market who had been to an art museum in the past year) compared to the Isabella Stewart Gardner with 16%, the Worcester Art Museum (11%), and the Peabody Essex Museum (10%). All other art museums in the area had a total share less than 7%. The MFA was more than a local museum; it was also ranked in the top 50 museums or cultural attractions in the U.S. and the sixth-most-visited art museum in the nation.[14]

Within Boston, the MFA's competitive set, however, went beyond other art institutions. The other major nonart museums were the Museum of Science, which attracted 1.5 million visitors in 2004, and the New England Aquarium, which had 1.3 million. In addition, the MFA competed with myriad other museums and leisure activities for the scarce discretionary time of Boston's citizens and the packed schedules of Boston's visitors. For residents, a trip to the MFA competed against personal leisure activities at home (reading a book, listening to music, spending time with family) and outside the home (going to a restaurant, shopping, attending a sports event). For visitors to the city, the museum competed with all of Boston's attractions including the Freedom Trail, Faneuil Hall, Fenway Park, and the *U.S.S. Constitution.*

Visitors

The MFA estimated that approximately 37% of its revenues were directly or indirectly related to visitor attendance. When visitors came to the MFA, they could purchase a $15 general admission ticket to the core galleries or a combination ticket that included admission to the core galleries and a special exhibition. This ticket varied in price. For example, a $22 ticket to the forthcoming Ansel Adams exhibition included admission to the exhibition and admission to all of the museum's galleries. On Wednesday evenings the admission fee was "pay as you wish," with the museum offering three free community days each year. Membership rates were $70 for an individual membership and $95 for a dual/family membership. There were additional memberships available up to $2,500, with increased membership privileges at each level. Those with individual memberships received free admission to the MFA's core collection and two admission tickets for special exhibitions. Additionally, members received parking and restaurant discounts. The MFA estimated that approximately

13% of attendance came from adults paying full price and 21% from members. Another 31% of the museum's attendees had free admission (those under 17, university members, and others), and another 35% paid less than the full admission rate (school groups, special admission nights' visitors, students, seniors, etc.). Museum attendance peaked in 1999 at about 1.7 million visitors and fell to 1 million in 2004. Over the same period, member retention rates fell from 79% to 72%. Similarly, special-exhibition attendance fell from 47% of total attendance in 1999 to 34% in 2005.

The MFA launched a three-pronged effort to address the attendance issue:

- Market research to understand the customer and thereby retain and expand the audience

- Analysis of special exhibitions

- Visitor intercepts to understand visitors' experience once they arrived at the MFA and thereby better retain them

Indeed, these efforts represented key initiatives in achieving the audience goals stated in the strategic plan.

Retaining and Expanding the Audience

There were two major groups of visitors to the MFA: residents in the Greater Boston area and visitors to the city. While the museum recognized that the MFA would not often drive a visit to Boston, they believed they could do more to bring visitors to the museum once in Boston.

To better understand the MFA's existing and potential audience, in December 2004, the MFA conducted a market research study with an Internet panel of 300 adults living in the Boston area (demographics of the Boston market are summarized in Exhibit 6). The study sought to determine the size of the potential market for art museums and confirm the hypothesis that a significant opportunity existed to grow the audience. The study defined six customer segments. Segments one and two consisted of those that either would not consider visiting an art museum or did not currently visit and were unlikely to do so in the future. These segments represented 21% and 5% of the population, respectively. Segments three through six were composed of people with varying levels of intent to visit an art museum. In segment three, respondents considered visiting art museums (23%) but ultimately ended up not attending; those in segment four visited less than once a year (32%); segment five consisted of those who visited every six months or so (13%); and in segment six were respondents who visited more than once over a six-month period (6%).

In March 2005, the MFA commissioned a follow-up research study Internet panel of 1,516 adults who represented the Boston area and belonged to segment three or higher (would at least consider attending an art museum). The goal was to probe their attitudes and behaviors about leisure-time activities, art museum attendance in general, and specifically perceptions of the MFA. The study found that less than 35% of the potential audience visited an art museum (based on those who had participated in a given activity several times a year or more) and less than 20% visited the MFA.

EXHIBIT 6

BOSTON MARKET DEMOGRAPHICS

POPULATION 2004	5,749,197	
AGE		Percent
5 to 19 years	1,113,863	19.4
20 to 24 years	333,761	5.8
25 to 34 years	791,051	13.8
35 to 44 years	978,405	17.0
45 to 54 years	877,699	15.3
55 to 59 years	359,210	6.2
60 to 64 years	238,762	4.2
65 to 74 years	342,562	6.0
75 to 84 years	256,548	4.5
85 years and over	84,144	1.5
RACE		
White	4,922,258	85.6
Black or African American	354,512	6.2
American Indian and Alaska Native	31,267	0.5
Asian	300,004	5.2
Native Hawaiian and Other Pacific Islander	n/a	n/a
Some other race	213,762	3.7
Population 25 years and over	**3,928,381**	
Less than 9th grade	167,630	4.3
9th to 12th grade, no diploma	276,576	7.0
High school graduate (including equivalency)	1,071,186	27.3
Some college, no degree	604,818	15.4
Associate degree	291,171	7.4
Bachelor's degree	899,647	22.9
Graduate or professional degree	617,353	15.7
Percent high school graduate or higher		88.7
Percent bachelor's degree or higher		38.6
Total households	**2,232,151**	
Less than $35,000	637,456	28.6
$35,000 to $49,999	295,513	13.2
$50,000 to $74,999	431,169	19.3
$75,000 to $99,999	313,464	14.0
$100,000 to $149,999	331,736	14.9
$150,000 to $199,999	106,646	4.8
$200,000 or more	108,034	4.8
Median household income (dollars)	58,918	
Mean household income (dollars)	77,531	

Note: Results based on the Boston-Worcester—Lawrence, MA—NH—ME—CT consolidated metropolitan statistical area (CMSA). A CMSA is a geographic entity defined by the federal Office of Management and Budget for use by federal statistical agencies. An area becomes a CMSA if it meets the requirements to qualify as a metropolitan statistical area, it has a population of 1 million or more, component parts are recognized as primary metropolitan statistical areas, and local opinion favors the designation.

Source: U.S. Census Bureau, Fact Finder, www.factfinder.census.gov.

(Exhibit 7 summarizes the range of leisure pursuits.) Generally, the study found that respondents tended to be largely white (mirroring the Boston market) and well educated and liked to learn. Those who frequented art museums more regularly were more passionate about learning, were more likely to have attended art museums as children, and were more avid readers (generally they were more active people engaged in many different activities). (Exhibit 8 provides a summary of findings.) The study recommended a two-tiered approach that would increase repeat visits, especially among segment four patrons, and a longer-term strategy to attract segment three people to the museum.

In addition to Boston-area residents, the MFA estimated that over 300,000 tourists visited the MFA in 2003, representing about 30% of total museum attendees. Approximately 40% of tourists were from the Northeast; about half were repeat visitors (had visited the MFA within the past year). Another 35% of tourist visitors were domestic visitors outside of the Northeast; about 30% were repeat visitors. Another 30% of tourists were international; 25% of this group were repeat visitors. The demographics of he MFA's tourist visitors closely matched those of its core patrons—high average incomes (in excess of $75,000), predominantly white, and traveling without children.

Special Exhibitions

Interesting special exhibitions were seen as a significant driver of a visit to the MFA. While art museums had always had special exhibitions, generally speaking, the era of the "blockbuster exhibition" began with the King Tut exhibit in the 1970s and continued on with exhibitions such as "Van Gogh's Van Goghs," which attracted 821,000 visitors at the Los Angeles County Museum of Art. The MFA's most successful exhibition (in terms of attendance) was Monet, which had brought 566,000 visitors to the MFA and was highly successful on the road. It was one of the leading exhibitions ever held at the Royal Academy in London, where it drew 739,000 visitors. Yet with the exception of exceptional years and exhibitions, special-exhibition attendance remained erratic. The MFA, however, did not expect every special exhibition to be an attendance blockbuster. The MFA mounted about a dozen special exhibitions annually, knowing that many of the exhibitions lacked broad attendance appeal but offered substantive artistic merit and opportunities for learning. For example, the MFA's exhibition of Meiji prints drew only 36,000 visitors but was both exquisite and scholarly.

Special exhibitions were also perceived as a way for the MFA to increase its accessibility to new audiences. The "Art of the Guitar" exhibition brought 140,000 visitors to the museum. The Ritts exhibition brought over 250,000 visitors. In the summer of 2005, the MFA reached out to a male audience with its exhibition "Speed, Style, and Beauty: Cars from the Ralph Lauren Collection." With a goal of 140,000 attendees, the MFA also reached out beyond its traditional media—taking out ads in *Sports Illustrated*, *Car Collector,* and *Sports Car Market.* It also promoted the exhibition with car clubs, inviting car-club members to a black-tie gala and offering "hoods-up" nights, during which hoods of the cars would be lifted and what was under the hood could be viewed. When the exhibition concluded, 197,000 people had seen it, making

EXHIBIT 7   LIKELY ART MUSEUM ATTENDANCE

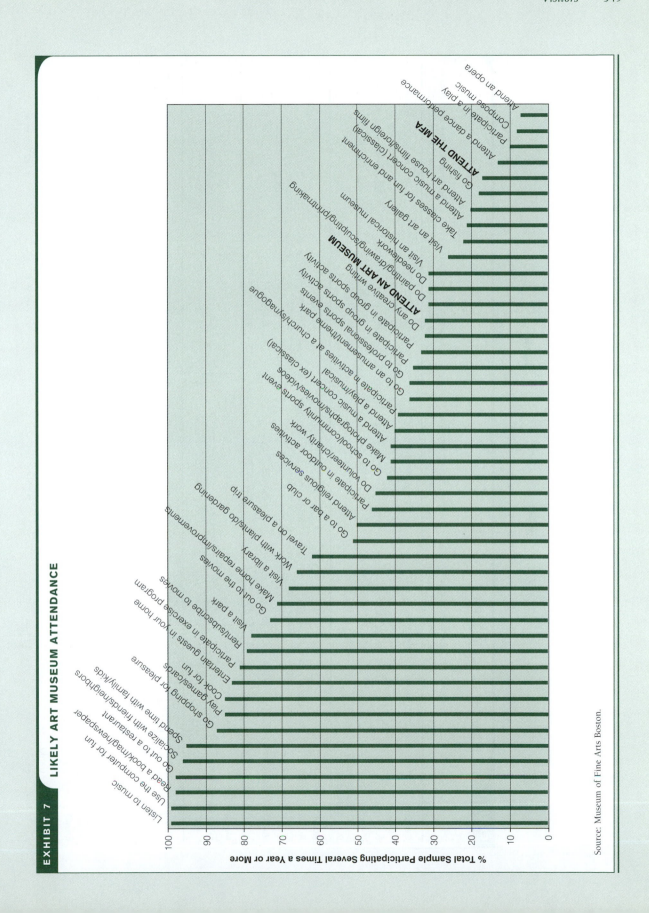

Source: Museum of Fine Arts Boston.

EXHIBIT 8   SEGMENT DESCRIPTIONS

	(Segment 3) Considered/did not attend (23%)	(Segment 4) Visit less than 1/year (32%)	(Segment 5) Visits every 6 months (13%)	(Segment 6) More than once in six months (6%)
Gender	42% male/58% female	41% male/59% female	48% male/52% female	48% male/52% female
Age	49% over 45	54% over 45	54% over 45	67% over 45
Education	74% some college or more	90% some college or more	91% some college or more	92% some college or more
Income (% over $100K)	11%	17%	22%	23%
% Without children in household	62%	70%	72%	70%
Activity score	1,896	2,246	2,819	3,086
Activities (Top 5)	Computer, listen to music, read, restaurant, time with family/kids	Listen to music, restaurant, computer, read, time with family/kids	Restaurant, computer, listen to music, read, socialize with friends or neighbors	Listen to music, read, computer, socialize with friends or neighbors, restaurant
Visit Art Museum (rank)	#44 out of 45	#36 out of 45	#16 out of 45	#7 out of 45
Visit Art Gallery (rank)	#42 out of 45	#38 out of 45	#19 out of 45	#14 out of 45
Media score	473	571	734	951
Top 5 publications	Community paper, Globe, Herald, Good Housekeeping, Providence Journal	Globe, Community paper, Herald, USA Today, Good Housekeeping	Globe, Community paper, Time, Newsweek, National Geographic	Globe, Community paper, National Geographic, New York Times, Boston Magazine
Attitudes (top 5)	Family single most important thing; Financial security very important; Rather spend quite evening at home than go to party; More important to understand inner self than be famous, powerful, or wealthy; Like to learn even if of no use	Family single most important thing; Financial security very important; Like to learn about things even if they may be of no use; Like to learn about art, culture, history; Most important to understand inner self than to be famous, powerful, or wealthy	Like to learn about art, culture, history; Like to learn about things even if they may be of no use; Financial security very important; Family single most important thing; More important to understand inner self than to be famous, powerful, or wealthy	Like to learn about art, culture, history; Like to learn about things even if they may be of no use; Financial security very important; Like doing things that are new and different; Like lot of variety in life
Visited art museums growing up (rank)	#40 out of 46	#30 out of 46	#21 out of 46	#12 out of 46
Like to learn about art, culture, history (rank)	#15 out of 46	#4 out of 46	#1 out of 46	#1 out of 46
Like to learn even if no use (rank)	#5 out of 46	#3 out of 46	#2 out of 46	#2 out of 46

MFA perceptions (top 5)	Is high quality; Gives me opportunity to learn; Is something anyone can enjoy; Intellectually stimulating experience; Is for old people	Is high quality; Gives me opportunity to learn; Intellectually stimulating experience; Is boring; Is something anyone can enjoy	Is high quality; Gives me opportunity to learn; Intellectually stimulating experience; Is boring; Is a place where I feel comfortable	Is high quality; Gives me opportunity to learn; Intellectually stimulating experience; Is a place where I feel comfortable: Is something anyone can enjoy
MFA gives opportunity to learn (rank)	#2 out of 23	#2 out of 23	#2 out of 23	#2 out of 23
Place where feel comfortable (rank)	#19 out of 23	#8 out of 23	#5 out of 23	#4 out of 23
Is intimidating (rank)	#17 out of 23	#14 out of 23	#16 out of 23	#19 out of 23
Motivations/ Decisions to Visit				
Came to the MFA to see something specific in the main galleries		27%	41%	46%
I was the main decision-maker to visit an art museum		29%	39%	56%
Advance Planning				
Spur of moment		28%	17%	29%
A few days		34%	41%	39%
A week or more		38%	42%	33%

Activity score is a sum of responses across all activities that constitute several times a year or more. Top 5 activities based on several times a year. Media score is sum of respondents who report reading on survey list.

Source: Museum of Fine Arts Boston.

EXHIBIT 9

MFA SPECIAL EXHIBITIONS–RANKED BY ATTENDANCE

Gund Exhibitions	Attendance	Fiscal Year
Monet in the 20th Century	565,992	1999
John Singer Sargent	318,707	2000
Van Gogh: Face to Face	316,049	2001
Picasso: the Early Years 1892–1906	283,423	1998
Herb Ritts: Work	253,649	1997
Gauguin—Tahiti	241,124	2004
Mary Cassatt: Modern Woman	230,750	1999
Pharaohs of the Sun: Akhenaten, Nefertiti, Tutankhamen	209,344	2000
Speed, Style and Beauty: Cars from the Ralph Lauren Collection	197,000	2005
Impressionist Still Life	179,416	2002
Gauguin and the School of Pont-Aven	162,856	1997
Art Deco: 1910–1939	154,935	2005
Dangerous Curves: Art of the Guitar	140,217	2001
Rembrandt's Journey: Painter–Draftsman–Etcher	140,085	2004
Impressions of Light	137,616	2003
Tales from the Land of Dragons: 1,000 Years of Chinese Paintings	120,754	1997
American Folk	81,636	2001
Edward Weston: Photography and Modernism	76,088	2000
Jasper Johns to Jeff Koons: Four Decades of Art from the Broad Collection	75,694	2003
The Look: Images of Glamour and Style	75,655	2002
Thomas Gainsborough, 1727–1788	74,884	2004
A Grand Design: The Art of the Victoria and Albert Museum	71,889	1998

Source: Museum of Fine Arts Boston.

---

it the ninth-best-attended Gund Gallery show. (Exhibit 9 ranks the MFA's special exhibitions in the Gund Gallery in terms of attendance. Exhibits 10 and 11 provide images from the Ritts and Ralph Lauren Cars exhibitions, respectively.)

The unpredictability of special-exhibition attendance made it difficult to create reliable revenue forecasts for the MFA. In 2005, Courtney Cole, director of strategic research and analysis, began building a two-stage model that would first predict special-exhibition attendance levels and then its financial contribution. Attendance levels were predicted based on survey information and the advertising budget associated with a given exhibit. Specifically, the MFA used a museum intercept survey to determine the percentage of people who would be extremely likely to attend an exhibition (based on a general description provided as part of the survey), given the opportunity.

The next stage of the model calculated contribution based on projected revenues and costs. On the revenue side, the model incorporated direct revenue (such as admissions, sponsorships if any, and audio guides) and allocated ancillary revenues (such as parking, food, and membership revenues). On the cost side, the model again incorporated both direct and indirect costs. Direct costs included expenses associated with items loaned to the MFA from other art institutions (shipping, crating,

EXHIBIT 10   IMAGES FROM "HERB RITTS: WORK" EXHIBITION

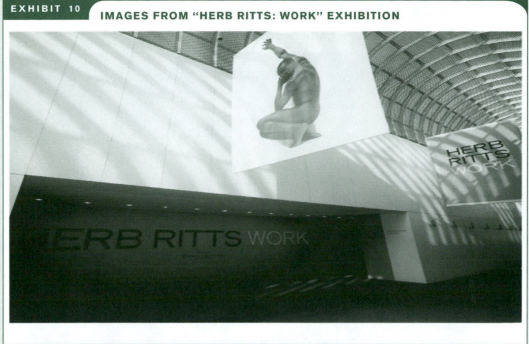

Source: Museum of Fine Arts Boston.

insurance), costs to mount the exhibition (carpentry, photography, conservation), sponsorship event costs, and direct salary expenses (temporary staff, additional guards, consultants). While the model remained under development, early indications suggested a predictive value of over 80%. Notably, however, the predictive model was but one of several criteria the MFA used in determining its special-exhibition

EXHIBIT 11 **IMAGES FROM "SPEED, STYLE, AND BEAUTY: CARS FROM THE RALPH LAUREN COLLECTION"**

Source: Museum of Fine Arts Boston.

schedule. Other factors included intellectual contribution, curatorial interest and support, artistic importance and merit, and the opportunity to work with and cultivate donors.

A significant issue for the museum was how and when to reach both local visitors and those attending special exhibitions. Kim French noted, "I believe the MFA and museums generally do an excellent job marketing special exhibitions in newspapers, magazines, and other media, but as a whole we are less able to reach out to visitors and create the awareness of a visit to the MFA as a viable option in their overly extended personal leisure time."

Visitor Experience

One of the MFA's goals was to engage, educate, and delight visitors. Achieving this goal was integral to repeat visits to the museum. To attack the problem, the MFA commissioned visitor-experience research. The museum prerecruited 31 visitors (15 members and 16 individuals who had not visited the MFA within a two-year period). The visitors were observed by eight trained observers in teams of two. With the goal of training MFA staff to conduct their own observations, each team consisted of one MFA staff member and one consultant. Findings and ideas were then generated in debriefing sessions. The research revealed some key deficiencies in the visitor's experience in the museum. The most important finding was that visitors had a very difficult time navigating their way through the museum. They found the entrance disorienting and unwelcoming and experienced difficulty in getting maps from the information desk (both finding the desk and waiting in line for help were issues). Some visited the MFA with a specific purpose in mind—these individuals experienced frustration with the time it took to locate an exhibit. Others visited the museum without a specific purpose. These visitors felt overwhelmed by the scale and complexity of the museum, and the museum failed to help them make choices. Once in the galleries, visitors again became disoriented and found a dearth of directions to assist them. The galleries seemed lacking in a logical layout (e.g., chronological) that would intuitively assist them in navigating the museum.

Compounding the challenge was that infrequent visitors had the least ability to navigate the museum and were often those in most need of support, as they tended to be less familiar with the art. They were also most likely to be intimidated by the museum and were uncertain of what was "appropriate museum behavior."

The study also found that visitors approached the museum and art differently. Some visitors never read the labels associated with a particular artwork, others skimmed the materials, and others read every label. Similarly, some visitors glanced at the art while others studied it closely. However, most visitors wanted to be able to plan and direct (redirect) their own visit, without heavy reliance on a map or a guided tour.

Visitors were favorably impressed by galleries that combined mixed media (for example, paintings and furniture), with some visitors noting that they had never visited the furniture galleries but really liked the juxtaposition of the two media, which had deepened their appreciation of both. Visitors were also curious in learning more about a particular piece (the artist, techniques, or the story behind a piece), the museum (role of the curator, collections in storage, or conservation techniques), and museum operations (the need to limit light, climate-control devices, or touching art works).

The museum put together a cross-functional team, called the Your Museum Team (in the spirit of the strategic plan), that consisted of staff from curatorial, communications, museum learning, membership/visitor services, HR, strategic research and analysis, and protective services. Focused on initiatives related to orientation, customer service, and on-site communications, the team undertook numerous initiatives such as hiring two visitor services representatives who provided phone coverage and enhanced customer service, the installation of 15 "You are Here" signs at critical decision-making points throughout the museum to help orient visitors, and the development and installation of signs to better direct visitors to amenities such as restrooms, elevators, and restaurants. A secret-shopper program was initiated to monitor customer service levels. In the next fiscal year, the team planned to focus on four key areas: staff training and recognition, on-site communications, interpretation of art in the galleries, and measurement of visitor satisfaction.

Building the New MFA

In February 2002, the MFA unveiled its new master plan. The first phase of the master plan had several components, the most visible of which was the construction of a new east wing intended to house the MFA's Art of the America collection, effectively expanding gallery space for the collection by 50%. The new wing called for four floors of gallery space including learning galleries and a restaurant. Pavilions on either side of the central building had two floors of gallery space, as well as a 150-seat auditorium, classrooms, and offices. A glass-enclosed walkway was planned to create easy access between the American galleries and the museum's major collections.

The existing major special-exhibition gallery, the Gund Gallery, on the second floor of the west wing, was to be converted to house the Contemporary Art collection, effectively increasing that collection's space by 200%. The Gund Gallery would remain a special-exhibitions venue but would be relocated to a new space beneath the east courtyard. By the completion of phase one, the MFA expected to physically grow by 27%, from 531,000 sq. ft. to 677,000 sq. ft. In announcing the new building, Rogers noted that the new MFA would be a "landmark building for the city of Boston that makes a strong statement about the value of contemporary art and builds bridges to our surrounding community and audiences that have not been served."

At the time of the announcement, the MFA launched a $425 million fund-raising campaign to support phase one of its master site plan. In September, the fund-raising goal was raised to $500 million. The museum had designated $305 million to establish a building and renovation fund that included construction costs as well as expenses for art relocation and reinstallation, professional fees, and improved landscaping of the grounds. Another $140 million was designated to endow programs and staff positions, with the remaining $65 million to support museum operations and project contingencies.

Notwithstanding the challenges, under Jacoby's stewardship, the capital campaign had proven effective. In July 2005, having raised $245 million through the work of the external relations department and the generosity of MFA donors, the museum announced the end of its quiet phase of development. By September, $302 million had been raised, a figure that included 76 donations of more than $1 million, 14 gifts of $5 million or more, and $6.2 million through a federal government grant.

As museum director Malcolm Rogers walked through the museum, he noted:

This is a unique moment in the museum's history. We are building a new wing to house our American collection. Not only will this showcase our extraordinary collection, it will allow us to reorganize our existing collections and exhibit many pieces that have been in storage due to a lack of exhibit space. We will undoubtedly get focus and attention in 2010 when the new wing opens, but we need to develop a strategy that will allow us to take full advantage of the opening and then carry us forward once the focus has shifted away.

"But even as we get closer to the big event, we need to make progress on improving our core attendance," remarked Rogers. "We are bound to have cycles that correlate with the economy, but the secular trend should be pointing upwards." This concern was especially important given the experience of museums around the country that were also facing overall declines in attendance. As the MFA's leadership team assembled in the museum's conference room, the critical questions on their mind were: What do we do about attendance? When and how should we go about fixing the problem?

G.I. JOE: Marketing an Icon

Billy Lagor, Hasbro's brand manager for G.I. JOE, grinned broadly as he gazed about his office. Every square inch of wall space was covered with shelves that contained G.I. JOE action figure toys, accessories, vehicles, and other "G.I. JOE" paraphernalia. It was a young boy's dream, and it was Lagor's dream as well. "This is a great job for someone who has energy and capacity because you can really add value to the company," said Lagor (HBS '03). "But because we're small and lean, we have to be thoughtful about where to focus our resources."

In the winter of 2003, Lagor faced a set of decisions that would ultimately determine the 2004 marketing plan for the G.I. JOE brand. Under consideration were three different ways to market the military action figure:

- *Use Traditional Media.* This option would involve marketing Hasbro's G.I. JOE line the same way that most classic toys were marketed—using traditional forms of marketing. The marketing mix would rely heavily on television advertising (particularly in the Saturday morning hours), print, and ongoing product innovation. The plan would also focus on maintaining strong relationships with Hasbro's biggest retail partners.

- *Supplement Traditional Media with Limited Entertainment.* This option would involve supplementing traditional forms of marketing with a limited entertainment component. Specifically, the team was considering producing and launching a short, animated DVD—perhaps bundled with G.I. JOE merchandise—to sustain interest in the action figure.

- *Use Non-Traditional Forms of Marketing.* This option would involve embracing a number of non-traditional forms of marketing, such as DVDs, video games, trading cards, books, and even a full-length feature film. In recent years, some of the most high-profile brands in the boys' toys category had achieved blockbuster sales by flooding the market with multiple forms of entertainment. Pokémon was the most obvious example; licensed brands such as Harry Potter and Star Wars had also benefited from these types of product synergies.

As Lagor reflected on the various options, he remarked:

> *In making this decision, there are several things we need to consider. First, we need to determine the long-term strategy for the brand and figure out which approach would best deliver that strategy. This involves making sure we understand the trade-offs—the risks and rewards—associated with each one of the options. A big part of the decision boils down to, what type of brand is G.I. JOE today, and what type of brand do we want it to become? We also need to focus on execution, in particular, weighing the changing dynamics in the category, retail environment, and kids market. We can develop the greatest strategy in the world, but if we aren't capable of executing well, it won't do us a bit of good.*

Lagor also recognized how high the stakes were for Hasbro. G.I. JOE was one of the company's most well-known brands, and as caretaker of the brand, he knew how important it was to get it right. "For a lot of people in this country—everyone from little boys to full-grown men—G.I. JOE is an icon," said Lagor. "And because kids' tastes come and go in this industry, when you have a brand that has demonstrated any kind of longevity, you want to be sure you're maximizing the brand over the long term. The question is: are we taking full advantage of the brand potential of G.I. JOE?"

The Toy Industry

The $20.9 billion toy industry included everything from crayons to stuffed animals. Historically, the industry had grown by 5% to 7% each year; however, the category had only been up 1% in 2003, and analysts were projecting no more than 2% to 3% growth in the near future. Some sub-categories within the industry were doing better than others; for example, the games/puzzles sub-category was booming, while the outdoor and sports sub-category was stagnant. (please see Exhibit 1).

In 2003, the industry was led by two companies, Hasbro and Mattel. Ten years ago, these two companies had accounted for a combined 15% of the toy category; by 2003, they had increased their share to 40%. (please refer to Exhibit 2). Much of this share capture had come through acquisitions in the 1980s and 1990s; however, the pace and scale of acquisitions had slowed in recent years.

Aside from Hasbro and Mattel, there was tremendous fragmentation in the market, with dozens of smaller companies constantly jockeying for market share. The cumulative share of the top 10 brands had steadily decreased over time (please see Exhibit 3), and one brand's gain almost always came at another brand's loss. For example, in recent years, the success of MGA Entertainment's Bratz doll had come at the expense of Mattel's Barbie franchise. Similarly, the blockbuster success of the Yu-Gi-Oh franchise had occurred at the expense of other properties in the 6-to-11 year-old age group for boys, such as Pokémon and Harry Potter.

EXHIBIT 1

TOY MARKET: GROWTH AND DECLINE IN SELECT SUB-CATEGORIES

Sub-Category	$ Volume (mm), 2003	Change in $ Volume (2003 vs. 2002)	% Change
Games/Puzzles	$2,466	$511	26%
Arts & Crafts	$2,368	$310	15%
Infant/Preschool	$2,843	$110	4%
Learning & Exploration	$494	$105	27%
Trading Cards & Accessories	$240	−$11	−5%
Action Figures & Accessories	$1,291	−$63	−5%
Dolls	$2,598	−$119	−4%
Plush	$1,397	−$120	−8%
Building Sets	$713	−$124	−15%
Vehicles	$2,080	−$194	−9%
Outdoor & Sports Toys	$2,357	−$292	−11%

Source: Adapted from "Traditional Toy Overview: 2002 and First-Half 2003," prepared for Hasbro by NPD Group. Note: 2003 data refers to August 2002 to July 2003. 2002 data refers to August 2001 to July 2002.

"There's no question that this is a tough market," said Lagor, "and it's only getting tougher. There's so much seasonality in this category to begin with—a huge percentage of our sales take place during the fourth quarter holiday season. But now there's a lot of pressure on margins as well." One reason for this was that competition for shelf space had become increasingly severe, as toy distribution was now heavily concentrated with retail giants such as Wal-Mart and Target. In 2003, for example, Wal-Mart and Target accounted for over 50% of Hasbro sales; the top five retailers accounted for over 75%. In this context, retailer relationships were key. "Because we've got a strong historical track record and because we manage a lot of leading brands, this gives us some leverage in terms of placement in the stores," noted Lagor. "On the other

EXHIBIT 2

TOY MANUFACTURERS: MARKET SHARE (2003)

Toy Manufacturer	U.S. Market Share	Worldwide Market Share
Mattel	22%	18.2%
Hasbro	16%	11%
Leapfrog	3%	3%
MGA	2%	1.6%
Other	57%	66.2%

Source: Adapted from multiple sources, including J.P. Morgan, "Toy Industry 101: 2004 Edition." and "Traditional Toy Overview" prepared for Hasbro by NPD Group.

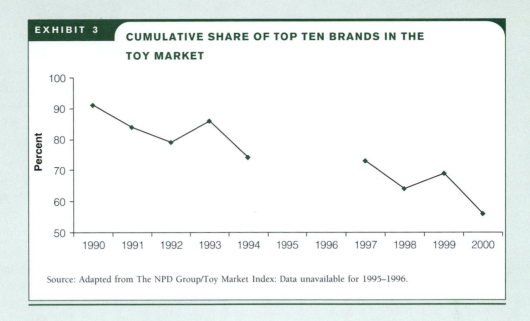

EXHIBIT 3

CUMULATIVE SHARE OF TOP TEN BRANDS IN THE TOY MARKET

Source: Adapted from The NPD Group/Toy Market Index: Data unavailable for 1995–1996.

hand, the retailers have imposed a lot of price pressure on the market, and we've felt that too."

Meanwhile, product lifecycles within the industry were getting shorter. Close to 70% of industry sales were driven by toys released in the previous 3 to 4 years (please see Exhibit 4). Between 1982 and 2001, there were roughly 50 boys' brands that reached $10 million in sales but did not last three years. Conversely, in the same period, only seven brands lasted over 8 years: G.I. JOE, *Star Wars*, TRANSFORMERS, Power Rangers, Teenage Mutant Ninja Turtles, Masters of the Universe, and World Wrestling Federation. Lagor explained:

> *There are lots of factors behind the shrinking product lifecycles we've seen in this industry. One factor has to do with something called "age compression."*

EXHIBIT 4

PERCENT OF DOLLAR SALES IN 2003, BY PRODUCT INTRODUCTION YEAR (SKUS)

	% of Dollar Sales in 2003
Toys introduced in 2003	18%
Toys introduced in 2002	21%
Toys introduced in 2001	17%
Toys introduced in 2000	11%
Toys introduced in 1999	9%
Toys introduced 1996–1998	12%
Toys introduced 1991–1995	9%
Toys introduced before 1990	3%

Source: Adapted from the NPD Group/NPD Funworld/Consumer Panel.

It used to be that kids would play with toys until they hit 10 or 12-years of age. But nowadays, we see a lot of kids abandoning toys at a much earlier age—say, 7 or 8 years old—because they're more interested in playing with video games and computers.[1] This means that if you're selling something like an action figure, you've got a much smaller window of time in which to target these kids. And then even if you manage to grab their attention, it's difficult to sustain that attention for a long period of time before they've moved on to more mature forms of entertainment.

Another factor has to do with how toys are purchased nowadays. Today, there are so many toys for kids to choose from, that the volume has turned up on the "nag factor." Kids are playing an increasingly large role in decision-making when it comes to purchasing toys. This has had a lot of implications for the toy industry because when an adult chooses a toy, they tend to choose something classic, like PLAY-DOH modeling compound or MR. POTATO HEAD. But when a kid chooses a toy, they tend to choose whatever's hot that day.

How Toys Were Marketed

As the industry had evolved, the ways in which companies marketed toys had evolved as well. Prior to the 1980s, most toy manufacturers had adopted a traditional consumer goods approach to marketing toys. The focus had been on developing classic toy brands with long-term staying power—brands like Crayola crayons, PLAY-DOH, MR. POTATO HEAD, and Slinky. These toys had been marketed in a traditional, formulaic fashion. Advertising had typically consisted of TV spots shown primarily during Saturday morning cartoon shows, coupled with print advertisements. In addition, manufacturers would work with their multiple retail partners to gain shelf space and point-of-sale support.

During the 1980s and 1990s, however, the runaway success of properties like the Cabbage Patch Kids had led manufacturers to shift their emphasis toward discovering, producing, and launching the next big "hit." Rather than market these hits in such a way as to achieve long-term staying power, manufacturers had positioned them with the goal of creating a short-term "must have" attitude among kids that would spike sales over the holiday season. As blockbusters such as Teenage Mutant Ninja Turtles and Power Rangers began to dominate the toy scene, "evergreen" brands like PLAY-DOH received less attention. Of course, fads were a double-edged sword for toymakers; while they drove sales and earning to new heights, they could also be cause for disappointment when they went from being hits to being duds.

Some of the biggest successes during this era had included licensed properties; in this regard, the 1990s had been a decade in which licensing played an increasingly large role in the toy industry. "The conventional wisdom is that more than 90% of new products fail in this market," remarked Lagor, "so the nice thing about acquiring a license is that you know you're getting a property that kids are already familiar with, that they already have an emotional connection to. You still need strong R&D and marketing, but you don't have to build a brand from scratch. The downside is, you don't own the intellectual property, so you not only have to pay for use of the brand, you've also got less control over the direction of the brand."

In a typical licensing deal, the manufacturer would pay an upfront lump sum for the license, in addition to ongoing royalties. Competition for movie and animation licenses was significant; this often resulted in fierce bidding wars between the various toy manufacturers. As a result, by the late-1990s, licensing fees had risen to as high as 20% of sales and minimum royalty guarantees had shifted much of the risk to the manufacturer. This was in spite of the fact that movies were lasting for shorter periods of time at the box office, shortening the selling period for toys.

By the end of the 1990s, the line between toys and other forms of entertainment—movies, television shows, video games, etc.—had become nearly impossible to distinguish, as toymakers had become more reliant than ever on the entertainment industry as a source for intellectual property. It was now standard practice for a new movie release (e.g., Spider Man) to be accompanied by licensed toys and other merchandise, and the sales of these products were heavily dependent on the success with which the movies were marketed.

At the same time, toy manufacturers were also actively seeking to produce new forms of entertainment as a way to boost interest in their existing toy franchises. Often, this entertainment was packaged in the form of in-pack or direct-to-video DVDs. For example, Mattel had recently begun creating DVDs designed to strengthen sales of its Barbie line in the face of heavy competition from Bratz—and in the process had sold an average 3 million units per title.

Lagor remarked:

We've done a lot of market research on this, and we think the entertainment component is particularly important when it comes to boys' toys. Boys have different play patterns than girls. Girls will invent storylines about their dolls or their stuffed animals on their own, based on what they've observed in everyday situations. Boys are much less likely to do this. They need someone to give them a storyline, along with information about the characters, the action figures, and the context, in order to maintain interest in the toys. That's one reason why we're considering increasing the entertainment component in the marketing of the G.I. JOE brand.

Hasbro, Inc.

Hasbro was the nation's second-largest toymaker, responsible for such popular toy and game brands as TONKA, PLAYSKOOL, and Monopoly. (Please see Exhibit 5 for a list of Hasbro's selected brands and products.) The company was founded in 1923, when Henry and Helal Hassenfeld had formed Hassenfeld Brothers to distribute fabric remnants. By the 1940s, the company had expanded into toys, and in 1952, it became the first company to use television to advertise a toy, MR. POTATO HEAD.

During the 1950s and 60s, MR. POTATO HEAD was joined by a number of other successful product launches, including LITE-BRITE, and G.I. JOE. The marketing plan

---

EXHIBIT 5   **HASBRO: SELECTED BRANDS AND PRODUCTS**

Games and Puzzles

Milton Bradley	Battleship
	Yahtzee
	Scrabble
	Twister
Parker Brothers	Clue
	Monopoly
	Trivial Pursuit
	Risk
Tiger Electronics	Furby
	VideoNow
	Hitclips
Wizards of the Coast	Dungeons and Dragons
	Harry Potter Trading Cards
	Magic: The Gathering
	NeoPets
Boys' Toys	BeyBlade
	G.I. JOE
	Transformers
	Star Wars action figures
	Tonka
Preschool Toys	Playskool
	Mr. Potato Head
Creative Play	Easy-Bake Oven
	Lite-Brite
	Play-Doh
	Spirograph
	Tinkertoys
Girls' Toys	My Little Pony
	Raggedy Ann and Raggedy Andy
Other	Super Soaker water products
	Nerf (soft play toys)
	Shrek 2 toys

Source: Hasbro.

---

for these products was based primarily on television advertising, coupled with careful management of Hasbro's many retail partners. Although not all of Hasbro's toy launches were successful, the toys that did achieve popularity tended to become company mainstays. Moreover, success tended to breed success—as Hasbro accumulated a growing portfolio of popular toys, it became easier for the company to achieve stable revenues, to negotiate with retail partners, and to launch product extensions.

In 1968, the firm went public and changed its name to Hasbro Industries, and by 1980, Hasbro's new CEO Stephen Hassenfeld, grandson of one of the founders, had taken over leadership of the company. During the 1980s, Hasbro concentrated on beefing up its toy and game portfolio by targeting specific children's markets. Some of these toys were developed internally; examples included the highly successful G.I. JOE 3.75″ relaunch and MY LITTLE PONY, one of the hottest girls' toys of the decade. Other toys were added to the Hasbro product portfolio through acquisitions. Popular board games such as THE GAME OF LIFE and CANDYLAND, for example, were added when Hasbro acquired Milton Bradley and its preschool division, PLAYSKOOL.

When Stephen Hassenfeld passed away in 1989, his brother Alan took over as Chairman and CEO of the company. Under his guidance, the acquisitions continued apace. Some of the most prominent of these included:

- *Tonka* (cars and trucks), which owned *Parker Brothers* (board games and puzzles including MONOPOLY and TRIVIAL PURSUIT) and *Kenner* (action figures, creative play, girls toys)

- *OddzOn Products* (sports toys, KOOSH balls)

- *Tiger Electronics* (FURBY, GIGAGAPETS)

- *Galoob Toys* (MICRO MACHINES)

- *Wizards of the Coast* (Pokémon and MAGIC: THE GATHERING trading card games)[2]

During the 1990s, the company was also able to successfully outbid other toy manufacturers for a number of high-profile licenses, including the rights to produce all action figures and games for the Star Wars prequels, toys and games related to select Disney television and movie properties,[3] and NFL-related toys and games. By the end of the decade, Hasbro's licenses accounted for a full 25% of the company's revenue, despite the fact that these licenses represented just a tiny fraction of the total number of brands in Hasbro's brand portfolio.

In many respects, the aggressive acquisition and licensing strategy paid off. Whereas Hasbro had been just a $100 million (sales) player with single-digit market share in the early 1980s, twenty years later, it was a $3 billion player with 16% market share. (Please refer to Exhibit 6 for the firm's income statement and Exhibit 7 for a breakdown of revenues by selected products.)

But in other respects, the strategy had come at a cost. When Hasbro had sealed the Star Wars deal in 1997, for example, the company had agreed to $590 million in royalty guarantees. The end result was that Hasbro had been left with more than $100 million in unsold Star Wars inventory in 2000. Even the company's most successful hits had come at a price. For example, the Wizards of the Coast acquisition had given Hasbro the Pokémon trading card property, with blockbuster results: In 2000, Pokémon had accounted for a significant portion of Hasbro game revenues, and had helped propel the company to $3.8 billion in revenues. A year later, however, demand for Pokémon games had dropped sharply. This sales drop, coupled with a decline in the popularity of other products like FURBY, had caused company revenues to plummet to $2.9 billion in a single year. The one-year revenue decline of $0.9 billion

EXHIBIT 6	HASBRO FINANCIAL STATEMENTS ($ THOUSANDS)		
	2001	**2002**	**2003**
Boys Toys	657,300	871,400	962,500
Games and Puzzles	1,259,600	1,121,200	1,207,100
Electronic Toys	213,900	118,000	266,500
Preschool Toys	222,000	225,400	215,500
Creative Play	211,600	195,500	198,100
Girls Toys	111,900	122,500	104,000
Other	180,039	162,230	184,957
Net Revenues	**$2,856,339**	**$2,816,230**	**$3,138,657**
Cost of Sales	**$1,223,483**	**$1,099,162**	**$1,287,962**
Gross Profit	**$1,632,856**	**$1,717,068**	**$1,850,695**
Expenses			
Amortization	121,652	94,576	76,053
Royalties	209,725	296,152	248,423
Research & Development	125,633	153,775	143,183
Advertising	290,829	296,549	363,876
Selling, Distribution, Admin.	673,687	656,725	674,544
Total Expenses	**$1,421,526**	**$1,497,777**	**$1,506,079**
Operating Profit	**$211,330**	**$219,291**	**$344,616**
Non-operating (income) Expense			
Interest expense	103,688	77,499	52,462
Other expense, net	11,443	37,704	48,090
Total non-operating (income) expense	115,131	115,203	100,552
Earning before income taxes and cumulative effect of accounting change	96,199	104,088	244,064
Income taxes	35,401	29,030	69,049
Net earnings before cumulative effect of accounting change	60,798	75,058	175,015
Cumulative effect of accounting change, net of tax	(1,066)	(245,732)	(17,351)
Net Earnings (loss)	**$59,732**	**$ (170,674)**	**$157,664**

Source: Hasbro 2003 annual report.

was a stark reminder of the risks and rewards of competing in a market in which tastes changed quickly and hits faded fast.

G.I. JOE

Since its inception, G.I. JOE had been one of the company's most reliable properties. "The toy industry has evolved in some radical ways over the past forty years, and Hasbro has changed dramatically as well," noted Lagor. "But G.I. JOE has been one of those brands that has managed to endure despite all the changes in the market. The brand has stayed current with today's boys but it has also stayed true to its core message—a REAL AMERICAN HERO."

EXHIBIT 7   SELECTED HASBRO BRANDS: SALES DATA ($ THOUSANDS)

	1991	1992	1993	1994	1995	1996	1997	1998	1999	2000	2001	2002	2003
Play-Doh	42,308	43,046	42,400	44,129	52,593	51,879	64,949	67,028	63,896	73,750	69,008	87,770	110,213
Star Wars-Hasbro only	—	—	282	199	33,049	137,448	464,504	237,133	418,749	160,491	62,099	220,416	75,402
Beyblade	—	—	—	—	—	—	—	—	—	—	—	62,362	312,074
G.I. JOE	**99,809**	**109,913**	**123,023**	**79,375**	**40,102**	**35,357**	**31,801**	**32,530**	**34,272**	**42,838**	**68,457**	**103,243**	**87,866**
Transformers	8,820	1,894	60,295	34,776	6,821	56,596	58,455	83,563	57,613	50,915	57,348	85,775	135,218
My Little Pony	27,830	10,884	1,887	2,322	109	183	174	9,729	3,751	672	2	3,405	60,945
Easy-Bake Oven	—	—	—	—	—	—	—	—	47,402	47,883	40,384	47,000	40,587
Tonka	—	—	27,459	37,404	60,978	52,185	49,452	41,402	37,311	46,568	47,949	65,590	44,525
Lite Brite	—	—	—	—	—	—	—	—	15,761	15,244	14,147	23,923	24,202
Nerf	57,621	127,303	100,747	81,803	100,290	116,698	89,478	76,257	66,805	44,441	33,169	59,200	53,583
Pokémon – Hasbro only	—	—	—	—	—	—	—	3,170	857,163	627,050	251,839	95,798	47,116
NeoPets	—	—	—	—	—	—	—	—	—	—	—	2,608	45,404
Super Soaker	38,577	188,147	89,675	65,310	59,058	63,067	66,824	89,101	82,907	58,424	48,805	48,915	32,273

Source: Hasbro. The data in this exhibit has been disguised for competitive reasons.

Based on a concept from Stan Weston, G.I. JOE was introduced in 1964, and was the first mass-produced doll for boys. "At the time of its introduction, dolls were for girls, not boys," Alan Hassenfeld recalled. "And yet my father made the gutsy decision to support the launch of what people were calling a boy's doll." Of course, what G.I. JOE *was* and how it was *marketed* were two different things—when G.I. JOE was actually launched, then-president Merrill Hassenfeld had admonished his sales force, "If I over-hear you calling G.I. JOE a doll, we're not shipping any to you." Instead, G.I. JOE was marketed as a 12-inch "action figure" with 21 moving parts. Within a year, Hasbro was selling $23 million worth of G.I. JOE toys, a remarkable sales figure in the 1964 toy market.

Over the next thirty years, the brand received a number of product extensions, updates, and revivals. In 1970, the G.I. JOE line went from being a set of individual military figures (e.g., ACTION SOLDIER and ACTION MARINE) to being part of an ADVENTURE TEAM that battled everything from spies and aliens to environmental hazards. In 1978, G.I. JOE was discontinued but was then reintroduced in 1982 as a team of "Real American Heroes," supported by a comic book (which provided an entirely new avenue for marketing the toy), a highly successful daily cartoon show, and range of licensed merchandise. For this re-launch, the G.I. JOE team shrank to $3\frac{3}{4}$ inch size and featured a wide range of characters, including a field commander (DUKE), Ninja Master (SNAKE EYES), and an infamous group of villains (COBRA, led by the evil COBRA COMMANDER). (Please see Exhibit 8 for G.I. JOE action figures through the years.)

Sales over the years had fluctuated. For example, in the late-1960s and 1970s, sales had slumped, whereas in the mid-1980s, G.I. JOE product sales had climbed to $185 million. "Remember, the 1980s were the years when the product line was buoyed by one of the most successful toy cartoons of that decade," Lagor noted. In the mid 1990s, Joe's sales had faded again, to the point where Hasbro decided to pull the $3\frac{3}{4}$ inch action figures, leaving only the 12 inch Joes (which tended to appeal to aging adult collectors) on the shelves. Then in the spring of 2002, Hasbro had relaunched the $3\frac{3}{4}$ inch figures (with increased advertising support), to strong success. (Please see Exhibit 7 for G.I. JOE sales over time.) Lagor commented:

> *This is part of what makes G.I. JOE a fascinating brand. Even when sales have dropped and other brands have come and gone, G.I. JOE brand awareness has remained incredibly high, and the brand has always been able to recover. What this tells us is how strong the brand is. Everyone—regardless of their age or gender—knows who G.I. JOE is and what he stands for. There's a lot of affection for this brand.*

Al Verrecchia, Hasbro CEO (who joined Hasbro as a junior accountant in 1965) added, "Little boys have been playing with toy soldiers since the beginning of time. It may be retro [to adults], but it's not retro to the child that was born yesterday."

By 2003, the complete G.I. JOE product line consisted of an extensive set of per-sonalities, vehicles, and accessories, including African American figures, Native American characters, Asian American and female action figures. (Please see Exhibits 9 and 10

EXHIBIT 8   G.I. JOE ACTION FIGURES THROUGH THE YEARS

1964 Packaging

1964 G.I. JOE

1974 Man of Action with Kung Fu Grip

Source: Hasbro.

for a sample of the 2003 G.I. JOE product line.) The average G.I. JOE buyer owned 9.9 products, and of the roughly 10 million boys aged 5 through 12 in the U.S., 42% reported owning a G.I. JOE.[4] (Another 40% of boys in this age group did not own a G.I. JOE, but owned other action figures.) More specifically, G.I. JOE consumers could be broken down into three age segments:

- *Boys age 5–7.* Most G.I. JOE consumers acquired their first G.I. JOE product at this age; 46% of boys within this group reported that they owned at least one G.I. JOE. In testing the most recent G.I. JOE line, Hasbro had learned that 84% of these buyers either loved or liked the new line "a lot."

- *Boys age 8–10.* Ownership of G.I. JOE figures tended to peak at this age, with 48% of all boys in this group reporting that they owned at least one G.I. JOE. Hasbro had learned that 50% of these consumers either loved or liked the new line a lot.

EXHIBIT 9

G.I. JOE: A SAMPLE OF THE CURRENT PRODUCT LINE

Source: Hasbro.

EXHIBIT 10

SELECTED G.I. JOE PRODUCTS FROM THE 2003 LINE, WITH APPROXIMATE RETAIL PRICES

Mainline Product	Approx. Retail Price	G.I. JOE Exclusives	Approximate Retail Price
G.I. JOE Realistic Military			
Basic Military Asst	$9.99	**Toys "R" Us Exclusives**	
Alpha Asst	$9.99	3³⁄₄" Awe Striker	$12.99
Bravo Asst	$14.99	12" JOE vs. Cobra	$14.99
Echo Asst	$29.99	3³⁄₄" Tiger Force	$19.99
40th Anniv. Wv1	$39.99	101st Airborne Freefall	$24.99
40th Anniv Wv2	$39.99	3³⁄₄" Arctic Snowcat	$19.99
Vehicles			
WW II Jeep	$59.99	**Wal-Mart Exclusives**	
G.I. JOE Hummv	$99.99	Life Apollo Astronaut	$29.99
Night Attack Chopper	$29.99	Spy Troops 2	
		Home for the Holidays	
		Target Exclusives	
		Timeless wooden foot locker	$34.99
Accessories			
G.I. JOE Figure gear	$8.99	**K-Mart Exclusives**	
G.I. JOE Weapon Tech	$9.99	Search and rescue accessories	$5.99
12" foot locker	$12.99	12" Navy Jeep	$29.99
3³⁄₄ inch Figures		**Kay Bee Exclusives**	
Mission Single pack	$4.99	Everyday Heroes	$12.99
Single Figure pack	$3.99	12" Fall Promo Figure	$7.99
Basic Figure 2-pack	$6.99		
Bravo Vehicle	$15.99		
G.I. JOE – Regular			
2-pack Ninja	$19.99		
Barrel Roll w/ Parachute	$22.99		
Elite Asst	$22.99		
"Evilution" Asst	$14.99		
Night Attack Chopper	$29.99		

Source: Hasbro

- *Boys age 11–12.* Interest in the G.I. JOE brand tended to dip sharply among this age group, with 22% of all boys in this group reporting that they owned at least one G.I. JOE. Just 41% of these consumers reported loving or liking the new line a lot. (Please see Exhibit 11 for additional information about the consumer profile.)

In addition to these youth segments, there was also an adult segment of collectors who purchased G.I. JOEs on a regular basis. This collector segment—which primarily consisted of males between the ages of 20 and 55—was responsible for an estimated 25% of total G.I. JOE sales. Derryl DePriest, Marketing Director for G.I. JOE, considered himself one of these collectors: "I became a collector after graduate school.

EXHIBIT 11a

TOP-SELLING PROPERTIES AMONG BOYS AGED 6–11 IN 2003

Rank	Property
1	Yu-Gi-Oh!
2	Beyblade
3	Lego
4	Hot Wheels
5	Nikko

Source: Adapted from The NPD Group/NPD Funworld/Consumer Panel.

EXHIBIT 11b

G.I. JOE CONSUMER PROFILE

6–7 Year Olds	8–11 Year Olds

Favorite Games and Toys

6–7 Year Olds	8–11 Year Olds
Boggle, Battleship, Clue Jr.	*Battleship, Monopoly, Clue, Scrabble*
Cars and Trucks	*Cars and Trucks*
Trains	*Trains*
Play Guns	*Building Sets*

Use of Technology

6–7 Year Olds	8–11 Year Olds
uses a computer at home	*uses a computer, goes on the Internet*
has a VCR in their bedroom	*has and uses a stereo, CD player, radio*
owns a Nintendo handheld system	*uses a videogame system—Sony, Nintendo*

Movie Consumption

6–7 Year Olds	8–11 Year Olds
rents video cassettes, watches children's DVDs	*rents DVDs*
likes animation films	*likes thrillers, science fiction*

Television Favorites

6–7 Year Olds	8–11 Year Olds
Digimon	*Major League sports*
Samurai Jack	*ESPN*
Pokémon	*Time Squad*
Bob the Builder	*Comedy Central*
Spiderman	*Grim & Evil*

Opinions

6–7 Year Olds	8–11 Year Olds
likes listening to commercials	*doesn't buy things he's seen in ads*
buys things seen in ads	*doesn't think TV is bad*
learns from TV	*loves playing sports during free time*
likes TV ads	

Source: Adapted from Spectra Advantage 03A-Simmons 2002 Kid Survey.

It was the thrill of rediscovering my childhood. As a kid I knew that G.I. JOE was very special. I just never really stopped being passionate about G.I. JOE."

The collectors were a hardcore group—they held regular conventions, hosted websites, and communicated with each other online. Avid collectors spent tens of thousands of dollars each year collecting G.I. JOE toys and would typically spend two to three hours a day working with their collections. Collector groups, both official and unofficial, often organized G.I. JOE conventions around the world, including diorama-building contests. At the Fall 2003 convention in San Francisco, the display of an original 1963 prototype G.I. JOE had been protected by an armed guard. The prototype was expected to fetch $250,000 at an upcoming auction. As Brian Savage, who ran the International G.I. JOE Collectors Club (which had thousands of members), put it, "We like to say that G.I. JOE has saved the world millions of times—one backyard at a time."

G.I. JOE Team's Marketing Strategy

As Lagor considered the possibilities for marketing G.I. JOE, he was mindful of the tremendous opportunities associated with managing a brand with such broad iconic appeal. "G.I. JOE is a national symbol of heroism, not just for young boys, but for adults too," he noted. At the same time, Lagor recognized the importance of proceeding with caution, particularly in the context of a recent shift in the company's overall product strategy.

Over the past several years, the company had made a conscious move to mitigate severe spikes in revenue by adopting a more conservative portfolio management approach. This strategic shift had involved a renewed commitment to growing the company's "core" brands—brands that had either demonstrated their longevity by sustaining relatively stable revenues over a long period of time, or had displayed evergreen potential. As part of this change in strategy, Hasbro had begun repackaging, modernizing, and/or bringing out of retirement many of its classic brands such CANDY LAND, TRIVIAL PURSUIT, MY LITTLE PONY, and SUPER SOAKER.

The company had also begun reducing its reliance on licensing, with a particular eye on limiting its exposure to volatile film properties. The company still pursued licenses; however, revenues from licensed products had been reduced to less than 10% of revenues. "For example, we decided to pay for some Disney licenses, but we agreed to forego the Batman license, which was picked up by Mattel," Lagor said. "We learned a lot from *Star Wars* and other licensing deals and have really switched our focus to Hasbro-owned brands."

Alan Hassenfeld explained:

Core brands are like children. If you don't treat them with tender loving care, they become wayward on you. In recent years, we were so focused on things like BATMAN or Disney products, we lost our focus on brands like PLAYSKOOL, PLAY-DOH and TINKER TOY. We have a rich portfolio of our own brands that we need to take care of. Rather than squeeze all the juice out of a brand, we need to make sure we're investing for the long run.

Given this, the G.I. JOE brand had taken on added importance within the company. G.I. JOE was one of Hasbro's most long-standing properties, but although it enjoyed almost universal brand awareness (90% among the general American public), there was, as Lagor put it, "a sense that we haven't really fulfilled the potential of the brand." Certainly, G.I. JOE had demonstrated two of the key characteristics of a core brand—longevity and extendibility. It was also a property that was unencumbered by external licensing agreements. The question that the G.I. JOE marketing team was now asking itself was, how big could the Joe franchise become?

An obvious point of comparison was Mattel's line of Barbie products. In the toy industry, Barbie was one of the few properties (along with Lego) that had achieved mega-brand status. The best-selling toy in the history of the industry, Barbie dominated the fashion doll segment with roughly 50% market share. After more than forty years on the market, Mattel was still selling roughly 1.5 million Barbies each week; this amounted to more than two Barbie sales per *second*. Moreover, the Barbie franchise, which was supported by a $100 million marketing budget, was bringing in $780 million in annual sales—even in what was considered a "down" year for the property. (Please see Exhibit 12 for revenues for Barbie and other non-Hasbro brands.)

By comparison, the G.I. JOE product line was on course to bring in roughly $88 million in revenues in 2003, supported by an $10 million advertising budget. "Can G.I. JOE become a mega-brand and compete in the same league as Barbie or Lego?" asked Lagor. "What we need to decide is how big we think this brand can and should become, and what kind of marketing strategy will get us there."

The G.I. JOE marketing team was currently considering three different options.

Traditional Marketing Approach

The first option was to continue to use traditional forms of advertising (print, TV, web sites) and continuous product innovation to stimulate both retailer and consumer interest in the G.I. JOE brand. Already, G.I. JOE had enjoyed forty years of longevity supported by traditional advertising,[5] and the company had a number of other brands (e.g., MR. POTATO HEAD, PLAY-DOH) that had demonstrated sustainability using this marketing approach. In addition, in recent years, several industry blockbusters had emerged on the basis of nothing more than traditional advertising campaigns. Examples included Bratz, MGA Entertainment's fashion doll phenomenon, as well as Hasbro's FURBY, an interactive stuffed animal.

As Lagor considered this option, he was reminded of something Alan Hassenfeld had once said: "The key to this business is shipping the market 90% complete and leaving 10% hunger out there to live another day. Retailers can always find something new, but we can't. If we want to live to fight another day, then we need to keep the market hungry."

If Hasbro were to adopt a traditional marketing approach, the goal would be to make sure that G.I. JOE dominated the "green aisle" (military) in the stores the same way that Barbie dominated the "pink aisle" (dolls). Although G.I. JOE had, by far, the strongest brand recognition in its sub-category, copycat brands in the green aisle were

EXHIBIT 12   **SELECTED NON-HASBRO BRANDS: SALES DATA ($ THOUSANDS)**

	1991	1992	1993	1994	1995	1996	1997	1998	1999	2000	2001	2002	2003
Barbie	579,368	574,154	644,561	790,352	956,003	1,204,289	1,329,475	1,329,448	1,020,524	990,036	927,931	998,022	780,884
Lego	283,584	313,364	293,730	292,268	325,245	361,473	354,565	422,260	487,302	482,946	610,593	512,268	373,371
Bratz	—	—	—	—	—	—	—	—	—	—	22,608	179,705	496,541
Hot Wheels	73,004	86,119	122,108	113,410	154,897	180,172	335,046	407,909	326,977	308,744	359,611	374,965	290,113
Matchbox	46,858	47,902	47,164	54,237	61,859	58,398	73,292	81,960	76,866	84,500	62,308	121,488	92,325
Care Bears	7,118	6,936	1,249	—	—	—	—	—	—	—	—	28,719	164,758
Harry Potter	—	—	—	—	—	—	—	—	—	33,600	213,808	204,692	74,882
Power Rangers	—	—	—	—	475,762	166,855	126,328	127,294	138,636	121,156	132,903	157,778	133,043
Yu-Gi-Oh!	—	—	—	—	—	—	—	—	—	—	—	279,287	600,850
Batman	29,865	148,635	117,768	91,996	182,346	154,204	164,602	94,320	53,932	39,899	21,657	48,713	50,101
Ninja Turtles	383,268	219,069	97,103	43,732	19,722	13,147	11,719	3,910	3,189	2,377	174	90	58,544

Source: Adapted from The NPD Group/NPD Funworld/Toy Market Index (2001 and prior) & Consumer Panel (2002 and forward).

creating both price pressure and competition for shelf space for the G.I. JOE line. Given Hasbro's high quality standards for G.I. JOE, competing primarily on price was not an option. Thus, successful execution of this strategy depended on getting all of the fundamentals right—i.e., managing the overall "Joe" brand experience through advertising, pricing, merchandising, strong retailer support, product line management, etc. Lagor noted, "While Mattel has traditionally been great at managing its long-term mega-brands, Hasbro has excelled at continuously producing and marketing innovative products."

Manage the G.I. JOE brand with Limited Forms of Entertainment

The second option was to supplement the traditional marketing approach with limited forms of entertainment. For example, Hasbro was currently running a collection of 60-second animated television commercials to promote a wide range of G.I. JOE characters. The footage used to create these TV commercials could theoretically be converted into a 44-minute narrative feature that could fit on a DVD. The DVD could then be bundled with selected G.I. JOE merchandise. The goal would be to give boys a concrete storyline to guide their G.I. JOE play activities.

"The DVD would fill in the kinds of details that boys need to enrich their play," explained Lagor. "It would provide kids with information about the characters' different personalities and backgrounds, and it would introduce them to the villains, the equipment, and the vehicles. It would also give them lots of story and plot ideas that they could take with them into the sandbox."

The combination of traditional advertising coupled with a DVD was an approach used by Mattel to market Barbie. For example, when Mattel had launched a holiday season "Nutcracker Barbie," it had also introduced a Nutcracker DVD.

"One advantage is that we would own the content," said Lagor, "no royalties, no licensing fees." Plus, the 44-minute format would give the G.I. JOE marketing team the added option of buying television time to air the complete feature in two 30-minute segments, leaving time for the standard eight minutes of advertising. The downside was the expense. Producing a G.I. JOE a 44-minute DVD could cost the company between $1 and 2 million. As Lagor noted, "Given an annual marketing budget of $10 million, that's a huge expense to swallow, particularly when the return on this kind of investment has never really been demonstrated."

Manage the Brand with Multiple Forms of Entertainment

The third option under consideration was to adopt a non-traditional marketing approach involving a number of different product forms, including toys, trading cards, video games, DVDs, books, a content-rich website, and even a full-length feature film. Under this option, the marketing of G.I. JOE would not necessarily be geared toward selling the toys per se; rather, it would be geared toward promoting the G.I. JOE "story" in all of its various forms.

In recent years, some of the biggest successes in the boys' toys category had adopted this type of strategy. Pokémon, and more recently, Yu-GI-Oh, were perhaps the most high-profile examples, but a number of licensed brands had also achieved blockbuster toy success by using multiple forms of entertainment. For example, toys associated with *Star Wars*, Spider Man, Harry Potter, Disney/Pixar's *Toy Story*, and Rugrats had all averaged four-year returns of over $130 million in sales.

Hasbro had already received inquiries from a major Hollywood producer who was interested in creating a full-length, live-action G.I. JOE feature film. Lagor could not help but be excited about the prospect:

> *The potential upside is huge. Even the strongest advertising and promotion plan can't compare to the boost from having a strong movie franchise. In a good movie year, total licensed toys can exceed $250 million. This would be a big step towards establishing G.I. JOE as a mega-brand.*
>
> *Of course, this option would require a significant amount of effort to work with Hollywood to maintain the vision of the brand. If we were to hand over creative control to top directors and producers, we would want them to feel creatively unconstrained, but we would also want to make sure to keep the core of our brand identity intact. There would be some areas in which we'd have a voice, but other areas in which we'd have none. In addition, whenever you invest resources in a movie, there is never a guarantee for success; there would even be a possibility that the movie wouldn't be released.*

The idea was appealing nonetheless. Hasbro would bear no licensing fees or costs for the movie; in fact, the company would probably generate royalties from the film (for a typical film, annual royalties tended to amount to several million dollars). By contrast, if the company were to try to produce a weekly cartoon series, it would not only have to bear the cost of producing the cartoons, there would be no guarantee that the series would be picked up by a network. "Not only are cartoons expensive," Lagor said, "but they require lots of work with networks who are constantly being pursued by many companies with many ideas. The networks could turn down our show for any number of reasons—maybe we don't hit the right demographics or maybe we don't fit their current programming direction."

DePriest described some of the other risks with an entertainment-focused approach:

> *If we were to make investments in the entertainment side of things, it would become G.I. JOE VS. COBRA programming, which is an area in which we don't have a lot of experience. When we won the StarWars and Pokémon licenses, the entertainment piece was executed by our partners. If we decide to invest in a storyline or a DVD or a cartoon series, we'd be taking a calculated risk that this is the way kids want the military delivered.*

As Lagor considered his three options, he commented:

> *G.I. JOE is a core brand. Having said that, it's hard to know when to be aggressive and when to pull back. We want to make sure we're maximizing the potential*

of the brand, but we also want to make sure we don't burn out the brand either. Nothing is a sure thing in this market, but it's important that we weigh the risks and rewards before making a decision. The G.I. JOE brand has a rich history and an incredible future—we have millions of boys who grew up with G.I. JOE . . . and we need to ensure that there will be millions more to come.

Strategic Inflection: TiVo in 2005

Even for the usually unflappable Mike Ramsay, chairman and chief executive officer of TiVo Inc., the first six months of 2005 had been an amazing roller coaster. Ramsay had pioneered the digital video recording business (DVR) in 1997 and driven TiVo to a market-leading position. Nonetheless, many observers believed that TiVo's world was falling apart in the first quarter of 2005. Ramsay, who had been the visionary leader and founder of the company, announced that he would soon retire as CEO. In addition, his second in command at the company was leaving, with no apparent successor in the wings. Then, within weeks, TiVo's most important distribution partner, DirecTV, announced it would shift away from TiVo to an in-house DVR. Despite the fact that TiVo had exceeded unit growth, market share, and revenue expectations in 2004, analysts were speculating that TiVo would not survive. As the stock dove to a three-year low, takeover rumors were rampant.

But TiVo struck back quickly. In March 2005, TiVo and Comcast, the largest cable company in the United States, agreed to a new distribution arrangement that would offer TiVo to Comcast's 21.5 million customers in late 2006 or early 2007. Moreover, Ramsay promised Wall Street that the company would become profitable by the end of 2005, despite racking up a half billion dollars in losses since its founding in 1997. When the company announced its first-quarter earnings in May 2005, it was close to break-even, improving its relationship with investors. At the end of June, the company named Tom Rogers, a seasoned media veteran, as the new president and CEO. Rogers, trained as a lawyer, had been chairman and CEO of Primedia, as well as president of NBC Cable. He also knew TiVo well, having served as vice chairman of the TiVo Board since the fall of 2003.

Yet Rogers and Ramsay, who planned to remain on the TiVo Board, knew that the roller-coaster ride was hardly over. Rogers commented that he was "firmly convinced" TiVo could extend its brand and technology to "the mass market," despite having only

Professors David B. Yoffie and Pai Ling Yin and Research Associate Barbara J. Mack prepared this case. HBS cases are developed solely as the basis for class discussion. Cases are not intended to serve as endorsements, sources of primary data, or illustrations of effective or ineffective management.

three million customers. And Ramsay argued that TiVo should become "the portal to entertainment services in the home. We aren't really in the 'DVR' business," suggested Ramsay, "we're in the user interface and entertainment services business. Our challenge is how to get from 'here to there.'" TiVo remained a highly differentiated product in 2005, offering an array of "cool" new features, with extraordinary customer loyalty. But at the same time, TiVo was facing growing competitive challenges. Its competitors could not yet offer many of TiVo's more advanced features, yet EchoStar (Dish Network), Motorola, ReplayTV, Scientific Atlanta, and others had significantly narrowed the gap on basic DVR technology. In addition, TiVo had two critical holes in its product line: most competitors offered multiple tuners (to watch and record two shows at once), and many were also offering DVRs compatible with high-definition television, one of the fastest-growing segments in home entertainment. But TiVo would be unable to match these offerings for at least 18 months, except through its deteriorating relationship with DirecTV. Moreover, start-ups such as Akimbo and 2Wire were exploring opportunities to offer Web-based alternatives to TiVo. Even Microsoft was entering the fray, with Home Media Center software that allowed a PC to provide DVR functionality, as well as Internet protocol TV (IPTV) technology that sought to deliver on-demand content over the Web.

Despite the challenges, management remained confident that there was considerable upside for TiVo. Though the company had struggled with the issue of financial discipline, management felt that the Comcast deal might represent a new era for TiVo. As Ramsay said, "We need a new mind-set today. Last year our challenge was, should we be mass market or upmarket? We couldn't do it all. Today, our biggest problem may be, how do we scale this business?"

What Is TiVo?

TiVo was a leading provider of DVR technology and services, selling directly to consumers as well as through original equipment manufacturers (OEMs) and licensees. Former Silicon Graphics, Inc. executives Ramsay and Jim Barton—who had been working on a joint venture with Time-Warner to create the first large-scale interactive TV system—founded TiVo in 1997. At its simplest, the TiVo product was a hard-disk-based replacement for the videocassette recorder (VCR).[1] DVRs—an emerging consumer electronics (CE) category—were similar to VCRs except that TV programs were recorded on hard disks rather than on cassette tapes. Also referred to as PVRs (personal video recorders), DVRs changed the way that consumers experienced television. In addition to viewing programs at their convenience, users could pause live TV, fast forward through commercials, and hit instant replay during sporting events. (See Exhibit 1 for a glossary of terms.)

The mechanics of TiVo were fairly simple. TiVo users could access two weeks of electronic program guide (EPG) information and record shows the "old-fashioned way" by simply clicking on the program. They could also tell TiVo to record an entire season of a favorite show, using TiVo's "Season Pass" feature. As an extension of the user choice feature, consumers could go to the "Wishlist" and ask TiVo to record a

EXHIBIT 1 **GLOSSARY OF TERMS**

Term	Definition
CPU	The central processing unit was the "brains" of a computer.
DVD	DVD stood for digital video disc or digital versatile disc and was a type of optical disc-storage medium that could store a full-length feature film.
DVD-DVR	DVD-DVR was a consumer electronics device that combined a digital video-disc player with a digital video recorder.
DVR	DVR stood for digital video recorder. A DVR was similar to a VCR (videocassette recorder) except that it recorded digitally onto a hard drive instead of onto videocassette tape. This meant that it could store dozens of hours of programming and perform many functions that a VCR could not, such as pausing and rewinding live TV. DVRs were sometimes referred to as PVRs (see below).
EPG	EPGs, or electronic programming guides, were available on most cable and satellite services as well as most DVRs. EPGs allowed consumers to see from 3 to 14 days of programming in advance and, in the case of DVRs, to click on a show to record it or double click to record it every time the show was shown. Stand-alone DVRs required a connection to a phone line to download the EPG each evening. EPGs were also referred to as IPGs (see below).
GB	Gigabyte was a unit used to measure the capacity of hard drives.
IPG	IPG was an abbreviation for interactive programming guide. (See EPG above.) IPGs could have more advanced features than EPGs.
IR Blaster	A feature of most DVRs but usually lacking in DVD-DVRs, an IR (infrared) blaster was a small bulb on a wire that acted like a remote control to change channels on cable or satellite set-top boxes. Without an IR blaster, consumers had to set the recording device to the correct channel before recording.
MPEG	MPEG, a digital compression standard, stood for Motion Picture Experts Group.
MSO	MSO, an abbreviation for multiple services operator—meaning a cable operator with more than one network—was a term commonly used for all cable operators.
PVR	PVR stood for personal video recorder. Also referred to as DVR (see above).
STB	STB was an abbreviation for set-top box, which meant any piece of hardware (generally in the shape of a VCR) that was placed on top of (or beside or beneath) the television.
SVOD	SVOD stood for subscription video on demand, which provided consumers with continuous access to certain content (e.g., HBO shows) for a monthly fee.
VOD	VOD stood for video on demand, a service that allowed consumers to pay for a movie or other content and watch it on their cable or satellite TV at their convenience.

Source: Casewriter research, adapted from Webopedia Web site, http://www.webopedia.com, and The Online ITV Dictionary, http://itvdictionary.com/broadband.html, accessed May 7, 2003.

particular show, actor, director, or style of programming, whenever it might be playing. Based on historical viewing habits and whether a consumer gave a show or genre a positive or negative rating, TiVo would use spare hard-disk space to record programs that he or she might enjoy. This feature was particularly valuable in the age of cable and satellite TV, when sifting through hundreds of channels to find the most interesting shows had become a daunting task. TiVo also offered a unique conflict resolution system: if there were conflicts between recording preferences, TiVo would automatically seek alternative times to record a program.

After purchasing a TiVo machine with 40 to 140 hours of recording time, the consumer would install the machine and activate the service, which cost either $12.95 per month or a one-time, lifetime fee of $299. Installing TiVo was not always easy; TiVo needed to connect to the TV and to a phone jack or the Internet.[2] Up to six cables were involved,[3] and most users needed help from the customer service desk during installation.[4] However, once the TiVo unit had been set up and activated, it received high marks from consumers for its user-friendly interface and rich feature set.

TiVo was compatible with cable, satellite, and over-the-airwaves TV systems. In early 2002, TiVo launched its second-generation product, the TiVo Series2, which featured a more robust processor and increased memory, creating an opportunity to offer new services such as digital music, digital pictures, and broadband video on demand (VOD).

TiVo and DirecTV

In addition to offering stand-alone boxes, TiVo offered boxes through a partnership with DirecTV, the largest U.S. satellite TV operator, with which it launched an integrated DirecTV/DVR set-top box. Initially, DirecTV sold Microsoft's UltimateTV DVRs but switched to TiVo's Series2 technology. (See Exhibit 2 for TiVo subscriber history.) By 2005, TiVo offered customers a basic TiVo DVR with two tuners for as little as $100 and a high-definition TV (HDTV) tuner that sold for as much as

---

EXHIBIT 2   **TIVO SUBSCRIBER HISTORY, 1999–2005**

For Quarter Ended	Net New Additions			Total Cumulative Subscriptions			Percent of TiVo Service Cumulative Subscriptions Paying Recurring Fees
	TiVo Svc	DirecTV	TOTAL	TiVo Svc	DirecTV	TOTAL	
1999 June			1,000			1,000	
1999 Sept.			1,500			2,500	
1999 Dec.			15,500			18,000	
2000 March			14,000			32,000	
2000 June			16,000			48,000	
2000 Sept.			25,000			73,000	
2000 Dec.			63,000			136,000	
2001 Jan.			18,000			154,000	
2001 April	22,000	13,000	35,000	160,000	29,000	189,000	36
2001 July	22,000	18,000	40,000	182,000	47,000	229,000	37
2001 Oct.	24,000	27,000	51,000	206,000	74,000	280,000	39
2002 Jan.	40,000	60,000	100,000	246,000	134,000	380,000	41
2002 April	24,000	18,000	42,000	270,000	152,000	422,000	34
2002 July	21,000	21,000	42,000	291,000	173,000	464,000	33
2002 Oct.	30,000	16,000	46,000	321,000	189,000	510,000	34
2003 Jan.	74,000	40,000	114,000	396,000	228,000	624,000	34
2003 April	37,000	42,000	79,000	433,000	270,000	703,000	34
2003 July	34,000	56,000	90,000	467,000	326,000	793,000	34
2003 Oct.	59,000	150,000	209,000	526,000	476,000	1,002,000	34
2004 Jan.	130,000	200,000	330,000	656,000	676,000	1,332,000	34
2004 April	68,000	196,000	264,000	724,000	872,000	1,596,000	34
2004 Oct.	103,000	316,000	419,000	890,000	1,413,000	2,303,000	34
2005 Jan.	251,000	447,000	698,000	1,141,000	1,860,000	3,001,000	34

Note: The "Percent of TiVo Service Cumulative Subscriptions Paying Recurring Fees" excludes DirecTV subscribers.

Source: Casewriter research, adapted from company reports and press releases, TiVo Web site, http://www.tivo.com, accessed May 17, 2005.

$999. TiVo designed the boxes and had rights to share data and advertising revenues, but DirecTV took responsibility for manufacturing, marketing, installing, and servicing TiVo DVR accounts.[5] DirecTV offered a basic DVR subscription price of $4.95 per month with free service to subscribers of DirecTV's premium package.[6] DirecTV paid a monthly fee per household to TiVo. The average monthly fee to TiVo was $3.00 in mid-2003 but was expected to drop close to $1.00 in 2005.

Despite extremely low churn, very high satisfaction with TiVo among DirecTV customers, and more than 2 million customers, the DirecTV management decided to sell its 4% stake in TiVo in 2004, resign from TiVo's board, and offer customers an alternative DVR in late 2005. Although DirecTV had a contract to sell TiVo through 2007, the satellite company's new owner, News Corp., owned a 77% stake in a TiVo competitor called NDS.[7] While it would still support TiVo and was, in fact, extending its advertising agreements with TiVo, DirecTV announced plans to push customers to buy NDS DVRs instead. DirecTV plans called for the NDS DVR to offer new features, such as the ability to record pay-per-view shows and allow customers to pay the fees when they watched the program. In spite of ugly skirmishes in the press, the TiVo team maintained that the venture with DirecTV was not over. "The outside perception is that DTV is gone," said one insider. "The reality is that DTV is paying every month for two million subscribers, and they added 425,000 in the last quarter [of 2004]. We seem to be doing a lot of business for a relationship that is supposed to be dead."[8]

TiVo Technology

The TiVo DVR was essentially a computer with a large hard disk, read-write MPEG digital video chips for encoding and decoding, a modem, and other components. The product was designed to keep costs low, and manufacturing was outsourced. The biggest portion of the bill of materials was the hard disk at 33%, though the MPEG components were also expensive. The TiVo DVR ran on a MIPS CPU core with a Linux operating system.

TiVo took security and privacy very seriously. The TiVo DVR's microprocessor, containing cryptography software, was soldered into the box. This made TiVo difficult, though not impossible, to hack. The DVRs would call in—usually through the public switched telephone network—for EPG information and/or any software updates. Although TiVo was able to download data to the DVRs, TiVo was not able to upload all data residing on the DVR. Instead, every night TiVo would upload anonymous batch files that would be aggregated across the TiVo user base, allowing the company to analyze viewing habits at a very granular level. Showcases were distributed to the TiVo DVRs via broadcast whenever possible. Periodically, TiVo bought 30 minutes of very early morning broadcast time on the Discovery Channel. TiVos that had access to the Discovery Channel would automatically record any showcases, giving TiVo an inexpensive method for transferring large files to the DVRs.

TiVo management believed strongly that TiVo should be a platform technology where third parties could add value. Yet TiVo management's view of this platform evolved over time. Through 2004, Barton, a company cofounder whose role was chief technical officer and senior vice president of research and development, explained,

"Our future lies not with APIs [application program interfaces] but with protocols. For example, we now have a music protocol that allows TiVo to play digital music on your television. In the future, other services will interact with, but not sit on top of, the DVR." In 2005, TiVo sought to open the system further. Engineering created a new software layer, called Home Media Engine (HME), that allowed third parties to write applications. One of the company's bigger challenges with regard to its technology platform was that TiVo was not originally built to be an extensible system that could be easily adapted to different hardware and software environments. Moreover, TiVo was not modular: additional engineering work and therefore significant costs came into play whenever TiVo wanted to extend its technology to a new OEM, CE device, or set-top box. The biggest technical challenge for the near term was to turn TiVo into a software and service layer that could work on existing Motorola set-top boxes in the Comcast network.

To build greater differentiation in its product, TiVo continued to innovate in a number of categories. In the spring of 2003, TiVo shipped its first premium service application—the Home Media Option (HMO)—which enabled users to view digital photos, listen to and catalog digital music, and schedule programs to be recorded from anywhere the user had Internet access. TiVo originally offered the HMO at $99 but in 2004 started offering the features at no additional charge beyond the monthly fees or lifetime subscriptions. Once the HMO software was downloaded via broadband or telephone line and activated at the TiVo Web site, the TiVo DVR was capable of linking over wired or wireless (802.11b) networks with either Apple or Wintel PCs. Users with HMO could do remote scheduling over the Internet and use their TVs to view digital photos or listen to digital music. TiVo did not store the images or songs on its hard disk; rather, it pulled the pictures and music over the network and "published" on the TiVo platform. In addition, households with more than one TiVo unit could record programs on one TiVo and then transfer the programs to another for viewing. In theory, HMO also created an opportunity for new services such as broadband VOD, where content could be streamed directly to TVs. TiVo sought to offer further differentiation in 2005 with its TiVo to Go technology. Once customers had HMO, they could download a software program for their personal computers from the TiVo Web site that could transfer any TiVo recorded program to their computer or laptop.

TiVo also sold services to advertisers and networks. TiVo's "showcases" were long-form (four to six minutes) commercials designed to be entertaining, as TiVo subscribers had to choose to "opt in" to watch them. TiVo's audience-measurement services allowed buyers to analyze viewer behavior at a micro level, for example, whether commercials or shows did better at certain times or in certain markets. For other forms of advertising, TiVo could also insert digital messages into programming; a network, for example, might preview a new program and pay TiVo to insert a message allowing for the instant recording of the show when it ran.

TiVo Manufacturing and Licensees

Having filed for patents early in the company's life, TiVo had been awarded several significant patents, including one for personal video recording software and hardware design and two for core DVR functions and home networking capabilities. Several other aspects of TiVo's system were patent protected, including the scheduling and optimization of disk space—that is, what was recorded when—and resolving recording conflicts. By 2005, TiVo had approximately 70 patents related to DVR technology, with 106 pending. While TiVo did not want to expend resources in its early days to enforce its intellectual property, in 2004 TiVo sued EchoStar, the second-largest DVR distributor, for patent infringement. EchoStar countersued, and the case was still undecided.

In deciding where to position itself in the value chain, TiVo management initially focused on software and service. To entice brand-name CE firms to manufacture and distribute TiVo, the company subsidized CE manufacturers up to $200 per box. After TiVo discontinued CE subsidies in 2002 in an effort to conserve cash, management discovered that there was not enough profit in the TiVo Series2 box for CE manufacturers to make their required margins. To alleviate the situation, TiVo reduced the number of parts, outsourced to a very efficient contracting firm, and started selling boxes. The great majority of the TiVo-manufactured DVRs were sold through national CE retailers such as Best Buy and Circuit City, major regional retailers such as The Good Guys, and online retailer Amazon.com. Approximately 15% of TiVo boxes were sold directly to consumers through TiVo's own Web site. TiVo's agreement with one of its major retailers stipulated that TiVo would share a portion of the TiVo service revenue generated from the TiVo-manufactured DVRs. CE retailers generally had product margins ranging from 15% to 30%, with those margins trending toward the lower end during recessions.[9]

In addition to the retailer deals, TiVo worked with manufacturers to gain broader distribution for the TiVo technology. TiVo signed up a number of prominent licensees, ranging from Japanese partners Toshiba and Pioneer to Korea's Humax. Toshiba, for example, offered a DVD recorder with TiVo's "basic-service" option, which included record, pause, rewind, and instant replay. The basic-service option allowed licensees to include "entry-level" DVR functionality—with no monthly fee—in high-end integrated CE devices such as a combination DVD player with a built-in DVR. This version of the TiVo service would not have access to popular TiVo features such as WishList and Season Pass. TiVo offered consumers a 45-day free trial for the full service at the time of installation, hoping to spur adoption of TiVo's $mo. monthly service. Humax, by comparison, offered an integrated DVD recorder with the full TiVo service. Toshiba pricing came in between $229 and $499, while Humax pricing ran from $199 to $349.[10] When a company licensed TiVo's DVR technology, it generally paid an up-front license fee of several million dollars, with annual maintenance fees set at about 15% to 20% of the up-front license fee. TiVo devoted engineering resources to then make TiVo's technology compatible with the CE's product.

End Users: Consumers

The U.S. market for TVs, TV-related devices, and TV services was large, with around 105 million households owning a TV in 2005. While cable and satellite services and devices such as VCRs and DVD players had made significant inroads into many households, DVR penetration remained low in 2005, at 8%. (See Exhibit 3 for cable and satellite TV DVR penetration rates for U.S. households.) However, the segment was growing rapidly,

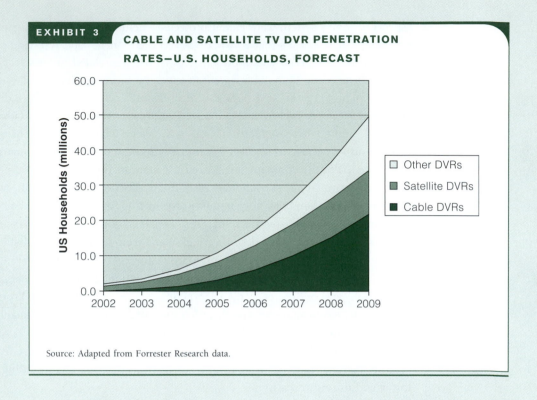

EXHIBIT 3

CABLE AND SATELLITE TV DVR PENETRATION RATES—U.S. HOUSEHOLDS, FORECAST

Source: Adapted from Forrester Research data.

roughly doubling between mid-2004 and mid-2005. Some analysts expected as many as 40% of U.S. homes would have DVRs by 2009.[11] Price sensitivity was an important issue for DVRs. Some industry observers believed that the price of DVR devices needed to be significantly below $200 before growth would accelerate, citing adoption patterns for consumer devices such as DVD players.[12] With that in mind, TiVo had aggressively cut prices on hardware as well as sought new sources of service revenues. (See Exhibit 4 for TiVo's lines of business.)

To build awareness of the TiVo brand and educate consumers about TiVo's "personal TV service," TiVo spent over $250 million on a wide range of sales and marketing efforts in 2000 and 2001.[13] On the advertising front, the company initially tried to list all of TiVo's features and benefits in a 30-second ad, but the task proved too difficult. Eventually the ads focused on how TiVo could help consumers overcome a specific TV-related problem.[14] Despite a spike in brand recognition following the advertising, TiVo management found that consumers were still confused about the use of a DVR—in particular, they were unclear about what TiVo could and could not do. Even the name of the device was not settled at that point—half of the manufacturers and market analysts used "PVR," while the other half used "DVR." In addition, TiVo discovered that consumers were surprised they had to pay a monthly service fee to use a product that they had purchased in a retail store.

Although the average consumer had not fully grasped the DVR concept yet, the existing TiVo users were ardent fans. According to some polls, up to 97% of TiVo users were "very satisfied" and said that they would recommend TiVo to a friend. Many

EXHIBIT 4	TYPES OF REVENUE GENERATED BY TIVO'S LINES OF BUSINESS	

Product or Service	Customer	Types of Revenue Generated
TiVo DVR	Consumers	*Hardware revenues Services revenues* (either a lifetime fee amortized over 48 months or a recurring monthly fee)
Showcases (advertising services)	Networks/Studios/ Advertisers	*Services revenues* (the company intended to use a CPM-like model to charge for advertising services revenues)
Audience research services	Networks/Advertisers	*Services revenues* (research services)
DVR technology	OEMs and CE manufacturer Licensees	*Technology revenues,* which included 1) license fees—both up-front fees, which ranged from several million dollars for object code up to $10 million for source code; 2) per unit license fees; and 3) engineering service fees, which were charged by the man-hour for the engineering services necessary to help OEMs and licensees adapt the TiVo technology to the licensees/OEMs' hardware.
		Service revenues, whenever TiVo received a percentage of the monthly fees paid by consumers to the CE or OEM, e.g., DirecTV paid TiVo a monthly per subscriber fee for each of DirecTV's DVR subscribers.

Source: TiVo Inc.

stated that TiVo had changed their lives. Numerous celebrities also sang the praises of TiVo, including Oprah Winfrey, who often spoke of "TiVo-ing" a favorite show. TiVo found that its core consumer segment consisted of "discriminating enthusiasts," people comfortable with technology, but not necessarily "techies," whose lives revolved around their passions. The typical discriminating enthusiast was married, between 25 and 45 years old, and had a household income of $70,000 to $100,000. Families with young children were particularly fond of TiVo, not only because of its "TV-on-demand" aspect but the parental controls as well.

In spite of TiVo's growing fan base, market research on consumer willingness to pay a monthly fee for DVR devices offered conflicting results. One study showed that while 25% of consumers were interested in getting television programs whenever they wanted them, a mere 5% said that they were willing to pay a monthly fee for a DVR product.[15] However, another study indicated that consumers were willing to pay cable operators between $5 and $10 a month for DVR service and that there was high satisfaction with the service.[16] Once consumers subscribed to TiVo, they seemed to believe the service was worth continuing. TiVo's churn rate—the rate at which customers gave up their subscriptions—was extremely low. At less than 1% per month and about 10% per year, it was lower than churn rates for other subscription services such as cell phone service (about 33% per year), cable TV service (about 30% per year), and DirecTV (about 18% per year).[17]

Advertisers

Although advertising rose and fell with the tides of the U.S. economy, advertising expenditures in the U.S. totaled approximately $168 billion in 2004, 35% of which was allocated to broadcast and cable TV.[18] Spending on advertising in the U.S. as a whole hovered at around 1% of gross domestic product. TV advertising was more important for broadcast networks than for cable operators because TV stations typically received up to 90% of their revenues from advertising, while cable system operators received 65% to 70% of their revenues from subscriber fees.[19] In addition, cable operators generated revenues from installation charges and sales of VOD movies and events. About one-third of cable advertising revenues went to the cable operators and two-thirds to the cable networks, content generators such as Nickelodeon.

DVRs raised important questions for advertisers. In 2004, researchers estimated that 88% of consumers skipped ads with their DVRs.[20] By 2005, roughly 2% of TV ads were being skipped, and more than 10% might be skipped by 2009.[21] Some analysts believed that advertising would need to expand beyond the traditional 30-second commercials and away from broadcast TV as the anchor medium. To keep the consumer interested, advertising innovations included 1) "mini-movies" that were highly entertaining commercials, often shown on the advertiser's Web site (Anheuser-Busch was a pioneer in this area), and 2) the enhanced use of product placement in popular TV series (e.g., the reality TV series "Survivor" and "The Apprentice").[22] Overall, the trends signaled a move to more "opt-in" advertising, where consumers chose to see commercials as an integral part of the entertainment package. According to TiVo Vice President Stuart West, "Total TV advertising was roughly $60 billion. If we are successful, we could capture hundreds of millions of this revenue by the end of the decade."

TiVo's "showcase" service, dubbed "advertainment" by some, fit in with this trend. Showcases provided specialized digital content meant to entertain subscribers while promoting an advertiser's product. Subscribers could choose whether to "opt in" and could be given other choices as well, for example, to enter a contest or receive a free product or brochure. TiVo frequently sold showcases in combination with its audience-measurement service, an offering aimed at networks and advertisers. The audience-measurement service allowed second-by-second analysis of viewing patterns within TV programs or ads. Networks and advertisers could see what percentage of viewers opted to watch a showcase and how many times they watched it. TiVo charged a few hundred thousand dollars to place content over three to six months but was moving toward a cost-per-viewer fee so that revenues would reflect the size of the subscriber base. Showcase and audience-research revenues were relatively small, although showcase revenues reached about $5 million in fiscal year 2004.

In 2004, TiVo announced a new advertising initiative, introducing a feature that would let television viewers send personal information directly to advertisers when they viewed commercials. For example, after watching an ad for a car or vacation, users could use the remote control to tell TiVo to release their contact information and request that a brochure be sent to their home. "Advertising is a substantial growth area," noted Kimber Sterling, former director of advertising and research sales at TiVo. Sterling noted that advertising was "not material revenue for us yet."[23] Some TiVo users might prefer to skip ads entirely, but others would watch long-form commercials, particularly if they were about cars or Hollywood films.

TiVo's Competitive Environment

Content Distributors

The three major types of TV distributors were the terrestrial TV stations, the cable operators, and the satellite companies. The Big Three (ABC, CBS, and NBC) broadcasters' share of the prime-time television audience had declined for several decades. Cable grabbed the lion's share of U.S. TV households, while satellite was also gaining rapidly.

The battle between cable and satellite had important implications for TiVo. The multiple services operators (MSOs) were at a critical juncture in their history, having spent billions of dollars upgrading their systems to carry digital signals in the past decade. Over the next several years, the cable industry was projected to go through a massive change, as millions of subscribers switched their analog set-top boxes for new digital boxes. Cable operators averaged around $40 per analog (or basic) subscriber and $60 per digital subscriber, providing a significant incentive for urging consumers to make the switch.

MSOs were initially slow to adopt DVRs. Comcast, for example, had urged the cable industry to adopt VOD instead of DVRs. (See Exhibit 5 for cable and satellite operators' VOD, HDTV, and DVR activity.) Taken to an extreme, if all content were available "on demand," consumers would have no need for DVR products. AOL Time-Warner was developing a large VOD system set to debut in mid-2005. Dubbed "Mystro TV," the system would store programming in the central "hubs" of cable networks, allowing the networks to control the features (e.g., there would be no ability to skip ads). The two largest roadblocks to developing the service were that 1) cable hubs would need significant centralized storage capacity (compared to the TiVo system where capacity was decentralized), and 2) licensing agreements with studios and networks would be necessary.

By 2005, the cable industry had reversed course. Competition from TiVo and satellite DVRs as well as the growing acceptance of the category led cable companies to promote DVRs aggressively. One challenge was that the cable industry was highly fragmented, and cable set-top boxes could vary slightly from locale to locale. Most MSOs sold their DVR-capable set-top boxes directly through their local subsidiary. There were two major DVR providers to the cable industry: Motorola and Scientific Atlanta. Comcast and RCN, for example, used a Motorola DVR, while Time-Warner, Cox, and other cable operations offered Scientific Atlanta's Explorer 8,000—the first integrated set-top box for the cable industry. Some MSOs used both technologies. While both the Motorola and Scientific Atlanta boxes lacked TiVo's advanced features, some versions had multiple tuners and could record in high definition. Most cable companies gave away the hardware for free, with an $8–$10 monthly subscription.

Both U.S. satellite operators provided DVR capabilities. DirecTV's competitor, EchoStar, offered DVR capability based on OpenTV's technology. EchoStar's Dish Network was estimated to be the second-largest provider of DVR devices, after TiVo (and DirecTV). Similar to the Motorola and Scientific Atlanta boxes, the Dish Network

EXHIBIT 5   CABLE AND SATELLITE OPERATORS' VOD, HDTV, AND DVR ACTIVITY (MID-2005)

Cable Operator	Millions of Subscribers		Market Share (households)	Current VOD/HD Activity		Current DVR Activity		
	Basic/Digital (households in millions)	Broadband		Deployment VOD	Deployment HDTV	Deployment DVR	Pricing	Comments
Comcast/AT&T	21.3/6.8	6.0	24%	Yes	Yes	Comcast in 2004 TiVo deal in 2005	$9.95/month	"Most bullish on VOD" (EVP, Marketing)
DirecTV	13.0 satellite	Partners Verizon, BellSouth, Qwest	15%	PPV	Yes	Yes	$4.99/month, free to premium subscribers	Note: ongoing relationship with TiVo, but conflict over NDS
Time-Warner Cable	10.9/4.7	3.7	12%	Yes	Yes	Yes	$8.95/month	"SVOD substantially reduces churn" by as much as 40% (EVP, Marketing)
Dish Networks	10.5 satellite	EarthLink option	12%	PPV	Yes	Yes	Packages start at $19.99/month	
Charter Communications	5.9/2.6	1.9	7%	Yes	Yes	Yes	$9.99/month	"Not sure DVR and VOD need to coexist" (VP, Marketing)
Cox Communications	6.3/2.3	2.4	7%	Yes	Yes	Yes	$9.95/month	"We're very encouraged by what we see with DVR" (VP, video product management)
Adelphia	5.0/1.8	0.9	6%	Yes	Yes	Yes	$8.45/month	Note: in bankruptcy, possible acquisition by Comcast/TW in 2005
Cablevision	2.9/1.6	1.4	4%	Yes	Yes	No	N/A	

Note: SVOD refers to subscription video on demand, which provided consumers with continuous access to certain content for a monthly fee. Comcast was experimenting with three types of VOD: (1) movie based; (2) an SVOD offering that provided access to Showtime content anytime; and (3) free VOD, which offered about 750 hours a month of programming.

Source: Smith Barney, TiVo Report, January 17, 2005; "US Cable Subscriber Statistics," *eMarketer Report*, April 1, 2003; "Deploy and Conquer," *Cable World*, April 7, 2003, http://www.seachangeinternational.com/newsevents/articles/2003/Cable_World_April_7_2003.pdf, accessed July 20, 2003; Shirley Brady, "Mystro Wants to Play," *Cable World*, July 2, 2003, http://cableworld.com/microsites, accessed July 23, 2003; and "4Q 2002 Research Notes," Leichtman Research Group, Inc. Report, p. 5. Also, http://www.tnstelecoms.com/press-1-31-05.html.

DVRs had limited functionality, but Dish had become an aggressive distributor, occasionally giving its products away for free with no monthly charge.

In 2005, a new content distributor was entering the equation: telecommunications companies. Many analysts assumed that the future existence of the telephone companies could depend on their ability to enter the video market, bundling video with phone and Internet access. SBC, Verizon, and others hoped to bring brand recognition and very deep pockets to the battle for video distribution. Several telcos were aggressively laying fiber-optic networks to offer superior bandwidth coupled with IPTV. And unlike the cable companies, which had made prior commitments to set-top box providers for their aggressive rollouts of digital video, most telcos were still early in the testing phases.

Content Providers

Filmed entertainment content providers had become more concentrated following several acquisitions and mergers in the late 1990s and early 2000s. The industry's top nine companies owned a variety of entertainment assets ranging from Hollywood studios to television networks to theme parks. The four major U.S. TV broadcast networks, which attracted about 40% of prime-time viewers, were each owned by one of these top entertainment companies. Seven of the top nine companies also owned cable TV operations.

The TV and movie content providers were somewhat conflicted regarding DVR technology. Several Hollywood studios sued TiVo competitor ReplayTV over its "send show" feature, which allowed consumers to record and then send shows to others. Replay's "commercial advance" feature also allowed consumers to skip commercials with the push of a button rather than fast forward as TiVo did. At the same time, several large players had significant ownership positions in DVR companies—for example, AOL and NBC had invested in TiVo's equity; News Corp., which owned TiVo competitor NDS, had acquired a controlling interest in Hughes Electronics, which owned DirecTV. Sony also manufactured and sold DVRs in Japan and the U.S. Smaller players such as Liberty Media, which had controlling interest of OpenTV, were also involved with DVR technologies.

Equipment and Technology Competitors

In addition to cable and satellite DVR offerings, there were several other types of DVR producers. (See Exhibit 6 for DVR competitors and Exhibit 7 for product features of selected DVR products.) These included stand-alone DVR providers, technology component (e.g., software and chips) suppliers, and PC manufacturers. ReplayTV was the only major competitor in the stand-alone DVR product category. Founded at about the same time as TiVo, ReplayTV sold the DVRs most often compared with TiVo's, with some reviewers preferring TiVo's features and some preferring ReplayTV's.

Initially, ReplayTV did not charge a monthly service fee, instead charging more for the DVR unit, which included lifetime service. In 2002 Replay began charging a monthly service fee—$9.95—for the first time. Management said that although they and consumers believed that paying one price for the hardware and the service up

EXHIBIT 6   DVR COMPETITORS (EXCLUDES PURE DVR TECHNOLOGY PROVIDERS, AS OF MAY 2005)

Product	Company	Parent Company	DVR Technology Used	Box Manufacturer	Hard-Drive Capacity	Price of Hardware	Monthly Subscription Fee
Stand-alone DVRs:							
TiVo Series2	TiVo	N/A	TiVo	TiVo (contract mfr.)	40GB–140GB	$199–$349	$mo. or $299 lifetime
ReplayTV	ReplayTV	D&M Holdings	ReplayTV	Various	40GB–320GB	$149–$799	$mo. or $299 lifetime
Stand-alone DVD-DVRs							
DMRE85HS (DVD-DVR)	Panasonic	Matsushita	N/A	Self	120GB	$399	None
DVR 10—HD (DVD-DVR)	RCA	N/A	N/A	Thomson	80GB	$399	None
Satellite and Cable Integrated Set-top Boxes							
HDVR2	DirectTV (satellite)	Hughes Electronics	TiVo	Hughes, Samsung, RCA, Philips	40GB	$99	$4.99; free to premium subscribers
DishPVR508 and 721	Dish Network (satellite)	EchoStar Com-munications	OpenTV	N/A	40GB–250GB	$299 to $699 with rebate	$4.98–$9.99; free to premium subscribers
Digital Video Recorder	Time-Warner Cable	AOL Time-Warner	Scientific Atlanta 8000 with Keen and MetaByte Networks technology	Scientific Atlanta	40GB–80GB (2 tuners)	$650 list (free to digital subscribers)	$9.95
PCs w/DVR Software							
Media Center PC	Microsoft	N/A	Microsoft (Ultimate TV)	Various (e.g., Hewlett-Packard)	80GB–250GB hard drive	$1,399–$1,999	None

Source: Casewriter research, adapted from company Web sites (http://www.tivo.com, http://www.digitalnetworksna.com/replaytv, http://www.rca.com, http://www.panasonic.com, http://www.directv.com, http://www.dishnetwork.com, http://www.timewarnercable.com, http://www.microsoft.com), accessed May 17, 2005.

EXHIBIT 7 PRODUCT FEATURES OF SELECTED DVR PRODUCTS

	TiVo Series2	TiVo Series2	TiVo Series2	DirecTV with TiVo	ReplayTV 5,504	ReplayTV 5,508	Replay TV 5,516	ReplayTV 5,532	EchoStar's Dish PVR 508	EchoStar's Dish PVR 721	EchoStar's PVR 942 HD	Example Cable: Time-Warner Scientific Atlanta 8,000
Pricing—Hardware	$199	$249	$349	$149 or $99 after rebate	$149 or $99 after rebate	$299 or $199 after rebate	$449 or $349 after rebate	$799 or $599 after rebate	$299 with rebate	$549	$699	Equipment leased free of charge (cost to cable company $300)
Pricing—Service	$mo./mo., $6.95 boxes 2-6 or $299 lifetime	$mo./mo., $6.95/mo boxes 2-6 or $299 lifetime	$mo./mo., $6.95/mo boxes 2-6 or $299 lifetime	$4.99/mo. Free to premium subscribers	$mo./mo. or $299 lifetime	$mo./mo. or $299 lifetime	$mo./mo. or $299 lifetime	$12.95/mo. or $299 lifetime	$4.98–$9.99/mo. Free to premium subscribers	$4.98–$9.99/mo. Free to premium subscribers	$4.98–$9.99/mo. Free to premium subscribers	$9.95/mo.
Hard-disk recording, VCR style (e.g., by date, time)	x	x	x	x	x	x	x	x	x	x	x	x
Amount of program guide data	14 days	14 days	14 days	14 days	12 days	12 days	12 days	12 days	9 days	9 days	9 days	7 days
Skip forward 30 seconds	x	x	x	x	x	x	x	x	x	x	x	x
Two tuners	No	Yes	Yes	Yes	No	No	No	No	No	Yes	Yes	x
Storage capacity (GB)	40 GB	80 GB	140 GB	40 GB	40 GB	80 GB	160 GB	320 GB	40-80 GB	120 GB	250 GB	?
Ability to "suggest" shows to user based on user's viewing habits	x	x	x	x	No	No	No	No	No	No	No	No
DVR is integrated into cable or satellite receiver	No	No	No	No	No	No	No	No	x	x	No	x
Ability to display digital photos	No	No	x	No	x	x	x	No	No	No	No	No
Ability to play digital music (mp3 files)	No	No	x	No	No	No	No	No	No	No	No	No
Source of DVR technology	TiVo	TiVo	TiVo	TiVo	ReplayTV	ReplayTV	ReplayTV	Replay TV	OpenTV	OpenTV	Open TV	Scientific Atlanta

Note: Two tuners enabled a user to record two live programs at once, record live while watching live, or record two programs live while watching one prerecorded.

Source: Casewriter research, adapted from "Dish Network PVR Brochures," Dish Network Web site, http://www.pvrcmpare.com/featurechart.html, accessed May 17, 2005; TiVo Web site, http://www.tivo.com/2.0asp, accessed May 17, 2005; TiVo Inc. Form 10-K for year ended January 31, 2005, accessed May 17, 2005.

593

front was much simpler, CE retailers wanted the DVR unit priced lower, and the only way to do that was to charge a separate service fee.

Scientific Atlanta's combination cable receiver/DVR set-top boxes were powered by MetaByte Networks software and Keen Personal Media software. Keen received 80 cents per DVR. OpenTV's middleware platform was used by dozens of large and small set-top box manufacturers. Consumers could also turn their PCs into DVRs. It was possible to buy software packages that required a monthly subscription fee of about $5 in order to receive an EPG. Finally, consumers could buy PCs configured with Microsoft's Windows XP Media Center designed to offer DVR capabilities. Hewlett-Packard and Gateway, for example, made Media Center PCs priced from $1,000 to $2,000. The Sony Vaio also included DVR capability.

TiVo confronted a rash of new entrants. Two of the most aggressive were 2Wire and Akimbo. 2Wire was founded shortly after TiVo in 1998. Its MediaPortal set-top box was an elegant video and entertainment system with some features superior to those of the current TiVo. 2Wire could offer an integrated satellite and digital television receiver, high-definition DVR, digital media server, multi-room entertainment networking, and broadband media services such as Internet movie, messaging, and online music. In January 2005, 2Wire and SBC formed a joint venture called SBC Media Solution to develop set-top boxes for SBC's video services. They planned to deploy in the second half of 2005, in cooperation with satellite broadcasts from Dish Network.

Akimbo was a more recent entrant, founded in 2002. Akimbo's focus was VOD services over the Internet, rather than through cable or satellite. The Akimbo Player was a set-top box that enabled a user to view programming from the Internet on a television set. The device, which licensed digital rights management software and an operating system from Microsoft, had on-screen menus for browsing downloaded content and stored up to 200 hours of digital-quality video. Akimbo followed a subscription model similar to TiVo's. It required an up-front hardware cost of $229.99, sold through the company Web site and Amazon.com, and had a monthly subscription fee of $9.99 or a lifetime subscription fee of $199.99. Premium content was available at an additional cost. Although there were only a few hundred units sold as of February 2005, Akimbo had signed contracts with content providers such as A&E, the History Channel, National Geographic, CinemaNow, Turner Classic Movies, and iFilm, as well as adult content providers.

Competitive Positioning in 2005

TiVo's growth depended partly on its actions in retail channels. TiVo had responded to competitors' DVR products with mail-in rebates and service enhancements. In August 2004, TiVo offered boxes between $99 (after rebate) and $299. The box had a new design and was sold by some of the largest retailers in the U.S. The new low prices led to a surge in TiVo unit volumes in late 2004. To address the high-definition market, TiVo required an integrated set-top box. Without integration or direct access to a high-definition set-top box, TiVo could not record programs in high definition, even if high definition was available. The same was true for dual tuners: unless TiVo had direct access to a set-top box that could get multiple channels simultaneously, it could only record one channel at a time.

In addition to consumer features, TiVo had potential advantages over other DVRs for advertisers. Through showcases, the capability to provide interactive ads with specific TV programs, and the ability to collect fine-grained data on consumer viewing habits, TiVo was seeing a growing roster of advertisers.[24] TiVo advertisers included GM, Coca-Cola, Universal Pictures, Nissan, Fox, Walt Disney, and Charles Schwab. TiVo was also active on the TV show ratings front. In October, TiVo's Season Pass Hot 100 rankings showed that "Desperate Housewives" was the first new fall show to hit the number one spot in TiVo's weekly ratings. As the TiVo subscriber base had grown to over 3 million accounts, the Season Pass ratings were carrying more significance for networks.[25]

Pending actions by the Federal Communications Commission (FCC) could have a big impact on TiVo. The FCC was debating whether to force the cable industry to make their set-top boxes less proprietary and more open to third parties. TiVo, along with companies such as Intel and Microsoft, had been lobbying for a requirement that would allow television manufacturers, PC companies, and other TV peripherals manufacturers of devices such as DVRs to build plug-and-play open standards that could communicate with the cable networks without a separate set-top box. Many cable companies, on the other hand, were lobbying to delay or minimize the degree of openness for any new standards. TiVo announced in January 2005 that it would ship an integrated DVR with a cable card, eliminating the need for a set-top box, in early 2006. A "one-way" cable card was necessary for TiVo's stand-alone box to support high-definition and multiple tuners that were available directly from the MSOs. A "two-way" cable card would be necessary for TiVo to support premium services such as pay-per-view. One-way cable cards became available for many markets in 2005. For two-way cable cards TiVo would have to wait and see if the new FCC chairman, Kevin Martin, would be supportive in the face of intense industry pressure.[26]

The Future for TiVo

Despite continuing rave reviews from critics and consumers about its product, TiVo management faced daunting challenges. By the summer of 2005, DirecTV was announcing that it planned to replace TiVo as soon as possible with NDS DVRs. Roughly 70% of TiVo's 3.3 million users were DirecTV subscribers. Even though DirecTV had signed a new advertising services agreement with TiVo the prior April that would allow both companies to sell and distribute TiVo's advanced advertising capabilities,[27] News Corp. appeared anxious to accelerate the transition. On the one hand, a DirecTV customer only generated a net present value (NPV) of around $25 to $35 per customer (compared with roughly $250 NPV for a stand-alone customer). On the other hand, DirecTV created a volume platform, with 14 million potential customers.

The new agreement with Comcast offered an opportunity to replace and expand on DirecTV's customer base. But the Comcast deal was different for TiVo: While DirecTV sold an integrated satellite-TiVo box, Comcast wanted to adapt TiVo software to run on existing hardware, mostly Motorola boxes. TiVo could either use the existing Motorola operating system with a TiVo interface and application or scoop it out and replace it with a Linux kernel with TiVo inside. TiVo was obliged to deliver on the technical front, and Comcast would cover marketing. They also concluded an advertising agreement that would span all DVRs deployed with the TiVo system. Although the deal was not exclusive, it would run for seven years from the first deployment, with an option to extend year by year for another eight years. Similar to the DirecTV deal, Comcast would pay TiVo under one dollar per subscriber, per month as well as pay nonrecurring engineering (NRE) expenses for TiVo to adapt its software.

TiVo had one immediate, pressing objective: deliver the solution for Comcast. Ramsay had promised to drive the company to positive earnings by the end of 2005, but new CEO Rogers told Wall Street in August that was unrealistic. Long-term strategy at TiVo was still very much open for debate. Management actively debated at least four options: 1) aggressively pursue the stand-alone business; 2) focus on OEM (Comcast-like) deals with other cable companies, and possibly telcos, with the hope of making TiVo into an advertising platform business versus a DVR hardware-services business; 3) become a content distributor; and 4) seek new markets outside of the U.S., where DVRs were still in their nascent stages.

Stand-alone DVRs

If TiVo could make the stand-alone DVR business work, some managers argued, it could be a home run. One way to segment the market, according to Matt Wisk, TiVo's chief marketing officer, was to construct three large segments:

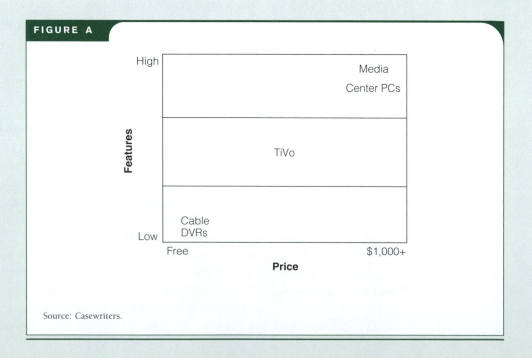

FIGURE A

Source: Casewriters.

Although many cable companies largely gave away their DVRs for free, they were generally low-function products that could not match TiVo's differentiation. At the high end, Microsoft and PC companies would offer very expensive, general purpose PCs that could also function as DVRs. In the middle, TiVo might have an opportunity to build a profitable business. CEO Rogers also viewed three key customer segments for TiVo to address: the 40 million or so analog cable customers, who were unlikely to move to digital cable anytime soon; the middle market of cable, satellite, and potential telco customers who would receive digital television, largely through dedicated set-top boxes; and the growing base of home-theater customers, who were early adopters of high-definition, multiple-tuner DVRs and other leading-edge technologies.

To serve these segments with a stand-alone box, one of the biggest challenges was making the business model work. First, TiVo had to solve the problem of "subscriber acquisition cost," or SAC. In 2005, the company was working hard to pare those costs down from a SAC of $180 to $125 per user. (See Exhibit 8 for TiVo subscriber acquisition cost.) One TiVo executive stated, "The brand is better established now, and the box cost has come down in manufacturing. It is getting easier to offer rebates. Also, our retailers are very supportive, and the existing customers' word of mouth is spreading. If we can build ancillary revenue streams, the proposition gets much easier."[28] A further consideration was the "average revenue per subscriber (user)," or ARPU. Between 2003 and 2004, TiVo had made significant gains, moving from an ARPU of $7.45 per subscription per month to $8.57. In 2005, the company made a modest gain—reaching $8.76. However, the picture was quite different with the DirecTV subscribers; there the ARPU had fallen from a high of $6.06 per month in 2003 to $1.52 in early 2005. (See Exhibit 9 for TiVo average revenue per subscriber.)

Another big advantage of the stand-alone business was the opportunity to innovate and establish a strong branded product. Distribution partners, such as DirecTV or Comcast, had long development cycles and limited flexibility for introducing new innovations. For example, TiVo to Go was not available to DirecTV customers and was only possible for the stand-alone system. At the same time, one manager noted, "Is it realistic for TiVo to aggressively sell our stand-alone system in direct competition with

---

EXHIBIT 8   **TIVO SUBSCRIBER ACQUISITION COST**

(in thousands except for SAC)	2005	2004	2003
Sales and marketing expenses	37,367	18,947	48,117
Rebates, revenues share, other payments to channel	54,696	9,159	9,780
Hardware revenues	(111,275)	(72,882)	(45,620)
Cost of hardware revenues	120,323	74,836	44,647
Total acquisition cost	**101,111**	**30,060**	**56,924**
TiVo-owned subscription gross additions	555	282	164
Subscription acquisition cost	**182**	**106**	**347**

Source: Company Annual Report, 2004.

EXHIBIT 9

TIVO AVERAGE REVENUE PER SUBSCRIBER (IN THOUSANDS EXCEPT ARPU DATA)

	2005	2004	2003
TiVo-Owned ARPU			
Service and technology revenues	115,476	77,357	60,170
Less: Technology revenues	(8,130)	(15,797)	(20,909)
Total service revenues	107,166	61,560	39,261
Less: DirecTV-related service revenues	(21,071)	(11,624)	(12,557)
TiVo-owned related service revenues	86,095	49,936	26,704
Average TiVo-owned revenues per month	7,175	4,161	2,225
Average TiVo-owned per month subscriptions	819	486	299
TiVo-owned ARPU per month	$8.76	$8.57	$7.45
TiVo-DirecTV ARPU			
Service and technology revenues	115,476	77,357	60,170
Less: Technology revenues	(8,130)	(15,797)	(20,909)
Total service revenues	107,166	61,560	39,261
Less: TiVo-owned related service revenues	(86,095)	(49,936)	(26,704)
DirecTV-related service revenues	21,071	11,624	12,557
Average DirecTV revenues per month	1,756	969	1,046
Average DirecTV subscriptions	1,154	377	173
DirecTV ARPU per month	$1.52	$2.57	$6.06

Source: Company Annual Report, 2004.

Comcast? Will retailers, such as Best Buy, continue to push TiVo if Comcast is giving away the hardware for free?" In addition, another manager emphasized that a retail, stand-alone business was dependent on the FCC and the cable card initiative. "There is no other way to make retail successful," he noted. "Should we count on it?"

Comcast and Advertising

While the economics of selling a stand-alone box with an ARPU of $12.95/month was clearly more attractive than an ARPU of $1/month or less for a Comcast box, Comcast and other cable and telecommunications companies offered a very high-volume distribution channel with a very low SAC. Moreover, if more Comcast-like deals could be signed, where the cable or telco would cover all development costs through NRE, incremental margin for each subscriber would be very high. In addition, if TiVo could achieve significant volumes (tens of millions), it could become the advertising platform for TV. TiVo's existing technology allowed for fine-grained data mining of viewer watching habits that went far beyond Nielson. In combination with TiVo's advertising management system, which allowed it to place ads in programming, store special advertising on the hard disk, and target those ads, it might develop a large, alternative revenue stream.

At the same time, many questions surrounded this strategy, for example, would others sign on? Since most cable companies were risk adverse, would TiVo be able to innovate and maintain its edge? Advertising on TiVo DVRs was a tiny business (projected to be roughly $5 million in 2005). Could this become a significant business for TiVo?

Content Distribution

For years, TiVo had debated the merits of entering the content distribution business directly. As a first step, TiVo announced a strategic partnership with Netflix, Inc. in the fall of 2004. The two companies hoped to work with Hollywood studios to obtain rights to distribute content digitally. Then, during the summer of 2005, TiVo struck a trial deal with the Independent Film Channel to broadcast several of the cable channel's shows over broadband. For many in the entertainment world, delivering content over the Internet was the Holy Grail. Ramsay, in particular, was intrigued by the notion of the "long tail" of content—the thousands of programs that were rarely broadcast over mass media but could be delivered on demand over the Internet to consumers with specialized interests.

By using the Internet, TiVo, in effect, could bypass the existing methods of distribution. Brodie Keast, TiVo's executive vice president for the consumer division, commented:

> We all know that broadband connectivity and home networking are increasing rapidly. If homes have both broadband and wireless, you can deliver content to the living room, and consumers will have the opportunity to define their own personal "network." In addition, producers won't be constrained by the big networks as much as in the past. People often approach us and say, "I have a great idea, but the networks don't want to do it—will you let me do this on TiVo?" Taking advantage of some of these opportunities would put us in direct competition with the networks, but it might be the best way to provide a unique service. On the other hand, pursuing this opportunity might spread us too thin. The key question is this: Since we intend over the long haul to be a television services company and the center of home entertainment, would pursuing the opportunity to be a content distributor and/or producer be helpful in terms of achieving our long-term goal?

Ramsay, TiVo's chief executive officer, added, "In the future, the consumer won't necessarily know where content comes from. You might search—in several different places—for a program that you want to watch and then record it. Eventually the pipes will become subordinated to the content providers."

Howard Look, vice president of TiVo developer studios, investigated the economics of TiVo's participation in content distribution. Look had broken down the costs into several categories including capital costs—for servers, the network, hosting, racks, and so on—as well as delivery costs, development costs, and costs for acquiring content. Regarding content acquisition, fees had to be paid both to the primary rights holder as well as to an aggregator in many cases. (Examples of aggregators included MovieLink and Shockwave.) As part of his exercise, Look had to estimate the number of TiVo

Series2 subscribers, the percentage of Series2 subscribers who would have home networking, and the rate at which relevant Series2 subscribers would choose to download content. Look estimated that it would take the company six to nine months to get into the business once a decision was made.

Look discussed the various types of video content that TiVo could broadcast:

When you think about content, you first think about "A" movies. This is the most expensive content. Studios take a 50%–60% share and aggregators take 30%–33%. Generally, you can charge consumers something similar to the cost they would pay to rent the movie from a movie rental chain. Another category of content is the thousands of hours of content that have been aggregated by various cable channels such as Discovery, PBS, and National Geographic. A third category is the work of independent producers. Aaron Sorkin is a good example of a producer who wants to distribute his content in an unconventional way; other producers have also come to us with show ideas. Other content categories include both short- and long-form adult video content and "niche" opportunities such as Australian rugby. Two content questions we would need to answer are what content would our subscribers value most and whether we should partner with a large aggregator. Such a partnership would expand our pool of content very efficiently, but our share of the revenues would be smaller.

As TiVo management debated the idea of becoming a content distributor, several questions were raised for discussion, including the extent to which satellite and cable operators—some of which were the company's customers—would be unhappy with a TiVo move into content distribution; whether TiVo would use its own brand or create another brand; whether the company should consider entering the content distribution business to drive TiVo adoption even if the business was not highly profitable; and whether TiVo would deliver content just to TiVo customers or to others as well.

International

A fourth option was for TiVo to explore opportunities outside the United States. The international opportunity was obvious: if DVRs become a worldwide phenomena, then better to be early than to be late. At the same time, one TiVo executive noted, "We cannot do big engineering projects in every country."[29] In early 2005, TiVo was working on projects in Asia, the largest of which was known as TGC, Inc. (which stood for TiVo Greater China) and covered China, Hong Kong, Taiwan, and Singapore. TiVo was the largest shareholder of this venture, holding a 40% stake, with VCs and industry players holding the rest. The goals were to drive lower-cost platforms for TiVo, to explore other platforms, and to exploit the service market. The company was also considering activity in Japan, where the hard-disk recorder market was strong but the software was perhaps not as good. There was a sense that the brand would work well in Japan, but the company was not making announcements yet.

EXHIBIT 10

TIVO FINANCIAL PERFORMANCE 2000–2004 (IN THOUSANDS EXCEPT PER SHARE DATA AND SUBSCRIPTIONS)

Year Ended	Jan. 31, 2005	Jan. 31, 2004	Jan. 31, 2003	Jan. 31, 2002	Jan. 31, 2001	Dec. 31, 2000
Service revenues	107,166	61,560	39,261	19,297	989	3,782
Technology revenues	8,310	15,797	20,909	100	–	–
Hardware revenues	111,275	72,882	45,620	–	–	–
Rebates, revenue share and other payments to channel	(54,696)	(9,159)	(9,780)	–	(630)	(5,029)
Net revenues	**172,055**	**141,080**	**96,010**	**19,397**	**359**	**(1,247)**
Cost of service revenues	29,360	17,705	17,119	19,852	1,719	18,734
Cost of technology revenues	6,575	13,609	8,033	62		
Cost of hardware revenues	120,323	74,836	44,647			
Research and development	37,634	22,167	20,714	27,205	2,544	25,070
Sales and marketing	37,367	18,947	48,117	104,897	13,946	151,658
General and administrative	16,593	16,296	14,465	18,875	1,395	15,537
Loss from operations	**(75,797)**	**(22,480)**	**(57,085)**	**(151,494)**	**(19,245)**	**(212,246)**
Interest income, net	1,548	498	4,483)	2,163	672	7,928
Interest expense and other	(5,459)	(9,587)	(27,569)	(7,374)	(17)	(522)
Net loss attributable to common stockholders	**(79,842)**	**(32,018)**	**(82,261)**	**(160,723)**	**(19,013)**	**(206,354)**
Net loss per common share—basic and diluted	**(0.99)**	**(0.48)**	**(1.61)**	**(3.74)**	**(0.47)**	**(5.55)**
Weighted average common shares used to calculate basic and diluted	80,264	66,784	51,219	42,956	40,850	37,175
Total subscribers—stand-alone TiVo	1,141,000	656,000	396,000	246,000		
Total subscribers—DirecTV TiVo	1,860,000	676,000	228,000	134,000		
Total cumulative subscriptions	3,001,000	1,332,000	624,000	380,000		

Note: For year-end statistics, earnings per share are based on basic shares outstanding.

Source: SEC documents, TiVo financial statements.

International expansion had the further problem of stretching resources that were already too thin.

Decision Time

For new CEO Rogers, Ramsay in his new capacity on the board, and the TiVo team, it was time to make decisions. In the near term, they had to deliver the Comcast solution. But unless they started investing immediately in their longer-term strategic initiatives, the opportunities could be lost. Ultimately the key question was, what was the ideal mix of these various strategic options? With only a few hundred employees, they could not do everything. As Ramsay put it, "As the founder, I encouraged creativity around the product and brought its value to customers. But now we need creativity around business models, and that area has not always been clear."[30] Yet as the team focused on reaching that goal, they had to focus on their best opportunities

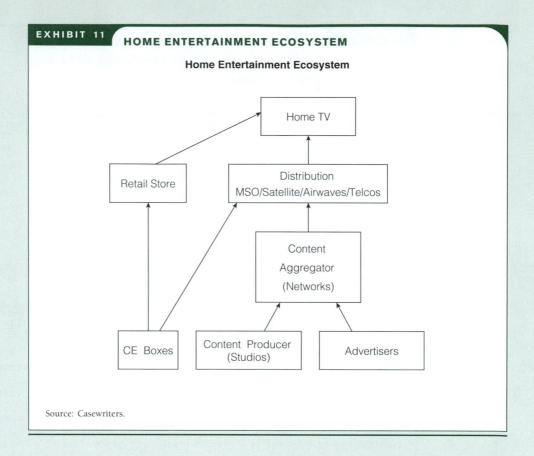

EXHIBIT 11   **HOME ENTERTAINMENT ECOSYSTEM**

Home Entertainment Ecosystem

Source: Casewriters.

and simultaneously solve the problem of a disintegrating relationship with DirecTV, aggressive competitors such as EchoStar, and the emergence of new players such as Akimbo. (See Exhibit 10 for TiVo financial performance and Exhibit 11 for home entertainment ecosystem.)

The Brand in the Hand: Mobile Marketing at adidas

Nick Drake, Global Media manager (Global Media Group) for adidas, arrived at the company's headquarters to present a bold new marketing strategy, based around mobile phones. "We call it the Brand in the Hand," he told the senior marketing executives who had gathered to present their strategy for the upcoming year. The Global Media Group had been arguing that mobile marketing was the surest, and perhaps only, way for adidas to break free from the advertising clutter and fragmentation of traditional media. "Mobile is the most personal medium available," Drake explained. "People run their whole lives off of mobile. It's business, it's personal, it's information gathering. It's on 24/7. With mobile, you have the customer's complete attention."

The Global Media Group predicted that mobile media would eventually replace most forms of print media, and by taking advantage of this trend early, adidas had a chance to surpass its competitors. Uli Becker, adidas head of Global Communications, was not so sure. "Prove it to me," he said. He gave the Global Media Group one year to test various mobile marketing concepts in order to demonstrate how handheld devices could provide a positive brand experience without annoying potential customers by intruding into their personal lives.

A few months later, adidas entered into a promising agreement to market a new line of footwear and clothing by Missy Elliott, hip-hop's leading female artist. The Global Media Group proposed a mobile component that would appeal to "hundreds of thousands" of young Americans and provide a long-term connection between the adidas brand and Missy Elliott fans.

Richard Ivey School of Business
The University of Western Ontario

David Wesley prepared this case under the supervision of Professors Andy Rohm and Fareena Sultan solely to provide material for class discussion. The authors do not intend to illustrate either effective or ineffective handling of a managerial situation. The authors may have disguised certain names and other identifying information to protect confidentiality.

Ivey Management Services is the exclusive representative of the copyright holder and prohibits any form of reproduction, storage, or transmittal without its written permission. This material is not covered under authorization from CanCopy or any reproduction rights organization. To order copies or request permission to reproduce materials, contact Ivey Publishing, Ivey Management Services, c/o Richard Ivey School of Business, The University of Western Ontario, London, Ontario, Canada, N6A 3K7; phone (519) 661-3208; fax (519) 661-3882; e-mail cases@ivey.uwo.ca.

Copyright © 2005, Northeastern University, College of Business Administration. One time permission to reproduce granted by Ivey Management Services on September 27, 2006.

soccer team in 2002. The company likewise increased advertising spending for important soccer events, such as the World Cup. In 2003, Nike edged out adidas for the first time in the European soccer market with a 34 per cent market share, compared to 30 per cent for adidas.[2]

In 2004, Nike spent a total of $1.4 billion on advertising and promotion, compared to approximately $900 million by adidas. Therefore, adidas had to be more effective and focused in its advertising spending. "Our goal is to be the leading sport brand," explained Rich Prenderville, head of Global Media. "And that means we have to use our money in smarter ways."

Breaking through the Clutter

For adidas, television remained the primary communications medium. While the company was gradually moving away from print media and replacing it with online and mobile advertising, digital advertising remained a lesser component of larger integrated campaigns. Noted Prenderville:

> *Print for us has become a poor environment in regard to clutter. If you look at the magazine* FHM, *for example, in some issues you need to go to page 48 before you get any editorial. Unless you have the inside front or back covers, you just become part of the clutter.*

Adidas traditionally advertised at sporting events and through sponsorship of sports teams and players. These events reinforced the brand's value to an existing customer base, but did little to attract consumers outside the sporting sphere. Meanwhile, urban environments were fast becoming saturated with advertising messages as companies vied for attention. Not only were consumers harder to reach, but clutter had made many people hostile to the perceived intrusions that advertising made in their lives. In an effort to break free of clutter, consumers sought refuge in new technologies, such as digital video recorders and popup blockers that offered ways to avoid unwanted messages.

In this environment, consumers on average received no more than eight minutes of adidas advertising per year through all forms of broadcast media. Given the scarcity of time available to directly address consumers, adidas had to ensure that its messages were meaningful and memorable. Grabbing the attention of potential consumers meant seeking innovative ways to deliver advertising. For example, in 2002, the company created a special billboard for the World Cup soccer tournament in Japan, featuring a giant foot extended toward a large boulevard. Half way down the boulevard a giant soccer ball sat atop a crushed car. The advertisement received extensive coverage by international news media as part of their World Cup coverage.

Another early attempt to penetrate clutter was the "living billboard." In September 2003, adidas Japan created a vertical soccer field where two "players" were suspended on bungee cords down the side of the billboard five times a day for 20 minutes. According to one observer:

> *Hundreds of people stopped to take photos and cheer the two players on. Then, by talking about the event to others, the bystanders spread the word about it. The resulting buzz just got bigger and bigger.*[3]

For a time, the living billboard received coverage on local and international news media, and drew millions of visitors.

The Role of Digital Media

A more pressing dilemma was the move away from traditional media forms, in favor of digital media, such as mobile devices, video games and the Internet. As late as 2003, adidas devoted its entire marketing budget to traditional media. Based on the assumption that more than half of all media consumption would be digital by 2007 (see Exhibit), adidas decided to gradually shift its marketing efforts toward new media. In particular, 12- to 24-year-olds, who made up the core of adidas's target audience, devoted a large portion of their time to using online instant messengers, downloading music and communicating with friends via e-mail. "We're not walking away from TV," noted Prenderville. "We're still spending about three-quarters of our budget on traditional media, such as TV, out of home (billboards), and cinema." The Global Media Group saw new media as offering richer, more personal, transactional experiences than television or print.

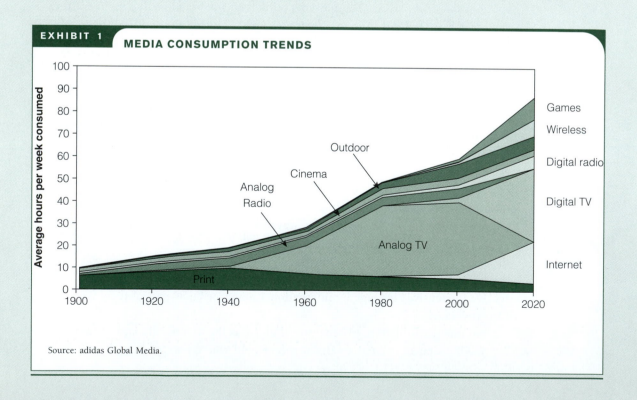

EXHIBIT 1   MEDIA CONSUMPTION TRENDS

Source: adidas Global Media.

"It is an environment in which consumers are entirely focused and want to receive a message," Drake explained.

By 2005, adidas was spending between 15 and 25 per cent of its marketing budget on new media, more than any of its competitors. Regional subsidiaries were required to spend at least 10 per cent of their budgets on new media. Production for online was relatively inexpensive, since it often adapted existing creative from traditional media. At the same time, online costs for website takeovers and banner advertising increased substantially and, as a result, consumed a larger portion of new media advertising budgets.

Reaching Internet users with an impactful message became increasingly difficult amid the clutter of banner ads and popup windows. One way to stand out was to "take over" a popular web portal. For between $200,000 and $500,000 a day, advertisers could rent the Yahoo homepage. In early 2004, adidas took over the Yahoo portal to promote its "Impossible is Nothing Campaign" featuring female boxing star, Laila Ali, daughter of Muhammad Ali (see Exhibit 2). Users could stream a short film to their computer featuring Laila Ali and her father.

According to Tara Moss of adidas America:

Our objective was to extend the "Impossible Is Nothing" adidas brand campaign online to effectively increase our reach to 12- to 24-year-old consumers. We sought to harness the emotional concepts of improvement, challenge and achievement, bringing them to life in an inspirational narrative.[4]

The Yahoo takeover far exceeded expectations, reaching more than twice the number of customers initially hoped for. It was also one of the most successful advertisements placed on Yahoo with more than 5 million downloads. Of those downloads, the average user viewed more than 22 seconds of the 30 second clip. Visitors to the site were directed to adidas's online retail representative (finishline.com), but the site was unable to handle the unexpectedly high number of visitors and crashed part way through the day. As a direct result of the takeover, adidas sold several thousand pairs of shoes.[5]

At adidas, the failure of some competitors to adapt to rapid technological change created opportunities to deliver advertising messages through "softer points," such as mobile devices. In the words of one analyst, "Advertisers will have to keep moving if they want to reach young people who wait at the corner, playing with the keypads on their mobile phones."[6]

According to the Global Media Group, adidas needed to invest heavily in interactive media in order to gain an advantage over better funded competitors, such as Nike. "The ideal scenario," Drake explained, "is to have intuitive marketing, where you completely understand what consumers want, when they want it and how they want it. And the only way to do that is to collect data. The amount of data that we are talking about is phenomenal."

Pushing unwanted content (popularly known as spam) on users proved unpopular when it was tested in Korea and Europe using SMS advertising.[7] "We have to be careful," explained Drake.

EXHIBIT 2   **YAHOO WEB PORTAL TAKEOVER**

Personalize   Finance   Shop   **YAHOO!**®   Mail   Messenger   HotJobs   ? Help

Yahoo! Personals - A romantic Valentine's date could be yours. Enter Project: Real Valentines.

Web	Images	Yellow Pages	Products

Search the **Web**: [   ]   Yahoo! Search   • **Advanced**
• **Preferences**

New!   Yahoo! Valentine's Day Guide

Shop   Auctions, Autos, Classifieds, Real Estate, Shopping, Travel
Find   HotJobs, Maps, People Search, Personals, Yellow Pages
Connect   Chat, GeoCities, Greetings, Groups, Mail, Messenger, Mobile

Organize   Addresses, Briefcase, Calendar, My Yahoo!, PayDirect, **Photos**
Fun   Games, Horoscopes, Kids, **Movies**, Music, Radio, TV
Info   Finance, Health, News, Sports, Weather   **More Yahoo!...**

Personal Assistant   **Sign In**

Get free email with SpamGuard!
Yahoo! Mail - **Sign up now**

LAUNCH Hot New Videos
Watch: Kylie Minogue - Norah Jones
Plus: Videos, Radio, Photos & **more**

IMPOSSIBLE IS NOTHING
adidas
ALI vs. ALI
>> CLICK TO SEE MORE

Visit IIN Homepage - Replay Animation - Ad Feedback

Make Yahoo! your home page - **Yahoo! Toolbar with Pop-Up Blocker**

Yahoo! Business Services
• Web Hosting   • Sell Online
• Get a Domain   • Market Online

Yahoo! Premium Services
• SBC Yahoo! DSL   • Personals
• Live Sports   • PC Games

Web Site Directory - Sites organized by subject   Suggest your site

Business & Economy
B2B, Finance, Shopping, Jobs...

Regional
Countries, Regions, US States...

Computers & Internet
Internet, WWW, Software, Games...

Society & Culture
People, Environment, Religion...

News & Media
Newspapers, TV, Radio...

Education
College and University, K-12...

Entertainment
Movies, Humor, Music...

Arts & Humanities
Photography, History, Literature...

Recreation & Sports
Sports, Travel, Autos, Outdoors...

Science
Animals, Astronomy, Engineering...

In The News   3:23pm ET, Wed Feb 11

• Disney to study Comcast merger offer
• Edwards courts workers in Wisconsin
• 15 Palestinians die in Gaza Strip clash
• Iran marks Islamic revolution anniversary
• Detained bin Laden driver to stand trial
• Report: Smoking damages sexual health
• Use of camera phones prompting bans
• **Markets:** Dow ⬆ 1.0% • Nasdaq ⬆ 0.4%

News - **Elections** - **Sports** - **Stocks** - **Weather**

Marketplace

• Valentine flowers + free vase $29.99

    Send the freshest flowers direct from the grower. Satisfaction guaranteed and save 30-55%

• The top rated laptop and business cases - All shipped free - Today only
• Get a degree online - Boost your salary - Bachelor's, Master's, Postgrad and more
• Mortgage Calculator - Free mortgage quotes - Mortgage rates for Wednesday 2/11/04
• Personalized new Ultra golf balls - $9.99 dozen plus free ground shipping in USA

Shopping - **Computers** - **Electronics** - **Travel**

Source: Yahoo.com web archive.

To me, the phone is sacrosanct. If your personal life can appear in the same manner as a business question can, it can be intrusive. With computers you are more prepared to receive messages like this. You can read the heading, and choose to disregard it. In terms of consumer reaction to messages like this, people are very aware of what is intrusive.

After its Korea experience, adidas adopted an "opt-in" policy for all Internet and mobile advertising. In order to receive communications from adidas, users had to request it. The most challenging aspect of such a policy was developing compelling content that would attract users.

Personal Mobile Gateway

Personal mobile gateways (PMGs) allowed cellular phone users to manage personal data, such as addresses, e-mail, etc. Analysts expected PMGs to quickly replace personal digital assistants, such as Palm Pilots and Pocket PCs, by allowing everything to run off a single platform. PMGs on cellular phones would also add functionality to control household devices such as TVs, Internet, refrigerators and heart rate monitors. Adidas envisioned a platform that would allow users to manage a variety of fitness and sports programs, such as tracking exercise activity or accessing professional sports statistics.

In its current form, a PMG allowed content, such as news, music, games and applications, to be delivered directly to cellular telephones. Adidas divided content into three tiers, based on production cost and user value. Free content provided an incentive for consumers to interact with the adidas brand and usually included inexpensive media, such as wallpapers. Any production costs associated with free content were viewed as advertising expense. Cost-plus content charged a small fee to cover the expense of creating the content, such as ring tones. Finally, fee-based content provided extra value that customers were willing to pay for, such as an interview with a sports celebrity. In contrast, Nike charged users for all content downloaded to cellular phones, including wallpapers sporting the Nike logo as their central feature (see Exhibit 3). The Global Media Group debated whether or not adidas should follow the same model as Nike. "Usually marketing is about giving something for free," Drake explained. "Should marketers be selling marketing content? It's still an open debate."

The Brand in the Hand

When Drake joined the adidas Global Media Group in 2003, he was already convinced that wireless information services were quickly becoming the primary communication and entertainment medium for younger consumers. Drake had just finished working on the Vodafone account for a U.K.-based media agency, where his task had been to re-brand Vodafone's J-Sky service as Vodafone Live, an early attempt to develop a global third-generation (3G) brand.[8]

EXHIBIT 3   NIKE MOBILE DOWNLOADS

Source: nikefootball.com, December 2004.

Japan was the first to implement 3G cellular telephony in 2001, with transfer speeds as high as 2 megabits per second. Such speeds were comparable to cable modems and wireless broadband.[9] With the advent of 3G in Europe, wireless providers prepared to deliver rich content to phones. Users would be able to browse the web, watch movie clips and sporting events, download music and play games. For adidas, advanced mobile technology created new opportunities to have its brand in the hands of consumers.

By 2003, 70 per cent of Europeans owned cellular phones. The majority of these phones provided basic voice and text features. Beyond portability, most provided little beyond traditional landline phones. However, some 28 per cent of mobile phone users were equipped with a newer technology, known as 2.5G, and the number of

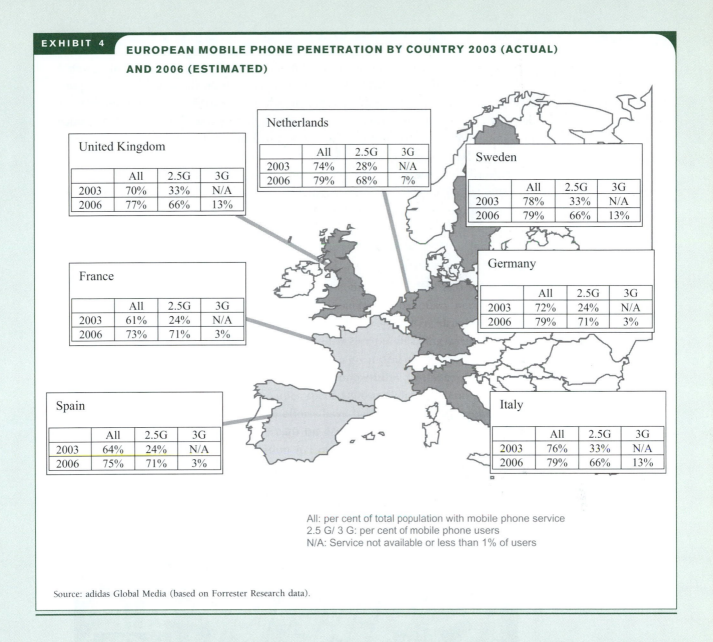

EXHIBIT 4   EUROPEAN MOBILE PHONE PENETRATION BY COUNTRY 2003 (ACTUAL) AND 2006 (ESTIMATED)

United Kingdom

	All	2.5G	3G
2003	70%	33%	N/A
2006	77%	66%	13%

Netherlands

	All	2.5G	3G
2003	74%	28%	N/A
2006	79%	68%	7%

Sweden

	All	2.5G	3G
2003	78%	33%	N/A
2006	79%	66%	13%

France

	All	2.5G	3G
2003	61%	24%	N/A
2006	73%	71%	3%

Germany

	All	2.5G	3G
2003	72%	24%	N/A
2006	79%	71%	3%

Spain

	All	2.5G	3G
2003	64%	24%	N/A
2006	75%	71%	3%

Italy

	All	2.5G	3G
2003	76%	33%	N/A
2006	79%	66%	13%

All: per cent of total population with mobile phone service
2.5 G/ 3 G: per cent of mobile phone users
N/A: Service not available or less than 1% of users

Source: adidas Global Media (based on Forrester Research data).

subscribers with access to advanced features continued to increase at a steady pace. Although 2.5G phones often included color screens and enhanced audio, they were still too slow to provide delivery of rich multimedia content. They could, however, allow users to download wallpaper, ringtones, and stripped-down Internet text, as well as send picture messages using built-in digital cameras.

With the implementation of 3G, the situation had begun to change dramatically, especially among younger consumers. While the number of Europeans with cellular phones was not expected to increase much over time, subscribers were trading in older phones for newer ones with 2.5G or 3G capabilities. By 2006, most cellular phones in Europe would be either 2.5G or 3G equipped (see Exhibit 4).

For the Global Media Group, mobile media offered several advantages over traditional media. For one, advertising could be delivered directly to a targeted audience in much the same way as direct mail. And while mobile media devices had the portability of print, they were much more time-sensitive, providing continuous on-time delivery of content. Furthermore, as the technology progressed, it began to approach the richness of TV and some wireless providers had already begun delivering television content to 3G-equipped cellular telephones.

Nevertheless, measuring the effectiveness of mobile marketing in a rapidly changing technology environment was a challenge. Without solid evidence to support the transition to new technologies, advocates found it difficult to convince other managers that Internet and mobile marketing was not just hype, particularly after the dot-com-inspired stock market decline of 2000.[10] Without strong company backing, supporters of new media had to be willing to take greater risks. The Global Media Group wanted adidas to break free of the idea that television was the center of marketing communications and embrace the potential of mobile technology.

The Global Media Group viewed Coca-Cola's Flaschenpost[11] campaign in Europe as an example of the potential of mobile marketing. In Germany, Austria, and Hungary, customers who purchased Coca-Cola products received unique codes imprinted on product boxes, cans and bottles (see Exhibit 5). The codes could then be used to

EXHIBIT 5   **"FLASCHENPOST" FOR COCA-COLA**

Source: adidas Global Media.

TABLE 1	YOUTH SPENDING ON MOBILE MEDIA BY REGION			
	2003 (actual)		**2006 (projected)**	
Region	Total Spending ($ millions)	% Leisure Spending	Total Spending ($ millions)	% Leisure Spending
North America	250	<0.1	4,500	5
Asia-Pacific	6,250	13.5	16,000	7.5
Europe	6,900	9.2	8,500	9

Source: w2forum Mobile Youth 2003.

download free mobile content. During the campaign, more than six million free wallpapers and ringtones were downloaded to mobile phones. "That's the kind of number we're interested in," explained Drake.

> *They put their entire marketing budget into this (€ 8 million) and it was hugely impactful and very successful. That's where we have to take adidas. The small steps we are taking now must show our chief marketing officer that we can achieve this.*

When adidas announced its mobile marketing initiative to regional subsidiaries, most were enthusiastic. Only the company's U.S. subsidiary was reluctant, due to the relative paucity of spending on mobile media by American youth compared to other regions of the world (see Table 1). However, once adidas Global Media presented its strategy, along with growth projections by medium, adidas America agreed to support the plan.

Global Brands vs. Regional Preferences

Technology adoption among developed countries varied from region to region, with the Far East (particularly Japan) leading the world in mobile technology, followed by Europe, and finally North America. The lag in technology adoption in the U.S. cellular phone market provided an opportunity for adidas to test new products in Europe before launching them in North America. Noted Drake:

> *The U.S. is our key market. Everything that we test in Europe is done so that we have a better practice for the U.S. The battle can be won or lost in the U.S.*

While consumers around the world enjoyed sports, movies, and music, advertising had to be tailored to the regional tastes reflected through these forms of entertainment. For instance, the endorsement of soccer superstar David Beckham[12] had a major impact on sports fans in Europe, but had little impact on Americans, who were more interested in baseball and basketball, or on Canadians obsessed with hockey.

With that in mind, adidas partnered with MTV, the most well-known music entertainment channel on television. With its vast audience and global reach, MTV became an important part of the adidas campaign. "MTV is a source of cool," Drake explained.

> *We can try to integrate adidas into MTV programming, but we also need an element where consumers can react and take action. For example, we can mix songs and tones with mobile applications.*

Mobile messaging had to be both fun and interactive in order to compel people to use it. Therefore, adidas sought methods that gave customers a "hook," and then relied on viral marketing to convince others to use the service or product.[13]

Moving Beyond Text Messages

Ringtones and Wallpaper   Adidas's first attempt at interactive mobile marketing was in Sweden in 2002, with a campaign called "Colours." Using very simple banners and wallpaper, users could click on an icon to download to their phones wallpaper that featured the adidas logo. The wallpaper was collectable and enabled discounts in stores, which proved to be the main driver for consumers. By tracking the number of clicks, adidas was able to determine that campaign had been more effective than anticipated. From that experience, adidas marketing executives came to believe that mobile marketing could be an effective weapon.

Another pilot involved a ring tone[14] program in the United Kingdom, in which users could download ring tones to their cell phones for a small fee. Adidas advertised the ring tones on interactive TV for 10 days, which resulted in 600,000 downloads. While the profit from the ring tones was miniscule, it helped create brand awareness and helped establish the effectiveness of such tools in reaching consumers.

As a first step, adidas wanted consumers to feel comfortable with the company logo on their cellular phones. Ultimately, adidas envisioned its own broadband channel that could be accessed through an adidas icon. Once accessed, subscribers would enter a virtual "adidas world" that would include a number of multimedia services aimed at increasing brand awareness and product purchases.

Video Games   According to the Global Media Group's research, video games were one of the few ways that adidas could provide a brand experience specifically aimed at the 12- to 24-year-old demographic. "Gaming is the biggest growth area among youth consumers," Drake observed. In response, mobile companies and mobile handset manufacturers invested more in developing gaming technology than any other service area.

In recognition of the trends, adidas hired a software development firm to create an arcade-style soccer game applet that could be downloaded for a fee of € 1.99. The game offered three areas of play: trick play, in which a player kicks the ball in the air and tries to prevent it from hitting the ground; free kicks, which require players to bend the ball around a wall of opposing players; and penalties. As players completed each level of play, they progressed to increasingly difficult levels.

The intent of the game applet was to create a complete brand experience for users by linking brand icons, such as David Beckham, to company products. Moreover, the acquisition of virtual equivalents of certain products, such as particular styles of soccer shoe, allowed players to improve their performance in certain areas. As a result, adidas hoped that players would realize the benefits offered by the real products represented in the game. Finally, Vodafone Live subscribers could post high scores or exchange scores with other subscribers.

The Road to Lisbon

One of the more important sporting events in Europe was the Union of European Football Associations (UEFA) Championship, a soccer event also known as the European Cup. Once every four years, the European Cup brought 16 of Europe's national teams together to compete for the title of European champion. In 2004, Portugal played host to the largest ever UEFA event and the largest sporting event ever hosted by Portugal. More than one million event tickets were sold to fans in 100 countries, and television broadcasts of the 31 games reached a cumulative audience of approximately seven billion viewers.[15]

Adidas sponsored the event with its "Road to Lisbon" (R2L) campaign, featuring 13 of Europe's greatest soccer stars as they travelled together across Europe on motorized scooters to their final destination, the European Cup (Euro 2004) in Lisbon. The centerpiece of the campaign was a short film that featured the soccer greats as they stopped in various locations along the way.

The company also invested heavily in television ads to build awareness, complemented by an Internet site from which the company promoted the mobile component. Although advertising was prohibited within one square mile of the stadium, adidas sent out "scooter squads" to other areas of Lisbon to remind people of the campaign.

The success of the R2L campaign was rounded out with an upset win by the adidas-sponsored Greek team at the Euro 2004 championship. In addition to the publicity generated by the event, sales of adidas-licensed sales of replica jerseys and Euro 2004 jerseys surpassed 2.5 million units.

Adidas's media campaigns were designed to follow three steps: impact, involvement, and activation. The first step, "impact," meant that the campaign had to be relevant to its target audience. In this respect, R2L tapped into the affinity Europeans had for soccer. Second, "involvement" meant that the advertising had personal relevance and interactivity for the consumer. For instance, by downloading wallpaper or ring tones, consumers received a benefit that made them want to participate in the marketing campaign. However, neither of these prerequisites were any benefit to adidas if they did not increase sales. "Activation," the final and most important step, involved purchases of adidas products as a direct result of advertising and promotion.

R2L Mobile Marketing

To complement the campaign, the company created a Road to Lisbon website that included downloaded polyphonic ringtones featuring music from the company's television commercial. Adidas charged less than $1 per ringtone, which included a small profit margin. In its first month, 10,000 ringtones were downloaded.

Members of Club Nokia[16] in Germany were sent text messages advertising clips from the Road to Lisbon commercial that could be inserted into conversations. Of the

EXHIBIT 6   **ADIDAS MATCH CENTRE**

Road to Lisbon   Match Centre 2.0

To get the adidas Match Centre, users entered the keyword "adidas." The Match Centre provided users with live scores, statistics and European soccer news.

A simple menu structure included:

- *Live Scores*
- *Results of Previous Matches*
- *Group Tables*
- *News*
- *adidas Zone*

Source: company files.

120,000 messages sent, 10 per cent responded by downloading clips, such as crowds cheering or booing.

Adidas created a more useful and interactive product with its Euro 2004 Java ticker applet.[17] The ticker could be downloaded to cellular phones and offered real-time scores for the championship matches (see Exhibit 6). The applet was promoted through soccer websites across Europe, such as football365.com in the United Kingdom, and it was available in five languages (English, French, German, Spanish and Swedish).

Additionally, some phone service providers, such as Vodafone, promoted the applet on their websites in order to encourage subscribers to use newer forms of multimedia services.

The applet could be downloaded to 2.5G phones using an advertised code at a cost of € 5.00 for two months' use, which was charged directly to the user's monthly mobile phone bill. The applet then connected with a third-party information provider that adidas had hired to feed scores and other information to users for a flat fee. Any earnings generated from subscription fees also went to the information provider rather than adidas.

Actual subscriptions to the Euro 2004 applet far exceeded pre-launch projections of 30,000 subscribers. When the mobile provider's tracking site failed halfway through the campaign, the company already had more than 63,000 subscribers. Although users could still download the applet, the mobile phone provider was never able to restore tracking or collect additional subscription fees. Nevertheless, adidas viewed this early effort in branded cellular phone services as a qualified success. Although user profiles were not collected, the Global Media Group was concerned about the lack of focus on the key 12- to 24-year-old consumer. "From the testing we did," Drake explained, "the applet was too factual and appealed mainly to hardcore football geeks. Kids want something that is more lighthearted; something that's a bit cooler; something that will give them an advantage over their friends."

Some believed that the R2L mobile effort could have been even more successful had it been cross-promoted on food and beverage containers, for example. The cost of such promotion, however, was very high. With R2L, adidas was "testing the waters" to see what could be achieved on mobile devices, without spending a significant amount of money. According to Prenderville, new media had to be approached cautiously. "We will continue to migrate to digital media, such as mobile devices," he explained. "However, for senior management to have faith in new media, we need to have a gradual transition. We have to make sure that the tools we are using have critical mass before we invest money in them."

A second generation program called "Match Centre" provided up-to-date regional league scores for the Italian, French, German, Spanish and U.K. leagues. The applet was promoted on sports websites (see Exhibit 7). By clicking on a banner ad, users were taken to an instruction page that explained how to enter a text code into their phone (see Exhibit 8). Once the code was entered, a download link was sent to the phone, and any associated fees were automatically charged to the user's phone bill.

Although Match Centre appeared to be popular among soccer fans, the Global Media Group was unsure how much the service would appeal to younger consumers. According to Drake:

> *We have found a way to impart information; we have found a way to demonstrate products, and we can align it all with the current brand concept. We've achieved all of that. Has it made a positive impact on the football fan? We think yes, as future research will demonstrate. But we still haven't been able to engage youth in a meaningful way.*

EXHIBIT 7   U.K. SOCCER WEBSITE WITH ADIDAS MATCH CENTRE ADVERTISEMENT

Football | Betting | Casino | Poker | T-Shirts 365 | Games | | Sunday League   *rivals.*

YOUR SPORT. YOUR TEAM. YOUR PASSION.

Rivals.net | | | | February 7,

Rivals Menu

Rivals Football

Football365
Rugby
F1
Cricket
Horse Racing
Golf

Football Shop
Rivals Casino
Rivals Poker
Games
Mobile Channel
Text Alerts
Fantasy Manager
Competitions

Video Highlights
Replica Kit

Contact the Editor
Set as Homepage

Site Services

Competitions
Replica Kit

▼ TOP STORIES

Harper/Curtis - A Taste For Coke

Kevin Harper and John Curtis have left Pompey for Stoke and Nottingham Forest respectively...

RELATED ▶ **pompey-fans.com** | **Forum**

Ganea On The Mend

Wolves striker Vio Ganea is ready to put a summer of hell behind him by stepping back into training this week...

RELATED ▶ **wolvescentral.com** | **Forum**

Daly Linked With Hartlepool

Hartlepool United could be set for a surprise swoop for Jon Daly, as Neale Cooper looks to bolster his squad for a promotion push...

RELATED ▶ **HattersMatters.com** | **Forum**

Chairman To Step Down?

Cambridge United chairman Gary Harwood is going to consider his future at the helm of the U's later this month...

RELATED ▶ **amberarmy.co.uk** | **Forum**

▼ FOOTBALL HEADLINES

RIVALS	**LATEST HEADLINES**
CHELSEA	That Ashley Cole Rumour
PALACE	Zamora Move Fails
NORWICH	City Sign Stuart
NEWCASTLE	Bellamy Is Pissed Off
EVERTON	Rooney's Coming Home
CREWE	Murdock Reaction
WATFORD	Jones Extends Loan Deal
BRISTOL	Talk Is Cheap
CAMBRIDGE	Konte Off To Hibs
GRIMSBY	Unjustified Expectations
LINCOLN	Stamped Out

Sport-e.com
Get the latest replica shirts for only £30 at sport-e.com!   ▶▶ Buy N

ADIDAS MATCH CENTRE
Text ADIDAS to 83900 for your FREE* Mobile Match Centre.   ▶▶ Sign

FANTASY MANAGER
Play Premier Fantasy Manager and WIN the chance to join the European football jet-set!   ▶▶ Sign

LEGENDS T-SHIRT
Check out our new Sticker Legends T-Shirt   ▶▶ Sign

VIDEO HIGHLIGHTS
The great new PC video highlights service. Sign up and get a 1 month free trial!   ▶▶ Sign

Latest Football Odds
Checkout the latest prices from the Number 1 football betting service.   ▶▶ Mor

About Rivals.net Terms and Conditions Privacy Policy Sales and Sponsorship Media Centre   *rivals.*

Source: rivals.net, February 2005.

EXHIBIT 8   ADIDAS MATCH CENTRE SIGN-UP WEBPAGE

RELAX, LET ME TAKE CARE OF YOUR MOBILE

MOBILE LOUNGE .co.uk

| ringtones | games | sms services | wallpapers | slide shows | java tickers | **Nuts** | help | compatibility |

Premiership Match Centre

GET YOUR FREE* ADIDAS F50 PREMIERSHIP MOBILE MATCH CENTRE

The adidas f50 Premiership Mobile Match Centre is the most essential piece of football kit for any football fan! To keep up to date with all the latest footy news and scores on the move

Text **ADIDAS** to **83900** now!

Live Scores - Get the goals as they hit the net!
Breaking News - All the latest news as it breaks!
Latest Results - See all the latest results and scorers!
Premiership Table - Updated within hours of each match!
Latest Fixtures - Check out the fixtures for the next 7 days!
adidas Zone - Win a pair of adidas F50s signed by Djibril Cisse!

You will be sent a wap download link in a message. Highlight the link, connect to the wapsite and follow the instructions on your phone to install. This application will be valid for the **entire** duration of 2004/05 Premiership season and the first 30 days after you connect to the server will be **FREE OF CHARGE***. Thereafter you will receive one text message each 30 days charged at £5 unless you unsubscribe from the service**. To unsubscribe text ADIDAS STOP to 83900. You can resubscribe at any time by texting ADIDAS START to 83900.

When you start the application for the first time go to the Breaking News section and read the "Welcome to the Match Centre" story which tells you how to work the application. Alternatively select 'Connect' and the application will download the latest information. As long as you are connected the application will check for the latest news and scores every minute.

Please check your phone is compatible before ordering as refunds cannot be given for incompatible orders. The adidas f50 Premiership Match Centre is only available to UK customers of Vodafone, O2, T Mobile & Orange. The application will ONLY work on the following handsets:

Nokia: 3650, 3660, 6600, 7600, 7610, 7650, n-Gage
Nokia: 6230, 6650, 6800, 6810, 6820, 3100, 3200, 3300, 5100, 6220, 6610, 6610i, 7210, 7250, 7250i
More phones to follow shortly...

Tip: If you are promoted each time the application checks for updates you can stop this but the solution is different for each phone.
Nokia 6600 - Go to Menu > Manager. Scroll to Adidas Prem and select Options > Settings. In Network Access, click into this and change the setting to Ask first time.
Nokia 3650 - Go to Applications and scroll down to Adidas Prem and select Options > Settings > Settings (again) > Network Connection. Change this to Allowed.

**Please note that you will be charged by your network for the amount of GPRS data downloaded each month, depending on your network's tariff, even during the first 30 days.

IN ASSOCIATION WITH
Football365.com

We are only interested in the 12- to 24-year-olds, which is an age in which we can make a favorable impression. Although they have greater spending power, we are less interested in older consumers because they already have brand loyalty.

In future generations of Match Centre, adidas planned to incorporate "cooler" elements, such as photos and video.

Urban Cool

Basketball

Basketball had traditionally been dominated by Nike and its affiliation with basketball star Michael Jordan. The affinity American urban youth had for basketball resulted in a large market share for Nike among American teens. For adidas, breaking into this market was a critical part of its U.S. product strategy. The Global Media Group sought to adjust the R2L tools to provide the same benefits to basketball fans in the United States, such as real-time basketball scores and other basketball data on a mobile Java ticker. Drake explained:

Right now we are limited by the bandwidth in the U.S., which means that we can only deliver text. But it is only a matter of time before the technology will allow us to deliver more information. The problem for us is not delivering information to the consumer, but combining it with product and brand messaging.

Drake believed that mobile phones could prove to be an important way to deliver marketing messages to basketball fans in American cities:

In my opinion, the basketball fan is inclined to look for personalization and for the latest technology, something that can demonstrate urban cool. And we think the mobile phone is a cool item. Therefore, an investment in that will be a big part of their income.

One option involved creating an adidas-branded mobile phone. To realize the concept, adidas would have to work with cellular phone manufacturers to include features important to its target market. Secondly, it had to develop appealing add-on content, such as sports tickers, games, and ringtones.

Hip-Hop Music

Adidas based its U.S. brand strategy around "urban centers of cool," where hip-hop (rap) music stars strongly influenced style fashion trends. Although Reebok was arguably the most aggressive company when it came to sponsoring hip-hop, the first music group to endorse a line of footwear was Run DMC with its 1986 hit song "My adidas." At the time, marketers were only beginning to look at the cultural phenomenon of hip-hop, so when Run DMC subsequently asked adidas to underwrite a concert tour, company executives were hesitant. One observer noted:

> *They were skeptical about the marketing potential of rap musicians until they were convinced to attend a Run DMC concert. At a crucial moment, while the rap group was performing the song, one of the members yelled out, "Okay, everybody in the house, rock your adidas!" and three thousand pairs of sneakers shot into the air. The adidas executives couldn't reach for their checkbooks fast enough.*[18]

By 2003, the hip-hop cultural phenomenon had reached 45 million Americans, who spent more than $10 billion on hip-hop music and related merchandise. Of this number, an estimated 80 per cent were Caucasian between the ages of 13 and 34, with a total spending power of roughly $1 trillion.[19] The influence of hip-hop even extended to other countries, particularly the United Kingdom, Germany, and Japan, where fans imitated the clothing and lifestyle choices of their favorite hip-hop stars.

Respect M.E.: The Missy Elliott Campaign

Five-time Grammy nominee Missy Elliott was the best-selling female hip-hop star of all time with more than 7 million albums sold. In 2001, she signed a one-year deal to promote Reebok shoes before appearing in television commercials for the Gap and Sprite. After her contract with Reebok expired, she signed a deal with adidas to create her own line of adidas-branded clothing and footwear.

Known as Respect M.E., the line ranged from "Run DMC style" sneakers priced at $70 to Missy Elliott "Remix" boots for $120. Adidas even set aside its long-standing guidelines for style and color in order to accommodate Missy's unique fashion.

The Missy Elliot line was launched well into the fiscal year, when advertising budgets had already been allocated to various campaigns. With limited marketing support available to Respect M.E., adidas decided to promote the line in three ways: mobile, online, and a face-to-face event at the music awards in Miami, Florida. Mobile was viewed as a particularly inexpensive media that would allow adidas to "stretch the budget" while reaching a wide audience.

The objectives of the mobile campaign were to:

- Show the product line,

- Create consumer demand,

- Drive traffic to retail outlets,

- Help consumers locate the products,

- Grow the existing database of Missy fans and capture SMS data,

- Alert fans to product line activity, such as Missy press updates and appearances, and

- Enable users to download exclusive Respect M.E. mobile content onto their handsets for viral promotion.

EXHIBIT 9   RESPECT M.E. REGISTRATION SITE AND SAMPLE WALLPAPER

Source: company files.

The Missy Elliott campaign was adidas's most ambitious mobile effort yet, one that the Global Media Group hoped would attract "hundreds of thousands" of potential customers. It included a broad variety of content, such as monophonic, polyphonic and true-tone ringtones, voice tones,[20] and adidas-branded wallpapers. Adidas decided to initially price content at $1.99 (except true tones, which sold for $2.99). Users were required to register on the Respect M.E. website by entering personal data and a valid credit card number (see Exhibit 9). Once registered, any downloads were charged to the user's credit card. Finally, any profits generated from the site would be donated to Missy Elliott's "Break the Cycle" charity.[21]

Cell phones that accessed the site could also be used to browse the Respect M.E. collection, find the nearest adidas store by inputting a postal code, sign up for product and content alerts, chat with Missy Elliott once a week, send a notification to another cell phone about Respect M.E., and enter a contest to win a vacation with Missy Elliott.

The delivery of exclusive product previews of the new Respect M.E. line was a key component of the campaign. "People generally like to show their friends what's coming and what's new," Drake reasoned. "And if brands are considered cool, they definitely want to show their friends before it becomes available."

To encourage traffic to the site during its initial launch, adidas offered for free the first 10,000 wallpapers downloaded from the site. Also, for each message sent to a friend about the Missy Elliott site, members received credits that could be used to download content, also for free. Finally, Missy Elliot created an exclusive track for adidas, which was advertised on various blogging sites.

Santa Fe Relocation Services: Regional Brand Management

A Branding Challenge

I n April 2005, Hong Kong-based Santa Fe Relocation Services (Santa Fe) faced a branding challenge. Santa Fe was a full-service relocation company operating throughout the Asia-Pacific region. The company offered household goods moving services and a range of value-added support services to expatriate workers and their families. Chief operating officer Keith Meader searched for ways to differentiate and position Santa Fe as a premium service provider in a competitive and price-sensitive market.

Santa Fe Relocation Services

Background

Economic development in Asia in recent decades had created international opportunities for skilled workers. Representative posts, operating offices, and manufacturing facilities had sprung up throughout the region, and foreigners had been called upon to offer their skills and experience. To paraphrase one Santa Fe manager, the "global workforce" had been called upon to mobilize and send its members to—and within—Asia.[1] Naturally, this worker migration fuelled demand for relocation services.

Santa Fe was established in Hong Kong in 1980 to meet this demand. Initially, the company restricted its activities to household goods packing and moving services. Santa Fe served individuals and families, and sold its services either to those individuals and families or to their employers.

In 1988, Santa Fe was acquired by the East Asiatic Company Limited (EAC), a Danish corporation with interests in various industries. This gave Santa Fe more

Nigel Goodwin prepared this case under the supervision of Professor Niraj Dawar solely to provide material for class discussion. The authors do not intend to illustrate either effective or ineffective handling of a managerial situation. The authors may have disguised certain names and other identifying information to protect confidentiality.

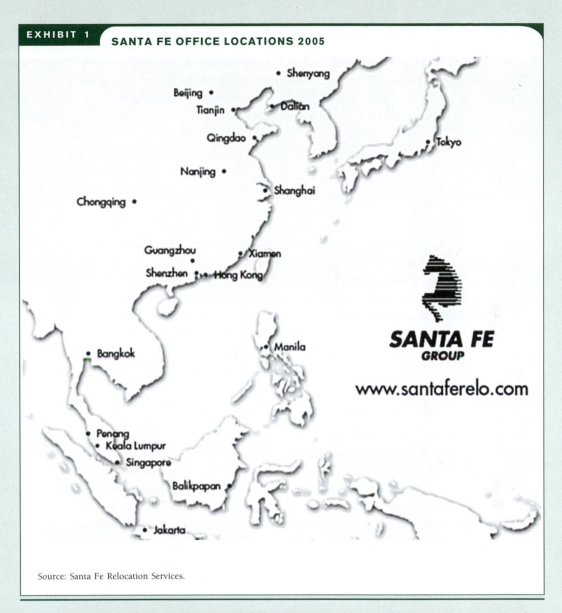

EXHIBIT 1   SANTA FE OFFICE LOCATIONS 2005

Source: Santa Fe Relocation Services.

financial strength and facilitated the company's organic growth into Singapore and Thailand. In 2000, Santa Fe acquired the Asian branch of another moving company, Global Silverhawk, and integrated it under the Santa Fe brand. The Global Silverhawk acquisition expanded Santa Fe's operations in Hong Kong, Singapore and Thailand and also gave the company a presence in the new markets of Indonesia, Japan, Malaysia, and the Philippines (see Exhibit 1).

As Santa Fe grew, it built a reputation for quality. In fact, the company's stated vision was to lead the market on this metric. In the company's words,

> A strong brand...is sustained by the employees' dedicated and unrelenting commitment to quality and customer service, and underpinned by comprehensive quality procedures and operational processes.[2]

Packing and moving crews were led by English-speaking supervisors and trained according to ISO quality standards. Their compensation was tied to performance and customer comments, and with a low employee turnover rate, the teams retained many experienced workers. Handheld computers were used during pre-move surveys, ensuring detailed and accurate inventory and providing volume and weight estimates on location. In addition, clients had access to shipping dates, country profiles, and various forms through the company's Web site. These measures led to high customer satisfaction rates and minimized claims for damaged or lost goods.

Santa Fe contributed DKK468 million to EAC's 2004 revenue.[3] This was a nine per cent increase over 2003 when measured in local currencies. Santa Fe grew in China, Hong Kong, Japan, the Philippines, Singapore, and Thailand in 2004, while performance remained flat in Indonesia and declined in Malaysia. The company handled over 17,000 international, domestic, and local relocations in 2004 with the help of over 1,000 employees.[4]

Santa Fe projected six per cent revenue growth in 2005 (as measured in local currencies). Demand for relocation services would be driven by improving economic conditions, increasing foreign direct investment and greater political stability across the Asia-Pacific region. China's fulfillment of its World Trade Organization commitments would further bolster demand. In addition to China, Santa Fe's key markets of Hong Kong, Japan, and Singapore were expected to show particular strength.

Business Model

Santa Fe moved households from other regions to Asia, between Asian countries, or from Asia to other regions. These three types of moves were referred to as inbound, regional, and outbound, respectively.

Santa Fe handled regional moves from start to finish with its own people and resources. Each Santa Fe office had its own sales and operations personnel, and the different offices co-ordinated on regional moves. Since the company had teams in the Asian region only, inbound and outbound moves were conducted in partnership with overseas moving companies. As Santa Fe stated:

> As an Asian specialist, we stick to one simple philosophy in delivering services globally: create and maintain partnerships with the best providers outside of Asia. This choice to work with the best companies around the world is one of our greatest strengths. We know who the best partners are, and our clients benefit from their proven quality.[5]

Santa Fe sold outbound services under its own name. The company co-ordinated all aspects of an outbound move at the point of origin, including the pre-move survey, quotation, confirmation, insurance, packing, removal of debris, freight, customs clearance, and when necessary, storage. The partner company was then responsible for delivering and unpacking the household goods at the destination. The partnership arrangement was reversed for inbound moves, with the overseas firm making the sale and co-ordinating the operations.

Santa Fe and many of its partner firms were members of the Overseas Moving Network International (OMNI). OMNI promoted close co-operation between its 260 members in 70 countries. OMNI restricted each member to operations on only one continent, but facilitated interactions between members and thus enabled worldwide coverage. Most countries covered by OMNI were served by more than one member. Therefore, Santa Fe was able to choose between partners when moving families overseas. Likewise, overseas partners could choose between Santa Fe and Santa Fe's competitors for inbound operations.

Quality service from OMNI members was assured. Members were audited biannually on standards set by the Brussels-based International Association of Moving Companies (FIDI). The audit was conducted by international consulting firm Cap Gemini Ernst & Young and covered all aspects of international relocation work, from equipment, facilities and staffing to processes, administration and customer service. Some members had also achieved ISO9001 accreditation, proving their commitment to quality, customer satisfaction, and continuous performance improvement.

The company was unwilling to sell to overseas clients directly if those clients were already being served by Santa Fe's overseas partners. The OMNI partnership model simply did not justify or allow such action. If Santa Fe were to expand beyond its home continent and participate directly in another with its own on-the-ground operations, it would no longer qualify for OMNI membership. These actions would eliminate Santa Fe's inbound demand and leave it unable to deliver on its outbound business. The company would have to rebuild its sales and operations from the ground up. "That's simply not a move we're willing to contemplate," Meader said emphatically.[6]

Support Services

Moving a worker to a new office in a new country involved more than simply packing and transporting household goods. An expatriate worker needed to socialize and settle into the new environment as quickly as possible. The old home had to be sold or rented, temporary accommodation had to be arranged, and a new home had to be found. Also, expatriates often had to contend with new cultures and languages. This was exacerbated by the emotional hardship of leaving behind family, friends, and a community, and starting fresh in an unfamiliar place. The entire experience could be overwhelming.

The process could be further complicated by the involvement of a spouse and children. A survey conducted jointly by several industry organizations found that 60 per cent of expatriate workers were married, and 86 per cent of those married expatriates were accompanied by their spouses.[7] Specific to the American market, a different source held that 75 per cent of expatriates from the United States were married (see Exhibits 2 and 3).[8]

Conversely, while a smooth transition enabled an employee to add value soon after landing at the new location, a failed overseas assignment could be very costly. In Santa Fe's estimation, it could cost US$300,000 or more to move an employee with

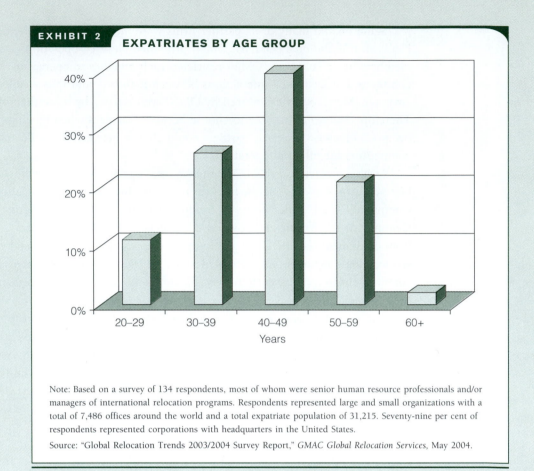

EXHIBIT 2   **EXPATRIATES BY AGE GROUP**

Note: Based on a survey of 134 respondents, most of whom were senior human resource professionals and/or managers of international relocation programs. Respondents represented large and small organizations with a total of 7,486 offices around the world and a total expatriate population of 31,215. Seventy-nine per cent of respondents represented corporations with headquarters in the United States.

Source: "Global Relocation Trends 2003/2004 Survey Report," *GMAC Global Relocation Services,* May 2004.

a family, send them back, and lose opportunities and productivity. The aforementioned survey identified partner dissatisfaction, family concerns, inability to adapt, and poor job performance as key contributors to assignment failure.

Organizations generally recognized it was in their best interest to make worker relocations as smooth, easy and comfortable as possible and assigned responsibility to their human resources departments. However, many organizations lacked the necessary resources and experience. Seeking to relieve themselves of this burden while ensuring consistency and success, many organizations operating in Asia and around the world chose to outsource the work to support service providers. The most commonly outsourced support services in the relocation value chain were language training, intercultural services, destination services, and visa and immigration applications.[9] Some support service providers specialized in one or two tasks while others offered a comprehensive service line.

In approximately 1995, Santa Fe realized there were not enough support service providers in the Asian market, particularly in mainland China. While moving household goods, Santa Fe often heard stories of expatriates' other difficulties and suspected the current customer base might have other unmet needs. Seeing an opportunity, Santa Fe began offering its own value-added support services in China. In

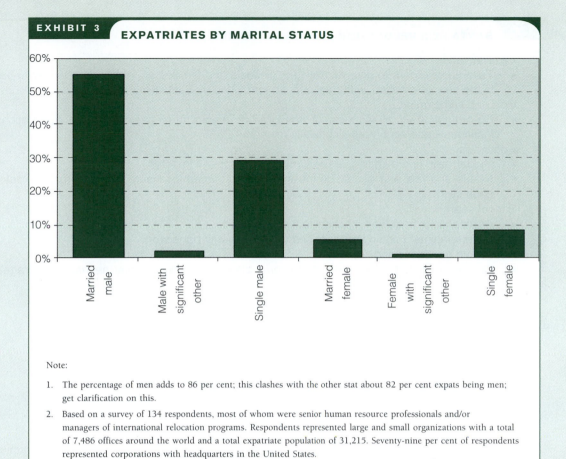

EXHIBIT 3   **EXPATRIATES BY MARITAL STATUS**

Note:

1. The percentage of men adds to 86 per cent; this clashes with the other stat about 82 per cent expats being men; get clarification on this.

2. Based on a survey of 134 respondents, most of whom were senior human resource professionals and/or managers of international relocation programs. Respondents represented large and small organizations with a total of 7,486 offices around the world and a total expatriate population of 31,215. Seventy-nine per cent of respondents represented corporations with headquarters in the United States.

Source: "Global Relocation Trends 2003/2004 Survey Report," *GMAC Global Relocation Services*, May 2004.

the following years, Santa Fe expanded its range of support services (see Exhibit 4) and introduced them in its other countries of operation.

By the end of 2000, Santa Fe had achieved full geographic coverage for a wide range of support services and had completed its transition from a traditional moving company to a full-service relocation provider. Meader thought the expanded service line gave Santa Fe a much stronger sales proposition. The support services were a compelling sales feature that attracted new customers and drove demand for the original household goods services. Furthermore, the support services offered Santa Fe better margins.

Santa Fe either delivered the support services with its own staff or outsourced to other providers, depending on the specific service and location. For example, Santa Fe provided visa and immigration services in-house in Hong Kong, Singapore, and China but outsourced those services elsewhere. Handyman services were usually provided in-house while familiarization services were conducted by consultants who were hired as necessary. Cross-cultural and language training programs were always outsourced as they required specialists. When service delivery was outsourced, Santa Fe still managed and co-ordinated the activities.

EXHIBIT 4   **SANTA FE'S RELOCATION SUPPORT SERVICES**

Before an assignment

Familiarization
- Tailored city tours to give relocating individuals and families an introduction to day-to-day life in the new destination, with transportation provided by Santa Fe

Visa and immigration
- Co-ordination of all aspects of immigration, employment pass and visa applications for individuals and accompanying family members

Home search
- Guidance in home finding, lease signing, and property transfer
- Needs analysis and access to multiple listing sources to ensure a good property match for each client

School search
- Assistance in matching a school to a child's needs
- Accompaniment on school visits and assistance with paperwork

Household goods moving
- Cost estimates, packing, freight, customs clearance, delivery, any necessary storage, and unpacking at the destination

Furniture rental
- Short- and long-term hire of furniture, soft furnishings, basic kitchen items, and linens

Settling-in assistance
- Help with small details to make customers more comfortable
- Neighborhood tours, shopping for essentials, connection of utilities, opening of bank accounts, and registration with embassies and local authorities

Maid and handyman services
- Residence cleaning and repairs prior to moving in
- Residence cleaning after moving out

Cross-cultural training
- Education about different cultures, business environments, customs and communication styles, as well as language training
- Custom-made programs for individuals or whole families

During an assignment

Ongoing support
- General ongoing support as needed and invitations to social events

Tenancy management
- Support in dealing with landlords and utility companies
- Minor repairs and preventative maintenance

Ongoing visa tracking
- Tracking of visa status and notification of necessary follow-up actions

After an assignment

Departure programme
- Termination of rental and lease agreements
- Cancellation of home insurance and utilities
- Recovery of security and utility deposits

Household goods moving
- Managing the movement of household goods to new destinations, as described above

Furniture rental
- Rental service as described above, if household goods are moved out before a client is actually ready to leave

Source: Santa Fe Relocation Services.

The Market

Consumers and Decision-makers

People in many different professions relocated to, from, and within Asia for reasons of employment. As a premium service provider, Santa Fe primarily catered to employees of multinational corporations. These corporations managed significant expatriate populations and generally paid for employee relocations. The expatriates, being executives, managers, bankers, and other skilled professionals, expected to be treated well; concurrently, corporations recognized the impact of the relocation process on employee productivity. Naturally, Santa Fe was particularly interested in multinational corporations that were expanding their Asian operations. Most of the expatriates were from the United States or other western countries, although some were already living in Asia.

While the expatriate was the consumer of the moving and support services and the corporate employer paid the bill, the choice of service provider could be made by either party. In the past, 80 per cent of the revenue Santa Fe generated itself in Asia was derived from corporations and 20 per cent from employees; by April 2005, the ratio had shifted to 70 per cent from corporations and 30 per cent from employees.[10]

In the corporate-centric scenario, a corporation hired one or more service providers to serve all its expatriate employees over a defined period of time. A typical contract lasted two or three years and covered household goods moving services as well as any outsourced support services. This was typically the case in the American market, with Santa Fe's OMNI partners deriving almost all of their American revenue in this way. Moreover, many American corporations centralized the decision-making authority at the head office level. Many Asian-based corporations also followed the corporate-centric scenario, although they often delegated authority to their local offices.

The alternative was the employee-centric scenario, in which a corporation gave each expatriate employee a sum of money or a higher salary and asked the employee to make the necessary arrangements. This shifted both the burden and the decision-making authority to the individual. The employee-centric scenario was becoming increasingly common in Asia.

Buying Behavior

The broader market for relocation services, encompassing all market segments, was very price-driven. Relocation was seen as an unpleasant but necessary task, and many people just wanted to do it as cheaply as possible. "But this is not always the case; it's not always about providing the cheapest service," remarked Bryce Burns, Santa Fe's general manager for sales and marketing. "If it were, we would not be in business."[11]

The customers in Santa Fe's target segment still considered the price but placed a higher emphasis on service quality. They wanted smooth, reliable, hassle-free moving so long as the price was still reasonable. Many of the expatriates had heard "horror stories" about other people suffering broken or lost goods, delayed or misdirected shipments, and other problems, and they naturally wanted to avoid such issues themselves. Their employers, meanwhile, wanted to ensure smooth transitions and future productivity.

Santa Fe's revenue from support services grew 67 per cent in the preceding year, on a worldwide basis, but still accounted for only five per cent of the company's total. Few expatriates or corporations were aware that a moving company like Santa Fe even offered support services as it was unusual for one company to be active in both fields. Meanwhile, relocation services specialists enjoyed more awareness and controlled more market share.

Also, in spite of the expressed interest in a smooth, hassle-free moving process, many expatriates and corporations were unwilling to pay for the additional services. "The total cost of the relocation is still very important," remarked Santa Fe's group manager for relocation services, Yves Therien, "and it's very hard to up-sell from the basic household goods moving services."[12]

Of the customer segments, American corporations were most likely to pay for support services and were becoming increasingly aware of and receptive to these services. Asian corporations had given support services a cool reception, with low awareness and even lower acceptance. While American corporations often viewed these services as a cost-effective way to outsource unnecessary tasks, Asian corporations sometimes viewed them as a threat to human resources jobs and consequently rejected them.

Expatriates who made their own relocation arrangements were even less likely to pay for support services. These expatriates received lump sums or higher salaries to cover their relocation expenses, and they were motivated to contain their expenses and pocket the remaining money.

Expatriates moving from western countries to Asia faced much greater challenges than expatriates moving within Asia or returning home to the West. Therefore, Santa Fe's overseas partners often sold support services and then contracted Santa Fe to actually deliver the services. Support services were especially popular among western expatriates relocating to China, which was viewed as a particularly difficult environment for newcomers.

Santa Fe still faced downward pricing pressure on all its services despite its focus on the premium market segment. Widespread concern over the state of the global economy in previous years had forced many corporations to reduce their budgets for overseas relocations. Expatriate assignments had become shorter, often with durations of one year or less,[13] and the benefits had been reduced. In particular, corporations were less inclined to offer family-related benefits on shorter assignments, and it became more common for expatriates to leave their children at home.[14] Individuals and corporations alike compared service providers and searched for the best possible deals. In extreme cases, expatriate assignments were cancelled in favor of local hiring.

Santa Fe Branding

Strategy

Meader believed in the power of branding in reaching out to a market. As stated by Santa Fe's parent company, "A strong brand helps to secure new business, maintain customer loyalty and provide a sound basis for entering new markets and offering new services."[15] However, Meader thought Santa Fe's brand could be much clearer, stronger, and more effective in reaching the company's key market segments.

According to Burns, Santa Fe was trying to position itself as "a high quality company at a higher-than-average cost."[16] Meader wanted the market to understand that while Santa Fe was not the most affordable service provider, it consistently delivered the best possible customer service experience. He wanted people to see that the difficult process of relocating could be simplified and the extra cost was justified. Unfortunately, he was concerned that many potential customers were scared away by Santa Fe's pricing and failed to consider the true value proposition. Santa Fe needed to overcome this crucial communication challenge.

Meader was certain the company had positive word-of-mouth advertising and personal recommendations from past customers. The company's solid customer satisfaction reviews supported his belief. As one previous customer attested, "Moving isn't about transportation, it's about relying on strangers to care for our personal belongings. Santa Fe has earned our trust."[17] Santa Fe needed to communicate that reputation and that trust through its brand.

As an additional challenge, Santa Fe had been a mover of household goods since its establishment in 1980. In recent years, it had tried to move beyond its core service and be recognized, as Burns commented, as "a one-stop shop for expatriates and HR professionals within our target market."[18] However, this concept was unusual in the market, and the company's rebranding effort had been only moderately successful. As Burns explained,

> *In the last few years, we changed more than the market realized. We need to let people know. Right now, they say, 'Santa Fe is a moving company. Oh, and they do some other stuff, too.' And that's only if they know about our other services at all.*[19]

Meader had to consider how a relocation service line could be incorporated under a household goods moving brand, and what implications that might have.

Marketing

Santa Fe attempted to get its message out through various marketing materials and promotional efforts. The company took a direct marketing approach to reach corporations in Asia, with sales representatives from Santa Fe approaching human resources personnel from the corporations through phone calls, personal sales visits, presentations, and e-mail campaigns. Santa Fe sales personnel also built networks with current and potential corporate clients by joining various industry associations. Occasionally, corporations proactively sought moving and relocation services by issuing requests for proposals (RFPs); Santa Fe gladly responded, but such customer-led situations were an exception.

The company armed its sales representatives with a group-wide presentation on CD-ROM discs. A sales representative would open the presentation on a prospective customer's computer and click on various icons on a main screen to reveal video clips, graphics, and text. This interactive presentation had been developed by a professional design agency, and Meader thought it was a powerful sales tool. Sales representatives also distributed printed brochures that had recently been expanded to highlight the value-added services and shift the focus away from standard household goods moving.

In addition, Santa Fe sponsored a global conference of the Employee Relocation Council (ERC) in Hong Kong in March 2005. The ERC was an international body of human resources professionals and the vendors who served them. This sponsorship was considered a key way for Santa Fe to spread the message that it had become a full-service relocation company. Santa Fe planned to sponsor the same conference again in 2006. The company would also sponsor similar industry conferences overseas in the future, but the ERC conference was considered the most important due to its broad relocation scope.

Naturally, Santa Fe took a more mass-market approach in reaching out to individuals in Asia. The company placed ads in magazines read by expatriates and on a well-known expatriate Web site, www.asiaxpat.com, and also sponsored events, teams, non-profit arts groups, and charities that were popular among the expatriate community. Similar to its corporate marketing strategy, the company relied on its own employees going out into the community and networking.

Santa Fe did not have any employees developing advertising campaigns and marketing materials on a full-time basis. Most of this work was performed by Burns, in addition to his other duties, or on an ad hoc basis by various people in the other offices.

Overseas sales were generated by developing and maintaining relationships with OMNI partners. According to Burns, relationships between OMNI members were mutually beneficial and often long-standing. "Our bosses know their bosses, and they have established client referral relationships," he explained. "Although it's becoming more competitive, it's still a personal network."[20]

Santa Fe's managers and executives developed and maintained these relationships by periodically travelling overseas and meeting with partner firms' representatives. More recently, Santa Fe had hired an experienced relocation industry professional to represent Santa Fe overseas and to liaise with those partners on a full-time basis. This person had also been instructed to promote the value-added services to the partner firms. In addition, Santa Fe placed advertisements in industry publications to maintain a level of awareness with overseas OMNI members.

Finally, Santa Fe looked to its Web site as a tool for marketing as well as customer retention. Located at www.santaferelo.com, the site provided destination guides and allowed customers to electronically request services and initiate relocations. It also allowed customers to log in and view information on their past business with Santa Fe. Employers that owned residential properties for employee use and contracted Santa Fe to manage those properties could also log in to view related information. An updated version of this tenancy management system, with additional features and content, was due for launch in October 2005.

Regional Co-ordination

Corporations buying relocation services in Asia typically did so at a local or domestic level rather than at a regional level. Santa Fe consequently gave each of its offices a great deal of autonomy over sales, marketing, and branding activities. Offices referred opportunities and co-ordinated on larger pitches when appropriate, but such opportunities were rare.

Burns was largely responsible for designing the company's marketing materials, but personnel at the other offices often customized these materials for their own use. The colors, scripts, font sizes, and even versions of the logo used in marketing materials varied widely from office to office (see Exhibit 5). Meader wondered whether more consistency in marketing materials would reinforce the brand or whether local adaptation was more effective in reaching local markets. He also wondered whether periodic changes to the logo would keep the brand fresh, but he noted that Santa Fe's chief competitor, Crown Relocations (Crown), was more consistent with its own logo.

Competition

Moving and Full-service Relocation Companies

The industry's size, the different types of relocations, and the diversity of players made it difficult to measure Santa Fe's competitive success. An independent study published several years earlier had found that Santa Fe appeared to have captured the largest share of household goods moving business sold in Hong Kong. Crown was thought to be close behind, but competitors' market share dropped off quickly after that. Santa Fe had seen no estimates for the other countries in the region or for the support services business.

Crown was Santa Fe's most direct competitor, with a similar service range and comparable pricing. Crown was also headquartered in Hong Kong and had strength in Asia, although it was actually a global company with over 100 wholly owned offices in 42 countries. Crown also specialized in serving expatriates from multinational corporations. In addition, the company recently began offering fine arts moving services and had opened a wine storage facility in Hong Kong. Crown managed 30,000 relocations per year and stated its philosophy as "Helping you begin life's next chapter."

Household goods moving companies, which provided household goods packing and moving services only, were also strong competitors. Among these companies, Santa Fe considered Asian Tigers Group (Asian Tigers) and Allied Pickfords as its closest competitors. Asian Tigers was a specifically Asian company, as its name

EXHIBIT 5   **SAMPLE MARKETING MATERIALS**

Source: Santa Fe Relocation Services.

suggested, and a member of OMNI, so it was in competition for referrals from overseas partners as well as for business sold directly in Asia. Allied Pickfords, by comparison, was a global company, managing over 50,000 international relocations each year through 800 offices in 40 countries. These companies priced their services lower than did Santa Fe and Crown.

On the surface, it was difficult to tell the difference between Santa Fe, Crown, Asian Tigers, and Allied Pickfords. Each company offered household goods packing and moving services, and each one billed itself as a high quality provider. Furthermore, there were myriad local and domestic household goods movers in each Asian country attracting customer attention. It was only when one considered the support services that there were any obvious differences. Meader believed his company's competitive advantage was its track record of high quality and customer satisfaction, but this voice was easily lost in the larger crowd of competitors. He believed Santa Fe did a better job of branding and marketing than Asian Tigers and Allied Pickfords did, but he admitted that Crown outgunned Santa Fe with more effective and more consistent marketing materials.

Support Service Companies and Niche Players

Some large, American support service companies posed a new and rising threat, extending their global reach and entering the Asian market. The biggest names included Prudential Real Estate & Relocation Services (Prudential) and Cendant Corporation (Cendant). Prudential, for example, helped corporate clients set and manage relocation policy. Prudential also assisted expatriates with home sales and new home searches. Relocation support companies could also co-ordinate household goods moving, although they typically did not have their own capabilities for this service and outsourced the work to moving companies.

These support service providers had long operating histories and were part of much larger companies. Prudential was one of many operating units of Prudential Financial, a well-known and diversified financial services company. Cendant, meanwhile, was a global powerhouse in the real estate and travel industries. Its brands included Orbitz for travel services, Avis and Budget for car rentals, Century 21 for real estate brokerage, and Days Inn and Ramada for hotels.

The Santa Fe team thought their primary advantage over Prudential, Cendant and other relocation support specialists was their on-the-ground presence in Asia, which helped them focus on their target market.

Finally, Santa Fe had to contend with specialized, niche players in the support services industry. For example, real estate agents provided home search services while law firms and the larger accounting firms assisted with visa and immigration applications. While these companies were indirect competitors with limited service offerings, collectively they posed a threat.

Competitive Dynamics

The variety of companies and business models made this industry very complex. Companies sold different combinations of relocation services and then delivered those services in-house or outsourced them to other service providers. For example, Santa Fe would compete for home search business in Hong Kong, but outsource the service delivery to realtors who had been in competition for the business in the first place. Relocation service companies could therefore be either competitors or service delivery partners, depending on their service scope and geographic coverage.

The balance was expected to shift in favor of greater competition over time. The large support service companies based in the United States had traditionally outsourced much of their Asian work to Santa Fe and other regional players. However, the American companies were extending their reach, building their own capabilities in Asia and increasingly coming into direct competition with their Asian counterparts. For example, Cendant and Prudential had established their own Asian presence in recent years and had therefore become sources of direct competition.

The Work Ahead

Meader carefully considered the threefold challenge before him. Principally, Santa Fe had to differentiate and gain brand recognition in a crowded market. The company's expanded service line might help, but Meader was unsure how this service line could be incorporated under the original household moving brand and what implications that might have. Finally, the new branding strategies and tactics would have to be managed across a diverse geographic region. In short, Meader knew he had a lot of work to do.

Appendix A

Marketing Plan Worksheets

These worksheets will assist you in writing a formal marketing plan. Worksheets are a useful planning tool because they help ensure that important information is not omitted from the marketing plan. Answering the questions on these worksheets will enable you to:

1. Organize and structure the data and information that you collect during the situation analysis.

2. Use this information to better understand a firm's strengths and weaknesses and to recognize the opportunities and threats that exist in the marketing environment.

3. Develop goals and objectives that capitalize on strengths.

4. Develop a marketing strategy that creates competitive advantages.

5. Outline a plan for implementing the marketing strategy.

These worksheets are available in electronic format on our text's website at http://www.thomsonedu.com/marketing/ferrell. After downloading these worksheets, you will be able to change the outline or marketing ferrell information that is relevant to your situation. Remember that there is no one best way to organize a marketing plan. We designed our outline to serve as a starting point and to be flexible enough to accommodate the unique characteristics of your situation.

As you complete the worksheets, it might be useful to refer back to the text of the chapters. In completing the situation analysis section, be sure to be as comprehensive as possible. The viability of your SWOT analysis depends on how well you have identified all the relevant environmental issues. Likewise, as you complete the SWOT analysis, you should be honest about the firm's characteristics. Do not depend on strengths that the firm really does not possess. Honesty is also important for your listing of weaknesses.

I. **Executive Summary**

   The executive summary is a synopsis of the overall marketing plan. It should provide an overview of the entire plan including goals/objectives, strategy elements, implementation issues, and expected outcomes. The executive summary is easier to write if you do it last, after you have written the entire marketing plan.

II. **Situation Analysis**

   A. **The Internal Environment (refer to Exhibit 4.3)**

   Review of marketing goals and objectives

Identify the firm's current marketing goals and objectives.

Explain how these goals and objectives are being achieved.

Explain how these goals and objectives are consistent or inconsistent with the firm's mission, recent trends in the external environment, and recent trends in the customer environment.

Review of current marketing strategy and performance

Describe the firm's current marketing strategy with respect to products, pricing, distribution, and promotion. Which elements of the strategy are working well? Which elements are not?

Describe the firm's current performance (sales volume, market share, profitability, awareness, and brand preference) compared to other firms in the industry. Is the performance of the industry as a whole improving or declining? Why?

If the firm's performance is declining, what is the most likely cause (for example, environmental changes, flawed strategy, poor implementation)?

Review of current and anticipated organizational resources

Describe the current state of the firm's organizational resources (for example, financial, capital, human, experience, relationships with key suppliers/customers). How are the levels of these resources likely to change in the future?

If resource levels are expected to change, how can the firm leverage additional resources to meet customer needs better than competitors?

If additional resources are not available, how can the firm compensate for future resource constraints (lack of resources)?

Review of current and anticipated cultural and structural issues

In terms of marketing strategy development and implementation, describe the positive and negative aspects of the current and anticipated culture of the firm. Examples could include:

    The firm's overall customer orientation (or lack there of)
    The firm's emphasis on short-term versus long-term planning
    Willingness of the firm's culture to embrace change
    Internal politics and power struggles
    The overall position and importance of the marketing function
    Changes in key executive positions
    General employee satisfaction and morale

Explain whether the firm's structure is supportive of the current marketing strategy.

B. **The Customer Environment (refer to Exhibit 4.4)**

Who are the firm's current and potential customers?

Describe the important identifying characteristics of the firm's current and potential customers with respect to demographics, geographic location, psychographic profiles, values/lifestyles, and product usage characteristics (heavy versus light users).

Identify the important players in the purchase process for the firm's products. These might include purchasers (actual act of purchase), users (actual product user), purchase influencers (influence the decision or make recommendations), and the bearer of financial responsibility (who pays the bill?).

What do customers do with the firm's products?

How are the firm's products connected to customer needs? What are the basic benefits provided by the firm's products?

How are the firm's products purchased (quantities and combinations)? Is the product purchased as a part of a solution or alongside complementary products?

How are the firm's products consumed or used? Are there special consumption situations that influence purchase behavior?

Are there issues related to disposition of the firm's products, such as waste (garbage) or recycling, which must be addressed by the firm?

Where do customers purchase the firm's products?

Identify the merchants (intermediaries) where the firm's products are purchased (for example, store-based retailers, e-commerce, catalog retailers, vending, wholesale outlets, and/or direct from the firm).

Identify any trends in purchase patterns across these outlets (for example, how has e-commerce has changed the way the firm's products are purchased?).

When do customers purchase the firm's products?

How does purchase behavior vary based on different promotional events (communication and price changes) or customer services (hours of operation, delivery)?

How does purchase behavior vary based on uncontrollable influences such as seasonal demand patterns, time-based demand patterns, physical/social surroundings, or competitive activities?

Why (and how) do customers select the firm's products?

Describe the advantages of the firm's products relative to competing products. How well do the firm's products fulfill customers' needs relative to competing products?

Describe how issues such as brand loyalty, value, commoditization, and relational exchange processes affect customers' purchase behaviors.

Why do potential customers not purchase the firm's products?

Identify the needs, preferences, and requirements of noncustomers that are not being met by the firm's products.

What are the features, benefits, and advantages of competing products that cause noncustomers to choose them over the firm's products?

Explain how the firm's pricing, distribution, and/or promotion are out of sync with noncustomers. Outside of the product, what causes noncustomers to look elsewhere?

Describe the potential for converting noncustomers into customers.

C. **The External Environment (refer to Exhibit 4.5)**

Competition

Identify the firm's major competitors (brand, product, generic, and total budget).

Identify the characteristics of the firm's major competitors with respect to size, growth, profitability, target markets, products, and marketing capabilities (production, distribution, promotion, pricing).

What other major strengths and weaknesses do these competitors possess?

List any potential future competitors not identified above.

Economic Growth and Stability

Identify the general economic conditions of the country, region, state, or local area where the firm's target customers are located. How are these economic conditions related to customers' ability to purchase the firm's products?

Describe the economics of the industry within which the firm operates. These issues might include the cost of raw materials, patents, merger/acquisition trends, sales trends, supply/demand issues, marketing challenges, and industry growth/decline.

Political Trends

Identify any political activities affecting the firm or the industry with respect to changes in elected officials (domestic or foreign), potential regulations favored by elected officials, industry (lobbying) groups or political action committees, and consumer advocacy groups.

What are the current and potential hot-button political or policy issues at the national, regional, or local level that may affect the firm's marketing activities?

Legal and Regulatory Issues

Identify any changes in international, federal, state, or local laws and regulations affecting the firm's or industry's marketing activities with respect to recent court decisions; recent rulings of federal, state, or local government entities; recent decisions by regulatory and self-regulatory agencies; and changes in global trade agreements or trade law.

Technological Advancements

How have recent technological advances affected the firm's customers with respect to needs/wants/preferences, access to information, the timing and location of purchase decisions, the ability to compare competing product offerings, or the ability to conduct transactions more effectively and efficiently?

Have customers embraced or rejected these technological advances? How is this issue related to customers' concerns over privacy and security?

How have recent technological advances affected the firm or the industry with respect to manufacturing, process efficiency, distribution, supply chain effectiveness, promotion, cost-reduction, or customer relationship management?

What future technologies offer important opportunities for the firm? Identify any future technologies that may threaten the firm's viability or its marketing efforts.

Sociocultural Trends

With respect to the firm's target customers, identify changes in society's demographics, values, and lifestyles that affect the firm or the industry.

Explain how these changes are affecting (or may affect) the firm's products (features, benefits, and branding), pricing (value), distribution and supply chain (convenience, and efficiency), promotion (message content, delivery, and feedback), and people (human resource issues).

Identify the ethical and social responsibility issues that the firm or industry faces. How do these issues affect the firm's customers? How are these issues expected to change in the future?

III. SWOT Analysis

A. Strengths

Strength 1: _____

Strength 2: _____

(Repeat as needed to develop a complete list of strengths.)

How do these strengths enable the firm to meet customers' needs?
How do these strengths differentiate the firm from its competitors?

B. Weaknesses

Weakness 1: _____

Weakness 2: _____

(Repeat as needed to develop a complete list of weaknesses.)

How do these weaknesses prevent the firm from meeting customers' needs?
How do these weaknesses negatively differentiate the firm from its competitors?

C. Opportunities (external situations independent of the firm—not strategic options)

Opportunity 1: _____

Opportunity 2: _____

(Repeat as needed to develop a complete list of opportunities.)

How are these opportunities related to serving customers' needs?

What is the time horizon of each opportunity?

D. **Threats (external situations independent of the firm)**

Threat 1: _____

Threat 2: _____

(Repeat as needed to develop a complete list of threats.)

How are these threats related to serving customers' needs?

What is the time horizon of each threat?

E. **The SWOT Matrix**

Strengths:	Opportunities:
•	•
•	•
•	•
•	•
Weaknesses:	Threats:
•	•
•	•
•	•
•	•

F. **Developing Competitive Advantages**

Describe ways that the firm can match its strengths to its opportunities to create capabilities in serving customers' needs.

Are these capabilities and competitive advantages grounded in the basic principles of operational excellence, product leadership, and/or customer intimacy? If so, how are these capabilities and advantages made apparent to customers?

Can the firm convert its weaknesses into strengths or its threats into opportunities? If not, how can the firm minimize or avoid its weaknesses and threats?

Does the firm possess any major liabilities (unconverted weaknesses that match unconverted threats) or limitations (unconverted weaknesses or threats that match opportunities)? If so, are these liabilities and limitations apparent to customers?

Can the firm do anything about its liabilities or limitations, especially those that impact the firm's ability to serve customers' needs?

G. **Developing a Strategic Focus**

What is the overall strategic focus of the marketing plan? Does the strategic focus follow any particular direction such as aggressiveness, diversification, turnaround, defensiveness, or niche marketing?

Describe the firm's strategic focus in terms of a strategy canvas. How does the firm's strategic thrust provide sufficient focus and divergence from other firms in the industry?

IV. **Marketing Goals and Objectives**

A. **Marketing Goal A:** _____
(Should be broad, motivational, and somewhat vague.)

Objective A1: _____
(Must contain a specific and measurable outcome, a time frame for completion, and identify the person/unit responsible for achieving the objective.)

Objective A2: _____
(Must contain a specific and measurable outcome, a time frame for completion, and identify the person/unit responsible for achieving the objective.)

B. **Marketing Goal B:** _____
(Should be broad, motivational, and somewhat vague.)

Objective B1: _____
(Must contain a specific and measurable outcome, a time frame for completion, and identify the person/unit responsible for achieving the objective.)

Objective B2: _____
(Must contain a specific and measurable outcome, a time frame for completion, and identify the person/unit responsible for achieving the objective.)

(Repeat as needed to develop a complete list of goals and objectives.)

V. **Marketing Strategy**

A. **Primary (and Secondary) Target Market**

Primary target market: _____

Identifying characteristics (demographics, geography, values, and psychographics):

Basic needs, wants, preferences, or requirements:

Buying habits and preferences:

Consumption/disposition characteristics:

Secondary target market (optional): _____

Identifying characteristics (demographics, geography, values, and psychographics):

Basic needs, wants, preferences, or requirements:

Buying habits and preferences:

Consumption/disposition characteristics:

B. **Product Strategy**

Brand name, packaging, and logo design:

Major features and benefits:

Differentiation/positioning strategy:

Supplemental products (including customer service strategy):

Connection to value (core, supplemental, and experiential/symbolic attributes):

C. **Pricing Strategy**

Overall pricing strategy and pricing objectives:

Price comparison to competition:

Connection to differentiation/positioning strategy:

Connection to value (monetary costs):

Profit margin and breakeven:

Specific pricing tactics (for example, discounts, incentives, and financing):

D. **Distribution/Supply Chain Strategy**

Overall supply chain strategy (including distribution intensity):

Channels and intermediaries to be used:

Connection to differentiation/positioning strategy:

Connection to value (nonmonetary costs):

Strategies to ensure channel support (for example, slotting fees and guarantees):

Tactics designed to increase time, place, and possession utility:

E. **Integrated Marketing Communication (Promotion) Strategy**

Overall IMC strategy, IMC objectives, and budget:

Consumer promotion elements

Advertising strategy:

Public relations/publicity strategy:

Personal selling strategy:

Consumer sales promotion (pull) strategy:

Trade (channel) promotion elements

Advertising strategy:

Public relations/publicity strategy:

Personal selling strategy;

Trade sales promotion (push) strategy:

VI. **Marketing Implementation**

A. **Structural Issues**

Describe the overall approach to implementing the marketing strategy.

Describe any changes to the firm's structure needed to implement the marketing strategy (for example, add/delete positions, and change lines of authority, change reporting relationships).

Describe any necessary internal marketing activities in the following areas: employee training, employee buy-in and motivation to implement the marketing strategy, overcoming resistance to change, internal communication and promotion of the marketing strategy, and coordination with other functional areas.

B. **Tactical Marketing Activities (be *very* specific—this lays out the details of the marketing strategy and how it will be executed)**

Specific Tactical Activities	Person/Department Responsible	Required Budget	Completion Date
Product Activities 1. 2. 3.			
Pricing Activities 1. 2. 3.			
Distribution/Supply Chain Activities 1. 2. 3.			
IMC (Promotion) Activities 1. 2. 3.			

VII. **Evaluation and Control**

A. **Formal Controls**

Describe the types of *input controls* that must be in place before the marketing plan can be implemented. Examples include financial resources, capital expenditures, additional research and development, and additional human resources.

Describe the types of *process controls* that will be needed during the execution of the marketing plan. Examples include management training, management commitment to the plan and to employees, revised employee evaluation/compensation systems, enhanced employee authority, and internal communication activities.

Describe the types of *output controls* that will be used to measure marketing performance and compare it to stated marketing objectives during and after the execution of the marketing plan.

Overall performance standards (these will vary based on the goals and objectives of the marketing plan): Examples include dollar sales, sales volume, market share, share of customer, profitability, customer satisfaction, customer retention, or other customer-related metrics.

Product performance standards (these are optional and will vary based on the product strategy): Examples include product specifications, core product quality, supplemental product quality, experiential quality, new product innovation, branding, and positioning.

Price performance standards (these are optional and will vary based on the pricing strategy): Examples include revenue targets, supply/demand balance, price elasticity, yield management, or metrics based on specific price adjustments.

Supply Chain performance standards (these are optional and will vary based on the distribution strategy): Examples include distribution effectiveness/efficiency, supply chain integration, value (time, place, and possession utility), relationship maintenance (collaboration and conflict), outsourcing, and/or direct distribution performance.

IMC (promotion) performance standards (these are optional and will vary based on the IMC strategy): Examples include communication objectives; brand awareness, recognition, or recall; campaign reach, frequency, and impressions; purchase intentions; and public relations, sales, and sales promotion effectiveness.

B. **Informal Controls**

Describe issues related to *employee self-control* that can influence the implementation of the marketing strategy. Examples include employee satisfaction, employee commitment (to the firm and the marketing plan), and employee confidence in their skills. If any of these controls are lacking, how can they be enhanced to support the implementation of the marketing plan?

Describe issues related to *employee social control* that can influence the implementation of the marketing strategy. Examples include shared organizational values, work-group relationships, and social or behavioral norms. If any of these controls are lacking, how can they be enhanced to support the implementation of the marketing plan?

Describe issues related to *cultural control* that can influence the implementation of the marketing strategy. Examples include organizational culture and organizational rituals. If any of these controls are lacking, how can they be enhanced to support the implementation of the marketing plan?

C. **Implementation Schedule and Timeline**

Activities	*Month* *Week*	1	2	3	4	1	2	3	4	1	2	3	4
Product Activities													
Pricing Activities													
Supply Chain Activities													
IMC Activities													

D. **Marketing Audits**

Explain how marketing activities will be monitored. What are the specific profit- and time-based measures that will be used to monitor marketing activities?

Describe the marketing audit to be performed, including the person(s) responsible for conducting the audit.

If it is determined that the marketing strategy does not meet expectations, what corrective actions might be taken to improve performance (overall or within any element of the marketing program)?

If the marketing plan, as currently designed, shows little likelihood of meeting the marketing objectives, which elements of the plan should be reconsidered and revised?

Appendix B

Example Marketing Plan

This example marketing plan was written using the worksheets in Appendix A. As a result, this plan is consistent with the outline of the textbook. Florida State University MBA students wrote this plan as a part of their course requirements. The text's authors edited the plan prior to its inclusion here. Furthermore, this plan is meant to be an example and nothing more. We do not suggest that this plan is ideal, feasible, or capable of generating desired goals and objectives. This plan is intended for classroom discussion and to demonstrate how a finished marketing plan might look and read. You should consult with your instructor regarding the format, layout, and other specific requirements that are needed in your particular situation.

Background on the Assignment

Students were assigned the task of developing a marketing plan for the launch of a new over-the-counter (OTC) pain medication. The fictitious client is VirPharm, Inc., a midsized Florida-based pharmaceutical company that specializes in quality-of-life prescription and OTC medications for the consumer market. VirPharm has been quite successful with a range of products in recent years. However, the big push at VirPharm has been to transition its prescription medications to the OTC market as patents expire and generic competition enters the market.

The task is to continue VirPharm's past successes by developing a plan to move Boprex from the prescription market to the OTC market. As a prescription medication, butoprofen (the active ingredient in Boprex) has been prescribed by doctors to treat rheumatoid arthritis, osteoarthritis, and migraine headache. However, as a nonsteroidal anti-inflammatory drug (NSAID), butoprofen is also suitable to treat general pain and fever. The use of Boprex by doctors has been declining steadily over the years as more powerful treatments for arthritis and migraine have come into favor. VirPharm recently received Federal Drug Administration (FDA) approval to market Boprex as an OTC treatment for rheumatoid arthritis, osteoarthritis, and migraine headache as well as a general-purpose analgesic (pain reliever) and antipyretic (fever reducer).

Bryan Chappelle, Rodney Foote, Douglas Hodges, Melinda Phillips, and Brian Taylor (Florida State University MBA Class of 2007) developed this marketing plan under the supervision of Dr. Michael Hartline as a part of their course requirements. This marketing plan is intended for classroom discussion rather than to illustrate effective or ineffective strategic planning.

In planning for the launch of Boprex to the OTC market, students were given three positioning options:

1. Launch as a treatment for rheumatoid arthritis and osteoarthritis. The key issues are the following:

   a. Strong competition from more effective prescription medications and well-known OTC drugs claiming similar benefits

   b. Age- and lifestyle-related target market issues

   c. Potential for higher profit margin, but with a smaller target market (lower volume)

2. Launch as a treatment for migraine headache. The key issues are the following:

   a. Strong competition from more effective prescription medications and well-known OTC drugs claiming similar benefits

   b. Consumer education regarding migraines versus headaches, as well as the need for immediate pain relief availability

   c. Potential for higher profit margin, but with a smaller target market (lower volume)

3. Launch as a general-purpose pain reliever and fever reducer. The key issues are the following:

   a. Intense competition from very strong OTC drugs such as aspirin, acetaminophen, ibuprofen, and naproxen sodium

   b. Overcoming fairly strong consumer loyalty to branded pain medications

   c. Potential for very high volume due to wide target market applicability but with a lower profit margin

Students were assigned the task of choosing one of these options after conducting extensive research on the industry, the market, and the competition. This comprised the first half of the marketing plan (situation analysis, SWOT analysis, goals, and objectives). The next task was to develop a marketing program to launch Boprex in a manner consistent with the chosen positioning option. Students were required to make decisions regarding the entire marketing program.

Marketing Plan for the OTC Launch of Boprex

Executive Summary

VirPharm, Inc. is a midsized pharmaceutical company that manufactures several quality of life OTC and prescription drugs. Its primary objective is to grow its market share for several of its products. VirPharm has realized success through Hapizine, an antidepressant; however, the patent for this drug will soon expire, exposing its market share to generic competition. VirPharm recently received approval to sell its NSAID, Boprex, in the OTC market to treat general pain and migraines as well as to act as an anti-inflammatory.

Currently, Boprex ranks sixth in its market for sales, and this strategic marketing plan aims to increase the market share that the drug holds through its introduction into the OTC market. VirPharm intends to leverage its strengths in a highly saturated and competitive market to accomplish this goal. Its primary competitors are other OTC NSAIDS, aspirin, and acetaminophen. Among other weaknesses, there is weak product differentiation in the market as a whole. Currently there are three primary outlets for OTC pain relief: mass merchant retailers (Wal-Mart, Target, Costco, and others), drugstores (Walgreens, CVS, Rite-Aid, and others) and grocery stores.

There are several challenges in the NSAID marketplace right now. NSAIDs are currently under attack in the media due to negative heart-related side effects. In addition, there are many competitors already in this market, and brand loyalty is difficult to overcome. However, VirPharm has several strengths that it intends to leverage to overcome these challenges. It have a market-leading sales force and a highly motivated workforce. Cost of production is comparatively low for its products.

VirPharm will explore new markets not currently exploited by its competitors. The name of the product will be changed to Releven (pronounced ree lee ven). This newly packaged product will be priced competitively in the marketplace, higher than private-label competition but slightly lower than many of its brand-name competitors. The primary target market will be young executives, 21 to 40 years old, with a predominant focus on pain relief associated with day-to-day overexertion rather than just headache relief. Another target market will be the older generation, which is increasing in population. VirPharm will focus its efforts to market Releven to the age range of 50 to 75 years old for particularly active seniors. Releven will be differentiated from other products through its use of new distribution channels, specifically office-supply website/stores and online distribution. VirPharm expects to capture 20 percent of the OTC pain reliever's market share within two years of the product launch. This represents $438 million in revenue in 2008.

Situation Analysis

The Internal Environment

Marketing Goals and Objectives   VirPharm has specific marketing goals and objectives that have brought historical success, which will provide the foundation for future successes. The primary objective set forth for VirPharm involves the focus of efforts to grow the sales and market share of each product that it manufactures. VirPharm engages in the manufacturing of a number of quality-of-life prescription and OTC drugs for the consumer market, which has brought brand-preference and leading market-share positions with several of its offerings.

As with any publicly traded company, one of the underlying missions of the organization must include the maximization of shareholder wealth. VirPharm's leading marketing objective has resulted in the predominant driver in the alignment of the organization's mission, particularly as it relates to the subsequent impact on shareholder value. In addition, the marketing objective to grow sales and market share allows the organization the flexibility to respond to external environmental changes as well as consumer needs and wants. VirPharm is somewhat uniquely structured by engaging in both the prescription and the OTC market, which allows the organization additional flexibility in market preferences and requirements.

Current Marketing Strategy and Performance   The main objective for VirPharm is focused on the marketing efforts used to grow sales and market-share position through the products that the company produces. The objective is primarily fostered through a strategy in which profits resulting from their successes are funneled back through research and development (R&D) to create new and improved products for the markets that they choose to serve. In addition, VirPharm has followed a transitional approach into the OTC market from its respective prescription product line as patents expire, such as the recently expired patent of the antidepressant Hapizine, which is the most successful in the marketplace. In combination with drug performance, the prescription drug market depends heavily on the medical profession's endorsement for success, whereas the OTC market depends heavily on relationships with trade, wholesalers, mass retailers, and drug stores.

Recent performance by VirPharm has been fairly successful with a sales growth rate of 23.4 percent and a net income growth of just over 19 percent. This recent performance has translated into a 2006 revenue level of $8.6 billion and net income of $474.2 million. One of the drivers for the increased growth by VirPharm has been its strong brand preference, which has pushed it to one of the top pharmaceutical providers in both the prescription and OTC drug markets. For the six different product lines that VirPharm offers in the prescription drug market that account for 75 percent of the business, it is approximately the second or third largest player overall and appears to be maintaining that position, without much concern for a recently expired patent on Hapizine, which is number one in the market. The primary concern involves Boprex, which has been in decline the last few years and currently finds itself as the sixth preferred drug in its market. In regard to the macroposition of the OTC market, VirPharm is holding approximately the second largest position.

VirPharm has experienced aggressive growth in sales and has established itself in the top tier of the various product categories that it services, which can be largely attributed to its "best in the industry" sales force. However, VirPharm has come to the recent realization that it will need to address the periodic decline in the market position of one of its prescription drugs, Boprex. This respective decline in Boprex has been primarily the result of more powerful NSAIDs, from competitors that provide Vioxx, Celebrex, and Bextra.

Current and Anticipated Organizational Resources   The overall resources for Vir-Pharm are described as good and led by a highly motivated sales force that has been recognized as a leader in the pharmaceutical industry, as well as good working relationships with both suppliers and customers. As a midsized company competing with a large number of major firms, VirPharm has been able to develop a strong reputation for employee integrity, customer satisfaction, and commitment. Conversely, as a midsized player in the industry, VirPharm has realized some limitation on consumer and trade budgets, which operate at nearly half the rate of the major competitors.

While the resource levels and relationships are expected to be virtually unchanged in the future, VirPharm must be cautious in some of the variability that it has experienced with its offshore suppliers, particularly those in China. The use of suppliers in this region has allowed VirPharm to leverage its market position through lower costs of raw materials. Current alternatives to these resources will lead VirPharm to source supplies and materials from more expensive vendors located in Europe and Puerto Rico.

Any potential threats related to offshore suppliers that sustain competitive leverages might need to be combated with a potential merger regarding a larger player in the pharmaceutical industry. VirPharm has entertained these very possibilities and has engaged discussions with leading firms such as GlaxoSmithKline, Aventis, Pfizer, and Procter & Gamble. Results from a merger with any of these respective firms would allow VirPharm greater access to resources, specific expertise to be leveraged, supplier leverage, and the ability to focus on the core of what it has established.

Current and Anticipated Cultural and Structural Issues   The current organizational culture and structure at VirPharm are depicted as very customer driven, with a foundation that is particularly employee oriented. This culture is best depicted by a sales force that is nearly half of the entire organization's population and by the embracing of an ethical means of doing business through its Code of Integrity. The organization's philosophy recognizes that it operates in a customer- and market-driven industry and that success will not be realized if it does not have the internal motivation and commitment to the firm by its most valued asset: the employees.

The Customer Environment

Current and Potential Customers   A study published by ABC News, *USA Today*, and Stanford University Medical Center in May 2005 found that more than half of Americans live with chronic or recurrent pain. Nearly six in ten said their last pain experience was moderate or worse, and two in ten rated their pain as severe. Fifty-seven percent of seniors, age 55 years and older, experience pain often, compared to 43 percent of people ages 31 to 55 years old and 17 percent of adults 30 years old and younger. Back and knee pain account for 37 percent of pain locations, followed by headaches/migraines at nine percent and leg and shoulder at seven percent each. Together, these account for 60 percent of all pain by location. To eliminate this pain, 84 percent of respondents said they use OTC drugs, and 81 percent use home remedies such as heating pads, ice packs, and hot baths or showers.

American Demographics concluded that the four major uses for OTC pain relievers are headaches, sore muscles, arthritis, and heart-attack prevention. In 1996, an estimated 177 million Americans used an OTC pain reliever for one problem or another. This number is expected to grow to 205 million by 2010. Exhibit B.1 indicates how American consumers use OTC pain relievers.

Customer's Need for Pain Relievers   Headaches and migraines are the number-one reason why people take OTC pain relievers. Migraines affect 13 percent of the U.S. population, or 29.5 million people, and are most prevalent in people between 20 and

EXHIBIT B.1

OTC PAIN-RELIEF USAGE

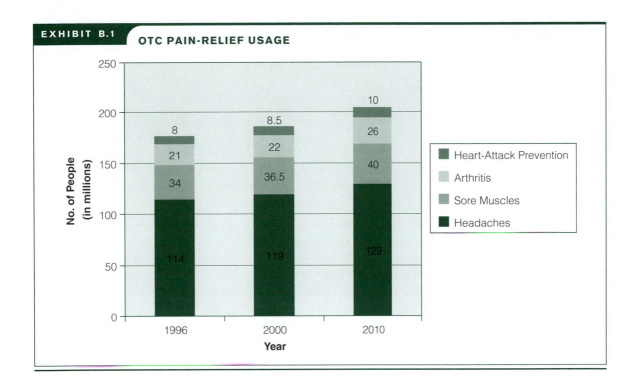

40 years old. This results in one in every four households having a migraine sufferer. Approximately 60 percent of adults have taken an OTC pain reliever for a headache in the past six months. This number has been declining over the past few years due to the acceptance of headaches as a legitimate and sometimes serious medical problem. Individuals have begun seeing doctors for prescription medications that are more effective than typical analgesics for specific types of headaches.

The second most popular reason for taking pain relievers is sore muscles. This is also the fastest-growing reason for the use of OTC pain relievers, specifically NSAIDs. In the early 1990s, this reason grew by 17 percent in the young adult—age segment from 18 to 24 years old. This was initially believed to be due to their more active lifestyle, but the market segment of ages 65 years and older has grown by 17 percent, too. The aggressive marketing of ibuprofen as an antidote for sore muscles can be credited for this increase. Prior to this marketing campaign, individuals believed that not much could be done for their achy muscles and that it was something they would have to live with. The aging baby-boomer generation could also help this segment along with the arthritis segment grow rapidly in the future.

Arthritis sufferers have also found relief from OTC pain relievers. Almost 43 million people have been diagnosed as having some form of arthritis, and an estimated 23.2 million live with chronic joint symptoms but have not been diagnosed by a physician. This is equivalent to one in three adults. Some types of arthritis include osteoarthritis, a degenerative joint disease; rheumatoid arthritis, which attacks the joint lining causing it to become inflamed; and juvenile arthritis, which affects children. Arthritis affects people of all ages, including over 300,000 children, and is the

---

EXHIBIT B.2 **FREQUENCY OF PURCHASE OF OTC PAIN RELIEVERS**

How often have you purchased an OTC pain-relief drug in the past 6 months?

	Frequency	Percent	Cumulative Percent
0 times	370	30.8	30.8
1–2 times	520	43.3	74
3–4 times	175	14.6	88.6
5–6 times	79	6.6	95.2
7+ times	56	4.7	99.8
Don't know	2	0.2	100
Total	1,202	100	

---

most prevalent chronic health problem and the leading cause of disability among Americans over the age of 15 years. Arthritis also affects women more than men, with 25.9 million women being physician-diagnosed compared with 16.8 million men.

Customer Purchase Patterns   Customers typically purchase pain relievers at supermarkets such as Publix, Albertson's, and Winn Dixie while doing their weekly grocery shopping. NSAIDs can also be purchased at pharmacies such as Walgreen's, Eckerd, or Target. Individuals may buy OTC pain relievers after surgery or to help eliminate pain after they have used all their prescription painkillers. Purchases typically occur no more than one to two times per month as indicated in Exhibit B.2.

A number of issues play a role in the consumers' selection of which OTC pain reliever to use. Some consumers look for the lowest price, in which case most private label pain relievers such as Wal-Mart's Equate brand cost considerably less than such name brands as Tylenol or Excedrin. Other consumers look for the absence of certain side effects such as gastrointestinal bleeding or effects on one's liver. Few OTC pain relievers can be taken during pregnancy, and others cannot be used in conjunction with certain prescription drugs. When consumers have multiple symptoms, such as a headache with a stuffy head or congestion, they often choose a medication that will solve all their problems. Products such as Tylenol Sinus serve to eliminate headaches and clear congestion. As an added benefit, the user does not need to be concerned with possible side effects of mixing medications. Once consumers find a pain reliever that works well, they tend to buy only this brand in the future.

Rationale of Noncustomers   Aspirin and ibuprofen should not be taken by consumers taking blood pressure medications like ace inhibitors and/or beta-blockers. Some people have allergic reactions to aspirin, which can cause wheezing, hives, facial swelling, and/or shock. Other individuals have a holistic approach to medicine and prefer not to take any sort of medication. Because of these reasons, many individuals experiment with alternative means of pain relief. Sports creams, like Ben-Gay and Icy Hot, along with ice packs can be used to eliminate achy muscles and reduce swelling. Electric heating pads are commonly used to reduce lower-back pain, and acupuncture has grown in popularity in recent years as an alternative to medications as well.

Competition

VirPharm's likely competition for Boprex can be categorized into three groups. These three groups of competitors—products that treat rheumatoid arthritis and osteo-arthritis, migraines, and general fever and pain—are grouped by the common ailment that they are intended to remedy.

For the treatment of arthritis, competition exists in both the prescription market and the OTC market. The most common prescription competitors are Vioxx, Celebrex, and Bextra, whereas the OTC competitors are Aleve, Excedrin, and aspirin. New competitors on the prescription front, while not publicly well known, are Enbrel, Remicade, and Avara.[1] For the treatment of migraines, competition exists in both the prescription and OTC markets. Common prescription medications for the treatment of migraines are Imitrex, Axert, and Midrin. The OTC counterparts are Excedrin Migraine and Advil Migraine. Next, there is strong competition in the OTC market for a general fever/pain reliever from many well-known brand names and private-label brands. Bayer and Excedrin are the major brand players in the aspirin segment. Acetaminophen is a competing product, most often associated with the Tylenol brand. Next, there is ibuprofen, with common brand names of Motrin and Advil. Finally, there is a rather recent entry to the market, Aleve, which employs naproxen sodium as its active ingredient. Finally, VirPharm could look at a different market for the product, such as offering the product as a multisymptom treatment. In this arena, competition comes from many of the same organizations, which supply multisymptom products such as Tylenol Cold, Advil Cold & Sinus, and Nyquil.

Analysis of Major Competitors   Because it will compete for shelf space, for market share, and against drugs promoting various types of symptom relief, Boprex will compete against several different drug types, specifically aspirin, ibuprofen, naproxen sodium, and acetaminophen. Each of these drugs carries unique qualities to provide symptom relief, with uniquely corresponding side effects. Exhibit B.3 summarizes these symptom-relief and side-effect combinations.

Competing Nondrug Therapies   In response to the high cost of prescription and nonprescription drugs and in conjunction with these drugs' side effects, the use of nondrug therapies for the treatment of pain and other ailments is thriving. Nondrug therapies are also the first option by choice for some people because they choose not to introduce drugs into their bodies. Examples of these therapies include exercise, weight control, the use of hot and cold packs, attitude, education, and assistive devices.[2] Advantages to these methods can take the form of improved health, lower cost, and the ability to maintain the treatment indefinitely unlike many drugs. Some disadvantages may include the continuance of pain or discomfort during the healing process that could be avoided with the use of medication.

Economic Growth and Stability

According to the Beige Book, the U.S. economy continues to expand in each of the Federal Reserve Board districts.[3] The Fed's report further states that consumer prices are stable, and employment is noted as moderately increasing across the districts. The

---

EXHIBIT B.3   **STRENGTHS AND WEAKNESSES OF COMPETING DRUGS**

Drug Type (Common Brands)	Strengths/Major Symptoms Relieved	Weaknesses/Side Effects
Aspirin (Bayer, Excedrin, St. Joseph's)	Preventive care for cardiovascular issues; reduces inflammation; trusted pain reliever	Can cause stomach irritation; not suitable for infants or use during the last three months of pregnancy
Ibuprofen (Motrin, Advil)	Effective pain reliever and fever reducer; reduces inflammation; trusted, with strong brand names; formulas available for adults, children, and infants	Like all NSAIDs, can cause stomach irritation; may have cardiovascular side effects; not recommended for prolonged use
Naproxen sodium (Aleve, Naprosyn)	Long-lasting pain and fever relief from minimal dosage; excellent at reducing inflammation	Like all NSAIDs, can cause stomach irritation; may have cardiovascular side effects; not recommended for prolonged use; not as well known as other NSAIDs
Acetaminophen (Tylenol)	Excellent pain and fever reducer; very high brand loyalty; does not cause stomach irritation; formulas available for adults, children, and infants; can be used during all stages of pregnancy	Does not reduce inflammation; dosage must be repeated every four hours; long-term use may cause liver damage
COX-2 inhibitors (Celebrex, Vioxx, Bextra)	Highly effective at reducing inflammation; significant arthritis pain relief; does not cause stomach irritation	Documented cardiovascular health issues (especially Vioxx); only Celebrex is currently on the market

---

Atlanta district, in which VirPharm resides, has experienced a shortage of labor in some specialized fields. Consumers are generally confident in the economy because the consumer confidence index has increased in five of the previous six months.[4] For the state of Florida, consumer confidence rose sharply in the most recently measured period.[5]

The global dollar volume for phamaceutical sales is approximately $550 billion. In the United States, sales grew to approximately $250 billion, a growth rate of nearly nine percent. The United States accounts for 46 percent of the world's pharmaceutical market. Taking a broader look across the industry, no fewer than 19 blockbuster drugs are expected to hit patent crisis by 2008. Analysis suggests that 150 new compounds will be needed by 2007–2008 in the United States alone to plug this gap.

In the OTC market, global sales recently totaled $47 billion, with $15.1 billion in the United States.[6] The OTC market has been growing dramatically as more customers are turning to self-diagnosis and treatment. There are currently more than 100,000 OTC products that consumers can choose from. The trend to use OTC medications has also been supported by physicians, who have been prescribing them more frequently than in the past. Some drugs that move from prescription to OTC enjoy greater attention from physicians. For example, after Claritin moved from prescription to OTC, 42 percent of purchasers in the first six months were advised to do so by their physicians. There are currently more than 600 OTC drugs that were once available only by prescription. When drugs move to the OTC market, their prices typically drop. However, these drugs also enjoy a dramatic increase in demand while demand for comparable OTC and prescription drugs sharply declines.[7]

Political Trends

A great deal of political attention has recently centered on COX-2 inhibitors, sold via prescription under the Vioxx, Bextra, and Celebrex brands. After Vioxx was found to double the rate of heart attacks among its users, Merck voluntarily withdrew the product from the market. Similarly, Pfizer withdrew Bextra when its use was associated with life-threatening skin reactions. Celebrex continues to be sold legally in the United States. The fallout of the COX-2 controversy has placed a great deal of scrutiny on the entire pain relief market, particularly with OTC NSAIDs.

Price controls and advertising regulations are also hot-button political issues. The United States and New Zealand are the only current nations where direct-to-consumer (DTC) drug advertising is permitted by the government.[8] Some politicians, such as Senator Bill Frist, are very direct regarding their stance on advertising by drug manufacturers. Senator Frist stated that drug advertisements add "fuel to America's skyrocketing drug costs" and asked companies to wait two years before advertising new drugs.[9] A secondary objective of such a probationary period on advertising is to prevent unnecessary prescriptions of drugs, where drug awareness created by advertising is inflating the number of prescriptions being written.

Drug manufacturers marshal a great deal of resources to lobby Congress to extend their patents and block generic competition. In the seven years leading up to 2005, pharmaceutical companies spent $800 million in federal lobbying and campaign contributions.[10] These efforts have helped to fend off the importation of drugs from companies that place caps on drug prices. In 2004, lobbying efforts helped pass the Medicare Modernization Act of 2003, which sets up a government-based reliable purchaser for the pharmaceutical companies.[11]

Drug importation is also a hotly contested political debate in the industry. While technically illegal and forbidden by the FDA, the practice of acquiring prescription and nonprescription drugs from nondomestic markets is very popular in the United States. Politicians, including the president, have stated their positions regarding the importation of nondomestic drugs into the United States. President George W. Bush stated, "If it's [drug importation] safe, then it makes sense." Bush continued by stating that "there's a lot of pressure in Congress for importation and so I think it makes sense for us to make sure we can do so in a safe way."[12] Although the importation of nondomestic drugs seemed to have the president's support, the FDA has yet to clear the way for the process to become legal. The FDA claims foreign drug providers may import drugs that are either counterfeit or untested. Those not in support of importing foreign drugs, especially U.S. pharmaceutical companies, side with the FDA and restate the safety concerns with foreign drugs. Those in support of foreign drug importation denounce this stance because they suspect that the pharmaceutical companies are only taking this position to maintain artificially high profit margins.

Legal and Regulatory Issues

Pharmaceutical firms have recently faced a number of challenges relating to regulation as well as to consumer perception. As a result of the COX-2 controversy, the FDA in June 2005 distributed letters to promoters of NSAIDs that called for changes in the labeling of such products. This new labeling was intended to inform consumers of "the potential for increased risk of cardiovascular events and the well-described, serious, and potentially life threatening gastrointestinal (GI) bleeding associated with these drugs."[13] In addition, the FDA warned that NSAIDs should not be used in conjunction with aspirin "because this may increase bleeding or lead to decreased renal function."[14] Though recent publicity has created a scare among consumers and a number of lawsuits, "the FDA has reaffirmed the safety of OTC NSAIDs and stressed that short-term use of low doses of OTC NSAIDs is not associated with any increased serious CV [cardiovascular] risk."[15] One challenge for manufacturers is that "OTC medicines have intended use for short periods of time, while prescription NSAIDs can be for long-term or chronic use as directed by a physician."[16] In addition to not being recommended for long-term use, OTC NSAIDs are also recommended at lower starting and maintenance doses than prescription NSAIDs. However, OTC medicines do not require a doctor's visit or prescription and therefore offer an additional level of convenience.

Additional regulations have been passed to enhance patient safety. The Prescription Drug Marketing Act of 1987 aids in the reduction of counterfeiting prescription drugs. Furthermore, in 2004 the FDA announced a ruling requiring hospitals to use bar codes on prescription medications that they distribute. The purpose of this is to minimize the chance of error within drug dispensing. Recently, the FDA went one step further to begin trials of radio-frequency identification (RFID) as a stronger means of tracking and controlling the nation's drug supply. Concerns are looming, however, regarding potential radio interference with lifesaving equipment within hospitals.[17]

Medicare reform offers other implications to VirPharm and the transition of Boprex from a prescription status. For example, the Medicare Prescription Drug Improvement and Modernization Act of 2003 impacts manufacturers of OTC drugs. "The Medicare compromise pumps $400 billion over ten years into the purchase of prescription drugs."[18] Even though patients may find comparable or improved relief from OTC medications, financial support encourages the use of prescription drugs. However, the 2005 introduction of the OTC Medicine Tax Fairness Act could level the playing field. If this bill passes, the new law would amend the medical and dental expense income tax deduction so that nonprescription or OTC drugs would be allowed as a deductible expense. In the meantime, OTC medications still qualify as reimbursable expenses through pretax dollars. The ability of consumers to pay for Boprex with pretax dollars offers them greater choice in their health while providing greater opportunity to VirPharm.

Technological Advancements

As in most industries, technological advancements have affected consumer activity in a number of ways. The Internet has created an abundance of information, not all of which is reliable. Consumers have easy access to information, much of which is promotional material presented in a manner to appear unbiased. Internet sources, however, can also offer educational and potentially useful information. For instance, sites such as www.rxlist.com and www.webmd.com provide useful information on uses and side effects of virtually all prescription and OTC pain relievers.

In addition to the impact to customers, technological advances also offer a number of opportunities and challenges pertaining to manufacturing, distribution, and promotional activities. Technology generates more extensive research, greater accuracy in manufacturing, more effective methods for tracking issues, and faster processes for development. With regard to distribution, technology has provided opportunities for environmentally friendly packaging while increasing safety mechanisms to prevent tampering. The most promising of these technologies is RFID. Potential benefits include inventory control, counterfeit deterrence, patient protection, and prompt communications relating to recalls. The cost to implement such technology, however, is significant and has prevented widespread implementation thus far. The FDA has developed a timeline in which drugs that are more likely to be duplicated by counterfeiters will be serialized sooner than others. The adoption of RFID technology affects drug manufacturers such as VirPharm and must be considered when developing packaging.

Technology influences not only marketing and distribution techniques but also the type of pain relief that is available and the delivery mechanism. In addition to traditional pain management, a number of technological advances are now available to patients seeking relief of acute and chronic pain. For example, neuromuscular stimulators run electrical currents through the body to generate healthy tissue and repair tissues that cause pain.[19] Facet rhizotomy, a procedure that uses an electrode to deaden the nerves that are causing pain in specific areas, is another specialized method of relief for joint pain.[20] Nerve blockers, magnetic therapies, infrared technology, and energy waves also represent technological advances for relief of localized pain.

In addition to new methods of pain relief, there are also new mechanisms for delivering medications. Beyond the traditional oral medications that include tablets, caplets, capsules, powders, and liquid forms, transdermal patch systems are gaining popularity. These systems have already been implemented in areas such as motion sickness, smoking cessation, and birth control. Furthermore, drug delivery may also be in the form of injections, inhalers, magnets, or lighting systems. Recognizing the effectiveness and convenience offered in alternative drug delivery systems creates future opportunities for makers of pain relief medications.

Sociocultural Trends

The changing values and demographics of today's society offer both opportunities and challenges to pharmaceutical firms. For instance, the increased size of an elderly population creates a large customer base for manufacturers of pharmaceutical products. In addition, this elderly population does not maintain the same lifestyles as those of past decades. They are remaining employed well into their 60s and 70s and are maintaining active lifestyles. Those in the workforce are increasingly using computers and keyboards, requiring manual dexterity and the ability to remain seated for hours at a time. Today's elderly population is not content to remain inactive. Active lifestyles create a market of on-the-go Americans who require effective pain relief to maintain the quality of life that they demand.

More active populations and dual-income households also result in consumers' placing an increased value on their time. The convenience of purchasing items and the convenience of dosing are both significant. Many want to purchase their pain relievers at the same place they purchase milk on the way home from work. This may be their local supermarket, a large supercenter, or the convenience store down the road. Shopping online is becoming increasingly common due to convenience as well. Busy schedules result in convenience being a critical aspect for today's shoppers.

Furthermore, patients are increasingly vocal about their health care, and they are active in seeking solutions to health issues. Television advertising of pharmaceuticals has risen, creating a new level of competition for drug manufacturers. A challenge for manufacturers of OTC medications is that, in recent years, there has been a significant increase in direct-to-consumer advertising of prescription drugs. "Ask your doctor if product X is right for you," suggests one commercial. With prescription medications promoting directly to consumers, manufacturers of OTC drugs are faced with increased competition from makers of similar products of prescription strength.

However, OTC drug manufacturers can take advantage of the growing trend of self-diagnosis and self-medication. With the diverse selection of vitamins, natural supplements, and OTC products that are available, consumers often self-diagnose their ailments and purchase products targeted to treat their symptoms. The inconveniences of visiting the doctor's office, coupled with increasing medical costs, have resulted in consumers' increasingly looking toward alternative solutions outside of conventional health care. The drawback to VirPharm, however, is that self-medication may result in a lack of compliance with recommended dosing. This presents a potential risk to consumers in that OTC NSAIDs are not intended for long-term use.

Another key sociocultural trend is access to and affordability of health insurance. According to the U.S. Census Bureau, over 46 million people in the United States were without health insurance coverage in 2006. Though the uninsured rate has hovered around 15 percent over the preceding 15 years, the number of uninsured has increased nearly 50 percent over the same timeframe.[21] This creates challenges for pricing OTC medications. Patients with excellent health insurance may find that the copayment on prescriptions drugs is actually less than the price of OTC medications.

SWOT Analysis

The SWOT Analysis for Boprex is provided in Exhibit B.4. Boprex has a number of strengths that can be matched with market opportunities to develop competitive advantages for VirPharm.

Developing Competitive Advantages

Shifting Boprex to the OTC medication is a huge opportunity for VirPharm. By moving OTC, VirPharm can take maximum advantage of its past R&D spending and use its remaining patent exclusivity to capture OTC dominance in the butoprofen pain-relief category. VirPharm will be able to tout Boprex as prescription-strength butoprofen at an OTC price. VirPharm has previous success in moving its prescription products to the OTC market, and that experience will be invaluable as VirPharm attempts this transition with Boprex. VirPharm's low manufacturing costs are also critical because the OTC market is very price competitive.

EXHIBIT B.4 — SWOT ANALYSIS FOR BOPREX

Strengths	M	•	I	=	R	Opportunities	M	•	I	=	R
Boprex approved to treat arthritis, migraine headache, and general pain	3		3		9	FDA has approved the transition of prescription NSAIDs into OTC market	3		3		9
Patent exclusivity for three years	3		3		9	Consumers will try new products as they become available	3		3		9
New product entry	3		2		6	NSAIDs can be used as general pain reliever and fever reducer	3		3		9
Prescription-strength pain relief available OTC	3		2		6	Potential market channels not currently exploited	3		3		9
Effective migraine treatment	3		2		6	Competing prescription pain relievers have been pulled from the market	3		2		6
Talented and motivated workforce	2		2		4	Weak product differentiation among OTC competitors	3		2		6
Lower cost of raw materials	3		1		3	U.S. population is increasingly seeking convenience of online shopping	2		3		6
Wide range of products	1		2		2	Increase in aging population	2		2		4
Weaknesses	**M**	**•**	**I**	**=**	**R**	**Threats**	**M**	**•**	**I**	**=**	**R**
Limited marketing budget	−3		3		−9	Competition from both prescription pain relievers and OTC pain relievers	−3		3		−9
Market position (number 6 in market)	−3		3		−9	Extremely crowded OTC market	−3		3		−9
Weak product differentiation	−3		3		−9	Consumer loyalty with existing competitors	−3		2		−6
Current brand name (new to market)	−3		2		−6	Negative publicity regarding NSAIDs	−2		3		−6
Midsized company	−2		2		−4	Declining doctor recommendation of NSAIDs	−1		3		−3
Boprex associated with gastrointestinal side effects	−1		3		−3	OTC NSAIDs not indicated for long-term use	−1		2		−2
Variability in offshore suppliers	−1		2		−2	Regulations on drug advertisements could intensify	−1		2		−2

In moving to OTC, VirPharm will be able to leverage its strength and newness in a market that consistently looks for the newest, most effective pain relief on the market. In addition, VirPharm can take advantage of the relatively weak differentiation among OTC competitors, as well as the relative softness in the market for COX-2 inhibitors. Furthermore, VirPharm can take advantage of marketing channels that are relatively underutilized by competing OTC firms.

Despite the tremendous opportunities, VirPharm must also be cognizant of its weaknesses in the crowded OTC market. Although being a midsized company does not allow for significant financial backing, it does allow VirPharm to react quickly to changing markets and customer requests. To compensate for its relatively small marketing budget, VirPharm's industry-leading sales force will work with physicians and pharmacists to emphasize the effectiveness and lower cost of Boprex. Likewise, VirPharm's promotional campaign will need to be lean, efficient, and cost effective.

Developing a Strategic Focus

The overall strategy of this marketing plan incorporates key opportunities in the industry into VirPharm's focus. The ability to transition VirPharm's prescription medication into an OTC medication offers an opportunity for market launch within the general pain-relief market. VirPharm will benefit from a large adult population, many of whom work beyond the age of 65 years. As a part of this launch, Boprex will be renamed Releven—a name that plays on the relief offered by prescription-strength butoprofen. The strategic focus is to position Releven as a medication that is stronger and more effective than traditional pain relievers and one that is easier to access than obtaining a prescription.

In terms of distribution and access, Releven will be offered for sale through traditional grocery, mass-merchandise, and drug store channels. However, VirPharm will also aggressively pursue nontraditional venues such as office-supply merchants and online stores. VirPharm will develop partnerships with companies such as Staples, Office Max, and Office Depot to offer Releven as an add-on item through online purchases. This partnership will assist corporate office-supply buyers to satisfy multiple office needs with a one-stop shop concept. Relven will gain an online presence and develop an "e-drug" status, and evolve as the preferred pain-relief product in the office environment. Realizing the weaknesses of VirPharm's limited marketing budget and its unrecognizable brand name, this approach to marketing and selling Releven will minimize marketing costs.

Marketing Goals and Objectives

Based on careful consideration of the situational and SWOT analysis, the following goals and objectives have been identified to provide the blueprint for an opportunity to transition Releven to the OTC market.

> **Goal** To launch and position Releven as the convenient, prescription-strength, OTC pain reliever.

Convenience is the driving theme of this marketing plan. One of the underlying demands of consumers for products in the OTC market involves convenience, whether it is off the shelf or the convenience of online ordering. In addition, Releven has the unique characteristic of its move to the OTC market. This will give consumers the confidence, satisfaction, and convenience of acquiring a prescription-strength medication without the need of physician direction.

> **Objective 1** Obtain a 20 percent share of the multipurpose pain-relief market within two years of launch.

Whereas most competing products are positioned as relief for specific ailments, Releven will be positioned as a broad-spectrum pain reliever for a number of different ailments (headaches, migraines, general aches, pains, and fever). This positioning will be focused on the adult population who suffers from overexertion at work—whether it be from tension, stress, computer strain, or noise—or at home from the physical exertion of exercise or household demands.

Objective 2   Garner 20 percent of sales from online ordering within one year of launch.

As strength continues to build in Releven's market share, the availability of non-traditional procurement options (online ordering and availability from office-supply retailers) will position Releven as a leader in the office environment. Online buyers will be able to meet their needs without leaving their office.

Marketing Strategy

A summary of our marketing strategy over time is shown in Exhibit B.5. The elements of this strategy will be discussed in the following sections.

EXHIBIT B.5   SUMMARY OF RELEVEN MARKETING STRATEGY

	Stage 1	Stage 2	Stage 3	Stage 4
Overall Marketing Goals	Transition Releven to the OTC market; position as a prescription-strength product for general pain relief.	Increase product awareness and market share through sales to users of prescription medications and other pain relievers.	Continually increase market share through increased office and online presence.	Having gained brand awareness, maximize profit through reduced promotional efforts.
Product Strategy	Releven will be offered in one form (capsule) and in one dosage strength (50 milligrams).	As patent expires, Releven will be offered in other forms; single-dose packaging will be offered.	The product will sustain an "e-drug" reputation and be perceived as *the* solution for general aches and pains.	The most popular forms of Releven will remain on the market; other forms will be dropped.
Pricing Strategy	Releven will be priced higher than generics and aspirin but lower than prescription medications and specialty products.	As patent expires, prices will be reduced to maintain market position.	Prices will remain consistent with the growth phase.	Lower costs through reduced promotional efforts will allow further price reductions.
Distribution Strategy	Obtain shelf space from traditional outlets such as drug stores and large retailers; primary focus on office-supply retailers and online merchants; trial packs distributed with office supplies.	Further penetration into nontraditional vendors such as shipping and photocopy centers; single-dose packs will be available through vending machines.	Maximum availability will be provided through traditional and nontraditional merchants.	Only most profitable channels and merchants will be retained; significant online presence will continue.
Promotion Strategy	Heavy use of in-store promotions; trial-sized packs available with office-related items.	Continued in-store promotions; online promotion via office-supply websites; promotion via vending services and providers of water cooler suppliers; TV advertising to attract older adults.	Heavy advertising on online news sites	To further reduce costs, online promotion will be reduced.

Primary Target Market

VirPharm's primary target market consists of men and women, ages 21 to 40 years old, who work in an office environment. Their ethnic background is increasingly diverse. These individuals are found in both urban and suburban locations. Most have some college, and many possess bachelor's and master's degrees. They typically remain single well into their 20s and often do not have children until their 30s. Once married, they maintain dual-income households and therefore have larger incomes but less free time. This segment represents an easily identifiable and measurable group. This is a substantial consumer group that is accessible through many diverse communication channels.

Although the primary focus is on young professionals, a second focus within the growth phase will include a target market of active, older adults. This target, which includes both men and women, ranges in age from 50 to 74 years old. The population of this segment continues to grow, and this group will be the largest consumer of pharmaceutical products in the future.

Identifying Characteristics   Most of the young professionals in our target market have Internet access through multiple locations including home and work. Many also maintain a home office or a laptop for working from home. The target maintains an on-the-go lifestyle where they work extended hours and are motivated to succeed in their career. They also sustain active social lives that include frequenting sports events, social gatherings, and restaurants and bars. Because of the lifestyle they lead, the target is seeking convenient access to medications because they have little time for doctor's visits or for filling prescriptions and they expect quick relief for their pain. The younger portion of this target was brought up with pagers, cell phones, and the Internet. They often have short attention spans and are accustomed to having information at their fingertips. To break into this market, it is essential to allow quick and easy access to Releven. Many in this segment have become accustomed to periodic headaches and muscle aches, and they choose to endure the pain rather than to address it.

The older target now leads an active lifestyle well beyond the typical retirement age. The nation's baby boomers represent a large percentage of the population and therefore a large consumer segment. Those in their 50s have yet to peak in their career. Many others remain employed well beyond the age of 65 years and have no intentions of retiring. These individuals also lead active lives including maintaining primary and sometimes secondary careers, participating in social activities such as bowling and sports events, and beautifying their homes through landscaping and gardening.

Basic Needs and Requirements   In terms of pain relief, the primary market seeks effective pain relief for general symptoms including headaches, eyestrain from the computer, and a miracle cure for hangovers. Because of the time constraints for this active generation, they are seeking prescription-strength medications that are available OTC. Others need relief but have failed to seek resolution due to lack of convenience. The younger group is more impressionable and more easily influenced by products that are perceived as popular and trendy. The older segment, on the other hand, simply has a need for effective treatment at a reasonable price. In terms of pain relief, the primary market is seeking effective pain relief for sporadic pain such as aching muscles and occasional arthritic pain.

Purchasing/Shopping Habits and Preferences The younger generation increasingly purchases items online. They seek quick and convenient access for all of their shopping needs. In addition to shopping online, many frequent their local convenience store. They are also willing to pay a little more to save time. Furthermore, younger professionals are of a generation that demonstrates items are affordable as long as one can pay the minimum payment. Financing is common and price is often less a factor than status. The reverse is more likely to be true with the older market. Given the increased cost of health-care coverage and of prescription medications, they are seeking a low-cost alternative for pain relief.

As mentioned previously, price is less of a factor for the primary target. They seek the best solution regardless of price. If a product costs a little more but is easily accessible or can be taken less frequently, that added convenience adds greater utility. Also within this group is a subsegment that tends to endure their pain rather than treat it. A focus of the marketing strategy is to sway nonusers of pain-relief medication by offering an effective alternative to relief, one that can be used conveniently, on a short-term basis, and with minimal side effects. The consumers that comprise the older segment are more price sensitive and more likely to be loyal to well-known medications that have maintained a long-term existence in the OTC market. They are exposed to media through TV and newspapers and are typically aware of publicity related to drug recalls and issues relating to products' being pulled from the market.

Product Strategy

One primary feature of Releven that will be emphasized repeatedly is its prescription-strength formula. In addition, it has been approved to treat osteoarthritis and migraine headaches along with providing general pain relief. At the outset, Releven will be offered in capsule form and in one dosage strength. To simplify the initial product offering, there will not be an "extra strength" formula or a formula positioned specifically for migraines or headaches. Instead, Releven will be offered for general relief of pain symptoms that arise from headaches, migraines, arthritis, and other aches and pains. Future offerings will include alternate product forms including tablets in varying dosages.

A key advantage for VirPharm is Releven's patent protection for three years after launch. This patent will help prevent imitations and generic substitutions in the immediate future. Our patent will also support our initial pricing structure for a full three years after launch.

Brand Name and Packaging The product previously referred to as Boprex will be designated as Releven in its OTC form. The name was selected to subtly communicate its purpose of providing relief. The capsule—which is white with red "Releven" on it— will initially be packaged in three different sizes: a Trial Pack with ten capsules, a Personal Relief Pack with 100 capsules, and an Office Pack with 250 capsules. While most competitors offer larger packages as Family Packs, our Office Pack is designed to maximize positioning in the office/work environment. Future packaging will include a single-dose (two capsules) that will be made available in vending machines throughout the United States.

Differentiation and Positioning   There are several features that differentiate Releven. First, it will be developed with an "office presence" that is positioned as the best solution for general pain relief among office workers. The focus will be on pain relief for many ailments related to an office environment, including eyestrain, headaches, and migraines. The office presence is further enhanced through distribution in office-supply stores and websites. Moreover, based on the distribution focus, Releven will be differentiated as an "e-drug" solution that is easily accessible through online shopping. It will be positioned as a solution for active, young professionals and will gain brand loyalty through the newness, prestige, and coolness factors.

Releven itself will not be sold with accompanying supplemental products. However, Releven is unique in that it will be sold as a supplemental product within office-supply stores. In addition to partnering with retailers such as Staples, Office Max, and Office Depot, VirPharm will partner with manufacturers of specific product lines to include free trial packages of Releven with their product offerings.

Pricing Strategy

Releven is positioned toward young professionals who, in their consumption habits, have demonstrated that price is not the number-one factor in selecting products. Convenience is critical to this market, and status is also desirable. By positioning Releven as the best solution for pain relief and by securing a significant office presence the affordability of Releven will not be the primary focus of its appeal.

Though price is not the most critical factor in marketing Releven, VirPharm can nonetheless capitalize on its access to cheaper raw materials and therefore lower its cost of production. The pricing strategy, while primarily dependent upon retailers, will position Releven as an affordable solution to pain relief. Revenues will be gained through both volume and substantial profit margins. With a list price of $5.63 for the 100-count Personal Relief Pack, we expect Releven to sell at an average retail price of $8.99. This price is comparable with Advil and Aleve and less expensive than migraine-specific medications. The ten-capsule Trial Pack will have a list price of $.83 and the 250-count Office Pack will list for $8.77.

Distribution Strategy

The overall distribution strategy contains multiple approaches. In the introduction phase, shelf space will be sought through such traditional venues as drug stores and other retailers such as grocery stores and mass-merchandise retailers. The primary focus, however, will be through office-supply retailers and websites. During the growth phase, access will be extended through less traditional venues such as shipping and photocopy centers. These venues attract the specific target market of young professionals.

Furthermore, Releven will be offered through online office retailers such as Staples.com, OfficeMax.com, and OfficeDepot.com. Company buyers of office supplies and/or technological equipment and supplies will be exposed to Releven through their regular buying activities. A third strategy will present single-dose packages through vending machines in offices, shopping centers, health clubs, golf courses, and bowling alleys. Given the primary venue of online retailers, the focus will be on national distribution.

Integrated Marketing Strategy

The overall integrated marketing communications directed specifically toward the consumer include advertising primarily through Internet advertising, outdoor advertising such as billboards, through add-on sales via online venues, and through in-store promotions at office suppliers. Additional TV advertising will allow Releven to enhance its initial brand-name recognition. Advertising efforts will include 50 percent to Internet advertising, 20 percent to outdoor advertising, and 30 percent to television advertising. VirPharm's advertising budget includes $125 million for consumer advertising, and an equivalent amount has been dedicated to trade-marketing activities.

The advertising strategy will be specific to the product, images of the target market, types of pain that it treats, and the relief that it provides. The strategy will focus on general-purpose pain relief on the days (and nights) that adults have exerted themselves. Exertions include stress from work, eyestrain from the computer, headaches caused by screaming children, and general aches and pains resulting from a late night. Images of a young professional working on a laptop or of a young man waking up after a rough night will be shown to illustrate the uses for Releven.

Sales promotions will include free trial packages that are offered with office supplies in retail stores and online. Further indirect advertising will be presented in the form of office-related items to increase brand awareness. Items will include pens, paperweights, mouse pads, and office calendars. These inexpensive items will be shared through the vending services and through contact with office managers.

Secondary Target Market and Marketing Program

Secondary Target Market   Although VirPharm's secondary market will include numerous retailers, the primary focus will be on obtaining shelf space in office-supply stores as well as in the warehouses of online suppliers. Other businesses such as shipping and photocopy centers will also be targeted. Finally, vending machine services will be targeted as an opportunity for more direct access to customers. The primary need of these merchants is to increase sales through increased use and visitation of their product offerings. With regard to the vending services, the goal is to increase sales because profitability is directly related to sales quantities.

Product Strategy   The general-purpose relief offered by Releven aligns well with the needs of office-supply customers. For online retailers, offering Releven as an add-on sales item is an easy way to increase sales. Because Releven will be positioned with a strong office presence, office suppliers will benefit from their affiliation with Releven.

Pricing Strategy   The primary pricing objective is to blend midsized profit margins with substantial sales volumes for profitability. Releven will be offered to retailers at a price higher than generics and aspirin but at a price that is lower than most specialized arthritis and migraine products. As mentioned previously, the list price to retailers and wholesalers is $5.63 for the 100-count Personal Relief Pack, $.83 for the ten-count Trial Pack, and $8.77 for the 250-count Office Pack.

Distribution Strategy   The overall distribution strategy contains multiple approaches. VirPharm will initially gain shelf space in major retailer stores through the use of slotting fees and discounts on other VirPharm OTC products. These incentives will be phased out by the end of the first year when Releven is established in the market. Freestanding display packs will also be offered to major retailers. Point-of-sale displays will be offered to office-supply stores, shipping and copy centers, and convenience stores to capture customers at the checkout. Distribution via vending machines will be outsourced to a third-party vending supply company. After the initial launch through both traditional and nontraditional venues, the primary distribution strategy will be online availability. Online intensity is expected to increase beyond 50 percent once initial distribution has created brand-name recognition.

Integrated Marketing Strategy   Given the utilization of the organization's sales staff and consulting firm, communications with the supply chain will be primarily through site visits and sales negotiations. The budget of $125 million dedicated to the trade-marketing activities will be consumed through consulting services, travel expenses of the sales staff, and trial packages that will be offered to a substantial number of retail locations.

Marketing Implementation

Given the specific focus and direction of the marketing plan, VirPharm will follow an initial structural approach that is somewhat centralized in nature. This choice is based on the specific strategy that has been derived and new, somewhat unfamiliar channels, as well as to provide efficient and effective use of limited human and financial resources. The charge of implementing this marketing plan will fall to the senior vice president of the Over-the-Counter Division. This sponsor will have responsibility for the overall plan and project and will be a "sounding board" to obtain feedback on issues and to help alleviate any discrepancies/conflicts that could jeopardize the plan and/or the organization's goals and values. Second, a key account manager from the Consumer Group will be assigned role of implementation leader. This person will be responsible for ensuring that timelines are met, recruiting internal talent, ensuring resources are adequate, and being responsible for the overall completion of the endeavor.

In addition to internal resources, VirPharm will also solicit the expertise of a consulting firm that is well versed in web-based selling, promotion, advertising, and procurement. Because the thrust of the marketing strategy is focused on end-user sales from the use of the Internet, this creates an unfamiliar strategy that VirPharm has not been previously employed. Therefore, it is essential that the use of an experienced and skilled resource be used to ensure that pitfalls are avoided and to provide

EXHIBIT B.6	TACTICAL IMPLEMENTATION ACTIVITIES		
Specific Activities	**Assigned Responsibility**	**Required Budget ($250M/100%)**	**Estimated Completion Time**
Product Activities	Implementation leader	$37.5M/15%	
1 Releven capsule, 50-mg dosing, Trial Pack of 10 capsules.	Marketing and R&D	$12.5M	Month 1
2 Develop 100-count Personal Relief and 250-count "Office" Packs.	Marketing and R&D	$8M	Month 2
3 Product will be offered in single-dose packages, which entails two capsules.	Marketing and R&D	$17M	Month 3
Pricing Activities		$25M/10%	
1 Initial Trial Packs are free for the first two months.	Wholesale group	$25M	Month 1
Distribution Activities		$62.5M/25%	
1 Obtain contracts with traditional venues such as drug stores and large retailers.	Consultant and wholesale group	$17M	Month 1
2 Obtain contracts with mass office-supply retailers and gain initial entrance through Trial Packs.	Wholesale group and marketing	$8M	Month 1
3 Gain entrance to vending sales by outsourcing vending to a third party; develop single-dose package for vending machines.	Wholesale group and marketing	$17M	Month 3
4 Work with office-supply retailers to provide product through their respective online ordering systems.	Consultant, marketing, wholesale group, and consumer group	$20.5M	Month 6
IMC Activities		$125M/$50%	
1 In-store promotions through Trial Pack offerings.	Wholesale group and marketing	$8M	Month 1
2 Television advertising to enhance awareness utility for the office professional, the active person, and the older adult; targeted time slots include sporting events, morning news, and afternoon daytime programming	Wholesale group and marketing	$37.5M	Month 1
3 Online advertising through Internet search engines and news portals, such as Google, Yahoo!, CNN, Fox News, and Bloomberg.	Consultant, marketing, wholesale group, and consumer group	$31.25M	Month 2
4 Work with office-supply retailers to advertise add-on sales through online ordering system.	Consultant, marketing, wholesale group, and consumer group	$31.25M	Month 6
5 Sponsorship of major television and sporting events.	Marketing	$17M	Month 12

general direction/feedback to the effort. One of the essential deliverables that the consultant will provide will be a scientific study on the buying habits of corporate buyers, the venues, and retailers that are most prevalent and preferred. A detailed listing of implementation activities is provided in Exhibit B.6.

Evaluation and Control

Output Controls

To ensure the proper implementation of VirPharm's marketing strategy for Releven, procedures must be in place to evaluate outcomes relative to the plan's stated

EXHIBIT B.7   THREE-MONTH IMPLEMENTATION SCHEDULE FOR RELEVEN LAUNCH

Month	May				June				July			
Week	1	2	3	4	1	2	3	4	1	2	3	4
Product Activities												
Finalize artwork, packaging, and label design	x	x										
Employee training and education on new strategy	x	x	x									
Produce packaging materials	x	x	x	x	x	x	x		x			
Production runs	x	x	x	x	x	x		x		x	x	x
Distribution Activities												
Finalize distribution issues with retailers and vending services firm	x	x	x									
Shipments to warehouses and distribution centers			x	x				x			x	x
Shipments to retailers				x	x			x	x			x
Pricing Activities												
5% discount on 100-count packs to retailers selling Releven online					x	x	x	x	x	x	x	x
10% discount on 250-count packs to retailers selling Releven online					x	x	x	x	x	x	x	x
IMC Activities												
Finalize website design			x									
Website testing				x								
Launch website					x							
Television advertising					x	x	x	x				
Online advertising					x	x	x					
In-store promotions at office supply centers					x	x	x	x	x	x	x	x
Free Trial Packs with online purchase (>$50) at office-supply retailers					x	x	x	x				
Free 250-count pack with online purchase (>$200) at office-supply retailers					x	x	x	x				

objectives. Recapping the objectives to be measured, VirPharm has established the following objectives for the launch of Releven into the OTC market:

> **Objective 1**   Obtain a 20 percent share of the multipurpose pain-relief market within two years of launch.

This objective will be assessed via a combination of internal and third-party research reports. Specifically, VirPharm will use the results of Nielsen's point-of-sale measurement reports to track sales and market share by region and type of merchant.

> **Objective 2**   Garner 20 percent of sales from online ordering within one year of launch.

This objective will be assessed via internal company sales records, along with support from members of the supply chain. We anticipate that 8 to 10 percent of sales will come from purely online vendors such as Drugstore.com and Amazon.com. The remaining 10 to 12 percent will come from online ordering at traditional brick-and-mortar stores such as Staples, Office Max, Office Depot, Wal-Mart, CVS, and Walgreens.

Implementation Timeline

Exhibit B.7 outlines a three-month schedule for the launch of Releven. Because a number of activities need to occur—such as finalizing product artwork, testing the website, and producing and distributing the medication—the product will not be sold until the first week of June. During this initial week of sales, most of our promotional activities will begin simultaneously. These include television ads, online banners, and promotional giveaways associated with office supply stores.

Final production of Releven will begin during the first week of May. This will provide sufficient supply to warehouses and retail shelf space prior to launch. After launch we anticipate that production will run continuously, though not in the high quantities necessary prior to launch.

This is only a three-month schedule because most of these activities revolve around the product launch. Marketing activities will continue in the future and will be adjusted based on effectiveness and product demand.

Endnotes

Chapter 1

1. These facts are from "Best Buy: How to Break Out of Commodity Hell," *BusinessWeek Online,* March 27, 2006 (http://www.businessweek.com/magazine/content/06_13/b3977007.htm); James V. Cammisa, "Midyear Industry Review and Outlook," Association of Travel Marketing Executives, July 28, 2005; Robert D. Hof, "Building an Idea Factory," *BusinessWeek Online,* October 11, 2004 (http://www.businessweek.com/magazine/content/04_41/b3903462.htm).

2. Peter Coy, "For Sale by Owner," *BusinessWeek Online*, May 5, 2006 (http://www.businessweek.com/the_thread/hotproperty/ archives/2006/05/for_sale_by_own.html).

3. Ronald Grover, "Will *Bubble* Burst a Hollywood Dogma?" *BusinessWeek Online,* January 24, 2006 (http://www.businessweek.com/bwdaily/dnflash/jan2006/nf20060124_4959_db011.htm).

4. Terril Y. Jones, "Dell Advancing to the Championship Round; The Texas Company Moves Aggressively to Expand Beyond PCs, with Its Sights Set on Big Rivals HP and IBM," *Los Angeles Times,* June 1, 2003, C1.

5. "Mrs. Fields Cookies and Hershey's Foods Assessed Largest Penalties to Date for COPPA Violations," *Computer and Internet Lawyer* 20 (May 2003): 30–31.

6. Laura Sydell, "Google Unveils Censored Search Engine in China," *All Things Considered,* January 25, 2006 (http://www.npr.org/templates/story/story.php?storyId=5172204).

7. Wenran Jiang, "Watchful and Wary: China's Hu Visits Bush," *BusinessWeek Online,* April 13, 2006 (http://www.businessweek.com/globalbiz/content/apr2006/gb20060413_186631.htm).

8. Eric Chabrow, "Retailers Agree to Online Tax," *InformationWeek,* February 10, 2003, 16.

9. American Marketing Association, http://www.marketingpower.com.

10. Ibid.

11. Jeffrey F. Rayport and Bernard J. Jaworski, *e-Commerce* (Boston: McGraw-Hill/Irwin, 2001), 3.

12. Mohanbir Sawhney, "Making New Markets," *Business 2.0,* May 1999, 116–121.

13. http://www.amazon.com.

14. This list is adapted from Philip Kotler, *A Framework for Marketing Management,* 2nd ed. (Upper Saddle River, NJ: Prentice Hall, 2003), 4–5.

15. http://www.americanlegacy.org.

16. Alabama Development Office, "Teamwork Drives Hyundai to Alabama!" *Developing Alabama,* Spring 2002.

17. These facts are from Molly Wood, "DRM This, Sony!" CNET.com, November 10, 2005 (http://www.cnet.com/4520-6033_1-6376177-1.html).

18. The Society of Competitive Intelligence Professionals (http://www.scip.org).

19. These facts are from Theresa Johnston, "View from the Top: Southwest Airlines' Kelleher Advises Managing in Good Times for the Bad," Stanford Graduate School of Business, April 2006 (http://www.gsb.stanford.edu/news/headlines/vftt_kelleher.shtml).

20. Hampton Inn's Satisfaction Guarantee (http://www.hamptoninn.com).

21. These facts are from Alex Halperin, "No Space for MySpace," *BusinessWeek Online,* May 12, 2006 (http://www.businessweek.com/technology/content/may2006/tc20060512_299340.htm); Jesse Hempel, "The MySpace Generation," *BusinessWeek,* December 12, 2005; Steve Rosenbush and Timothy Mullaney, "Social Networking's Gold Rush," *BusinessWeek Online,* April 19, 2006 (http://www.businessweek.com/technology/content/apr2006/tc20060419_514268.htm); "From MySpace

to Safer Space," *BusinessWeek Online,* April 11, 2006 (http://www.businessweek.com/technology/content/apr2006/tc20060411_341338.htm).

22. Michael Grigsby, "Getting Personal," *Marketing Research* 14 (Fall 2002): 18–22.

23. Grant Gross, "RFID and Privacy: Debate Heating up in Washington," *InfoWorld* (IDG News Service), May 28, 2004 (http://www.infoworld.com/article/04/05/28/HNrfidprivacy_1.html).

24. These facts are from Mark Kassof & Company, "McDonald's Arch McFlop," *Research Insights: Lessons from Marketing Flops,* Summer 1997.

25. These facts are from the Aflac corporate website (http://www.aflac.com) and "The 100 Best Companies to Work For 2006," *Fortune* (http://money.cnn.com/magazines/fortune/best companies).

26. These facts are from Parija Bhatnagar, "Wal-Mart's Challenge in China," CNNMoney.com, January 12, 2006 (http://money.cnn.com/2006/01/12/news/companies/walmart_china/index.htm); and Kerry Capell, "Tesco: California Dreaming?" *BusinessWeek Online,* February 16, 2006 (http://www.businessweek.com/bwdaily/dnflash/feb2006/nf20060216_6586_db016.htm).

27. From various sources, including http://www.fedex.com.

Chapter 2

1. We thank Dr. Elaine S. Potoker, Maine Maritime Academy, for her insight and suggestions on the concept of strategic planning as a funnel.

2. These facts are from Daren Fonda, "Who Says GM is Dead?" *Time,* May 22, 2006, 51–53; David Welch, "Is GM's Turnaround Temporary?" *Business Week Online,* May 12, 2006 (http://www.business week.com/autos/content/may2006/bw20060512_562538.htm); and David Welch, "GMAC: Is GM Selling Its Seed Corn?" *BusinessWeek Online,* April 4, 2006 (http://www.businessweek. com/print/autos/content/apr2006/bw20060404_121027.htm).

3. The Pfizer mission and vision statements are from http://www.pfizer.com/pfizer/are/mn_about_mission.jsp.

4. The Southwest Airlines mission statement is from http://www.southwest.com/about_swa/mission.html.

5. The Ben & Jerry's mission statement is from http://www.benandjerrys.com/our_company/our_mission.

6. "Johnson & Johnson Reincarnates a Brand," *Sales and Marketing Management,* January 16, 1984, 63; and Elyse Tanouye, "Johnson & Johnson Stays Fit by Shuffling Its Mix of Businesses," *Wall Street Journal,* December 22, 1992, A1, A4.

7. These facts are taken from "Turning Compassion into Action —Donor Dollars at Work: Hurricanes Katrina, Rita and Wilma," http://www.redcross.org/news/ds/hurricanes/support05/report.html.

8. This information is from http://www.sony.com.

9. This information is from http://www.3m.com.

10. These facts are from Kevin Allison, "More Than Price Behind Dell Fall," *Financial Times* (London, UK), May 10, 2006, 30; Louise Lee, "Dell: Burned by a Fire Sale," *BusinessWeek Online,* May 9, 2006 (http://www.businessweek.com/technology/content/may2006/tc20060509_664617.htm); Louise Lee, "Dell Goes High-End and Hip," *BusinessWeek Online,* March 23, 2006 (http://www.businessweek.com/technology/content/mar2006/tc20060323_034268.htm); Louise Lee, "From Servers to Service: Dell's Makeover," *BusinessWeek Online,* May 19, 2006 (http://www.businessweek.com/technology/content/may2006/tc20060519_475997.htm); and "Pressure from Hewlett-Packard Causes Dell to Undercut Earnings," *FinancialWire,* May 9, 2006, 1.

11. Howard Sutton, *The Marketing Plan in the 1990s* (New York: The Conference Board, Inc., 1990).

12. Ibid., 9.

13. Cindy Claycomb, Richard Germain, and Cornelia Droge, "The Effects of Formal Strategic Marketing Planning on the Industrial Firm's Configuration, Structure, Exchange Patterns, and Performance,"

Industrial Marketing Management 29 (May 2000): 219–234.

14. "Marketing Plan Help," *ABA Banking Journal* 95 (October 2003): 18.

15. Sutton, *The Marketing Plan in the 1990s,* 16.

16. Ibid., 17.

17. Bernard J. Jaworski and Ajay K. Kohli, "Market Orientation: Antecedents and Consequences," *Journal of Marketing* 57 (July 1993): 53–70.

18. Ibid; and Stanley F. Slater and John C. Narver, "Market Orientation and the Learning Organization," *Journal of Marketing* 59 (July 1995): 63–74.

19. These facts are from the Toyota website (http://www.toyota.com/about/environment/partnerships/index.html); and "Toyota-GM Partnership on Fuel Cells Imminent," Green Car Congress, July 11, 2005 (http://www.greencarcongress.com/2005/07/toyotagm_partne.html).

20. The material in this section is adapted from Robert S. Kaplan and David P. Norton, *The Strategy-Focused Organization* (Boston: Harvard Business School Press, 2001).

21. Descriptions of each perspective are adapted from "What is the Balanced Scorecard?" The Balanced Scorecard Institute (http://www.balancedscorecard.org/basics/bsc1.html).

22. Kaplan and Norton, *The Strategy-Focused Organization,* 8–17.

Chapter 3

1. Chad Terhune, "How Coke Beefed Up Results of a Marketing Test," *Wall Street Journal,* August 20, 2003, A1.

2. Betsy McKay and Chad Terhune, "Coca-Cola Settles Regulatory Probe; Deal Resolves Allegations by SEC That Firm Padded Profit by 'Channel Stuffing,'" *Wall Street Journal,* April 19, 2005, A3.

3. These facts are from Lester R. Brown, "Appetite for Destruction," *Fortune,* August 21, 2006, 36; Roland Jones, "Is a Hybrid Car Really Good for Your Wallet?" MSNBC.com, February 2, 2006

(http://www.msnbc.msn.com/id/8959811); Julia Layton and Karim Nice, "How Hybrid Cars Work," howstuffworks® (http://auto.howstuffworks.com/hybrid-car.htm); and Chris Woodyard, "Hybrid Buyers Stall Dealers to Claim Tax Credit," *USA Today,* December 22, 2005, B1.

4. Chad Terhune, "A Suit by Coke Bottlers Exposes Cracks in a Century-Old System," *Wall Street Journal,* March 13, 2006, A1.

5. James Bone, "Three Charged with Stealing Coca-Cola Trade Secrets," *Times Online,* July 6, 2006 (http://www.timesonline.co.uk/printfriendly/0,1-3-2259092-3,00.html).

6. Bonnie Thompson, "Do the Right Thing? Not with a Rival's Inside Information," *Advertising Age,* July 17, 2006, 4.

7. Lynn Brewer, Robert Chandler, and O. C. Ferrell, *Managing Risks for Corporate Integrity: How to Survive an Ethical Misconduct Disaster* (Mason OH: Texere/Thomson, 2006), 11.

8. Ibid.

9. Archie Carroll, "The Pyramid of Corporate Social Responsibility: Toward the Moral Management of Organizational Stakeholders," *Business Horizons* 34 (July/August 1991): 42.

10. Neil Weinberg, "Healing Thyself," *Forbes Online,* March 17, 2003 (http://www.forbes.com/forbes/2003/0317/064.html).

11. Debbie Thorne McAlister, O. C. Ferrell, and Linda Ferrell, *Business and Society* (Boston: Houghton Mifflin, 2003).

12. Ibid.

13. *Business Ethics,* January/February 1995, 13.

14. "Eye on Europe," *Business Ethics,* January/February 2002, 9.

15. These facts are from Sarah Ellison and Janet Adamy, "Panel Faults Food Packaging for Kid Obesity," *Dow Jones Reprints,* December, 7, 2005 (http://online.wsj.com/article/SB113387976454515095.html); "Kaiser Family Foundation Releases New Report on Role of Media in Childhood Obesity," Washington Panel Discussion to Explore Role of Media/Policy

Options, www.kff.org, February 24, 2004 (http://www.kff.org/entmedia/entmedia022404nr.cfm); and William M. Pride and O. C. Ferrell, "Supersizing Europeans," *Marketing* (Boston: Houghton Mifflin, 2006), 122.

16. Ronald Alsop, "Ranking Corporate Reputation," *Wall Street Journal,* December 6, 2005, B1.

17. "Andrea Jung," in Wikipedia, http://en.wikipedia.org/wiki/Andrea_Jung (as of April 25, 2006).

18. Oliver Ryan, "Avon Looks Ripe for a Rebound," *Fortune Online,* March 15, 2006 (http://money.cnn.com/magazines/fortune/fortune_archive/2006/03/20/8371795/index.htm).

19. "Worth Noting," *Business Ethics,* January/February 1999, 5.

20. Barry Newman, "An Ad Professor Huffs Against Puffs, but It's A Quixotic Enterprise," *Wall Street Journal,* January 24, 2003, A1.

21. McAlister, Ferrell, and Ferrell, *Business and Society.*

22. William T. Neese, O. C. Ferrell, and Linda Ferrell, "An Analysis of Mail and Wire Fraud Cases Related to Marketing Communication: Implications for Corporate Citizenship," working paper, 2003.

23. "Snapshot," *USA Today,* October 3, 2002.

24. Marty Bernstein, "Car Salespeople, Ad Execs Rank Low in Poll," *Automotive News,* May 26, 2003, 3M.

25. "13th Annual NACAA/CFA Consumer Complaint Survey Report," February 10, 2005 (http://www.consumerfed.org/pdfs/nacaacomplaintreport.pdf).

26. James Heckman, "Puffery Claims No Longer So Easy to Make," *Marketing News,* February 14, 2000, 6.

27. Archie B. Carroll, *Business and Society: Ethics and Stakeholder Management* (Cincinnati: South-Western, 1989), 228–230.

28. Sara Nathan, "Phony Jobs," *USA Today,* March 7, 2000, B1.

29. "Mott's Will Rewrite Some Labels Blamed for Misleading People," *Wall Street Journal,* August 2, 2000, B7.

30. Mary Foster, "Merck Suffers 2 Vioxx Setbacks," *BusinessWeek Online,* August 18, 2006 (http://www.businessweek.com/ap/financialnews/D8JIR3FG0.htm); and Heather Won Tesoriero, "Merck Is Handed Another Loss Over Vioxx," *Wall Street Journal,* April 22–23, 2006, A1.

31. Lisa Roner, "Drug-makers' Spoonful of Sugar," *Ethical Corporation,* October 2005, 27.

32. Consumer Fraud and Identity Theft Complaint Data January–December 2005, Federal Trade Commission 2006, Data from Consumer Sentinel and the Identity Theft Data Clearinghouse (http://www.consumer.gov/sentinel/pubs/Top10Fraud2005.pdf).

33. "About the Council of Better Business Bureaus," Better Business Bureau, September 21, 2006 (http://www.bbb.org/about/aboutCouncil.asp).

34. Jennifer Rewick, "Connecticut Attorney General Launches Probe of Priceline.com After Complaints," *Wall Street Journal,* October 2, 2000, B16.

35. McAlister, Ferrell, and Ferrell, *Business and Society.*

36. Brian Steinberg and Suzanne Vranica, "Brewers Are Urged to Tone Down Ads," *Wall Street Journal,* June 23, 2003, A1.

37. White Dog Café website (http://www.whitedogcafe.com/mission.html).

38. Constance E. Bagley, "The Ethical Leader's Decision Tree," *Harvard Business Review* (February 2003): 18–19.

39. Ethics Resource Center, *2005 National Business Ethics Survey: How Employees View Ethics in Their Organizations* (Washington, DC: Ethics Resource Center, 2005), 56.

40. "Ethics Is the Cornerstone of TI," (http://www.ti.com/corp/docs/company/citizen/ethics/brochure/index.shtml). Courtesy Texas Instruments, Inc.

41. "The TI Ethics Quick Test," (http://www.ti.com/corp/docs/company/citizen/ethics/quicktest.shtml). Courtesy Texas Instruments, Inc.

42. Ibid.

43. McAlister, Ferrell, and Ferrell, *Business and Society.*

44. Ibid.

45. Thomas A. Stewart, Ann Harrington, and Maura Griffin Sol, "America's Most Admired Companies: Why Leadership Matters," *Fortune,* March 3, 1998, 70–71.

46. "Corporate Culture Can Prevent Ethical Crises and Boost Profits, Study Says; Analysis by International Survey Research Provides Roadmap for Monitoring Ethics," *PR Newswire,* September 4, 2002.

47. Diane E. Kirrane, "Managing Values: A Systematic Approach to Business Ethics," *Training and Development Journal* 1 (November 1990): 53–60.

48. O. C. Ferrell, Isabelle Maignan, and Terry Loe, "Corporate Ethics + Citizenship = Profits," *The Bottom Line: Good Ethics Is Good Business* (Tampa, FL: University of Tampa, Center for Ethics, 1997).

49. Terry Loe, "The Role of Ethical Climate in Developing Trust, Market Orientation, and Commitment to Quality," unpublished dissertation, University of Memphis, 1996.

50. Isabelle Maignan, "Antecedents and Benefits of Corporate Citizenship: A Comparison of U.S. and French Businesses," unpublished dissertation, University of Memphis, 1997.

51. Ibid; and Loe, "The Role of Ethical Climate."

52. O. C. Ferrell, Isabelle Maignan, and Terry W. Loe, "The Relationship Between Corporate Citizenship and Competitive Advantage," in *Rights, Relationships, & Responsibilities: Business Ethics and Social Impact Management,* Vol. 1 (Kennesaw, GA: Kennesaw State University, Coles College of Business, 2003).

53. John C. Narver and Stanley Slater, "The Effect of Market Orientation on Business Profitability," *Journal of Marketing* 54 (October 1990), 20–35.

54. Isabelle Maignan and O. C. Ferrell, "Corporate Social Responsibility: Toward a Marketing Conceptualization," *Journal of the Academy of Marketing Science* 32 (January, 2004), 3–19.

55. Ibid.

56. Amy Merrick, "Gap Report Says Factory Inspections Are Getting Better," *Wall Street Journal,* July 13, 2005, B10.

57. Maignan and Ferrell, "Corporate Social Responsibility."

58. Christine Moorman, Gerald Zaltman, and Rohit Deshpande, "The Relationship Between Providers and Users of Market Research: The Dynamics of Trust Within and Between Organizations," *Journal of Marketing Research* 29 (August 1993), 314–328.

59. "The 1997 Cone/Roper Cause-Related Marketing Trends Report," *Business Ethics* 11 (March/April 1997), 14–16.

60. McAlister, Ferrell, and Ferrell, *Business and Society.*

61. Craig Smith, "Corporate Citizens and Their Critics," *New York Times,* September 8, 1996, 11.

62. The material on ethics compliance programs and the Federal Sentencing Guidelines for Organizations was adapted from Debbie Thorne LeClair, O. C. Ferrell, and John Fraedich, *Integrity Management: A Guide to Managing Legal and Ethical Issues in the Workplace* (Tampa, FL: University of Tampa Press, 1998).

63. "Krispy Kreme Problems," *(Fort Collins) Coloradoan,* August 11, 2005, D7.

64. Ronald Alsop, "Scandal-Filled Year Takes Toll on Firms' Good Names," *Wall Street Journal,* February 12, 2003.

65. R. Edward Freeman and David R. Gilbert, Jr., *Corporate Strategy and the Search for Ethics* (Englewood Cliffs, NJ: Prentice Hall, 1988), 7.

Chapter 4

1. These facts are from Parija Bhatnagar, "Home Depot Looking to Age Well," CNNMoney, January 17, 2006 (http://money.cnn.com/2006/01/17/news/companies/home_depot/index.htm);Alicia Clegg, "Mining the Golden Years," *BusinessWeek Online,* May 4, 2006 (http://www.businessweek.com/print/innovate/content/ may2006/id20060504_612679.htm); Karen E. Klein,

"Reaching Out to an Older Crowd," *BusinessWeek Online,* April 3, 2006 (http://www. businessweek.com/print/smallbiz/content/apr2006/ sb20060403_549646.htm); and Louise Lee, "Love Those Boomers," *BusinessWeek,* October 25, 2005.

2. These facts are from "RIM: Back from the Edge," *BusinessWeek Online,* March 6, 2006 (http://www.businessweek.com/magazine/content/06_10/b3974130.htm).

3. These facts are from Katrina Brooker, "The Pepsi Machine," *Fortune,* February 6, 2006, 68–72.

4. These facts are from Pamela Babcock, "America's Newest Export: White Collar Jobs," *HR Magazine* 49, no. 4 (2004); and Robert J. Grossman, "The Truth About the Coming Labor Shortage," *HR Magazine* 50, no. 3 (2005).

5. These facts are from Gail Edmondson, David Welch, and David Kiley, "Daimler Shakeup: Realignment in the Auto Industry," *BusinessWeek Online,* January 25, 2006 (http://www.businessweek.com/autos/content/jan2006/bw20060124_277216.htm).

6. These facts are from Charles Hutzler, "Adidas Hopes to Spread Brand in Beijing for the 2008 Olympics," *Miami Herald Online,* February 27, 2006 (http://www.miami.com/mld/miamiherald/business/13966024.htm).

7. These facts are from Cynthia Graber, "No Dumping: State Bans Techno-Trash, Donated Old Computers, TVs Add Up," *Boston Globe,* March 31, 2000, A1; Kendra Mayfield, "E-Waste: Dark Side of Digital Age," *Wired News,* January 10, 2003 (http://www.wired.com/news/technology/0,1282,57151,00.html); and Patricky McMahon, "E-Waste Flooding Landfills," *USA Today Online,* January 21, 2002 (http://www.usatoday.com).

8. Michael Levy and Barton A. Weitz, *Retailing Management,* 5th ed. (Boston: Irwin/McGraw-Hill, 2004).

9. Gary Gentile, "Disney to Sell Movies Through Internet Downloads," *San Jose Mercury News Online,* May 31, 2006 (http://www.mercurynews. com/mld/mercurynews/business/14705356.htm).

10. Mary Ellen Pinkham, "20 Surprising Uses for Vinegar," September 21, 2006 (http://www.ivillage.com/home/experts/clean/articles/0,258151_258168,00.html).

11. International Reciprocal Trade Association, "2004 Global Reciprocal Trade Statistics," September 21, 2006 (http://www.irta.com).

12. These facts are from "March of the Pinots," *BusinessWeek Online,* April 24, 2006 (http://www.businessweek.com/magazine/content/06_17/b3981101.htm); and W. Chan Kim and Renee Mauborgne, *Blue Ocean Strategy* (Boston: Harvard Business School Press, 2005), 24–35.

13. These facts are from Aaron Smith, "'Ask Your Doctor' Ads in FDA Crosshairs," CNNMoney, October 31, 2005 (http://money.cnn.com/2005/10/31/news/fortune500/dtc/index.htm).

14. These facts are from Dave Carpenter, "Gatorade Has Competition on the Run," *Los Angeles Times,* May 30, 2000, 3; Anthony Crupi, "Exercise[tv] Signs Up Gatorade," *MediaWeek,* May 15, 2006; and Kenneth Hein, "Gatorade Sweats the Visual Details to Refresh Connection with Consumers," *Brandweek,* March 3, 2003, 4.

15. This definition of competitive intelligence is adapted from The Society of Competitive Intelligence Professionals, http://www.scip.org/ci/.

16. Ibid.

17. This information is from http://www.inflationdata.com.

18. These facts are from Michael Mandel, "Why the Economy Is a Lot Stronger Than You Think," *BusinessWeek Online,* February 13, 2006 (http://www.businessweek.com/magazine/content/06_07/b3971001.htm); and Michael Mandel, "GDP: What's Counted, What's Not," *BusinessWeek Online,* February 13, 2006 (http://www.businessweek.com/magazine/content/06_07/b3971010.htm).

19. These facts are from The Sarbanes–Oxley Act Community Forum (http://www.sarbanes-oxley-forum.com/); and Amey Stone, "SOX: Not So Bad After All?" *BusinessWeek Online,* August 1, 2005

(http://www.businessweek.com/bwdaily/dnflash/aug2005/nf2005081_7739_db016.htm).

20. Kerry Capell, "Now, Will Europe Swallow Frankenfoods?" *BusinessWeek Online,* February 8, 2006 (http://www.businessweek.com/bwdaily/dnflash/feb2006/nf2006028_3575_db039.htm).

21. These facts are from RFID Journal, http://www.rfidjournal.com.

22. Administration on Aging website, http://www.aoa.dhhs.gov

23. *Minority Population Growth: 1995 to 2050,* U.S. Department of Commerce, Minority Business Development Agency, September 1999, 1–3; "More Diversity, Slower Growth," U.S. Census Bureau press release, March 18, 2004.

24. Joanne Muller, "Kmart con Salsa: Will It Be Enough?" *BusinessWeek Online,* August 30, 2002 (http://www.businessweek.com/bwdaily/dnflash/aug2002/nf20020830_7797.htm).

25. Chip Walker and Elissa Moses, "The Age of Self-Navigation," *American Demographics,* September 1996.

26. The organizational descriptions of corporate affairs are taken from websites of these companies: Blue-Scope Steel (http://www.bluescopesteel.com/navajo/display.cfm/objectID.464982A7-9F65-4FD1-8AC52566A9C4FB69); Microsoft (http://members.microsoft.com/careers/careerpath/legal/affairs.mspx); Pfizer (http://www.pfizer.com/pfizer/are/careers/mn_businesses_functions.jsp); and Philip Morris International (http://www.pmicareers.com/corporate/eng/philip_morris_functions/corporate_affairs.asp).

27. Yochi J. Dreazen, "'Do Not Call' Roster Debuts Today—Curbs on Telemarketers Set to Cut Calls Up to 80%; Violators Face Big Fines," *Wall Street Journal,* June 27, 2003, B2.

Chapter 5

1. These facts are from "Creativity Pays. Here's How Much," *BusinessWeek Online,* April 24, 2006 (http://www.businessweek.com/magazine/content/06_17/b3981410.htm); Robert D. Hof, "Building an Idea Factor," *BusinessWeek Online,* October 11, 2004 (http://www.businessweek.com/magazine/content/04_41/b3903462.htm); Matthew Maier, "Chewable Innovation," *Business 2.0,* April 20, 2006, via (http://money.cnn.com/magazines/business2/ business2_archive/2006/05/01/8375918/index.htm); and Jenna McGregor, "The World's Most Innovative Companies," *Business Week Online,* April 24, 2006 (http://www.businessweek. com/magazine/content/06_17/b3981401.htm).

2. Nigel Piercy, *Market-Led Strategic Change* (Oxford, UK: Butterworth-Heinemann, 1992), 257.

3. These facts are from Jena McGregor, "The World's Most Innovative Companies," *BusinessWeek,* April 24, 2006.

4. Mary C. Gilly and Mary Wolfinbarger, "Advertising's Second Audience," *Journal of Marketing* 62 (January 1998): 69–88.

5. This list and most of this section are based on E. K. Valentin, "SWOT Analysis from a Resource-Based View," *Journal of Marketing Theory and Practice* 9 (Spring 2001): 54–69.

6. Shelby D. Hunt, *A General Theory of Competition* (Thousand Oaks, CA: Sage, 2000), 67–68.

7. These facts are from the Bureau of Transportation Statistics, Airline Domestic Unit Costs (Cents per Mile), Table 11, 4th Quarter 2005; and Shawn Tully, "The Airlines' New Deal: It's Not Enough," *Fortune,* April 28, 2003, 79–82.

8. These facts are from Cora Daniels, "Mr. Coffee: The Man Behind the $4.75 Frappuccino Makes the 500," *Fortune,* April 14, 2003, 139–140; and Starbucks Company Fact Sheet (http://www.starbucks.com/aboutus/Company_Fact_Sheet_Feb06.pdf).

9. George Stalk, Philip Evans, and Lawrence E. Shulman, "Competing on Capabilities: The New Rules of Corporate Strategy," *Harvard Business Review* 70 (March–April 1992): 57–69.

10. This information is based on editorial reviews of MP3 players at CNET.com, June 7, 2006.

11. Michael Treacy and Fred Wiersema, *The Discipline of Market Leaders* (Reading, MA: Addison-Wesley, 1995).

12. These facts are from "Nordstrom Scores for Service," *Fortune,* November 15, 2005, via (http://money.cnn.com/2005/11/15/news/fortune500/customer_service/index.htm); and the Nordstrom website (http://www.nordstrom.com).

13. This material is based on Cornelis A. De Kluyver, *Strategic Thinking: An Executive Perspective* (Upper Saddle River, NJ: Prentice Hall, 2000), 53–56; Philip Kotler, *A Framework for Marketing Management,* 2nd ed. (Upper Saddle River, NJ: Prentice Hall, 2003), 67; and Arthur A. Thompson, Jr., and A. J. Strickland III, *Strategic Management: Formulation, Implementation, and Control,* 6th ed. (Boston: McGraw-Hill, 1997).

14. These facts are from Nanette Byrnes, "For Altria, Too Soon to Celebrate?" *BusinessWeek Online,* December 15, 2005 (http://www.businessweek.com/bwdaily/dnflash/dec2005/nf20051215_0993_db035.htm); and Patricia Sellers, "Altria's Perfect Storm," *Fortune,* April 28, 2003, 96–102.

15. These facts are from Kerry Capell, "VodaPhone: What Went Wrong," *BusinessWeek Online,* June 6, 2006 (http://www.businessweek.com/globalbiz/content/jun2006/gb20060606_579981. htm).

16. These facts are from Amy Barrett, "Why Merck Remains Unsettled," *BusinessWeek Online,* April 12, 2006 (http://www.businessweek.com/technology/content/apr2006/tc20060412_775867.htm).

17. The material in this section is adapted from W. Chan Kim and Renee Mauborgne, *Blue Ocean Strategy* (Boston: Harvard Business School Press, 2005).

18. The strategy canvas for Southwest Airlines is from Kim and Mauborgne, *Blue Ocean Strategy,* 38.

19. Ibid.

20. Ibid., 39.

21. Ibid., 29–37.

22. See Circuit City website (http://www. circuitcity. com).

23. These facts are from The Home Depot website (http://www.homedepot.com).

Chapter 6

1. These facts are from "Math Will Rock Your World," *BusinessWeek,* January 23, 2006; and Chris Taylor, "Imagining the Google Future," *Business 2.0,* February 1, 2006, via CNNMoney.com (http://money.cnn.com/magazines/business2/business2_archive/2006/01/01/8368125/index.htm).

2. Robert Berner, "The Ethnography of Marketing," *BusinessWeek Online,* June 12, 2006 (http://businessweek.com/innovate/content/jun2006/id20060612_919537.htm).

3. Philip Kotler, *A Framework for Marketing Management,* 2nd ed. (Upper Saddle River, NJ: Prentice-Hall, 2003), 7.

4. These facts are from "2006.6 Cadillac BLS," *BusinessWeek Online,* April 20, 2006 (http://www.businessweek.com/autos/content/apr2006/bw20060420_002969.htm); and Jean Halliday, "Cadillac Tries to Crash Out of Old Man Image," AdAge.com, January 29, 2003.

5. These facts are from Marty Bernstein, "Will Honda's Fit be a Hit?" *BusinessWeek Online,* April 27, 2006 (http://www.businessweek.com/autos/content/apr2006/bw20060427_337053.htm); and the Honda Fit website (http://automobiles.honda.com/models/model_overview. asp?ModelName=Fit&bhjs=1&bhqs=1).

6. "Can Fast Food Be Good Food?" Gothamist.com, March 17, 2005 (http://www.gothamist.com/archives/2005/03/17/can_fast_food_be_good_food.php).

7. These facts are from Matthew Boyle, "Joe Galli's Army," *Fortune,* December 30, 2002, 135.

8. Sophia Banay, "Super Spas 2006," *Forbes Online,* January 19, 2006 (http://www.forbes.com/travel/2006/01/18/luxury-spas-travel-cx_sb_0119feat_ls.html).

9. Judy Strauss, Adel El-Ansary, and Raymond Frost, *E-Marketing,* 3rd ed. (Upper Saddle River, NJ: Prentice Hall, 2003), 231–232.

10. These facts are from Andy Cross, "Pepsi Looks to Cash In in China," *The Motley Fool,* January 17, 2006 (http://www.fool.com/news/mft/2006/mft06011705.htm); Parija Bhatnagar, "Wal-Mart's Challenge in China," CNNMoney.com, January 12, 2006 (http://money.cnn.com/2006/01/12/news/companies/walmart_china/index.htm); "Starbucks Sees Big Opportunity in China," MSNBC.com (via Associated Press), February 14, 2006 (http://www.msnbc.msn.com/id/11341340/); and "Wal-Mart Poised for Major China Expansion," MSNBC.com (via Reuters), March 21, 2006 (http://www.msnbc.msn.com/id/11924811/).

11. This discussion is based on information obtained from the VALS website (http://www.sric-bi.com/VALS/).

12. These facts are from the PRIZM$_{NE}$ website (http://www.claritas.com/claritas/Default.jsp?ci=3&si=4&pn=prizmne_segments#18).

13. Danit Lidor, "Canon Aims Wide," *Forbes Online,* May 16, 2006 (http://www.forbes.com/infoimaging/2006/05/16/hp-printer-canon-cx_df_0516canon.html).

14. This material is adapted from Charles W. Lamb, Jr., Joseph F. Hair, Jr., and Carl McDaniel, *Marketing,* 7th ed. (Mason, OH: South-Western, 2004), 228–231; and Philip Kotler, *A Framework for Marketing Management,* 2nd ed. (Upper Saddle River, NJ: Prentice Hall, 2003), 181–185.

15. These facts are from the Littman website (http://www.littmann.com).

16. These facts are from the Follett Corporation website (http://www.follett.com).

17. These facts are from W. Chan Kim and Renee Mauborgne, *Blue Ocean Strategy* (Boston: Harvard Business School Press, 2005), 109–110; and Susan Yara, "The Price of a Perfect Smile," *Forbes Online,* June 6, 2006 (http://www.forbes.com/lifestyle/2006/06/01/teeth-cosmetic-cost_cx_sy_0602health.html).

Chapter 7

1. These facts are from Fred Mackerodt, "Defending a Brand Isn't Easy," *CEO Magazine,* April/May 2006, 54–55; and Andy Serwer, "Happy Birthday, Steinway," *Fortune,* March 17, 2003, 94–97.

2. This material is adapted from Charles W. Lamb, Jr., Joseph F. Hair, Jr., and Carl McDaniel, *Marketing,* 7th ed. (Mason, OH: South-Western, 2004), 294–295.

3. The Hampton Inn Guarantee (http://www.hamptoninn.com/en/hp/brand/about.jhtml).

4. *New Products Management for the 1980s* (New York: Booz, Allen & Hamilton, 1982), 14.

5. These facts are from "The Science of Desire," *BusinessWeek Online,* June 5, 2006 (http://www.businessweek.com/magazine/content/06_23/b3987083.htm).

6. These concepts are adapted from Jennifer Rice's Brand Blog, Mantra Brand Consulting (http://brand.blogs.com).

7. "Penney: Back in Fashion," *BusinessWeek Online,* January 9, 2006 (http://www.businessweek.com/magazine/content/06_02/b3966112.htm).

8. "J&J to Buy Pfizer Unit for $16B" CNNMoney (from Reuters), June 26, 2006 (http://money.cnn.com/2006/06/26/news/companies/pfizer_jnj.reut/index.htm).

9. David A. Aaker, *Managing Brand Equity: Capitalizing on the Value of a Brand Name* (New York: Free Press, 1991).

10. "Porsche Tops Quality Survey," CNNMoney, June 8, 2006 (http://money.cnn.com/2006/06/07/Autos/jdpower_iqs/index.htm).

11. "Beatles Lose Apple Court Battle," *BBC News Online,* May 8, 2006 (http://news.bbc.co.uk/2/hi/entertainment/4983796.stm).

12. BIOTA Spring Water website (http://biotaspringwater.com/bottle); and Bridget Finn, "Just One Word: Corn," *Business 2.0,* April 1, 2005, via CNNMoney (http://money.cnn.com/magazines/business2/business2_archive/2005/04/01/8256029/index.htm).

13. "Lunchmeats Launch in Reusable PP Containers," June 2, 2003, Packworld.com (http://www. packworld.com/cds_search.html?rec_id=14587& ppr_key=lunchmeat&sky_key=lunchmeat&term= lunchmeat).

14. Cecilia Blalock, "Label Foods for Choking Risks," August 27, 2003, Packworld.com (http://www. packworld.com/cds_search.html?rec_id=16586& ppr_key=choking&sky_key=choking&term= choking).

15. This material is adapted from Carol H. Anderson and Julian W. Vincze, *Strategic Marketing Management*, 2nd ed. (Boston: Houghton Mifflin, 2004), 249–253.

16. Kenji Hall, "Sony Sharpens Its Focus," *BusinessWeek Online*, June 7, 2006 (http://www. businessweek.com/globalbiz/content/jun2006/ gb20060607_941413.htm).

17. See Napster's FAQs (http://www.napster.com/faq/ subscribetonapster.html).

18. These facts are from Bill Britt, "Chevy Chase Does Turkish Cola Ads Aimed at Coke and Pepsi," *Advertising Age*, July 28, 2003, via AdAge.com (http://www.adage.com/abstract. php?article_id=38049).

19. These facts are from Timothy J. Mullaney, "Netflix," *BusinessWeek Online*, May 25, 2006 (http://www. businessweek.com/smallbiz/content/may2006/ sb20060525_268860.htm).

20. "Open-Source Ad Campaigns," *Business 2.0*, April 2006, 92.

21. These facts are from Brian Bremner, "Camera Makers' Many Negatives," *BusinessWeek Online*, February 10, 2006 (http://www.businessweek. com/bwdaily/dnflash/feb2006/nf20060210_ 8105_db016.htm).

22. Corporate Design Foundation, "Branding That Speaks to the Eyes," *BusinessWeek Online*, March 16, 2006 (http://www.businessweek.com/innovate/ content/mar2006/id20060316_504093.htm).

23. Peter Valdes-Dapena, "Shelby Mustangs: $20,000 Over Sticker," CNNMoney (Autos Section), May 19, 2006 (http://www.cnn.com/2006/AUTOS/05/ 17/shelby_over_sticker/index.html).

24. These facts are from Matthew Swibel, "Spin Cycle," *Forbes*, April 2, 2001, 118; and Randy Tucker, "Liquid Oxydol Aimed at Gen X," *Cincinnati Inquirer Online*, May 3, 2001 (http://www. enquirer.com/editions/2001/05/03/fin_liquid_ oxydol_aimed.html).

25. Reena Jana, "Nintendo's Brand New Game," *BusinessWeek Online*, June 22, 2006 (http://www. businessweek.com/innovate/content/jun2006/ id20060622_124931.htm); Next Generation, "Miyamoto Faces the Future," *BusinessWeek Online*, May 11, 2006 (http://www. businessweek.com/ innovate/content/may2006/id20060511_ 087395.htm); and Nintendo's Touch Generations website (http://us.touchgenerations.com).

Chapter 8

1. These facts are from Les Christie, "Oslo Beats Out Tokyo as Priciest City," CNNMoney, January 31, 2006 (http://money.cnn.com/2006/01/31/real_estate/ world_cities_most_expensive/index.htm); Charles Dubow, "Where Do iPods Cost Most—Or Least?" *BusinessWeek Online*, May 17, 2006 (http:// www.businessweek.com/globalbiz/content/ may2006/gb20060517_386795.htm); and Joseph Pisani, "What Things Cost," *BusinessWeek Online*, May 17, 2006 (http://images.business week. com/ss/ 06/05/what_things_ cost/source/1.htm).

2. Information obtained from http://www.rivalwatch. com.

3. See http://www.nwa.com/travel/cyber/overview. html for further information.

4. Valarie A. Zeithaml, "Consumer Perceptions of Price, Quality, and Value: A Means–End Model and Synthesis of Evidence," *Journal of Marketing* 52 (July 1988): 2–22.

5. This discussion is based on material from Charley Kyd, "Tempted to Cut Prices? It's Probably Time to *Raise* Them," *Today's Business*, Fall 2000, 3.

6. Material in this section is adapted from Mark M. Davis and Janelle Heineke, *Managing Services* (Boston: McGraw-Hill/Irwin, 2003), 379–382.

7. For further information, see the Southwest Airlines website (http://www.southwest.com).

8. "Stradivarius Tops Auction Record," *BBC News Online,* May 17, 2006 (http://news.bbc.co.uk/2/low/entertainment/4988838.stm).

9. These facts are from Aaron Smith, "Zocor and Zoloft Face Patent Expiration," CNNMoney, June 15, 2006 (http://money.cnn.com/2006/06/15/news/companies/zoloft_zocor/index.htm); and West Connor, "Lipitor Saving Tips," RxList.com, January 24, 2006 (http://www.rxlist.com/rxboard/lipitor.pl?noframes;read=4574).

10. Michael Gartenberg, "Motorola Launches the Q—First Take," Jupiter Research Weblogs, May 22, 2006 (http://weblogs.jupiterresearch.com/analysts/gartenberg/archives/015565.html).

11. These facts are from James Brightman, "Sony Expects Big Losses on PS3 Launch," *GameDaily,* May 1, 2006, via *BusinessWeek Online* (http://www.businessweek.com/innovate/content/may2006/id20060501_525587.htm); Arik Hesseldahl, "Toshiba's Battle with Blu-ray," *BusinessWeek Online,* June 23, 2006 (http://www.businessweek.com/technology/content/jun2006/tc20060622_113255.htm); and Arik Hesseldahl, "Microsoft's Red-Ink Game," *BusinessWeek Online,* November 22, 2005 (http://www.businessweek.com/technology/content/nov2005/tc20051122_410710.htm).

12. Mark Dixon Bunger, "eBay 2003: The World's Biggest Auto Showroom," Forrester Research, December 23, 2002; and Rob Hof, "The Future of eBay," *BusinessWeek Online,* May 4, 2006 (http://www.businessweek.com/the_thread/techbeat/archives/2006/05/the_future_of_e.html).

13. These facts are from "Sentencing in Archer Daniels Midland Price-Gouging Case," *Agribusiness Examiner,* July 21, 1999; and Steve Hargreaves, "Gas Prices Won't Slow Holiday Driving," CNNMoney, May 18, 2006 (http://money.cnn.com/2006/05/18/ news/economy/summer_driving/index.htm).

Chapter 9

1. "Barnes & Noble Reports 2005 Results," Barnes & Noble, press releases (http://www.barnesandnobleinc.com/press_releases/2006_2005_earnings_results.html); "Investor Relations," Barnes & Noble website (http://www.barnesandnobleinc.com/for_investors/for_investors.html); Tom Andel, "Logistics @ Barnesandnoble.com," *Material Handling Management,* January 2000, 39; "Barnes & Noble Implements 12 Solutions to Increase Distribution Center Efficiencies Nationwide," *Canadian Corporate News,* May 8, 2001 (www.comtextnews.com); "Barnes & Noble, Inc. Reports 2001 Consolidates EPS Increases 21% to $1.28," Barnes & Noble Inc., press release, March 21, 2002; "Barnes & Noble Selects Retek to Support Supply Chain Planning and Optimization," Barnes & Noble, news release, January 10, 2001; Herb Greenberg, "Dead Man Walking," *Fortune,* May 1, 2000, 304; and "Mezzanines Help Support Store and Web Demand," *Material Handling Management,* January 2000, 14SFC.

2. Deborah Catalano Ruriani, "Inventory Velocity: All the Right Moves," *Inbound Logistics,* November 2005, 36.

3. Del Monte Food 2005 Annual Report, 25.

4. Kevin O'Mara, Vice President of Research, AMR Research, "Describing the Businesses on AMR's 2005 Top 25 Best Demand-Driven Supply Network List," Nexus 2005 Supply Chain Conference, Winston-Salem, NC," in *Inbound Logistics,* November 2005, 10.

5. These facts are from the PayPal website (http://www.paypal.com).

6. These facts are from David Koenig, "Dell Recall Stems from Production Flaw," *BusinessWeek Online,* August 15, 2006 (http://www.businessweek.com/ap/financialnews/D8JH7QU80.htm).

7. Pallavi Gogoi, "General Mills' Far-Flung Search for Efficiency Ideas," *BusinessWeek,* July 28, 2003, 74.

8. The J.M. Smucker Company 2006 Annual Report, 11.

9. See Edward W. Davis and Robert E. Speckman, *The Extended Enterprise* (Upper Saddle River, NJ: Prentice Hall Financial Times, 2004).

10. Ibid., 15.

11. Robert Dawson, *Secrets of Power Negotiation,* 2nd ed. (Franklin Lakes, NJ: Career Press, 1999).

12. Davis and Speckman, *The Extended Enterprise,* 161.

13. This information is adapted from "Collaborative SCM: Adversaries to Allies," *Inbound Logistics,* July 2000, 124.

14. Category Management Report ©1995 by the Joint Industry Project on Efficient Consumer Response.

15. Ibid.

16. Affinity Internet, "Doing Business Online," 2005 Affinity eCommerce Survey, *USA Today Snapshots,* June 6, 2006.

17. These facts are from "New Shopping Carts May Talk to You," CNN.com, October 29, 2003 (http://www.cnn.com/2003/TECH/ptech/10/29/shoo.future.ap/index.html).

18. These facts are from Constance L. Hays, "What Wal-Mart Knows About Customers' Habits," *New York Times,* November 14, 2004; Skip Kaltenheuser, "Innovative Air Force Data Warehouse Integrates Millions of Parts into One-Stop Supply Chain Visibility," *World Trade Magazine Online,* January 1, 2005 (http://www.worldtrademag.com/CDA/ArticleInformation/features/BNP_Features_Item/0,3483,140201,00.html); "Wal-Mart Expands Its Teradata Warehouse to Optimize Decision Support Capabilities," Teradata press release, October 13, 2004 (http://www.teradata.com/t/page/128640/index.html); John Johnson, "RFID Watch: Transmissions from the RFID Front Lines: How They Did It," *DC Velocity,* January 2006 (http://www.dcvelocity.com); and Jim Wagner, "Wal-Mart RFID Tests Underway," *Wireless,* April 30, 2004 (http://www.internetnews.com).

19. The material in this section is based on Davis and Speckman, *The Extended Enterprise,* 109–129.

20. Lisa H. Harrington, "Balancing on the Rim," *Inbound Logistics,* January 2006, 168–170.

21. Leslie H. Harps, "EuroLogistics," *Inbound Logistics,* August 2000, 44–53.

22. Joseph O'Reilly, "LaserNetworks Banks on Same-Day Delivery, *Inbound Logistics,* April 2004, 74–77.

23. Bert Rosenbloom, *Marketing Channels: A Management View* (Hindsale, IL: Dryden, 1991), 103.

24. Attorney General of Washington (http://www.atg.wa.gov).

25. These facts are from Jonathan Collins, "FDA Clears Way for RFID Tagging," *RFID Journal Online,* November 15, 2004 (http://www.rfidjournal.com/article/articleview/1238/1/1/); and "FDA Eyes New Tactics Against Fakes," *CBS News Online,* October 3, 2003 (http://www.cbsnews.com/stories/2003/09/26/health/main575354.shtml).

Chapter 10

1. Enid Burns, "Marketers Push Toward Integrated Marketing Campaigns," *ClickZ Network,* June 14, 2006 (http://www.clickz.com/stats/sectors/advertising/article.php/3613506).

2. These facts are from "The End of TV (as You Know It)," *BusinessWeek Online,* November 21, 2005 (http://www.businessweek.com/magazine/content/05_47/b3960075.htm); "New York Times to Trim Page Size, Staff," CNNMoney, July 18, 2006 (http://money.cnn.com/2006/07/18/news/companies/nytimes.reut/index.htm); and David Schatsky, "The Media Industry Is Falling to Pieces," *TelevisionWeek,* January 30, 2006, 10.

3. Kenneth Hein, "Going Gets Tough, Sprite Gets Weird," *Brandweek,* May 1, 2006, 6.

4. These facts are from Harry Maurer, "Univision Picks a Buyer," *BusinessWeek,* July 10, 2006, 24; and Teresa Wiltz, "Spanglish: Pop Culture's Lingua Franca," *Washington Post,* January 26, 2003, G01.

5. Data from *Time* magazine Media Kit (http://www.time.com/time/mediakit/editions/national/index.html).

6. Data from Paul La Monica, "Super Bowl XL's Extra-Large Ad Sales," CNNMoney, January 3, 2006 (http://money.cnn.com/2006/01/03/news/companies/superbowlads/index.htm).

7. Stephanie Thompson, "Wrigley Slaps Kraft for Shortchanging Brands," *Advertising Age,* April 10, 2006, 3–4.

8. These facts are from Heather Green, "Reality Check for Podcasting," *BusinessWeek Online,* April 5, 2006 (http://www.businessweek.com/the_thread/blogspotting/archives/2006/04/reality_check_f.html); Heather Green, "Podbridge: Podcasting Metrics Please," *BusinessWeek Online,* February 17, 2006 (http://www.businessweek.com/the_thread/blogspotting/archives/2006/02/podcasting_metr.html); Heather Green, "The Business of Podcasting," *BusinessWeek Online,* November 30, 2005 (http://www.businessweek.com/the_thread/blogspotting/archives/2005/11/the_business_of_1.html); Olga Kharif, "Podcasts Calling," *BusinessWeek Online,* April 7, 2006 (http://www.businessweek.com/technology/content/apr2006/tc20060407_521419.htm); and Mike Shields, "Nielsen: Podcasting Remains a Niche Activity," *Adweek Online,* July 12, 2006 (http://www.adweek.com/aw/search/article_display.jsp?vnu_content_id=1002837819).

9. Xueming Luo, "Measuring Advertising Spending Inefficiency: A Comparison of Data Envelopment Analysis and Stochastic Frontier," *Marketing Theory and Applications,* Proceedings of the American Marketing Association Winter Educators' Conference, Ram Krishnan and Madhu Viswanathan, eds. (Scottsdale, AZ: American Marketing Association, 2001), 4–5.

10. These facts are from the New Belgium Brewery website (http://www.newbelgium.com).

11. These facts are from Ben & Jerry's website (http://www.benandjerrys.com) and the Lick Global Warming website (http://www.lickglobalwarming.org).

12. William C. Moncrief, Emin Babakus, David W. Cravens, and Mark W. Johnston, "Gender Differences in Sales Organizations," *Journal of Business Research* (September 2000): 245–257.

13. "Outstanding Training Initiatives," *Training,* March 2006, 64–65.

14. Rebecca Aronauer, "Train Anytime, Anywhere," *Sales and Marketing Management,* May 2006, 19; and Julia Chang, "No Instructor Required?" *Sales and Marketing Management,* May 2003, 26.

15. This information is from http://www.salesforce.com.

16. Promotion Marketing Association, "State of the Promotion Industry Report," © 2005 Promotion Marketing Association (http://www.pmalink.org/resources/pma2005report.pdf).

Chapter 11

1. These facts are from Mark Basham, "Good Things Brewing for Green Mountain Coffee," *Business Week Online,* April 8, 2002 (http://www.businessweek.com/investor/content/apr2002/pi2002048_1946.htm); Pallavi Gogoi, "Mickey D's New Brew," *BusinessWeek Online,* March 1, 2006 (http://www.businessweek.com/bwdaily/dnflash/mar2006/nf2006031_8259_db016.htm); "Green Mountain Coffee Roasters Included in Fortune Small Business List of America's Fastest-Growing Small Companies," *Forbes Online,* June 28, 2006 (http://www.forbes.com/businesswire/feeds/businesswire/2006/06/28/businesswire20060628005081r1.html); Green Mountain Coffee Roasters website (http://www.greenmountaincoffee.com); Hoover's Fact Sheet on Green Mountain Coffee (http://www.hoovers.com/green-mountain-coffee/--ID__45721--/free-co-factsheet.xhtml?cm_ven=PAID&cm_cat=BUS&cm_pla=CO1&cm_ite=Green_Mountain_Coffee_Roasters_Inc.); and "Learning on the Front Lines," *BusinessWeek Online,* July 10, 2006 (http://

www.businessweek.com/magazine/content/06_28/b3992011.htm).

2. Orville C. Walker, Jr., and Robert W. Ruekert, "Marketing's Role in the Implementation of Business Strategies: A Critical Review and Conceptual Framework," *Journal of Marketing* 51 (July 1987): 15–33.

3. Frank V. Cespedes, *Organizing and Implementing the Marketing Effort* (Reading, MA: Addison-Wesley, 1991), 19.

4. Robert Howard, "Values Make the Company: An Interview with Robert Haas," *Harvard Business Review* 68 (September–October 1990): 132–144.

5. See the New Belgium Brewery website (http://www.newbelgium.com).

6. Michael D. Hartline, James G. Maxham III, and Daryl O. McKee, "Corridors of Influence in the Dissemination of Customer-Oriented Strategy to Customer Contact Service Employees," *Journal of Marketing* 64 (April 2000): 35–50.

7. Ibid.

8. Cespedes, *Organizing and Implementing the Marketing Effort,* 622–623.

9. Robert W. Ruekert, Orville C. Walker, Jr., and Kenneth J. Roering, "The Organization of Marketing Activities: A Contingency Theory of Structure and Performance," *Journal of Marketing* 49 (Winter 1985): 13–25.

10. Hartline, Maxham, and McKee, "Corridors of Influence."

11. Michael Hammer and James Champy, *Reengineering the Corporation: A Manifesto for Business Revolution* (New York: Harper Business, 1993), 35.

12. Jena McGregor, "How Failure Breeds Success," *BusinessWeek Online,* July 10, 2006 (http://www.businessweek.com/magazine/content/06_28/b3992001.htm?chan=innovation_innovation+%2B+design_the+creative+corporation).

13. Myron Glassman and Bruce McAfee, "Integrating the Personnel and Marketing Functions: The Challenge of the 1990s," *Business Horizons* 35 (May–June 1992): 52–59.

14. Michael D. Hartline and O. C. Ferrell, "Service Quality Implementation: The Effects of Organizational Socialization and Managerial Actions on Customer-Contact Employee Behaviors," *Marketing Science Institute Working Paper Series,* Report No. 93–122 (Cambridge, MA: Marketing Science Institute, 1993).

15. Richard L. Oliver and Erin Anderson, "An Empirical Test of the Consequences of Behavior- and Outcome-Based Sales Control Systems," *Journal of Marketing* 58 (October 1994): 53–67.

16. Hartline, Maxham, and McKee, "Corridors of Influence."

17. FedEx Corporation website (http://www.fedex.com).

18. These facts are from Betsy Morris, "The New Rules," *Fortune,* July 24, 2006, 70–87; and Betsy Morris, "Tearing Up the Jack Welch Playbook," CNNMoney, July 11, 2006 (http://money.cnn.com/2006/07/10/magazines/fortune/rules.fortune/index.htm).

19. W. Chan Kim and Renee Mauborgne, *Blue Ocean Strategy* (Boston: Harvard Business School Press, 2005).

20. The material in this section has been adapted from L. J. Bourgeois III and David R. Brodwin, "Strategic Implementation: Five Approaches to an Elusive Phenomenon," *Strategic Management Journal* 5 (1984): 241–264; and Steven W. Floyd and Bill Wooldridge, "Managing Strategic Consensus: The Foundation of Effective Implementation," *Academy of Management Executive* 6 (November 1992): 27–39.

21. These facts are from Delroy Alexander, "Upgrade Edict by McDonald's Faces Challenge: Owner-Operators to Hire Law Firm," *Chicago Tribune,* September 3, 2003; and Pallavi Gogoi, "Mickey D's Makeover," *BusinessWeek Online,* May 15, 2006 (http://www.businessweek.com/magazine/content/06_20/b3984065.htm).

22. These facts are from Patricia O'Connell, "Samsung's Goal: Be Like BMW," *BusinessWeek Online,*

August 1, 2005 (http://www.businessweek.com/magazine/content/05_31/b3945107.htm); and Craig Smith, "Soaring Samsung Provides Proof of Marketing's Value," *Marketing,* September 25, 2003, 19.

23. Bourgeois and Brodwin, "Strategic Implementation: Five Approaches to an Elusive Phenomenon."

24. Hartline, Maxham, and McKee, "Corridors of Influence."

25. This information is from Mohammed Rafiq and Pervaiz K. Ahmed, "Advances in the Internal Marketing Concept: Definition, Synthesis and Extension," *Journal of Services Marketing* 14 (2000): 449–463.

26. Ibid.

27. Glassman and McAfee, "Integrating the Personnel and Marketing Functions."

28. Howard, "Values Make the Company."

29. Hartline and Ferrell, "Service Quality Implementation."

30. This section is based on material from Hartline, Maxham, and McKee, "Corridors of Influence"; and Bernard J. Jaworski, "Toward a Theory of Marketing Control: Environmental Context, Control Types, and Consequences," *Journal of Marketing* 52 (July 1988): 23–39

31. These facts are from Steve Miller, "Saturn Launches Rolled, Will New Models Rock?" *Brandweek,* April 17, 2006, 14.

32. Ibid; and Brian P. Niehoff, Cathy A. Enz, and Richard A. Grover, "The Impact of Top-Management Actions on Employee Attitudes and Perceptions," *Group & Organization Studies* 15 (September 1990): 337–352.

33. Michael D. Hartline and O. C. Ferrell, "The Management of Customer-Contact Service Employees: An Empirical Investigation," *Journal of Marketing* 60 (October 1996): 52–70.

34. Ibid.

35. Ben M. Enis and Stephen J. Garfein, "The Computer-Driven Marketing Audit," *Journal of Management Inquiry* (December 1992): 306–318; and Philip Kotler, William Gregor,
and William Rodgers, "The Marketing Audit Comes of Age," *Sloan Management Review* 30 (Winter 1989): 49–62.

36. Jaworski, "Toward a Theory of Marketing Control."

37. Ibid.

38. Hartline, Maxham, and McKee, "Corridors of Influence.

39. Jack R. Meredith and Scott M. Shafer, *Introducing Operations Management* (New York: Wiley, 2003), 458.

Chapter 12

1. These facts are from Mila D'Antonio, "Courting Customers," *1-t-1 Magazine Online,* July/August 2006 (http://www.1to1media.com/Issues.aspx?Publication=9221).

2. Jill Dyché, *The CRM Handbook* (Boston, MA: Addison-Wesley, 2002), 4–5.

3. Judy Strauss, Adel El-Ansary, and Raymond Frost, *E-Marketing,* 3rd ed. (Upper Saddle River, NJ: Prentice Hall, 2003), 407–408.

4. "Relationships Rule," *Business 2.0,* May 2000, 303–319; and Strauss, El-Ansary, and Frost, *E-Marketing,* 406.

5. This information is taken from the Regions website (http://www.regions.com/everyday_banking/relationship_money.shtml).

6. Cliff Edwards, "AMD + ATI: Imperfect Together?" *BusinessWeek Online,* July 25, 2006 (http://www.businessweek.com/technology/content/jul2006/tc20060725_893757.htm).

7. Adapted from Mary Jo Bitner, "Managing the Evidence of Service," *The Service Quality Handbook,* E. E. Scheuing and W. F. Christopher, eds. (New York: AMACOM, American Management Association, 1993).

8. These facts are from Brian Hindo, "Satisfaction Not Guaranteed," *BusinessWeek Online,* June 19, 2006 (http://www.businessweek.com/magazine/content/06_25/b3989041.htm).

9. This material is adapted from Valarie A. Zeithaml, A. Parasuraman, and Leonard L. Berry, *Delivering*

Quality Service: Balancing Customer Perceptions and Expectations (New York: Free Press, 2001).

10. Information in this section is based on James H. Myers, *Measuring Customer Satisfaction* (Chicago: American Marketing Association, 1999); and Valarie A. Zeithaml, Leonard L. Berry, and A. Parasuraman, "The Nature and Determinants of Customer Expectations of Service," *Journal of the Academy of Marketing Science* 21 (January 1993) 1–12.

11. A. Parasuraman, Leonard L. Berry, and Valarie A. Zeithaml, "Understanding Customer Expectations of Service," *Sloan Management Review* 32 (Spring 1991): 42.

12. Adapted from Strauss, El-Ansary, and Frost, *E-Marketing,* 435–437.

13. Susan Fournier and David Glen Mick, "Rediscovering Satisfaction," *Journal of Marketing* 63 (October 1999): 5–23.

Case 16

1. Geoff Edgers, "Furor Ahoy; MFA Exhibit of Koch's Collections Stirs Questions over Choices, Motives," *The Boston Globe,* August 31, 2005, p. A1.

2. Geoff Edgers, "MFA Takes a New Road; Car Show Seeks to Drive in Men," *The Boston Globe,"* February 20, 2005, p. A1.

3. Alberto Vilar, "What every journalist should know about . . . the next wave of arts funding," *Editor and Publisher,* January 6, 2003, p. 11.

4. These trends in philanthropy are widely discussed. See "The Corporate Givers," *BusinessWeek,* November 29, 2004; "The New Face of Philanthropy," *BusinessWeek,* December 2, 2002; and "What Some Recent Research Tells Us about Planned Giving (legacy marketing) in North America," *International Journal of Nonprofit and Voluntary Sector Marketing,* February 2005.

5. As noted in "Art Museums and the Public Trust," lecture given by MFA director Malcolm Rogers, September 29, 2004.

6. "Art Museums and the Public Trust," lecture given by MFA Director Malcolm Rogers, September 29, 2004.

7. For example, in 2004 the Louvre, with 7.5 million visitors, boasted the highest visitor attendance. The Metropolitan Museum of Art received 5 million visitors, and the Uffizi in Italy had 2 million visitors.

8. Geoff Edgers, "Malcolm, X; In 10 Unorthodox years, the MFA's Malcolm Rogers has Popularized, Polarized," *The Boston Globe,* September 12, 2004.

9. Geoff Edgers, "MFA Takes a New Road; Car Show Seeks to Drive in Men," *The Boston Globe,* February 20, 2005.

10. Geoff Edgers, "MFA Sending More Paintings to Vegas," *The Boston Globe,* April 28, 2005.

11. Geoff Edgers, "Malcolm, X; In 10 Unorthodox Years, the MFA's Malcolm Rogers has Popularized, Polarized," *The Boston Globe,* September 12, 2004.

12. Geoff Edgers, "Under Construction: An Art Renaissance," *The Boston Globe,* April 10, 2005.

13. Moira Cotlier, "Trying to profit from for-profit status," *Catalog Age,* May 2001, p. 61.

14. This was based on a ranking of top 50 museums or cultural attractions completed in 2000. Seven art museums were listed: The Smithsonian (34 million, including all eight museums under its auspices), the National Gallery of Art (5.13 million), the Metropolitan Museum of Art (4.7 million), the Museum of Fine Arts Houston (2.0 million), the Art Institute of Chicago (1.39 million), the Museum of Fine Arts Boston (1.35 million), and the Museum of Modern Art (1.2 million).

Case 17

1. In one recent survey, 46% of 7 and 8 year olds considered "playing with toys" as a favorite pastime, versus only 5% for 11 and 12 year olds. The older group cited reading, playing video games and listening to music, as being higher on their preference list.

2. MAGIC THE GATHERING and DUNGEONS AND DRAGONS are trademarks of Wizards of the Coast. SUPER SOAKER is a trademark of Larami Limited. KOOSH is a trademark of Oddzon, Inc. GI JOE,

PLAY-DOH, MR. POTATO HEAD, TONKA, PLAYSKOOL, EASY-BAKE, NERF, SPIROGRAPH, MY LITTLE PONY, LITE-BRITE, TRANS-FORMERS, TINKERTOY, GIGA PETS, HITCLIPS, POO-CHI, MICRO MACHINES, MONOPOLY, CANDY LAND, BATTLESHIP, TWISTER, YAHT-ZEE, CLUE, OUIJA, RISK and FURBY are trademarks of Hasbro and are used with permission. SCRABBLE is a trademark of Hasbro in the US and Canada and is used with permission. TRIVIAL PURSUIT is a trademark of Horn Abbot Ltd. and is manufactured under license by Hasbro. OPERA-TION is a trademark of Fleet Capital Corporation, licensed for use by Hasbro.

3. The Disney deal was signed in 2000.

4. Some of these figures have been disguised to protect proprietary company information.

5. One exception to this—for several years in the 1980s, the G.I. JOE product line had been supported by a cartoon series.

Case 18

1. There were over 500 million VCRs in the world in 2003. While introduced to allow consumers to watch TV shows they had previously recorded, the worldwide installed base of VCRs grew from fewer than 10 million in 1980 to over 200 million in 1990 as consumers began using their VCRs to watch prerecorded movies—with adult movies the first killer app. Jimmy Schaeffler, "Ten Trends in Consumer Electronics," *Satellite News*, Vol. 26, No. 13, March 31, 2003; David Backus and Luis Cabral, "Betamax and VHS," NYU Stern School Case, November 26, 2001, p. 2; and Peter Sealey, "Commercial Television: Rest in Peace," speech to the 2003 Association of National Advertisers, March 13, 2003.

2. Almost all DVRs included automatic access to an electronic programming guide (EPG); in order to update the EPG on a daily basis, DVRs either had an internal modem that allowed them to dial out on a phone line or used an Internet, cable, or satellite connection to access the EPG.

3. Dawn C. Chmielewski, "The Number of Cables Needed for TiVo Should Have Been a Clue," *The San Jose Mercury News,* June 19, 2003, p. 1E.

4. TiVo outsourced call center operations to a big call center operator. Customer service costs varied primarily with new subscribers.

5. TiVo had had a partnership with DirecTV since 1999, and under terms of the earlier agreement, TiVo had shouldered most of the marketing and operations costs and received a high proportion of the monthly subscriber fees generated.

6. Richard Shim, "DirecTV Cuts Fee for TiVo Service," CNET News.com Web site, September 3, 2002, http://news.com/2100-1040-956384.html, accessed July 2, 2003.

7. NDS has two share classes; Class A shares, which account for approximately 22.2% of all outstanding shares, are fully registered and publicly traded in the form of American Depository Receipts. News Corp. owns all of the Series B shares, which total approximately 77.8% of all outstanding shares and are not registered for trading. www.nds.com/investor_relations/investor_info.html.

8. Interview, March 22, 2005.

9. Joseph Palenchar, "Microsoft: See SPOT Run Despite Past Wristwatch-Pager Failures," TWICE Web site, March 10, 2003, http://www.twice.com, accessed April 30, 2003.

10. Based on price quotes on Amazon.com, July 20, 2005.

11. Jessica Hodgson, "TiVo Technology Could leave 10% of TV Ads Unwatched," *The Wall Street Journal,* June 23, 2005.

12. David Farina, Mary O'Toole, and Ralph Schackart, "TiVo Inc.," William Blair & Company, March 17, 2003, p. 10.

13. Through its IPO, the sale of convertible preferred stock, and subsequent stock offerings, TiVo raised approximately $280 million in capital during the 1999 to 2000 time frame.

14. Om Malik, "Ta-Ta TiVo," Red Herring Web site, January 29, 2003, http://www.redherring.com/investor/2003/01/tivo012903.html, accessed June 16, 2003.

15. "Research Notes 3Q 2002," Leichtman Research Group, Inc., p. 1.

16. David Farina, Mary O'Toole, and Ralph Schackart, "TiVo, Inc.," William Blair & Company, March 17, 2003, p. 13.

17. Ibid., p. 25; and Bob Parks, "Where the Customer Service Rep is King," *Business 2.0,* June 2003, http://www.business2.com/articles/mag/print/ 0,1643,49462,00.html, accessed July 1, 2003.

18. http://www.itfacts.biz/index.php?id=P2064.

19. Ibid., p. 12.

20. Paul Bond, "Households double up on digital video recorders," July 22, 2005, http://labs. news. yahoo.com/news?tmpl=story&u=/nm/20050722/ media_nm/television_survey_dc, accessed August 8, 2005.

21. Jessica Hodgson, "TiVo Technology Could leave 10% of TV Ads Unwatched," *The Wall Street Journal,* June 23, 2005.

22. Dr. Peter Sealey, "Commercial Television: Rest in Peace," speech to the 2003 Meeting of the Association of National Advertisers, March 13, 2003.

23. "TiVo to Let Viewers Contact Advertisers," *The New York Times,* July 19, 2005.

24. "Charles Schwab Joins TiVo's Growing Advertiser Roster with Showcase Featuring Golfer Phil Mickelson During U.S. Open," press release, June 14, 2004, www.tivo.com/5.3.1.1.asp? article=212.

25. "Desperate Housewives Towers Over Other New Fall Shows in TiVo Weekly Season Pass Ratings," TiVo press release, October 29, 2004.

26. "Statement of TiVo Chairman and CEO Mike Ramsay Regarding FCC Chairman Michael Powell," company press release, January 25, 2005.

27. "TiVo Signs New Advertising Services Agreement with DirecTV," TiVo press release, April 5, 2005.

28. Interviews, March 22, 2005.

29. Ibid.

30. Interview with Mike Ramsay, March 22, 2005.

Case 19

1. Arguably the United Kingdom's top professional soccer team, as well as its best known, Manchester United has consistently been one of the top 10 teams in the world since the 1950s.

2. "Nike Tackles Adidas at Home," News24.com, November 30, 2004.

3. "Welcome to the Matrix," *Asia Inc.,* December 2003.

4. "Like Father, Like Daughter," *iMedia Connection,* April 07, 2004.

5. Sales were directly traceable to the Yahoo takeover, and did not include indirect sales or longer term trends from increased brand awareness.

6. "Ad Agencies Sound Alert over the Mobile Phone Generation," *Financial Times,* November 8, 2004.

7. SMS: Short Message Service was a feature available with some wireless phones that allowed users to send and receive short text messages.

8. Vodafone was the world's largest cellular phone carrier with more than 150 million subscribers in 39 countries. J-Sky was the cellular brand for Japan-based J-Phone, the world's first wireless carrier to provide 3G. The company was acquired by Vodafone in 2001.

9. Regulatory delays and diverging standards delayed the introduction of 3G technology in the United States. However, by the end of 2004, all three major U.S. carriers had announced plans to make broadband cellular service available in urban centers. By 2008, most of the country would be linked to broadband cellular phone services.

10. In early 2000, the failure of prominent Internet companies, such as E-toys and Value America, caused many investors to reevaluate the market. As bearish sentiment began to take hold, the technology shares entered into an extended downward spiral. In March 2000, the technology-laden NASDAQ exchange peaked at 5,000. By year's end, approximately half of that index's value had been erased.

11. Flaschenpost: German for "message in a bottle."

12. As soccer's best-known icon, David Beckham was renowned for his long curving kicks. He helped lead the Manchester United soccer team to championship wins in 1996, 1997, 2000, 2001,

and 2003. In 2003, Beckham was traded to the Real Madrid team. His personal fortune was estimated to be greater than that of the Queen of England.

13. Viral marketing referred to "network-enhanced word-of-mouth." Users accessed content voluntarily and then solicited their friends to do the same, often through e-mails (viral e-mail) or text messages.

14. A ring tone is a music clip that plays when receiving phone calls. Ring tones could be customized to identify specific callers, or they could be used to help distinguish one phone from other nearby devices. Finally, ring tones added a personal element that reflected a sense of individuality.

15. This figure represents the cumulative number of viewers, including repeat viewers. Therefore, one person viewing all 31 games would be counted as 31 viewers.

16. Club Nokia was a marketing program in which subscribers agreed to receive promotional messages on their cellular phones in exchange for benefits such as product discounts and free cellular phone content or services.

17. An applet is a small self-contained computer application written in the Java programming language developed by Sun Microsystems, Inc. An applet has limited connectivity and can usually only interact with the site from which the applet originated. A ticker applet downloads and displays simple information, such as weather, news headlines and sports data.

18. "Simmons' Rush for Profits," *Black Enterprise,* December, 1992.

19. "Hip-hop's Bling Culture is Wooing Corporate America," *Marketing Week,* June 24, 2004.

20. Unlike ringtones, which used music to notify subscribers of incoming calls, voice tones utilized voice messages from Missy Elliott, such as "Yo, this is Missy Elliott. Why don't you show me some respect and pick up your phone." True tones were digital music samples similar to MP3 audio recordings.

21. "Break the Cycle" offered programs aimed at reducing domestic violence in the United States.

Case 20

1. Kim Froggatt, "Asia: A Decade of Growth in the Relocation Industry," www.santaferelo.com/ecs/data/misc/Newsletter/inside/feature_article.html, accessed April 11, 2005.

2. Annual Report 2004, *The East Asiatic Company Limited,* Copenhagen, March 31, 2005.

3. DKK is the Danish Krone, the principal currency for the East Asiatic Company Limited. Using a rate of DKK1 = HK$1.4265 at December 31, 2004, DKK468 million would be equivalent to HK$667.6 million; using a rate of DKK1 = US$0.18345, this would be equivalent to US$85.9 million.

4. Santa Fe also offered records management, freight forwarding and office moving services. Those services accounted for only a small portion of the company's revenue and are extraneous to this case.

5. "Worldwide Network," Santa Fe Relocation Services, www.santaferelo.com/ecs/html/other/WorldwideNetwork.html, accessed March 31, 2005.

6. Interview with Santa Fe Relocation Services Chief Operating Officer, Keith Meader, November 16, 2004.

7. "Global Relocation Trends 2003/2004 Survey Report," *GMAC Global Relocation Services,* Oak Brook, May 2004.

8. Elizabeth Kennedy, "Moving On Up," Women in Business, January 1, 2005.

9. "Global Relocation Trends 2003/2004 Survey Report," *GMAC Global Relocation Services,* Oak Brook, May 2004.

10. This was a ratio for the entire company, but it was not true of all offices or countries. For example, in mainland China, the employer was almost always the decision-maker and purchaser of relocation services.

11. Interview with Santa Fe Relocation Services General Manager of Sales and Marketing, Bruce Burns, April 6, 2005.

12. Interview with Santa Fe Relocation Services Group Manager of Relocation Services, Yves Therien, April 6, 2005.

13. "Global Relocation Trends 2003/2004 Survey Report," GMAC Global Relocation Services, Oak Brook, May 2004.

14. Ibid.

15. "Annual Report 2004," *The East Asiatic Company Limited*, Copenhagen, March 31, 2005.

16. Interview with Santa Fe Relocation Services General Manager of Sales and Marketing, Bruce Burns, April 6, 2005.

17. Customer quoted in "Annual Report 2004," *The East Asiatic Company Limited,* Copenhagen, March 31, 2005.

18. Interview with Santa Fe Relocation Services General Manager of Sales and Marketing, Bruce Burns, April 6, 2005.

19. Interview with Santa Fe Relocation Services General Manager of Sales and Marketing, Bruce Burns, November 16, 2004.

20. Interview with Santa Fe Relocation Services General Manager of Sales and Marketing, Bruce Burns, April 6, 2005.

Appendix B

1. "New Arthritis Drugs for Rheumatoid Arthritis and Osteoarthritis," HealingWell.com website (http://www.healingwell.com/library/arthritis/info4.asp), accessed October 8, 2006.

2. Surprisingly Simple (non-drug) Pain Relief for Arthritis, Vanderbilt Online Wellness Center (http://vanderbiltowc.wellsource.com/dh/content.asp?ID=1846), accessed October 8, 2006.

3. "Beige Book Summary," Federal Reserve Board (http://www.federalreserve.gov/FOMC/Beige Book/ 2006/20060118/default.htm), January 18, 2006.

4. The Conference Board website (http://www.conference-board.org/), accessed October 8, 2006.

5. Cathy Keen, "Florida Consumer Confidence Marks Big Gains in December," University of Florida press release (http://news.ufl.edu/2005/12/27/cc1205/), December 27, 2005.

6. Consumer Healthcare Products Association FAQs (http://www.chpa-info.org/ChpaPortal/PressRoom/FAQs/), accessed October 8, 2006.

7. "The Self Care Situation," University of California, San Francisco (http://pharmacy.ucsf.edu/ccsc/situation.php?print=yes), accessed October 8, 2006.

8. "Direct-to-Consumer Advertising," Source Watch website (http://www.sourcewatch.org/index.php?title=Direct-to-consumer_advertising), accessed October 8, 2006.

9. Ibid.

10. M. Asif Ismail, "Drug Lobby Second to None," The Center for Public Integrity (http://www.publicintegrity.org/rx/report.aspx?aid=723), July 7, 2005.

11. Ibid.

12. "The Issues: Rx Drug Imports," CBS News (http://www.cbsnews.com/stories/2004/09/09/evening news/main642415.shtml), September 9, 2004.

13. "Breast Cancer," About.com (http://breastcancer.about.com/od/dailylife/a/nsaids01.htm), accessed October 8, 2006.

14. "Internal Analgesic, Antipyretic, and Antirheumatic Drug Products for Over-the-Counter Human Use," FDA website (http://www.fda.gov/cder/otcmonographs/Internal_Analgesic/internal_analgesic(343).htm), accessed October 8,2006.

15. Consumer Healthcare Products Association FAQs, accessed October 8, 2006.

16. Ibid.

17. Bob Brewin, "Sidebar: FDA Mandate Could Have $7B Price Tag," *Computerworld* (http://www.computerworld.com/governmenttopics/government/policy/story/0,10801,90596,00.html), March 1, 2004.

18. Jonathan Cohn, *Medicare Reform: The Real Winners,"* CBS News (http://www.cbsnews.com/stories/2003/11/20/opinion/main584722.shtml), November 20, 2003.

19. Pain Management Technologies website (http://www.paintechnology.com), accessed October 8, 2006.

20. "Pain Management for the Neck and Spine," SpineUniverse.com (http://www.spineuniverse. com/displayarticle.php/article59.html), accessed October 8, 2006.

21. "Income Stable, Poverty Rate Increases, Percentage of Americans Without Health Insurance Unchanged," U.S. Census Bureau (http://www.census.gov/Press-Release/www/releases/archives/income_wealth/005647. html), August 30, 2005.

Name Index

Subject Index